Complete Book of
HOME PRESERVING
400 delicious and creative recipes for today

Edited by Judi Kingry and Lauren Devine

Robert
ROSE

Complete Book of Home Preserving
Text copyright © 2006, 2012 Jarden Corporation
Photographs copyright © 2006, 2012 Robert Rose Inc.
Cover and text design copyright © 2012 Robert Rose Inc.

Ball®, *Ball.* are registered trademarks of Ball Corporation, used under limited license to Jarden Corporation.

Bernardin®, **BERNARDIN** are trademarks used under license of Jarden Corporation NYSE: JAH

Library and Archives Canada Cataloguing in Publication
Complete book of home preserving: 300 delicious and creative recipes for today / edited by Judi Kingry
    & Lauren Devine.

Includes index.
ISBN 0-7788-0139-X (U.S. bound).   ISBN 0-7788-0131-4 (U.S. pbk).
ISBN 0-7788-0140-3 (Can. bound).   ISBN 0-7788-0137-3 (Can. pbk).

1. Canning and preserving. 2. Fruit—Preservation. 3. Vegetables—Preservation. 4. Cookery (Fruit). 5. Pickles.
6. Cookery (Vegetables). I. Kingry, Judi. II. Devine, Lauren. III. Ball Corporation/Bernardin Ltd.

TX601.B34 2006   641.4'2   C2005-906165-0
TX601.B468 2006   641.4'2   C2005-906166-9

Disclaimer
The recipes in this book have been carefully tested by our kitchen and our tasters. To the best of our knowledge, they are safe and nutritious for ordinary use and users. For those people with food or other allergies, or who have special food requirements or health issues, please read the suggested contents of each recipe carefully and determine whether or not they may create a problem for you. All recipes are used at the risk of the consumer.

We cannot be responsible for any hazards, loss or damage that may occur as a result of any recipe use.

For those with special needs, allergies, requirements or health problems, in the event of any doubt, please contact your medical adviser prior to the use of any recipe.

Design & Production: PageWave Graphics Inc.
Editors: Judith Finlayson and Sue Sumeraj
Proofreader: Sheila Wawanash
Indexer: Gillian Watts
Front cover photography: Mark T. Shapiro
Inside photography: Colin Erricson and Mark T. Shapiro
Food Stylist: Izabella Snider
Props Stylist: Charlene Erricson
Stock photography: © iStockphoto.com/Emilie Duchesne
Illustrations: Kveta

The publisher and editors wish to express their appreciation to the following suppliers of props used in the food photography:

Caban
396 St. Clair Avenue West
Toronto, Ontario
M5P 3N3
Tel: (416) 654-3316
www.caban.com

Parpar
649 St. Clair Avenue West
Toronto, Ontario
M6C 1A7
(416) 657-3333

Gourmet Settings Inc.
245 West Beaver Creek Road,
Unit 10
Richmond Hill, Ontario
L4B 1L1
Tel: 1-800-551-2649
www.gourmetsettings.com

Living 2
1766 Avenue Road
Toronto, Ontario
M5M 3Y9
416 256-9234

The publisher acknowledges the financial support of the Government of Canada through the Book Publishing Industry Development Program (BPIDP) for our publishing activities.

Published by: Robert Rose Inc.
120 Eglinton Avenue East, Suite 800, Toronto, Ontario, Canada M4P 1E2
Tel: (416) 322-6552 Fax: (416) 322-6936 www.robertrose.ca

Printed in Canada

29 FP 14

Contents

◆

Preserving the Good Things of Life Because You Can!

Home canning puts the pleasure of eating natural, delicious produce at your fingertips year-round. Preserving food in mason jars might sound old-fashioned, but it is as modern and practical as the latest health food trend or gourmet creation — and it's really quite simple! Home canners enjoy the rewards of numerous homemade meals and snacks, created from just one preserving session. When you preserve food at home, you create products that save you time in day-to-day food preparation, a real blessing given today's hectic lifestyles. Individual home-preserved jars can be opened and served as is, or used to simplify on-the-spot meal and snack preparation.

A Simple Step Beyond Cooking

Like baking, preserving food is a simple step beyond recipe preparation. For home canning, this step is called "heat processing." It is neither difficult nor time-consuming. In fact, the most popular home-preserved foods require less time than baking a cake or a casserole. Unlike baking, the results of home canning sessions do not require space in your refrigerator or freezer. Properly home-canned foods can be stored in your cupboard for up to a year.

During heat processing, mason jars filled with food and fitted with two-piece metal closures are heated, destroying harmful microorganisms that cause food spoilage and creating an airtight seal that prevents contamination during storage. Precise processing techniques, times and temperatures are determined by the acidity of the food being preserved. A full description of the process of home canning, with step-by-step instructions and all the details you need to know to preserve food safely, can be found in The Art and Science of Home Food Preservation, beginning on page 409.

If you're eager to jump right in, the Getting Started chapter (pages 8–18) gives detailed instructions on preparing five versatile home-canned foods: strawberry jam, mint jelly, salsa, corn relish and dill pickles. If you prefer to know all the details before you begin a project, take some time to peruse The Art and Science of Home Food Preservation, and especially the section called Boiling-Water Heat Processing, Step by Step (page 415), before you begin one of the Getting Started recipes.

Happy canning!

Home Canning Equipment

The majority of today's home-canned foods — jams and jellies, pickles, fruits and tomatoes — can be prepared and preserved using utensils you are likely to already have in your kitchen. To get started, of course, you will need canning jars and new two-piece metal closures, as well as a canner for heat-processing the filled jars.

Boiling-Water Canner

Most of the recipes in this book are heat-processed in a boiling-water canner. This is not something you necessarily need to run out and buy: most kitchens have pots that can double as boiling-water canners, especially if you're using smaller jars. A boiling-water canner is simply a large, deep pot equipped with a lid and a rack. Cooking equipment stores do stock commercial boiling-water canners, but before you purchase this specialized equipment, check to see if one of your existing pots might be a suitable substitute.

Any pot used as a boiling-water canner must be large enough to completely immerse the jars in water. Ideally, the pot will be at least 3 inches (7.5 cm) deeper than the height of the jars. This depth allows space for the jars to be covered by at least 1 inch (2.5 cm) of water, while leaving sufficient extra pot height (1 to 2 inches/ 2.5 to 5 cm) for the water to boil rapidly. The rack simply lifts the jars off the bottom of the pot, keeping them away from direct heat and allowing the boiling water to heat the entire jar. Racks designed specifically for boiling-water canners have handles that allow the rack to be elevated and hooked to the rim of the pot. When the rack is filled with jars, do not remove it from the pot. You can also use a cake cooling rack or tie extra screw bands together to cover the bottom of the pot. With this type of rack, a jar lifter is a definite asset.

5

Pressure Canner

To heat-process non-acidified vegetables, meat, poultry or fish — or recipes that include any of these foods — you'll need a special piece of equipment called a pressure canner. Pressure canners are available in cooking supply stores. They are tall, usually heavy, pots with two special features: a lid that can be locked in place and a pressure-regulating device. To learn more about pressure canners and how to use them, see Pressure Canning: Low-Acid Foods, page 379.

Canning Jars

Glass canning jars, often called mason jars, are the only containers recommended for safe home canning. Authentic canning jars have a unique threaded neck designed to engage with home canning screw bands. The top of the jar must be smooth and flat, without chips, to accommodate the sealing compound in the flange of the lid. The shape and volume capacity of canning jars must also comply with well-established heat processing methods and times. For more information on canning jars, see page 413.

Jar Lids and Screw Bands

Two-piece metal home-canning closures include a screw band and a flat metal lid with a channel filled with sealing compound. Flat lids are constructed of tin-plated steel that has been protected with food-safe coatings. The underside of the lid has a channel coated with a unique food-safe sealing compound specifically formulated for preserving food at home. The threaded metal screw band fits over the threaded neck of the jar and holds the lid in place during heat processing. Holding the lid securely in place during heat processing is the sole purpose of a screw band. For more information on lids and screw bands, see page 414.

Canning Utensils

While they are not essential, there are a number of specialty kitchen tools that make canning easier and safer. These include jar lifters, canning funnels, magnetic lid wands and nonmetallic spatulas. For more information on these useful utensils, see page 415.

Getting Started

To introduce you to the pleasures of preserving, this chapter provides detailed instructions for home canning five popular foods: jam, jelly, salsa, relish and pickles. It provides beginners with a jumpstart on making outstanding preserves without studying the science of preserving.

After reading through one or two of these simple recipes, we're certain you'll feel confident enough to try your hand at any of the more than 400 recipes included in this book. If you have questions, you'll find the answers in The Art and Science of Home Food Preservation, pages 409–419. Even if you aren't a beginner, reading through these recipes will provide many useful tips that will help you produce the best possible results when making preserves at home.

Strawberry Jam

A universal favorite, strawberry jam adds marvelous flavor and color to breakfasts, snacks and desserts. While freshly picked, locally grown strawberries produce the best jam, this recipe can be made using imported berries or unsweetened frozen berries. If using frozen berries, thaw them in the refrigerator just until they are soft enough to crush. Some ice crystals should remain.

TIPS

Powdered fruit pectin is sometimes sold in 49 g packages and sometimes in 57 g packages. The weight difference does not affect the performance of the product.

When preparing jars and lids, prepare a couple extra in case your yield is larger than you expect. If you don't have enough jars, place any leftover preserves in an airtight container, store in the refrigerator and use within a few weeks.

Before using jars, inspect them carefully for any chips, cracks or fractures. Discard any imperfect jars.

Makes about eight 8-ounce (250 mL) jars

7 cups	granulated sugar	1.75 L
8 cups	whole strawberries (approx.)	2 L
4 tbsp	lemon juice	60 mL
1	package (1.75 oz/49 to 57 g) regular powdered fruit pectin	1

1. Place 8 clean 8-ounce (250 mL) mason jars on a rack in a boiling-water canner. (You can also use a large, deep saucepan or stockpot that is at least 3 inches/7.5 cm deeper than the height of the jars.) Fill the jars and canner with cool water that reaches the top of the jars. Cover and bring water to a simmer over medium heat. Do not boil.

2. Prepare 8 two-piece closures. Set screw bands aside. Place lids in a small saucepan and cover with water. Heat just to a simmer over medium heat, but do not boil. Keep lids warm until ready to use. Do not heat screw bands.

3. Measure sugar into a bowl and set aside. (Sugar is added to the boiling jam all at once, so measuring it ahead of time prevents errors in quantities and eliminates cooking delays.)

4. In a colander placed over a sink, wash strawberries in cool running water. Drain thoroughly and, using a strawberry huller or the rounded end of a potato peeler, remove hulls.

5. In a glass pie plate or flat-bottomed bowl, place a single layer of strawberries. Using a potato masher, crush berries and transfer to a 1-cup (250 mL) liquid measure. As you accumulate each cup (250 mL), transfer crushed berries to a large, deep stainless steel saucepan. Repeat until you have 5 cups (1.25 L) of crushed strawberries.

6. Add lemon juice to crushed strawberries in saucepan. Whisk in pectin until dissolved. Bring to a full rolling boil over high heat, stirring frequently. Add sugar all at once and, stirring constantly, return to a full rolling boil that cannot be stirred down. Boil hard, stirring constantly, for 1 minute. Remove from heat and, using a large slotted metal spoon, skim off foam (see tip, opposite).

7. Fill one jar at a time. Remove jar from canner and empty hot water back into canner. (Do not dry jar.) Place jar on a tray or towel-covered counter and place a canning funnel in it. Ladle hot jam into hot jar, leaving ¼ inch (0.5 cm) headspace. Slide a nonmetallic utensil, such as a rubber spatula, down between

Measuring accurately is essential to success when making gelled products. Multi-cup glass or liquid measures are generally less accurate than single-cup (250 mL) glass measures.

When measuring dry ingredients, such as sugar, use measures that can be leveled off with a straight-edge tool. Do not use glass or liquid measures for dry ingredients.

Foam accumulates on the surface of soft spreads as air is released from the fruit during cooking. To reduce foaming, add up to ½ tsp (2 mL) butter or margarine to the recipe before cooking. This will reduce surface tension and thus reduce the buildup of air bubbles or foam.

the jam and the inside of jar two or three times to release air bubbles. Adjust headspace, if necessary, by adding hot jam. With a clean damp cloth or paper towel, wipe jar rim and threads to remove any food residue. Using a magnetic or nonmetallic utensil, lift hot lid from water and center it on jar. Place screw band on jar and, with your fingers, screw band down evenly and firmly, just until resistance is met, then increase to fingertip-tight. Do not over-tighten or use any tools to apply screw band. Return jar to canner rack and repeat until all jam is used.

8. When all jars are filled, lower rack into canner and ensure jars are completely covered by at least 1 inch (2.5 cm) of hot water. Cover canner and bring water to a full rolling boil over high heat. Process (continue boiling rapidly) for 10 minutes, starting timer only when water reaches a full rolling boil. At the end of the processing time, turn heat off and remove canner lid. Wait 5 minutes, then remove jars, without tilting. Place jars upright on a towel in a draft-free place and let cool, undisturbed, for 24 hours.

9. After 24 hours, check lids for seal. Remove screw bands and press down on the center of each lid with your finger. Sealed lids will be concave (they'll curve downward) and will show no movement when pressed. Jars that haven't sealed properly must be refrigerated immediately or reprocessed (see page 418). Rinse and dry screw bands. Wipe jars and, if desired, loosely reapply screw bands. Label jars and store in a cool, dry, dark place.

Variations

Vanilla Strawberry Jam: Add half a vanilla bean, split in half lengthwise, to the crushed strawberries. Cook as directed and remove vanilla bean before ladling jam into jars. The resulting jam will be enhanced with subtle yet distinct vanilla overtones.

Strawberry Balsamic Jam: Reduce the lemon juice to 1 tbsp (15 mL) and add 3 tbsp (45 mL) good-quality balsamic vinegar. Balsamic vinegar accents the strawberry flavor and gives the jam a robust taste.

Lemony Strawberry Jam: Add the grated zest of 1 large lemon to the crushed strawberries.

Peppered Strawberry Jam: Stir ½ tsp (2 mL) freshly ground black pepper into the cooked jam just before ladling it into the jars. Pepper accents and compliments strawberries' sweet flavor. Be sure to use freshly ground pepper, which delivers a fresher-quality flavor.

Mint Jelly

Mint jelly is a trans-lucent jewel. Not only does it have many uses in cooking, it makes a delicious spread for bread and a tasty condiment with lamb or pork. Used as a glaze for roast or grilled meat or stirred into marinades, mint jelly adds refreshing flavor to many foods.

TIPS

Cheesecloth can be found at many retailers, such as grocery stores and other stores that carry kitchen supplies. Look in the area where kitchen utensils are located.

For best results when cooking jelly, use a heavy-bottomed stainless steel saucepan that is at least three times deeper than the level of the recipe's juice and sugar combined. Jelly bubbles and boils up when it reaches a full rolling boil and therefore requires this extra pan depth.

Read a recipe all the way through, even before you go shopping for the ingredients. It's very important to have all of the ingredients and equipment ready before you start making preserves.

Makes about four 8-ounce (250 mL) jars

1½ cups	firmly packed mint leaves	375 mL
2¼ cups	water	550 mL
2 tbsp	lemon juice	30 mL
3½ cups	granulated sugar	875 mL
	Green food coloring (optional)	
1	pouch (3 oz/85 mL) liquid pectin	1

1. Place 4 clean 8-ounce (250 mL) mason jars on a rack in a boiling-water canner. (You can also use a large, deep saucepan or stockpot that is at least 3 inches/7.5 cm deeper than the height of the jars.) Fill the jars and canner with cool water that reaches the top of the jars. Cover and bring water to a simmer over medium heat. Do not boil.

2. Prepare 4 two-piece closures. Set screw bands aside. Place lids in a small saucepan and cover with water. Heat just to a simmer over medium heat, but do not boil. Keep lids warm until ready to use. Do not heat screw bands.

3. In a colander placed over a sink, rinse mint leaves thoroughly under cold running water. Shake off excess moisture and chop finely.

4. In a large stainless steel saucepan, combine mint and water. Bring to a boil over medium-high heat. Remove from heat, cover and let steep for 10 minutes. Pour liquid into a damp jelly bag or a cheesecloth-lined sieve set over a large glass measure. Let drip until you have 1¾ cups (425 mL) of mint-flavored liquid.

5. In a clean large, deep stainless steel saucepan, combine mint-flavored liquid, lemon juice and sugar. Over high heat, stirring constantly, bring to a full rolling boil that cannot be stirred down. Stir in liquid pectin, squeezing the full content from the pouch. Boil hard, stirring constantly, for 1 minute. Add a few drops of food coloring (if using). Remove from heat and, using a large slotted metal spoon, skim off foam (see tip, page 9).

A jar lifter is very helpful for handling hot, wet jars. Because they are bulky and fit loosely, oven mitts — even water-resistent types — are not a wise choice. When filling jars, an all-purpose rubber glove, worn on your helper hand, will allow you to steady the jar.

Place a clean towel on your work surface to absorb water from the hot jars as you take them out of the boiling-water canner to be filled, and again once the jars are processed. The towel prevents hot jars from coming into contact with cooler countertops. Significant temperature differences can cause jar breakage.

6. *Some jellies set up very quickly, so it is important to move quickly when transferring cooked jelly from the pot to the jars. Because jellies are pure liquids, bubble removal for each jar is not required.* Remove a jar from canner and empty hot water back into canner. (Do not dry jar.) Place jar on a tray or towel-covered counter and place a canning funnel in it. Quickly ladle or pour hot jelly into hot jar, leaving $\frac{1}{4}$ inch (0.5 cm) headspace. With a clean damp cloth or paper towel, wipe jar rim and threads to remove any food residue. Using a magnetic or nonmetallic utensil, lift a hot lid from water and center it on jar. Place screw band on jar and, with your fingers, screw band down evenly and firmly, just until resistance is met, then increase to fingertip-tight. Do not over-tighten or use any tools to apply screw bands. Return jar to canner rack and repeat until all jelly is used.

7. When all jars are filled, lower rack into canner and ensure jars are completely covered by at least 1 inch (2.5 cm) of hot water. Cover canner and bring water to a full rolling boil over high heat. Process (continue boiling rapidly) for 10 minutes, starting timer only when water reaches a full rolling boil. At the end of the processing time, turn heat off and remove canner lid. Wait 5 minutes, then remove jars, without tilting. Place jars upright on a towel in a draft-free place and let cool, undisturbed, for 24 hours.

8. After 24 hours, check lids for seal. Remove screw bands and press down on center of each lid with your finger. Sealed lids will be concave (they'll curve downward) and will show no movement when pressed. Jars that haven't sealed properly must be refrigerated immediately or reprocessed (see page 418). Rinse and dry screw bands. Wipe jars and, if desired, loosely reapply screw bands. Label jars and store in a cool, dry, dark place.

Simple "House" Salsa

Create a distinctive salsa to suit your family's taste preference, mild to fiery hot. If you can't wait for fresh tomato season, use canned tomatoes instead. Do not alter the quantities of vegetables and vinegar — they must be used as stated to assure the proper acidity for high-acid food processing. Adjust the flavor by substituting chopped jalapeños or other fresh hot peppers for some of the red or green bell peppers. Additional dried spices and/or hot pepper sauce may be added to the cooked mixture without affecting acidity.

TIPS

Refer to the Produce Purchase Guide on pages 426–429 to determine how much produce you'll need to buy to prepare this recipe.

Salsa is a versatile complement to entrées and snacks. Serve homemade salsa with steak fajitas, meatloaf, baked potatoes, nachos and main dish salads.

Makes eight to nine 8-ounce (250 mL) jars

1½ cups	chopped onions	375 mL
1 tbsp	chopped garlic	15 mL
1 cup	cider vinegar	250 mL
10 cups	coarsely chopped, seeded, cored plum tomatoes	2.5 L
2 cups	chopped, seeded red and/or green bell peppers	500 mL
1 cup	loosely packed chopped fresh cilantro or Italian parsley	250 mL
1 tbsp	dried oregano	15 mL
1 tbsp	granulated sugar	15 mL
1 tbsp	hot pepper sauce	15 mL
1½ tsp	ground cumin	7 mL
1½ tsp	salt	7 mL

1. Place 9 clean 8-ounce (250 mL) mason jars on a rack in a boiling-water canner. (You can also use a large, deep saucepan that is at least 3 inches/7.5 cm deeper than the height of the jars.) Fill the jars and canner with cool water that reaches the top of the jars. Cover and bring water to a simmer over medium heat. Do not boil.

2. Prepare 9 two-piece closures. Set screw bands aside. Place lids in a small saucepan and cover with water. Heat just to a simmer over medium heat, but do not boil. Keep lids warm until ready to use. Do not heat screw bands.

3. In a large stainless steel saucepan, combine onions, garlic and vinegar. Bring to a boil over high heat, stirring occasionally. Reduce heat and boil gently for 2 minutes. Stir in tomatoes and peppers, return mixture to a boil and cook for 3 minutes. Add cilantro, oregano, sugar, hot pepper sauce, cumin and salt. Return to a full boil, stirring constantly. Reduce heat and boil gently, stirring occasionally, just until peppers are tender, 3 to 5 minutes. Remove from heat.

4. Fill one jar at a time. Remove one jar from canner and empty hot water back into canner. (Do not dry jar.) Place jar on a tray or towel-covered counter and place a canning funnel in it. Ladle hot salsa into hot jar, leaving ½ inch (1 cm) headspace. Slide a nonmetallic utensil, such as a rubber spatula,

For best results, use firm plum tomatoes. Round or globe garden tomatoes may be used, but they need to be seeded, diced and drained in a colander for at least 30 minutes before adding to the recipe. Measure the required quantity of chopped tomatoes after draining.

Homemade salsas tend to be runnier than commercial salsas. If you wish to have a chunkier salsa, drain off the excess juice. This juice is a wonderful addition to stews, soups or salad dressings.

Salsa flavors mellow and blend during shelf storage. Optimum flavor is achieved after 3 to 4 weeks.

down between the salsa and the inside of jar two or three times to release air bubbles. Adjust headspace, if necessary, by adding hot salsa. With a clean damp cloth or paper towel, wipe jar rim and threads to remove any food residue. Using a magnetic or nonmetallic utensil, lift hot lid from water and center it on jar. Place screw band on jar and, with your fingers, screw band down evenly and firmly, just until resistance is met, then increase to fingertip-tight. Do not over-tighten or use any tools to apply screw band. Return jar to canner rack and repeat until all salsa is used.

5. When all jars are filled, lower rack into canner and ensure jars are completely covered by at least 1 inch (2.5 cm) of hot water. Cover canner and bring water to a full rolling boil over high heat. Process (continue boiling rapidly) for 15 minutes, starting timer only when water reaches a full rolling boil. At the end of the processing time, turn heat off and remove canner lid. Wait 5 minutes, then remove jars, without tilting. Place jars upright on a towel in a draft-free place and let cool, undisturbed, for 24 hours.

6. After 24 hours, check lids for seal. Remove screw bands and press down on the center of each lid with your finger. Sealed lids will be concave (they'll curve downward) and will show no movement when pressed. Jars that haven't sealed properly must be refrigerated immediately or reprocessed (see page 418). Rinse and dry screw bands. Wipe jars and, if desired, loosely reapply screw bands. Label jars and store in a cool, dry, dark place.

Variations

Year-round Salsa: In place of fresh tomatoes, substitute $6\frac{1}{3}$ cups (1.575 L) chopped, drained canned tomatoes and omit the salt. You will need one institutional-size can (100 oz/2.84 L) or 4 cans (each 28 oz/796 mL) whole tomatoes. Coarsely chop canned tomatoes and place in a sieve for 15 minutes to drain excess liquid before adding to the recipe. The salt content varies in canned tomatoes, so adjust seasonings accordingly.

Chipotle Salsa: For a smoky flavor, substitute 3 finely chopped drained canned chipotle peppers in adobo sauce for the hot pepper sauce.

Traditional Corn Relish

Serve this colorful, tangy relish to perk up the appetite appeal of sandwiches or stir into deli salads for added flavor and texture.

TIPS

For a hot and sweet relish, add ¼ to 1 tsp (1 to 5 mL) hot pepper flakes to the vegetable mixture along with the spices. Adjust the "heat" of this relish by increasing or decreasing hot pepper flakes.

Refer to the Produce Purchase Guide on pages 426–429 to determine how much produce you'll need to buy to prepare this recipe.

Makes about five pint (500 mL) jars

9 cups	frozen corn kernels, thawed	2.25 L
3 cups	finely chopped cabbage	750 mL
1 cup	finely chopped onion	250 mL
1 cup	finely chopped, seeded red bell pepper	250 mL
4 cups	white vinegar	1 L
3 cups	granulated sugar	750 mL
1 cup	water	250 mL
2 tbsp	dry mustard	30 mL
1 tbsp	celery seeds	15 mL
1 tbsp	mustard seeds	15 mL
1 tbsp	salt	15 mL
1 tbsp	ground turmeric	15 mL

1. In a large stainless steel saucepan, combine corn, cabbage, onion, red pepper, vinegar, sugar, water, dry mustard, celery seeds, mustard seeds, salt and turmeric. Bring to a boil over medium-high heat, stirring frequently. Reduce heat and boil gently, stirring occasionally, for about 25 minutes or until liquid is reduced and vegetables are tender-crisp.

2. Meanwhile, place 5 clean pint (500 mL) mason jars on a rack in a boiling-water canner. (You can also use a large, deep saucepan or stockpot that is at least 3 inches/7.5 cm deeper than the height of the jars.) Fill the jars and canner with cool water to within 1 inch (2.5 cm) of the top of the jars. Cover and bring water to a simmer over medium heat. Do not boil.

3. Prepare 5 two-piece closures. Set screw bands aside. Place lids in a small saucepan and cover with water. Heat just to a simmer over medium heat, but do not boil. Keep lids warm until ready to use. Do not heat screw bands.

4. Fill one jar at a time. Remove one jar from canner and empty hot water back into canner. (Do not dry jar.) Place jar on a tray or towel-covered counter and place a canning funnel in it. Ladle hot relish into hot jar, leaving ½ inch (1 cm) headspace. Slide a nonmetallic utensil, such as a rubber spatula, down between

TIP

A clear plastic ruler (kept solely for kitchen use) will help you determine the correct headspace. Each filled jar should be measured accurately, as the headspace can affect sealing and the preservation of the contents.

the relish and the inside of jar two or three times to release air bubbles. Adjust headspace, if necessary, by adding hot relish. With a clean damp cloth or paper towel, wipe jar rim and threads to remove any food residue. Using a magnetic or nonmetallic utensil, lift hot lid from water and center it on jar. Place screw band on jar and, with your fingers, screw band down evenly and firmly, just until resistance is met, then increase to fingertip-tight. Do not over-tighten or use any tools to apply screw band. Return jar to canner rack and repeat until all relish is used.

5. When all jars are filled, lower rack into canner and ensure jars are completely covered by at least 1 inch (2.5 cm) of hot water. Cover canner and bring water to a full rolling boil over high heat. Process (continue boiling rapidly) for 15 minutes, starting timer only when water reaches a full rolling boil. At the end of the processing time, turn heat off and remove canner lid. Wait 5 minutes, then remove jars, without tilting. Place jars upright on a towel in a draft-free place and let cool, undisturbed, for 24 hours.

6. After 24 hours, check lids for seal. Remove screw bands and press down on the center of each lid with your finger. Sealed lids will be concave (they'll curve downward) and will show no movement when pressed. Jars that haven't sealed properly must be refrigerated immediately or reprocessed (see page 418). Rinse and dry screw bands. Wipe jars and, if desired, loosely reapply screw bands. Label jars and store in a cool, dry, dark place.

Variation

Fresh Corn Relish: Fresh corn on the cob lends unique sweetness and flavor to this popular relish. To prepare fresh corn kernels, remove husks and silk from about 18 medium fresh ears of corn and blanch ears in boiling water for 5 minutes (begin counting blanching time after the water returns to a boil). Immediately plunge blanched ears into ice water. Cut kernels from ears, using a sharp knife. Measure 9 cups (2.25 L) of kernels and continue with recipe.

Pick-a-Vegetable Dill Pickles

Sandwiches and dill pickles go together like love and marriage. Serving your own homemade pickles every time you serve sandwiches adds a unique and welcome touch. Although cucumber pickles are the most common "dills," other vegetables are easily converted into crisp, tangy dill pickles that can be preserved year-round (see variations, page18). This recipe uses dill seeds instead of fresh dillweed flowers, another seasonal commodity that can be difficult to find.

TIPS

When packing fruits or vegetables into jars for pickles, pack tightly, without crushing. Leave room for the pickling liquid, since that is where the flavor comes from.

Ingredient quantities are approximate. Variations in the sizes of pickling cucumbers and jars dictate the number of pickles that can be placed in each jar. This, in turn, affects the quantity of liquid required.

Makes about six pint (500 mL) jars

30 to 36	medium 5-inch (13 cm) pickling cucumbers (approx 7 lbs/3.2 kg)	30 to 36
⅓ cup	pickling or canning salt	75 mL
	Ice water	
½ cup	finely chopped sweet red or green bell pepper	125 mL
2 tbsp	minced garlic	30 mL
1	jalapeño pepper, seeded and finely chopped (optional)	1
2 tbsp	dill seeds, divided	30 mL
1½ cups	granulated sugar	375 mL
2 tbsp	mustard seeds	30 mL
4 cups	white vinegar	1 L
1 cup	water	250 mL

1. With a soft brush, scrub pickling cucumbers in cool water. Rinse thoroughly in fresh water. Cut off a thin slice from each end of the cucumbers. Cut cucumbers lengthwise into quarters. You should have about 12 cups (3 L) of cucumber spears. Place spears in a large glass or stainless steel bowl and sprinkle with pickling salt. Add ice water to cover. Place a large clean inverted dinner plate over the cucumbers and weigh it down with a quart (1 L) jar filled with water or a plastic bag filled with water. (This will ensure the cucumbers remain submerged in salt water). Let stand in a cool place for 2 hours.

2. Place 6 clean pint (500 mL) mason jars on a rack in a boiling-water canner. (You can also use a large, deep saucepan or stockpot that is at least 3 inches/7.5 cm deeper than the height of the jars.) Fill the jars and canner with cool water to within 1 inch (2.5 cm) of the top of the jars. Cover and bring water to a simmer over medium heat. Do not boil.

3. Prepare 6 two-piece closures. Set screw bands aside. Place lids in a small saucepan and cover with water. Heat just to a simmer over medium heat, but do not boil. Keep lids warm until ready to use. Do not heat screw bands.

4. In a small bowl, combine red pepper, garlic, jalapeño pepper (if using) and 1 tbsp (15 mL) of the dill seeds. Mix well and set aside.

5. In a large stainless steel saucepan, combine sugar, mustard seeds, the remaining 1 tbsp (15 mL) dill seeds, vinegar and water. Bring to a boil over medium-high heat, stirring until sugar dissolves. Reduce heat and boil gently for 5 minutes.

When making pickles,
select uniformly sized
fruits and vegetables
and/or cut them into
pieces of similar size.
During processing, each
piece of produce should
be heated to the same
degree. If the pieces vary
too much in size, smaller
pieces will soften and
larger pieces may not be
heated sufficiently. In
addition to reduced
quality, inadequate heat
penetration can become
a safety issue.

Pickle fruits and
vegetables within
24 hours of harvest. If
your schedule does not
accommodate this brief
time window, refrigerate
the produce and use it
as soon as possible.

6. Transfer cucumbers to a colander placed over a sink and drain. Rinse thoroughly with cool running water and drain again, shaking off excess moisture. Add to pickling liquid and heat just until liquid begins to boil. Remove from heat.

7. Fill one jar at a time. Remove one jar from canner and empty hot water back into canner. (Do not dry jar.) Place jar on a tray or towel-covered counter. Place 2 tbsp (30 mL) pepper-dill mixture in jar. With a slotted spoon, transfer cucumber spears from hot liquid to jar, packing them snugly and leaving a generous $\frac{1}{2}$ inch (1 cm) headspace. Add hot pickling liquid to cover vegetables, leaving $\frac{1}{2}$ inch (1 cm) headspace. Slide a nonmetallic utensil, such as a rubber spatula, down between food and the inside of the jar two or three times to release air bubbles and settle the vegetables in the jar. Adjust headspace, if necessary, by adding hot pickling liquid. With a clean damp cloth or paper towel, wipe jar rim and threads to remove any food residue. Using a magnetic or nonmetallic utensil, lift hot lid from water and center it on jar. Place screw band on jar and, with your fingers, screw band down evenly and firmly, just until resistance is met, then increase to fingertip-tight. Do not over-tighten or use any tools to apply screw band. Return jar to canner rack and repeat until all vegetables are used.

8. When all jars are filled, lower rack into canner and ensure jars are completely covered by at least 1 inch (2.5 cm) of hot water. Cover canner and bring water to a full rolling boil over high heat. Process (continue boiling rapidly) for 10 minutes, starting timer only when water reaches a full rolling boil. At the end of the processing time, turn heat off and remove canner lid. Wait 5 minutes, then remove jars, without tilting. Place jars upright on a towel in a draft-free place and let cool, undisturbed, for 24 hours.

9. After 24 hours, check lids for seal. Remove screw bands and press down on the center of each lid with your finger. Sealed lids will be concave (they'll curve downward) and will show no movement when pressed. Jars that haven't sealed properly must be refrigerated immediately or reprocessed (see page 418). Rinse and dry screw bands. Wipe jars and, if desired, loosely reapply screw bands. Label jars and store in a cool, dry, dark place.

Continued on next page

Variations

Prepare approximately 12 cups (3 L) of one of these vegetables as directed below. Use in place of cucumbers.

Zucchini: Scrub and rinse zucchini; cut off stem end and a thin slice of blossom end. Cut in half lengthwise and into lengths appropriate to fit into jars, then cut zucchini halves into uniform-sized spears.

Mini-Carrots: Rinse mini-carrots and cut noticeably larger pieces in half. Or peel and rinse fresh carrots and cut into uniform sticks that are about 3 inches (7.5 cm) long.

Cauliflower: Wash and drain cauliflower; cut into small florets.

Asparagus: Rinse asparagus and break off tough end of each stalk. Cut into lengths appropriate for the jar you are using. The quantity of asparagus required will vary based on stalks' diameter.

Green or Yellow Beans: Wash thoroughly. Break off stem ends and leave whole.

Soft Spreads

Luscious raspberry jam slathered over hot whole-grain toast. Orchard-fresh oranges transformed into marmalade to enjoy with warm muffins. A glaze of red currant jelly to finish a succulent roast chicken. These are just a small sampling of the cornucopia of soft spreads contained in this chapter. Not only is it extremely satisfying to make your own, but when your family and friends sit down to enjoy these mouthwatering treats, you'll know they are experiencing flavors that just can't be store-bought.

• •

continued on next page

Conserves

Marmalades

Jellies

Gel Stage Tests

Soft spreads made without added pectin require a doneness test to ensure that a gel will form when the recipe cools. The most reliable gel stage test is the temperature test, but the sheet test and the refrigerator test will also work. If the test shows that the gel stage has not been reached, return the mixture to the heat to cook for a few minutes longer.

Temperature Test

Because elevation affects cooking temperatures, you must know the elevation of your home and/or the boiling temperature of water in your area to be able to use this test. Cook the soft spread until it reaches a temperature of 220°F (104°C), or 8°F (4°C) above the boiling point of water. Measure the temperature of soft spreads with a candy or jelly thermometer. Always insert the thermometer vertically into the soft spread and ensure that it does not contact the surface of the pot.

At or below 1,000 feet (305 m) above sea level, water boils at 212°F (100°C). At higher altitudes, subtract 2°F (1°C) for each added 1,000 feet (305 m) of elevation. For example, at 2,000 feet, you would cook the soft spread until it reaches a temperature of 218°F (103°C).

Sheet Test

Dip a cold metal spoon into the boiling soft spread. Lift the spoon and hold it horizontally and edge down so that the syrup runs off the edge. As the mixture cooks, the drops will become heavier and will drop off the spoon separately but two at a time. When the two drops join together and "sheet" off the spoon, the gel stage has been reached.

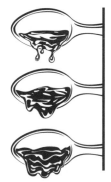

Beginning — Jelly drops are light and syrupy.

Drops become large and show signs of sheeting.

Sheeting (gel stage) jelly breaks from spoon in a sheet or flake.

Refrigerator Test

To prevent overcooking or scorching, remove the soft spread from the heat before performing this test. Chill two or three small saucers in the freezer. Place a teaspoonful (5 mL) of soft spread on the saucer and chill it in the freezer for 1 minute. Remove the saucer from the freezer and push the edge of the spread with your finger. A mixture that has reached the gel stage will be set, and the surface will wrinkle when the edge is pushed.

Jams

Jam, a thick mixture of fruit and sugar, boiled gently until the fruit is soft and almost formless, captures the taste of summer in a jar. Ideal as a spread for bread, jams also make wonderful fillings for pastries, cakes and cookies. They are becoming a standard ingredient for easy desserts, and many go well with cheese.

Jams with No Added Pectin

Jams prepared without added pectin have a softer, less set texture than jams prepared with added pectin. They must be cooked longer to evaporate moisture and concentrate fruit's natural pectin. Longer cooking produces a darker-colored product with a slightly caramelized flavor. Although jams with no added pectin generally require less added sugar in relation to the amount of fruit than those with added pectin, the longer cooking time reduces the yield and concentrates the sugar content. Before making any of the jams in this section, review the gel stage tests on page 21.

Old-Fashioned Jams

Old-fashioned jams are made just as your great-grandmother made them, without the use of commercial pectin. The only ingredients in these jams are fresh, sun-ripened fruit and sugar, although lemon juice or vinegar is sometimes added to help the jam set.

Apricot
Makes about nine 8-ounce (250 mL) jars

8 cups	chopped pitted peeled apricots	2 L
4 tbsp	lemon juice	60 mL
6 cups	granulated sugar	1.5 L

1. Prepare canner, jars and lids. *(For more information, see page 415.)*
2. In a large, deep stainless steel saucepan, combine apricots, lemon juice and sugar. Bring to a boil over medium heat, stirring constantly to dissolve sugar. Boil, stirring frequently, until mixture thickens. Remove from heat and test gel (see page 21). If gel stage has been reached, skim off foam.
3. Ladle hot jam into hot jars, leaving ¼ inch (0.5 cm) headspace. Remove air bubbles and adjust headspace, if necessary, by adding hot jam. Wipe rim. Center lid on jar. Screw band down until resistance is met, then increase to fingertip-tight.
4. Place jars in canner, ensuring they are completely covered with water. Bring to a boil and process for 10 minutes. Remove canner lid. Wait 5 minutes, then remove jars, cool and store. *(For more information, see pages 417–418.)*

TIPS

For long-boil soft spreads that do not use added pectin, use three parts fruit that is fully ripe to one part fruit that is slightly under-ripe. Under-ripe fruit generally has a higher pectin content, which helps these spreads form a gel.

When making long-boil jams, it is essential to maintain a close vigil on the boiling fruit mixture. As the spread thickens, it tends to stick to the pan and can easily burn if it is not stirred frequently and thoroughly. Using a heavy-bottomed, good-quality saucepan also helps to prevent scorching.

If your mixture has not reached the gel stage when first tested, return the pan to medium heat and cook, stirring constantly, for an additional 5 minutes. Repeat gel stage test and cooking as needed.

Berry

Makes about six 8-ounce (250 mL) jars

9 cups	crushed blackberries, blueberries, boysenberries, dewberries, gooseberries, loganberries, raspberries, youngberries or a combination of these berries	2.25 L
6 cups	granulated sugar	1.5 L

Elderberry

Makes about six 8-ounce (250 mL) jars

8 cups	crushed elderberries	2 L
¼ cup	white vinegar	50 mL
6 cups	granulated sugar	1.5 L

Strawberry

Makes about eight 8-ounce (250 mL) jars

8 cups	crushed hulled strawberries	2 L
6 cups	granulated sugar	1.5 L

Damson Plum

Makes about six 8-ounce (250 mL) jars

5 cups	coarsely chopped pitted Damson plums	1.25 L
3 cups	granulated sugar	750 mL
¾ cup	water	175 mL

Grape

Makes about six 8-ounce (250 mL) jars

8 cups	stemmed Concord, Muscadine or Scuppernong grapes	2 L
6 cups	granulated sugar	1.5 L

1. Using your fingers, pinch individual grapes, separating skins and pulp into two saucepans. Bring grape pulp to a boil over medium heat and boil, stirring frequently, until soft, about 10 minutes. Press pulp through a fine sieve and discard seeds. Set aside.

2. To the saucepan containing the grape skins, add enough water to prevent sticking. Bring to a boil over medium heat. Reduce heat, cover and boil gently until skins have softened and liquid is nearly evaporated, about 10 minutes. Combine skins and pulp in a large, deep stainless steel saucepan.

3. Continue following method for Old-Fashioned Apricot Jam, Steps 1 through 4.

Pineapple Jam

The taste of the tropics captured in this jam will add a ray of sunshine to winter meals. This jam also makes a wonderful, ready-to-use filling or topping for cakes.

TIP

If you have particularly hard water and use it in the boiling-water canner, it can leave a residue on jars. Use filtered or reverse-osmosis water to fill your canner instead.

Makes about three 8-ounce (250 mL) jars

4 cups	finely chopped peeled cored fresh pineapple	1 L
2½ cups	granulated sugar	625 mL
1	small lemon (unpeeled), seeded and thinly sliced	1
1 cup	water	250 mL

1. Prepare canner, jars and lids. *(For more information, see page 415.)*
2. In a large, deep stainless steel saucepan, combine pineapple, sugar, lemon and water. Bring to a boil over medium heat, stirring constantly to dissolve sugar. Boil, stirring frequently, until mixture thickens, about 15 minutes. Remove from heat and test gel (see page 21). If gel stage has been reached, skim off foam.
3. Ladle hot jam into hot jars, leaving ¼ inch (0.5 cm) headspace. Remove air bubbles and adjust headspace, if necessary, by adding hot jam. Wipe rim. Center lid on jar. Screw band down until resistance is met, then increase to fingertip-tight.
4. Place jars in canner, ensuring they are completely covered with water. Bring to a boil and process for 10 minutes. Remove canner lid. Wait 5 minutes, then remove jars, cool and store. *(For more information, see pages 417–418.)*

Apricot Red Currant Jam

Sweet apricots and tart red currants combine to create a delectable taste sensation that will brighten up your mornings.

TIP

To zest the lemon for this recipe, use a vegetable peeler to remove the yellow part of the peel in one long strip.

Makes about seven 8-ounce (250 mL) jars

5 cups	chopped pitted apricots (unpeeled)	1.25 L
4 cups	stemmed red currants	1 L
	Zest and juice of 1 large lemon (see tip, at left)	
7 cups	granulated sugar	1.75 L

1. Prepare canner, jars and lids. *(For more information, see page 415.)*
2. In a large, deep stainless steel saucepan, combine apricots, red currants and lemon zest and juice. Bring to a boil over medium-high heat. Gradually stir in sugar, stirring constantly to dissolve sugar. Boil hard, stirring frequently, until mixture thickens, about 15 minutes. Remove from heat and test gel (see page 21). If gel stage has been reached, skim off foam.

3. Ladle hot jam into hot jars, leaving ¼ inch (0.5 cm) headspace. Remove air bubbles and adjust headspace, if necessary, by adding hot jam. Wipe rim. Center lid on jar. Screw band down until resistance is met, then increase to fingertip-tight.

4. Place jars in canner, ensuring they are completely covered with water. Bring to a boil and process for 10 minutes. Remove canner lid. Wait 5 minutes, then remove jars, cool and store. *(For more information, see pages 417–418.)*

Raspberry Red Currant Jam

Most people find the seeds in red currants objectionable in soft spreads, but they love the sweet, tart taste of currants. This recipe offers the best of both worlds, using seeded currant pulp but leaving just a few seeds from the raspberries to provide an interesting texture.

TIP

To prepare red currant pulp, in a saucepan, heat 6 cups (1.5 L) red currants with ½ cup (125 mL) water over medium-high heat. Crush and stir until skins are softened, about 5 minutes. Press through a fine sieve or food mill to remove seeds.

Makes about four 8-ounce (250 mL) jars

2 cups	seeded red currant pulp (see tip, at left)	500 mL
2 cups	crushed red raspberries	500 mL
3 cups	granulated sugar	750 mL

1. Prepare canner, jars and lids. *(For more information, see page 415.)*

2. In a large, deep stainless steel saucepan, combine red currant pulp, raspberries and sugar. Bring to a boil over high heat, stirring constantly to dissolve sugar. Boil hard, stirring frequently, until mixture thickens, about 10 minutes. Remove from heat and test gel (see page 21). If gel stage has been reached, skim off foam.

3. Ladle hot jam into hot jars, leaving ¼ inch (0.5 cm) headspace. Remove air bubbles and adjust headspace, if necessary, by adding hot jam. Wipe rim. Center lid on jar. Screw band down until resistance is met, then increase to fingertip-tight.

4. Place jars in canner, ensuring they are completely covered with water. Bring to a boil and process for 10 minutes. Remove canner lid. Wait 5 minutes, then remove jars, cool and store. *(For more information, see pages 417–418.)*

Natural Summer Fruit Jams

Adding apples to berry and fruit jams extends the volume you produce. These recipes take advantage of apple's natural pectin content and mild flavor to create luscious, not-too-sweet spreads that are perfect for calorie-counters and those who don't have a home-grown berry patch or orchard.

TIP

Wash berries gently in small batches in a colander under cool running water to make sure you remove all dirt and grit and to avoid bruising the soft fruit.

Strawberry
Makes about eight 8-ounce (250 mL) jars

5	tart apples, such as Granny Smith, stem and blossom ends removed, chopped coarsely, cores intact	5
I	lemon or lime (unpeeled), finely chopped	I
	Water	
8 cups	halved hulled strawberries	2 L
5½ cups	granulated sugar	1.375 mL

1. In a large, deep stainless steel saucepan, combine apples, lemon and enough water to prevent sticking. Bring to a boil over high heat. Reduce heat, partially cover and boil gently, stirring occasionally, for 20 minutes, until mixture is very soft. Working in batches, transfer mixture to a fine sieve. With back of spoon, press mixture through sieve to yield 2 cups (500 mL) applesauce. Discard skins and cores.

2. Prepare canner, jars and lids. *(For more information, see page 415.)*

3. In a clean large, deep stainless steel saucepan, combine applesauce, strawberries and sugar. Bring to a boil over medium heat, stirring constantly to dissolve sugar. Boil, stirring frequently, until mixture thickens and mounds on a spoon, about 20 minutes. Remove from heat and skim off foam.

4. Ladle hot jam into hot jars, leaving ¼ inch (0.5 cm) headspace. Remove air bubbles and adjust headspace, if necessary, by adding hot jam. Wipe rim. Center lid on jar. Screw band down until resistance is met, then increase to fingertip-tight.

5. Place jars in canner, ensuring they are completely covered with water. Bring to a boil and process for 10 minutes. Remove canner lid. Wait 5 minutes, then remove jars, cool and store. *(For more information, see pages 417–418.)*

Blueberry
Makes about five 8-ounce (250 mL) jars

5	tart apples, stem and blossom ends removed, chopped coarsely, cores intact	5
2	limes (unpeeled), finely chopped	2
	Water	
4 cups	blueberries	I L
3 cups	granulated sugar	750 mL

For each of the following jams, follow the method for Strawberry Summer Fruit Jam, above, but use the quantity of fruit and sugar specified in the variation.

Raspberry

Makes about six 8-ounce (250 mL) jars

5	tart apples, stem and blossom ends removed, chopped coarsely, cores intact	5
1	lemon (unpeeled), finely chopped	1
	Water	
4 cups	raspberries	1 L
5 cups	granulated sugar	1.25 L

Red Currant

Makes about seven 8-ounce (250 mL) jars

5	tart apples, stem and blossom ends removed, chopped coarsely, cores intact	5
1	lemon (unpeeled), finely chopped	1
	Water	
6 cups	stemmed red currants	1.5 L
5½ cups	granulated sugar	1.375 L

Peach or Nectarine

Makes about seven 8-ounce (250 mL) jars

5	tart apples, stem and blossom ends removed, chopped coarsely, cores intact	5
2	lemons (unpeeled), finely chopped	2
	Water	
6 cups	chopped pitted peeled peaches or nectarines	1.5 L
5½ cups	granulated sugar	1.375 L

Plum

Makes about eight 8-ounce (250 mL) jars

5	tart apples, stem and blossom ends removed, chopped coarsely, cores intact	5
1	lemon (unpeeled), finely chopped	1
	Water	
6 cups	chopped pitted plums	1.5 L
5½ cups	granulated sugar	1.375 L

Spreadable Fieldberries

Light and luscious, these spreads showcase the natural sweetness and flavor of fruit because they are sweetened with frozen juice concentrates, with no added sugar. The addition of tart apples boosts the pectin content and adds body to these spreads. For best results, select fully ripe, sweet berries at the peak of quality and ripeness.

Cherry-Berries

Makes about seven 8-ounce (250 mL) jars

5	tart apples, peeled, cored and chopped	5
6 cups	halved hulled strawberries	1.5 L
3 cups	chopped pitted cherries	750 mL
3 cups	raspberries	750 mL
2	cans (each 12 oz/355 mL) undiluted frozen unsweetened apple juice concentrate, thawed	2

1. Prepare canner, jars and lids. (For more information, see page 415.)
2. In a large, deep stainless steel saucepan, combine apples, strawberries, cherries, raspberries and apple juice concentrate. Bring to a boil over medium-high heat, stirring constantly. Reduce heat and boil gently, stirring frequently while mashing fruit, until mixture thickens, about 45 minutes. Remove from heat and test gel (see page 21). If gel stage has been reached, skim off foam.
3. Ladle hot jam into hot jars, leaving ¼ inch (0.5 cm) headspace. Remove air bubbles and adjust headspace, if necessary, by adding hot jam. Wipe rim. Center lid on jar. Screw band down until resistance is met, then increase to fingertip-tight.
4. Place jars in canner, ensuring they are completely covered with water. Bring to a boil and process for 10 minutes. Remove canner lid. Wait 5 minutes, then remove jars, cool and store. (For more information, see pages 417–418.)

Blueberries

Makes about six 8-ounce (250 mL) jars

4	tart apples, peeled, cored and chopped	4
10 cups	blueberries	2.5 L
2	cans (each 12 oz/355 mL) undiluted frozen unsweetened grape juice concentrate, thawed	2

In Step 2, increase cooking time to about 60 minutes.

For each of the following jams, follow the method for Spreadable Cherry-Berries, above, but use the quantity of fruit and other ingredients specified in the variation and increase or decrease the cooking time in Step 2 as stated.

When making long-boil jams, it is essential to maintain a close vigil on the boiling fruit mixture. As the spread thickens, it tends to stick to the pan and can easily burn if it is not stirred frequently and thoroughly. Using a heavy-bottomed, good-quality saucepan also helps to prevent scorching.

If your mixture has not reached the gel stage when first tested, return the pan to medium heat and cook, stirring constantly, for an additional 5 minutes. Repeat gel stage test and cooking as needed.

Strawberries

Makes about seven 8-ounce (250 mL) jars

5	tart apples, peeled, cored and chopped	5
12 cups	halved hulled strawberries	3 L
2	cans (each 12 oz/355 mL) undiluted frozen unsweetened grape juice concentrate, thawed	2

In Step 2, decrease cooking time to about 30 minutes.

Rhuberries

Makes about six 8-ounce (250 mL) jars

4	tart apples, peeled, cored and chopped	4
5 cups	halved hulled strawberries	1.25 L
2 cups	finely chopped rhubarb	500 mL
2	cans (each 12 oz/355 mL) undiluted frozen unsweetened apple juice concentrate, thawed	2

In Step 2, increase cooking time to about 50 minutes.

Spicy Peaches

Makes about five 8-ounce (250 mL) jars

4	tart apples, peeled, cored and chopped	4
5 cups	chopped pitted peeled peaches	1.25 L
1	can (12 oz/355 mL) undiluted frozen unsweetened apple juice concentrate, thawed	1
½ tsp	grated lemon zest	2 mL
2 tbsp	lemon juice	30 mL
½ tsp	ground nutmeg	2 mL
½ tsp	ground ginger	2 mL

In Step 2, decrease cooking time to about 30 minutes.

Jams with Regular Powdered Fruit Pectin

Adding pectin to fruit mixtures shortens the cooking time to deliver a fresher-tasting product. Whether to use liquid or regular powdered pectin is a matter of preference, as the products produce similar results. When using a powdered fruit pectin, it is essential to fully dissolve the pectin in the fruit *before* adding the sugar. For best results, measure the sugar into a bowl so it can be added to the boiling jam all at once.

Powdered fruit pectin is sometimes sold in 49 g packages and sometimes in 57 g packages. The weight difference does not affect the performance of the product.

Traditional Jams

Traditional jams use powdered pectin to reduce the cooking time to 1 minute. There are two important things to remember when making jams with powdered fruit pectin. First, whisk the powdered pectin into the crushed fruit until it is dissolved, then bring the mixture to a boil, stirring frequently. This step is essential to dissolve the pectin. Then, and only then, add the sugar and return the mixture to a full rolling boil that cannot be stirred down.

Sweet Cherry

Makes about six 8-ounce (250 mL) jars

4 cups	chopped pitted sweet cherries	1 L
4 tbsp	lemon juice	60 mL
1/2 tsp	ground cinnamon (optional)	2 mL
1/2 tsp	ground cloves (optional)	2 mL
1/4 cup	amaretto liqueur (optional)	50 mL
1	package (1.75 oz/49 to 57 g) regular powdered fruit pectin	1
5 cups	granulated sugar	1.25 L

1. Prepare canner, jars and lids. *(For more information, see page 415.)*

2. In a large, deep stainless steel saucepan, combine cherries, lemon juice, cinnamon, cloves and amaretto liqueur, if using. Whisk in pectin until dissolved. Bring to a boil over high heat, stirring frequently. Add sugar all at once and return to a full rolling boil, stirring constantly. Boil hard, stirring constantly, for 1 minute. Remove from heat and skim off foam.

3. Ladle hot jam into hot jars, leaving 1/4 inch (0.5 cm) headspace. Remove air bubbles and adjust headspace, if necessary, by adding hot jam. Wipe rim. Center lid on jar. Screw band down until resistance is met, then increase to fingertip-tight.

4. Place jars in canner, ensuring they are completely covered with water. Bring to a boil and process for 10 minutes. Remove canner lid. Wait 5 minutes, then remove jars, cool and store. *(For more information, see pages 417–418.)*

For each of the following jams, follow the method for Traditional Sweet Cherry Jam, opposite, but use the quantity of fruit and other ingredients specified in the variation.

TIP

To cook black currants, in a large stainless steel saucepan, combine 8 cups (2 L) stemmed black currants and ¾ cup (175 mL) water. Bring to a boil over medium heat. Boil gently, crushing currants and stirring frequently, until skins are softened, about 15 minutes. Measure 5 cups (1.25 L).

TIP

To make plum pulp, in a large stainless steel saucepan, combine 8 cups (2 L) pitted plums and ½ cup (125 mL) water. Bring to a boil over medium heat. Reduce heat and boil gently, stirring occasionally, until plums are softened, about 5 minutes. Measure 6 cups (1.5 L) of pulp.

Apricot

Makes about eight 8-ounce (250 mL) jars

5 cups	finely chopped pitted fresh apricots	1.25 L
4 tbsp	lemon juice	60 mL
1	package (1.75 oz/49 to 57 g) regular powdered fruit pectin	1
7 cups	granulated sugar	1.75 L

Peach or Pear

Makes about six 8-ounce (250 mL) jars

4 cups	finely chopped pitted peeled peaches or finely chopped cored peeled fully ripe pears	1 L
2 tbsp	lemon juice	30 mL
1	package (1.75 oz/49 to 57 g) regular powdered fruit pectin	1
5 cups	granulated sugar	1.25 L

Berry or Black Currant

Makes about seven 8-ounce (250 mL) jars

5 cups	crushed blackberries, boysenberries, dewberries, loganberries, raspberries, youngberries or cooked black currants (see tip, at left)	1.25 L
1	package (1.75 oz/49 to 57 g) regular powdered fruit pectin	1
7 cups	granulated sugar	1.75 L

Mulberry

Makes about six 8-ounce (250 mL) jars

3 cups	crushed stemmed mulberries	750 mL
½ cup	lemon juice	125 mL
1	package (1.75 oz/49 to 57 g) regular powdered fruit pectin	1
6 cups	granulated sugar	1.5 L

Plum

Makes about eight 8-ounce (250 mL) jars

6 cups	cooked plum pulp (see tip, at left)	1.5 L
1	package (1.75 oz/49 to 57 g) regular powdered fruit pectin	1
8 cups	granulated sugar	2 L

Saskatoon Berry Jam

These earthy-flavored, purplish black berries grow wild throughout Western Canada and are now grown in a number of commercial operations. Make an effort to find them, as they add a new taste sensation to berry jam.

TIP

For 4½ cups (1.125 L) crushed Saskatoon berries, you'll need about 9 cups (2.25 L) whole berries.

For each of the following jams, follow the method for Saskatoon Berry Jam, above, but use the quantity of fruit and other ingredients specified in the variation.

Makes about seven 8-ounce (250 mL) jars

4½ cups	crushed Saskatoon berries (see tip, at left)	1.125 L
4 tbsp	lemon juice	60 mL
1	package (1.75 oz/49 to 57 g) regular powdered fruit pectin	1
6 cups	granulated sugar	1.5 L
2 tbsp	orange-flavored liqueur (optional)	30 mL

1. Prepare canner, jars and lids. *(For more information, see page 415.)*
2. In a large, deep stainless steel saucepan, combine berries and lemon juice. Whisk in pectin until dissolved. Bring to a boil over high heat, stirring frequently. Add sugar all at once and return to a full rolling boil, stirring constantly. Boil hard, stirring constantly, for 1 minute. Immediately stir in orange-flavored liqueur, if using. Remove from heat and skim off foam.
3. Ladle hot jam into hot jars, leaving ¼ inch (0.5 cm) headspace. Remove air bubbles and adjust headspace, if necessary, by adding hot jam. Wipe rim. Center lid on jar. Screw band down until resistance is met, then increase to fingertip-tight.
4. Place jars in canner, ensuring they are completely covered with water. Bring to a boil and process for 10 minutes. Remove canner lid. Wait 5 minutes, then remove jars, cool and store. *(For more information, see pages 417–418.)*

Strawberry Rhubarb Jam

Makes about six 8-ounce (250 mL) jars

2 cups	crushed hulled strawberries	500 mL
2 cups	chopped rhubarb	500 mL
4 tbsp	lemon juice	60 mL
1	package (1.75 oz/49 to 57 g) regular powdered fruit pectin	1
5½ cups	granulated sugar	1.375 L

Blueberry Lime Jam

Makes about six 8-ounce (250 mL) jars

4½ cups	crushed blueberries	1.125 L
	Grated zest and juice of 1 large lime	
1	package (1.75 oz/49 to 57 g) regular powdered fruit pectin	1
5 cups	granulated sugar	1.25 L

To peel and pit mangoes, make 4 lengthwise cuts to the pit. Cut into quarters, leaving about ¼ inch (0.5 cm) of fibrous flesh around the pit. Cut fruit from the peel and slice.

Mango Raspberry Jam

Makes about seven 8-ounce (250 mL) jars

3 cups	finely chopped pitted peeled mangoes (see tip, at left)	750 mL
1½ cups	crushed red raspberries	375 mL
2 tbsp	lemon juice	30 mL
I	package (1.75 oz/49 to 57 g) regular powdered fruit pectin	I
5½ cups	granulated sugar	1.375 L

Sweet Cherry Loganberry Jam

Makes about six 8-ounce (250 mL) jars

2 cups	chopped pitted dark sweet cherries	500 mL
2 cups	crushed loganberries	500 mL
I	package (1.75 oz/49 to 57 g) regular powdered fruit pectin	I
5 cups	granulated sugar	1.25 L

Heavenly Fig Jam

Start your day with a smile by sweetening your breakfast cereal with this delicious jam instead of sugar. Thought to be sacred by the ancients, figs were early symbols of peace and prosperity. Dried figs create a full-bodied yet mellow jam that is wonderful as a spread or a dessert sauce.

TIPS

For best results, measure the sugar into a bowl so it can be added to the boiling jam all at once.

Check your package of pectin for the expiration date and use only fresh pectin. Products that have expired may not set properly.

Makes about six 8-ounce (250 mL) jars

18 oz	dried figs	535 g
3¼ cups	water	800 mL
⅓ cup	orange juice	75 mL
1 tbsp	lemon juice	15 mL
1	package (1.75 oz/49 to 57 g) regular powdered fruit pectin	1
3½ cups	granulated sugar	875 mL
⅓ cup	orange-flavored liqueur (optional)	75 mL

1. Prepare canner, jars and lids. *(For more information, see page 415.)*

2. In a large, deep stainless steel saucepan, combine figs and water. Bring to a boil over medium-high heat, stirring frequently. Reduce heat, cover and boil gently until softened, about 20 minutes. Let cool slightly. Transfer to a food processor fitted with a metal blade and purée. Measure 3 cups (750 mL).

3. Return puréed figs to saucepan and add orange juice and lemon juice. Whisk in pectin until dissolved. Bring to a boil over high heat, stirring frequently. Add sugar all at once and return to a full rolling boil, stirring constantly. Boil hard, stirring constantly, for 1 minute. Immediately stir in orange-flavored liqueur, if using. Remove from heat and skim off foam.

4. Ladle hot jam into hot jars, leaving ¼ inch (0.5 cm) headspace. Remove air bubbles and adjust headspace, if necessary, by adding hot jam. Wipe rim. Center lid on jar. Screw band down until resistance is met, then increase to fingertip-tight.

5. Place jars in canner, ensuring they are completely covered with water. Bring to a boil and process for 10 minutes. Remove canner lid. Wait 5 minutes, then remove jars, cool and store. *(For more information, see pages 417–418.)*

Kiwi Daiquiri Jam

Now that kiwifruit are available year-round, this lovely emerald treat can be made anytime you need to add a touch of summer to your kitchen.

TIPS

The alcohol content of rum evaporates quickly when added to boiling jams, but if you prefer a liquor-free product, substitute 1 tsp (5 mL) rum flavoring.

Powdered fruit pectin is sometimes sold in 49 g packages and sometimes in 57 g packages. The weight difference does not affect the performance of the product.

Makes about four 8-ounce (250 mL) jars

2 cups	crushed peeled kiwifruit	500 mL
⅔ cup	unsweetened pineapple juice	150 mL
⅓ cup	lime juice	75 mL
1	package (1.75 oz/49 to 57 g) regular powdered fruit pectin	1
3 cups	granulated sugar	750 mL
¼ cup	rum	50 mL
	Green food coloring (optional)	

1. Prepare canner, jars and lids. *(For more information, see page 415.)*
2. In a large, deep stainless steel saucepan, combine kiwifruit, pineapple juice and lime juice. Whisk in pectin until dissolved. Bring to a boil over high heat, stirring frequently. Add sugar all at once and return to a full rolling boil, stirring constantly. Boil hard, stirring constantly, for 1 minute. Immediately stir in rum and tint with a few drops of green food coloring, if using. Remove from heat and skim off foam.
3. Ladle hot jam into hot jars, leaving ¼ inch (0.5 cm) headspace. Remove air bubbles and adjust headspace, if necessary, by adding hot jam. Wipe rim. Center lid on jar. Screw band down until resistance is met, then increase to fingertip-tight.
4. Place jars in canner, ensuring they are completely covered with water. Bring to a boil and process for 10 minutes. Remove canner lid. Wait 5 minutes, then remove jars, cool and store. *(For more information, see pages 417–418.)*

Orange Plum Jam

The flavor of orange infuses this summer favorite with a delightfully intriguing note.

TIPS

For best results, measure the sugar into a bowl so it can be added to the boiling jam all at once.

Refer to the Produce Purchase Guide on pages 426–429 to determine how much produce you'll need to buy to prepare this recipe.

Makes about six 8-ounce (250 mL) jars

5 cups	finely chopped pitted plums	1.25 L
2 tbsp	grated orange zest	30 mL
1	package (1.75 oz/49 to 57 g) regular powdered fruit pectin	1
5½ cups	granulated sugar	1.375 L
¼ cup	orange-flavored liqueur (optional)	50 mL

1. Prepare canner, jars and lids. *(For more information, see page 415.)*

2. In a large, deep stainless steel saucepan, combine plums and orange zest. Whisk in pectin until dissolved. Bring to a boil over high heat, stirring frequently. Add sugar all at once and return to a full rolling boil, stirring constantly. Boil hard, stirring constantly, for 1 minute. Immediately stir in orange-flavored liqueur, if using. Remove from heat and skim off foam.

3. Ladle hot jam into hot jars, leaving ¼ inch (0.5 cm) headspace. Remove air bubbles and adjust headspace, if necessary, by adding hot jam. Wipe rim. Center lid on jar. Screw band down until resistance is met, then increase to fingertip-tight.

4. Place jars in canner, ensuring they are completely covered with water. Bring to a boil and process for 10 minutes. Remove canner lid. Wait 5 minutes, then remove jars, cool and store. *(For more information, see pages 417–418.)*

Rhubarb Orange Jam

Citrus and rhubarb marry to produce a robust jam that is quick and easy to prepare. It is amazing on crumpets and wonderful as a filling for layer cakes.

TIP

Check your package of pectin for the expiration date and use only fresh pectin. Products that have expired may not set properly.

Makes about seven 8-ounce (250 mL) jars

2	oranges	2
5 cups	finely chopped rhubarb	1.25 L
1	package (1.75 oz/49 to 57 g) regular powdered fruit pectin	1
6 cups	granulated sugar	1.5 L

1. Prepare canner, jars and lids. *(For more information, see page 415.)*
2. Using a vegetable peeler, remove peel from half of one orange. Cut peel into very thin slivers, about 1 inch (2.5 cm) long, and set aside. Squeeze juice from both oranges into a measure, adding water if necessary, to yield 1 cup (250 mL).
3. In a large, deep stainless steel saucepan, combine orange juice, slivered orange peel and rhubarb. Whisk in pectin until dissolved. Bring to a boil over high heat, stirring frequently. Add sugar all at once and return to a full rolling boil, stirring constantly. Boil hard, stirring constantly, for 1 minute. Remove from heat and skim off foam.
4. Ladle hot jam into hot jars, leaving ¼ inch (0.5 cm) headspace. Remove air bubbles and adjust headspace, if necessary, by adding hot jam. Wipe rim. Center lid on jar. Screw band down until resistance is met, then increase to fingertip-tight.
5. Place jars in canner, ensuring they are completely covered with water. Bring to a boil and process for 10 minutes. Remove canner lid. Wait 5 minutes, then remove jars, cool and store. *(For more information, see pages 417–418.)*

Mom's Apple Pie in a Jar

If you're a fan of apple pie — and who isn't? — you will love this luscious apple jam. Serve it on bread or use it more creatively in mini-tarts or as a dessert topping. You're certain to receive rave reviews for its good taste.

TIPS

For best results, measure the sugar into a bowl so it can be added to the boiling jam all at once.

Refer to the Produce Purchase Guide on pages 426–429 to determine how much produce you'll need to buy to prepare this recipe.

Makes about six 8-ounce (250 mL) jars

¾ cup	raisins or dried cranberries	175 mL
6 cups	chopped cored peeled Granny Smith or other tart apples	1.5 L
	Grated zest and juice of 1 lemon	
1 cup	unsweetened apple juice	250 mL
1	package (1.75 oz/49 to 57 g) regular powdered fruit pectin	1
9 cups	granulated sugar	2.25 L
1 tsp	ground cinnamon	5 mL
½ tsp	ground nutmeg	2 mL

1. Prepare canner, jars and lids. *(For more information, see page 415.)*

2. In a food processor fitted with a metal blade, pulse raisins until finely chopped. Set aside.

3. In a large, deep stainless steel saucepan, combine apples and lemon zest and juice. Bring to a boil over high heat, stirring frequently. Reduce heat and boil gently, stirring occasionally, until apples begin to soften, about 10 minutes. Remove from heat and whisk in pectin until dissolved. Stir in raisins. Return to high heat and bring to a boil, stirring frequently. Add sugar all at once and return to a full rolling boil, stirring constantly. Boil hard, stirring constantly, for 1 minute. Remove from heat and stir in cinnamon and nutmeg. Skim off foam.

4. Ladle hot jam into hot jars, leaving ¼ inch (0.5 cm) headspace. Remove air bubbles and adjust headspace, if necessary, by adding hot jam. Wipe rim. Center lid on jar. Screw band down until resistance is met, then increase to fingertip-tight.

5. Place jars in canner, ensuring they are completely covered with water. Bring to a boil and process for 10 minutes. Remove canner lid. Wait 5 minutes, then remove jars, cool and store. *(For more information, see pages 417–418.)*

Carrot Cake Jam

Sweetened with crushed pineapple and spices, this sunny fall jam tastes just like carrot cake. It makes a perfect gift for any occasion.

TIPS

Turn this delicious jam into a conserve by stirring in ¼ cup (50 mL) chopped pecans or walnuts immediately after completing the 1-minute boil. Stir thoroughly and remove from heat.

Powdered fruit pectin is sometimes sold in 49 g packages and sometimes in 57 g packages. The weight difference does not affect the performance of the product.

Makes about six 8-ounce (250 mL) jars

1½ cups	finely grated peeled carrots	375 mL
1½ cups	chopped cored peeled pears	375 mL
1¾ cups	canned pineapple, including juice	425 mL
3 tbsp	lemon juice	45 mL
1 tsp	ground cinnamon	5 mL
½ tsp	ground nutmeg	2 mL
½ tsp	ground cloves	2 mL
1	package (1.75 oz/49 to 57 g) regular powdered fruit pectin	1
6½ cups	granulated sugar	1.625 L

1. Prepare canner, jars and lids. *(For more information, see page 415.)*

2. In a large, deep stainless steel saucepan, combine carrots, pears, pineapple with juice, lemon juice, cinnamon, nutmeg and cloves. Bring to a boil over high heat, stirring frequently. Reduce heat, cover and boil gently for 20 minutes, stirring occasionally. Remove from heat and whisk in pectin until dissolved. Bring to a boil over high heat, stirring frequently. Add sugar all at once and return to a full rolling boil, stirring constantly. Boil hard, stirring constantly, for 1 minute. Remove from heat and skim off foam.

3. Ladle hot jam into hot jars, leaving ¼ inch (0.5 cm) headspace. Remove air bubbles and adjust headspace, if necessary, by adding hot jam. Wipe rim. Center lid on jar. Screw band down until resistance is met, then increase to fingertip-tight.

4. Place jars in canner, ensuring they are completely covered with water. Bring to a boil and process for 10 minutes. Remove canner lid. Wait 5 minutes, then remove jars, cool and store. *(For more information, see pages 417–418.)*

Jams with Liquid Pectin

Unlike soft spreads made with powdered pectin, when making jams with liquid pectin, the fruit, lemon juice (if required) and sugar are brought to a boil before the pectin is added. To form a good gel, it is essential to bring the fruit–sugar mixture to a full rolling boil that cannot be stirred down, stir in the entire contents of the liquid pectin pouch, then boil hard for 1 minute longer.

Quick Jams

Jams made with liquid pectin need the least cooking time of all cooked jams. Liquid pectin is predissolved and ready to bond with a briefly cooked mixture of fruit and sugar.

TIP

Some brands of liquid pectin direct you to stir in the pectin *after* boiling the fruit–sugar mixture for 1 minute. It is advisable to follow the directions given by the brand you are using when preparing these recipes.

For each of the following jams, follow the method for Quick Apricot Jam, above, but use the quantity of fruit and other ingredients specified in the variation.

Apricot

Makes about six 8-ounce (250 mL) jars

3½ cups	finely chopped pitted fresh apricots	875 mL
⅓ cup	lemon juice	75 mL
5¾ cups	granulated sugar	1.425 L
I	pouch (3 oz/85 mL) liquid pectin	I

1. Prepare canner, jars and lids. *(For more information, see page 415.)*
2. In a large, deep stainless steel saucepan, combine apricots, lemon juice and sugar. Over high heat, stirring constantly, bring to a full rolling boil that cannot be stirred down. Stir in pectin. Boil hard, stirring constantly, for 1 minute. Remove from heat and skim off foam.
3. Ladle hot jam into hot jars, leaving ¼ inch (0.5 cm) headspace. Remove air bubbles and adjust headspace, if necessary, by adding hot jam. Wipe rim. Center lid on jar. Screw band down until resistance is met, then increase to fingertip-tight.
4. Place jars in canner, ensuring they are completely covered with water. Bring to a boil and process for 10 minutes. Remove canner lid. Wait 5 minutes, then remove jars, cool and store. *(For more information, see pages 417–418.)*

Berry

Makes about eight 8-ounce (250 mL) jars

4 cups	crushed blackberries, boysenberries, dewberries or youngberries	I L
2 tbsp	lemon juice	30 mL
7 cups	granulated sugar	1.75 L
I	pouch (3 oz/85 mL) liquid pectin	I

TIP

Check your package of pectin for the expiration date and use only fresh pectin. Products that have expired may not set properly.

Bumbleberry

Makes about five 8-ounce (250 mL) jars

1 cup	crushed blueberries	250 mL
1 cup	crushed raspberries	250 mL
1 cup	crushed hulled strawberries	250 mL
6 cups	granulated sugar	1.5 L
1	pouch (3 oz/85 mL) liquid pectin	1

Blueberry

Makes about eight 8-ounce (250 mL) jars

4½ cups	crushed blueberries	1.125 L
4 tbsp	lemon juice	60 mL
7 cups	granulated sugar	1.75 L
2	pouches (each 3 oz/85 mL) liquid pectin	2

Gooseberry

Makes about six 8-ounce (250 mL) jars

3¾ cups	crushed gooseberries	925 mL
2 tbsp	lemon juice	30 mL
6 cups	granulated sugar	1.5 L
1	pouch (3 oz/85 mL) liquid pectin	1

TIP

To make 2 cups (500 mL) raspberry pulp, working in batches, push 4 to 5 cups (1 to 1.25 L) raspberries through a fine sieve. Discard seeds.

Raspberry

Makes about six 8-ounce (250 mL) jars

2 cups	seeded raspberry pulp (see tip, at left)	500 mL
2 cups	crushed raspberries (including seeds)	500 mL
6½ cups	granulated sugar	1.625 L
1	pouch (3 oz/85 mL) liquid pectin	1

Strawberry

Makes about eight 8-ounce (250 mL) jars

3¾ cups	crushed hulled strawberries	925 mL
4 tbsp	lemon juice	60 mL
7 cups	granulated sugar	1.75 L
1	pouch (3 oz/85 mL) liquid pectin	1

continued on next page

For each of the following jams, follow the method for Quick Apricot Jam, page 40, but use the quantity of fruit and other ingredients specified in the variation.

Peach

Makes about eight 8-ounce (250 mL) jars

4 cups	finely chopped pitted peeled peaches	I L
4 tbsp	lemon juice	60 mL
7½ cups	granulated sugar	1.875 L
I	pouch (3 oz/85 mL) liquid pectin	I

Cinnamon Pear

Makes about six 8-ounce (250 mL) jars

4 cups	chopped cored peeled fully ripe pears, such as Bartlett	I L
⅓ cup	lemon juice	75 mL
7½ cups	granulated sugar	1.875 mL
I tsp	ground cinnamon	5 mL
I	pouch (3 oz/85 mL) liquid pectin	I

Add the cinnamon along with the sugar.

Cherry

Makes about six 8-ounce (250 mL) jars

4 cups	finely chopped pitted sweet or tart cherries	I L
2 tbsp	lemon juice (if using sweet cherries)	30 mL
6¼ cups	granulated sugar	1.55 L
2	pouches (each 3 oz/85 mL) liquid pectin	2

TIP

If using tart cherries to make this jam, omit the lemon juice.

Sundae in a Jar

One taste of this spread and you'll think you are indulging in an ice cream sundae. Use it as a jam, as a dessert topping or on ice cream. Add a sliced banana and enjoy a split!

TIP

To make 2½ cups (625 mL) crushed strawberries, you'll need about 4 cups (1 L) whole strawberries. To make 1⅓ cups (325 mL) crushed raspberries, you'll need about 2 cups (500 mL) whole raspberries.

If you are a fan of chocolate fondue, you are sure to love this classy peach jam. With a hint of chocolate liqueur, this soft-set jam makes a wonderful topping for ice cream and crêpes. **Follow the method for Sundae in a Jar, above.**

Makes about six 8-ounce (250 mL) jars

2½ cups	crushed hulled strawberries	625 mL
1⅓ cups	crushed raspberries	325 mL
6 cups	granulated sugar	1.5 L
1	pouch (3 oz/85 mL) liquid pectin	1
⅓ cup	chocolate-flavored liqueur	75 mL

1. Prepare canner, jars and lids. *(For more information, see page 415.)*
2. In a large, deep stainless steel saucepan, combine strawberries, raspberries and sugar. Over high heat, stirring constantly, bring to a full rolling boil that cannot be stirred down. Stir in pectin. Boil hard, stirring constantly, for 1 minute. Stir in chocolate-flavored liqueur. Remove from heat and skim off foam.
3. Ladle hot jam into hot jars, leaving ¼ inch (0.5 cm) headspace. Remove air bubbles and adjust headspace, if necessary, by adding hot jam. Wipe rim. Center lid on jar. Screw band down until resistance is met, then increase to fingertip-tight.
4. Place jars in canner, ensuring they are completely covered with water. Bring to a boil and process for 10 minutes. Remove canner lid. Wait 5 minutes, then remove jars, cool and store. *(For more information, see pages 417–418.)*

Peach Fondue

Makes about seven 8-ounce (250 mL) jars

4 cups	finely chopped pitted peeled peaches	1 L
4 tbsp	lemon juice	60 mL
5½ cups	granulated sugar	1.375 L
1	pouch (3 oz/85 mL) liquid fruit pectin	1
⅓ cup	chocolate-flavored liqueur	75 mL

Easy Grape Jam

Using seedless grapes to prepare grape jam produces a delicious whole-grape jam and eliminates the steps needed separate skin, pulp and seeds.

TIP

Check your package of pectin for the expiration date and use only fresh pectin. Products that have expired may not set properly.

Makes about eight 8-ounce (250 mL) jars

3½ lbs	Sovereign or other seedless blue grapes	1.6 kg
½ cup	water	125 mL
7½ cups	granulated sugar	1.875 L
1	pouch (3 oz/85 mL) liquid pectin	1

1. Prepare canner, jars and lids. *(For more information, see page 415.)*
2. In a large, deep stainless steel saucepan, combine grapes and water. Bring to a boil over medium heat, stirring frequently. Partially cover, reduce heat and boil gently, stirring occasionally, for 5 minutes. Remove from heat and measure 4½ cups (1.125 L) grapes and liquid.
3. Return grape mixture to saucepan and add sugar. Over high heat, stirring constantly, bring to a full rolling boil that cannot be stirred down. Stir in pectin. Boil hard, stirring constantly, for 1 minute. Remove from heat and skim off foam.
4. Ladle hot jam into hot jars, leaving ¼ inch (0.5 cm) headspace. Remove air bubbles and adjust headspace, if necessary, by adding hot jam. Wipe rim. Center lid on jar. Screw band down until resistance is met, then increase to fingertip-tight.
5. Place jars in canner, ensuring they are completely covered with water. Bring to a boil and process for 10 minutes. Remove canner lid. Wait 5 minutes, then remove jars, cool and store. *(For more information, see pages 417–418.)*

Autumn Cranberry Pear Jam

With a hint of cinnamon, and dried cranberries for dazzle, this jam is the perfect way to warm up chilly autumn days.

TIP

Be sure to use fully ripe, juicy pears that can easily be crushed to give you the proper measurement and allow for enough liquid to dissolve the sugar.

Makes about six 8-ounce (250 mL) jars

3 cups	crushed cored peeled pears	750 mL
⅔ cup	coarsely chopped dried cranberries	150 mL
¼ cup	unsweetened apple juice	50 mL
¼ cup	bottled lemon juice	50 mL
5½ cups	granulated sugar	1.375 L
1 tsp	ground cinnamon	5 mL
1	pouch (3 oz/85 mL) liquid pectin	1

1. Prepare canner, jars and lids. *(For more information, see page 415.)*
2. In a large, deep stainless steel saucepan, combine pears, cranberries, apple juice, lemon juice, sugar and cinnamon. Over high heat, stirring constantly, bring to a full rolling boil that cannot be stirred down. Stir in pectin. Boil hard, stirring constantly, for 1 minute. Remove from heat and skim off foam.

3. Ladle hot jam into hot jars, leaving ¼ inch (0.5 cm) headspace. Remove air bubbles and adjust headspace, if necessary, by adding hot jam. Wipe rim. Center lid on jar. Screw band down until resistance is met, then increase to fingertip-tight.
4. Place jars in canner, ensuring they are completely covered with water. Bring to a boil and process for 10 minutes. Remove canner lid. Wait 5 minutes, then remove jars, cool and store. (*For more information, see pages 417–418.*)

Spiced Golden Plum Jam

Adding a hint of island spice to plentiful golden plums produces a delicious jam with exotic overtones.

TIPS

A jar lifter is very helpful for handling hot, wet jars. Because they are bulky and fit loosely, oven mitts — even water-resistent types — are not a wise choice. When filling jars, an all-purpose rubber glove, worn on your helper hand, will allow you to steady the jar.

If desired, add 4 tbsp (60 mL) dark rum immediately after adding the liquid pectin. Stir well.

Makes about seven 8-ounce (250 mL) jars

I	cinnamon stick (about 4 inches/10 cm), broken into pieces	I
4 to 6	cardamom pods	4 to 6
3½ lbs	golden plums, halved and pitted	1.6 kg
½ cup	unsweetened apple juice	125 mL
6⅔ cups	granulated sugar	1.65 L
I	pouch (3 oz/85 mL) liquid pectin	I

1. Prepare canner, jars and lids. (*For more information, see page 415.*)
2. Tie cinnamon stick and cardamom pods in a square of cheesecloth, creating a spice bag.
3. In a large, deep stainless steel saucepan, combine plums, apple juice and spice bag. Bring to a boil over medium heat, stirring frequently. Partially cover, reduce heat and boil gently, stirring occasionally, for 5 minutes. Remove from heat and discard spice bag. Measure 4½ cups (1.125 L) of the cooked mixture.
4. Return plum mixture to saucepan and add sugar. Over high heat, stirring constantly, bring to a full rolling boil that cannot be stirred down. Stir in pectin. Boil hard, stirring constantly, for 1 minute. Remove from heat and skim off foam.
5. Ladle hot jam into hot jars, leaving ¼ inch (0.5 cm) headspace. Remove air bubbles and adjust headspace, if necessary, by adding hot jam. Wipe rim. Center lid on jar. Screw band down until resistance is met, then increase to fingertip-tight.
6. Place jars in canner, ensuring they are completely covered with water. Bring to a boil and process for 10 minutes. Remove canner lid. Wait 5 minutes, then remove jars, cool and store. (*For more information, see pages 417–418.*)

Freezer Jams

Making freezer jam is extremely easy: You just chop or crush the fruit and stir in sugar and freezer jam pectin. You can serve the delicious result immediately or freeze it for future use. Better yet, since most freezer jams require no cooking, they retain the beautiful color and flavor of just-picked fruit. There's only one risk — you may get addicted!

Most powdered and liquid pectin products include recipes for single-fruit, no-cook freezer spreads. Unfortunately, many of those recipes require relatively high proportions of sugar to fruit. Our recipes use special powdered freezer jam pectin, sold in pouches where food and home canning supplies are stocked. Using this product, we've been able to develop recipes that require a limited amount of added sweetener — just enough to enhance the fruit's natural sweet flavor without overpowering it.

> If you prefer, an equal amount of Splenda No Calorie Sweetener® may be substituted for the granulated sugar in these recipes. Other artificial sweeteners are not suitable substitutes.

··

Blueberry Nectarine Freezer Jam

In this recipe, we've heated the crushed blueberries to soften the skins and enhance the flavor. Heat also inactivates an enzyme that tends to weaken pectin. This jam is delicious spooned over pound cake or angel food cake, as well as slathered on bread.

Makes about five 8-ounce (250 mL) jars

1 cup	crushed blueberries	250 mL
1½ cups	granulated sugar	375 mL
1	pouch (1.59 oz/45 g) freezer jam pectin	1
3 cups	finely chopped pitted peeled nectarines	750 mL
1 tbsp	grated lemon zest	15 mL
1 tsp	lemon juice	5 mL

1. In a glass pie plate, heat blueberries in a microwave oven on High, stopping the microwave several times to stir and crush the berries, until the mixture reaches a boil, about 2 minutes.

2. In a medium bowl, combine sugar and pectin, stirring until well blended. Add blueberries, nectarines and lemon zest and juice. Stir for 3 minutes.

3. Ladle jam into plastic or glass freezer jars, leaving ½ inch (1 cm) headspace. Apply lids tightly. Let jam stand at room temperature until thickened, about 30 minutes. Serve immediately, if desired. For longer storage, refrigerate for up to 3 weeks or freeze for up to 1 year.

Raspberry Chipotle Freezer Jam

Accenting sweet fruit with smoky heat creates a spread that can be served as a sweet or a savory complement to both entrées and side dishes.

TIP

Chipotle peppers in adobo sauce freeze well. Separate any extra peppers into batches of two and freeze them, with sauce, in small freezer bags.

Makes about five 8-ounce (250 mL) jars

1½ cups	granulated sugar	375 mL
1	pouch (1.59 oz/45 g) freezer jam pectin	1
2	chipotle peppers in adobo sauce (see tip, at left)	2
4 cups	crushed red raspberries	1 L

1. In a medium bowl, combine sugar and pectin, stirring until well blended. Set aside.
2. If desired, remove seeds from chipotle peppers. In a mini-chopper or with a knife, finely chop peppers, getting as close as possible to a purée. Combine peppers and 2 tbsp (30 mL) adobo sauce. Add pepper mixture and raspberries to pectin mixture. Stir for 3 minutes.
3. Ladle jam into plastic or glass freezer jars, leaving ½ inch (1 cm) headspace. Apply lids tightly. Let jam stand at room temperature until thickened, about 30 minutes. Serve immediately, if desired. For longer storage, refrigerate for up to 3 weeks or freeze for up to 1 year.

Blushing Peach Almond Freezer Conserve

Luscious peaches and sweet cherries combine with crunchy almonds to make a divine crêpe filling, croissant spread or ice cream topping.

TIP

To toast almonds, place on a baking sheet and bake in a preheated 350°F (180°C) oven, stirring occasionally, for about 5 minutes or until golden.

Makes about five 8-ounce (250 mL) jars

1½ cups	granulated sugar	375 mL
1	pouch (1.59 oz/45 g) freezer jam pectin	1
3½ cups	finely chopped pitted peeled peaches	875 mL
4 tbsp	chopped drained maraschino cherries	60 mL
1 tbsp	lemon juice	15 mL
3 tbsp	slivered almonds, toasted	45 mL
¼ tsp	almond extract	1 mL

1. In a medium bowl, combine sugar and pectin, stirring until well blended. Add peaches, cherries, lemon juice, almonds and almond extract. Stir for 3 minutes.
2. Ladle jam into plastic or glass freezer jars, leaving ½ inch (1 cm) headspace. Apply lids tightly. Let jam stand at room temperature until thickened, about 30 minutes. Serve immediately, if desired. For longer storage, refrigerate for up to 3 weeks or freeze for up to 1 year.

Tropical Breeze Freezer Jam

Liven up breakfasts and teatime with this tasty jam, made with seasonally fresh pineapple.

TIP

You can use either sweetened or unsweetened coconut in this recipe.

Makes about five 8-ounce (250 mL) jars

1½ cups	granulated sugar	375 mL
1	pouch (1.59 oz/45 g) freezer jam pectin	1
2 cups	finely chopped drained canned pineapple	500 mL
1 cup	mashed banana	250 mL
¾ cup	chopped seeded drained mandarin orange segments	175 mL
¼ cup	flaked or shredded coconut	50 mL

1. In a medium bowl, combine sugar and pectin, stirring until well blended. Add pineapple, banana, oranges and coconut. Stir for 3 minutes.

2. Ladle jam into plastic or glass freezer jars, leaving ½ inch (1 cm) headspace. Apply lids tightly. Let jam stand at room temperature until thickened, about 30 minutes. Serve immediately, if desired. For longer storage, refrigerate for up to 3 weeks or freeze for up to 1 year.

For each of the following jams, follow the method for Tropical Breeze Freezer Jam, above, but use the quantity of sugar, pectin and fruit specified in the variation.

Fieldberry Feast Freezer Jam

Makes about five 8-ounce (250 mL) jars

1½ cups	granulated sugar	375 mL
1	pouch (1.59 oz/45 g) freezer jam pectin	1
2 cups	crushed hulled strawberries	500 mL
1 cup	crushed red raspberries	250 mL
1 cup	crushed blackberries	250 mL

Variation

If desired, substitute blueberries for the blackberries and/or use black raspberries instead of red.

TIP

Wash berries gently in small batches in a colander under cool running water to make sure you remove all dirt and grit and to avoid bruising the soft fruit.

Peach Melba Freezer Jam

Makes about five 8-ounce (250 mL) jars

1½ cups	granulated sugar	375 mL
1	pouch (1.59 oz/45 g) freezer jam pectin	1
2½ cups	finely chopped pitted peeled peaches	625 mL
1 cup	crushed raspberries	250 mL
1 tbsp	lemon juice	15 mL

TIP
Refer to the Produce Purchase Guide on pages 426–429 to determine how much produce you'll need to buy to prepare this recipe.

Strawberry Kiwi Freezer Jam

Makes about five 8-ounce (250 mL) jars

1 1/2 cups	granulated sugar	375 mL
1	pouch (1.59 oz/45 g) freezer jam pectin	1
2 cups	crushed hulled strawberries	500 mL
2 cups	diced peeled kiwifruit	500 mL

Variations

Gingered Strawberry Kiwi Freezer Jam: Add ¾ tsp (4 mL) minced crystallized ginger to fruit mixture before stirring.

Margarita-Style Strawberry Kiwi Freezer Jam: Increase strawberries to 3 cups (750 mL) and decrease kiwifruit to 1 cup (250 mL). Add the grated zest of 1 small lime and 2 tbsp (30 mL) tequila with the fruit mixture before stirring.

Strawberry Banana Freezer Jam: Substitute 2 cups (500 mL) mashed bananas for the kiwifruit.

Mango Raspberry Freezer Jam

Makes about five 8-ounce (250 mL) jars

1 1/2 cups	granulated sugar	375 mL
1	pouch (1.59 oz/45 g) freezer jam pectin	1
3 cups	finely chopped pitted peeled mangoes	750 mL
1 cup	crushed red raspberries	250 mL

Gingery Peach Pear Freezer Jam

Makes about five 8-ounce (250 mL) jars

1 1/2 cups	granulated sugar	375 mL
1	pouch (1.59 oz/45 g) freezer jam pectin	1
3 cups	crushed pitted peeled peaches	750 mL
1 cup	grated cored peeled pears	250 mL
1 tbsp	grated gingerroot	15 mL
	Grated zest and juice of 1 small lemon	

Plum Orange Freezer Jam

Orange adds flavor and texture to this tasty spread, which is sure to become a breakfast favorite.

TIPS

Be sure to wash jars and lids and rinse thoroughly before filling with freezer jam.

Freezer jams make excellent dessert sauces.

Makes about five 8-ounce (250 mL) jars

10	medium blue plums, halved and pitted	10
½ cup	water	125 mL
1	small orange	1
1½ cups	granulated sugar	375 mL
½ tsp	ground mace or nutmeg	2 mL
1	pouch (1.59 oz/45 g) freezer jam pectin	1

1. In a medium saucepan, combine plums and water. Bring to a boil over medium heat. Reduce heat, cover and boil gently until plums are softened and most of the liquid is evaporated, about 5 minutes. Measure 3¾ cups (925 mL) cooked plums and liquid.

2. Grate 1 tsp (5 mL) zest from orange and cut orange in half. Using a spoon, scoop out ¼ cup (50 mL) orange pulp and chop finely. Add orange zest and pulp to plums.

3. In a medium bowl, combine sugar, mace and pectin, stirring until well blended. Add fruit mixture. Stir for 3 minutes.

4. Ladle jam into plastic or glass freezer jars, leaving ½ inch (1 cm) headspace. Apply lids tightly. Let jam stand at room temperature until thickened, about 30 minutes. Serve immediately, if desired. For longer storage, refrigerate for up to 3 weeks or freeze for up to 1 year.

Spiced Apple Pear Freezer Butter

This spread, which keeps the quantity of sugar and the cooking time to a minimum, resembles old-fashioned fruit butters with sparkling fresh fruit flavor.

TIP

Refer to the Produce Purchase Guide on pages 426–429 to determine how much produce you'll need to buy to prepare this recipe.

Makes about five 8-ounce (250 mL) jars

4 cups	chopped cored peeled apples	1 L
4 cups	chopped cored peeled pears	1 L
¼ cup	water	50 mL
1 cup	granulated sugar	250 mL
1	pouch (1.59 oz/45 g) freezer jam pectin	1
¾ tsp	ground cinnamon	4 mL
¼ tsp	ground cloves (optional)	1 mL
¼ tsp	ground nutmeg	1 mL
¼ tsp	ground allspice	1 mL
½ cup	lightly packed brown sugar	125 mL

1. In a medium saucepan, combine apples, pears and water. Bring to a boil over medium heat. Reduce heat, cover and boil gently until fruit is softened, about 5 minutes. Using a potato masher, crush fruit. Measure 4 cups (1 L).

2. In a medium bowl, combine granulated sugar, pectin, cinnamon, cloves, if using, nutmeg and allspice, stirring until well blended. Add brown sugar and cooked fruit. Stir for 3 minutes.

3. Ladle jam into plastic or glass freezer jars, leaving ½ inch (1 cm) headspace. Apply lids tightly. Let jam stand at room temperature until thickened, about 30 minutes. Serve immediately, if desired. For longer storage, refrigerate for up to 3 weeks or freeze for up to 1 year.

Fruit Butters

Fruit butters, as their name implies, are smooth, creamy spreads. They are made by slowly cooking fruit pulp and sugar to a thick but spreadable consistency. Spices or a second fruit are often added to enhance the flavor.

Among their many uses, these soft spreads make an excellent filling for layer cakes and the basis for a delicious trifle. Just spread the fruit butter of your choice on sliced pound cake, then layer with fresh fruit, vanilla pudding and, if desired, whipped cream. They also make an excellent filling for sandwich cookies. Simply spread butter on a plain cookie and top with a second cookie. Fruit butters can also be substituted for some of the fat in many baking recipes to produce delicious baked goods that are lower in fat.

Cooking Butters

Butters are cooked over medium to medium-high heat. To prevent scorching, stir butters frequently, especially as they thicken and reach the doneness point. Cooking times will vary depending on the diameter of the saucepan, the type of fruit and the intensity of the heat. Most butters will need 30 to 60 minutes of cooking time. Butters cook best in a wide-diameter, heavy-bottomed stainless steel saucepan. The extended cooking time evaporates moisture, thickening the fruit mixture and creating a spreadable, buttery texture.

Testing Fruit Butters for Doneness

Butters are cooked until they thicken and begin to hold their shape on a spoon. To assess doneness, spoon a small quantity of cooked mixture onto a chilled plate. When liquid does not separate, creating a rim around the edge, and the mixture holds a buttery, spreadable shape, the butter is ready to ladle into jars and process.

Sweet Apple Cider Butter

Apple cider adds an extra layer of flavor to traditional apple butter. Apple butters are excellent accompaniments for meat pies and make delicious enhancements for roast pork.

TIPS

As butter thickens, stir frequently to prevent sticking or scorching.

You can adjust the taste and texture of this butter by using different varieties of apples.

A clear plastic ruler (kept solely for kitchen use) will help you determine the correct headspace. Each filled jar should be measured accurately, as the headspace can affect sealing and the preservation of the contents.

Makes about eight 8-ounce (250 mL) jars or four pint (500 mL) jars

6 lbs	apples, peeled, cored and quartered	2.7 kg
2 cups	sweet apple cider	500 mL
3 cups	granulated sugar	750 mL
1 ½ tsp	ground cinnamon	7 mL
½ tsp	ground cloves	2 mL

1. In a large stainless steel saucepan, combine apples and apple cider. Bring to a boil over medium-high heat. Reduce heat and boil gently, stirring occasionally, until apples are soft, about 30 minutes.
2. Working in batches, transfer apple mixture to a food mill or a food processor fitted with a metal blade and purée just until a uniform texture is achieved. Do not liquefy. Measure 12 cups (3 L) of apple purée.
3. In a clean large stainless steel saucepan, combine apple purée, sugar, cinnamon and cloves. Stir until sugar dissolves. Bring to a boil over medium-high heat, stirring frequently. Reduce heat and boil gently, stirring frequently, until mixture thickens and holds its shape on a spoon (see Testing Fruit Butters for Doneness, page 52).
4. Meanwhile, prepare canner, jars and lids. *(For more information, see page 415.)*
5. Ladle hot butter into hot jars, leaving ¼ inch (0.5 cm) headspace. Remove air bubbles and adjust headspace, if necessary, by adding hot butter. Wipe rim. Center lid on jar. Screw band down until resistance is met, then increase to fingertip-tight.
6. Place jars in canner, ensuring they are completely covered with water. Bring to a boil and process for 10 minutes. Remove canner lid. Wait 5 minutes, then remove jars, cool and store. *(For more information, see pages 417–418.)*

Variations

If you prefer a butter that is less sweet than Sweet Apple Cider Butter, substitute 1 cup (250 mL) honey for the 3 cups (750 mL) granulated sugar.

Traditional Apple Butter: Prepare above recipe as indicated, but replace apple cider with 3 cups (750 mL) water and increase sugar to 6 cups (1.5 L). If using very sweet apples, start with 5 cups (1.25 L) sugar, cook until thickened, then taste and add remaining sugar if desired.

Cranapple Butter

Use this butter in place of traditional cranberry jelly when serving turkey or poultry.

TIPS

When measuring wet ingredients, use a liquid measuring cup (with a handle and spout and graduated markings for measures). Smaller measuring cups (1 or 2 cups/250 or 500 mL) are more accurate than many of the larger cups (4 or 8 cups/1 or 2 L), so it is better to use a smaller one several times than to use one larger cup.

As butter thickens, stir frequently to prevent sticking or scorching.

Makes about nine 8-ounce (250 mL) jars or four to five pint (500 mL) jars

6 lbs	apples, cored, peeled and chopped	2.7 kg
8 cups	cranberry juice cocktail	2 L
4 cups	granulated sugar	1 L
1 tbsp	ground cinnamon	15 mL
1 tsp	ground nutmeg	5 mL

1. In a large stainless steel saucepan, combine apples and cranberry juice cocktail. Bring to a boil over medium-high heat. Boil, stirring occasionally, until apples are soft, about 15 minutes.

2. Working in batches, transfer apple mixture to a food mill or a food processor fitted with a metal blade and purée just until a uniform texture is achieved. Do not liquefy.

3. In a clean large stainless steel saucepan, combine apple purée, sugar, cinnamon and nutmeg. Bring to a boil over medium-high heat. Boil, stirring frequently, until mixture thickens and holds its shape on a spoon (see Testing Fruit Butters for Doneness, page 52).

4. Meanwhile, prepare canner, jars and lids. *(For more information, see page 415.)*

5. Ladle hot butter into hot jars, leaving 1/4 inch (0.5 cm) headspace. Remove air bubbles and adjust headspace, if necessary, by adding hot butter. Wipe rim. Center lid on jar. Screw band down until resistance is met, then increase to fingertip-tight.

6. Place jars in canner, ensuring they are completely covered with water. Bring to a boil and process for 10 minutes. Remove canner lid. Wait 5 minutes, then remove jars, cool and store. *(For more information, see pages 417–418.)*

Crabapple Butter

When your crabapple tree produces a bumper crop, use this recipe to turn the harvest bounty into delicious butter. It will be appreciated throughout the year.

TIPS

As butter thickens, stir frequently to prevent sticking or scorching.

If you have particularly hard water and use it in the boiling-water canner, it can leave a residue on jars. Use filtered or reverse-osmosis water to fill your canner instead.

Makes about six 8-ounce (250 mL) jars

4 lbs	crabapples, stems and blossom ends removed, quartered	1.8 kg
1 cup	water	250 mL
	Grated zest and juice of 1 orange	
2 cups	granulated sugar	500 mL
1½ tsp	ground cinnamon	7 mL
½ tsp	ground cloves	2 mL
½ tsp	ground ginger	2 mL

1. In a large stainless steel saucepan, combine crabapples and water. Bring to a boil over medium-high heat. Reduce heat, cover and boil gently, stirring occasionally, until crabapples are soft, 20 to 30 minutes.

2. Working in batches, transfer crabapple mixture to a food mill and purée just until a uniform texture is achieved. Do not liquefy. Measure 6 cups (1.5 L) of crabapple purée.

3. In a clean large stainless steel saucepan, combine crabapple purée, orange zest and juice, sugar, cinnamon, cloves and ginger. Stir until sugar dissolves. Bring to a boil over medium-high heat. Reduce heat and boil gently, stirring frequently, until mixture thickens and holds its shape on a spoon (see Testing Fruit Butters for Doneness, page 52).

4. Meanwhile, prepare canner, jars and lids. *(For more information, see page 415.)*

5. Ladle hot butter into hot jars, leaving ¼ inch (0.5 cm) headspace. Remove air bubbles and adjust headspace, if necessary, by adding hot butter. Wipe rim. Center lid on jar. Screw band down until resistance is met, then increase to fingertip-tight.

6. Place jars in canner, ensuring they are completely covered with water. Bring to a boil and process for 10 minutes. Remove canner lid. Wait 5 minutes, then remove jars, cool and store. *(For more information, see pages 417–418.)*

Silky Apricot Butter

Use this rich butter as a cake filling, dessert topping or condiment. The rich flavors will be a welcome addition to any meal.

TIPS

If desired, this butter can be prepared with unpeeled apricots. It will have a coarser texture but a more robust flavor.

As butter thickens, stir frequently to prevent sticking or scorching.

Makes about six 8-ounce (250 mL) jars or three pint (500 mL) jars

2 lbs	apricots, peeled, halved and pitted	900 g
½ cup	water	125 mL
3 cups	granulated sugar	750 mL
2 tbsp	lemon juice	30 mL

1. In a large stainless steel saucepan, combine apricots and water. Bring to a boil over medium-high heat. Reduce heat and boil gently, stirring occasionally, until apricots are soft, about 20 minutes.

2. Working in batches, transfer apricot mixture to a food mill or a food processor fitted with a metal blade and purée just until a uniform texture is achieved. Do not liquefy. Measure 6 cups (1.5 L) of apricot purée.

3. In a clean large stainless steel saucepan, combine apricot purée and sugar. Stir until sugar dissolves. Bring to a boil over medium-high heat, stirring frequently. Reduce heat and boil gently, stirring frequently, until mixture thickens and holds its shape on a spoon (see Testing Fruit Butters for Doneness, page 52). Stir in lemon juice.

4. Meanwhile, prepare canner, jars and lids. *(For more information, see page 415.)*

5. Ladle hot butter into hot jars, leaving ¼ inch (0.5 cm) headspace. Remove air bubbles and adjust headspace, if necessary, by adding hot butter. Wipe rim. Center lid on jar. Screw band down until resistance is met, then increase to fingertip-tight.

6. Place jars in canner, ensuring they are completely covered with water. Bring to a boil and process for 10 minutes. Remove canner lid. Wait 5 minutes, then remove jars, cool and store. *(For more information, see pages 417–418.)*

Peach Butter

Smooth and golden, this butter tastes like summer. Spreading it on toast on a cold, dreary morning is sure to chase away the winter blues.

TIPS

As butter thickens, stir frequently to prevent sticking or scorching.

When preparing jars and lids, prepare a couple extra in case your yield is larger than you expect. If you don't have enough jars, place any leftover butters in an airtight container, store in the refrigerator and use within a few weeks.

Before using jars, inspect them carefully for any chips, cracks or fractures. Discard any imperfect jars.

Makes about eight 8-ounce (250 mL) jars or four pint (500 mL) jars

4½ lbs	peaches, peeled, pitted and coarsely chopped	2 kg
½ cup	water	125 mL
	Grated zest and juice of 1 lemon	
4 cups	granulated sugar	1 L

1. In a large stainless steel saucepan, combine peaches, water and lemon zest and juice. Bring to a boil over medium-high heat. Reduce heat and boil gently, stirring occasionally, until peaches are soft, about 20 minutes.

2. Working in batches, transfer peach mixture to a food mill or a food processor fitted with a metal blade and purée just until a uniform texture is achieved. Do not liquefy. Measure 8 cups (2 L) of peach purée.

3. In a clean large stainless steel saucepan, combine peach purée and sugar. Stir until sugar dissolves. Bring to a boil over medium-high heat, stirring frequently. Reduce heat and boil gently, stirring frequently, until mixture thickens and holds its shape on a spoon (see Testing Fruit Butters for Doneness, page 52).

4. Meanwhile, prepare canner, jars and lids. *(For more information, see page 415.)*

5. Ladle hot butter into hot jars, leaving ¼ inch (0.5 cm) headspace. Remove air bubbles and adjust headspace, if necessary, by adding hot butter. Wipe rim. Center lid on jar. Screw band down until resistance is met, then increase to fingertip-tight.

6. Place jars in canner, ensuring they are completely covered with water. Bring to a boil and process for 10 minutes. Remove canner lid. Wait 5 minutes, then remove jars, cool and store. *(For more information, see pages 417–418.)*

Variations

For a more sophisticated fruit butter, reduce the sugar to 3 cups (750 mL). When butter has begun to thicken but doesn't quite mound on a spoon, add 1 cup (500 mL) of your favorite spirit, such as amaretto liqueur or a sweet wine, and continue cooking, stirring frequently, until mixture mounds on a spoon.

Pear Butter: Substitute 7 lbs (3.2 kg) pears, peeled, cored and coarsely chopped, for the peaches. Combine with water, lemon juice and zest, cook and purée. Measure 8 cups (2 L) pear purée. Stir in sugar, grated zest and juice of 1 orange and 1 tsp (5 mL) grated nutmeg. Cook as indicated above until thickened.

Lemon Prune Honey Butter

Lift your spirits from winter's doldrums by rekindling the joys of preserving. Made from ingredients that are available year-round, this tasty butter, like all those made from dried fruit, cooks relatively quickly. However, before you begin cooking, the dried fruit must be rehydrated and puréed (Step 1).

TIP

As butter thickens, stir frequently to prevent sticking or scorching.

Makes about three 8-ounce (250 mL) jars

3 cups	pitted prunes	750 mL
1 ¼ cups	water, divided	300 mL
	Grated zest and juice of 2 lemons	
⅔ cup	liquid honey	150 mL
½ tsp	ground cinnamon	2 mL
¼ tsp	ground cloves	1 mL
¼ tsp	ground allspice	1 mL
¼ tsp	ground nutmeg	1 mL
2 tbsp	brandy (optional)	30 mL

1. In a large stainless steel saucepan, combine prunes, 1 cup (250 mL) of the water and lemon zest and juice. Stir well. Bring to a boil over medium-high heat. Reduce heat, cover and boil gently, stirring occasionally, until prunes are soft, about 15 minutes.

2. Working in batches, transfer prune mixture to a food mill or a food processor fitted with a metal blade and purée just until a uniform texture is achieved. Do not liquefy.

3. Meanwhile, prepare canner, jars and lids. *(For more information, see page 415.)*

4. In a clean large stainless steel saucepan, combine prune purée, remaining ¼ cup (50 mL) water, honey, cinnamon, cloves, allspice and nutmeg. Stir well. Bring to a boil over high heat, stirring constantly. Boil hard, stirring constantly, for 1 minute. Stir in brandy, if using, and remove from heat.

5. Ladle hot butter into hot jars, leaving ¼ inch (0.5 cm) headspace. Remove air bubbles and adjust headspace, if necessary, by adding hot butter. Wipe rim. Center lid on jar. Screw band down until resistance is met, then increase to fingertip-tight.

6. Place jars in canner, ensuring they are completely covered with water. Bring to a boil and process for 10 minutes. Remove canner lid. Wait 5 minutes, then remove jars, cool and store. *(For more information, see pages 417–418.)*

Honeyed Yellow Tomato Butter

Similar to plum sauce, this savory butter makes an ideal dipping sauce for chicken fingers or a tasty glaze for barbecued fish.

TIP

Cheesecloth can be found at many retailers, such as grocery stores and other stores that carry kitchen supplies. Look in the area where kitchen utensils are located.

Makes about three 8-ounce (250 mL) jars

5 lbs	yellow tomatoes, cored and quartered	2.3 kg
I	I-inch (2.5 cm) piece peeled gingerroot	I
I tbsp	whole allspice	15 mL
2	cinnamon sticks (each about 4 inches/10 cm), broken into pieces	2
2 cups	granulated sugar	500 mL
I cup	liquid honey	250 mL

1. In a large stainless steel saucepan, crush tomatoes with a potato masher. Bring to a boil over medium-high heat. Reduce heat and boil gently, stirring occasionally, until tomatoes are soft, 20 to 30 minutes.

2. Working in batches, press tomatoes through a food mill or sieve to seperate pulp from skin and seeds. Discard skin and seeds. Measure 8 cups (2 L) of tomato pulp.

3. Meanwhile, tie gingerroot, allspice, and cinnamon sticks in a square of cheesecloth, creating a spice bag.

4. In a clean large stainless steel saucepan, combine tomato purée, sugar, honey and spice bag. Stir until sugar dissolves. Bring to a boil over medium-high heat, stirring frequently. Reduce heat and boil gently, stirring frequently, until mixture thickens and mounds on a spoon (see Testing Fruit Butters for Doneness, page 52). Discard spice bag.

5. Meanwhile, prepare canner, jars and lids. *(For more information, see page 415.)*

6. Ladle hot butter into hot jars, leaving ¼ inch (0.5 cm) headspace. Remove air bubbles and adjust headspace, if necessary, by adding hot butter. Wipe rim. Center lid on jar. Screw band down until resistance is met, then increase to fingertip-tight.

7. Place jars in canner, ensuring they are completely covered with water. Bring to a boil and process for 10 minutes. Remove canner lid. Wait 5 minutes, then remove jars, cool and store. *(For more information, see pages 417–418.)*

Blueberry Bonanza

This recipe uses the same blueberries to make two different products: a thick old-fashioned berry butter and a luscious silky blueberry syrup. Once the juice is extracted for the syrup, the remaining blueberry pulp is used to make a lightly spiced butter.

TIPS

To clean blueberries without rinsing, place 2 to 3 cups (500 to 750 mL) on a clean tea towel and discard any shriveled berries or visible debris. Grasp the towel on both ends, lift it and gently roll the berries back and forth by raising first your left hand, then your right hand, tilting the towel slightly.

If blueberries are to be frozen for later use in preserving, do not rinse. Clean using the towel method and freeze in recipe-sized batches.

As butter thickens, stir frequently to prevent sticking or scorching.

Makes about four 8-ounce (250 mL) jars of syrup and five 8-ounce (250 mL) jars of butter

12 cups	blueberries	3 L
	Water	
6 cups	granulated sugar, divided	1.5 L
2 cups	corn syrup	500 mL
	Grated zest of 1 lemon	
	Juice of 2 lemons	
1 tsp	ground nutmeg	5 mL
1/2 tsp	ground cinnamon	2 mL

1. In a stainless steel saucepan, combine blueberries with 3 cups (750 mL) water. Bring to a boil over medium-high heat, stirring and crushing mixture with a potato masher. Reduce heat and boil gently, stirring occasionally, for 5 minutes.

2. Transfer blueberries to a dampened jelly bag or a strainer lined with several layers of dampened cheesecloth set over a deep bowl. Let drip until 5 cups (1.25 L) juice has been collected, adding water if necessary to yield the required quantity. Set juice aside. Purée remaining pulp and juice in a blender or a food processor fitted with a metal blade. Set purée aside.

3. Prepare canner, jars and lids. *(For more information, see page 415.)*

Blueberry Syrup

4. In a clean large, deep stainless steel saucepan, combine 1 cup (250 mL) water and 3 cups (750 mL) of the granulated sugar. Bring to a boil over high heat, stirring to dissolve sugar. Stir in blueberry juice, corn syrup and half of the lemon juice; return to a boil. Reduce heat to medium-high and boil steadily, stirring occasionally, until mixture is slightly thickened, about 35 minutes. Remove from heat and skim off foam.

5. Ladle hot syrup into hot jars, leaving 1/4 inch (0.5 cm) headspace. Wipe rim. Center lid on jar. Screw band down until resistance is met, then increase to fingertip-tight.

6. Place jars in canner, ensuring they are completely covered with water. Bring to a boil and process for 10 minutes. Remove canner lid. Wait 5 minutes, then remove jars, cool and store. *(For more information, see pages 417–418.)*

Stick blenders make quick work of the purée step required in butters. Cook the fruit as directed until softened, then purée the mixture in the saucepan and proceed as directed.

Berries can be frozen before use in soft spreads. If you pick the berries on a day that is too hot to do your preserving, measure out the required amount of berries, prepare and freeze for up to 3 months. When you plan to make your recipe, thaw prepared berries in the refrigerator just long enough so that berries can be crushed. Some ice crystals should remain.

Blueberry Butter

7. Meanwhile, in a separate clean large stainless steel saucepan, combine blueberry purée, remaining 3 cups (750 mL) sugar, lemon zest, remaining lemon juice, nutmeg and cinnamon. Bring to a boil over medium-high heat, stirring frequently. Reduce heat to medium and boil, stirring frequently, until mixture thickens and holds its shape on a spoon (see Testing Fruit Butters for Doneness, page 52).

8. Ladle hot butter into hot jars, leaving ¼ inch (0.5 cm) headspace. Remove air bubbles and adjust headspace, if necessary, by adding hot butter. Wipe rim. Center lid on jar. Screw band down until resistance is met, then increase to fingertip-tight.

9. Place jars in canner, ensuring they are completely covered with water. Bring to a boil and process for 10 minutes. Remove canner lid. Wait 5 minutes, then remove jars, cool and store. *(For more information, see pages 417–418.)*

Profiterole-Style Blueberry Macaroons
Use Blueberry Bonanza to turn store-bought macaroons into a spectacular dessert. Cut macaroons in half and fill with Blueberry Butter, then arrange on individual serving plates and drizzle with Blueberry Syrup.

Preserves

Unlike jams, which have a soft, consistent texture, preserves offer chunks of fruit suspended in a soft jelly. Like jams, preserves make delicious spreads for breads, but they are even better spooned over frozen desserts or cakes.

Preserves with No Added Pectin

Preserves made with no added pectin require a longer cooking time and must be stirred frequently to prevent scorching. Before making any of the preserves in this section, review the gel stage tests on page 21.

Choose-a-Berry Preserves

Use blackberries, loganberries or red or black raspberries, or a combination of these berries, in this recipe.

TIP

If your mixture has not reached the gel stage when first tested, return the pan to medium heat and cook, stirring constantly, for an additional 5 minutes. Repeat gel stage test and cooking as needed.

Makes about four 8-ounce (250 mL) jars

8 cups	berries	2 L
4 cups	granulated sugar	1 L

1. In a large, deep stainless steel saucepan, combine berries and sugar. Stir well. Set aside until berries release their juice, about 10 minutes.
2. Prepare canner, jars and lids. *(For more information, see page 415.)*
3. Bring berry mixture to a boil over medium heat, stirring to dissolve sugar. Boil hard, stirring frequently, until mixture thickens, 10 to 15 minutes. Remove from heat and test gel (see page 21). If gel stage has been reached, remove from heat and skim off foam.
4. Ladle hot preserves into hot jars, leaving ¼ inch (0.5 cm) headspace. Remove air bubbles and adjust headspace, if necessary, by adding hot preserves. Wipe rim. Center lid on jar. Screw band down until resistance is met, then increase to fingertip-tight.
5. Place jars in canner, ensuring they are completely covered with water. Bring to a boil and process for 15 minutes. Remove canner lid. Wait 5 minutes, then remove jars, cool and store. *(For more information, see pages 417–418.)*

Fig Preserves

Fig preserves make a wonderful condiment to serve with sharp cheese dishes or pork.

TIPS

When measuring wet ingredients, use a liquid measuring cup (with a handle and spout and graduated markings for measures). Smaller measuring cups (1 or 2 cups/250 or 500 mL) are more accurate than many of the larger cups (4 or 8 cups/1 or 2 L), so it is better to use a smaller one several times than to use one larger cup.

Refer to the Produce Purchase Guide on pages 426–429 to determine how many figs you'll need to buy to prepare this recipe.

Makes about six 8-ounce (250 mL) jars

8 cups	firm fresh figs	2 L
8 cups	boiling water	2 L
2⅔ cups	granulated sugar	650 mL
4 cups	water	1 L
1	lemon (unpeeled), seeded and thinly sliced	1

1. In a large glass or stainless steel bowl, combine figs and boiling water. Cover and let stand at room temperature for 15 minutes. Transfer to a colander placed over a sink and drain. Rinse with cold water and drain again.

2. In a large, deep stainless steel saucepan, combine sugar, 4 cups (1 L) water and lemon slices. Bring to a boil over high heat, stirring to dissolve sugar. Boil hard, stirring occasionally, for 10 minutes. Using a slotted spoon, remove and discard lemon slices. Reduce heat to medium-high and return syrup to a boil. Add 2 cups (500 mL) of the figs and boil until figs are transparent. Using a slotted spoon, remove figs to a shallow pan and repeat with remaining figs, working in 2 cup (500 mL) batches, until all figs are transparent. Boil syrup until thickened. Pour thickened syrup over figs. Cover and let stand at room temperature for at least 8 hours or overnight.

3. Prepare canner, jars and lids. *(For more information, see page 415.)*

4. In a large stainless steel saucepan, bring fig mixture to a boil over medium-high heat, stirring frequently. Remove from heat and skim foam, if necessary.

5. Ladle hot preserves into hot jars, leaving ¼ inch (0.5 cm) headspace. Remove air bubbles and adjust headspace, if necessary, by adding hot preserves. Wipe rim. Center lid on jar. Screw band down until resistance is met, then increase to fingertip-tight.

6. Place jars in canner, ensuring they are completely covered with water. Bring to a boil and process for 10 minutes. Remove canner lid. Wait 5 minutes, then remove jars, cool and store. *(For more information, see pages 417–418.)*

Brandied Apricot Preserves

In specialty stores, a small jar of liqueur-laced apricot preserves is likely to cost a small fortune. Because it's so easy to make your own, you can enjoy these gourmet delights at a reasonable cost.

TIP

Allowing a fruit–sugar mixture to stand releases the fruit's natural juices. It also firms the remaining fruit solids and helps them retain their shape in the thick gel, creating a preserve.

Makes about six 8-ounce (250 mL) jars

5 cups	sliced pitted fresh apricots	1.25 L
2 cups	chopped cored peeled tart apples	500 mL
2 cups	granulated sugar	500 mL
½ cup	liquid honey	125 mL
2 tbsp	lemon juice	30 mL
1 cup	brandy	250 mL

1. In a large stainless steel saucepan, combine apricots, apples, sugar, honey and lemon juice. Stir to mix well. Cover and let stand at room temperature for 40 minutes.
2. Meanwhile, prepare canner, jars and lids. *(For more information, see page 415.)*
3. Bring reserved apricot mixture to a boil over medium heat, stirring to dissolve sugar. Reduce heat and boil gently, stirring frequently, until mixture thickens, about 25 minutes. Remove from heat and test gel (see page 21). If gel stage has been reached, skim off foam. Stir in brandy and return to medium heat. Boil gently, stirring constantly, for 5 minutes. Remove from heat and skim off foam.
4. Ladle hot preserves into hot jars, leaving ¼ inch (0.5 cm) headspace. Remove air bubbles and adjust headspace, if necessary, by adding hot preserves. Wipe rim. Center lid on jar. Screw band down until resistance is met, then increase to fingertip-tight.
5. Place jars in canner, ensuring they are completely covered with water. Bring to a boil and process for 10 minutes. Remove canner lid. Wait 5 minutes, then remove jars, cool and store. *(For more information, see pages 417–418.)*

Raspberry Cherry Preserves

If you're lucky enough to have more raspberries than you know what to do with, this is the recipe for you.

Makes about four 8-ounce (250 mL) jars

3 cups	seedless raspberry pulp (see tip, page 65 top)	750 mL
4 cups	granulated sugar	1 L
3 cups	pitted sweet cherries, including juice	750 mL

1. Prepare canner, jars and lids. *(For more information, see page 415.)*
2. In a glass or stainless steel bowl, combine raspberry pulp and sugar. Set aside.

You'll need about 10 cups (2.5 L) of raspberries to yield 3 cups (750 mL) of pulp. Working in batches, press raspberries through a fine sieve to remove seeds and create seedless pulp.

3. In a large, deep stainless steel saucepan, bring cherries with juice to a boil over medium heat, stirring frequently. Reduce heat and boil gently, stirring occasionally, until cherries are tender, about 5 minutes. Stir in raspberry mixture and return to a boil over medium-high heat. Boil hard, stirring constantly, until mixture thickens, about 7 minutes. Remove from heat and test gel (see page 21). If gel stage has been reached, skim off foam.

4. Ladle hot preserves into hot jars, leaving ¼ inch (0.5 cm) headspace. Remove air bubbles and adjust headspace, if necessary, by adding hot preserves. Wipe rim. Center lid on jar. Screw band down until resistance is met, then increase to fingertip-tight.

5. Place jars in canner, ensuring they are completely covered with water. Bring to a boil and process for 10 minutes. Remove canner lid. Wait 5 minutes, then remove jars, cool and store. *(For more information, see pages 417–418.)*

Strawberry Margarita Preserves

This mouthwatering combination of fruit-flavored spirits with strawberries and apples creates a product with the pizzazz of an expensive gourmet spread. These preserves also make a great topping for cheesecake.

TIPS

Refer to the Produce Purchase Guide on pages 426–429 to determine how much produce you'll need to buy to prepare this recipe.

Use care when using alcoholic beverages near a hot stove.

Makes about six 8-ounce (250 mL) jars

6 cups	halved hulled strawberries	1.5 L
2 cups	chopped cored peeled tart apples	500 mL
¼ cup	lemon juice	50 mL
4 cups	granulated sugar	1 L
½ cup	tequila	125 mL
½ cup	orange-flavored liqueur	125 mL
2 tbsp	strawberry schnapps (optional)	30 mL

1. Prepare canner, jars and lids. *(For more information, see page 415.)*

2. In a large, deep stainless steel saucepan, combine strawberries, apples and lemon juice. Bring to a boil over high heat, stirring constantly. Add sugar, stirring until dissolved. Reduce heat and boil gently, stirring frequently, until mixture thickens, about 25 minutes. Remove from heat and test gel (see page 21). If gel stage has been reached, stir in tequila, orange-flavored liqueur and strawberry schnapps, if using. Return to medium-high heat and bring to a boil, stirring constantly. Boil hard, stirring constantly, for 5 minutes. Remove from heat and skim off foam.

3. Ladle hot preserves into hot jars and process as in Steps 4 and 5 of Raspberry Cherry Preserves, above.

Cranberry Grape Preserves

Cranberries add zip and a pleasant chunky twist to traditional grape jam.

TIP

When preparing jars and lids, prepare a couple extra in case your yield is larger than you expect. If you don't have enough jars, place any leftover preserves in an airtight container, store in the refrigerator and use within a few weeks.

Makes about five 8-ounce (250 mL) jars

4 cups	unsweetened grape juice	I L
4 cups	chopped cranberries, thawed if frozen	I L
I tsp	finely grated orange zest	5 mL
5 cups	granulated sugar	1.25 L

1. Prepare canner, jars and lids. *(For more information, see page 415.)*
2. In a large, deep stainless steel saucepan, combine grape juice, cranberries and orange zest. Bring to a boil over medium-high heat and, maintaining boil, gradually stir in sugar. Boil hard, stirring frequently, until mixture thickens, about 12 minutes. Remove from heat and test gel (see page 21). If gel stage has been reached, skim off foam.
3. Ladle hot preserves into hot jars, leaving ¼ inch (0.5 cm) headspace. Remove air bubbles and adjust headspace, if necessary, by adding hot preserves. Wipe rim. Center lid on jar. Screw band down until resistance is met, then increase to fingertip-tight.
4. Place jars in canner, ensuring they are completely covered with water. Bring to a boil and process for 10 minutes. Remove canner lid. Wait 5 minutes, then remove jars, cool and store. *(For more information, see pages 417–418.)*

Plum Preserves

For a quick, show-stopping dessert, spoon this distinctive preserve over a store-bought cheesecake.

Makes about five 8-ounce (250 mL) jars

5 cups	pitted halved tart plums	1.25 L
4 cups	granulated sugar	I L
I cup	water	250 mL

1. Prepare canner, jars and lids. *(For more information, see page 415.)*
2. In a large, deep stainless steel saucepan, combine plums, sugar and water. Bring to a boil over medium heat, stirring to dissolve sugar. Increase heat to high and boil hard, stirring frequently, until mixture thickens. Remove from heat and test gel (see page 21). If gel stage has been reached, skim off foam.

3. Ladle hot preserves into hot jars, leaving ¼ inch (0.5 cm) headspace. Remove air bubbles and adjust headspace, if necessary, by adding hot preserves. Wipe rim. Center lid on jar. Screw band down until resistance is met, then increase to fingertip-tight.

4. Place jars in canner, ensuring they are completely covered with water. Bring to a boil and process for 15 minutes. Remove canner lid. Wait 5 minutes, then remove jars, cool and store. *(For more information, see pages 417–418.)*

Rhubarb Red Currant Preserves

These tangy-sweet preserves with a hint of spice elevate a simple piece of toast to gourmet fare.

TIPS

The two oranges you used for the zest should make ⅔ cup (150 mL) juice. If you don't have quite enough, add water to make the required amount.

If your mixture has not reached the gel stage when first tested, return the pan to medium heat and cook, stirring constantly, for an additional 5 minutes. Repeat gel stage test and cooking as needed.

Makes about five 8-ounce (250 mL) jars

7½ cups	finely chopped rhubarb	1.875 L
	Grated zest of 2 oranges	
⅔ cup	freshly squeezed orange juice (see tip, at left)	150 mL
3 cups	granulated sugar	750 mL
2 cups	stemmed red currants	500 mL
1 tsp	ground nutmeg	5 mL

1. In a large stainless steel saucepan, combine rhubarb, orange zest, orange juice and sugar. Stir well. Cover and let stand at room temperature for 1 to 4 hours or until rhubarb releases its juice.

2. Prepare canner, jars and lids. *(For more information, see page 415.)*

3. Bring rhubarb mixture to a boil over high heat, stirring constantly. Reduce heat and boil gently, stirring occasionally, for 15 minutes, until rhubarb is softened. Stir in red currants and nutmeg. Boil gently, stirring frequently, until currants are soft and mixture thickens, about 10 minutes. Remove from heat and test gel (see page 21). If gel stage has been reached, skim off foam.

4. Ladle hot preserves into hot jars, leaving ¼ inch (0.5 cm) headspace. Remove air bubbles and adjust headspace, if necessary, by adding hot preserves. Wipe rim. Center lid on jar. Screw band down until resistance is met, then increase to fingertip-tight.

5. Place jars in canner, ensuring they are completely covered with water. Bring to a boil and process for 10 minutes. Remove canner lid. Wait 5 minutes, then remove jars, cool and store. *(For more information, see pages 417–418.)*

Bar-le-Duc (Currant Preserves)

Bar-le-Duc is an exquisite suspension of currants in soft jelly that originated in a village of the same name in France. Hand-seeded white currants were used in the original recipe, but today's cooks make these sweet and saucy preserves using red or white currants with seeds, as well as with other small berries such as loganberries or elderberries.

Makes about five 8-ounce (250 mL) jars

11 cups	stemmed red or white currants, divided	2.75 L
1/3 cup	water	75 mL
7 cups	granulated sugar, divided	1.75 L

1. In a medium saucepan, combine 3 cups (750 mL) of the currants and water. Bring to a boil over medium heat, crushing currants with a potato masher. Reduce heat, cover and boil gently for 5 minutes.

2. Transfer currant mixture to a dampened jelly bag or a strainer lined with several layers of dampened cheesecloth set over a glass measure. Let drip until 1 cup (250 mL) juice has been collected, adding water as necessary to yield the required quantity.

3. Transfer juice to a large, deep stainless steel saucepan. Add remaining 8 cups (2 L) currants and 4 cups (1 L) of the sugar. Bring to a boil over high heat, stirring to dissolve sugar. Boil hard, stirring occasionally, for 5 minutes. Remove from heat, cover and let stand in a cool place (70 to 75°F/21 to 23°C) for at least 12 hours or overnight.

4. Prepare canner, jars and lids. *(For more information, see page 415.)*

5. Add remaining 3 cups (750 mL) sugar to currant mixture. Bring to a boil over medium-high heat, stirring to dissolve sugar. Boil hard, stirring frequently, until mixture thickens, about 10 minutes. Remove from heat and test gel (see page 21). If gel stage has been reached, skim off foam.

6. Ladle hot preserves into hot jars, leaving 1/4 inch (0.5 cm) headspace. Remove air bubbles and adjust headspace, if necessary, by adding hot preserves. Wipe rim. Center lid on jar. Screw band down until resistance is met, then increase to fingertip-tight.

7. Place jars in canner, ensuring they are completely covered with water. Bring to a boil and process for 15 minutes. Remove canner lid. Wait 5 minutes, then remove jars, cool and store. *(For more information, see pages 417–418.)*

Ginger Pear Preserves

Pears with lime and gingerroot combine to make a delicately flavored preserve with an exotic island taste.

TIP

If your mixture has not reached the gel stage when first tested, return the pan to medium heat and cook, stirring constantly, for an additional 5 minutes. Repeat gel stage test and cooking as needed.

Makes about seven 8-ounce (250 mL) jars

5½ cups	finely chopped cored peeled pears	1.375 L
	Grated zest and juice of 3 limes	
2⅓ cups	granulated sugar	575 mL
1 tbsp	grated gingerroot	15 mL

1. Prepare canner, jars and lids. *(For more information, see page 415.)*
2. In a large stainless steel saucepan, combine pears, lime zest and juice, sugar and gingerroot. Bring to a boil over medium heat, stirring to dissolve sugar. Boil, stirring frequently, until mixture thickens, about 15 minutes. Remove from heat and test gel (see page 21). If gel stage has been reached, skim off foam.
3. Ladle hot preserves into hot jars, leaving ¼ inch (0.5 cm) headspace. Remove air bubbles and adjust headspace, if necessary, by adding hot preserves. Wipe rim. Center lid on jar. Screw band down until resistance is met, then increase to fingertip-tight.
4. Place jars in canner, ensuring they are completely covered with water. Bring to a boil and process for 10 minutes. Remove canner lid. Wait 5 minutes, then remove jars, cool and store. *(For more information, see pages 417–418.)*

Quince Preserves

An ancient Roman symbol of love, the yellow-skinned quince looks and tastes like a cross between an apple and a pear. This fragrant fruit is better cooked than raw and is the perfect choice for preserves.

TIP

When preparing quince, discard all gritty parts.

Makes about four 8-ounce (250 mL) jars

3 cups	granulated sugar	750 mL
8 cups	water	2 L
7 cups	quartered cored peeled quince	1.75 L

1. Prepare canner, jars and lids. *(For more information, see page 415.)*
2. In a large stainless steel saucepan, combine sugar and water. Bring to a boil over high heat, stirring to dissolve sugar. Boil hard, stirring frequently, for 5 minutes. Stir in quince. Reduce heat and boil gently, stirring frequently, until fruit is transparent and syrup thickens. Remove from heat and test gel (see page 21). If gel stage has been reached, skim off foam.
3. Ladle hot preserves into hot jars and process as in Steps 3 and 4 of Ginger Pear Preserves, above.

Tomato Preserves

When you've eaten all the fresh tomatoes you want and your vines continue to produce fruit, this recipe is a wonderful solution. Use this sweet, spicy preserve as you would any fruit spread and enjoy the delicious diversion.

TIPS

You can buy prepared pickling spice at well-stocked supermarkets or make your own (see page 217).

To peel tomatoes, place them in a pot of boiling water for 30 to 60 seconds or until the skins start to crack. Immediately dip in cold water. The skins will slip off easily.

Botanically, tomatoes are a fruit (a berry, the edible, seed-containing part of a plant). Legally, however, tomatoes are vegetables, thanks to a U.S. Supreme Court ruling that favored their "common use" over their botanical origin.

Makes about six 8-ounce (250 mL) jars

1 tbsp	pickling spice (see tip at left)	15 mL
1	½-inch (1 cm) piece peeled gingerroot	1
4 cups	granulated sugar	1 L
2	medium lemons (unpeeled), seeded and thinly sliced	2
¾ cup	water	175 mL
6 cups	peeled small yellow, green or red tomatoes (see tip, at left)	1.5 L

1. Tie pickling spice and gingerroot in a square of cheesecloth, creating a spice bag.

2. In a large, deep stainless steel saucepan, combine sugar, lemon slices, water and spice bag. Bring to a boil over high heat, stirring to dissolve sugar. Reduce heat and boil gently, stirring occasionally, for 15 minutes. Add tomatoes and boil gently, stirring frequently, until tomatoes are transparent. Remove from heat, cover and let stand in a cool place (70 to 75°F/21 to 23°C) for 12 to 18 hours.

3. Prepare canner, jars and lids. *(For more information, see page 415.)*

4. Using a slotted spoon, transfer tomatoes and lemon slices to a glass or stainless steel bowl and set aside. Discard spice bag. Bring syrup to a boil over high heat, stirring constantly. Boil hard, stirring constantly, until thickened, about 3 minutes. Add reserved tomatoes and lemons. Bring back to a boil and boil hard, stirring constantly, for 1 minute. Remove from heat and skim off foam.

5. Ladle hot preserves into hot jars, leaving ¼ inch (0.5 cm) headspace. Remove air bubbles and adjust headspace, if necessary, by adding hot preserves. Wipe rim. Center lid on jar. Screw band down until resistance is met, then increase to fingertip-tight.

6. Place jars in canner, ensuring they are completely covered with water. Bring to a boil and process for 20 minutes. Remove canner lid. Wait 5 minutes, then remove jars, cool and store. *(For more information, see pages 417–418.)*

Preserves with Regular Powdered Fruit Pectin

Adding pectin to preserves reduces the cooking time and helps the fruit retain its chunky texture. When using a powdered fruit pectin, it is essential to fully dissolve the pectin in the fruit *before* adding the sugar. For best results, measure the sugar into a bowl so it can be added to the boiling jam all at once.

Powdered fruit pectin is sometimes sold in 49 g packages and sometimes in 57 g packages. The weight difference does not affect the performance of the product.

Apple Preserves

Spoon these preserves into baked mini-tart shells for instant bite-sized apple pies.

TIPS

Check your package of pectin for the expiration date and use only fresh pectin. Products that have expired may not set properly.

Refer to the Produce Purchase Guide on pages 426–429 to determine how many apples you'll need to buy to prepare this recipe.

Makes about six 8-ounce (250 mL) jars

6 cups	sliced cored peeled apples	1.5 L
1 cup	water	250 mL
1 tbsp	lemon juice	15 mL
1	package (1.75 oz/49 to 57 g) regular powdered fruit pectin	1
1	medium lemon (unpeeled), seeded and thinly sliced	1
4 cups	granulated sugar	1 L
2 tsp	ground nutmeg	10 mL

1. Prepare canner, jars and lids. *(For more information, see page 415.)*
2. In a large, deep stainless steel saucepan, combine apples, water and lemon juice. Bring to a boil over high heat, stirring occasionally. Reduce heat, cover and boil gently, stirring occasionally, for 10 minutes. Remove from heat and whisk in pectin until dissolved. Return to high heat and bring to a boil, stirring frequently. Add lemon slices, sugar and nutmeg. Return to a full rolling boil, stirring constantly. Boil hard, stirring constantly, for 1 minute. Remove from heat and skim off foam.
3. Ladle hot preserves into hot jars, leaving ¼ inch (0.5 cm) headspace. Remove air bubbles and adjust headspace, if necessary, by adding hot preserves. Wipe rim. Center lid on jar. Screw band down until resistance is met, then increase to fingertip-tight.
4. Place jars in canner, ensuring they are completely covered with water. Bring to a boil and process for 10 minutes. Remove canner lid. Wait 5 minutes, then remove jars, cool and store. *(For more information, see pages 417–418.)*

Strawberries-on-Top Preserves

The berries float to the top of this preserve, but they are easily stirred into the delicate, translucent jelly before serving.

TIPS

If using frozen unsweetened strawberries, thaw just until berries can be separated and halved. Use partially thawed berries as directed in Step 1, but let stand in the refrigerator for 4 hours, stirring occasionally.

Small strawberries may be left whole.

Makes about six 8-ounce (250 mL) jars

5 cups	halved hulled strawberries (see tip, at left)	1.25 L
6¼ cups	granulated sugar	1.55 L
2 tsp	finely grated lemon zest	10 mL
4 tbsp	lemon juice, divided	60 mL
1 cup + 2 tbsp	water, divided	280 mL
1	package (1.75 oz/49 to 57 g) regular powdered fruit pectin	1

1. In a large, deep stainless steel saucepan, combine strawberries, sugar, lemon zest, 2 tbsp (30 mL) of the lemon juice and 2 tbsp (30 mL) of the water. Stir well. Let stand at room temperature for 3 hours.

2. Prepare canner, jars and lids. *(For more information, see page 415.)*

3. Bring strawberry mixture to a boil over high heat, stirring constantly. Boil hard, stirring occasionally, for 2 minutes. Remove from heat.

4. In another large stainless steel saucepan, combine remaining 1 cup (250 mL) water and remaining 2 tbsp (30 mL) lemon juice. Whisk in pectin until dissolved. Bring to a boil over high heat, stirring constantly. Boil hard, stirring constantly, for 1 minute. Add to hot strawberry mixture and stir for 3 minutes.

5. Ladle hot preserves into hot jars, leaving ¼ inch (0.5 cm) headspace. Remove air bubbles and adjust headspace, if necessary, by adding hot preserves. Wipe rim. Center lid on jar. Screw band down until resistance is met, then increase to fingertip-tight.

6. Place jars in canner, ensuring they are completely covered with water. Bring to a boil and process for 10 minutes. Remove canner lid. Wait 5 minutes, then remove jars, cool and store. *(For more information, see pages 417–418.)*

Quick Cinnamon Grape Preserves

This easy-to-make preserve blends the mouth-watering flavor of grapes with a hint of cinnamon. It is excellent slathered on toast, but just as good served with cheese.

TIPS

The grape skins add freshness to the intense grape flavor. If you prefer a smoother texture, finely chop the skins.

For best results, measure the sugar into a bowl so it can be added to the boiling preserves all at once.

Makes about nine 8-ounce (250 mL) jars

16 cups	stemmed Concord grapes	4 L
1 cup	water	250 mL
1	cinnamon stick (about 6 inches/15 cm)	1
1	package (1.75 oz/49 to 57 g) regular powdered fruit pectin	1
7 cups	granulated sugar	1.75 L

1. Prepare canner, jars and lids. *(For more information, see page 415.)*
2. Using your fingers, pinch individual grapes, separating skins and pulp. Place skins in a bowl and pulp in a medium stainless steel saucepan. Chop skins (see tip, at left). Add water to pulp and bring to a boil over medium-high heat. Reduce heat, cover and boil gently, stirring occasionally, for 5 minutes, until pulp is heated through. Press pulp through a fine sieve into a large, deep stainless steel saucepan. Discard seeds.
3. Add skins and cinnamon stick to pulp. Whisk in pectin until dissolved. Bring to a boil over high heat, stirring constantly. Add sugar and return to a full rolling boil, stirring constantly. Boil hard, stirring constantly, for 1 minute. Remove from heat and skim off foam. Discard cinnamon stick.
4. Ladle hot preserves into hot jars, leaving ¼ inch (0.5 cm) headspace. Remove air bubbles and adjust headspace, if necessary, by adding hot preserves. Wipe rim. Center lid on jar. Screw band down until resistance is met, then increase to fingertip-tight.
5. Place jars in canner, ensuring they are completely covered with water. Bring to a boil and process for 10 minutes. Remove canner lid. Wait 5 minutes, then remove jars, cool and store. *(For more information, see pages 417–418.)*

Preserves with Liquid Pectin

Unlike soft spreads made with powdered pectin, when making preserves with liquid pectin, the fruit, lemon juice (if required) and sugar are brought to a boil before the pectin is added. To form a good gel, it is essential to bring the fruit–sugar mixture to a full rolling boil that cannot be stirred down, stir in the entire contents of the liquid pectin pouch, then boil hard for 1 minute longer.

··

Cranberry Raspberry Preserves

Whole cranberries add chunkiness and robust flavor to raspberry jam. The butter in this recipe reduces foaming and gives the preserves an extra sheen. Do not increase the specified quantity.

TIPS

Wash berries gently in small batches in a colander under cool running water to make sure you remove all dirt and grit and to avoid bruising the soft fruit.

Some brands of liquid pectin direct you to stir in the pectin *after* boiling the fruit–sugar mixture for 1 minute. It is advisable to follow the directions given by the brand you are using when preparing these recipes.

Makes about six 8-ounce (250 mL) jars

2½ cups	raspberries	625 mL
2 cups	cranberries	500 mL
1 cup	finely chopped cored peeled apple	250 mL
3½ cups	granulated sugar	875 mL
1 cup	liquid honey	250 mL
½ tsp	butter or margarine	2 mL
1	pouch (3 oz/85 mL) liquid pectin	1

1. In a large, deep stainless steel saucepan, combine raspberries, cranberries, apple, sugar, honey and butter. Stir well. Let stand at room temperature for 15 minutes.
2. Meanwhile, prepare canner, jars and lids. *(For more information, see page 415.)*
3. Over medium heat, stirring frequently, bring fruit mixture to a full rolling boil that cannot be stirred down. Stir in pectin. Boil hard, stirring constantly, for 1 minute. Remove from heat and skim off foam.
4. Ladle hot preserves into hot jars, leaving ¼ inch (0.5 cm) headspace. Remove air bubbles and adjust headspace, if necessary, by adding hot preserves. Wipe rim. Center lid on jar. Screw band down until resistance is met, then increase to fingertip-tight.
5. Place jars in canner, ensuring they are completely covered with water. Bring to a boil and process for 10 minutes. Remove canner lid. Wait 5 minutes, then remove jars, cool and store. *(For more information, see pages 417–418.)*

Elderberry Peach Preserves

*Peaches suspended
in elderberry jelly
delight the eye as
well as the taste buds.
These preserves are
luscious on bread, but
also make a pleasing
dessert or breakfast
sauce.*

TIP

If the juice yield from
the berries does not
quite equal the required
quantity, you can add
up to ¼ cup (50 mL)
water or unsweetened
apple juice.

Makes about eight 8-ounce (250 mL) jars

6½ cups	elderberries	1.625 L
2 cups	coarsely chopped pitted peeled peaches	500 mL
½ cup	lemon juice	125 mL
7 cups	granulated sugar	1.75 L
2	pouches (each 3 oz/85 mL) liquid pectin	2

1. In a large, deep stainless steel saucepan, crush elderberries. Bring to a boil over medium heat, stirring occasionally. Boil gently, stirring frequently, for 5 minutes.

2. Transfer to a dampened jelly bag or a strainer lined with several layers of dampened cheesecloth set over a deep bowl. Let juices drip until 1½ cups (375 mL) juice has been collected. Discard solids.

3. Prepare canner, jars and lids. *(For more information, see page 415.)*

4. In a large, deep stainless steel saucepan, combine elderberry juice, peaches, lemon juice and sugar. Over high heat, stirring constantly, bring to a full rolling boil that cannot be stirred down. Stir in pectin. Boil hard, stirring constantly, for 1 minute. Remove from heat and skim off foam.

5. Ladle hot preserves into hot jars, leaving ¼ inch (0.5 cm) headspace. Remove air bubbles and adjust headspace, if necessary, by adding hot preserves. Wipe rim. Center lid on jar. Screw band down until resistance is met, then increase to fingertip-tight.

6. Place jars in canner, ensuring they are completely covered with water. Bring to a boil and process for 10 minutes. Remove canner lid. Wait 5 minutes, then remove jars, cool and store. *(For more information, see pages 417–418.)*

Summer Solstice Preserves

Deeply robust in flavor, this luscious preserve is too good to limit its use to spreading on bread. Serve it over cake or use it as a filling for a layer cake or other sweets.

TIP

Refer to the Produce Purchase Guide on pages 426–429 to determine how much produce you'll need to buy to prepare this recipe.

Makes about five 8-ounce (250 mL) jars

3 cups	halved pitted red tart cherries	750 mL
1 cup	blueberries	250 mL
4½ cups	granulated sugar	1.125 L
2 tbsp	lemon juice	30 mL
1	pouch (3 oz/85 mL) liquid pectin	1
2 tbsp	Kirsch or cherry brandy (optional)	30 mL

1. In a large, deep stainless steel saucepan, combine cherries, blueberries, sugar and lemon juice. Stir to mix well. Let stand at room temperature for 20 minutes.
2. Meanwhile, prepare canner, jars and lids. *(For more information, see page 415.)*
3. Over high heat, stirring constantly, bring fruit mixture to a full rolling boil that cannot be stirred down. Stir in pectin. Boil hard, stirring constantly, for 1 minute. Stir in Kirsch, if using. Remove from heat and skim off foam.
4. Ladle hot preserves into hot jars, leaving ¼ inch (0.5 cm) headspace. Remove air bubbles and adjust headspace, if necessary, by adding hot preserves. Wipe rim. Center lid on jar. Screw band down until resistance is met, then increase to fingertip-tight.
5. Place jars in canner, ensuring they are completely covered with water. Bring to a boil and process for 10 minutes. Remove canner lid. Wait 5 minutes, then remove jars, cool and store. *(For more information, see pages 417–418.)*

Black Forest Preserves

Let your creativity soar! The fabulous flavor of this preserve makes it a tasty accompaniment to cheese. Tuck it into ice cream balls for tartufo or spread it between cake layers or cookie sandwiches.

Makes about seven 8-ounce (250 mL) jars

6½ cups	granulated sugar	1.625 L
⅓ cup	sifted unsweetened cocoa powder	75 mL
3 cups	firmly packed coarsely chopped pitted sweet black cherries	750 mL
½ cup	lemon juice	125 mL
2	pouches (each 3 oz/85 mL) liquid pectin	2
4 tbsp	amaretto liqueur (or ½ tsp/2 mL almond extract)	60 mL

1. Prepare canner, jars and lids. *(For more information, see page 415.)*
2. In a small bowl, combine sugar and cocoa powder. Stir well and set aside.

3. In a large, deep stainless steel saucepan, combine cherries and lemon juice. Stir in reserved cocoa mixture. Over high heat, stirring constantly, bring to a full rolling boil that cannot be stirred down. Stir in pectin. Boil hard, stirring constantly, for 1 minute. Stir in amaretto liqueur. Remove from heat and skim off foam.

4. Ladle hot preserves into hot jars, leaving ¼ inch (0.5 cm) headspace. Remove air bubbles and adjust headspace, if necessary, by adding hot preserves. Wipe rim. Center lid on jar. Screw band down until resistance is met, then increase to fingertip-tight.

5. Place jars in canner, ensuring they are completely covered with water. Bring to a boil and process for 10 minutes. Remove canner lid. Wait 5 minutes, then remove jars, cool and store. *(For more information, see pages 417–418.)*

Kiwi Preserves

With its pale green color and tropical flavor, this delectable preserve is a show-stopping sweet to spoon over fresh-baked breads or simple desserts such as angel food cake.

TIP

Check your package of pectin for the expiration date and use only fresh pectin. Products that have expired may not set properly.

Makes about three 8-ounce (250 mL) jars

4	kiwifruit, peeled and thinly sliced	4
3 cups	granulated sugar	750 mL
¾ cup	unsweetened pineapple juice	175 mL
¼ cup	lime juice	50 mL
1	pouch (3 oz/85 mL) liquid pectin	1

1. Prepare canner, jars and lids. *(For more information, see page 415.)*

2. In a large, deep stainless steel saucepan, combine kiwifruit, sugar, pineapple juice and lime juice. Over high heat, stirring constantly, bring to a full rolling boil that cannot be stirred down. Stir in pectin. Boil hard, stirring constantly, for 1 minute. Remove from heat and skim off foam.

3. Ladle hot preserves into hot jars, leaving ¼ inch (0.5 cm) headspace. Remove air bubbles and adjust headspace, if necessary, by adding hot preserves. Wipe rim. Center lid on jar. Screw band down until resistance is met, then increase to fingertip-tight.

4. Place jars in canner, ensuring they are completely covered with water. Bring to a boil and process for 10 minutes. Remove canner lid. Wait 5 minutes, then remove jars, cool and store. *(For more information, see pages 417–418.)*

Conserves

Conserves are luscious combinations of fresh and dried fruit and nuts, cooked to create a thick, sweet spread with a varied texture. They are especially nice served with specialty breads such as crumpets, English muffins, pancakes and waffles. Conserves also make excellent garnishes for meat and cheese trays as well as cakes and pies.

Conserves with No Added Pectin

Cooking fruit–sugar mixtures concentrates the naturally occurring pectin. To enhance the natural pectin content of fruit when making conserves with no added pectin, use 3 parts fruit that is fully ripe to 1 part fruit that is slightly underripe.

Before making any of the conserves in this section, review the gel stage tests on page 21.

··

Apple Cinnamon Conserve

Naturally sweetened by fruit, this luscious conserve does not need added sugar. Dried apples and raisins create the traditional chunky conserve texture.

TIP

If your mixture has not reached the gel stage when first tested, return the pan to medium heat and cook, stirring constantly, for an additional 5 minutes. Repeat gel stage test and cooking as needed.

Makes about six 8-ounce (250 mL) jars

4 cups	unsweetened applesauce	1 L
2½ cups	unsweetened crushed pineapple, drained	625 mL
1 cup	chopped dried apples	250 mL
¾ cup	golden raisins	175 mL
2 tbsp	lemon juice	30 mL
½ tsp	ground cinnamon	2 mL

1. Prepare canner, jars and lids. *(For more information, see page 415.)*
2. In a large stainless steel saucepan, combine applesauce, pineapple, dried apples, raisins, lemon juice and cinnamon. Bring to a boil over medium-high heat, stirring constantly. Reduce heat and boil gently, stirring frequently, until mixture thickens, about 15 minutes. Remove from heat and test gel (see page 21). If gel stage has been reached, skim off foam.
3. Ladle hot conserve into hot jars, leaving ¼ inch (0.5 cm) headspace. Remove air bubbles and adjust headspace, if necessary, by adding hot conserve. Wipe rim. Center lid on jar. Screw band down until resistance is met, then increase to fingertip-tight.
4. Place jars in canner, ensuring they are completely covered with water. Bring to a boil and process for 10 minutes. Remove canner lid. Wait 5 minutes, then remove jars, cool and store. *(For more information, see pages 417–418.)*

Peach Almond Conserve

Maraschino cherries and almonds, combined with summer's favorite orchard fruit, create an inexpensive yet exquisite conserve that has been a favorite family recipe for generations.

TIPS

Refer to the Produce Purchase Guide on pages 426–429 to determine how much produce you'll need to buy to prepare this recipe.

Read a recipe all the way through, even before you go shopping for the ingredients. It's very important to have all of the ingredients and equipment ready before you start making preserves.

Makes about ten 8-ounce (250 mL) jars

1 tsp	whole cloves	5 mL
1 tsp	whole allspice	5 mL
1	cinnamon stick (about 4 inches/10 cm), broken into pieces	1
8 cups	crushed pitted peeled peaches	2 L
2 cups	finely chopped seeded oranges (unpeeled)	500 mL
7 cups	granulated sugar	1.75 L
1 cup	halved drained maraschino cherries	250 mL
½ cup	slivered almonds	125 mL

1. Prepare canner, jars and lids. *(For more information, see page 415.)*
2. Tie cloves, allspice and cinnamon stick pieces in a square of cheesecloth, creating a spice bag.
3. In a large, deep stainless steel saucepan, combine peaches, oranges and spice bag. Bring to a boil over high heat, stirring constantly. Reduce heat and boil gently, stirring occasionally, for 15 minutes, until fruit is softened. Add sugar, increase heat to medium-high and return to a boil, stirring to dissolve sugar. Boil hard, stirring frequently, until mixture thickens, about 15 minutes. Stir in cherries and almonds; return to a boil. Boil, stirring constantly, for 5 minutes. Remove from heat and test gel (see page 21). If gel stage has been reached, discard spice bag and skim off foam.
4. Ladle hot conserve into hot jars, leaving ¼ inch (0.5 cm) headspace. Remove air bubbles and adjust headspace, if necessary, by adding hot conserve. Wipe rim. Center lid on jar. Screw band down until resistance is met, then increase to fingertip-tight.
5. Place jars in canner, ensuring they are completely covered with water. Bring to a boil and process for 10 minutes. Remove canner lid. Wait 5 minutes, then remove jars, cool and store. *(For more information, see pages 417–418.)*

Cranberry Conserve

A food processor makes quick work of chopping the orange in this traditional cranberry favorite.

TIP

Walnuts, pecans, hazelnuts and blanched almonds are all excellent choices for conserves. Use whatever nut you prefer. However, when adding nuts to a recipe, always check to be sure they are not stale. To bring out their flavor, you can toast the required quantity of chopped nuts in a dry frying pan or toaster oven for 3 to 4 minutes before adding them to the conserve.

Makes about four 8-ounce (250 mL) jars

I	orange (unpeeled), seeded and finely chopped	I
2 cups	water	500 mL
4 cups	cranberries	I L
½ cup	raisins	125 mL
3 cups	granulated sugar	750 mL
½ cup	chopped nuts (see tip, at left)	125 mL

1. Prepare canner, jars and lids. *(For more information, see page 415.)*

2. In a large, deep stainless steel saucepan, combine orange and water. Bring to a boil over high heat. Reduce heat, partially cover and boil gently until peel is tender, about 5 minutes. Add cranberries, raisins and sugar, stirring until sugar dissolves. Return to a boil over medium-high heat, stirring frequently. Boil hard, stirring frequently, until mixture thickens, 10 to 15 minutes. Stir in nuts and cook, stirring constantly, for 5 minutes. Remove from heat and test gel (see page 21). If gel stage has been reached, skim off foam.

3. Ladle hot conserve into hot jars, leaving ¼ inch (0.5 cm) headspace. Remove air bubbles and adjust headspace, if necessary, by adding hot conserve. Wipe rim. Center lid on jar. Screw band down until resistance is met, then increase to fingertip-tight.

4. Place jars in canner, ensuring they are completely covered with water. Bring to a boil and process for 15 minutes. Remove canner lid. Wait 5 minutes, then remove jars, cool and store. *(For more information, see pages 417–418.)*

Blueberry Citrus Conserve

Citrus fruits enhance the rich, earthy flavor of blueberries in this luscious royal blue conserve. Serve it with bread or as a condiment with ham or smoked meats.

Makes about four 8-ounce (250 mL) jars

4 cups	granulated sugar	I L
2 cups	water	500 mL
I	small lemon (unpeeled), seeded and thinly sliced	I
½	orange (unpeeled), seeded and thinly sliced	½
½ cup	raisins	125 mL
4 cups	blueberries	I L

1. Prepare canner, jars and lids. *(For more information, see page 415.)*

For best results, cut lemon and orange in half, then use a sharp knife to slice halves into paper-thin slices.

2. In a large, deep stainless steel saucepan, combine sugar and water. Bring to a boil over high heat, stirring to dissolve sugar. Add lemon and orange slices and raisins. Reduce heat and boil gently for 5 minutes. Add blueberries, increase heat to high and return to a boil. Boil hard, stirring constantly, for 5 to 10 minutes, until mixture thickens. Remove from heat and test gel (see page 21). If gel stage has been reached, skim off foam.

3. Ladle hot conserve into hot jars, leaving ¼ inch (0.5 cm) headspace. Remove air bubbles and adjust headspace, if necessary, by adding hot conserve. Wipe rim. Center lid on jar. Screw band down until resistance is met, then increase to fingertip-tight.

4. Place jars in canner, ensuring they are completely covered with water. Bring to a boil and process for 15 minutes. Remove canner lid. Wait 5 minutes, then remove jars, cool and store. *(For more information, see pages 417–418.)*

Apricot Orange Conserve

While this sunny conserve adds delicious highlights to breakfast menus, it also makes an excellent filling for cookies and cakes.

TIP

If your mixture has not reached the gel stage when first tested, return the pan to medium-high heat and cook, stirring constantly, for an additional 5 minutes. Repeat gel stage test and cooking as needed.

Makes about six 8-ounce (250 mL) jars

3½ cups	chopped pitted peeled apricots	875 mL
2 tbsp	finely grated orange zest	30 mL
1½ cups	orange juice	375 mL
2 tbsp	lemon juice	30 mL
3½ cups	granulated sugar	875 mL
½ cup	chopped walnuts or pecans	125 mL

1. Prepare canner, jars and lids. *(For more information, see page 415.)*

2. In a large, deep stainless steel saucepan, combine apricots, orange zest, orange juice and lemon juice. Stir in sugar until dissolved. Bring to a boil over high heat, stirring constantly. Boil hard, stirring frequently, until mixture thickens, about 15 minutes. Stir in nuts and cook for 5 minutes, stirring constantly. Remove from heat and test gel (see page 21). If gel stage has been reached, skim off foam.

3. Ladle hot conserve into hot jars, leaving ¼ inch (0.5 cm) headspace. Remove air bubbles and adjust headspace, if necessary, by adding hot conserve. Wipe rim. Center lid on jar. Screw band down until resistance is met, then increase to fingertip-tight.

4. Place jars in canner, ensuring they are completely covered with water. Bring to a boil and process for 10 minutes. Remove canner lid. Wait 5 minutes, then remove jars, cool and store. *(For more information, see pages 417–418.)*

Gooseberry Conserve

Raisins and orange add texture and flavor to this tangy, sweet spread. For added color, substitute Thompson raisins or dried cranberries for the golden raisins.

Makes about six 8-ounce (250 mL) jars

6 cups	stemmed gooseberries	1.5 L
1 cup	golden raisins	250 mL
¾ cup	chopped seeded orange pulp	175 mL
4 cups	granulated sugar	1 L

1. Prepare canner, jars and lids. *(For more information, see page 415.)*
2. In a large, deep stainless steel saucepan, combine gooseberries, raisins, orange pulp and sugar. Bring to a boil over medium-high heat, stirring to dissolve sugar. Reduce heat and boil gently, stirring frequently, until mixture thickens, about 30 minutes. Remove from heat and test gel (see page 21). If gel stage has been reached, skim off foam.
3. Ladle hot conserve into hot jars, leaving ¼ inch (0.5 cm) headspace. Remove air bubbles and adjust headspace, if necessary, by adding hot conserve. Wipe rim. Center lid on jar. Screw band down until resistance is met, then increase to fingertip-tight.
4. Place jars in canner, ensuring they are completely covered with water. Bring to a boil and process for 15 minutes. Remove canner lid. Wait 5 minutes, then remove jars, cool and store. *(For more information, see pages 417–418.)*

Nutty Plum Conserve

As deeply rich in flavor as it is in color, this conserve is a luxurious addition to breakfast and lunch menus.

TIP

If your mixture has not reached the gel stage when first tested, return the pan to medium heat and cook, stirring constantly, for an additional 5 minutes. Repeat gel stage test and cooking as needed.

Makes about eight 8-ounce (250 mL) jars

5 lbs	blue prune plums, halved and pitted	2.3 kg
6¾ cups	granulated sugar	1.675 L
4 cups	seedless raisins	1 L
2 tbsp	grated orange zest	30 mL
½ cup	freshly squeezed orange juice	125 mL
¼ cup	bottled lemon juice	50 mL
2 cups	coarsely chopped walnuts or pecans	500 mL

1. In a large, deep stainless steel saucepan, combine plums, sugar, raisins, orange zest, orange juice and lemon juice. Bring to a boil over medium-high heat, stirring constantly. Reduce heat and boil gently, stirring frequently, until mixture thickens, about 35 minutes. Stir in nuts and boil gently for 5 minutes. Remove from heat and test gel (see page 21). If gel stage has been reached, skim off foam.
2. Meanwhile, prepare canner, jars and lids. *(For more information, see page 415.)*

3. Ladle hot conserve into hot jars, leaving ¼ inch (0.5 cm) headspace. Remove air bubbles and adjust headspace, if necessary, by adding hot conserve. Wipe rim. Center lid on jar. Screw band down until resistance is met, then increase to fingertip-tight.

4. Place jars in canner, ensuring they are completely covered with water. Bring to a boil and process for 10 minutes. Remove canner lid. Wait 5 minutes, then remove jars, cool and store. *(For more information, see pages 417–418.)*

Sour Cherry Walnut Conserve

Cherries and walnuts produce a luscious conserve worthy of a royal table. If you prefer a tart flavor, omit the amaretto liqueur, which adds a touch of sweetness.

TIP

Toasting nuts freshens them and intensifies their flavor. Toast nuts in a toaster oven or place in a dry heavy skillet over medium heat and stir until they release their aroma, about 4 minutes.

Makes about seven 8-ounce (250 mL) jars

3	oranges	3
3	lemons	3
5 cups	pitted sour cherries, with juice	1.25 L
2 cups	chopped cored peeled tart apples	500 mL
¾ cup	water	175 mL
3½ cups	granulated sugar	875 mL
¾ cup	chopped toasted walnuts (see tip, at left)	175 mL
¼ cup	amaretto liqueur (optional)	50 mL

1. Prepare canner, jars and lids. *(For more information, see page 415.)*

2. Using a zester or grater, grate zest from oranges and 1 of the lemons. Set aside. Cut oranges and lemons in half. Remove seeds. Working over a large, deep stainless steel saucepan, use a spoon to scoop pulp into saucepan. Add grated zest, cherries, apples and water. Bring to a boil over medium-high heat, stirring constantly. Reduce heat and boil gently, stirring occasionally, until cherries are softened, about 10 minutes. Stir in sugar until dissolved and boil gently, stirring frequently, until mixture thickens, about 35 minutes. Remove from heat and stir in walnuts and amaretto liqueur, if using. Return to a boil over medium-high heat. Boil hard, stirring constantly, for 4 minutes. Remove from heat and test gel (see page 21). If gel stage has been reached, skim off foam.

3. Ladle hot conserve into hot jars, leaving ¼ inch (0.5 cm) headspace. Remove air bubbles and adjust headspace, if necessary, by adding hot conserve. Wipe rim. Center lid on jar. Screw band down until resistance is met, then increase to fingertip-tight.

4. Place jars in canner, ensuring they are completely covered with water. Bring to a boil and process for 10 minutes. Remove canner lid. Wait 5 minutes, then remove jars, cool and store. *(For more information, see pages 417–418.)*

Ambrosia Conserve

The sweet, light flavors of ambrosia come alive in this conserve. If you close your eyes when you taste it, you won't believe it isn't the real thing.

TIPS

You can use either sweetened or unsweetened coconut in this recipe.

A clear plastic ruler (kept solely for kitchen use) will help you determine the correct headspace. Each filled jar should be measured accurately, as the headspace can affect sealing and the preservation of the contents.

Makes about six 8-ounce (250 mL) jars

5 cups	chopped cored peeled fresh pineapple	1.25 L
	Grated zest and juice of 2 medium oranges	
5 cups	granulated sugar	1.25 L
1 cup	flaked coconut (see tip, at left)	250 mL
1 cup	chopped drained maraschino cherries	250 mL
½ cup	slivered almonds	125 mL

1. Prepare canner, jars and lids. *(For more information, see page 415.)*
2. In a large, deep stainless steel saucepan, combine pineapple and orange zest and juice. Bring to a boil over high heat, stirring constantly. Reduce heat and boil gently, stirring occasionally, for 10 minutes, until pineapple is softened. Add sugar, increase heat to medium-high and return to a boil, stirring to dissolve sugar. Boil hard, stirring frequently, until mixture thickens, about 15 minutes. Stir in coconut, cherries and almonds; return to a boil. Boil, stirring frequently, until mixture thickens, about 5 minutes. Remove from heat and test gel (see page 21). If gel stage has been reached, skim off foam.
3. Ladle hot conserve into hot jars, leaving ¼ inch (0.5 cm) headspace. Remove air bubbles and adjust headspace, if necessary, by adding hot conserve. Wipe rim. Center lid on jar. Screw band down until resistance is met, then increase to fingertip-tight.
4. Place jars in canner, ensuring they are completely covered with water. Bring to a boil and process for 15 minutes. Remove canner lid. Wait 5 minutes, then remove jars, cool and store. *(For more information, see pages 417–418.)*

Conserves with Regular Powdered Fruit Pectin

Using pectin to make conserves saves time and energy and reduces the overall cooking time, delivering a fresher-tasting soft spread. When using a powdered fruit pectin, fully dissolve the pectin in the fruit *before* adding the sugar.

Cranberry Carrot Conserve

With all the delicious flavor of a favorite dessert, this colorful spread can also be used as a topping for cheesecake. It makes a perfect gift for any occasion.

TIPS

Toasting nuts freshens them and intensifies their flavor. Toast nuts in a toaster oven or place in a dry heavy skillet over medium heat and stir until they release their aroma, about 4 minutes.

For best results, measure the sugar into a bowl so it can be added to the boiling jam all at once.

Makes about six 8-ounce (250 mL) jars

1½ cups	finely grated peeled carrots	375 mL
1¾ cups	canned crushed pineapple, with juice	425 mL
3 tbsp	lemon juice	45 mL
1½ cups	chopped cored peeled pears	375 mL
⅓ cup	dried cranberries	75 mL
1 tsp	ground cinnamon	5 mL
½ tsp	ground nutmeg	2 mL
1	package (1.75 oz/49 to 57 g) regular powdered fruit pectin	1
6½ cups	granulated sugar	1.625 L
¼ cup	toasted chopped pecans (see tip, at left)	50 mL

1. Prepare canner, jars and lids. *(For more information, see page 415.)*

2. In a large, deep stainless steel saucepan, combine carrots, pineapple and lemon juice. Bring to a boil over high heat, stirring constantly. Reduce heat, cover and boil gently, stirring occasionally, for 20 minutes. Stir in pears, cranberries, cinnamon and nutmeg. Whisk in pectin until dissolved. Bring to a boil over high heat, stirring frequently. Add sugar all at once and return to a full rolling boil, stirring constantly. Boil hard, stirring constantly, for 1 minute. Stir in pecans. Remove from heat and skim off foam.

3. Ladle hot conserve into hot jars, leaving ¼ inch (0.5 cm) headspace. Remove air bubbles and adjust headspace, if necessary, by adding hot conserve. Wipe rim. Center lid on jar. Screw band down until resistance is met, then increase to fingertip-tight.

4. Place jars in canner, ensuring they are completely covered with water. Bring to a boil and process for 10 minutes. Remove canner lid. Wait 5 minutes, then remove jars, cool and store. *(For more information, see pages 417–418.)*

Zesty Grape Conserve

Perk up your peanut butter sandwiches with this spicy grape jam. Or serve it with turkey as an alternative to traditional cranberry sauce.

TIPS

When cutting or seeding hot peppers, wear rubber gloves to keep your hands from being burned.

If you prefer the flavor of cumin, substitute 2 tsp (10 mL) ground cumin for the coriander.

Check your package of pectin for the expiration date and use only fresh pectin. Products that have expired may not set properly.

Makes about eight 8-ounce (250 mL) jars

7 cups	stemmed Concord grapes	1.75 L
1 cup	water	250 mL
2 cups	crushed cored peeled fully ripe pears	500 mL
2	large jalapeño peppers, seeded and finely chopped	2
1 cup	dried cranberries or raisins	250 mL
1 tbsp	ground coriander (optional) (see tip, at left)	15 mL
1	package (1.75 oz/49 to 57 g) regular powdered fruit pectin	1
7 cups	granulated sugar	1.75 L

1. Prepare canner, jars and lids. *(For more information, see page 415.)*

2. Using your fingers, pinch individual grapes, separating skins and pulp. Place skins in a bowl and pulp in a medium saucepan. Add water to grape pulp and bring to a boil. Cover and boil gently, stirring occasionally, for 5 minutes. Press pulp through a fine sieve. Discard seeds. Set pulp aside.

3. In a large, deep stainless steel saucepan, combine grape skins with just enough water to cover. Bring to a boil over medium-high heat. Reduce heat, cover and boil gently until skins are softened, about 5 minutes. Remove from heat and stir in grape pulp, pears, jalapeño peppers, cranberries and coriander, if using. Whisk in pectin until dissolved. Bring to a boil over high heat, stirring frequently. Add sugar all at once and return to a full rolling boil, stirring constantly. Boil hard, stirring constantly, for 1 minute. Remove from heat and skim off foam.

4. Ladle hot conserve into hot jars, leaving ¼ inch (0.5 cm) headspace. Remove air bubbles and adjust headspace, if necessary, by adding hot conserve. Wipe rim. Center lid on jar. Screw band down until resistance is met, then increase to fingertip-tight.

5. Place jars in canner, ensuring they are completely covered with water. Bring to a boil and process for 10 minutes. Remove canner lid. Wait 5 minutes, then remove jars, cool and store. *(For more information, see pages 417–418.)*

Spring Conserve

As soon as rhubarb lifts its tender stalks skyward, assemble the ingredients for this sweet treat. Fresh-picked, imported or thawed frozen strawberries all work well in this recipe.

TIPS

Refer to the Produce Purchase Guide on pages 426–429 to determine how much produce you'll need to buy to prepare this recipe.

For best results, measure the sugar into a bowl so it can be added to the boiling conserve all at once.

Makes about seven 8-ounce (250 mL) jars

1½ cups	canned crushed pineapple, including juice	375 mL
1½ cups	crushed hulled strawberries	375 mL
1¼ cups	finely chopped rhubarb	300 mL
½ cup	golden raisins	125 mL
	Grated zest and juice of 1 lemon	
1	package (1.75 oz/ 49 to 57 g) regular powdered fruit pectin	1
6½ cups	granulated sugar	1.625 L
½ cup	chopped pecans	125 mL

1. Prepare canner, jars and lids. *(For more information, see page 415.)*

2. In a large, deep stainless steel saucepan, combine pineapple, strawberries, rhubarb, raisins and lemon zest and juice. Whisk in pectin until dissolved. Bring to a boil over high heat, stirring frequently. Add sugar all at once and return to a full rolling boil, stirring constantly. Boil hard, stirring constantly, for 1 minute. Stir in pecans. Remove from heat and skim off foam.

3. Ladle hot conserve into hot jars, leaving ¼ inch (0.5 cm) headspace. Remove air bubbles and adjust headspace, if necessary, by adding hot conserve. Wipe rim. Center lid on jar. Screw band down until resistance is met, then increase to fingertip-tight.

4. Place jars in canner, ensuring they are completely covered with water. Bring to a boil and process for 15 minutes. Remove canner lid. Wait 5 minutes, then remove jars, cool and store. *(For more information, see pages 417–418.)*

Conserves with Liquid Pectin

Unlike soft spreads made with powdered pectin, when making conserves with liquid pectin, the fruit, lemon juice (if required) and sugar are brought to a boil before the pectin is added. To form a good gel, it is essential to bring the fruit–sugar mixture to a full rolling boil that cannot be stirred down, stir in the entire contents of the liquid pectin pouch, then boil hard for 1 minute longer.

Cranberry Peach Conserve

Drive your taste buds wild with this classy new twist to peach conserve. Dried cranberries add color and flavor to sweet peaches. Add almonds or leave them out, whichever you prefer.

TIP

Toasting nuts freshens them and intensifies their flavor. Toast nuts in a toaster oven or place in a dry heavy skillet over medium heat and stir until they release their aroma, about 4 minutes.

Makes about six 8-ounce (250 mL) jars

4 cups	finely chopped pitted peeled peaches	1 L
½ cup	coarsely chopped dried cranberries	125 mL
5 cups	granulated sugar	1.25 L
2 tbsp	lemon juice	30 mL
2	pouches (each 3 oz/85 mL) liquid pectin	2
¼ cup	toasted slivered almonds (optional) (see tip, at left)	50 mL
¼ cup	amaretto liqueur (or ½ tsp/2 mL almond extract)	50 mL

1. Prepare canner, jars and lids. *(For more information, see page 415.)*
2. In a large, deep stainless steel saucepan, combine peaches, cranberries, sugar and lemon juice. Over high heat, stirring constantly, bring to a full rolling boil that cannot be stirred down. Stir in pectin. Boil hard, stirring constantly, for 1 minute. Remove from heat and stir in almonds, if using, and amaretto liqueur. Skim off foam.
3. Ladle hot conserve into hot jars, leaving ¼ inch (0.5 cm) headspace. Remove air bubbles and adjust headspace, if necessary, by adding hot conserve. Wipe rim. Center lid on jar. Screw band down until resistance is met, then increase to fingertip-tight.
4. Place jars in canner, ensuring they are completely covered with water. Bring to a boil and process for 10 minutes. Remove canner lid. Wait 5 minutes, then remove jars, cool and store. *(For more information, see pages 417–418.)*

Black Forest Macaroon Conserve

Spread this delicious conserve over ice cream or cake. The flavor combination of homemade black forest cake and chocolate macaroons is scrumptious.

TIPS

Some brands of liquid pectin direct you to stir in the pectin *after* boiling the fruit–sugar mixture for 1 minute. It is advisable to follow the directions given by the brand you are using when preparing these recipes.

Before using jars, inspect them carefully for any chips, cracks or fractures. Discard any imperfect jars.

A jar lifter is very helpful for handling hot, wet jars. Because they are bulky and fit loosely, oven mitts — even water-resistent types — are not a wise choice. When filling jars, an all-purpose rubber glove, worn on your helper hand, will allow you to steady the jar.

Makes about seven 8-ounce (250 mL) jars

4 cups	granulated sugar	1 L
1/3 cup	sifted cocoa powder	75 mL
3 1/2 cups	firmly packed coarsely chopped pitted sweet cherries	875 mL
2 tbsp	lemon juice	30 mL
2	pouches (each 3 oz/85 mL) liquid pectin	2
1/3 cup	unsweetened flaked coconut	75 mL
4 tbsp	Kirsch or cherry brandy (or 1 tsp/5 mL brandy extract)	60 mL

1. Prepare canner, jars and lids. *(For more information, see page 415.)*

2. In a medium bowl, combine sugar and cocoa powder.

3. In a large, deep stainless steel saucepan, combine cherries, lemon juice and cocoa mixture. Over high heat, stirring constantly, bring to a full rolling boil that cannot be stirred down. Stir in pectin. Boil hard, stirring constantly, for 1 minute. Remove from heat and add coconut and Kirsch; mix well. Skim off foam.

4. Ladle hot conserve into hot jars, leaving 1/4 inch (0.5 cm) headspace. Remove air bubbles and adjust headspace, if necessary, by adding hot conserve. Wipe rim. Center lid on jar. Screw band down until resistance is met, then increase to fingertip-tight.

5. Place jars in canner, ensuring they are completely covered with water. Bring to a boil and process for 10 minutes. Remove canner lid. Wait 5 minutes, then remove jars, cool and store. *(For more information, see pages 417–418.)*

Seasoned Pear Almond Conserve

Hints of lemon and ginger add zest to this pear conserve. Slivered almonds add flavor and crunch.

TIPS

Check your package of pectin for the expiration date and use only fresh pectin. Products that have expired may not set properly.

Place a clean towel on your work surface to absorb water from the hot jars as you take them out of the boiling-water canner to be filled, and again once the jars are processed. The towel prevents hot jars from coming into contact with cooler countertops. Significant temperature differences can cause jar breakage.

Makes about seven 8-ounce (250 mL) jars

3½ cups	finely chopped cored peeled ripe pears	875 mL
	Grated zest and juice of 2 large lemons	
6 cups	granulated sugar	1.5 L
½ cup	coarsely chopped slivered almonds	125 mL
I tsp	finely chopped gingerroot	5 mL
I	pouch (3 oz/85 mL) liquid pectin	I

1. Prepare canner, jars and lids. *(For more information, see page 415.)*

2. In a large, deep stainless steel saucepan, combine pears and lemon zest and juice. Stir in sugar and almonds. Cover and let stand at room temperature for 1 hour.

3. Add gingerroot to pear mixture and, over high heat, stirring constantly, bring to a full rolling boil that cannot be stirred down. Stir in pectin. Boil hard, stirring constantly, for 1 minute. Remove from heat and skim off foam.

4. Ladle hot conserve into hot jars, leaving ¼ inch (0.5 cm) headspace. Remove air bubbles and adjust headspace, if necessary, by adding hot conserve. Wipe rim. Center lid on jar. Screw band down until resistance is met, then increase to fingertip-tight.

5. Place jars in canner, ensuring they are completely covered with water. Bring to a boil and process for 10 minutes. Remove canner lid. Wait 5 minutes, then remove jars, cool and store. *(For more information, see pages 417–418.)*

Rhubarb Conserve

While it tastes great on bread, this conserve is also an excellent complement to a cheese tray.

TIPS

Preserve part of this recipe in 4-ounce (125 mL) jars (the processing time will stay the same). They make excellent gifts, just the right size to open and serve on a cheese tray.

A clear plastic ruler (kept solely for kitchen use) will help you determine the correct headspace. Each filled jar should be measured accurately, as the headspace can affect sealing and the preservation of the contents.

Makes about seven 8-ounce (250 mL) jars

4 cups	finely chopped rhubarb	1 L
¼ cup	water	50 mL
2	oranges (unpeeled), seeded and finely chopped	2
1	lemon (unpeeled), seeded and finely chopped	1
1 cup	raisins	250 mL
5 cups	granulated sugar	1.25 L
1¼ tsp	ground mace or nutmeg	6 mL
2	pouches (each 3 oz/85 mL) liquid pectin	2
½ cup	chopped walnuts	125 mL

1. Prepare canner, jars and lids. *(For more information, see page 415.)*

2. In a large, deep stainless steel saucepan, combine rhubarb and water. Partially cover and bring to a boil over medium heat. Boil gently for 2 minutes, until rhubarb is softened. Add oranges, lemon, raisins, sugar and mace, stirring until sugar dissolves. Over high heat, stirring constantly, bring to a full rolling boil that cannot be stirred down. Stir in pectin. Boil hard, stirring constantly, for 1 minute. Remove from heat and stir in walnuts. Skim off foam.

3. Ladle hot conserve into hot jars, leaving ¼ inch (0.5 cm) headspace. Remove air bubbles and adjust headspace, if necessary, by adding hot conserve. Wipe rim. Center lid on jar. Screw band down until resistance is met, then increase to fingertip-tight.

4. Place jars in canner, ensuring they are completely covered with water. Bring to a boil and process for 10 minutes. Remove canner lid. Wait 5 minutes, then remove jars, cool and store. *(For more information, see pages 417–418.)*

Marmalades

Marmalade is a golden suspension of fruit peel and pulp in a tart yet sweet jelly. These delicious spreads might best be described as citrus fruit preserves. Although the original European marmalades were made using quince — the Portuguese word *marmelada* means "quince jam" — today's most popular marmalade uses Seville oranges.

Marmalade can be made using any variety of citrus fruit, on its own or mixed. Tender fruits or vegetables may also be added. Toast with marmalade is a traditional breakfast favorite, but marmalade also makes a fantastic glaze for sweet and savory foods and is a marvelous addition to many marinades.

Traditional marmalades are made using the long-boil method and no added pectin. These products require longer boiling time, as well as a gel stage test (see page 21), for doneness. If you have not previously made a long-boil marmalade, start with one of our easier quick marmalades, prepared with added pectin.

Quick Marmalades

All the taste of Mom's traditional marmalade, but in half the time! Using powdered pectin is an easy way to make good old-fashioned marmalade in far less time than it usually takes. Be sure not to deviate from the quantities or method, as pectin requires a certain amount of sugar, acid and cooking time to form a proper gel.

Powdered fruit pectin is sometimes sold in 49 g packages and sometimes in 57 g packages. The weight difference does not affect the performance of the product.

Quick Strawberry Lemon Marmalade

Lemon shares the stage with strawberries, a summer favorite, in this sweet, red-hued marmalade.

TIPS

For best results, measure the sugar into a bowl so it can be added to the boiling marmalade all at once.

Using pectin in these recipes allows you to enjoy the beloved sweet flavor of marmalade with very little time by the hot stove.

Makes about seven 8-ounce (250 mL) jars

¼ cup	thinly sliced lemon peel	50 mL
	Water	
4 cups	crushed hulled strawberries	1 L
1 tbsp	lemon juice	15 mL
1	package (1.75 oz/49 to 57 g) regular powdered fruit pectin	1
6 cups	granulated sugar	1.5 L

1. Prepare canner, jars and lids. *(For more information, see page 415.)*
2. In a large, deep stainless steel saucepan, combine lemon peel and water to cover. Bring to a boil over medium-high heat and boil for 5 minutes, until peel is softened. Drain and discard liquid.
3. Add strawberries and lemon juice to peel and mix well. Whisk in pectin until dissolved. Bring to a boil over high heat, stirring constantly. Add sugar all at once and return to a full rolling boil, stirring constantly. Boil hard, stirring constantly, for 1 minute. Remove from heat and skim off foam.
4. Ladle hot marmalade into hot jars, leaving ¼ inch (0.5 cm) headspace. Remove air bubbles and adjust headspace, if necessary, by adding hot marmalade. Wipe rim. Center lid on jar. Screw band down until resistance is met, then increase to fingertip-tight.
5. Place jars in canner, ensuring they are completely covered with water. Bring to a boil and process for 10 minutes. Remove canner lid. Wait 5 minutes, then remove jars, cool and store. *(For more information, see pages 417–418.)*

Quick Lemon Ginger Marmalade

Lemon and gingerroot combine to make a tantalizing spread. This recipe uses added pectin to reduce the cooking time, making it ideal for today's busy cook.

TIPS

Check your package of pectin for the expiration date and use only fresh pectin. Products that have expired may not set properly.

If you have particularly hard water and use it in the boiling-water canner, it can leave a residue on jars. Use filtered or reverse-osmosis water to fill your canner instead.

Makes about seven 8-ounce (250 mL) jars

6	small lemons	6
½ tsp	baking soda	2 mL
2½ cups	water	625 mL
1 cup	coarsely grated gingerroot (about 12 oz/375 g)	250 mL
1	package (1.75 oz/49 to 57 g) regular powdered fruit pectin	1
6½ cups	granulated sugar	1.625 L

1. Prepare canner, jars and lids. *(For more information, see page 415.)*

2. Using a vegetable peeler, remove yellow lemon peel in long strips. Cut peel into thin slices. Set peel and fruit aside separately.

3. In a large, deep stainless steel saucepan, combine reserved lemon peel, baking soda and water. Bring to a boil over high heat. Reduce heat, cover and boil gently for 5 minutes, until peel is softened. Remove from heat and set aside.

4. Using a sharp knife, cut white pith from lemons. Working over a large bowl to catch juice and using a small, sharp knife, separate lemon segments from membrane. Place segments in bowl and squeeze membrane to remove as much juice as possible, collecting it in the bowl. Discard membrane and seeds. Measure 1 cup (250 mL) lemon segments and juice. Add to softened rind mixture with gingerroot. Whisk in pectin until dissolved. Bring to a boil over high heat, stirring constantly. Add sugar all at once and return to a full rolling boil, stirring constantly. Boil hard, stirring constantly, for 1 minute. Remove from heat and skim off foam.

5. Ladle hot marmalade into hot jars, leaving ¼ inch (0.5 cm) headspace. Remove air bubbles and adjust headspace, if necessary, by adding hot marmalade. Wipe rim. Center lid on jar. Screw band down until resistance is met, then increase to fingertip-tight.

6. Place jars in canner, ensuring they are completely covered with water. Bring to a boil and process for 10 minutes. Remove canner lid. Wait 5 minutes, then remove jars, cool and store. *(For more information, see pages 417–418.)*

Quick Red Onion Marmalade

Sweet red onion steals the show in this savory red marmalade.

TIPS

For best results, measure the sugar into a bowl so it can be added to the boiling marmalade all at once.

Read a recipe all the way through, even before you go shopping for the ingredients. It's very important to have all of the ingredients and equipment ready before you start making preserves.

Makes about five 8-ounce (250 mL) jars

1½ cups	thinly sliced halved red onion	375 mL
½ cup	finely chopped dried cranberries	125 mL
¼ cup	lightly packed brown sugar	50 mL
¼ cup	cider vinegar	50 mL
2 tsp	grated orange zest	10 mL
3 cups	unsweetened apple juice	750 mL
1	package (1.75 oz/49 to 57 g) regular powdered fruit pectin	1
4 cups	granulated sugar	1 L

1. Prepare canner, jars and lids. *(For more information, see page 415.)*

2. In a skillet, over medium heat, combine red onion, cranberries, brown sugar and vinegar. Cook, stirring, until onion is transparent, about 10 minutes.

3. In a large, deep stainless steel saucepan, combine cooked onion mixture, orange zest and apple juice. Whisk in pectin until dissolved. Bring to a boil over high heat, stirring frequently. Add sugar all at once and return to a full rolling boil, stirring constantly. Boil hard, stirring constantly, for 1 minute. Remove from heat and skim off foam.

4. Ladle hot marmalade into hot jars, leaving ¼ inch (0.5 cm) headspace. Remove air bubbles and adjust headspace, if necessary, by adding hot marmalade. Wipe rim. Center lid on jar. Screw band down until resistance is met, then increase to fingertip-tight.

5. Place jars in canner, ensuring they are completely covered with water. Bring to a boil and process for 15 minutes. Remove canner lid. Wait 5 minutes, then remove jars, cool and store. *(For more information, see pages 417–418.)*

Traditional Marmalades

Due to their extended cooking time, traditional marmalades have a slightly caramelized flavor that spells perfection to marmalade aficionados. Before making one of these long-boil marmalades, review the gel stage tests on page 21.

....

Orange Chili Marmalade

Chili peppers intensify the citrus flavor and add zest to this unique marmalade. Use it to add sparkle to cheese trays or serve it as a condiment with coconut-battered shrimp. And don't forget toast — it makes the traditional something special.

TIP

If your mixture has not reached the gel stage when first tested, return the pan to medium-high heat and cook, stirring constantly, for an additional 5 minutes. Repeat gel stage test and cooking as needed.

Makes about eight 8-ounce (250 mL) jars

2¼ lbs	oranges (unpeeled), seeded and thinly sliced	1 kg
	Grated zest and juice of 1 lemon	
6 cups	water	1.5 L
3	dried habanero chili peppers (or 6 dried Colorado or New Mexico chili peppers)	3
9 cups	granulated sugar	2.25 L

1. In a large, deep stainless steel saucepan, combine oranges, lemon zest and juice and water. Bring to a boil over high heat, stirring constantly. Reduce heat and boil gently, stirring occasionally, for 40 minutes. Add chili peppers, partially cover and boil gently, stirring occasionally, until fruit is very soft, about 30 minutes. Remove and discard chili peppers.

2. Meanwhile, prepare canner, jars and lids. *(For more information, see page 415.)*

3. Bring mixture to a boil over medium-high heat, stirring constantly. Maintaining boil, gradually stir in sugar. Boil hard, stirring occasionally, until mixture reaches gel stage, about 15 minutes. Remove from heat and test gel (see page 21). If gel stage has been reached, skim off foam.

4. Ladle hot marmalade into hot jars, leaving ¼ inch (0.5 cm) headspace. Remove air bubbles and adjust headspace, if necessary, by adding hot marmalade. Wipe rim. Center lid on jar. Screw band down until resistance is met, then increase to fingertip-tight.

5. Place jars in canner, ensuring they are completely covered with water. Bring to a boil and process for 10 minutes. Remove canner lid. Wait 5 minutes, then remove jars, cool and store. *(For more information, see pages 417–418.)*

Seville Orange Marmalade

Available only in the first quarter of each year, Seville oranges are not usually eaten as fruit but are reserved instead for making marmalade. They have a thick, rough skin and are highly acidic. Brandy adds a distinct, mature flavor to this delicious preserve.

TIPS

For a more tender result, after combining the pulp bag, juice and hot water, cover and set aside for 24 hours before continuing with Step 2.

When boiling the unsugared mixture in Step 2, check it frequently to ensure bubbles continue to gently break the surface.

If your mixture has not reached the gel stage when first tested, return the pan to medium-high heat and cook, stirring constantly, for an additional 5 minutes. Repeat gel stage test and cooking as needed.

Makes eleven to twelve 8-ounce (250 mL) jars

2¼ lbs	Seville oranges	1 kg
2	Clementine oranges	2
2	lemons	2
12½ cups	hot water	3.125 L
11½ cups	granulated sugar	2.875 L
⅓ cup	brandy (optional)	75 mL

1. Place a 12-inch (30 cm) square of dampened cheesecloth in a bowl. Cut Seville oranges, Clementine oranges and lemons in half crosswise. Squeeze juice from each half into cheesecloth-lined bowl. Using a spoon or grapefruit knife, scoop seeds and pulp into cheesecloth. Tightly tie cheesecloth around pulp and seeds, reserving juices that drip into bowl. Using a sharp knife, thinly slice peel crosswise.

2. In a large, deep stainless steel saucepan, combine sliced peel, pulp and seed bag, reserved juice and hot water. Bring to a boil over high heat. Reduce heat and boil gently, stirring occasionally, until peel is tender and mixture is reduced by nearly half, about 1½ hours. Remove from heat and transfer pulp bag to a sieve placed over a bowl. Press with a spoon to extract as much juice as possible. Discard pulp bag and add juice to cooked mixture. Measure 10 cups (2.5 L) and return to saucepan.

3. Meanwhile, prepare canner, jars and lids. *(For more information, see page 415.)*

4. Bring mixture to a boil over high heat, stirring constantly. Maintaining boil, gradually stir in sugar. Boil hard, stirring occasionally, until mixture reaches gel stage, about 15 minutes. Remove from heat and test gel (see page 21). If gel stage has been reached, add brandy, if using, and boil, stirring frequently, for 2 minutes. Skim off foam.

5. Ladle hot marmalade into hot jars, leaving ¼ inch (0.5 cm) headspace. Remove air bubbles and adjust headspace, if necessary, by adding hot marmalade. Wipe rim. Center lid on jar. Screw band down until resistance is met, then increase to fingertip-tight.

6. Place jars in canner, ensuring they are completely covered with water. Bring to a boil and process for 10 minutes. Remove canner lid. Wait 5 minutes, then remove jars, cool and store. *(For more information, see pages 417–418.)*

Blood Orange Marmalade

Create a unique "rose" marmalade with blood oranges. This blushed pink-golden marmalade has a unique color and a delightfully refreshing flavor. Cooking the orange–sugar mixture in two small batches shortens the boiling time and delivers a fresher taste.

TIPS

If you don't have two saucepans, use a single large, deep saucepan, but the cooking time will be at least doubled.

If you wish, you can add 4 tbsp (60 mL) orange-flavored liqueur to each saucepan when the marmalade has nearly reached the gel stage in Step 5. Continue cooking until the gel stage has been reached.

Makes about six 8-ounce (250 mL) jars

3 lbs	blood oranges	1.37 kg
	Water	
6 cups	granulated sugar, divided	1.5 L

1. Using a sharp knife, trim tops and bottoms from oranges. Score the peel of each orange lengthwise into quarters. Remove peel and set fruit aside. Place peel in a large stainless steel saucepan with enough water to cover generously . Bring to a boil over medium-low heat and boil for 10 minutes. Drain. Cover generously with fresh cold water and return to a boil. Boil for 10 minutes, until peel is softened. Drain. Using a spoon, scrape white pith from peel and discard. Using a sharp knife, cut peel into paper-thin strips.

2. Working over a large stainless steel saucepan to catch juice and using a small, sharp knife, separate orange segments from membrane. Place segments in saucepan and squeeze membrane to remove as much juice as possible, collecting it in the saucepan. Discard membrane and seeds.

3. Add cooked peel and 4 cups (1 L) water to segments. Bring to a boil over medium-high heat, stirring occasionally. Reduce heat and boil gently, stirring frequently, until peel is very soft when squeezed with fingers, about 30 minutes. Remove from heat and measure 6 cups (1.5 L), adding water as necessary to yield the required quantity. Mix well.

4. Meanwhile, prepare canner, jars and lids. *(For more information, see page 415.)*

5. Ladle 3 cups (750 mL) of the cooked mixture into a clean large, deep stainless steel saucepan. Ladle remaining mixture into a second saucepan. Bring both saucepans to a boil over medium-high heat. Maintaining boil, gradually stir 3 cups (750 mL) sugar into each saucepan. Boil hard, stirring constantly, until mixture reaches gel stage, about 12 minutes. Remove from heat and test gel (see page 21). If gel stage has been reached, skim off foam.

6. Ladle hot marmalade into hot jars, leaving ¼ inch (0.5 cm) headspace. Remove air bubbles and adjust headspace, if necessary, by adding hot marmalade. Wipe rim. Center lid on jar. Screw band down until resistance is met, then increase to fingertip-tight.

7. Place jars in canner, ensuring they are completely covered with water. Bring to a boil and process for 10 minutes. Remove canner lid. Wait 5 minutes, then remove jars, cool and store. *(For more information, see pages 417–418.)*

Ginger Pear Marmalade

The first cool days of autumn, when pears are freshly picked, are the ideal time to make this delicious marmalade.

TIPS

Look for crystallized ginger in Asian markets or well-stocked supermarkets.

If your mixture has not reached the gel stage when first tested, return the pan to high heat and cook, stirring constantly, for an additional 5 minutes. Repeat gel stage test and cooking as needed.

Makes about four 8-ounce (250 mL) jars

3	limes	3
8 cups	thinly sliced cored peeled firm ripe pears	2 L
4 cups	granulated sugar	I L
3 tbsp	chopped crystallized ginger (see tip, at left)	45 mL
I¼ cups	water	300 mL

1. Using a sharp knife, remove peel from limes and cut it into very thin strips. Set aside. Cut limes in half crosswise and squeeze juice into a large stainless steel saucepan. Add pears. Toss gently until pears are coated with lime juice. Add sugar and ginger. Stir until well combined. Cover and let stand at room temperature for 1 hour.

2. Meanwhile, prepare canner, jars and lids. *(For more information, see page 415.)*

3. In a small stainless steel saucepan, combine peel and water. Bring to a boil over medium heat and boil, stirring frequently, until peel is tender and most of the liquid has evaporated, about 15 minutes. Drain liquid into pear mixture; set peel aside.

4. Bring pear mixture to a full rolling boil over high heat, stirring frequently. Boil hard, stirring frequently, for 15 minutes. Add peel and boil until mixture reaches gel stage, about 5 minutes. Remove from heat and test gel (see page 21). If gel stage has been reached, skim off foam.

5. Ladle hot marmalade into hot jars, leaving ¼ inch (0.5 cm) headspace. Remove air bubbles and adjust headspace, if necessary, by adding hot marmalade. Wipe rim. Center lid on jar. Screw band down until resistance is met, then increase to fingertip-tight.

6. Place jars in canner, ensuring they are completely covered with water. Bring to a boil and process for 10 minutes. Remove canner lid. Wait 5 minutes, then remove jars, cool and store. *(For more information, see pages 417–418.)*

Variation

Substitute 2 lemons or 1 large orange for the lime.

Grapefruit Marmalade

Grapefruit provides a refreshing change from traditional orange and lemon marmalades.

TIPS

When preparing jars and lids, prepare a couple extra in case your yield is larger than you expect. If you don't have enough jars, place any leftover preserves in an airtight container, store in the refrigerator and use within a few weeks.

Before using jars, inspect them carefully for any chips, cracks or fractures. Discard any imperfect jars.

A jar lifter is very helpful for handling hot, wet jars. Because they are bulky and fit loosely, oven mitts — even water-resistent types — are not a wise choice. When filling jars, an all-purpose rubber glove, worn on your helper hand, will allow you to steady the jar.

Makes about three 8-ounce (250 mL) jars

1	large grapefruit	1
	Water	
	Granulated sugar	

1. Wash grapefruit, score skin into quarters and remove peel. With a spoon, scrape bitter white pith from peel and discard. Slice the peel thinly. In a large, deep stainless steel saucepan, combine peel with water to cover generously. Bring to a boil over medium-low heat and boil for 10 minutes. Drain and discard liquid. Return to saucepan.

2. Working over a bowl to catch juice and using a sharp knife, separate grapefruit segments from the membrane. Add segments and juice to peel in saucepan. Squeeze any juice from membrane into saucepan. Discard membrane and seeds. Add 4 cups (1 L) water to peel mixture. Bring to a boil over medium-high heat. Reduce heat and boil gently, stirring occasionally, for 10 minutes. Cover and let stand in a cool place (70 to 75°F/21 to 23°C) for 12 to 18 hours.

3. Prepare canner, jars and lids. *(For more information, see page 415.)*

4. Return saucepan to medium-high heat and bring to a boil, stirring frequently. Boil until peel is tender, about 15 minutes. Remove from heat and measure fruit mixture. Return to saucepan and bring back to a boil. Maintaining boil, gradually stir in 1 cup (250 mL) sugar for each cup (250 mL) of fruit. Boil hard, stirring frequently, until mixture reaches gel stage, about 30 minutes. Remove from heat and test gel (see page 21). If gel stage has been reached, skim off foam.

5. Ladle hot marmalade into hot jars, leaving ¼ inch (0.5 cm) headspace. Remove air bubbles and adjust headspace, if necessary, by adding hot marmalade. Wipe rim. Center lid on jar. Screw band down until resistance is met, then increase to fingertip-tight.

6. Place jars in canner, ensuring they are completely covered with water. Bring to a boil and process for 10 minutes. Remove canner lid. Wait 5 minutes, then remove jars, cool and store. *(For more information, see pages 417–418.)*

Morning Cheer Marmalade

Make this carrot delicacy any time of the year. The recipe combines always-plentiful carrots and oranges in a lightly spiced marmalade. Its intriguing ingredients make it an especially appropriate gift.

TIPS

If your mixture has not reached the gel stage when first tested, return the pan to medium-high heat and cook, stirring constantly, for an additional 5 minutes. Repeat gel stage test and cooking as needed.

Place a clean towel on your work surface to absorb water from the hot jars as you take them out of the boiling-water canner to be filled, and again once the jars are processed. The towel prevents hot jars from coming into contact with cooler countertops. Significant temperature differences can cause jar breakage.

Makes about six 8-ounce (250 mL) jars

½ tsp	whole allspice	2 mL
I	cinnamon stick (about 5 inches/13 cm), broken into pieces	I
5	oranges	5
I	tart apple, such as Granny Smith, peeled, cored and grated	I
4 cups	finely grated peeled carrots	I L
I½ cups	water	375 mL
4 cups	granulated sugar	I L
⅓ cup	lemon juice	75 mL
¼ cup	Scotch whisky (optional)	50 mL

1. Tie allspice and cinnamon stick pieces in a square of cheesecloth, creating a spice bag. Set aside.

2. Using a vegetable peeler, remove peel from each orange in one long strip. Cut peel into thin strips and set aside. Using a sharp knife, remove white pith from oranges and discard. Working over a large, deep stainless steel saucepan to catch juice and using a small, sharp knife, separate orange segments from membrane. Place segments in saucepan and squeeze membrane to remove as much juice as possible, collecting it in the saucepan. Discard membrane and seeds.

3. Add apple, carrots, water, reserved orange peel and reserved spice bag to saucepan. Bring to a boil over medium-high heat, stirring occasionally. Reduce heat, cover and boil gently, stirring occasionally, for 15 minutes. Maintaining boil, gradually stir in sugar and lemon juice. Boil hard, stirring frequently, until mixture reaches gel stage, about 30 minutes. Remove from heat and test gel (see page 21). If gel stage has been reached, stir in Scotch, if using. Discard spice bag and skim off foam.

4. Meanwhile, prepare canner, jars and lids. *(For more information, see page 415.)*

5. Ladle hot marmalade into hot jars, leaving ¼ inch (0.5 cm) headspace. Remove air bubbles and adjust headspace, if necessary, by adding hot marmalade. Wipe rim. Center lid on jar. Screw band down until resistance is met, then increase to fingertip-tight.

6. Place jars in canner, ensuring they are completely covered with water. Bring to a boil and process for 10 minutes. Remove canner lid. Wait 5 minutes, then remove jars, cool and store. *(For more information, see pages 417–418.)*

Cherry Marmalade

Sweet cherries create a special marmalade that will brighten any Sunday morning brunch.

TIP

A clear plastic ruler (kept solely for kitchen use) will help you determine the correct headspace. Each filled jar should be measured accurately, as the headspace can affect sealing and the preservation of the contents.

Makes about four 8-ounce (250 mL) jars

⅔ cup	chopped seeded orange (unpeeled)	150 mL
4 cups	pitted sweet cherries	I L
4 tbsp	lemon juice	60 mL
3½ cups	granulated sugar	875 mL

1. Prepare canner, jars and lids. *(For more information, see page 415.)*
2. In a large, deep stainless steel saucepan, combine orange, cherries and lemon juice. Bring to a boil over medium-high heat. Reduce heat, cover and boil gently, stirring frequently, until peel is tender, about 20 minutes. Maintaining boil, gradually stir in sugar. Boil hard, stirring frequently, until mixture reaches gel stage, about 30 minutes. Remove from heat and test gel (see page 21). If gel stage has been reached, skim off foam.
3. Ladle hot marmalade into hot jars, leaving ¼ inch (0.5 cm) headspace. Remove air bubbles and adjust headspace, if necessary, by adding hot marmalade. Wipe rim. Center lid on jar. Screw band down until resistance is met, then increase to fingertip-tight.
4. Place jars in canner, ensuring they are completely covered with water. Bring to a boil and process for 15 minutes. Remove canner lid. Wait 5 minutes, then remove jars, cool and store. *(For more information, see pages 417–418.)*

Prickly Pear Marmalade

Prickly pear is a member of the cactus family. It makes a sweet and fragrant addition to marmalade.

TIP

For this recipe, you'll need about 9 medium prickly pears.

Makes about six 8-ounce (250 mL) jars

3 cups	chopped seeded oranges (unpeeled)	750 mL
I cup	thinly sliced seeded lemons (unpeeled)	250 mL
4 cups	water	I L
4 cups	chopped seeded peeled prickly pears	I L
6 cups	granulated sugar	1.5 L

1. In a large, deep stainless steel saucepan, combine oranges, lemons and water. Bring to a boil over medium-high heat. Reduce heat and boil gently for 5 minutes. Cover and let stand in a cool place (70 to 75°F/21 to 23°C) for 12 to 18 hours.
2. Prepare canner, jars and lids. *(For more information, see page 415.)*

TIP

If your mixture has not reached the gel stage when first tested, return the pan to medium-high heat and cook, stirring constantly, for an additional 5 minutes. Repeat gel stage test and cooking as needed.

3. Bring orange mixture to a boil over medium-high heat. Boil, stirring frequently, until peel is tender, about 15 minutes. Stir in prickly pears. Maintaining boil, gradually stir in sugar. Boil hard, stirring frequently, until mixture reaches gel stage, about 30 minutes. Remove from heat and test gel (see page 21). If gel stage has been reached, skim off foam.

4. Ladle hot marmalade into hot jars, leaving ¼ inch (0.5 cm) headspace. Remove air bubbles and adjust headspace, if necessary, by adding hot marmalade. Wipe rim. Center lid on jar. Screw band down until resistance is met, then increase to fingertip-tight.

5. Place jars in canner, ensuring they are completely covered with water. Bring to a boil and process for 15 minutes. Remove canner lid. Wait 5 minutes, then remove jars, cool and store. *(For more information, see pages 417–418.)*

Easiest Ever Marmalade

A food processor speeds up preparation in this uniquely flavored, one-step marmalade. Maraschino cherries add a touch of brightness to the light amber color.

TIP

For ease in chopping citrus fruits in a food processor, quarter or coarsely chop before putting in the work bowl.

Makes about seven 8-ounce (250 mL) jars

3	small oranges (unpeeled), seeded	3
1	lemon (unpeeled), seeded	1
1	small grapefruit (unpeeled), seeded	1
2 cups	canned crushed pineapple, with juice	500 mL
6 cups	granulated sugar	1.5 L
½ cup	chopped drained maraschino cherries	125 mL

1. In a food processor fitted with a metal blade, working in batches, pulse oranges, lemon and grapefruit until finely chopped. Do not purée.

2. In a large, deep stainless steel saucepan, combine chopped fruit, pineapple with juice and sugar. Bring to a boil over medium-high heat, stirring to dissolve sugar. Boil hard, stirring constantly, until mixture begins to sheet from a metal spoon, about 20 minutes. Add cherries and boil until mixture reaches gel stage, about 5 minutes. Remove from heat and test gel (see page 21). If gel stage has been reached, skim off foam.

3. Prepare canner, jars and lids. *(For more information, see page 415.)*

4. Ladle hot marmalade into hot jars, leaving ¼ inch (0.5 cm) headspace. Remove air bubbles and adjust headspace, if necessary, by adding hot marmalade. Wipe rim. Center lid on jar. Screw band down until resistance is met, then increase to fingertip-tight.

5. Place jars in canner, ensuring they are completely covered with water. Bring to a boil and process for 10 minutes. Remove canner lid. Wait 5 minutes, then remove jars, cool and store. *(For more information, see pages 417–418.)*

Gingered Zucchini Marmalade

This delicious marmalade makes a great hostess gift. Label it "Mystery Marmalade" and see how many of your friends can guess the main ingredient.

TIPS

Cheesecloth can be found at many retailers, such as grocery stores and other stores that carry kitchen supplies. Look in the area where kitchen utensils are located.

If your mixture has not reached the gel stage when first tested, return the pan to medium-high heat and cook, stirring constantly, for an additional 5 minutes. Repeat gel stage test and cooking as needed.

Makes about four 8-ounce (250 mL) jars

2	oranges	2
2	lemons	2
3 tbsp	chopped gingerroot	45 mL
5 cups	shredded peeled zucchini	1.25 L
I	tart apple, cored and grated	I
4 cups	granulated sugar	I L

1. Using a vegetable peeler, remove peel from each orange in one long strip. Cut orange peel into thin strips and place in a large, deep stainless steel saucepan. Set aside. Remove white pith from oranges and peel and pith from lemon. Set fruit aside. Tie orange and lemon pith and peel and gingerroot in a square of cheesecloth, creating a spice bag. Add to saucepan.

2. Working over the saucepan to catch juice and using a small, sharp knife, separate orange and lemon segments from membrane. Place segments in saucepan and squeeze membrane to remove as much juice as possible, collecting it in the saucepan. Discard membrane and seeds.

3. Add zucchini, apple and sugar to saucepan and mix well. Bring to a boil over medium-high heat, stirring to dissolve sugar. Boil hard, stirring frequently, until mixture reaches gel stage, about 45 minutes. Remove from heat and test gel (see page 21). If gel stage has been reached, skim off foam. Discard spice bag.

4. Meanwhile, prepare canner, jars and lids. *(For more information, see page 415.)*

5. Ladle hot marmalade into hot jars, leaving ¼ inch (0.5 cm) headspace. Remove air bubbles and adjust headspace, if necessary, by adding hot marmalade. Wipe rim. Center lid on jar. Screw band down until resistance is met, then increase to fingertip-tight.

6. Place jars in canner, ensuring they are completely covered with water. Bring to a boil and process for 10 minutes. Remove canner lid. Wait 5 minutes, then remove jars, cool and store. *(For more information, see pages 417–418.)*

Jellies

Firm enough to hold its shape when spooned from the jar, yet tender enough to spread easily, jelly is a preserver's jewel. To make jelly, clear juice is cooked with the appropriate quantity of sugar, fruit pectin and acid. Pectin is added to most jelly recipes because few juices have enough natural pectin to create a "gel."

Juice for Jelly

Making the juice is the first step in making any fruit juice jelly. Although it is a simple procedure, it does take at least 2 hours, as the juice needs to drip undisturbed from the jelly bag to create the clear, translucent jellies we all expect.

Always prepare juice for jelly in small, recipe-sized batches. Select top-quality fruit and discard any damaged portions. If the yield of juice is slightly less than the quantity required for the recipe, add ½ cup (125 mL) boiling water to the remaining fruit pulp to extract additional juice. Alternatively, unsweetened apple or white grape juice may be added to homemade juice to extend the quantity.

If your schedule doesn't allow you to make jelly when fruit is at its peak, you can make the juice for jelly when fruit is fresh, then freeze it and make the jelly another day. Freeze juice in straight-sided containers filled to within ½ inch (1 cm) of the rim.

> Although it's tempting to squeeze the jelly bag because it speeds juice collection, doing so releases solids into the juice that may produce a cloudy jelly.

Berry Juice for Jelly

For each cup (250 mL) of berry juice, you'll need 3 to 3½ cups (750 to 875 mL) of raspberries, blackberries, boysenberries, youngberries, dewberries or loganberries. Use tender, ripe berries. Juice yield will vary depending upon the juiciness of the berries used.

TIP

Freezing raspberries and strawberries helps release their juices, as it weakens their tender cell structure. For berries that are very juicy, tender and plump, such as raspberries and strawberries, freezing can replace heating as a juice extraction method. Freeze unsweetened strawberries or raspberries for at least 24 hours. Thaw in refrigerator and thoroughly crush berries with a potato masher. Pour crushed mixture into a dampened jelly bag and proceed as directed in Step 2.

1. Gently wash and drain berries, handling carefully to avoid juice loss. Remove caps and stems. In a large stainless steel saucepan, combine berries and just enough water to prevent scorching, about ¼ to ½ cup (50 to 125 mL) water for every 4 cups (1 L) berries. Bring to a boil over medium-high heat, stirring frequently. Reduce heat, cover loosely and boil gently, stirring and crushing berries occasionally, just until berries are softened, 5 to 10 minutes.

2. Transfer berry mixture to a dampened jelly bag or a strainer lined with several layers of dampened cheesecloth set over a deep bowl. Let drip, undisturbed, for at least 2 hours or overnight to collect juice.

Variations

Blueberry Juice for Jelly: For each cup (250 mL) blueberry juice, substitute about 2 cups (500 mL) blueberries for the berries. Juice yield of blueberries will vary with individual harvest conditions.

Elderberry Juice for Jelly: For each cup (250 mL) elderberry juice, substitute about 1 lb (500 g) elderberries for the berries.

Strawberry Juice for Jelly: For each cup (250 mL) strawberry juice, substitute about 3¼ cups (800 mL) whole strawberries for the berries.

Red or Black Currant Juice for Jelly: For each cup (250 mL) currant juice, substitute about 1 lb (500 g) currants for the berries. Red currants yield slightly more juice than black.

Cherry Juice for Jelly: For each cup (250 mL) cherry juice, substitute about 1 lb (500 g) whole cherries for the berries.

Grape Juice for Jelly: For each cup (250 mL) grape juice, substitute about 14 oz (390 g) grapes for the berries.

Apple Juice for Jelly

For each cup (250 mL) of apple juice, you'll need about 4 small apples, or about 16 oz (454 g).

TIP

Once the fruit is prepared and placed in the dampened jelly bag or cheesecloth-lined sieve, make sure to let the juice drip for several hours. Do not squeeze the jelly bag, as that may cause the juice to be cloudy.

1. In a large stainless steel saucepan, place washed, quartered apples from which stem and blossom ends have been removed. (Do not core.) Add enough cold water to cover fruit, or about 1 cup (250 mL) for each 1 lb (500 g) apples. Bring to a boil over high heat, stirring frequently. Reduce heat, cover loosely and boil gently, stirring and crushing apples occasionally, just until apples are softened, about 30 minutes. (Do not overcook, as it reduces flavor, color and the strength of the pectin.)

2. Transfer apple mixture to a dampened jelly bag or a strainer lined with several layers of dampened cheesecloth set over a deep bowl. Let drip, undisturbed, for at least 2 hours or overnight to collect juice.

Variations

Crabapple Juice for Jelly: For each cup (250 mL) of crabapple juice, substitute 16 oz (454 g) crabapples for the apples.

Pear Juice for Jelly: For each cup (250 mL) of pear juice, substitute about 2 medium-large pears (or about 14 oz/390 g) for the apples.

Peach Juice for Jelly

For each cup (250 mL) of peach juice, you'll need about 3 medium peaches, or about 1 lb (500 g).

TIP

Cheesecloth can be found at many retailers, such as grocery stores and other stores that carry kitchen supplies. Look in the area where kitchen utensils are located.

1. In a large stainless steel saucepan, place washed, quartered peaches. (It is not essential to pit peaches; however, removing the pits before cooking reduces the bulk of solids that must fit in a jelly bag.) Add ½ cup (125 mL) water for each 1 lb (500 g) peaches. Bring to a boil over high heat, stirring frequently. Reduce heat, cover loosely and boil gently, stirring and crushing peaches occasionally, just until peaches are softened, about 20 minutes. (Do not overcook, as it reduces flavor, color and the strength of the pectin.)

2. Transfer peach mixture to a dampened jelly bag or a strainer lined with several layers of dampened cheesecloth set over a deep bowl. Let drip, undisturbed, for at least 2 hours or overnight to collect juice.

Variations

Nectarine Juice for Jelly: For each cup (250 mL) nectarine juice, substitute about 3 medium nectarines (or about 1 lb/500 g) for the peaches.

Plum Juice for Jelly: For each cup (250 mL) plum juice, substitute about 9 blue plums (or about 15 oz/420 g) for the peaches.

Fruit Jellies with Regular Powdered Fruit Pectin

Jellies made with added pectin are easy to prepare, provide a higher yield than old-fashioned long-boil recipes and deliver a fresher taste and brighter color. These recipes require precise measures of juice and sugar, but they do not require a gel stage test to determine doneness.

The following recipes are made with regular powdered fruit pectin. To create a translucent, tender jelly, it is essential to whisk powdered pectin into the juice until it is very well mixed. It is also important not to alter the quantity of ingredients, especially sugar. When making jelly with powdered pectin, the juice–pectin mixture must be brought to a boil and the pectin must be fully dissolved before the sugar is added. For best results, measure the sugar into a bowl so it can be added to the boiling jam all at once.

Powdered fruit pectin is sometimes sold in 49 g packages and sometimes in 57 g packages. The weight difference does not affect the performance of the product.

....

Traditional Jellies

Single-fruit jellies are simple, eye-catching, deliciously natural and very versatile soft spreads. While it's a bit of work to extract fresh fruit juice, the results are well worth the effort. Delicious on toast, these jellies also make fabulous glazes for both desserts and savory dishes. Few really interesting jellies are available commercially, and most that are lack the full-bodied flavor you can create at home.

Sour Cherry

Makes about five 8-ounce (250 mL) jars

3½ cups	Cherry Juice for Jelly (see variation, page 106), made with sour cherries	875 mL
1	package (1.75 oz/49 to 57 g) regular powdered fruit pectin	1
4½ cups	granulated sugar	1.125 L

1. Prepare canner, jars and lids. *(For more information, see page 415.)*
2. In a large, deep stainless steel saucepan, place cherry juice. Whisk in pectin until dissolved. Bring to a boil over high heat, stirring frequently. Add sugar all at once and return to a full rolling boil, stirring constantly. Boil hard, stirring constantly, for 1 minute. Remove from heat and quickly skim off foam.
3. Quickly pour hot jelly into hot jars, leaving ¼ inch (0.5 cm) headspace. Wipe rim. Center lid on jar. Screw band down until resistance is met, then increase to fingertip-tight.
4. Place jars in canner, ensuring they are completely covered with water. Bring to a boil and process for 10 minutes. Remove canner lid. Wait 5 minutes, then remove jars, cool and store. *(For more information, see pages 417–418.)*

For each of the following jellies, follow the method and processing time for Traditional Sour Cherry Jelly, opposite, but use the quantity of juice, sugar and pectin specified in the variation. Where lemon juice is called for, combine it with the fruit juice for jelly before adding the pectin.

Berry

Makes about five 8-ounce (250 mL) jars

3½ cups	Berry Juice for Jelly (see recipe, page 106), made with blackberries, boysenberries, dewberries or youngberries	875 mL
2 tbsp	lemon juice	30 mL
1	package (1.75 oz/49 to 57 g) regular powdered fruit pectin	1
5 cups	granulated sugar	1.25 L

Crabapple

Makes about seven 8-ounce (250 mL) jars

5 cups	Crabapple Juice for Jelly (see variation, page 107)	1.25 L
1	package (1.75 oz/49 to 57 g) regular powdered fruit pectin	1
7 cups	granulated sugar	1.75 L

Apple

Makes about seven 8-ounce (250 mL) jars

5 cups	Apple Juice for Jelly (see recipe, page 107)	1.25 mL
1	package (1.75 oz/49 to 57 g) regular powdered fruit pectin	1
7 cups	granulated sugar	1.75 L

Easy Apple

Makes about six 8-ounce (250 mL) jars

4 cups	unsweetened bottled apple juice	1 L
1	package (1.75 oz/49 to 57 g) regular powdered fruit pectin	1
5 cups	granulated sugar	1.25 L

If you're really busy and don't have time or the fruit to make your own juice for jelly, use bottled unsweetened juice from your grocery store.

Red Raspberry or Loganberry

Makes about six 8-ounce (250 mL) jars

4 cups	Berry Juice for Jelly (see recipe, page 106), made with raspberries or loganberries	1 L
4 tbsp	lemon juice	60 mL
1	package (1.75 oz/49 to 57 g) regular powdered fruit pectin	1
5½ cups	granulated sugar	1.375 L

continued on next page

For each of the following jellies, follow the method and processing time for Traditional Sour Cherry Jelly, page 108, but use the quantity of juice, sugar and pectin specified in the variation. Where lemon juice is called for, combine it with the fruit juice for jelly before adding the pectin.

TIP

Fruit juice cooked with sugar produces a considerable quantity of foam, which must be quickly skimmed off before hot jelly is poured into jars. To reduce foam, add ½ tsp (2 mL) butter or margarine to juice before bringing to a boil. Do not use a larger quantity.

If you're really busy and don't have time or the fruit to make your own juice for jelly, use bottled unsweetened juice from your grocery store.

Strawberry

Makes about five 8-ounce (250 mL) jars

3½ cups	Strawberry Juice for Jelly (see variation, page 106)	875 mL
1	package (1.75 oz/49 to 57 g) regular powdered fruit pectin	1
4½ cups	granulated sugar	1.125 L

Elderberry

Makes about five 8-ounce (250 mL) jars

3 cups	Elderberry Juice for Jelly (see variation, page 106)	750 mL
4 tbsp	lemon juice	60 mL
1	package (1.75 oz/49 to 57 g) regular powdered fruit pectin	1
4½ cups	granulated sugar	1.125 L

Red Currant

Makes about nine 8-ounce (250 mL) jars

6½ cups	Red Currant Juice for Jelly (see variation, page 106)	1.625 L
1	package (1.75 oz/49 to 57 g) regular powdered fruit pectin	1
7 cups	granulated sugar	1.75 L

Concord Grape

Makes about seven 8-ounce (250 mL) jars

5 cups	Grape Juice for Jelly (see variation, page 106), made with Concord grapes	1.25 L
1	package (1.75 oz/49 to 57 g) regular powdered fruit pectin	1
6 cups	granulated sugar	1.5 L

Easy Grape

Makes about five 8-ounce (250 mL) jars

3 cups	unsweetened bottled grape juice	750 mL
1	package (1.75 oz/49 to 57 g) regular powdered fruit pectin	1
4½ cups	granulated sugar	1.125 L

TIPS

Powdered fruit pectin is sometimes sold in 49 g packages and sometimes in 57 g packages. The weight difference does not affect the performance of the product.

Check your package of pectin for the expiration date and use only fresh pectin. Products that have expired may not set properly.

For best results, measure the sugar into a bowl so it can be added to the boiling jelly all at once.

Peach
Makes about five 8-ounce (250 mL) jars

3 cups	Peach Juice for Jelly (see recipe, page 107)	750 mL
1/2 cup	lemon juice	125 mL
1	package (1.75 oz/49 to 57 g) regular powdered fruit pectin	1
5 cups	granulated sugar	1.25 L

Pear
Makes about six 8-ounce (250 mL) jars

4 cups	Pear Juice for Jelly (see variation, page 107)	1 L
2 tbsp	lemon juice	30 mL
1	package (1.75 oz/49 to 57 g) regular powdered fruit pectin	1
5 1/2 cups	granulated sugar	1.375 L

Plum
Makes about eight 8-ounce (250 mL) jars

5 1/2 cups	Plum Juice for Jelly (see variation, page 107)	1.375 L
1	package (1.75 oz/49 to 57 g) regular powdered fruit pectin	1
7 1/2 cups	granulated sugar	1.875 L

Pomegranate Jelly

Rich in antioxidants, pomegranates are an excellent fruit for making jelly. Their full-bodied flavor and brilliant crimson color bring life to the breakfast or dinner table.

TIP

For 3½ cups (875 mL) pomegranate juice, you'll need about 5 lbs (2.3 kg) of pomegranates. To juice pomegranates, roll room-temperature fruit on a counter top, pressing it firmly to soften without breaking the skin. Holding the pomegranate over a fine sieve set over a bowl, use a sharp knife to cut out blossom (crown) end, including the pith. (Juice will begin to spurt out as soon as you puncture the skin.) Using your hands, squeeze juice and seeds into sieve. Open the fruit and, using a small spoon, scrape remaining seeds into sieve. Use the back of a large spoon to press out any remaining juice from seeds. (Wear rubber gloves to keep your hands from being stained.)

Makes about six 8-ounce (250 mL) jars

3½ cups	freshly squeezed pomegranate juice (see tip, at left)	875 mL
I	package (1.75 oz/49 to 57 g) regular powdered fruit pectin	I
5 cups	granulated sugar	1.25 L

1. Prepare canner, jars and lids. *(For more information, see page 415.)*

2. Place pomegranate juice in a large, deep stainless steel saucepan. Whisk in pectin until dissolved. Bring to a boil over high heat, stirring frequently. Add sugar all at once and return to a full rolling boil, stirring constantly. Boil hard, stirring constantly, for 1 minute. Remove from heat and quickly skim off foam.

3. Quickly pour hot jelly into hot jars, leaving ¼ inch (0.5 cm) headspace. Wipe rim. Center lid on jar. Screw band down until resistance is met, then increase to fingertip-tight.

4. Place jars in canner, ensuring they are completely covered with water. Bring to a boil and process for 10 minutes. Remove canner lid. Wait 5 minutes, then remove jars, cool and store. *(For more information, see pages 417–418.)*

"Love Apple" (Tomato) Jelly

Once thought to have aphrodisiac powers, tomatoes were christened pommes d'amour *(love apples) by the French. This amber-colored savory jelly is a delicious accompaniment to cheese and crackers, but is also delicious on toast.*

TIPS

For best results when cooking jelly, use a heavy-bottomed stainless steel saucepan that is at least three times deeper than the level of the recipe's juice and sugar combined. Jelly bubbles and boils up when it reaches a full rolling boil and therefore requires this extra pan depth.

Check your package of pectin for the expiration date and use only fresh pectin. Products that have expired may not set properly.

Makes about seven 4-ounce (125 mL) jars

8 cups	sliced tomatoes	2 L
½ cup	water	125 mL
3	dried hot chili peppers	3
¾ cup	coarsely chopped fresh basil	175 mL
2 tbsp	lemon juice	30 mL
1	package (1.75 oz/49 to 57 g) regular powdered fruit pectin	1
3¼ cups	granulated sugar	800 mL

1. In a large stainless steel saucepan, combine tomatoes, water, chili peppers and basil. Bring to a boil over medium heat. Reduce heat and boil gently, stirring and crushing tomatoes occasionally, until tomatoes are softened, about 25 minutes.

2. Transfer tomato mixture to a dampened jelly bag or a strainer lined with several layers of dampened cheesecloth set over a deep bowl. Let drip, undisturbed, for about 2 hours. Measure 1¾ cups (425 mL) tomato juice. If you do not have the required amount, add ½ cup (125 mL) boiling water to the remaining pulp in the jelly bag to extract additional juice. (Or add unsweetened apple or white grape juice to extend the juice to the required measure.)

3. Meanwhile, prepare canner, jars and lids. *(For more information, see page 415.)*

4. Transfer tomato juice to a large, deep stainless steel saucepan. Add lemon juice. Whisk in pectin until dissolved. Bring to a boil over high heat, stirring frequently. Add sugar all at once and return to a full rolling boil, stirring constantly. Boil hard, stirring constantly, for 1 minute. Remove from heat and quickly skim off foam.

5. Quickly pour hot jelly into hot jars, leaving ¼ inch (0.5 cm) headspace. Wipe rim. Center lid on jar. Screw band down until resistance is met, then increase to fingertip-tight.

6. Place jars in canner, ensuring they are completely covered with water. Bring to a boil and process for 10 minutes. Remove canner lid. Wait 5 minutes, then remove jars, cool and store. *(For more information, see pages 417–418.)*

Variation

Gingered "Love Apple" Jelly: Substitute 2 tbsp (30 mL) finely chopped crystallized ginger for the chili peppers and basil.

Fruit Jellies with Liquid Pectin

Jellies made with liquid pectin require the least cooking time of all cooked jellies. Predissolved liquid pectin bonds readily with the boiling-hot juice–sugar mixture to produce a clear, translucent jelly that tastes like fresh-picked fruit. And there is no need to worry about a gel stage test.

Unlike soft spreads made with powdered pectin, when making jellies with liquid pectin, the fruit, lemon juice (if required) and sugar are brought to a boil before the pectin is added. To form a good gel, it is essential to bring the fruit–sugar mixture to a full rolling boil that cannot be stirred down, stir in the entire contents of the liquid pectin pouch, then boil hard for 1 minute longer.

Quick Jellies

These recipes are the easiest way to make delicious jelly and require the least cooking time. Be sure that the juice–sugar mixture comes to a full rolling boil that cannot be stirred down before you begin counting the 1-minute cooking time. Failure to fully boil the mixture can lead to gel failure.

TIP

Some brands of liquid pectin direct you to stir in the pectin *after* boiling the fruit–sugar mixture for 1 minute. It is advisable to follow the directions given by the brand you are using when preparing these recipes.

Berry

Makes about seven 8-ounce (250 mL) jars

4 cups	Berry Juice for Jelly (see recipe, page 106)	1 L
7½ cups	granulated sugar	1.875 L
2	pouches (each 3 oz/85 mL) liquid pectin	2

1. Prepare canner, jars and lids. *(For more information, see page 415.)*
2. In a large, deep stainless steel saucepan, combine berry juice and sugar. Over high heat, stirring constantly, bring to a full rolling boil that cannot be stirred down. Stir in pectin. Boil hard, stirring constantly, for 1 minute. Remove from heat and quickly skim off foam.
3. Quickly pour hot jelly into hot jars, leaving ¼ inch (0.5 cm) headspace. Wipe rim. Center lid on jar. Screw band down until resistance is met, then increase to fingertip-tight.
4. Place jars in canner, ensuring they are completely covered with water. Bring to a boil and process for 10 minutes. Remove canner lid. Wait 5 minutes, then remove jars, cool and store. *(For more information, see pages 417–418.)*

For each of the following jellies, follow the method and processing time for Quick Berry Jelly, opposite, but use the quantity of juice, sugar and pectin specified in the variation. Where lemon juice is called for, combine it with the fruit juice for jelly and the sugar.

TIP

Berries can be frozen before use in jams or jellies. If you pick the berries on a day that is too hot to do your preserving, measure out the required amount of berries, prepare and freeze for up to 3 months. When you plan to make your preserves, thaw prepared berries in the refrigerator overnight and use both the thawed berries and the accumulated juice in the recipe.

Elderberry

Makes about seven 8-ounce (250 mL) jars

3 cups	Elderberry Juice for Jelly (see variation, page 106)	750 mL
½ cup	lemon juice	125 mL
7 cups	granulated sugar	1.75 L
2	pouches (each 3 oz/85 mL) liquid pectin	2

Black Raspberry

Makes about six 8-ounce (250 mL) jars

3 cups	Berry Juice for Jelly (see recipe, page 106), made with black raspberries	750 mL
4 tbsp	lemon juice	60 mL
5 cups	granulated sugar	1.25 L
1	pouch (3 oz/85 mL) liquid pectin	1

Strawberry

Makes about seven 8-ounce (250 mL) jars

3¾ cups	Strawberry Juice for Jelly (see variation, page 106)	925 mL
4 tbsp	lemon juice	60 mL
7½ cups	granulated sugar	1.875 L
2	pouches (each 3 oz/85 mL) liquid pectin	2

Red Currant

Makes about eight 8-ounce (250 mL) jars

5 cups	Red Currant Juice for Jelly (see variation, page 106)	1.25 L
7 cups	granulated sugar	1.75 L
1	pouch (3 oz/85 mL) liquid pectin	1

Cherry

Makes about seven 8-ounce (250 mL) jars

3½ cups	Cherry Juice for Jelly (see variation, page 106)	875 mL
4 tbsp	lemon juice (use for sweet cherries only)	60 mL
7 cups	granulated sugar	1.75 L
2	pouches (each 3 oz/85 mL) liquid pectin	2

continued on next page

For each of the **following jellies,** follow the method and processing time for Quick Berry Jelly, page 114, but use the quantity of juice, sugar and pectin specified in the variation. Where lemon juice is called for, combine it with the fruit juice for jelly and the sugar.

TIP

Fruit juice cooked with sugar produces a considerable quantity of foam, which must be quickly skimmed off before hot jelly is poured into jars. To reduce foam, add ½ tsp (2 mL) butter or margarine to juice before bringing to a boil. Do not use a larger quantity.

Concord Grape

Makes about seven 8-ounce (250 mL) jars

4 cups	Grape Juice for Jelly (see variation, page 106), made with Concord grapes	I L
7 cups	granulated sugar	1.75 L
I	pouch (3 oz/85 mL) liquid pectin	I

Apple

Makes about eight 8-ounce (250 mL) jars

5 cups	Apple Juice for Jelly (see recipe, page 107)	1.25 L
7½ cups	granulated sugar	1.875 L
I	pouch (3 oz/85 mL) liquid pectin	I

Crabapple

Makes about eight 8-ounce (250 mL) jars

5 cups	Crabapple Juice for Jelly (see variation, page 107)	1.25 L
7½ cups	granulated sugar	1.875 L
I	pouch (3 oz/85 mL) liquid pectin	I

Peach

Makes about seven 8-ounce (250 mL) jars

3½ cups	Peach Juice for Jelly (see recipe, page 107)	875 mL
4 tbsp	lemon juice	60 mL
7½ cups	granulated sugar	1.875 L
2	pouches (each 3 oz/85 mL) liquid pectin	2

Plum

Makes about seven 8-ounce (250 mL) jars

4 cups	Plum Juice for Jelly (see variation, page 107)	I L
6½ cups	granulated sugar	1.625 L
I	pouch (3 oz/85 mL) liquid pectin	I

Zesty Watermelon Jelly

If you enjoy watermelon, you'll love this beautiful pink jelly. Lemongrass adds a unique flavor.

TIP

For best results when cooking jelly, use a heavy-bottomed stainless steel saucepan that is at least three times deeper than the level of the recipe's juice and sugar combined. Jelly bubbles and boils up when it reaches a full rolling boil and therefore requires this extra pan depth.

Makes about five 8-ounce (250 mL) jars

6 cups	chopped watermelon, rind removed	1.5 L
½ cup	white balsamic, white wine or apple cider vinegar	125 mL
4 tbsp	lemon juice	60 mL
5 cups	granulated sugar	1.25 L
1	stem lemongrass, chopped	1
2	pouches (each 3 oz/85 mL) liquid pectin	2

1. In a large stainless steel saucepan, crush watermelon with a potato masher. Cover and heat gently over medium-low heat for 5 minutes. Remove from heat and crush thoroughly.

2. Transfer to a dampened jelly bag or a strainer lined with several layers of dampened cheesecloth set over a deep bowl. Let drip, undisturbed, for 2 hours. Measure 2 cups (500 mL) watermelon juice. If you do not have the required amount, crush more watermelon or add up to ¼ cup (50 mL) unsweetened white grape juice.

3. Meanwhile, prepare canner, jars and lids. *(For more information, see page 415.)*

4. Transfer watermelon juice to a clean large, deep stainless steel saucepan. Stir in vinegar, lemon juice, sugar and lemongrass. Over high heat, stirring constantly, bring to a full rolling boil that cannot be stirred down. Stir in pectin. Boil hard, stirring constantly, for 1 minute. Remove from heat and quickly skim off foam.

5. Quickly pour hot jelly into hot jars, leaving ¼ inch (0.5 cm) headspace. Wipe rim. Center lid on jar. Screw band down until resistance is met, then increase to fingertip-tight.

6. Place jars in canner, ensuring they are completely covered with water. Bring to a boil and process for 10 minutes. Remove canner lid. Wait 5 minutes, then remove jars, cool and store. *(For more information, see pages 417–418.)*

Jelly Bean Jelly

Root Beer, Bubble Gum, Mint Chocolate Chip Jelly! Translucent spreads that taste like your favorite jelly beans make super breakfast treats for the young-at-heart. Better yet, these kid-pleasing gems are a snap to make. They start with unsweetened apple or white grape juice, which you cook with sugar and liquid pectin. Flavoring oil concentrate — available at candy supply and gourmet kitchen stores — adds the unique taste. Adjust the jelly tint with a few drops of coloring, or substitute an unsweetened fruit juice of a natural color that matches a chosen flavor, such as cherry juice for cinnamon-flavored jelly. The potential for variety is limitless!

Makes about eight 4-ounce (125 mL) jars or three 8-ounce (250 mL) jars (plus a bit for tasting)

2 cups	unsweetened apple juice or white grape juice	500 mL
3½ cups	granulated sugar	875 mL
1	pouch (3 oz/85 mL) liquid pectin	1
¼ to ¾ tsp	flavoring oil concentrate (see box, below)	1 to 4 mL
	Food coloring (optional)	

1. Prepare canner, jars and lids. *(For more information, see page 415.)*

2. In a large, deep stainless steel saucepan, combine apple juice and sugar. Over high heat, stirring constantly, bring to a full rolling boil that cannot be stirred down. Stir in pectin. Boil hard, stirring constantly, for 1 minute. Stir in flavoring oil concentrate and food coloring, if using. Remove from heat and quickly skim off foam.

3. Quickly pour hot jelly into hot jars, leaving ¼ inch (0.5 cm) headspace. Wipe rim. Center lid on jar. Screw band down until resistance is met, then increase to fingertip-tight.

4. Place jars in canner, ensuring they are completely covered with water. Bring to a boil and process for 10 minutes. Remove canner lid. Wait 5 minutes, then remove jars, cool and store. *(For more information, see pages 417–418.)*

Highly concentrated, non-alcoholic, unsweetened flavorings are sold in very small bottles. A little goes a long way, and the quantity required varies by flavor. Start with ¼ tsp (1 mL) and adjust to taste. Here's a guide for three Jelly Bean Jellies.
- Root Beer: ¾ tsp (4 mL) flavoring oil concentrate
- Mint Chocolate Chip: ¼ tsp (1 mL) flavoring oil concentrate, plus 6 drops green food coloring
- Bubble Gum: ½ tsp (2 mL) flavoring oil concentrate, plus 4 drops red and 2 drops yellow food coloring

Fruit Jellies with No Added Pectin

Jellies made without added pectin need to cook longer, have lower yields per quantity of fresh fruit used and may have a slightly caramelized flavor. Most fruits do not contain enough natural pectin and/or acid to easily convert to jellies without the addition of pectin. Apples, crabapples and Concord grapes are the exceptions.

The biggest problem in making jellies with no added pectin lies in determining when the jelly is done. A gel stage test (see page 21) is essential. These jellies must be monitored very closely to avoid over- or undercooking. Undercooked jellies that do not set may be used as sauces and may sometimes be redeemed with a second boiling. There is no remedy to salvage an overcooked product.

Before cooking any long-boil jelly recipe, it is a good idea to determine whether your fruit juice has sufficient levels of pectin and acid to allow it to form a gel when you boil it with sugar.

Acid Test
Mix 1 tsp (5 mL) lemon juice, 3 tbsp (45 mL) water and ½ tsp (2 mL) sugar. Taste this mixture and compare it to the taste of your fruit juice. If the juice is sweeter, adjust the acid by adding 1 tbsp (15 mL) strained lemon juice for each 1 cup (250 mL) fruit juice.

Pectin Test
In a closed container, gently shake 1 tsp (5 mL) fruit juice with 1 tbsp (15 mL) rubbing alcohol. *Do not taste.* Adequate pectin is present when the mixture forms a solid jelly-like mass that can be picked up with a fork. If this mass does not form, the fruit juice lacks enough natural pectin to form a gel in a long-boil jelly recipe. Use the juice in a recipe that calls for added powdered or liquid pectin.

Old-Fashioned Jellies

Jellies made without added pectin must be watched carefully to determine the gelling point. Be sure to review the gel stage tests (page 21) before starting one of these recipes. Remember to remove pan from heat when performing the sheet test or refrigerator test.

For each of the following jellies, follow the method for Old-Fashioned Crabapple Jelly, above, but use the quantity of juice and sugar specified in the variation.

Crabapple

Makes about six 8-ounce (250 mL) jars

4 cups	Crabapple Juice for Jelly (see variation, page 107)	1 L
1 tbsp	lemon juice	15 mL
4 cups	granulated sugar	1 L

1. Prepare canner, jars and lids. (For more information, see page 415.)
2. In a large, deep stainless steel saucepan, combine crabapple juice, lemon juice and sugar. Bring to a boil over medium-high heat, stirring to dissolve sugar. Boil hard, stirring frequently, until mixture begins to sheet from a metal spoon (see page 21), about 25 minutes. Remove from heat and test gel (see page 21). If gel stage has been reached, skim off foam.
3. Quickly pour hot jelly into hot jars, leaving ¼ inch (0.5 cm) headspace. Wipe rim. Center lid on jar. Screw band down until resistance is met, then increase to fingertip-tight.
4. Place jars in canner, ensuring they are completely covered with water. Bring to a boil and process for 10 minutes. Remove canner lid. Wait 5 minutes, then remove jars, cool and store. (For more information, see pages 417–418.)

Apple

Makes about four 8-ounce (250 mL) jars

4 cups	Apple Juice for Jelly (see recipe, page 107)	1 L
2 tbsp	lemon juice	30 mL
3 cups	granulated sugar	750 mL

Grape

Makes about four 8-ounce (250 mL) jars

4 cups	Grape Juice for Jelly (see variation, page 106), made with Concord grapes	1 L
3 cups	granulated sugar	750 mL

Wine Jellies

Wine jellies are boiled slightly longer than other fruit jellies — 2 minutes versus the 1 minute normally recommended for a soft spread made with added fruit pectin. The slight increase in cooking time concentrates the unique wine flavor and evaporates a bit more of the alcohol, which can interfere with gel formation.

....

Herbes de Provence Wine Jelly

Herbes de Provence is a blend of dried herbs used most commonly in southern France but now widely available in North America. The herbs include basil, marjoram, summer savory, thyme, lavender, rosemary, sage and oregano. If you can't find a blend, you can make your own, which allows you to adjust individual herbs to suit your taste.

TIP

Squeezing the jelly bag is an exception to the rule for making juice for jelly. In this recipe, it is acceptable because there is no pulp that will be expressed into the juice.

Makes about four 4-ounce (125 mL) jars or two 8-ounce (250 mL) jars

2 cups	dry white wine	500 mL
2 tbsp	herbes de Provence	30 mL
2 cups	granulated sugar	500 mL
I	pouch (3 oz/85 mL) liquid pectin	I

1. In a large stainless steel saucepan, combine wine and herbs. Bring to a boil over high heat. Remove from heat, cover and let steep for 20 minutes.

2. Transfer to a dampened jelly bag or a strainer lined with several layers of dampened cheesecloth set over a deep bowl. Let drip, undisturbed, for 20 minutes. Measure 1¾ cups (425 mL) infused wine. If you do not have the required amount, squeeze the bag (see tip, at left).

3. Meanwhile, prepare canner, jars and lids. *(For more information, see page 415.)*

4. Transfer infused wine to a clean large, deep stainless steel saucepan. Stir in sugar. Over high heat, stirring constantly, bring mixture to a full rolling boil that cannot be stirred down. Stir in pectin. Boil hard, stirring constantly, for 2 minutes. Remove from heat and quickly skim off foam.

5. Quickly pour hot jelly into hot jars, leaving ¼ inch (0.5 cm) headspace. Wipe rim. Center lid on jar. Screw band down until resistance is met, then increase to fingertip-tight.

6. Place jars in canner, ensuring they are completely covered with water. Bring to a boil and process for 10 minutes. Remove canner lid. Wait 5 minutes, then remove jars, cool and store. *(For more information, see pages 417–418.)*

Variation

Lavender Wine Jelly: Substitute 1 tbsp (15 mL) dried lavender flowers for the herbes de Provence.

Red Wine Jelly

While wine jellies make elegant spreads, they're even better as glazes for desserts, roasts and grilled entrées. For best flavor, select a robust, dry red wine.

TIP

For best results, measure the sugar into a bowl so it can be added to the boiling jelly all at once.

Makes about six 8-ounce (250 mL) jars

3¼ cups	dry red wine	800 mL
½ cup	lemon juice	125 mL
1	package (1.75 oz/49 to 57 kg) regular powdered fruit pectin	1
4½ cups	granulated sugar	1.125 L

1. Prepare canner, jars and lids. *(For more information, see page 415.)*
2. In a large, deep stainless steel saucepan, combine wine and lemon juice. Whisk in pectin until dissolved. Bring to a boil over high heat, stirring frequently. Add sugar all at once and return to a full rolling boil, stirring constantly. Boil hard, stirring constantly, for 2 minutes. Remove from heat and quickly skim off foam.
3. Quickly pour hot jelly into hot jars, leaving ¼ inch (0.5 cm) headspace. Wipe rim. Center lid on jar. Screw band down until resistance is met, then increase to fingertip-tight.
4. Place jars in canner, ensuring they are completely covered with water. Bring to a boil and process for 10 minutes. Remove canner lid. Wait 5 minutes, then remove jars, cool and store. *(For more information, see pages 417–418.)*

Inferno Wine Jelly

This hot-sweet jelly, flecked with red and green pepper, makes a beautiful gift. Spread it on crackers with cream cheese or serve it by itself on French bread.

TIP

For a milder jelly, reduce the quantity of dried chili peppers or omit them entirely.

Makes about seven 4-ounce (125 mL) jars

½ cup	minced seeded red bell pepper	125 mL
2 tbsp	minced seeded jalapeño pepper	30 mL
3	dried hot chili peppers, halved lengthwise	3
1½ cups	sweet white wine, such as Sauternes	375 mL
3 tbsp	lemon juice	45 mL
3½ cups	granulated sugar	875 mL
1	pouch (3 oz/85 mL) liquid pectin	1

1. Prepare canner, jars and lids. *(For more information, see page 415.)*
2. In a large, deep stainless steel saucepan, combine red pepper, jalapeño pepper, chili peppers, wine and lemon juice. Stir in sugar. Over high heat, stirring constantly, bring to a full rolling boil that cannot be stirred down. Stir in pectin. Boil hard, stirring constantly, for 2 minutes. Remove from heat and quickly skim off foam.

3. Quickly pour hot jelly into hot jars, leaving ¼ inch (0.5 cm) headspace. Wipe rim. Center lid on jar. Screw band down until resistance is met, then increase to fingertip-tight.

4. Place jars in canner, ensuring they are completely covered with water. Bring to a boil and process for 10 minutes. Remove jars, cool (see suspension tip, page 130) and store. *(For more information, see pages 417–418.)*

Berry Wine Jelly

This fabulous rose-hued jelly is a regal accent for cheese trays, an intriguing glaze on poultry or pork and a show-stopper gift for tea and breakfast lovers.

TIPS

You don't need to precook the fruit to make the juice for this jelly. The berries release their flavor along with their juice as they are crushed with the wine.

Some brands of liquid pectin direct you to stir in the pectin *after* boiling the fruit–sugar mixture for 1 minute. It is advisable to follow the directions given by the brand you are using when preparing these recipes.

Makes about six 4-ounce (125 mL) jars

1 cup	raspberries or sliced hulled strawberries	250 mL
2½ cups	dry white wine	625 mL
3½ cups	granulated sugar	875 mL
1	pouch (3 oz/85 mL) liquid pectin	1

1. In a large stainless steel saucepan or bowl, combine berries and wine. Crush berries and transfer to a dampened jelly bag or a strainer lined with several layers of dampened cheesecloth set over a deep bowl. Let drip, undisturbed, for 1 hour. Measure 2½ cups (625 mL) berry wine.

2. Meanwhile, prepare canner, jars and lids. *(For more information, see page 415.)*

3. Transfer berry wine to a large, deep stainless steel saucepan. Stir in sugar. Over high heat, stirring constantly, bring to a full rolling boil that cannot be stirred down. Stir in pectin. Boil hard, stirring constantly, for 2 minutes. Remove from heat and quickly skim off foam.

4. Quickly pour hot jelly into hot jars, leaving ¼ inch (0.5 cm) headspace. Wipe rim. Center lid on jar. Screw band down until resistance is met, then increase to fingertip-tight.

5. Place jars in canner, ensuring they are completely covered with water. Bring to a boil and process for 10 minutes. Remove canner lid. Wait 5 minutes, then remove jars, cool and store. *(For more information, see pages 417–418.)*

Savory Jellies

Not all jellies are designed for bread. Savory jellies — served with cheese, as a condiment or as a glaze for meat, poultry or fish — are gaining in popularity. They can also be used as an ingredient in marinades. The delicious possibilities are limitless.

....

Fresh Herb Jelly

You can customize the flavor of this versatile yet easy-to-make jelly by using different fresh herbs or herb combinations. Herb jelly is a tasty companion to cheese and crackers and makes a delicious glaze for roast and grilled meat.

TIPS

Use fresh parsley, basil, thyme and/or dill for this jelly. Reduce quantity to 1 cup (250 mL) for stronger herbs such as rosemary and savory.

Check your package of pectin for the expiration date and use only fresh pectin. Products that have expired may not set properly.

Makes about five 8-ounce (250 mL) jars

2 cups	loosely packed coarsely chopped herbs (see tip, at left)	500 mL
1½ cups	unsweetened apple juice or dry white wine	375 mL
1 cup	water	250 mL
1 cup	white wine vinegar	250 mL
1	package (1.75 oz/49 to 57 g) regular powdered fruit pectin	1
5¼ cups	granulated sugar	1.3 L

1. In a large stainless steel saucepan, combine herbs, apple juice, water and vinegar. Bring to a boil over medium heat. Remove from heat, cover and let steep for 15 minutes. Stir well, pressing herbs to extract flavor.

2. Transfer herb mixture to a dampened jelly bag or a strainer lined with several layers of dampened cheesecloth set over a deep bowl. Let drip, undisturbed, for 30 minutes. Measure 3¼ cups (800 mL) herbed juice.

3. Meanwhile, prepare canner, jars and lids. *(For more information, see page 415.)*

4. Transfer herb juice to a clean large, deep stainless steel saucepan. Whisk in pectin until dissolved. Bring to a boil over high heat, stirring frequently. Add sugar all at once and return to a full rolling boil, stirring constantly. Boil hard, stirring constantly, for 1 minute. Remove from heat and quickly skim off foam.

5. Quickly pour hot jelly into hot jars, leaving ¼ inch (0.5 cm) headspace. Wipe rim. Center lid on jar. Screw band down until resistance is met, then increase to fingertip-tight.

6. Place jars in canner, ensuring they are completely covered with water. Bring to a boil and process for 10 minutes. Remove canner lid. Wait 5 minutes, then remove jars, cool and store. *(For more information, see pages 417–418.)*

Green Pepper Jelly

If you enjoy a mild pepper jelly, this recipe should top your list. The addition of jalapeño peppers adds just the right kick, without extinguishing your taste buds.

TIPS

The best way to seed peppers is to trim off the stem end and then cut the pepper in half lengthwise. Scrape out the seeds and veins, using a spoon.

Powdered fruit pectin is sometimes sold in 49 g packages and sometimes in 57 g packages. The weight difference does not affect the performance of the product.

For best results, measure the sugar into a bowl so it can be added to the boiling jelly all at once.

Makes about seven 4-ounce (125 mL) jars

4	green bell peppers, stemmed and seeded	4
2	jalapeño peppers, stemmed, seeded and deveined	2
2	cloves garlic	2
⅔ cup	white vinegar	150 mL
2 tbsp	lemon juice	30 mL
1	package (1.75 oz/49 to 57 g) regular powdered fruit pectin	1
3⅔ cups	granulated sugar	900 mL
4 to 5	drops green food coloring (optional)	4 to 5

1. In a blender or a food processor fitted with a metal blade, purée green peppers, jalapeño peppers and garlic until smooth.

2. Transfer purée to a dampened jelly bag or a strainer lined with several layers of dampened cheesecloth set over a deep bowl. Let drip, undisturbed, for 30 minutes. Measure 1½ cups (375 mL) pepper juice. If you do not have the required amount, add ½ cup (125 mL) boiling water to the remaining pulp in the jelly bag to extract additional juice.

3. Meanwhile, prepare canner, jars and lids. *(For more information, see page 415.)*

4. Transfer pepper juice to a large, deep stainless steel saucepan. Add vinegar and lemon juice. Whisk in pectin until dissolved. Bring to a boil over high heat, stirring frequently. Add sugar all at once and return to a full rolling boil, stirring constantly. Boil hard, stirring constantly, for 1 minute. Remove from heat, stir in food coloring, if using, and quickly skim off foam.

5. Quickly pour hot jelly into hot jars, leaving ¼ inch (0.5 cm) headspace. Wipe rim. Center lid on jar. Screw band down until resistance is met, then increase to fingertip-tight.

6. Place jars in canner, ensuring they are completely covered with water. Bring to a boil and process for 10 minutes. Remove canner lid. Wait 5 minutes, then remove jars, cool and store. *(For more information, see pages 417–418.)*

Balsamic Red Pepper Jelly

The combination of red wine and balsamic vinegars creates a pleasing gourmet flavor. Serve this jelly with cream cheese and crackers as an hors d'oeuvre. Or use it as a glaze for roast poultry or fish.

TIPS

If you prefer a spicier jelly, do not seed and devein the jalapeño peppers.

Check your package of pectin for the expiration date and use only fresh pectin. Products that have expired may not set properly.

For best results when cooking jelly, use a heavy-bottomed stainless steel saucepan that is at least three times deeper than the level of the recipe's juice and sugar combined. Jelly bubbles and boils up when it reaches a full rolling boil and therefore requires this extra pan depth.

Makes about seven 4-ounce (125 mL) jars

5	medium red bell peppers, stemmed and seeded	5
3	medium jalapeño peppers, stemmed, seeded and deveined (see tip, at left)	3
2	cloves garlic	2
½ cup	red wine vinegar	125 mL
3 tbsp	balsamic vinegar	45 mL
2 tbsp	lemon juice	30 mL
1	package (1.75 oz/49 to 57 g) regular powdered fruit pectin	1
3¼ cups	granulated sugar	800 mL

1. Finely dice enough red pepper to measure ½ cup (125 mL) and set aside. In a blender or a food processor fitted with a metal blade, purée remaining red peppers, jalapeño peppers and garlic until smooth.

2. Transfer purée to a dampened jelly bag or a strainer lined with several layers of dampened cheesecloth set over a deep bowl. Let drip, undisturbed, for 30 minutes. Measure 1½ cups (375 mL) pepper juice. If you do not have the required amount, add ½ cup (125 mL) boiling water to the remaining pulp in the jelly bag to extract additional juice.

3. Meanwhile, prepare canner, jars and lids. *(For more information, see page 415.)*

4. Transfer pepper juice to a large, deep stainless steel saucepan. Add reserved diced red pepper, red wine vinegar, balsamic vinegar and lemon juice. Whisk in pectin until dissolved. Bring to a boil over high heat, stirring frequently. Add sugar all at once and return to a full rolling boil, stirring constantly. Boil hard, stirring constantly, for 1 minute. Remove from heat and quickly skim off foam.

5. Quickly pour hot jelly into hot jars, leaving ¼ inch (0.5 cm) headspace. Wipe rim. Center lid on jar. Screw band down until resistance is met, then increase to fingertip-tight.

6. Place jars in canner, ensuring they are completely covered with water. Bring to a boil and process for 10 minutes. Remove canner lid. Wait 5 minutes, then remove jars, cool and store. *(For more information, see pages 417–418.)*

Roasted Garlic Jelly

Enjoy the sweet but subtle flavor of roasted garlic in this sophisticated jelly. Use it as a glaze for meat, or spread it over warm toasted bread.

TIPS

White balsamic vinegar creates a lovely light-colored jelly, but it is difficult to find. More commonly available dark balsamic vinegar may be substituted, but the resulting jelly will be dark in color and will have a more robust flavor.

Cheesecloth can be found at many retailers, such as grocery stores and other stores that carry kitchen supplies. Look in the area where kitchen utensils are located.

Makes about nine 4-ounce (125 mL) jars

• *Preheat oven to 425°F (220°C)*

3	medium heads garlic	3
1 tbsp	olive oil, divided	15 mL
1 tbsp	balsamic vinegar, divided	15 mL
1 cup	dry white wine	250 mL
2/3 cup	water	150 mL
1/2 cup	white balsamic vinegar (see tip, at left)	125 mL
1 tsp	whole black peppercorns, crushed	5 mL
3 tbsp	lemon juice	45 mL
3 cups	granulated sugar	750 mL
2	pouches (each 3 oz/85 mL) liquid pectin	2

1. Using a sharp knife, cut off tops of garlic heads, exposing cloves. Place each head on a small square of aluminum foil set on a baking sheet. Top each head with 1 tsp (5 mL) olive oil and 1 tsp (5 mL) balsamic vinegar. Scrunch foil loosely around garlic heads and roast in preheated oven until garlic is golden and very soft, 45 to 60 minutes. Let stand until cool enough to handle. Separate cloves, pinching each one to extract the soft roasted garlic. Discard skins.

2. In a medium stainless steel saucepan, combine roasted garlic, wine, water, white balsamic vinegar and peppercorns. Bring to a boil over medium heat. Reduce heat and boil gently for 5 minutes. Cover, remove from heat and let steep for 15 minutes.

3. Transfer garlic mixture to a dampened jelly bag or a strainer lined with several layers of dampened cheesecloth set over a deep bowl. Let drip, undisturbed, for about 30 minutes. Measure 1 2/3 cups (400 mL) garlic juice. If you do not have the required amount, add up to 1/4 cup (50 mL) dry white wine or water.

4. Meanwhile, prepare canner, jars and lids. *(For more information, see page 415.)*

5. Transfer garlic juice to a large, deep stainless steel saucepan. Stir in lemon juice and sugar. Over high heat, stirring constantly, bring to a full rolling boil that cannot be stirred down. Stir in pectin. Boil hard, stirring constantly, for 1 minute. Remove from heat and quickly skim off foam.

6. Quickly pour hot jelly into hot jars, leaving 1/4 inch (0.5 cm) headspace. Wipe rim. Center lid on jar. Screw band down until resistance is met, then increase to fingertip-tight.

7. Place jars in canner, ensuring they are completely covered with water. Bring to a boil and process for 10 minutes. Remove canner lid. Wait 5 minutes, then remove jars, cool (see Jelly Particle Suspension Tip, page 130) and store. *(For more information, see pages 417–418.)*

Sun-Dried Tomato Jelly

With the rich flavor of sun-dried tomatoes, this burgundy jelly is the perfect accompaniment to white meat. It is also delicious spread on freshly baked bread as an appetizer.

TIPS

Do not use sun-dried tomatoes that have been packed in oil in this recipe. The dried tomatoes will reconstitute as they cook in Step 1.

A jar lifter is very helpful for handling hot, wet jars. Because they are bulky and fit loosely, oven mitts — even water-resistent types — are not a wise choice. When filling jars, an all-purpose rubber glove, worn on your helper hand, will allow you to steady the jar.

Place a clean towel on your work surface to absorb water from the hot jars as you take them out of the boiling-water canner to be filled, and again once the jars are processed. The towel prevents hot jars from coming into contact with cooler countertops. Significant temperature differences can cause jar breakage.

Makes about five 8-ounce (250 mL) jars

7 cups	sliced cored plum tomatoes	1.75 L
10	sun-dried tomatoes, coarsely chopped (see tip, at left)	10
2	dried hot chili peppers	2
¼ cup	dried basil	50 mL
⅓ cup	balsamic vinegar	75 mL
½ cup	lemon juice	125 mL
5 cups	granulated sugar	1.25 L
2	pouches (each 3 oz/85 mL) liquid pectin	2

1. In a large stainless steel saucepan, combine plum tomatoes, sun-dried tomatoes, chili peppers, basil and vinegar. Bring to a boil over medium heat. Reduce heat and boil gently, stirring occasionally and crushing fresh tomatoes, for 30 minutes, until sun-dried tomatoes are softened. Remove from heat, cover and let steep for 15 minutes.

2. Transfer to a dampened jelly bag or a strainer lined with several layers of dampened cheesecloth set over a deep bowl. Let drip, undisturbed, for about 30 minutes. Measure 2 cups (500 mL) tomato juice.

3. Meanwhile, prepare canner, jars and lids. *(For more information, see page 415.)*

4. Transfer tomato juice to a clean large, deep stainless steel saucepan. Stir in lemon juice and sugar. Over high heat, stirring constantly, bring to a full rolling boil that cannot be stirred down. Stir in pectin. Boil hard, stirring constantly, for 1 minute. Remove from heat and quickly skim off foam.

5. Quickly pour hot jelly into hot jars, leaving ¼ inch (0.5 cm) headspace. Wipe rim. Center lid on jar. Screw band down until resistance is met, then increase to fingertip-tight.

6. Place jars in canner, ensuring they are completely covered with water. Bring to a boil and process for 10 minutes. Remove canner lid. Wait 5 minutes, then remove jars, cool and store. *(For more information, see pages 417–418.)*

**Ginger Pear Marmalade (page 99),
Quick Red Onion Marmalade (page 95),
Seville Orange Marmalade (page 97)**

Strawberry Jam (page 8)

Cranapple Butter (page 54)

Blueberry Bonanza (page 60)

Easy Grape Jam (page 44)

Habanero Gold (page 131)

Cranberry Raspberry Preserves (page 74)

Spirited Pears (page 155)

Apple Wedges in Cinnamon Red Hot Syrup (page 159)

Berry Wine Jelly (page 123),
Rhubarb Conserve (page 91)

Easy Jalapeño Jelly

Eliminate the juice-making step and still produce a translucent jelly? This unique recipe does! Flecked with tiny bits of peppers, this zesty jelly adds a jewel-like flair to cheese trays. Spread it on a block of warmed cream cheese and serve with crackers.

TIPS

If you prefer a hotter jelly, tie the jalapeño seeds in a square of cheesecloth, creating a spice bag. Add with the sugar and cook as directed. Discard the spice bag just before adding the pectin.

When cutting or seeding hot peppers, wear rubber gloves to keep your hands from being burned.

Makes about five 8-ounce (250 mL) jars

12 oz	jalapeño peppers, stemmed, seeded and deveined (see tip, at left)	350 g
2 cups	cider vinegar, divided	500 mL
6 cups	granulated sugar	1.5 L
2	pouches (each 3 oz/85 mL) liquid pectin	2
	Green food coloring (optional)	

1. Prepare canner, jars and lids. *(For more information, see page 415.)*
2. In a blender or a food processor fitted with a metal blade, purée peppers and 1 cup (250 mL) of the vinegar until smooth.
3. In a large, deep stainless steel saucepan, combine pepper purée, remaining 1 cup (250 mL) vinegar and sugar. Bring to a boil over high heat and boil, stirring constantly, for 10 minutes. Stir in pectin. Boil hard, stirring constantly, for 1 minute. Remove from heat, stir in food coloring, if using, and quickly skim off foam.
4. Quickly pour hot jelly into hot jars, leaving ¼ inch (0.5 cm) headspace. Wipe rim. Center lid on jar. Screw band down until resistance is met, then increase to fingertip-tight.
5. Place jars in canner, ensuring they are completely covered with water. Bring to a boil and process for 10 minutes. Remove canner lid. Wait 5 minutes, then remove jars, cool and store. *(For more information, see pages 417–418.)*

Variation

Easy Red Pepper Jelly: Substitute 2 cups (500 mL) coarsely chopped seeded red bell peppers for the jalapeño peppers. Adjust the color as desired, using red and yellow food coloring.

Jelly Particle Suspension Tip

The following savory jelly recipes create translucent jellies with colorful particles suspended throughout. To enhance the suspension of these solids, it may be necessary to gently manipulate the jar after processing. This procedure can be used *only* with jellies prepared in 4- or 8-ounce (125 or 250 mL) jars that have been processed for 10 minutes in a boiling-water canner.

To enhance particle suspension, cool the processed jars upright for 15 to 30 minutes or just until the lids pop down but the jelly is not fully set. As soon as the lids are concave, carefully and gently twist and/or tilt — *do not shake and do not invert* — individual jars to distribute solids throughout the jelly. The sealed jar must not be inverted, as this might prevent the formation of a vacuum seal. Repeat as needed during the cooling and setting time until solids are nicely suspended in the jelly.

Some recipes recommend stirring jelly for several minutes to suspend particles within the jelly before pouring it into jars. This process is *not recommended*, as it interferes with the natural gelling process and can, in fact, "break the gel," which, in turn, may result in gel failure of the completed product.

Red Pepper and Garlic Jelly

This tasty jelly is dressed up with flecks of red bell pepper. If you prefer a milder garlic flavor, use small rather than large cloves.

TIP

To finely chop the pepper for this recipe, cut into ⅛ inch (0.25 cm) slices. Cut the slices into ¼ inch (0.5 cm) pieces. If desired, pepper can be chopped in a hand-turned mechanical chopper, but take care to avoid puréeing it.

Makes about three 8-ounce (250 mL) jars

1 cup	finely chopped seeded red bell pepper	250 mL
3	large cloves garlic, cut into thin slivers	3
¾ cup	cider vinegar	175 mL
3 cups	granulated sugar	750 mL
1	pouch (3 oz/85 mL) liquid pectin	1

1. Prepare canner, jars and lids. *(For more information, see page 415.)*
2. In a large, deep stainless steel saucepan, combine red pepper, garlic and vinegar. Stir in sugar. Over high heat, stirring constantly, bring to a full rolling boil that cannot be stirred down. Stir in pectin. Boil hard, stirring constantly, for 1 minute. Remove from heat and quickly skim off foam.
3. Quickly pour hot jelly into hot jars, leaving ¼ inch (0.5 cm) headspace. Wipe rim. Center lid on jar. Screw band down until resistance is met, then increase to fingertip-tight.
4. Place jars in canner, ensuring they are completely covered with water. Bring to a boil and process for 10 minutes. Remove jars, cool (see Jelly Particle Suspension Tip, above) and store. *(For more information, see pages 417–418.)*

Habanero Gold

This recipe makes a fiery golden, translucent jelly with colorful suspended fruit and vegetables. Serve it with cheese or melt it onto grilled or sautéed dishes to add sparkling flavor highlights.

TIPS

For the most attractive jelly, cut fruit and vegetables into ⅛-inch (0.25 cm) slices, then cut the slices into ¼-inch (0.5 cm) pieces.

To make a tamer yet still tasty version of this beautiful apricot-red pepper suspension, substitute a mixture of jalapeño and Scotch bonnet peppers for the habanero peppers. To add a touch more heat in either version, include the hot pepper seeds.

When cutting or seeding hot peppers, wear rubber gloves to keep your hands from being burned.

Makes about three 8-ounce (250 mL) jars

⅓ cup	finely sliced dried apricots	75 mL
¾ cup	white vinegar	175 mL
¼ cup	finely chopped red onion	50 mL
¼ cup	finely chopped seeded red bell pepper	50 mL
¼ cup	finely chopped seeded habanero peppers (see tips, at left)	50 mL
3 cups	granulated sugar	750 mL
1	pouch (3 oz/85 mL) liquid pectin	1

1. In a large, deep stainless steel saucepan, combine apricots and vinegar. Cover and let stand at room temperature for at least 4 hours or overnight.
2. Prepare canner, jars and lids. *(For more information, see page 415.)*
3. Add red onion, red pepper and habanero peppers to apricots. Stir in sugar. Over high heat, stirring constantly, bring to a full rolling boil that cannot be stirred down. Stir in pectin. Boil hard, stirring constantly, for 1 minute. Remove from heat and quickly skim off foam.
4. Quickly pour hot jelly into hot jars, leaving ¼ inch (0.5 cm) headspace. Wipe rim. Center lid on jar. Screw band down until resistance is met, then increase to fingertip-tight.
5. Place jars in canner, ensuring they are completely covered with water. Bring to a boil and process for 10 minutes. Remove jars, cool (see Jelly Particle Suspension Tip, opposite) and store. *(For more information, see pages 417–418.)*

Basil Banana Pepper Jelly

Almost any variety of pepper will work in this jelly, but using both hot and mild peppers and a combination of colors creates the best flavor and appearance. Look for color, but don't be afraid to use peppers with lots of flavor and heat. Sugar and vinegar tame the heat, which is less noticeable when the jelly is used as a marinade or glaze.

TIPS

Try a combination of red and green chilies.

Check your package of pectin for the expiration date and use only fresh pectin. Products that have expired may not set properly.

Makes about three 8-ounce (250 mL) jars

½ cup	thinly sliced seeded mild banana peppers	125 mL
¼ cup	thinly sliced partially seeded red or green chili peppers (see tip, at left)	50 mL
¼ cup	finely chopped red onion	50 mL
3 to 4	large fresh basil leaves, cut into thin ribbons	3 to 4
¼ tsp	dried basil	1 mL
¾ cup	white vinegar	175 mL
3 cups	granulated sugar	750 mL
1	pouch (3 oz/85 mL) liquid pectin	1

1. Prepare canner, jars and lids. *(For more information, see page 415.)*
2. In a large, deep stainless steel saucepan, combine banana peppers, chili peppers, red onion, fresh and dried basil and vinegar. Stir in sugar. Over high heat, stirring constantly, bring to a full rolling boil that cannot be stirred down. Stir in pectin. Boil hard, stirring constantly, for 1 minute. Remove from heat and quickly skim off foam.
3. Quickly pour hot jelly into hot jars, leaving ¼ inch (0.5 cm) headspace. Wipe rim. Center lid on jar. Screw band down until resistance is met, then increase to fingertip-tight.
4. Place jars in canner, ensuring they are completely covered with water. Bring to a boil and process for 10 minutes. Remove jars, cool (see Jelly Particle Suspension Tip, page 130) and store. *(For more information, see pages 417–418.)*

Zesty Red Onion Jelly

To create jelly with the most pleasing pink hue, prepare this recipe using freshly harvested red onions. Cold-storage red onions will deliver the desired flavor, but they fall short on supplying the beautiful shade of rose obtained with fresher produce.

TIPS

To finely chop the red onion for this recipe, cut into ⅛-inch (0.25 cm) slices and cut the slices into ¼-inch (0.5 cm) pieces.

To julienne the lemon zest, using a sharp knife, cut a wide strip of paper-thin yellow peel from lemon. Cut into thin strips.

Makes about three 8-ounce (250 mL) jars

1 cup	finely chopped red onion (see tip, at left)	250 mL
2 tsp	finely julienned lemon zest (see tip, at left)	10 mL
¾ cup	white vinegar	175 mL
3 cups	granulated sugar	750 mL
1	pouch (3 oz/85 mL) liquid pectin	1

1. Prepare canner, jars and lids. *(For more information, see page 415.)*
2. In a large, deep stainless steel saucepan, combine red onion, lemon zest and vinegar. Stir in sugar. Over high heat, stirring constantly, bring to a full rolling boil that cannot be stirred down. Stir in pectin. Boil hard, stirring constantly, for 1 minute. Remove from heat and quickly skim off foam.
3. Quickly pour hot jelly into hot jars, leaving ¼ inch (0.5 cm) headspace. Wipe rim. Center lid on jar. Screw band down until resistance is met, then increase to fingertip-tight.
4. Place jars in canner, ensuring they are completely covered with water. Bring to a boil and process for 10 minutes. Remove jars, cool (see Jelly Particle Suspension Tip, page 130) and store. *(For more information, see pages 417–418.)*

Curry Raisin Jelly

Very little manipulation is required to obtain the suspension in this jelly. In our test kitchen, it came out of the canner looking marvelous. It's an easy way to give plain grilled meats an exotic touch. Or try stirring it into hot cooked rice to serve with Asian dishes.

TIP

Curry powder gives the jelly a slightly cloudy look. For a more translucent jelly, infuse the vinegar with the flavor of whole spices, such as black pepper, coriander, cumin seeds, cloves, hot peppers and cinnamon — the quantity will vary according to your personal preference. In a stainless steel saucepan, combine desired spices and vinegar. Heat just to the boiling point over medium heat. Cover pan tightly and remove from heat. Let steep for 15 minutes. Strain and discard spices.

Makes about three 8-ounce (250 mL) jars

3 cups	granulated sugar	750 mL
1 to 2 tsp	curry powder (see tip, at left)	5 to 10 mL
½ cup	golden raisins	125 mL
½ cup	very finely chopped Spanish onion or sweet Vidalia onion	125 mL
¾ cup	white vinegar	175 mL
1	pouch (3 oz/85 mL) liquid pectin	1

1. Prepare canner, jars and lids. *(For more information, see page 415.)*

2. In a large, deep stainless steel saucepan, combine sugar and curry powder. Stir in raisins, onion and vinegar. Over high heat, stirring constantly, bring to a full rolling boil that cannot be stirred down. Stir in pectin. Boil hard, stirring constantly, for 1 minute. Remove from heat and quickly skim off foam.

3. Quickly pour hot jelly into hot jars, leaving ¼ inch (0.5 cm) headspace. Wipe rim. Center lid on jar. Screw band down until resistance is met, then increase to fingertip-tight.

4. Place jars in canner, ensuring they are completely covered with water. Bring to a boil and process for 10 minutes. Remove jars, cool (see Jelly Particle Suspension Tip, page 130) and store. *(For more information, see pages 417–418.)*

Variation

For a spectacular flavor, use freshly ground garam masala instead of curry powder. Garam masala is available at gourmet and Asian food shops.

Soft Spreads Problem Solver

CONDITION	CAUSE	PREVENTION/SOLUTION
Soft spread is tough or stiff.	There was too much natural pectin in fruit.	Use fruit that is fully ripe, not under-ripe.
	Soft spread was cooked too long.	When commercial pectin is not added, use a gel stage test (see page 21) to check doneness before filling jars.
	Too much sugar was used.	If commercial pectin is not used, ¾ cup to 1 cup (175 mL to 250 mL) sugar for each cup (250 mL) of juice or fruit should be adequate. Use standard dry measuring cups and level sugar even with the top edge of the cup.
Soft spread ferments (bubbles are apparent in or on top of spread). *If spoilage is evident, do not use.*	Soft spread was not brought to the correct temperature before filling jars and/or was under-processed, preventing all spoilage microorganisms, such as yeasts, from being destroyed.	Bring soft spread to a full rolling boil when using commercial pectin or to 220°F (104°C) when preparing a recipe with no added pectin. Fill jars and apply and adjust lids and screw bands one at a time. Process in a boiling-water canner. Refer to recipe for correct processing time.
Soft spread weeps (liquid forms at the top).	Syneresis, or "weeping," occurs in quick-setting soft spreads and is due to an imbalance of acid and pectin in fruit mixture or the quality of pectin in the fruit.	None.
	Storage conditions were not ideal.	Store soft spreads in a dry, dark place between 50 and 70°F (10 and 21°C).
Soft spread contains glass-like particles (crystals in grape spreads).	Too much sugar was used.	Follow recipe instructions and sugar measurements. Use standard dry measuring cups and level sugar even with the top edge of the cup.

CONDITION	CAUSE	PREVENTION/SOLUTION
Soft spread contains glass-like particles (crystals in grape spreads). (continued)	The mixture may have been undercooked. When the cooking time is too short, sugar does not dissolve completely and does not mix thoroughly with the juice or fruit.	Follow cooking instructions closely.
	The mixture may have been cooked too slowly or for too long. Long, slow cooking results in too much evaporation of the water content of the fruit.	Follow cooking instructions closely.
	Undissolved sugar that was sticking to the pan washed into the soft spread as it was poured.	Carefully wipe side of pan free of sugar crystals with a spatula during cooking or with a damp cloth before filling jars. Instead of pouring, ladle soft spread into jars.
	For grape products: crystals were formed by tartaric acid, a natural substance in grapes from which cream of tartar is made.	Allow grape juice to stand in the refrigerator for 12 to 24 hours. Ladle juice from bowl, being careful not to disturb sediment that may have settled on the bottom, and strain through a dampened jelly bag or several layers of dampened cheesecloth.
Soft spread made with no added pectin is too soft.	Proportions of sugar, juice or fruit, acid and pectin were not in balance.	Follow instructions precisely for soft spreads with no added pectin.
	Too large a batch was made at one time.	Use no more than 4 to 6 cups (1 L to 1.5 L) of juice or fruit in each batch. Never make a double batch.
	Fruit was too ripe.	Fruit selected should be fully ripe but not over-ripe. Using some slightly under-ripe (but not green) fruit will help because it has more natural pectin to aid with gelling.
	Soft spread was not boiled to the correct temperature.	Use a gel stage test (see page 21) to check doneness before packing jars.

CONDITION	CAUSE	PREVENTION/SOLUTION
Soft spread is cloudy.	Fruit used was too green or under-ripe.	Fruit should be firm and fully ripe.
	Fruit was cooked too long before being strained to collect juice.	Fruit should be cooked only until it is tender.
	Some fruit pulp may have been extracted when juice was squeezed from fruit.	To obtain the clearest jelly possible, let juice drain through a dampened jelly bag or several layers of dampened cheesecloth. Do not squeeze jelly bag.
	Soft spread was ladled into jars too slowly.	Work quickly to fill jars before soft spread starts to set.
	Soft spread mixture was allowed to stand before it was ladled into jars.	When cooking time is complete, ladle soft spread into jars and process immediately.
Soft spread made with added pectin is too soft.	Proportions of sugar, juice or fruit, acid and pectin were not in balance.	Measure precisely and make one recipe at a time. Never make a double batch.
	Too large a batch was made at one time.	Use no more than 4 to 6 cups (1 L to 1.5 L) of juice or fruit in each batch.
	Fruit used was too ripe.	Fruit selected should be fully ripe but not over-ripe. Using some slightly under-ripe (but not green) fruit will help because it has more natural pectin to aid with gelling.
	Soft spread was not boiled at a "full rolling boil" for the time indicated in the recipe.	Bring soft spread to a full rolling boil that cannot be stirred down and boil hard for the time indicated in the recipe.
	The wrong type of pectin was used, the wrong quantity of pectin was used and/or proportions of ingredients used were not according to the recipe.	Use only the type and quantity of pectin called for in the recipe. Pectin types are not inter-changeable. Ingredients must be added in the order specified in the recipe (the order depends on the type of pectin you are using).

CONDITION	CAUSE	PREVENTION/SOLUTION
Soft spread made with added pectin is too soft. *(continued)*	Fruit was puréed, not crushed or chopped, and therefore too much natural pectin was broken down, causing excess liquid.	Crush or chop fruit according to the recipe instructions; do not purée in a blender or food processor, unless specified in recipe.
Jelly or soft spread is filled with bubbles. *If spoilage is evident, do not use.*	If bubbles are moving when the jar is stationary, the soft spread is spoiling.	Process all soft spreads in a boiling-water canner for the time indicated in the recipe.
	If bubbles are not moving when the jar is stationary, air was trapped in the soft spread as it gelled.	Ladle soft spread quickly into the jar, holding the ladle near the rim of the jar or funnel. Use nonmetallic utensils to free bubbles before applying lid.
Soft spread or fruit mixture has mold. *Do not use.*	Mixture was not fully heated to a temperature high enough to destroy molds before jars were filled.	Bring soft spread to a full rolling boil that cannot be stirred down and boil hard for the time indicated in the recipe before filling jars.
	Food was not processed long enough to destroy molds, allowing them to grow on the surface of the food.	Process all filled jars in a boiling-water canner for the time indicated in the recipe.
	Headspace was too great to allow creation of an adequate vacuum seal.	Leave 1/4 inch (0.5 cm) headspace in soft spreads.
Fruit floats in soft spread: mixture gels, but fruit solids and clear jelly separate into layers.	Immature fruit or porous, textured fruit was used.	Use fully ripe, freshly picked fruit and berries, either fresh or frozen. Some imported out-of-season fruits are firm-textured and tend to float more easily.
	Sugar content of soft spread is too high.	Measure carefully and be sure to cook mixture at a full rolling boil for the time indicated in the recipe before filling jars.
	Air in fruit — may be dependent on growing season.	None.

Fabulous Fruits

Fruits can be preserved whole or halved in syrup, their own or store-bought juice, water or various liqueurs. They can also be made into pie fillings, sauces, juices and syrups.

● ●

Preserving Fruit

When preserving, always use the highest-quality fruit, harvested or purchased at its seasonal peak. Look for bright, richly colored fruit that feels heavy for its size. It should be plump and tender. Do not use overripe or diseased fruit, and avoid any that has mold, bruises or other blemishes.

If you've acquired fruit for canning and can't get to work immediately, store it in the refrigerator to slow the process of deterioration. Once you're ready to get started, wash the fruit well to remove dirt or soil, which may contain harmful microorganisms. Be sure to follow the guidelines in your recipe for preparing the fruit. These steps can play a significant role in producing the best-quality results.

Adding Spices and Flavorings

Spices, herbs and other flavorings such as liqueurs can be used to add flavor and flair to various preserved fruits. Because ground spices may affect the appearance of the final product, whole spices are often tied in a square of cheesecloth to create a spice bag. This bag is cooked with the fruit and removed prior to canning.

Wines and spirits impart unique flavors to fruit and are often added during the final stages of cooking. It is not necessary to buy the most expensive brand, but the flavor and color should complement the ingredients in the recipe.

As always, when adding spices, herbs and/or flavorings, follow the recipe to ensure the best results.

Peeling Fruit

To peel fruits such as peaches and apricots, place them in a pot of boiling water for 30 to 60 seconds or until the skins start to crack. Immediately dip in cold water. The skins will slip off easily.

Preventing Fruit from Browning

When fruit is cut, peeled, pitted or stemmed, the flesh is exposed to oxygen and a reaction occurs that causes the exposed areas to turn brown. Light-colored fruits, such as apples, apricots, peaches and pears, are particularly susceptible to browning, but cherries may also darken when pitted, as will grapes after they are stemmed.

This reaction (oxidation) can be prevented by treating fruit with an antioxidant such as citric acid. You can use a commercial produce protector containing ascorbic acid (vitamin C) or a mixture of ascorbic and citric acids. Follow the manufacturer's instructions. You can also submerge cut fruit in a mixture of ¼ cup (50 mL) lemon juice and 4 cups (1 L) water.

Equipment and Utensils

To can fruit, you will need all the standard kitchen equipment, as well as basic home canning supplies. Other utensils that will help with preparation include:
- Food processor or blender
- Zester
- Peeler
- Corer
- Jelly bag and stand

- Cheesecloth
- Thermometer
- Pitting spoon (grapefruit spoon)
- Cherry pitter
- Melon baller

While not essential, a kitchen scale is useful when recipe ingredients are listed by weight.

Most grocery stores and fruit markets have scales you can use when purchasing fruit. The Produce Purchase Guide (pages 426–429) provides weight and volume equivalents and will help you figure out the right amount of fruit to purchase for most recipes.

Packing Fruit into Jars

There are two basic methods for packing fruit into jars: raw-pack and hot-pack. Some fruits, such as cherries, can be packed either raw or hot; others, such as figs, require a specific method. Our recipes have been written to incorporate the appropriate method(s).

Fruits in Syrup

One of the simplest — and nicest — ways to preserve fruit is to can whole, halved or sliced fruit in a simple syrup, in fruit juice or even in water. Canning liquids that contain sugar help fruit hold its plump shape and maintain its bright color and delicious flavor, but if you're watching your sugar and/or caloric intake, unsweetened juice and water are safe alternatives.

Sweetened Syrups

Sugar syrup is the most common medium for canning fruit, as it helps fruit maintain its flavor, color and texture. Traditionally, fruit was preserved in heavy syrup, but because more and more people prefer lighter syrups with fewer calories, we've included recipes for ultra-light and extra-light syrups. A combination of sugar syrup and one sweetened with honey or corn syrup can also be used.

Here's how to make syrups for canning: In a stainless steel saucepan, combine sugar, other sweetener (if using) and water (see the chart below for recommended measurements). Bring to a boil over medium-high heat, stirring until sugar is dissolved. Reduce heat to low and keep warm until needed, taking care not to boil the syrup down.

TYPE OF SYRUP	GRANULATED SUGAR	OTHER SWEETENERS	WATER	SYRUP YIELD
Ultra-Light	½ cup (125 mL)		5 cups (1.25 L)	5¼ cups (1.3 L)
Extra-Light	1¼ cups (300 mL)		5½ cups (1.375 L)	6 cups (1.5 L)
Light	2¼ cups (550 mL)		5¼ cups (1.3 L)	6½ cups (1.625 L)
Medium	3¼ cups (800 mL)		5 cups (1.25 L)	7 cups (1.75 L)
Heavy	4¼ cups (1.05 L)		4¼ cups (1.05 L)	7 cups (1.75 L)
Corn Syrup	1½ cups (375 mL)	1 cup (250 mL) corn syrup	3 cups (750 mL)	6 cups (1.5 L)
Honey	1 cup (250 mL)	1 cup (250 mL) liquid honey	4 cups (1 L)	5 cups (1.25 L)

Allow 1 to 1½ cups (250 to 375 mL) syrup for each quart (1 L) jar of fruit. Each recipe indicates what type of syrup works best. In general, you can use even the lightest syrups with any kind of fruit, but the heavier syrups don't work well with everything. If you are watching your sugar intake or have special dietary needs, try using ultra-light or extra-light syrup.

Syrups Sweetened with Artificial Sweeteners

As a general rule, we don't recommend using artificial sweeteners when preserving fruit, as these products can produce a variety of negative effects. For instance, sweeteners containing saccharin may become bitter and present off-flavors during processing, and those containing aspartame may also lose strength during processing or storage.

Most sugar replacements tend to produce some degree of off-flavor when heated. For home canning, sucralose — Splenda® — is known to be the most stable when heated, and thus mimics the sweetness of sugar with the least noticeable flavor differences. When using sucralose, start by substituting it for sugar in the extra-light recipe at left. If this syrup is not sweet enough for your taste, increase the sucralose to the level of sugar in the light recipe. Then test one or two jars to make sure the flavor suits your preference once the fruit is processed. Remember, you can always add sweetness, but it is impossible to remove it. If you are watching your sugar intake, for the best quality, it may

be preferable to preserve fruit in water or unsweetened fruit juice and add sweetener to taste just before serving.

Unsweetened Liquids

While fruit is usually packed in sugar syrup, fruit juices such as unsweetened apple, pineapple or white grape juice — or juice from the fruit itself — can make good packing liquids. Unsweetened fruit juice provides flavor without additional sugar. Water may also be used, although it will yield a less flavorful result. When canned without the addition of sugar, fruit will be less flavorful, will have a dull color and won't hold its shape as well. If you're preserving fruits using fruit juice or water, use the same amount of juice or water as you would syrup. You must use the hot-pack method (see below).

Hot-Pack Method for Preserving Fruit in Juice or Water

The hot-pack method is required for fruits preserved in fruit juice or water. If you choose to pack your fruit in fruit juice or water rather than syrup, here's how to do it: In a stainless steel saucepan, combine fruit with just enough water to prevent sticking. Bring to a boil over medium-high heat, then reduce heat and boil gently until hot throughout. In a separate saucepan, heat fruit juice or water just to a boil. Pack hot fruit into hot jars to within a generous ½ inch (1 cm) of top of jar. Ladle hot juice over fruit, leaving ½ inch (1 cm) headspace, and heat-process as directed in the recipe.

Apples in Syrup

If you plan to use these preserved apples for baking — they are delicious in cobblers, pies and other desserts — be sure to pack them in an ultra-light or extra-light syrup, or in apple juice. When packing apples in syrup, use the hot-pack method only, as specified in the recipe.

TIPS

For best results when preserving apples in syrup, use a light or medium syrup (see page 142).

If you prefer, halve the apples or cut them into 1/4-inch (0.5 cm) slices.

**Makes about eight pint (500 mL) jars
or four quart (1 L) jars**

10 to 12 lbs	apples, stemmed, peeled, cored and quartered (see tip, at left), treated to prevent browning (see page 140) and drained	4.5 to 5.5 kg
1	batch hot syrup (see tip, at left)	1

1. Prepare canner, jars and lids. *(For more information, see page 415.)*
2. In a large stainless steel saucepan, combine apples and syrup. Bring to a boil over medium-high heat. Reduce heat to medium-low and boil gently for 5 minutes, until heated through.
3. Using a slotted spoon, pack hot apples into hot jars to within a generous 1/2 inch (1 cm) of top of jar. Ladle hot syrup into jar to cover apples, leaving 1/2 inch (1 cm) headspace. Remove air bubbles and adjust headspace, if necessary, by adding hot syrup. Wipe rim. Center lid on jar. Screw band down until resistance is met, then increase to fingertip-tight.
4. Place jars in canner, ensuring they are completely covered with water. Bring to a boil and process both pint (500 mL) and quart (1 L) jars for 20 minutes. Remove canner lid. Wait 5 minutes, then remove jars, cool and store. *(For more information, see pages 417–418.)*

Crabapples in Syrup

Select round, smaller, freshly picked crabapples that are uniform in size. Do not use crabapples that have fallen from the tree.

Makes eight pint (500 mL) jars or four quart (1 L) jars

5 lbs	stemmed whole crabapples (unpeeled)	2.3 kg
1	batch hot light or medium syrup (see page 142)	1

1. Prepare canner, jars and lids. *(For more information, see page 415.)*
2. Prick crabapples with a fork to prevent them from bursting. In a large stainless steel saucepan, over medium-low heat, warm crabapples, one layer at a time, in syrup until heated through and tender, 10 to 20 minutes, stirring occasionally to prevent scorching. Do not overcook.

TIP

A clear plastic ruler (kept solely for kitchen use) will help you determine the correct headspace. Each filled jar should be measured accurately, as the headspace can affect sealing and the preservation of the contents.

3. Using a slotted spoon, pack hot crabapples into hot jars to within a generous ½ inch (1 cm) of top of jar. Ladle hot syrup into jar to cover crabapples, leaving ½ inch (1 cm) headspace. Remove air bubbles and adjust headspace, if necessary, by adding hot syrup. Wipe rim. Center lid on jar. Screw band down until resistance is met, then increase to fingertip-tight.

4. Place jars in canner, ensuring they are completely covered with water. Bring to a boil and process both pint (500 mL) and quart (1 L) jars for 20 minutes. Remove canner lid. Wait 5 minutes, then remove jars, cool and store. *(For more information, see pages 417–418.)*

Pears in Syrup

Bartlett pears are considered best for canning. Kieffer pears and similar varieties are satisfactory if properly ripened and cooked in water instead of syrup until almost tender, drained and then packed in jars with a light syrup.

TIPS

Pears should be harvested when full-grown and stored in a cool place (60 to 75°F/15 to 18°C) until ripe but not soft.

Select fully ripe pears that are crisp and firm.

Makes eight pint (500 mL) jars or four quart (1 L) jars

8 to 12 lbs	ripe but firm pears (see tips, at left), peeled, cored, halved, treated to prevent browning (see page 140) and drained	3.6 to 5.5 kg
1	batch hot light or medium syrup (see page 142)	1

1. Prepare canner, jars and lids. *(For more information, see page 415.)*

2. In a large stainless steel saucepan, over medium-low heat, warm pears, one layer at a time, in syrup until heated through, about 5 minutes.

3. Using a slotted spoon, pack hot pears, cavity side down and overlapping layers, into hot jars to within a generous ½ inch (1 cm) of top of jar. Ladle hot syrup into jar to cover pears, leaving ½ inch (1 cm) headspace. Remove air bubbles and adjust headspace, if necessary, by adding hot syrup. Wipe rim. Center lid on jar. Screw band down until resistance is met, then increase to fingertip-tight.

4. Place jars in canner, ensuring they are completely covered with water. Bring to a boil and process pint (500 mL) jars for 20 minutes and quart (1 L) jars for 25 minutes. Remove canner lid. Wait 5 minutes, then remove jars, cool and store. *(For more information, see pages 417–418.)*

Variation

Pears Exotica: These pears make a light, refreshing dessert after a heavy meal and are a great garnish for roast meats. When making the syrup, replace ¾ cup (175 mL) of the water with white wine vinegar. Place a 2-inch (5 cm) strip of lemon zest, 1 bay leaf and 6 pink and green peppercorns in each jar before filling with pears and syrup. Process as directed above.

Fresh Berries in Syrup

Use the raw-pack method for red and black raspberries and other berries, such as blackberries, that don't hold their shape well when heated. Use the hot-pack method for firmer berries, such as blueberries, currants, elderberries, gooseberries and huckleberries. Whatever type of berry you use, be sure to select ripe, sweet berries that are uniform in color.

TIPS

You can double or triple this recipe to suit your needs. A wide range is provided for the weight of berries because of the differing sizes and densities of the different types of fruit. The range in the quantity of sugar when using the hot-pack method allows you to sweeten the fruit to suit your preference.

If you're canning elderberries, add 1 to 2 tbsp (15 to 30 mL) lemon juice to each quart jar before packing the fruit. It will improve the flavor.

Makes about eight pint (500 mL) jars or four quart (1 L) jars

6 to 12 lbs	fresh berries, stemmed or capped, if necessary	2.7 to 5.5 kg
1	batch hot light or medium syrup (see page 142), if using raw-pack method	1
	or	
1 to 2 cups	granulated sugar, if using hot-pack method	250 to 500 mL

Raw-Pack Method

1. Prepare canner, jars and lids. *(For more information, see page 415.)*
2. Ladle ½ cup (125 mL) hot syrup into each hot jar. Fill jar with berries to within a generous ½ inch (1 cm) of top of jar. Gently shake jar to pack berries closely without crushing. Add hot syrup to cover berries, if necessary, leaving ½ inch (1 cm) headspace. Remove air bubbles and adjust headspace, if necessary, by adding hot syrup. Wipe rim. Center lid on jar. Screw band down until resistance is met, then increase to fingertip-tight.
3. Place jars in canner, ensuring they are completely covered with water. Bring to a boil and process pint (500 mL) jars for 15 minutes and quart (1 L) jars for 20 minutes. Remove canner lid. Wait 5 minutes, then remove jars, cool and store. *(For more information, see pages 417–418.)*

Hot-Pack Method

1. Place berries in a large, deep stainless steel saucepan or stockpot. Add sugar (see tip, at left). Stir well, cover and set aside in a cool place for 2 hours.
2. Prepare canner, jars and lids. *(For more information, see page 415.)*
3. Transfer berry mixture to the stovetop and heat over medium-low heat, stirring occasionally, until sugar dissolves and berries are heated through.
4. Ladle hot berries and liquid into hot jars, leaving ½ inch (1 cm) headspace. Remove air bubbles and adjust headspace, if necessary, by adding hot liquid or boiling water. Wipe rim. Center lid on jar. Screw band down until resistance is met, then increase to fingertip-tight.
5. Place jars in canner, ensuring they are completely covered with water. Bring to a boil and process both pint (500 mL) and quart (1 L) jars for 15 minutes. Remove canner lid. Wait 5 minutes, then remove jars, cool and store. *(For more information, see pages 417–418.)*

When using the hot-pack method, choose the amount of sugar you add to the berries to suit your preference. We recommend using 2 cups (500 mL), but you can reduce that quantity to as little as 1 cup (250 mL) if you are watching your sugar intake. However, you should be aware that the sugar helps maintain the color, shape and flavor of the fruit.

If using gooseberries, snip off heads and tails, using scissors.

Variations

Grapefruit in Syrup (raw-pack): Substitute 8 to 10 lbs (3.6 to 4.5 kg) grapefruit, peeled and sectioned, for the berries. Be sure to cut deep enough when peeling to remove the bitter white pith, and remove the membrane when sectioning. Discard seeds. Use light syrup and do not ladle any into the jar before filling. Pack grapefruit sections into hot jars to within ½ inch (1 cm) of top of jar. Ladle hot syrup into the jar to cover grapefruit, leaving ½ inch (1 cm) headspace. Process both pint (500 mL) and quart (1 L) jars for 10 minutes.

Berries for Use in Baking Recipes (hot-pack): Packing berries in water allows you to use them in place of fresh or frozen berries in any baking recipe. In a large stainless steel saucepan, combine berries with just enough water to prevent sticking. Cook over medium-low heat, stirring occasionally, until berries are heated through. Ladle hot berries and liquid into hot jars, leaving ½ inch (1 cm) headspace. If there is not enough liquid to cover berries, add boiling water. Remove air bubbles and adjust headspace, if necessary, by adding boiling water. Process both pint (500 mL) and quart (1 L) jars for 15 minutes.

Cherries in Syrup

Select mature, bright, uniformly colored cherries.

TIPS

If your cherries are unpitted, prick them with a pin to prevent bursting or shrinking. If they have been pitted, treat them to prevent browning (see page 140).

Prepare light or medium syrup (see page 142) for sweet cherries and medium or heavy syrup (see page 142) for sour cherries.

The range in the quantity of sugar when using the hot-pack method allows you to sweeten fruit to suit your preference.

Makes about eight pint (500 mL) jars or four quart (1 L) jars

8 to 10 lbs	fresh cherries, pitted if desired (see tip, at left)	3.6 to 4.5 kg
1	batch hot syrup (see tip, at left), if using raw-pack method	1
	or	
2 to 3 cups	granulated sugar, if using hot-pack method	500 to 750 mL

Raw-Pack Method

1. Prepare canner, jars and lids. *(For more information, see page 415.)*
2. Ladle ½ cup (125 mL) hot syrup into each hot jar. Fill jar with cherries to within a generous ½ inch (1 cm) of top of jar. Gently shake jar to pack cherries closely without crushing. Add hot syrup to cover cherries, if necessary, leaving ½ inch (1 cm) headspace. Wipe rim. Remove air bubbles and adjust headspace, if necessary, by adding hot syrup. Center lid on jar. Screw band down until resistance is met, then increase to fingertip-tight.
3. Place jars in canner, ensuring they are completely covered with water. Bring to a boil and process both pint (500 mL) and quart (1 L) jars for 25 minutes. Remove canner lid. Wait 5 minutes, then remove jars, cool and store. *(For more information, see pages 417–418.)*

Hot-Pack Method

1. Prepare canner, jars and lids. *(For more information, see page 415.)*
2. In a large stainless steel saucepan, combine cherries, sugar and, if your cherries are unpitted, just enough water to prevent sticking. Cook over medium-low heat, stirring occasionally, until sugar dissolves and mixture is heated through.
3. Ladle hot cherries and liquid into hot jars, leaving ½ inch (1 cm) headspace. If there is not enough liquid to cover berries, add boiling water. Remove air bubbles and adjust headspace, if necessary, by adding boiling water. Wipe rim. Center lid on jar. Screw band down until resistance is met, then increase to fingertip-tight.
4. Place jars in canner, ensuring they are completely covered with water. Bring to a boil and process pint (500 mL) jars for 15 minutes and quart (1 L) jars for 20 minutes. Remove canner lid. Wait 5 minutes, then remove jars, cool and store. *(For more information, see pages 417–418.)*

Plums in Syrup

Select plump, freshly harvested, fully ripe plums. Purple or prune plums are the most popular variety for home canning; however, Damson and Greengage, as well as other meaty plum varieties, are also suitable for canning.

TIPS

Plums may be blanched and peeled, but they are usually preserved unpeeled. They may be left whole or cut in half and the pit removed. Pricking whole plums does not prevent the peel from cracking, but it does help to prevent the fruit from bursting.

When raw-packing plums, we recommend using a light or medium syrup (see page 142). When hot-packing plums, we recommend a medium or heavy syrup (see page 142).

Makes about eight pint (500 mL) jars or four quart (1 L) jars

6 to 10 lbs	plums (see tips, at left)	2.7 to 4.5 kg
1	batch hot syrup (see tip, at left)	1

Raw-Pack Method

1. Prepare canner, jars and lids. *(For more information, see page 415.)*
2. Using a fork, prick whole plums in several places. Pack plums into hot jars to within a generous $\frac{1}{2}$ inch (1 cm) of top of jar. Ladle hot syrup into jar to cover plums, leaving $\frac{1}{2}$ inch (1 cm) headspace. Remove air bubbles and adjust headspace, if necessary, by adding hot syrup. Wipe rim. Center lid on jar. Screw band down until resistance is met, then increase to fingertip-tight.
3. Place jars in canner, ensuring they are completely covered with water. Bring to a boil and process pint (500 mL) jars for 20 minutes and quart (1 L) jars for 25 minutes. Remove canner lid. Wait 5 minutes, then remove jars, cool and store. *(For more information, see pages 417–418.)*

Hot-Pack Method

1. Prepare canner, jars and lids. *(For more information, see page 415.)*
2. Using a fork, prick whole plums in several places. In a large stainless steel saucepan, one layer at a time, warm plums in hot syrup over medium-low heat until heated through, about 2 minutes per layer. Using a slotted spoon, transfer each batch to a bowl and keep hot. After all the plums have been heated, remove saucepan from heat and return plums to the syrup. Cover and let stand for 30 minutes. Return to a boil before packing.
3. Using a slotted spoon, pack hot plums into hot jars to within a generous $\frac{1}{2}$ inch (1 cm) of top of jar. Ladle hot syrup into jar to cover plums, leaving $\frac{1}{2}$ inch (1 cm) headspace. Remove air bubbles and adjust headspace, if necessary, by adding hot syrup. Wipe rim. Center lid on jar. Screw band down until resistance is met, then increase to fingertip-tight.
4. Place jars in canner, ensuring they are completely covered with water. Bring to a boil and process pint (500 mL) jars for 20 minutes and quart (1 L) jars for 25 minutes. Remove canner lid. Wait 5 minutes, then remove jars, cool and store. *(For more information, see pages 417–418.)*

Peaches in Syrup

Select firm, fully ripe peaches with a healthy golden color and no green.

TIPS

To peel peaches (and apricots) and treat them to prevent browning, see page 140.

Use light or medium syrup (see page 142) for raw-pack peaches and medium or heavy syrup (see page 142) when using the hot-pack method.

Peaches (and apricots and nectarines) may be canned in water, apple juice or white grape juice instead of syrup (see Hot-Pack Method for Preserving Fruit in Juice or Water, page 143).

Fruits such as peaches naturally trap an abundance of air in their juicy cell structure. Hot-packing heats the fruit to exhaust some of this air prior to packing and thus helps to prevent fruit shrinkage and floating upward in the jar during and after processing. Thus, for peaches, hot-packing is the preferred method.

Makes about eight pint (500 mL) jars or four quart (1 L) jars

8 to 12 lbs	peaches, peeled, halved, pitted, treated to prevent browning and drained	3.6 to 5.5 kg
1	batch hot syrup (see tip, at left)	1

Raw-Pack Method

1. Prepare canner, jars and lids. *(For more information, see page 415.)*
2. Pack peaches, cavity side down and overlapping layers, into hot jars to within a generous ½ inch (1 cm) of top of jar. Ladle hot syrup into jar to cover peaches, leaving ½ inch (1 cm) headspace. Remove air bubbles and adjust headspace, if necessary, by adding hot syrup. Wipe rim. Center lid on jar. Screw band down until resistance is met, then increase to fingertip-tight.
3. Place jars in canner, ensuring they are completely covered with water. Bring to a boil and process pint (500 mL) jars for 25 minutes and quart (1 L) jars for 30 minutes. Remove canner lid. Wait 5 minutes, then remove jars, cool and store. *(For more information, see pages 417–418.)*

Hot-Pack Method

1. Prepare canner, jars and lids. *(For more information, see page 415.)*
2. In a large stainless steel saucepan, one layer at a time, warm peaches in hot syrup over medium-low heat until heated through, about 1 minute per layer.
3. Using a slotted spoon, pack hot peaches, cavity side down and overlapping layers, into hot jars to within a generous ½ inch (1 cm) of top of jar. Ladle hot syrup into jar to cover peaches, leaving ½ inch (1 cm) headspace. Remove air bubbles and adjust headspace, if necessary, by adding hot syrup. Wipe rim. Center lid on jar. Screw band down until resistance is met, then increase to fingertip-tight.
4. Place jars in canner, ensuring they are completely covered with water. Bring to a boil and process pint (500 mL) jars for 20 minutes and quart (1 L) jars for 25 minutes. Remove canner lid. Wait 5 minutes, then remove jars, cool and store. *(For more information, see pages 417–418.)*

TIP

For a hint of distinctive flavor, add a well-rinsed fresh mint leaf or two when packing peaches in syrup.

Variations

Apricots in Syrup: Substitute 8 to 10 lbs (3.6 to 4.5 kg) firm ripe apricots, halved and pitted, for the peaches. Peel only if using the hot-pack method. Treat to prevent browning and drain. Use light or medium syrup. If using the raw-pack method, process pint (500 mL) jars for 25 minutes and quart (1 L) jars for 30 minutes. If using the hot-pack method, process pint (500 mL) jars for 20 minutes and quart (1 L) jars for 25 minutes.

Nectarines in Syrup: Substitute 8 to 10 lbs (3.6 to 4.5 kg) ripe nectarines, halved and pitted, for the peaches. Do not peel. Treat to prevent browning and drain. Use a light or medium syrup. If using the raw-pack method, process pint (500 mL) jars for 25 minutes and quart (1 L) jars for 30 minutes. If using the hot-pack method, process pint (500 mL) jars for 20 minutes and quart (1 L) jars for 25 minutes.

Grapes in Syrup

Select ripe, plump grapes that are free of bruises and soft spots and use the raw-pack method as outlined in the recipe.

TIP

A jar lifter is very helpful for handling hot, wet jars. Because they are bulky and fit loosely, oven mitts — even water-resistent types — are not a wise choice. When filling jars, an all-purpose rubber glove, worn on your helper hand, will allow you to steady the jar.

Makes about eight pint (500 mL) jars or four quart (1 L) jars

| 1 | batch hot light or medium syrup (see page 142) | 1 |
| 8 lbs | grapes, stemmed, treated to prevent browning (see page 140) and drained | 3.6 kg |

1. Prepare canner, jars and lids. *(For more information, see page 415.)*
2. Ladle ½ cup (125 mL) syrup into each hot jar. Fill jar with grapes to within a generous ½ inch (1 cm) of top of jar. Gently shake jar to pack grapes closely without crushing. Add hot syrup to cover grapes, if necessary, leaving ½ inch (1 cm) headspace. Remove air bubbles and adjust headspace, if necessary, by adding hot syrup. Wipe rim. Center lid on jar. Screw band down until resistance is met, then increase to fingertip-tight.
3. Place jars in canner, ensuring they are completely covered with water. Bring to a boil and process pint (500 mL) jars for 15 minutes and quart (1 L) jars for 20 minutes. Remove canner lid. Wait 5 minutes, then remove jars, cool and store. *(For more information, see pages 417–418.)*

Pineapple in Syrup

Select fully ripe pineapples with a yellowish-brown peel.

TIPS

Pineapple may also be cut lengthwise into wedges or 1-inch (2.5 cm) chunks.

For the best results, use light syrup. Pineapples are naturally very sweet.

A clear plastic ruler (kept solely for kitchen use) will help you determine the correct headspace. Each filled jar should be measured accurately, as the headspace can affect sealing and the preservation of the contents.

If you have particularly hard water and use it in the boiling-water canner, it can leave a residue on jars. Use filtered or reverse-osmosis water to fill your canner instead.

Makes about eight pint (500 mL) jars or four quart (1 L) jars

12 lbs	pineapple, peeled, cored and cut into ½-inch (1 cm) slices	5.5 kg
1	batch hot light syrup (see page 142)	1

1. Prepare canner, jars and lids. *(For more information, see page 415.)*
2. In a large stainless steel saucepan, one layer at a time, warm pineapple in hot syrup over medium-low heat until heated through, about 1 minute per layer.
3. Using a slotted spoon, pack hot pineapple into hot jars to within a generous ½ inch (1 cm) of top of jar. Ladle hot syrup into jar to cover pineapple, leaving ½ inch (1 cm) headspace. Remove air bubbles and adjust headspace, if necessary, by adding hot syrup. Wipe rim. Center lid on jar. Screw band down until resistance is met, then increase to fingertip-tight.
4. Place jars in canner, ensuring they are completely covered with water. Bring to a boil and process pint (500 mL) jars for 15 minutes and quart (1 L) jars for 20 minutes. Remove canner lid. Wait 5 minutes, then remove jars, cool and store. *(For more information, see pages 417–418.)*

Variations

Figs in Syrup: Substitute 10 lbs (4.5 kg) fully ripened whole figs (with stems and peels) for the pineapple. Blanch figs for 2 minutes in rapidly boiling water and drain before starting Step 2. Use a light or medium syrup. Increase cooking time (Step 2), warming figs in hot syrup for about 5 minutes per layer. Before packing the figs, add 1½ tsp (7 mL) bottled lemon juice to each pint (500 mL) jar and 1 tbsp (15 mL) to each quart (1 L) jar. Process pint (500 mL) jars for 45 minutes and quart (1 L) jars for 50 minutes.

Guavas in Syrup: Substitute 8 lbs (3.6 kg) slightly soft ripe guavas, peeled, halved and seeded, for the pineapple. Use a light syrup. Instead of Step 2, in a large stainless steel saucepan, bring syrup to a boil over medium-high heat. Remove from heat and add guavas, stirring to combine. Let stand for 30 minutes. Using a slotted spoon, remove guavas from syrup and transfer to a glass or stainless steel bowl. Return syrup to a boil over medium-high heat. Process pint (500 mL) jars for 15 minutes and quart (1 L) jars for 20 minutes.

Mangoes in Syrup: Substitute 12 to 14 lbs (5.5 to 6.4 kg) firm but ripe mangoes, peeled, quartered and sliced, for the pineapple. Use a light or medium syrup. Increase cooking time (Step 2), warming mangoes in hot syrup for 2 minutes per layer. Process pint (500 mL) jars for 15 minutes and quart (1 L) jars for 20 minutes.

Papayas in Syrup: Substitute 12 to 14 lbs (5.5 to 6.4 kg) papayas, peeled, seeded and cubed, for the pineapple. Use a medium or heavy syrup. Increase cooking time (Step 2), warming papayas in syrup for 2 to 3 minutes per layer. Before packing the fruit, add 1½ tsp (7 mL) bottled lemon juice to each pint (500 mL) jar and 1 tbsp (15 mL) to each quart (1 L) jar. Process pint (500 mL) jars for 15 minutes and quart (1 L) jars for 20 minutes.

Strawberries in Syrup

Select firm ripe red berries that have do not have white flesh or hollow centers. Strawberries tend to fade or lose flavor when canned.

TIP
Refer to the Produce Purchase Guide on pages 426–429 to determine how much produce you'll need to buy to prepare this recipe.

Makes about eight pint (500 mL) jars or four quart (1 L) jars

16 cups	hulled strawberries	4 L
2 to 3 cups	granulated sugar	500 to 750 mL

1. In a large stainless steel saucepan, combine strawberries and sugar. Stir gently to ensure all berries are coated with sugar. Cover and set aside in a cool place for 5 to 6 hours.
2. Prepare canner, jars and lids. *(For more information, see page 415.)*
3. Transfer saucepan to stovetop and heat over medium-low heat, stirring occasionally, until sugar dissolves and strawberries are heated through.
4. Ladle hot strawberries and liquid into hot jars, leaving ½ inch (1 cm) headspace. Remove air bubbles and adjust headspace, if necessary, by adding boiling water. Wipe rim. Center lid on jar. Screw band down until resistance is met, then increase to fingertip-tight.
5. Place jars in canner, ensuring they are completely covered with water. Bring to a boil and process pint (500 mL) jars for 10 minutes and quart (1 L) jars for 15 minutes. Remove canner lid. Wait 5 minutes, then remove jars, cool and store. *(For more information, see pages 417–418.)*

Variation

Rhubarb in Syrup: Substitute 16 cups (4 L) sliced rhubarb (1-inch/ 2.5 cm slices) for the strawberries. Toss with 2 to 4 cups (500 mL to 1 L) sugar, cover and set aside for 3 to 4 hours. When cooking, bring to a boil over medium heat and boil for 30 seconds. Continue with Steps 4 and 5. Process both pint (500 mL) and quart (1 L) jars for 15 minutes.

Spirited Fruits

Fruit with added pizzazz! Alcoholic beverages bring out the full-bodied flavor of fruit without overpowering its natural flavor. These spirited fruits are useful to have on hand as a no-fuss solution to brighten up any occasion.

Spirited Apricots

Among their many uses, apricots preserved in spirits are an excellent complement to honey-glazed ham. Just drain the apricots, pour over ham and, with a cooking brush, baste with the spirited syrup throughout the baking time. Bake at 325°F (160°C) for 30 to 40 minutes, or until bubbly.

TIP

To peel apricots (and peaches) and treat them to prevent browning, see page 140.

Makes about seven 8-ounce (250 mL) jars

1 cup	granulated sugar	250 mL
2 cups	water	500 mL
4 cups	sliced pitted peeled apricots, treated to prevent browning and drained	1 L
Per Jar		
1 tbsp	rum, brandy or white wine	15 mL
	or	
1 ½ tsp	apricot brandy, amaretto liqueur or port wine	7 mL

1. Prepare canner, jars and lids. *(For more information, see page 415.)*
2. In a large stainless steel saucepan, over medium-high heat, combine sugar and water. Bring to a boil, stirring to dissolve sugar. Add apricots, stirring constantly, and return to a boil. Reduce heat and boil gently for 5 minutes.
3. Using a slotted spoon, pack apricots into hot jars to within a generous ½ inch (1 cm) of top of jar and add the rum or spirit of your choice. Ladle hot syrup into jar to cover apricots, leaving ½ inch (1 cm) headspace. Remove air bubbles and adjust headspace, if necessary, by adding hot syrup. Wipe rim. Center lid on jar. Screw band down until resistance is met, then increase to fingertip-tight.
4. Place jars in canner, ensuring they are completely covered with water. Bring to a boil and process for 20 minutes. Remove canner lid. Wait 5 minutes, then remove jars, cool and store. *(For more information, see pages 417–418.)*

For each of the following **Spirited Fruits,** follow the method for Spirited Apricots, opposite, but use the quantity of fruit and other ingredients specified in the variation and reduce processing time if indicated. For all of these Spirited Fruits, the yield will be about seven 8-ounce (250 mL) jars.

Spirited Pears

I cup	granulated sugar	250 mL
2 cups	water	500 mL
8½ cups	quartered peeled cored pears, treated to prevent browning (see page 140) and drained	2.125 L
Per Jar		
I tbsp	rum, brandy or red wine	15 mL
	or	
1½ tsp	Kahlúa, cognac or crème de menthe	7 mL

Spirited Peaches

I cup	granulated sugar	250 mL
2 cups	water	500 mL
7 cups	sliced pitted peeled peaches, treated to prevent browning and drained	1.75 L
Per Jar		
I tbsp	rum or brandy	15 mL
	or	
1½ tsp	Dubonnet or peach schnapps	7 mL

Spirited Blueberries

I cup	granulated sugar	250 mL
2 cups	water	500 mL
12 cups	blueberries, washed and drained	3 L
Per Jar		
I tbsp	rum, brandy or vodka	15 mL
	or	
1½ tsp	Grand Marnier or other orange-flavored liqueur	7 mL

I. Reduce processing time to 15 minutes.

Spirited Cherries

TIP

If you prefer to pit your cherries before preserving them, use 7½ cups (1.875 L) unpitted cherries for this recipe.

I cup	granulated sugar	250 mL
2 cups	water	500 mL
5 cups	cherries with pits (see tip, at left), washed and drained	1.25 L
Per Jar		
I tbsp	rum, brandy or vodka	15 mL
	or	
1½ tsp	Kirsch, cherry brandy or amaretto liqueur	7 mL

I. Reduce processing time to 10 minutes.

Fruits of Distinction

What could be better than the fabulous flavor of fruit enhanced by the addition of luscious ingredients such as nuts, wine and liqueurs? These specialty recipes make superb gifts and will garner many compliments from your guests. They also make decorative edible garnishes on serving platters for parties or holiday festivities.

Crimson Honey Grapefruit

Nature's sweetener, honey, is an ideal complement to tart and tangy grapefruit segments. The addition of cranberry cocktail adds appealing color as well as flavor.

TIPS

To prepare grapefruit segments, remove the peel and pith (the bitter white part), using a sharp knife. Holding the fruit over a bowl, slide the knife down each side of a segment, separating it from the membrane and skin, reserving juice. Remove any seeds with the tip of a knife. Repeat until you have the required quantity of segments.

If you cannot find frozen cranberry concentrate, substitute any red frozen juice from concentrate.

Makes about seven 8-ounce (250 mL) jars

16 cups	grapefruit segments, including juice (see tip, at left)	4 L
1 ¼ cups	frozen cranberry cocktail concentrate, thawed and undiluted (see tip, at left)	300 mL
⅔ cup	liquid honey	150 mL

1. Prepare canner, jars and lids. *(For more information, see page 415.)*
2. In a large stainless steel saucepan, combine grapefruit and juice, cranberry cocktail concentrate and honey. Bring to a boil over medium-high heat. Reduce heat and boil gently until honey completely dissolves.
3. Using a slotted spoon, pack hot grapefruit into hot jars to within a generous ½ inch (1 cm) of top of jar. Ladle hot cranberry syrup into jar to cover grapefruit, leaving ½ inch (1 cm) headspace. Remove air bubbles and adjust headspace, if necessary, by adding hot syrup. Wipe rim. Center lid on jar. Screw band down until resistance is met, then increase to fingertip-tight.
4. Place jars in canner, ensuring they are completely covered with water. Bring to a boil and process for 10 minutes. Remove canner lid. Wait 5 minutes, then remove jars, cool and store. *(For more information, see pages 417–418.)*

Oranges in Cointreau

Spooned over ice cream or cake, this mouthwatering delicacy transforms simple sweets into special desserts. You can also use these orange slices as an edible garnish. Use the leftover syrup to sweeten beverages so nothing in the jar goes to waste.

TIPS

To prepare the oranges, cut ½ inch (1 cm) off each end. Using a sharp knife, cut oranges into ⅛-inch (0.25 cm) slices, creating circles. Or cut in half lengthwise and then cut into ⅛-inch (0.25 cm) slices, creating semi-circles. Carefully remove any seeds.

Cointreau is an orange-flavored liqueur. If you don't have it, you can substitute an equal quantity of Triple Sec, Grand Marnier or curaçao.

Makes about eight 8-ounce (250 mL) jars

10	whole cloves	10
5	cinnamon sticks (each about 4 inches/10 cm), broken in half	5
3½ cups	granulated sugar	875 mL
⅔ cup	water	150 mL
9	navel oranges, trimmed, sliced and seeded (see tip, at left)	9
¾ cup	Cointreau (see tip, at left)	175 mL
½ cup	dry white wine	125 mL

1. Prepare canner, jars and lids. *(For more information, see page 415.)*
2. Tie cloves and cinnamon stick pieces in a square of cheesecloth, creating a spice bag.
3. In a large stainless steel saucepan, combine sugar, water and spice bag. Bring to a boil over medium-high heat, stirring to dissolve sugar. Reduce heat and boil gently for 10 minutes, stirring occasionally. Remove spice bag and discard. Add orange slices, Cointreau and wine. Over medium-low heat, slowly return to a boil, occasionally stirring gently so as not to damage orange slices. Remove from heat.
4. Using a slotted spoon, carefully pack hot orange slices, loosely in layers, into hot jars to within a generous ½ inch (1 cm) of top of jar. Ladle hot syrup into jar to cover orange slices, leaving ½ inch (1 cm) headspace. Remove air bubbles and adjust headspace, if necessary, by adding hot syrup. Wipe rim. Center lid on jar. Screw band down until resistance is met, then increase to fingertip-tight.
5. Place jars in canner, ensuring they are completely covered with water. Bring to a boil and process for 15 minutes. Remove canner lid. Wait 5 minutes, then remove jars, cool and store. *(For more information, see pages 417–418.)*

Brandied Apple Rings

Apples have never looked so appetizing! Cut into perfect rings, with an edge of red peel, these apples make dumplings, strudels and pies even more attractive. Use them in place of regular apples and follow your recipe's instructions. You can cut the rings in half lengthwise or as needed. You can also enjoy these rings chilled on their own or with a dollop of whipped cream.

TIP

If food coloring is used, the intensity of the color will increase during storage.

Makes about six pint (500 mL) jars

4 cups	granulated sugar	1 L
3 cups	water	750 mL
1 tbsp	red food coloring (optional)	15 mL
4½ lbs	firm red apples, cored, cut into ¼-inch (0.5 cm) rings, treated to prevent browning (see page 140) and drained	2 kg
1 cup	brandy	250 mL

1. Prepare canner, jars and lids. *(For more information, see page 415.)*
2. In a large stainless steel saucepan, combine sugar and water. Bring to a boil over medium-high heat, stirring occasionally. Reduce heat and boil gently, stirring to dissolve sugar, about 5 minutes. Add food coloring, if using, and apple rings and return to a boil. Reduce heat and boil gently, stirring occasionally, until apples are slightly tender and, if using food coloring, the desired shade of red, about 15 minutes. Remove from heat.
3. Using a slotted spoon, remove apple rings from syrup and place in a large glass or stainless steel bowl. Return syrup to a boil over high heat. Remove from heat and stir in brandy.
4. Pack apple rings loosely into hot jars to within a generous ½ inch (1 cm) of top of jar. Ladle hot syrup into jar to cover apple rings, leaving ½ inch (1 cm) headspace. Remove air bubbles and adjust headspace, if necessary, by adding hot syrup. Wipe rim. Center lid on jar. Screw band down until resistance is met, then increase to fingertip-tight.
5. Place jars in canner, ensuring they are completely covered with water. Bring to a boil and process for 15 minutes. Remove canner lid. Wait 5 minutes, then remove jars, cool and store. *(For more information, see pages 417–418.)*

Apple Wedges in Cinnamon Red Hot Syrup

You'll love the beautiful red color and flavor of these cinnamon-spiked apples. They are the perfect accent for any fall or holiday meal and are particularly delicious as an accompaniment to roast pork.

TIPS

For this and other apple recipes, use firm, crisp apples that are good for cooking, such as Golden Delicious, Granny Smith, Jonagold, Lady or Rome Beauty.

Firm, crisp apples such as Granny Smith are preferable. Be sure apples are allowed to come to room temperature before you prepare this recipe.

Makes about eight pint (500 mL) jars

1 1/2 cups	granulated sugar	375 mL
1/2 cup	cinnamon red hot candies	125 mL
2	cinnamon sticks (each about 4 inches/10 cm)	2
2 tsp	whole cloves	10 mL
1 tsp	ground ginger	5 mL
2 cups	water	500 mL
1 1/2 cups	vinegar	375 mL
2/3 cup	light corn syrup	150 mL
2 tbsp	red food coloring (optional)	30 mL
24	medium apples, peeled, cored, cut lengthwise into eighths, treated to prevent browning (see page 140) and drained	24

1. Prepare canner, jars and lids. *(For more information, see page 415.)*

2. In a large stainless steel saucepan, combine sugar, cinnamon candies, cinnamon sticks, cloves, ginger, water, vinegar, corn syrup and red food coloring, if using. Bring to a boil over medium-high heat, stirring frequently. Add apples and stir gently over medium heat until apples are heated through, about 6 minutes. Discard cinnamon sticks. Turn heat off, but leave saucepan on heating element while filling jars.

3. Using a slotted spoon, pack hot apples into hot jars to within a generous 1/2 inch (1 cm) of top of jar. Ladle hot syrup into jar to cover apples, leaving 1/2 inch (1 cm) headspace. Remove air bubbles and adjust headspace, if necessary, by adding hot syrup. Wipe rim. Center lid on jar. Screw band down until resistance is met, then increase to fingertip-tight.

4. Place jars in canner, ensuring they are completely covered with water. Bring to a boil and process for 15 minutes. Remove canner lid. Wait 10 minutes, then remove jars, cool and store. *(For more information, see pages 417–418.)*

Apples Studded with Cherries and Raisins

In this recipe, tart apples are combined with sweet dried cherries and raisins. Try adding some of this delectable mixture to bread stuffing the next time you roast poultry. You'll need about 1/2 cup (125 mL) per 1 cup (250 mL) of stuffing.

TIP

When preparing jars and lids, prepare a couple extra in case your yield is larger than you expect. If you don't have enough jars, place any leftover preserves in an airtight container, store in the refrigerator and use within a few weeks.

Makes about eight pint (500 mL) jars or four quart (1 L) jars

8 lbs	medium-sized tart apples (such as Granny Smith), cored, cut lengthwise into eighths, treated to prevent browning (see page 140) and drained	3.6 kg
2 cups	granulated sugar	500 mL
1/2 cup	dried cherries	125 mL
1/2 cup	golden raisins	125 mL
2 tbsp	grated lemon zest	30 mL
2 tsp	ground cinnamon	10 mL
1 tsp	ground nutmeg	5 mL
2 cups	water	500 mL
1 tbsp	lemon juice	15 mL

1. Prepare canner, jars and lids. *(For more information, see page 415.)*
2. In a large stainless steel saucepan, combine apples and sugar. Toss gently to coat apples. Cover and set aside for 20 minutes. Add dried cherries, raisins, lemon zest, cinnamon, nutmeg, water and lemon juice. Bring to a boil over medium-high heat, stirring occasionally. Reduce heat and boil gently for 5 minutes.
3. Using a slotted spoon, pack hot fruit into hot jars to within a generous 1/2 inch (1 cm) of top of jar. Ladle hot syrup into jar to cover fruit, leaving 1/2 inch (1 cm) headspace. Remove air bubbles and adjust headspace, if necessary, by adding hot syrup. Wipe rim. Center lid on jar. Screw band down until resistance is met, then increase to fingertip-tight.
4. Place jars in canner, ensuring they are completely covered with water. Bring to a boil and process both pint (500 mL) and quart (1 L) jars for 20 minutes. Remove canner lid. Wait 10 minutes, then remove jars, cool and store. *(For more information, see pages 417–418.)*

Spiced Crabapples

Serve these for dessert or as a complement to meat. They are particularly delicious alongside roast pork.

TIPS

Crabapples are pricked prior to canning to reduce bursting when they are heated.

Before using jars, inspect them carefully for any chips, cracks or fractures. Discard any imperfect jars.

A clear plastic ruler (kept solely for kitchen use) will help you determine the correct headspace. Each filled jar should be measured accurately, as the headspace can affect sealing and the preservation of the contents.

Makes about six pint (500 mL) jars

1	cinnamon stick (about 4 inches/10 cm), broken into pieces	1
1 tbsp	whole allspice	15 mL
1 tbsp	whole cloves	15 mL
4½ cups	granulated sugar	1.125 L
3 cups	water	750 mL
2½ cups	white vinegar	625 mL
8 cups	stemmed crabapples, pricked with a fork	2 L

1. Tie cinnamon stick pieces, allspice and cloves in a square of cheesecloth, creating a spice bag.

2. In a large stainless steel saucepan, combine sugar, water, vinegar and spice bag. Bring to a boil over medium-high heat, stirring occasionally to dissolve sugar. Cover, reduce heat and boil gently for 10 minutes. Add crabapples and return to a boil, stirring occasionally. Reduce heat and boil gently, uncovered, for 10 to 20 minutes or until crabapples are tender. Do not overcook. Remove from heat and discard spice bag.

3. Meanwhile, prepare canner, jars and lids. *(For more information, see page 415.)*

4. Using a slotted spoon, pack hot crabapples into hot jars to within a generous ½ inch (1 cm) of top of jar. Ladle hot syrup into jar to cover crabapples, leaving ½ inch (1 cm) headspace. Remove air bubbles and adjust headspace, if necessary, by adding hot syrup. Wipe rim. Center lid on jar. Screw band down until resistance is met, then increase to fingertip-tight.

5. Place jars in canner, ensuring they are completely covered with water. Bring to a boil and process for 20 minutes. Remove canner lid. Wait 5 minutes, then remove jars, cool and store. *(For more information, see pages 417–418.)*

Blackberries in Framboise

Framboise is a raspberry brandy with an irresistible aroma. It infuses these blackberries with delectable flavor, while the cinnamon and nutmeg add an enticing hint of spice.

TIPS

Wash berries gently in small batches in a colander under cool running water to make sure you remove all dirt and grit and to avoid bruising the soft fruit.

The flavor of freshly grated nutmeg is superior to that of commercially prepared ground nutmeg. If you do not have a small nutmeg grater, any fine grater will work. Just mind that you don't grate your fingers as the nutmeg seed becomes smaller in size!

Makes about four 8-ounce (250 mL) jars

6 cups	blackberries, divided	1.5 L
	Water	
2 cups	granulated sugar	500 mL
1	cinnamon stick (about 4 inches/10 cm), broken into pieces	1
1 tbsp	grated lemon zest	15 mL
½ tsp	freshly grated nutmeg (see tip, at left)	2 mL
½ cup	framboise or other raspberry liqueur	125 mL

1. In a stainless steel saucepan, place 2 cups (500 mL) of the blackberries. Using a potato masher, crush slightly. Add 3 tbsp (45 mL) water. Cover and boil gently over medium-low heat until fruit is soft, about 2 minutes. Strain through a dampened jelly bag or a strainer lined with several layers of dampened cheesecloth set over a glass measure to collect ½ cup (125 mL) blackberry juice.

2. Meanwhile, prepare canner, jars and lids. *(For more information, see page 415.)*

3. In a large stainless steel saucepan, combine sugar, cinnamon stick pieces, lemon zest, nutmeg and 2 cups (500 mL) water. Bring to a boil over medium-high heat, stirring occasionally. Reduce heat and boil gently for 5 minutes. Strain and return syrup to saucepan. Add blackberry juice, remaining blackberries and framboise. Bring to a boil over medium-high heat, stirring constantly but gently so as not to crush blackberries.

4. Using a slotted spoon, pack hot blackberries into hot jars to within a generous ½ inch (1 cm) of top of jar. Ladle hot syrup into jar to cover blackberries, leaving ½ inch (1 cm) headspace. Remove air bubbles and adjust headspace, if necessary, by adding hot syrup. Wipe rim. Center lid on jar. Screw band down until resistance is met, then increase to fingertip-tight.

5. Place jars in canner, ensuring they are completely covered with water. Bring to a boil and process for 10 minutes. Remove canner lid. Wait 5 minutes, then remove jars, cool and store. *(For more information, see pages 417–418.)*

Honey-Orange Slices

These honey-spiced orange slices will remind you of sipping a hot cup of spiced orange-flavored tea. Among their many uses, they make an excellent addition to salad greens, tossed with a raspberry or balsamic vinaigrette and sprinkled with candied walnuts.

TIPS

A jar lifter is very helpful for handling hot, wet jars. Because they are bulky and fit loosely, oven mitts — even water-resistent types — are not a wise choice. When filling jars, an all-purpose rubber glove, worn on your helper hand, will allow you to steady the jar.

Place a clean towel on your work surface to absorb water from the hot jars as you take them out of the boiling-water canner to be filled, and again once the jars are processed. The towel prevents hot jars from coming into contact with cooler countertops. Significant temperature differences can cause jar breakage.

Makes about three 8-ounce (250 mL) jars

3	cinnamon sticks (each about 4 inches/10 cm), broken into pieces	3
1½ tsp	whole cloves	7 mL
1½ tsp	whole allspice	7 mL
2½ lbs	oranges, halved lengthwise and thinly sliced, ends and seeds discarded	1.14 kg
	Water	
1¼ cups	granulated sugar	300 mL
1¼ cups	liquid honey	300 mL
3 tbsp	lemon juice	45 mL

1. Tie cinnamon stick pieces, cloves and allspice in a square of cheesecloth, creating a spice bag. Set aside.

2. In a large stainless steel saucepan, combine oranges with water to cover. Bring to a boil over medium-high heat. Reduce heat and boil gently until peel is tender, about 15 minutes. Drain and set aside.

3. In a clean large stainless steel saucepan, combine sugar, honey and lemon juice. Bring to a boil over medium-high heat, stirring occasionally to dissolve sugar. Add reserved spice bag and oranges and bring to a boil. Reduce heat and boil gently until orange slices are well glazed, about 40 minutes. Discard spice bag.

4. Meanwhile, prepare canner, jars and lids. *(For more information, see page 415.)*

5. Using a slotted spoon, pack hot oranges into hot jars, leaving slightly more than ½ inch (1 cm) headspace. Ladle hot syrup into jar to cover oranges, leaving ½ inch (1 cm) headspace. Remove air bubbles and adjust headspace, if necessary, by adding hot syrup. Wipe rim. Center lid on jar. Screw band down until resistance is met, then increase to fingertip-tight.

6. Place jars in canner, ensuring they are completely covered with water. Bring to a boil and process for 10 minutes. Remove canner lid. Wait 5 minutes, then remove jars, cool and store. *(For more information, see pages 417–418.)*

Honey-Spiced Peaches

These zesty peaches
add a burst of spicy
fruit flavor to any
oatmeal or bran muffin
mix. Add about 1 cup
(250 mL) drained,
coarsely chopped
peaches to the batter
just before baking.

TIPS

To peel peaches and
treat them to prevent
browning, see page 140.

You can also pack the
peaches into 8-ounce
(250 mL) jars, using half
the quantity of spices per
jar. Processing time is
the same as for pint
(500 mL) jars.

Makes about six pint (500 mL) jars

1 cup	granulated sugar	250 mL
4 cups	water	1 L
2 cups	liquid honey	500 mL
8 lbs	small peaches, peeled, halved, pitted, treated to prevent browning and drained	3.6 kg
6	cinnamon sticks (each about 4 inches/10 cm)	6
1½ tsp	whole allspice	7 mL
¾ tsp	whole cloves	4 mL

1. Prepare canner, jars and lids. *(For more information, see page 415.)*
2. In a large stainless steel saucepan, combine sugar, water and honey. Bring to a boil over medium-high heat, stirring until sugar dissolves. Reduce heat to low, add peaches one layer at a time and warm until heated through, about 3 minutes per layer.
3. Using a slotted spoon, pack hot peaches, cavity side down, into hot jars to within a generous ½ inch (1 cm) of top of jar. Add 1 cinnamon stick, ¼ tsp (1 mL) allspice and ⅛ tsp (0.5 mL) cloves to each jar. Ladle hot syrup into jar to cover peaches, leaving ½ inch (1 cm) headspace. Remove air bubbles and adjust headspace, if necessary, by adding hot syrup. Wipe rim. Center lid on jar. Screw band down until resistance is met, then increase to fingertip-tight.
4. Place jars in canner, ensuring they are completely covered with water. Bring to a boil and process for 25 minutes. Remove canner lid. Wait 5 minutes, then remove jars, cool and store. *(For more information, see pages 417–418.)*

Variation

For a delightfully different flavor, substitute 1 large star anise for the cinnamon stick, cloves and allspice in each jar. Use small stars when packing into 8-ounce (250 mL) jars.

Cinnamon Kumquats

These sweet morsels can be eaten like candy or used to garnish special desserts. But don't waste the syrup. It makes an excellent dessert sauce and is delicious poured over pancakes.

TIPS

For best results, use small, firm, oval-shaped kumquats. Large kumquats do not hold their shape as well. Scrub with a soft brush under running water and drain well before using.

If you have particularly hard water and use it in the boiling-water canner, it can leave a residue on jars. Use filtered or reverse-osmosis water to fill your canner instead.

Makes about six 8-ounce (250 mL) or three pint (500 mL) jars

2½ lbs	kumquats (see tip, at left), stems completely removed	1.14 kg
2 tbsp	baking soda	30 mL
	Boiling water	
2	cinnamon sticks (each about 4 inches/10 cm)	2
6 cups	granulated sugar	1.5 L

1. In a large stainless steel saucepan, combine kumquats and baking soda. Add boiling water to cover and set aside for 5 minutes. Transfer to a colander placed over a sink and drain thoroughly. Rinse three times in cold running water. Prick each kumquat twice with a toothpick to prevent bursting.

2. In clean large stainless steel saucepan, combine kumquats, 8 cups (2 L) water and cinnamon sticks. Bring to a boil over high heat. Reduce heat to low and heat gently for 7 minutes. (Be careful not to boil, as boiling may cause the fruit to burst.) Add sugar and cook over medium-low heat, stirring constantly but gently, until sugar has dissolved and liquid has almost returned to a boil. Discard cinnamon sticks.

3. Meanwhile, prepare canner, jars and lids. *(For more information, see page 415.)*

4. Using a slotted spoon, pack kumquats loosely into hot jars to within a generous ½ inch (1 cm) of top of jar. Ladle hot syrup into jar to cover kumquats, leaving ½ inch (1 cm) headspace. Remove air bubbles and adjust headspace, if necessary, by adding hot syrup. Wipe rim. Center lid on jar. Screw band down until resistance is met, then increase to fingertip-tight.

5. Place jars in canner, ensuring they are completely covered with water. Bring to a boil and process both 8-ounce (250 mL) and pint (500 mL) jars for 15 minutes. Remove canner lid. Wait 5 minutes, then remove jars, cool and store. *(For more information, see pages 417–418.)*

Variation

Minted Kumquats: Replace the 2 cinnamon sticks with 1 cup (250 mL) fresh mint leaves and stems, tied tightly with string. When packing kumquats, place a fresh mint leaf in each jar.

Summer Fruit Cocktail

This lightly sweetened fruit cocktail is delightfully accented with honey and mint. It is best served alone as a simple dessert, accompanied by a tall glass of iced tea, finished with a sprig of mint to complement the flavors of the fruit.

TIPS

Refer to the Produce Purchase Guide on pages 426–429 to determine how much fruit you'll need to buy to prepare this recipe.

To peel peaches and treat peaches and pears to prevent browning, see page 140.

Makes about five pint (500 mL) jars

2 cups	water	500 mL
1¼ cups	granulated sugar	300 mL
¼ cup	liquid honey	50 mL
6 cups	chopped pitted peeled peaches, treated to prevent browning and drained	1.5 L
3 cups	chopped cored peeled pears, treated to prevent browning and drained	750 mL
2 cups	stemmed seedless grapes	500 mL
1 cup	drained maraschino cherries, halved	250 mL
5	fresh mint sprigs	5

1. Prepare canner, jars and lids. *(For more information, see page 415.)*
2. In a large stainless steel saucepan, combine water, sugar and honey. Bring to a boil over high heat, stirring occasionally. Add peaches, pears and grapes; return to a boil, stirring occasionally. Reduce heat and boil gently for 5 minutes. Stir in cherries. Remove from heat.
3. Place 1 mint sprig in each hot jar. Ladle hot fruit and syrup into hot jars, leaving ½ inch (1 cm) headspace. Remove air bubbles and adjust headspace, if necessary, by adding hot syrup. Wipe rim. Center lid on jar. Screw band down until resistance is met, then increase to fingertip-tight.
4. Place jars in canner, ensuring they are completely covered with water. Bring to a boil and process for 20 minutes. Remove canner lid. Wait 5 minutes, then remove jars, cool and store. *(For more information, see pages 417–418.)*

Autumn Glory Compote

Made into pie, pumpkins are a significant component of Thanksgiving celebrations. Using them in this delectable compote transforms them into a delicious treat that can be savored throughout the year.

TIPS

When making this recipe, it is best to use a pie pumpkin rather than a jack-o-lantern pumpkin. Jack-o-lantern pumpkins tend to be more watery and less flavorful.

Because they are so firm, pumpkins and pineapples can be difficult to cut into pieces. To prepare pumpkin, cut into quarters (or smaller pieces, if necessary), scoop out the seeds with a large spoon and, using a sharp knife, cut the flesh from the rind. Cube. Peel the pineapple, cut it into quarters and remove the core. Cube.

Makes about four pint (500 mL) jars

2	cinnamon sticks (each about 4 inches/10 cm), broken into pieces	2
5 cups	cubed seeded peeled pie pumpkin (¾-inch/2 cm cubes) (see tips, at left)	1.25 L
5 cups	cubed cored peeled fresh pineapple (¾-inch/2 cm cubes) (see tip, at left)	1.25 L
	Grated zest and juice of 2 lemons	
1 cup	coarsely chopped dried apricots	250 mL
1 cup	golden raisins	250 mL
2½ cups	granulated sugar	625 mL
½ cup	water	125 mL

1. Prepare canner, jars and lids. *(For more information, see page 415.)*
2. Tie cinnamon stick pieces in a square of cheesecloth, creating a spice bag.
3. In a large stainless steel saucepan, combine pumpkin and pineapple. Add lemon zest and juice, apricots, raisins, sugar, water and spice bag. Bring to a boil over medium-high heat, stirring occasionally. Reduce heat and boil gently, stirring constantly, until heated through, about 5 minutes. Discard spice bag.
4. Using a slotted spoon, pack hot pumpkin mixture into hot jars to within a generous ½ inch (1 cm) of top of jar. Ladle hot syrup into jar to cover pumpkin mixture, leaving ½ inch (1 cm) headspace. Remove air bubbles and adjust headspace, if necessary, by adding hot syrup. Wipe rim. Center lid on jar. Screw band down until resistance is met, then increase to fingertip-tight.
5. Place jars in canner, ensuring they are completely covered with water. Bring to a boil and process for 25 minutes. Remove canner lid. Wait 5 minutes, then remove jars, cool and store. *(For more information, see pages 417–418.)*

Curried Fruit Compote

Curry powder adds a distinct flavor to the summer fruits in this compote. It is excellent served with grilled chicken breasts or as a side dish with chicken salad for a special brunch.

TIPS

Refer to the Produce Purchase Guide on pages 426–429 to determine how much fruit you'll need to buy to prepare this recipe.

To peel peaches and apricots and treat them to prevent browning, see page 140.

Makes about eight pint (500 mL) jars or four quart (1 L) jars

3 cups	granulated sugar	750 mL
3 tbsp	curry powder	45 mL
4 cups	water	1 L
4 tbsp	lemon juice	60 mL
7 cups	cubed seeded peeled cantaloupe (1-inch/2.5 cm cubes)	1.75 L
6¾ cups	sliced pitted peeled peaches, treated to prevent browning and drained	1.675 L
5 cups	cubed cored peeled pineapple (1-inch/2.5 cm cubes)	1.25 L
4 cups	halved pitted peeled apricots, treated to prevent browning and drained	1 L
8	thin lime slices	8

1. Prepare canner, jars and lids. *(For more information, see page 415.)*

2. In a large stainless steel saucepan, combine sugar, curry powder, water and lemon juice. Bring to a boil over medium-high heat, stirring occasionally to dissolve sugar. Reduce heat to medium-low and add cantaloupe, peaches, pineapple and apricots. Heat gently, stirring occasionally, just until fruit is heated through, about 5 minutes.

3. Using a slotted spoon, pack hot fruit into hot jars to within a generous ½ inch (1 cm) of top of jar. Add a lime slice to each pint jar or 2 lime slices to each quart jar. Ladle hot syrup into jar to cover fruit, leaving ½-inch (1 cm) headspace. Remove air bubbles and adjust headspace, if necessary, by adding hot syrup. Wipe rim. Center lid on jar. Screw band down until resistance is met, then increase to fingertip-tight.

4. Place jars in canner, ensuring they are completely covered with water. Bring to a boil and process for 30 minutes. Remove canner lid. Wait 5 minutes, then remove jars, cool and store. *(For more information, see pages 417–418.)*

Pear Port Compote

Like fine wine, this compote improves with age. Make this recipe during the winter months, and you'll have the perfect hostess gift for Easter brunch or Thanksgiving dinner. Spoon the compote into cooked tart shells or piecrusts or serve warmed with whipped cream.

TIPS

When preparing jars and lids, prepare a couple extra in case your yield is larger than you expect. If you don't have enough jars, place any leftover preserves in an airtight container, store in the refrigerator and use within a few weeks.

Before using jars, inspect them carefully for any chips, cracks or fractures. Discard any imperfect jars.

Makes about five pint (500 mL) jars

1 cup	dark raisins	250 mL
1 cup	golden raisins	250 mL
½ cup	coarsely chopped dried apricots	125 mL
	Grated zest and juice of 1 orange	
	Grated zest and juice of 1 lemon	
½ cup	lightly packed brown sugar	125 mL
2 tsp	ground cinnamon	10 mL
2 tsp	ground nutmeg	10 mL
½ tsp	ground ginger	2 mL
¼ tsp	salt	1 mL
10 cups	coarsely chopped cored peeled pears (preferably Bartlett), treated to prevent browning (see page 140) and drained	2.5 L
1 cup	slivered blanched almonds (optional)	250 mL
¼ cup	port wine	50 mL

1. In a large stainless steel saucepan, combine dark and golden raisins, apricots, orange zest and juice, lemon zest and juice, brown sugar, cinnamon, nutmeg, ginger and salt. Gently fold in pears and bring to a boil over medium-high heat, stirring occasionally. Reduce heat, cover and boil gently for 20 minutes, stirring occasionally. Uncover, increase heat to medium and cook, stirring frequently, until mixture thickens, about 15 minutes. Stir in almonds, if using, and port wine. Cook, stirring constantly, for 5 minutes.

2. Meanwhile, prepare canner, jars and lids. *(For more information, see page 415.)*

3. Ladle hot compote into hot jars, leaving ½ inch (1 cm) headspace. Remove air bubbles and adjust headspace, if necessary, by adding compote. Wipe rim. Center lid on jar. Screw band down until resistance is met, then increase to fingertip-tight.

4. Place jars in canner, ensuring they are completely covered with water. Bring to a boil and process for 20 minutes. Remove canner lid. Wait 5 minutes, then remove jars, cool and store. *(For more information, see pages 417–418.)*

Fruit Pie Fillings

Few things smell as sweet as a fruit pie baking in the oven. Having homemade pie fillings on hand takes most of the work out of making pies, while delivering all the fresh fruit flavor. But pie fillings are not just for pies anymore. Try making small tarts with cherry pie filling, or use a jar of peach pie filling to produce a quick and easy cobbler.

Apple Pie Filling

Since apple pie is a North American tradition, homemade apple pie filling is a wonderful staple to have on hand. In addition to the classic pie, it allows you to quickly turn out luscious desserts such as apple turnovers, apple crisp or apple dumplings. The addition of cinnamon and nutmeg adds warmth to sweet or tart apple slices.

TIP

ClearJel® is a cooking starch that is acceptable for use in home canning. Not all cooking starches are suitable for home canning, as reheating causes some to lose viscosity. Making mixtures too thick can interfere with required heat penetration during heat processing. For more information, see page 431.

Makes about seven pint (500 mL) jars

12 cups	sliced peeled cored apples, treated to prevent browning (see page 140) and drained	3 L
2¾ cups	granulated sugar	675 mL
¾ cup	ClearJel® (see tip, at left)	175 mL
1½ tsp	ground cinnamon	7 mL
½ tsp	ground nutmeg	2 mL
1¼ cups	cold water	300 mL
2½ cups	unsweetened apple juice	625 mL
½ cup	lemon juice	125 mL

1. Prepare canner, jars and lids. *(For more information, see page 415.)*
2. In a large pot of boiling water, working with 6 cups (1.5 L) at a time, blanch apple slices for 1 minute. Remove with a slotted spoon and keep warm in a covered bowl.
3. In a large stainless steel saucepan, combine sugar, ClearJel®, cinnamon, nutmeg, water and apple juice. Bring to a boil over medium-high heat, stirring constantly, and cook until mixture thickens and begins to bubble. Add lemon juice, return to a boil and boil for 1 minute, stirring constantly. Remove from heat. Drain apple slices and immediately fold into hot mixture. Before processing, heat, stirring, until apples are heated through.
4. Ladle hot pie filling into hot jars, leaving 1 inch (2.5 cm) headspace. Remove air bubbles and adjust headspace, if necessary, by adding hot filling. Wipe rim. Center lid on jar. Screw band down until resistance is met, then increase to fingertip-tight.
5. Place jars in canner, ensuring they are completely covered with water. Bring to a boil and process for 25 minutes. Remove canner lid. Wait 5 minutes, then remove jars, cool and store. *(For more information, see pages 417–418.)*

Blueberry Pie Filling

Putting in some work during the summer means you can enjoy the mouthwatering flavor of blueberry pie year-round. This filling can also be used as the fruit layer in parfaits, between the pudding layer and the whipped cream.

TIP

We suggest using food coloring to enhance the color of this filling because blueberries tend to have a dull blue color that does not color the gel as well. The addition of food coloring enlivens the overall color of the pie filling, making it more appetizing.

Makes about four pint (500 mL) jars

	Water	
7 cups	blueberries	1.75 L
1²⁄₃ cups	granulated sugar	400 mL
²⁄₃ cup	ClearJel® (see tip, opposite)	150 mL
12	drops blue food coloring (optional) (see tip, at left)	12
4	drops red food coloring (optional)	4
1 tsp	grated lemon zest (optional)	5 mL
2 tbsp	lemon juice	30 mL

1. Prepare canner, jars and lids. *(For more information, see page 415.)*
2. Fill a large stainless steel saucepan halfway with water and bring to a full rolling boil over high heat. Add blueberries and blanch for 1 minute. Drain well and return to pot. Cover to keep warm.
3. In a large stainless steel saucepan, combine sugar and ClearJel®. Whisk in 2 cups (500 mL) water. Add blue and red food coloring, if using. Bring to a boil over medium-high heat, stirring occasionally. Reduce heat and boil gently, stirring constantly, until mixture thickens and begins to bubble. Stir in lemon zest, if using, and lemon juice and cook for 1 minute, stirring constantly. Remove from heat. Fold in heated blueberries.
4. Ladle hot pie filling into hot jars, leaving slightly more than 1 inch (2.5 cm) headspace. Remove air bubbles and adjust headspace, if necessary, by adding hot filling. Wipe rim. Center lid on jar. Screw band down until resistance is met, then increase to fingertip-tight.
5. Place jars in canner, ensuring they are completely covered with water. Bring to a boil and process for 30 minutes. Remove canner lid. Wait 5 minutes, then remove jars, cool and store. *(For more information, see pages 417–418.)*

Raspberry Pie Filling

The delicate flavor of raspberries in this pie filling is unforgettable. For something a little different, try using this filling to make a dessert crêpe. Fill warmed crêpes with a whipped topping or pudding. Top with the raspberry filling and drizzle with chocolate syrup. It's easy, elegant and delicious!

TIP

If using fresh raspberries, wash and drain thoroughly. If using frozen raspberries, measure whole berries, thaw, drain and reserve the liquid. Measure liquid and substitute for an equal quantity of the water called for in the recipe.

Makes about five pint (500 mL) jars

1¾ cups	granulated sugar	425 mL
⅔ cup	ClearJel® (see tip, page 170)	150 mL
2 cups	cool water	500 mL
	Blue food coloring (optional)	
	Red food coloring (optional)	
2 tbsp	lemon juice	30 mL
7 cups	raspberries (see tip, at left)	1.75 L

1. Prepare canner, jars and lids. *(For more information, see page 415.)*

2. In a large stainless steel saucepan, combine sugar and ClearJel®. Whisk in water. Add blue and red food coloring, if using, a few drops at a time, until the desired color is achieved. Bring to a boil over medium-high heat, stirring constantly. Add lemon juice, return to a boil and cook for 1 minute, stirring constantly. Reduce heat to low. Quickly fold in raspberries and return to a boil over medium-high heat, stirring frequently and gently until mixture boils. Remove from heat.

3. Ladle hot pie filling into hot jars, leaving 1 inch (2.5 cm) headspace. Remove air bubbles and adjust headspace, if necessary, by adding hot filling. Wipe rim. Center lid on jar. Screw band down until resistance is met, then increase to fingertip-tight.

4. Place jars in canner, ensuring they are completely covered with water. Bring to a boil and process for 30 minutes. Remove canner lid. Wait 5 minutes, then remove jars, cool and store. *(For more information, see pages 417–418.)*

Rhubarb Strawberry Pie Filling

Tart and sweet, there is no better combination than rhubarb and strawberries. Our favorite way to enjoy these complex flavors is in a simple but striking lattice-topped pie.

TIPS

To ensure they maintain their shape and texture, select a variety of apples suitable for cooking, such as Golden Delicious, Granny Smith, Jonagold, Lady or Rome Beauty.

If using fresh strawberries, wash and drain thoroughly. If using frozen strawberries, measure whole berries, thaw, drain and reserve the liquid. Measure liquid and substitute for an equal quantity of the water called for in the recipe.

Makes about five pint (500 mL) jars

3	large apples (see tip, at left), peeled and finely chopped	3
1 tbsp	grated orange zest	15 mL
¼ cup	freshly squeezed orange juice	50 mL
7 cups	sliced rhubarb (1-inch/2.5 cm slices)	1.75 L
2 cups	granulated sugar	500 mL
4 cups	halved hulled strawberries (see tip, at left)	1 L

1. Prepare canner, jars and lids. *(For more information, see page 415.)*
2. In a large stainless steel saucepan, combine apples and orange zest and juice. Stir to coat apples thoroughly. Stir in rhubarb and sugar. Bring to a boil over medium-high heat, stirring constantly. Reduce heat and boil gently, stirring frequently, until rhubarb is tender, about 12 minutes. Add strawberries and return to a boil. Remove from heat.
3. Ladle hot pie filling into hot jars, leaving 1 inch (2.5 cm) headspace. Remove air bubbles and adjust headspace, if necessary, by adding hot filling. Wipe rim. Center lid on jar. Screw band down until resistance is met, then increase to fingertip-tight.
4. Place jars in canner, ensuring they are completely covered with water. Bring to a boil and process for 15 minutes. Remove canner lid. Wait 5 minutes, then remove jars, cool and store. *(For more information, see pages 417–418.)*

Tart Cherry Pie Filling

Not only does this mouthwatering filling make a to-die-for pie, it is also an excellent topping for coffee cake. If you need a housewarming gift, it makes a nice addition to a food basket.

TIPS

You can store the extra cherry juice in the refrigerator for up to 3 weeks or freeze it for up to 1 year. Use it to flavor punches and lemon-lime soda. Or drink the juice alone, adding sweetener to taste.

Failing to heat the cherries and sauce to a full boil can lead to liquid escaping from the jar during processing and/or seal failure.

Makes about eight pint (500 mL) jars or four quart (1 L) jars

10 lbs	frozen tart red cherries, thawed in the refrigerator for 24 hours	4.5 kg
3½ cups	granulated sugar	875 mL
1 cup	ClearJel® (see tip, page 170)	250 mL
½ tsp	ground cinnamon	2 mL
¼ cup	lemon juice	50 mL

1. In a colander placed over a large bowl, drain thawed cherries, stirring occasionally, until you have collected 8 cups (2 L) of juice, about 2 hours. Set liquid and cherries aside.

2. Meanwhile, prepare canner, jars and lids. *(For more information, see page 415.)*

3. In a large stainless steel saucepan, whisk together 4 cups (1 L) cherry liquid (see tip, at left), sugar, ClearJel® and cinnamon. Bring to a boil over medium-high heat, stirring constantly, and boil until thickened and mixture begins to bubble. Add lemon juice, return to a boil and boil for 1 minute, stirring constantly. Add reserved cherries all at once. Return to a boil over medium-high heat, stirring constantly and gently. Remove from heat.

4. Ladle hot pie filling into hot jars, leaving 1 inch (2.5 cm) headspace. Remove air bubbles and adjust headspace, if necessary, by adding hot filling. Wipe rim. Center lid on jar. Screw band down until resistance is met, then increase to fingertip-tight.

5. Place jars in canner, ensuring they are completely covered with water. Bring to a boil and process both pint (500 mL) and quart (1 L) jars for 35 minutes. Remove canner lid. Wait 5 minutes, then remove jars, cool and store. *(For more information, see pages 417–418.)*

Variation

Sweet Black Cherry Pie Filling: This luscious filling is wonderful in Black Forest cake or spread generously over an angel food cake. Substitute sweet black cherries for the tart red cherries. Drain thawed sweet cherries until you have collected 7 cups (1.75 L) juice. Decrease the sugar to 2½ cups (625 mL) and increase the lemon juice to ⅓ cup (75 mL).

Peach Pie Filling

Peach lovers will enjoy
this homemade filling
in a hot cobbler or pie
any time of the year.
For a quick dessert, cut
squares of thinly rolled
puff pastry dough and
spoon peach filling
into the center of each
square. Fold in half
and seal the sides with
a fork. Cut a slit in the
top and place on
baking sheets. Bake in
a 400°F (200°C) oven
for about 20 minutes,
until golden brown.

TIPS

Choose peach varieties
that are firm and good for
cooking, such as Red
Haven and Redskin.

To ensure they maintain
their shape and texture,
select a variety of apples
suitable for cooking, such
as Golden Delicious,
Granny Smith, Jonagold,
Lady or Rome Beauty.

To peel peaches and
treat peaches and apples
to prevent browning,
see page 140.

Makes about four pint (500 mL) jars

1	cinnamon stick (about 3 inches/7.5 cm), broken into pieces	1
2 tsp	whole cloves	10 mL
12 cups	sliced pitted peeled peaches, treated to prevent browning and drained	3 L
2 cups	finely chopped cored peeled apples, treated to prevent browning and drained	500 mL
2⅔ cups	granulated sugar	650 mL
1 cup	golden raisins	250 mL
2 tbsp	grated lemon zest	30 mL
½ cup	lemon juice	125 mL
¼ cup	white vinegar	50 mL
½ tsp	ground nutmeg	2 mL

1. Tie cinnamon stick pieces and cloves in a square of cheesecloth, creating a spice bag.

2. In a large stainless steel saucepan, combine peaches, apples, sugar, raisins, lemon zest and juice, vinegar, nutmeg and spice bag. Bring to a boil over medium-high heat, stirring frequently. Reduce heat, cover and boil gently, stirring occasionally, until thickened.

3. Meanwhile, prepare canner, jars and lids. (For more information, see page 415.)

4. Ladle hot pie filling into hot jars, leaving 1 inch (2.5 cm) headspace. Remove air bubbles and adjust headspace, if necessary, by adding hot filling. Wipe rim. Center lid on jar. Screw band down until resistance is met, then increase to fingertip-tight.

5. Place jars in canner, ensuring they are completely covered with water. Bring to a boil and process for 15 minutes. Remove canner lid. Wait 5 minutes, then remove jars, cool and store. (For more information, see pages 417–418.)

Brandied Fruit Mincemeat

Full of dried fruits, citrus and spices, this meatless mincemeat is the perfect ending to holiday meals. Add it to piecrusts or tart shells for a special dessert. Served with a scoop of butter pecan ice cream, it's utterly delectable.

TIPS

Since dried fruit is most often sold by weight, we've added approximate weights for the fairly lengthy list of ingredients required for this recipe. Bulk food markets offer a wide range of these foods.

To seed and grind oranges and lemons, first halve the fruit lengthwise. Using the tip of a knife, remove seeds. Then cut into quarters or eighths. Grind fruit (pulp and peel) in a food processor or food grinder until a fine to medium texture is achieved.

Read a recipe all the way through, even before you go shopping for the ingredients. It's very important to have all of the ingredients and equipment ready before you start making preserves.

Makes about eight pint (500 mL) jars or four quart (1 L) jars

8 cups	diced cored peeled tart apples (such as Granny Smith)	2 L
4 cups	cranberries	1 L
2¾ cups	golden raisins (14 oz/390 g)	675 mL
2 cups	dark raisins (10 oz/284 g)	500 mL
2¼ cups	dried currants (11 oz/ 315 g)	550 mL
2½ cups	chopped dried figs (15 oz/420 g)	625 mL
1⅓ cups	ground seeded oranges (see tip, at left)	325 mL
1 cup	ground seeded lemons (see tip, at left)	250 mL
1 cup	mixed candied (glacé) peel	250 mL
2 cups	lightly packed brown sugar	500 mL
4 cups	apple cider	1 L
1 tbsp	ground cinnamon	15 mL
2 tsp	ground allspice	10 mL
2 tsp	ground nutmeg	10 mL
1 tsp	ground cloves	5 mL
1 tsp	ground ginger	5 mL
¾ cup	brandy	175 mL
½ cup	dry sherry	125 mL

1. In a stainless steel saucepan, combine apples, cranberries, golden and dark raisins, currants, figs, ground oranges and lemons, candied peel, brown sugar and apple cider. Bring to a boil over medium-high heat, stirring frequently. Reduce heat and boil, stirring occasionally, for 30 minutes.

2. Meanwhile, prepare canner, jars and lids. *(For more information, see page 415.)*

3. In a small bowl, combine cinnamon, allspice, nutmeg, cloves and ginger. Whisk in brandy and sherry. Remove fruit mixture from heat and stir in brandy–spice mixture. Return mixture to a boil over medium heat, stirring frequently, and cook for 10 minutes.

4. Ladle hot mincemeat into hot jars, leaving ½ inch (1 cm) headspace. Remove air bubbles and adjust headspace, if necessary, by adding hot mincemeat. Wipe rim. Center lid on jar. Screw band down until resistance is met, then increase to fingertip-tight.

5. Place jars in canner, ensuring they are completely covered with water. Bring to a boil and process for 30 minutes. Remove canner lid. Wait 5 minutes, then remove jars, cool and store. *(For more information, see pages 417–418.)*

Pear Mincemeat

This tasty mincemeat is easy to make and is wonderful to have on hand for a quick dessert. Add it to an unbaked pie shell and top with a crust. After crimping or folding the edges under, cut slits in the top to make a design and bake at 350°F (180°C) for 40 minutes or until crust is golden brown. You'll be positively salivating as the tantalizing aroma fills the kitchen while it bakes.

TIP

A jar lifter is very helpful for handling hot, wet jars. Because they are bulky and fit loosely, oven mitts — even water-resistent types — are not a wise choice. When filling jars, an all-purpose rubber glove, worn on your helper hand, will allow you to steady the jar.

Makes five pint (500 mL) jars

1 cup	dried currants	250 mL
1 cup	sultana raisins	250 mL
½ cup	coarsely chopped dried apricots	125 mL
	Grated zest and juice of 1 lemon	
	Grated zest and juice of 1 orange	
½ cup	lightly packed brown sugar	125 mL
2 tsp	ground cinnamon	10 mL
2 tsp	ground nutmeg	10 mL
½ tsp	ground ginger	2 mL
Pinch	salt	Pinch
10 cups	chopped cored peeled pears, treated to prevent browning (see page 140) and drained	2.5 L
1 cup	slivered blanched almonds	250 mL
¼ cup	rum (optional)	50 mL

1. In a large stainless steel saucepan, combine currants, raisins, apricots, lemon zest and juice, orange zest and juice, brown sugar, cinnamon, nutmeg, ginger and salt. Fold in pears, being careful not to bruise or break them. Bring to a boil over medium-high heat. Lower heat, cover and boil gently, stirring occasionally, for 30 minutes, until slightly thickened. Uncover and cook, stirring occasionally, until thick enough to mound on a spoon, about 15 minutes. Add almonds and rum, if using, and boil gently for 5 minutes.

2. Meanwhile, prepare canner, jars and lids. *(For more information, see page 415.)*

3. Ladle hot mincemeat into hot jars, leaving ½ inch (1 cm) headspace. Remove air bubbles and adjust headspace, if necessary, by adding hot mincemeat. Wipe rim. Center lid on jar. Screw band down until resistance is met, then increase to fingertip-tight.

4. Place jars in canner, ensuring they are completely covered with water. Bring to a boil and process for 20 minutes. Remove canner lid. Wait 5 minutes, then remove jars, cool and store. *(For more information, see pages 417–418.)*

Fruit Sauces

There are so many ways to use these delicious sauces! We've provided ideas to accompany each recipe, and we're sure our suggestions will inspire you to think of more.

Raisin Sauce

This old-fashioned favorite is sure to bring back memories of special occasions and family gatherings. If you have a sweet tooth, serve a warmed spoonful over bread pudding. It also makes a wonderful accompaniment to poultry, ham or grilled meats.

TIP

When measuring wet ingredients, use a liquid measuring cup (with a handle and spout and graduated markings for measures). Smaller measuring cups (1 or 2 cups/250 or 500 mL) are more accurate than many of the larger cups (4 or 8 cups/1 or 2 L), so it is better to use a smaller one several times than to use one larger cup.

Makes about five 8-ounce (250 mL) jars

1½ cups	raisins, divided	375 mL
3	medium apples, peeled, cored and quartered	3
4½ cups	orange juice	1.125 L
1 cup	corn syrup	250 mL
½ cup	white vinegar	125 mL
1 tbsp	dry mustard	15 mL
1½ tsp	salt	7 mL
½ tsp	ground allspice	2 mL

1. Prepare canner, jars and lids. *(For more information, see page 415.)*
2. In a blender or a food processor fitted with a metal blade, working in batches, purée 1 cup (250 mL) of the raisins with the apples. Add orange juice, corn syrup, vinegar, mustard, salt and allspice. Process until smooth.
3. Pour puréed mixture into a large stainless steel saucepan and bring to a boil over high heat. Reduce heat and boil gently, stirring occasionally, for 10 minutes. Stir in remaining ½ cup (125 mL) raisins. Boil gently, stirring occasionally, until thickened, about 10 minutes.
4. Ladle hot sauce into hot jars, leaving ¼ inch (0.5 cm) headspace. Remove air bubbles and adjust headspace, if necessary, by adding hot sauce. Wipe rim. Center lid on jar. Screw band down until resistance is met, then increase to fingertip-tight.
5. Place jars in canner, ensuring they are completely covered with water. Bring to a boil and process for 10 minutes. Remove canner lid. Wait 5 minutes, then remove jars, cool and store. *(For more information, see pages 417–418.)*

Jellied Cranberry Sauce

Homemade cranberry sauce is the perfect complement to turkey, whether it is a holiday or not.

TIPS

Fresh or frozen cranberries can be used in this recipe. If using frozen, be sure to partially thaw the cranberries in the refrigerator before getting started.

If you like, tie a cinnamon stick, broken into pieces, and 1 tsp (5 mL) whole cloves into a square of cheesecloth and cook with the cranberries. Discard spice bag when cooking is completed.

To serve jellied sauce as a mold, pack sauce in straight-sided canning jars. To serve, hold jar under warm running water. With a plastic spatula, loosen edges and tip jellied sauce onto a serving plate.

Makes about two pint (500 mL) jars

4¼ cups	cranberries (see tip, at left)	1.05 L
1¾ cups	water	425 mL
2 cups	granulated sugar	500 mL

1. Prepare canner, jars and lids. *(For more information, see page 415.)*
2. In a large stainless steel saucepan, combine cranberries and water. Bring to a boil over medium-high heat. Reduce heat and boil gently, stirring occasionally, until skins burst, about 5 minutes. Remove from heat and let cool for 5 minutes.
3. Working in batches, transfer cranberry mixture to a food mill or a food processor fitted with a metal blade and purée until smooth.
4. Return cranberry purée to saucepan. Add sugar and bring to a boil over medium heat, stirring until sugar dissolves. Increase heat to high and boil hard until mixture begins to sheet from a metal spoon (see page 21). Remove from heat and test gel (see page 21). If gel stage has been reached, skin off foam.
5. Ladle hot sauce into hot jars, leaving ¼ inch (0.5 cm) headspace. Wipe rim. Center lid on jar. Screw band down until resistance is met, then increase to fingertip-tight.
6. Place jars in canner, ensuring they are completely covered with water. Bring to a boil and process for 15 minutes. Remove canner lid. Wait 5 minutes, then remove jars, cool and store. *(For more information, see pages 417–418.)*

Whole Berry Cranberry Sauce

The whole berries in this cranberry sauce add texture and flavor. Thanksgiving dinner just wouldn't be the same without it!

TIP

When preparing jars and lids, prepare a couple extra in case your yield is larger than you expect. If you don't have enough jars, place any leftover preserves in an airtight container, store in the refrigerator and use within a few weeks.

Makes about eight 8-ounce (250 mL) jars or four pint (500 mL) jars

4 cups	granulated sugar	I L
4 cups	water	I L
8 cups	fresh cranberries	2 L
	Grated zest of I large orange (optional)	

1. Prepare canner, jars and lids. *(For more information, see page 415.)*
2. In a large stainless steel saucepan, combine sugar and water. Bring to a boil over high heat, stirring to dissolve sugar. Boil hard for 5 minutes. Add cranberries and return mixture to a boil. Reduce heat and boil gently, stirring occasionally, until all berries burst and liquid begins to sheet from a metal spoon (see page 21), about 15 minutes. Stir in orange zest, if using, during the last few minutes of cooking.
3. Ladle hot sauce into hot jars, leaving ¼ inch (0.5 cm) headspace. Remove air bubbles and adjust headspace, if necessary, by adding hot sauce. Wipe rim. Center lid on jar. Screw band down until resistance is met, then increase to fingertip-tight.
4. Place jars in canner, ensuring they are completely covered with water. Bring to a boil and process for 15 minutes. Remove canner lid. Wait 5 minutes, then remove jars, cool and store. *(For more information, see pages 417–418.)*

Cranberry Rum Sauce

This uniquely flavored condiment is wonderful with scones, toasted crumpets or English muffins. But don't save it just for tea or dessert. It also makes a deliciously different accompaniment to poultry, pork or game.

Makes about six 8-ounce (250 mL) jars

3	cinnamon sticks (each about 4 inches/I0 cm), broken in half	3
8	whole allspice	8
6	whole cloves	6
2 cups	granulated sugar	500 mL
I½ cups	water	375 mL
8 cups	cranberries (fresh or frozen)	2 L
2	large apples, peeled, cored and chopped	2
¾ cup	rum	175 mL

1. Prepare canner, jars and lids. *(For more information, see page 415.)*
2. Tie cinnamon stick pieces, allspice and cloves in square of cheesecloth, creating a spice bag.

Before using jars, inspect them carefully for any chips, cracks or fractures. Discard any imperfect jars.

3. In a large stainless steel saucepan, combine sugar, water and spice bag. Bring to a boil over high heat, stirring constantly, until sugar dissolves. Reduce heat and boil gently for 5 minutes, stirring occasionally. Add cranberries and apples. Return to a boil and boil gently, stirring constantly, until cranberry skins burst, about 5 minutes. Crush mixture using a potato masher. Add rum and return to a boil. Remove from heat and discard spice bag.

4. Ladle hot sauce into hot jars, leaving ¼ inch (0.5 cm) headspace. Remove air bubbles and adjust headspace, if necessary, by adding hot sauce. Wipe rim. Center lid on jar. Screw band down until resistance is met, then increase to fingertip-tight.

5. Place jars in canner, ensuring they are completely covered with water. Bring to a boil and process for 15 minutes. Remove canner lid. Wait 5 minutes, then remove jars, cool and store. *(For more information, see pages 417–418.)*

Sunshine Citrus Dessert Sauce

Sweet as sunshine, this sauce adds an enticing sweet and spicy citrus flavor, as well as vivid color, to ice cream and angel food cake.

TIPS

Use any small sweet oranges, such as honey tangerines or mandarins, in place of the clementines.

A jar lifter is very helpful for handling hot, wet jars. Because they are bulky and fit loosely, oven mitts — even water-resistent types — are not a wise choice. When filling jars, an all-purpose rubber glove, worn on your helper hand, will allow you to steady the jar.

Makes about seven 8-ounce (250 mL) jars

1¼ cups	granulated sugar	300 mL
⅓ cup	orange juice	75 mL
¼ cup	liquid honey	50 mL
3	pieces gingerroot (each about ¼ inch/0.5 cm thick)	3
1	cinnamon stick (about 4 inches/10 cm)	1
9 cups	peeled clementine orange segments (see tip, at left), pith and seeds removed	2.25 L

1. Prepare canner, jars and lids. *(For more information, see page 415.)*

2. In a large stainless steel saucepan, combine sugar, orange juice, honey, gingerroot and cinnamon stick. Bring to a boil over medium-high heat, stirring constantly until sugar dissolves. Add orange segments and return to a boil. Reduce heat and boil gently until orange segments are heated through, about 5 minutes. Discard gingerroot pieces and cinnamon stick.

3. Using a slotted spoon, pack hot orange segments into hot jars to within a generous ¼ inch (0.5 cm) of top of jar. Ladle hot syrup into jar to cover oranges, leaving ¼ inch (0.5 cm) headspace. Remove air bubbles and adjust headspace, if necessary, by adding hot syrup. Wipe rim. Center lid on jar. Screw band down until resistance is met, then increase to fingertip-tight.

4. Place jars in canner, ensuring they are completely covered with water. Bring to a boil and process for 10 minutes. Remove canner lid. Wait 5 minutes, then remove jars, cool and store. *(For more information, see pages 417–418.)*

Applesauce

Kids of all ages will love this delicious homemade applesauce for breakfast, lunch or dinner.

TIPS

If you prefer a tart flavor, use half tart and half sweet apples when making this applesauce and reduce the quantity of sugar as desired. Tart apple varieties include Granny Smith and Jonathon. Sweeter varieties include Golden Delicious, Rome and Fuji. Gala and Pink Lady make a nice tart/sweet combination.

Adding sugar to applesauce is optional. If the sugar is omitted in this recipe, the yield will be slightly reduced. However, lemon juice is not an optional addition. Lemon juice is added to help preserve the apples' natural color and to assure the acidity of the finished product, since different varieties and harvesting conditions can produce apples of lower acidity.

Makes about eight pint (500 mL) jars or four quart (1 L) jars

12 lbs	apples, peeled, cored, quartered, treated to prevent browning (see page 140) and drained	5.5 kg
	Water	
3 cups	granulated sugar (optional)	750 mL
4 tbsp	lemon juice	60 mL

1. Prepare canner, jars and lids. *(For more information, see page 415.)*
2. In a large stainless steel saucepan, combine apples with just enough water to prevent sticking. Bring to a boil over medium-high heat. Reduce heat and boil gently, stirring occasionally, for 5 to 20 minutes, until apples are tender (time will depend upon the variety of apple and their maturity). Remove from heat and let cool slightly, about 5 minutes.
3. Working in batches, transfer apples to a food mill or a food processor fitted with a metal blade and purée until smooth.
4. Return apple purée to saucepan. Add sugar, if using, and lemon juice; bring to a boil over medium-high heat, stirring frequently to prevent sticking. Maintain a gentle boil over low heat while filling jars.
5. Ladle hot applesauce into hot jars, leaving ½ inch (1 cm) headspace. Remove air bubbles and adjust headspace, if necessary, by adding hot applesauce. Wipe rim. Center lid on jar. Screw band down until resistance is met, then increase to fingertip-tight.
6. Place jars in canner, ensuring they are completely covered with water. Bring to a boil and process both pint (500 mL) and quart (1 L) jars for 20 minutes. Remove canner lid. Wait 5 minutes, then remove jars, cool and store. *(For more information, see pages 417–418.)*

Variations

Spiced Applesauce: In Step 4, add 4 tsp (20 mL) ground spices, such as cinnamon, nutmeg or allspice, to the sauce with the sugar and lemon juice.

Chunky Applesauce: In Step 4, coarsely crush half of the cooked apples and purée the remainder. Combine before adding the sugar.

Maple Strawberry Smooch

This sauce is lightly sweetened and flavored with maple syrup to give desserts a gentle "kiss of maple sweetness." Spoon it over cake, frozen desserts or fruit salad. Or stir it into hot cereal to both sweeten and add flavor.

TIP

For 4¾ cups (1.175 L) puréed strawberries, you'll need about 8 cups (2 L) of whole strawberries. Prepare strawberries by washing and hulling them. Working in batches, purée strawberries in a food processor fitted with a metal blade until smooth.

Makes about six 8-ounce (250 mL) jars

4¾ cups	puréed strawberries (see tip, at left)	1.175 L
1½ cups	pure maple syrup	375 mL
1 cup	unsweetened apple juice	250 mL
3 tbsp	lemon juice	45 mL
1	package (1.75 oz/49 to 57 g) regular powdered fruit pectin	1

1. Prepare canner, jars and lids. *(For more information, see page 415.)*
2. In a large stainless steel saucepan, combine puréed strawberries, maple syrup, apple juice and lemon juice. Bring to a boil over medium-high heat, stirring frequently. Add pectin, stirring constantly until dissolved. Bring to a full rolling boil and boil hard for 1 minute. Remove from heat.
3. Ladle hot smooch into hot jars, leaving ¼ inch (0.5 cm) headspace. Remove air bubbles and adjust headspace, if necessary, by adding hot smooch. Wipe rim. Center lid on jar. Screw band down until resistance is met, then increase to fingertip-tight.
4. Place jars in canner, ensuring they are completely covered with water. Bring to a boil and process for 10 minutes. Remove canner lid. Wait 5 minutes, then remove jars, cool and store. *(For more information, see pages 417–418.)*

Strawberry Sauce

In less than an hour, you can transform delicious sun-ripened berries into a versatile sauce for breakfast, brunch and dessert. Homemade berry sauces are show-stoppers served over breakfast fare such as pancakes or waffles, but they are just as wonderful as toppers for fruit, ice cream and other desserts.

TIPS

The sauces, especially the blueberry sauce (opposite), will be very liquid after cooking and processing. They will set up to a thicker consistency during storage.

You can substitute thawed unsweetened berries from your freezer for fresh berries in all of these berry recipes.

Makes about six 8-ounce (250 mL) jars

9 cups	halved hulled strawberries	2.25 L
²⁄₃ cup	unsweetened apple juice	150 mL
1 tbsp	grated orange zest	15 mL
1 ½ cups	granulated sugar	375 mL
²⁄₃ cup	corn syrup	150 mL
½ cup	orange juice	125 mL

1. Prepare canner, jars and lids. *(For more information, see page 415.)*
2. In a large stainless steel saucepan, combine strawberries, apple juice and orange zest. Bring to a gentle boil over medium heat, crushing berries with a potato masher. While maintaining a constant but gentle boil, gradually add sugar, stirring until completely dissolved. Continue boiling gently while gradually stirring in corn syrup and orange juice. Bring to a full rolling boil over high heat, stirring constantly. Boil hard for 15 minutes.
3. Ladle hot sauce into hot jars, leaving ¼ inch (0.5 cm) headspace. Remove air bubbles and adjust headspace, if necessary, by adding hot sauce. Wipe rim. Center lid on jar. Screw band down until resistance is met, then increase to fingertip-tight.
4. Place jars in canner, ensuring they are completely covered with water. Bring to a boil and process for 10 minutes. Remove canner lid. Wait 5 minutes, then remove jars, cool and store. *(For more information, see pages 417–418.)*

Raspberry Sauce

Raspberries are the most elegant choice in the berry family. Use this high-quality raspberry sauce on New York–style cheesecake or to garnish crème brûlée. For a quick and easy decoration, place sauce in a squeeze bottle and use the tip to decorate a dessert plate.

Makes about six 8-ounce (250 mL) jars

10 cups	raspberries	2.5 L
I cup	unsweetened apple juice	250 mL
I tbsp	grated orange zest	15 mL
I ½ cups	granulated sugar	375 mL
⅔ cup	corn syrup	150 mL
½ cup	orange juice	125 mL

I. Follow method for Strawberry Sauce, opposite. In Step 2, reduce boiling time to 12 minutes.

Blueberry Sauce

Lemon pound cake smothered with luscious blueberry sauce is not only delicious, it looks appealing too. But don't limit this sauce to cakes; try adding a tablespoon (15 mL) to vanilla yogurt for rich fruit flavor.

TIP

To clean blueberries without rinsing, place 2 to 3 cups (500 to 750 mL) on a clean tea towel and discard any shriveled berries or visible debris. Grasp the towel on both ends, lift it and gently roll the berries back and forth by raising first your left hand, then your right hand, tilting the towel slightly.

Makes about six 8-ounce (250 mL) jars

7 cups	blueberries	1.75 mL
2¾ cups	unsweetened apple juice	675 mL
I tbsp	grated lemon zest	15 mL
I ¼ cups	granulated sugar	300 mL
⅔ cup	corn syrup	150 mL
¼ cup	lemon juice	50 mL

I. Follow method for Strawberry Sauce, opposite.

Danish Cherry Sauce

This delectable cherry sauce is a perfect complement to cheesecake. If you are looking for something lighter, try a couple of spoonfuls over cubed or sliced angel food cake.

TIP

To thicken this sauce before serving, combine 1 tbsp (15 mL) cornstarch and 2 tbsp (30 mL) water in a saucepan. Add 1 pint (500 mL) Danish Cherry Sauce. Bring to a boil over medium-high heat and cook, stirring, until sauce thickens, about 2 minutes. Do not add cornstarch before canning.

Makes about three pint (500 mL) jars

1 ½ cups	granulated sugar	375 mL
3	cinnamon sticks (each about 4 inches/10 cm)	3
1 ½ tsp	almond extract	7 mL
1 cups	water	250 mL
¾ cup	corn syrup	175 mL
7 ½ cups	pitted sweet or sour cherries	1.875 L

1. Prepare canner, jars and lids. *(For more information, see page 415.)*
2. In a large stainless steel saucepan, combine sugar, cinnamon sticks, almond extract, water and corn syrup. Bring to a boil over medium-high heat, stirring constantly. Reduce heat to a gentle boil. Add cherries and boil gently, stirring, until heated through. Discard cinnamon sticks.
3. Ladle hot cherries and syrup into hot jars, leaving ½ inch (1 cm) headspace. Remove air bubbles and adjust headspace, if necessary, by adding hot syrup. Wipe rim. Center lid on jar. Screw band down until resistance is met, then increase to fingertip-tight.
4. Place jars in canner, ensuring they are completely covered with water. Bring to a boil and process for 10 minutes. Remove canner lid. Wait 5 minutes, then remove jars, cool and store. *(For more information, see pages 417–418.)*

Peach Rum Sauce

A spoonful of this delicately flavored, luscious sauce turns ordinary desserts into memorable treats. It's particularly good warmed and served with ice cream.

Makes about seven 8-ounce (250 mL) jars

6 cups	chopped pitted peeled peaches, treated to prevent browning and drained (see tip, opposite)	1.5 L
2 cups	lightly packed brown sugar	500 mL
2 cups	granulated sugar	500 mL
¾ cup	rum	175 mL
1 tsp	grated lemon zest	5 mL

1. Prepare canner, jars and lids. *(For more information, see page 415.)*
2. In a large stainless steel saucepan, combine peaches, brown sugar, granulated sugar, rum and lemon zest. Bring to a boil over high heat, stirring constantly, until sugar dissolves. Reduce heat and boil gently, stirring occasionally, until thickened, about 20 minutes.

To peel peaches and treat them to prevent browning, see page 140.

3. Ladle hot sauce into hot jars, leaving ¼ inch (0.5 cm) headspace. Remove air bubbles and adjust headspace, if necessary, by adding hot sauce. Wipe rim. Center lid on jar. Screw band down until resistance is met, then increase to fingertip-tight.

4. Place jars in canner, ensuring they are completely covered with water. Bring to a boil and process for 10 minutes. Remove canner lid. Wait 5 minutes, then remove jars, cool and store. *(For more information, see pages 417–418.)*

Pineapple Topping

Fresh or canned pineapple can be used to make this simple but delicious dessert topping. Since it has only two ingredients, it's easy to keep on hand to spruce up last-minute desserts. It's particularly good served over moist yellow cake.

TIP

To crush fresh pineapple, peel, cut into quarters and remove the core. Coarsely chop into large pieces. Place in a food processor and pulse several times until pineapple is a medium texture.

Makes about five 8-ounce (250 mL) jars

5 cups	crushed fresh or canned pineapple (see tip, at left), including juice	1.25 L
4 cups	granulated sugar	1 L

1. Prepare canner, jars and lids. *(For more information, see page 415.)*

2. In a large, deep stainless steel saucepan, combine pineapple and sugar. Slowly bring to a boil over medium heat, stirring constantly, until sugar dissolves. Boil hard, stirring frequently, for 30 minutes. Remove from heat and test gel (see page 21). If gel stage has been reached, skim off foam, if necessary.

3. Ladle hot topping into hot jars, leaving ¼ inch (0.5 cm) headspace. Remove air bubbles and adjust headspace, if necessary, by adding hot topping. Wipe rim. Center lid on jar. Screw band down until resistance is met, then increase to fingertip-tight.

4. Place jars in canner, ensuring they are completely covered with water. Bring to a boil and process for 15 minutes. Remove canner lid. Wait 5 minutes, then remove jars, cool and store. *(For more information, see pages 417–418.)*

Chocolate Raspberry Sundae Topper

This incredible sauce has limitless potential! It is decadent, rich and fantastically versatile. Serve it over ice cream, cheesecake or fruit. It makes a sure-to-be-appreciated hostess gift.

TIP

Due to their low acidity, most homemade chocolate sauce recipes are not suitable for safe home canning. This specially tested recipe was developed in our test kitchens to answer requests from numerous chocolate-loving home canners. It pairs cocoa powder with high-acid fruit to deliver a luscious fruit sauce with delightful chocolate overtones.

Makes about six 8-ounce (250 mL) jars

½ cup	sifted unsweetened cocoa powder	125 mL
1	package (1.75 oz/49 to 57 g) regular powdered fruit pectin	1
4½ cups	crushed red raspberries	1.125 L
4 tbsp	lemon juice	60 mL
6¾ cups	granulated sugar	1.675 L

1. Prepare canner, jars and lids. *(For more information, see page 415.)*

2. In a medium glass bowl, combine cocoa powder and pectin, stirring until evenly blended. Set aside.

3. In a large stainless steel saucepan, place crushed raspberries and lemon juice. Whisk in pectin mixture until dissolved. Bring to a boil over high heat, stirring frequently. Add sugar all at once and return to a full rolling boil, stirring constantly. Boil hard for 1 minute, stirring constantly. Remove from heat and skim off foam.

4. Ladle hot sundae topper into hot jars, leaving ¼ inch (0.5 cm) headspace. Remove air bubbles and adjust headspace, if necessary, by adding hot sundae topper. Wipe rim. Center lid on jar. Screw band down until resistance is met, then increase to fingertip-tight.

5. Place jars in canner, ensuring they are completely covered with water. Bring to a boil and process for 10 minutes. Remove canner lid. Wait 5 minutes, then remove jars, cool and store. *(For more information, see pages 417–418.)*

Fruit Juices

There is simply no comparison between the flavor of commercial fruit juice and that of homemade. Although it takes time to make your own juice, the results are worth it. In addition to superb flavor, you are in complete control of how much sugar gets added — or doesn't get added, as the case may be. And drinking a glass or two of cold fresh fruit juice is a pleasant way to get some of your daily servings of fruit.

Berry Juice

This recipe works for all kinds of berries: boysenberries, blueberries, raspberries, loganberries, strawberries, blackberries and so on. Berry juice is full of flavor and is extremely nutritious. In addition to making a refreshing drink, it's a delicious replacement for water in gelatin desserts, adding an extra boost of flavor to an everyday favorite.

TIPS

Select sweet, ripe berries of uniform color.

To crush berries easily, use a potato masher. If you don't have one, use a wooden spoon, plastic spatula or fork.

For average sweetness, add 1 to 2 cups (250 to 500 mL) of sugar for each 16 cups (4 L) of juice.

Berries
Water
Granulated sugar (optional)

1. In a large stainless steel saucepan, crush berries. Add a small amount of water to prevent sticking and bring to a boil over medium-high heat. Reduce heat and boil gently, stirring occasionally, until berries are soft.

2. Transfer to a dampened jelly bag or a strainer lined with several layers of dampened cheesecloth set over a deep bowl. Let drip, undisturbed, for at least 2 hours.

3. Meanwhile, prepare canner, jars and lids. *(For more information, see page 415.)*

4. In a clean large stainless steel saucepan, combine berry juice with sugar to taste (see tip, at left). Heat to 190°F (88°C) over medium-high heat. Do not boil. Keep juice at 190°F (88°C) for 5 minutes, adjusting heat as needed.

5. Ladle hot juice into hot jars, leaving ¼ inch (0.5 cm) headspace. Wipe rim. Center lid on jar. Screw band down until resistance is met, then increase to fingertip-tight.

6. Place jars in canner, ensuring they are completely covered with water. Bring to a boil and process both pint (500 mL) and quart (1 L) jars for 15 minutes. Remove canner lid. Wait 5 minutes, then remove jars, cool and store. *(For more information, see pages 417–418.)*

Apple Juice

What better way to get your apple a day and keep the doctor away than by drinking a glass of homemade apple juice? During the winter, serve this delicious juice warm, with the addition of a cinnamon stick. Cozy up next to the fireplace and enjoy.

TIP

For a clearer juice, after Step 2, cover and refrigerate juice for 24 to 48 hours to allow sediment to settle. Being careful not to disturb the sediment, ladle or pour juice into a large stainless steel saucepan. Discard sediment.

Makes about six quart (1 L) jars

24 lbs	apples, stemmed and chopped (about 72 apples)	10.9 kg
8 cups	water	2 L

1. In a large stainless steel saucepan, combine apples and water. Bring to a boil over medium-high heat. Reduce heat and boil gently, stirring occasionally, until apples are tender.
2. Working in batches, transfer to a dampened jelly bag or a strainer lined with several layers of dampened cheesecloth set over a deep bowl. Let drip, undisturbed, for at least 2 hours.
3. Meanwhile, prepare canner, jars and lids. *(For more information, see page 415.)*
4. In a clean large stainless steel saucepan, heat apple juice to 190°F (88°C) over medium-high heat. Do not boil. Keep juice at 190°F (88°C) for 5 minutes, adjusting heat as needed.
5. Ladle hot juice into hot jars, leaving ¼ inch (0.5 cm) headspace. Wipe rim. Center lid on jar. Screw band down until resistance is met, then increase to fingertip-tight.
6. Place jars in canner, ensuring they are completely covered with water. Bring to a boil and process for 10 minutes. Remove canner lid. Wait 5 minutes, then remove jars, cool and store. *(For more information, see pages 417–418.)*

Grape Juice

Grape juice is a favorite of kids and adults alike, and homemade tastes unlike any store-bought brand. Give this recipe a try — we promise you will love it!

TIP

Select sweet, well-colored grapes that are firm. The selected grapes should be of ideal quality for eating fresh or cooking.

	Stemmed grapes
	Boiling water
	Granulated sugar (optional)

1. In a large stainless steel saucepan, crush grapes. Add just enough boiling water to cover. Bring to a boil over medium-high heat, stirring occasionally. Reduce heat, cover and boil gently, stirring occasionally, until skins are soft, about 30 minutes.
2. Transfer to a dampened jelly bag or a strainer lined with several layers of dampened cheesecloth-lined sieve set over a deep bowl. Let drip, undisturbed, for at least 2 hours. Cover juice and refrigerate for 24 to 48 hours to allow sediment to settle.
3. Prepare canner, jars and lids. *(For more information, see page 415.)*

To crush grapes easily, use a potato masher. If you don't have one, a wooden spoon, plastic spatula or fork will do.

Decanting juice helps eliminate the formation of tartaric acid crystals in the juice during storage.

4. *Decant juice:* Ladle or pour juice into a clean saucepan, being careful not to disturb the sediment. Strain juice again through a dampened jelly bag or a cheesecloth-lined sieve set over a deep bowl.

5. In a clean large stainless steel saucepan, combine grape juice with sugar to taste, if desired. Heat to 190°F (88°C) over medium-high heat. Do not boil. Keep juice at 190°F (88°C) for 5 minutes, adjusting heat as needed.

6. Ladle hot juice into hot jars, leaving ¼ inch (0.5 cm) headspace. Wipe rim. Center lid on jar. Screw band down until resistance is met, then increase to fingertip-tight.

7. Place jars in canner, ensuring they are completely covered with water. Bring to a boil and process both pint (500 mL) and quart (1 L) jars for 15 minutes. Remove canner lid. Wait 5 minutes, then remove jars, cool and store. *(For more information, see pages 417–418.)*

Cranberry Juice

This homemade cranberry juice makes a regular martini into an extraordinary one! Add one part lemon-flavored vodka to one part cranberry juice, shake it up in a martini shaker with ice and serve in a martini glass with a twist of lemon peel. Your guests will be very impressed!

TIP

Select firm, deep red berries of ideal eating quality. Avoid cranberries that are soft or bruised.

Cranberries (fresh or frozen)
Water
Granulated sugar (optional)

1. In a large deep stainless steel saucepan, combine an equal measure of cranberries and water. Bring to a boil over medium-high heat. Reduce heat and boil gently, stirring occasionally, until cranberries burst, about 5 minutes.

2. Transfer to a dampened jelly bag or a strainer lined with several layers of dampened cheesecloth set over a deep bowl. Let drip, undisturbed, for at least 2 hours.

3. Meanwhile, prepare canner, jars and lids. *(For more information, see page 415.)*

4. In a clean large stainless steel saucepan, combine cranberry juice with sugar to taste, if desired. Heat to 190°F (88°C) over medium-high heat. Do not boil. Keep juice at 190°F (88°C) for 5 minutes, adjusting heat as needed.

5. Ladle hot juice into hot jars, leaving ¼ inch (0.5 cm) headspace. Wipe rim. Center lid on jar. Screw band down until resistance is met, then increase to fingertip-tight.

6. Place jars in canner, ensuring they are completely covered with water. Bring to a boil and process both pint (500 mL) and quart (1 L) jars for 15 minutes. Remove canner lid. Wait 5 minutes, then remove jars, cool and store. *(For more information, see pages 417–418.)*

Strawberry Lemonade Concentrate

The sweetness of fresh, ripe strawberries adds the perfect balance to tart lemons in this recipe. Preserving the freshness allows you to serve this summertime favorite at any special occasion throughout the year.

TIPS

Wash berries gently in small batches in a colander under cool running water to make sure you remove all dirt and grit and to avoid bruising the soft fruit.

To reconstitute, mix one part concentrate with one part water, tonic water or ginger ale; adjust concentrate to taste.

Makes about seven pint (500 mL) jars

6 cups	hulled strawberries	1.5 L
4 cups	freshly squeezed lemon juice	1 L
6 cups	granulated sugar	1.5 L

1. Prepare canner, jars and lids. *(For more information, see page 415.)*

2. In a blender or a food processor fitted with a metal blade, working in batches, purée strawberries until smooth. Transfer to a large stainless steel saucepan as completed. Add lemon juice and sugar and stir to combine. Heat to 190°F (88°C) over medium-high heat, stirring occasionally. Do not boil. Remove from heat and skim off foam.

3. Ladle hot concentrate into hot jars, leaving ¼ inch (0.5 cm) headspace. Wipe rim. Center lid on jar. Screw band down until resistance is met, then increase to fingertip-tight.

4. Place jars in canner, ensuring they are completely covered with water. Bring to a boil and process for 15 minutes. Remove canner lid. Wait 5 minutes, then remove jars, cool and store. *(For more information, see pages 417–418.)*

Sunshine Rhubarb Juice Concentrate

The natural tangy taste of rhubarb makes a great after-school drink for kids. You can also use the concentrate to make flavored ice cubes, a great addition to lemonade or lemon-lime soda.

TIPS

Cheesecloth can be found at many retailers, such as grocery stores and other stores that carry kitchen supplies. Look in the area where kitchen utensils are located.

To reconstitute, mix one part concentrate with one part water, tonic water or ginger ale; adjust concentrate to taste.

Makes about four pint (500 mL) jars

12 cups	sliced rhubarb (1-inch/2.5 cm slices)	3 L
4 cups	water	1 L
	Grated zest and juice of 1 lemon	
	Grated zest and juice of 1 orange	
1½ cups	granulated sugar	375 mL

1. In a large stainless steel saucepan, combine rhubarb, water, lemon zest and orange zest. Bring to a boil over medium-high heat, stirring constantly. Reduce heat, cover and boil gently until rhubarb is soft, about 10 minutes. Remove from heat and stir in lemon juice and orange juice.

2. Transfer to a dampened jelly bag or a strainer lined with several layers of cheesecloth set over a deep bowl. Let drip, undisturbed, for at least 2 hours.

3. Meanwhile, prepare canner, jars and lids. *(For more information, see page 415.)*

4. In a clean large stainless steel saucepan, combine rhubarb juice and sugar. Heat to 190°F (88°C) over medium-high heat, stirring to dissolve sugar. Do not boil. Remove from heat and skim off foam.

5. Ladle hot concentrate into hot jars, leaving ¼ inch (0.5 cm) headspace. Wipe rim. Center lid on jar. Screw band down until resistance is met, then increase to fingertip-tight.

6. Place jars in canner, ensuring they are completely covered with water. Bring to a boil and process for 10 minutes. Remove canner lid. Wait 5 minutes, then remove jars, cool and store. *(For more information, see pages 417–418.)*

Variation

For a basic rhubarb juice concentrate, omit the lemon and orange zest and juice, and reduce the sugar to 1 cup (250 mL).

Four Fruit Nectar

Bountiful fresh fruit flavor! This creative combination brings you summertime with every sip. For a healthy frozen treat, pour into small plastic or paper cups. Let the nectar partially freeze, then add a wooden stick. Freeze overnight and enjoy anytime!

TIPS

To make 4 cups (1 L) peach purée, peel, pit and halve 8 to 10 medium peaches. In a food processor fitted with a metal blade, working in batches, purée peaches until smooth.

To release the juice from oranges and grapefruit, roll each piece of fruit on the counter, using the palm of your hand. Cut in half horizontally. Over a strainer placed over a bowl, squeeze out the juice, using your hands or a juice reamer. (Another way to easily release juices is to cut the fruit in half and microwave it for about 30 seconds.) Choose fruits that are heavy for their size; they contain more juice.

Makes about eight pint (500 mL) jars or four quart (1 L) jars

4 cups	peach purée (see tip, at left)	1 L
4 cups	freshly squeezed orange juice (see tip, at left)	1 L
4 cups	unsweetened pineapple juice	1 L
4 cups	freshly squeezed grapefruit juice (see tip, at left)	1 L
2 cups	water	500 mL
½ cup	liquid honey	125 mL

1. Prepare canner, jars and lids. *(For more information, see page 415.)*

2. In a large stainless steel saucepan, combine peach purée, orange juice, pineapple juice, grapefruit juice, water and honey. Heat to 190°F (88°C) over medium-high heat. Do not boil. Remove from heat and skim off foam, if necessary.

3. Ladle hot nectar into hot jars, leaving ¼ inch (0.5 cm) headspace. Remove air bubbles and adjust headspace, if necessary, by adding hot nectar. Wipe rim. Center lid on jar. Screw band down until resistance is met, then increase to fingertip-tight.

4. Place jars in canner, ensuring they are completely covered with water. Bring to a boil and process both pint (500 mL) and quart (1 L) jars for 20 minutes. Remove canner lid. Wait 5 minutes, then remove jars, cool and store. *(For more information, see pages 417–418.)*

Fruit Syrups

Waffles and pancakes just wouldn't be the same without them. Not only do fruit syrups add flavor, texture and color to many breakfast and dessert dishes, homemade syrups make wonderful gifts. After perusing these appetizing recipes, you'll have difficulty deciding which one to make because they all look and taste so good.

••

Blueberry Syrup

Blueberry syrup is a traditional favorite with pancakes and waffles.

TIPS

To crush blueberries, place them one layer at a time (to keep juice from splattering) in a deep saucepan. Using a potato masher, or the back of a large spoon, crush gently.

Cheesecloth can be found at many retailers, such as grocery stores and other stores that carry kitchen supplies. Look in the area where kitchen utensils are located.

Makes about three pint (500 mL) jars

8 cups	blueberries, crushed (see tip, at left)	2 L
6 cups	water, divided	1.5 L
1 tbsp	grated lemon zest	15 mL
3 cups	granulated sugar	750 mL
2 tbsp	lemon juice	30 mL

1. In a large stainless steel saucepan, combine blueberries, 2 cups (500 mL) of the water and lemon zest. Bring to a gentle boil over medium heat and boil gently for 5 minutes.

2. Transfer to a dampened jelly bag or a strainer lined with several layers of cheesecloth set over a deep bowl. Let drip, undisturbed, for at least 2 hours.

3. Meanwhile, prepare canner, jars and lids. *(For more information, see page 415.)*

4. In a clean large stainless steel saucepan, combine sugar and remaining 4 cups (1 L) water. Bring to a boil over medium-high heat, stirring to dissolve sugar, and cook until temperature reaches 230°F (110°C), adjusting for altitude (see tips, page 196). Add blueberry juice. Increase heat to high, bring to a boil and boil for 5 minutes, stirring occasionally. Remove from heat and stir in lemon juice.

5. Ladle hot syrup into hot jars, leaving ¼ inch (0.5 cm) headspace. Wipe rim. Center lid on jar. Screw band down until resistance is met, then increase to fingertip-tight.

6. Place jars in canner, ensuring they are completely covered with water. Bring to a boil and process for 10 minutes. Remove canner lid. Wait 5 minutes, then remove jars, cool and store. *(For more information, see pages 417–418.)*

Apple-Cinnamon Syrup

Apples and cinnamon are a warm and inviting flavor combination. On a bleak February day, try adding this syrup to hot coffee or tea. It will bring back fond memories of recent winter holidays.

TIPS

This syrup is especially delicious when made from homemade apple juice. To make your own apple juice, see page 190.

At sea level, the temperature at which a syrup is formed from a mixture of sugar and water is 230°F (110°C), when the sugar concentration reaches 80%. This stage occurs just before the soft-ball stage when making candy. If you don't have a candy thermometer, you'll know your syrup is ready when a small amount dropped into cold water forms a thread, but not a ball.

To adjust for altitude, using a candy thermometer, establish the boiling point of water at your altitude. Subtract this temperature from the boiling point at sea level (212°F/100°C). Subtract the difference from 230°F (110°C), then cook until syrup reaches that temperature.

Makes about six pint (500 mL) jars

6 cups	unsweetened apple juice (see tip, at left)	1.5 L
3	cinnamon sticks (each about 4 inches/10 cm), broken in half	3
5 cups	granulated sugar	1.25 L
4 cups	water	1 L
3 cups	corn syrup	750 mL
¼ cup	lemon juice	50 mL

1. Prepare canner, jars and lids. *(For more information, see page 415.)*

2. In a large stainless steel saucepan, combine apple juice and cinnamon sticks. Bring to a boil over medium-high heat. Reduce heat and boil gently for 5 minutes. Remove from heat and set aside.

3. In a clean large stainless steel saucepan, combine sugar and water. Bring to a boil over medium-high heat, stirring to dissolve sugar, and cook until syrup reaches 230°F (110°C), adjusting for altitude (see tips, at left). Add apple juice, cinnamon sticks and corn syrup. Return to a boil and boil for 5 minutes, stirring occasionally. Remove from heat and discard cinnamon sticks. Stir in lemon juice.

4. Ladle hot syrup into hot jars, leaving ¼ inch (0.5 cm) headspace. Wipe rim. Center lid on jar. Screw band down until resistance is met, then increase to fingertip-tight.

5. Place jars in canner, ensuring they are completely covered with water. Bring to a boil and process for 10 minutes. Remove canner lid. Wait 5 minutes, then remove jars, cool and store. *(For more information, see pages 417–418.)*

Strawberry Syrup

In addition to traditional uses, this tasty syrup can be used to create edible designs on dessert plates. Just pour some syrup into a sealable plastic bag. Seal the bag, removing air, and cut off one corner to make a spout, then surround your dessert with fanciful designs.

TIP

Fruit syrup is typically thin. If you prefer a thicker syrup, combine 1 cup (250 mL) syrup and 1 tbsp (15 mL) cornstarch in a small saucepan. Bring to a boil over medium-high heat and cook, stirring, until syrup thickens, about 2 minutes. Do not add cornstarch before canning.

Makes about six 8-ounce (250 mL) jars or three pint (500 mL) jars

10 cups	strawberries, stemmed and crushed	2.5 L
3 cups	water, divided	750 mL
1	strip (2 inches/5 cm) lemon peel	1
2½ cups	granulated sugar	625 mL
3½ cups	corn syrup	875 mL
2 tbsp	lemon juice	30 mL

1. In a large stainless steel saucepan, combine strawberries, 1½ cups (375 mL) of the water and lemon peel. Bring to a gentle boil over medium heat and boil gently for 5 minutes.

2. Transfer to a dampened jelly bag or a strainer lined with several layers of cheesecloth set over a deep bowl. Let drip, undisturbed, for at least 2 hours.

3. Meanwhile, prepare canner, jars and lids. *(For more information, see page 415.)*

4. In a clean large stainless steel saucepan, combine sugar and remaining 1½ cups (375 mL) water. Bring to a boil over medium-high heat, stirring to dissolve sugar, and cook until temperature reaches 230°F (110°C), adjusting for altitude (see tips, opposite). Add strawberry juice and corn syrup. Increase heat to high, bring to a boil and boil for 5 minutes, stirring occasionally. Remove from heat and stir in lemon juice.

5. Ladle hot syrup into hot jars, leaving ¼ inch (0.5 cm) headspace. Wipe rim. Center lid on jar. Screw band down until resistance is met, then increase to fingertip-tight.

6. Place jars in canner, ensuring they are completely covered with water. Bring to a boil and process for 10 minutes. Remove canner lid. Wait 5 minutes, then remove jars, cool and store. *(For more information, see pages 417–418.)*

Pomegranate Syrup

Pomegranate juice, the basis for this delicious syrup, is becoming very popular as a healthy drink because it is naturally high in antioxidants. This luscious crimson syrup is elegant and practical, providing nutrients and taste in one great treat.

Makes about four 8-ounce (250 ml) jars

5 cups	pomegranate juice (see tip, page 112)	1.25 L
½ cup	lemon juice	125 mL
1 cup	granulated sugar	250 mL

1. Prepare canner, jars and lids. *(For more information, see page 415.)*
2. In a large stainless steel saucepan, combine pomegranate juice, lemon juice and sugar. Bring to a boil over medium-high heat, stirring to dissolve sugar. Reduce heat and boil gently, stirring occasionally, until reduced by half, about 30 minutes.
3. Ladle hot syrup into hot jars, leaving ¼ inch (0.5 cm) headspace. Wipe rim. Center lid on jar. Screw band down until resistance is met, then increase to fingertip-tight.
4. Place jars in canner, ensuring they are completely covered with water. Bring to a boil and process for 10 minutes. Remove canner lid. Wait 5 minutes, then remove jars, cool and store. *(For more information, see pages 417–418.)*

Blackberry Liqueur Syrup

The addition of Chambord, a raspberry liqueur, adds sensational flavor to this elegant sauce. Try it over puff pastries stuffed with lemon cream or lemon sorbet. It will impress even the most discriminating guest.

Makes about three 8-ounce (250 mL) jars

4 cups	blackberries	1 L
½ cup	Chambord or other raspberry liqueur	125 mL
¾ cup	granulated sugar	175 mL
1 tbsp	grated lemon zest	15 mL
1 tbsp	lemon juice	15 mL
1	pouch (3 oz/85 mL) liquid pectin	1

1. Prepare canner, jars and lids. *(For more information, see page 415.)*
2. In a large stainless steel saucepan, combine blackberries, Chambord and sugar. Cover and let stand for 2 hours, stirring occasionally to dissolve sugar. Add lemon zest and juice; bring to a boil over medium-high heat. Stir in liquid pectin and return to a full rolling boil. Boil hard for 1 minute, stirring constantly. Remove from heat. Skim off foam, if necessary.

3. Ladle hot syrup into hot jars, leaving ¼ inch (0.5 cm) headspace. Wipe rim. Center lid on jar. Screw band down until resistance is met, then increase to fingertip-tight.

4. Place jars in canner, ensuring they are completely covered with water. Bring to a boil and process for 10 minutes. Remove canner lid. Wait 5 minutes, then remove jars, cool and store. *(For more information, see pages 417–418.)*

Maple-Walnut Syrup

Serve this syrup warm over pancakes or Belgian waffles for a traditional but special breakfast or brunch.

TIP

If you have particularly hard water and use it in the boiling-water canner, it can leave a residue on jars. Use filtered or reverse-osmosis water to fill your canner instead.

Makes about four 8-ounce (250 mL) jars

1½ cups	corn syrup	375 mL
I cup	pure maple syrup	250 mL
½ cup	water	125 mL
½ cup	granulated sugar	125 mL
2 cups	walnut pieces	500 mL

1. Prepare canner, jars and lids. *(For more information, see page 415.)*

2. In a stainless steel saucepan, combine corn syrup, maple syrup and water. Add sugar and heat over medium heat, stirring until dissolved. Increase heat to medium-high and bring to a boil, stirring occasionally. Reduce heat and boil gently, stirring constantly, until syrup begins to thicken, about 15 minutes. Stir in walnuts and cook for 5 minutes.

3. Ladle hot syrup into hot jars, leaving ¼ inch (0.5 cm) headspace. Wipe rim. Center lid on jar. Screw band down until resistance is met, then increase to fingertip-tight.

4. Place jars in canner, ensuring they are completely covered with water. Bring to a boil and process for 10 minutes. Remove canner lid. Wait 5 minutes, then remove jars, cool and store. *(For more information, see pages 417–418.)*

Praline Syrup

Dark, sweet and nutty, this praline syrup, packaged elegantly in a jar, makes a great gift. Serve it warm, over vanilla ice cream, for a special treat.

TIP

For a lighter-flavored syrup, use light corn syrup and light brown sugar.

Makes about four 8-ounce (250 mL) jars

2 cups	dark corn syrup	500 mL
½ cup	water	125 mL
⅓ cup	lightly packed dark brown sugar	75 mL
1 cup	pecan pieces	250 mL
½ tsp	vanilla	2 mL

1. Prepare canner, jars and lids. *(For more information, see page 415.)*
2. In a stainless steel saucepan, combine corn syrup, water and sugar. Heat over medium heat, stirring constantly, until sugar dissolves. Increase heat to medium-high, bring to a boil and boil for 1 minute. Reduce heat and stir in pecans and vanilla. Boil gently, stirring constantly, for 5 minutes.
3. Ladle hot syrup into hot jars, leaving ¼ inch (0.5 cm) headspace. Wipe rim. Center lid on jar. Screw band down until resistance is met, then increase to fingertip-tight.
4. Place jars in canner, ensuring they are completely covered with water. Bring to a boil and process for 10 minutes. Remove canner lid. Wait 5 minutes, then remove jars, cool and store. *(For more information, see pages 417–418.)*

Spiced Honey

Jars of this luscious treat glow with golden honey, lemon slices, cloves and cinnamon sticks. Add a couple of drops to hot tea, stir and enjoy!

TIP

A jar lifter is very helpful for handling hot, wet jars. Because they are bulky and fit loosely, oven mitts — even water-resistent types — are not a wise choice. When filling jars, an all-purpose rubber glove, worn on your helper hand, will allow you to steady the jar.

Makes about three 8-ounce (250 mL) jars

1	lemon, end pieces removed and cut into 6 even slices	1
12	whole cloves	12
3	cinnamon sticks (each about 4 inches/10 cm)	3
2⅔ cups	liquid honey	650 mL

1. Prepare canner, jars and lids. *(For more information, see page 415.)*
2. Stud the peel of each lemon slice with 2 cloves. In a stainless steel saucepan, combine lemon slices, cinnamon sticks and honey. Bring to a boil over medium heat, stirring occasionally. Boil gently for 2 minutes.
3. Using tongs, remove lemon slices and transfer to hot jars, placing 2 in each jar. Add 1 cinnamon stick to each jar. Ladle hot honey into hot jars, leaving ¼ inch (0.5 cm) headspace. Wipe rim. Center lid on jar. Screw band down until resistance is met, then increase to fingertip-tight.
4. Place jars in canner and process as in Step 4 of Praline Syrup, above.

Salsa, Relish and Chutney

Salsa, relish and chutney are all members of the pickle family — fruit and/or vegetable mixtures that rely on the addition of acid, in the form of vinegar or citrus juice, to elevate the acidity of the ingredients, allowing them to be safely preserved in a boiling-water canner. These condiments can vary broadly in both spiciness and texture and are differentiated in certain ways. Chutney usually contains a higher proportion of fruit and has a saucier texture. Relish has less sauce than chutney, has a coarser texture and is more colorful because it is usually contains a mixture of vegetables. Salsa falls somewhere between the two, featuring a wide variety of fruits and vegetables in a chunky chili pepper–spiked sauce that is just the right consistency for dipping or spooning over entrées.

Tips for Salsa, Relish and Chutney

Peeling Tomatoes and Fruit

To peel tomatoes and fruits such as peaches and nectarines, place them in a pot of boiling water for 30 to 60 seconds or until the skins start to crack. Immediately dip in cold water. The skins will slip off easily.

Preventing Fruit from Browning

When fruit is cut, peeled, pitted or stemmed, the flesh is exposed to oxygen and a reaction occurs that causes the exposed areas to turn brown. Light-colored fruits, such as apples, apricots, peaches and pears, are particularly susceptible to browning, but cherries may also darken when pitted, as will grapes after they are stemmed.

This reaction (oxidation) can be prevented by treating fruit with an antioxidant such as citric acid. You can use a commercial produce protector containing ascorbic acid (vitamin C) or a mixture of ascorbic and citric acids. Follow the manufacturer's instructions. Alternatively, submerge cut fruit in a mixture of ¼ cup (50 mL) lemon juice and 4 cups (1 L) water.

Seeding and Chopping Hot Peppers

Removing the seeds and veins of hot peppers lessens the heat of the food you are preparing. If you like your foods hot, hot, hot, feel free to leave the seeds and veins in when preparing any of the recipes in this chapter.

The best way to seed peppers is to trim off the stem end and then cut the pepper in half lengthwise. Scrape out the seeds and veins, using a spoon. Remember, when chopping or seeding hot peppers, wear rubber gloves to keep your hands from being burned and wash your hands thoroughly immediately afterwards — and don't touch your eyes!

Salsa

Salsa has overtaken ketchup as the condiment of choice. The emerging popularity of Mexican food has introduced more and more people to tomato-based salsas, heat-infused mixtures that are deliciously rustic. These chunky mixtures remain an inspired dip for nachos and tortilla chips, but today's salsas contain a broad spectrum of ingredients and are no longer reserved for Mexican foods. Salsas such as Peach Salsa or Carrot Pepper Salsa include a variety of seasonings to wake up your taste buds and add pizzazz to all types of snacks and entrées.

Fresh Vegetable Salsa

Add excitement, flavor and texture to baked potatoes, while keeping the fat per serving to a bare minimum, by topping your potato with this delicious salsa instead of sour cream.

TIPS

If you don't mind heat, you can leave the seeds and veins in the jalapeños.

Always follow a tested home canning recipe for salsa. Do not add extra ingredients to the salsa prior to processing, as this can affect the acidity of the salsa, which is a critical factor in the safety of a home-canned product. You can always add ingredients before serving the salsa if you wish. Do not use salsa mixes unless they are specifically designed for home canning.

Makes about ten 8-ounce (250 mL) jars or five pint (500 mL) jars

7 cups	chopped cored peeled tomatoes	1.75 L
2 cups	coarsely chopped onion	500 mL
1 cup	coarsely chopped green bell pepper	250 mL
8	jalapeño peppers, seeded and finely chopped (see tip, at left)	8
3	cloves garlic, finely chopped	3
1	can (5.5 oz/156 mL) tomato paste	1
¾ cup	white vinegar	175 mL
½ cup	loosely packed finely chopped cilantro	125 mL
½ tsp	ground cumin	2 mL

1. In a large stainless steel saucepan, combine tomatoes, onions, green pepper, jalapeño peppers, garlic, tomato paste, vinegar, cilantro and cumin. Bring to a boil over medium-high heat, stirring constantly. Reduce heat and boil gently, stirring frequently, until thickened, about 30 minutes.

2. Meanwhile, prepare canner, jars and lids. *(For more information, see page 415.)*

3. Ladle hot salsa into hot jars, leaving ½ inch (1 cm) headspace. Remove air bubbles and adjust headspace, if necessary, by adding hot salsa. Wipe rim. Center lid on jar. Screw band down until resistance is met, then increase to fingertip-tight.

4. Place jars in canner, ensuring they are completely covered with water. Bring to a boil and process both 8-ounce (250 mL) and pint (500 mL) jars for 20 minutes. Remove canner lid. Wait 5 minutes, then remove jars, cool and store. *(For more information, see pages 417–418.)*

Summer Salsa

Fruit adds a sweet and mellow flavor to traditional tomato salsa. Use this tasty salsa to liven up grilled meat, fish or vegetables.

Fruit adds a sweet and mellow flavor to traditional tomato salsa. Use this tasty salsa to liven up grilled meat, fish or vegetables.

TIPS

To peel tomatoes and peaches and treat peaches and pears for browning, see page 202.

After chopping tomatoes, place them in a colander over a sink and drain off excess liquid. Then measure the 4 cups (1 L) required for this recipe.

We've suggested a range in the quantity of jalapeño peppers so you can suit your taste. If you like heat, use the maximum number. If you prefer a balance between sweetness and heat, we recommend 3.

Need a quick meal? Combine equal portions of mayonnaise and salsa. Spread over skinless chicken breasts, top with buttered bread crumbs and bake.

Makes about twelve 8-ounce (250 mL) jars or six pint (500 mL) jars

4 cups	chopped cored peeled tomatoes (see tips, at left)	1 L
2 cups	chopped pitted peeled peaches, treated to prevent browning and drained	500 mL
2 cups	chopped cored peeled pears, treated to prevent browning and drained	500 mL
1	red bell pepper, seeded and finely chopped	1
1 cup	chopped red onion	250 mL
3 to 4	jalapeño peppers, seeded and finely chopped (see tip, at left)	3 to 4
½ cup	loosely packed finely chopped cilantro	125 mL
½ cup	liquid honey	125 mL
	Grated zest and juice of 1 lemon	
¼ cup	balsamic vinegar	50 mL
1 tbsp	finely chopped fresh mint	15 mL

1. Prepare canner, jars and lids. *(For more information, see page 415.)*

2. In a large stainless steel saucepan, combine tomatoes, peaches, pears, red pepper, onion and jalapeño peppers. Bring to a boil over medium-high heat, stirring constantly. Add cilantro, honey, lemon zest and juice, vinegar and mint. Reduce heat and boil gently, stirring frequently, until slightly thickened, about 5 minutes.

3. Ladle hot salsa into hot jars, leaving ½ inch (1 cm) headspace. Remove air bubbles and adjust headspace, if necessary, by adding hot salsa. Wipe rim. Center lid on jar. Screw band down until resistance is met, then increase to fingertip-tight.

4. Place jars in canner, ensuring they are completely covered with water. Bring to a boil and process 8-ounce (250 mL) jars for 15 minutes and pint (500 mL) jars for 20 minutes. Remove canner lid. Wait 5 minutes, then remove jars, cool and store. *(For more information, see pages 417–418.)*

Variation

Quick 'n' Easy Party Dip: Stir 1½ cups (375 mL) of this or any other salsa into 16 oz (500 g) softened cream cheese or cubed processed cheese or a combination of both. Heat in a microwave oven for 5 minutes, stirring well after 3 minutes. Serve hot with tortilla chips, crackers or chunks of thick-crusted bread.

Spicy Tomato Salsa

Dried chili peppers, fresh jalapeño peppers and hot pepper flakes add multidimensional spice to this simple tomato salsa. The overall color scheme is red, but the jalapeños accent with a burst of deep green.

TIPS

Any dried chili can be used in this recipe, but you'll get the best results if you choose one with the heat level you prefer. We recommend mild chilies such as New Mexico, ancho or cascabel (also known as guajillo chilies). If you like more heat, you can substitute chipotle, cayenne or dried habanero chilies for some of the milder variety.

If you don't mind heat, you can leave the seeds and veins in the jalapeños.

Use homemade salsa instead of hollandaise sauce over eggs Benedict. It is much lower in fat!

Makes about twelve 8-ounce (250 mL) jars or six pint (500 mL) jars

9	dried chili peppers (see tip, at left)	9
	Hot water	
12 cups	diced cored peeled tomatoes (½-inch/1 cm dice)	3 L
3 cups	chopped red onions	750 mL
1½ cups	tightly packed finely chopped cilantro	375 mL
15	cloves garlic, finely chopped	15
6	jalapeño peppers, seeded and chopped (see tip, at left)	6
¾ cup	red wine vinegar	175 mL
1 tbsp	salt	15 mL
¾ tsp	hot pepper flakes	4 mL

1. In a heatproof glass or stainless steel bowl, combine dried chilies with hot water to cover. Weigh chilies down with a bowl or a weight to ensure they remain submerged, and soak until softened, about 15 minutes. Drain off half of the water. Transfer chilies and remaining water to a blender or a food processor fitted with a metal blade and purée until smooth.

2. Meanwhile, prepare canner, jars and lids. *(For more information, see page 415.)*

3. In a large stainless steel saucepan, combine chili purée, tomatoes, onions, cilantro, garlic, jalapeño peppers, vinegar, salt and hot pepper flakes. Bring to a boil over medium-high heat, stirring constantly. Reduce heat and boil gently, stirring frequently, until slightly thickened, about 10 minutes.

4. Ladle hot salsa into hot jars, leaving ½ inch (1 cm) headspace. Remove air bubbles and adjust headspace, if necessary, by adding hot salsa. Wipe rim. Center lid on jar. Screw band down until resistance is met, then increase to fingertip-tight.

5. Place jars in canner, ensuring they are completely covered with water. Bring to a boil and process both 8-ounce (250 mL) and pint (500 mL) jars for 15 minutes. Remove canner lid. Wait 5 minutes, then remove jars, cool and store. *(For more information, see pages 417–418.)*

Roasted Tomato–Chipotle Salsa

Not all markets stock cascabel chilies or chipotle chilies (which are dried, smoked jalapeños), but this unique salsa is so tasty it's well worth the extra shopping effort.

TIPS

In some locations, cascabel peppers are known as guajillo chilies. Either works well in this recipe.

Add pizzazz to fish and pork entrées by serving them with homemade salsa.

Stir salsa into cooked white, brown or yellow rice to create an eye-catching dish that will add appeal to any meal.

Toss cooked pasta and your favorite homemade salsa with grilled vegetables and grilled steak or chicken to make a delicious summer meal. Serve with grilled bread seasoned with olive oil, garlic and a touch of chili powder.

Makes about eight 8-ounce (250 mL) jars or four pint (500 mL) jars

• *Preheat broiler*

12	dried chipotle chili peppers, stems removed	12
12	dried cascabel chili peppers, stems removed	12
2 cups	hot water	500 mL
3 lbs	Italian plum tomatoes	1.37 kg
2	large green bell peppers	2
2	small onions	2
1	head garlic, broken into cloves	1
2 tsp	granulated sugar	10 mL
1 tsp	salt	5 mL
1 cup	white vinegar	250 mL

1. In a large dry skillet, over medium heat, working in batches, toast chipotle and cascabel chilies on both sides, about 30 seconds per side, until they release their aroma and are pliable. Transfer to a large glass or stainless steel bowl. When all chilies have been toasted, add hot water. Weigh chilies down with a bowl or a weight to ensure they remain submerged, and soak until softened, about 15 minutes. Working in batches, transfer chilies and soaking liquid to a blender or a food processor fitted with a metal blade and purée until smooth. Set aside.

2. Meanwhile, under a broiler, roast tomatoes, peppers, onions and garlic, turning to roast all sides, until tomatoes and peppers are blistered, blackened and softened, and onions and garlic are blackened in spots, about 15 minutes. Set onions and garlic aside until cool. Place tomatoes and peppers in paper bags. Secure openings and set aside until cool enough to handle, about 15 minutes. Peel and chop tomatoes, peppers, onions and garlic.

3. Prepare canner, jars and lids. *(For more information, see page 415.)*

4. In a large stainless steel saucepan, combine reserved chili purée, roasted vegetables, sugar, salt and vinegar. Bring to a boil over medium-high heat, stirring constantly. Reduce heat and boil gently, stirring frequently, until slightly thickened, about 15 minutes.

5. Ladle hot salsa into hot jars, leaving ½ inch (1 cm) headspace. Remove air bubbles and adjust headspace, if necessary, by adding hot salsa. Wipe rim. Center lid on jar. Screw band down until resistance is met, then increase to fingertip-tight.

6. Place jars in canner, ensuring they are completely covered with water. Bring to a boil and process 8-ounce (250 mL) jars for 15 minutes and pint (500 mL) jars for 20 minutes. Remove canner lid. Wait 5 minutes, then remove jars, cool and store. *(For more information, see pages 417–418.)*

Zesty Salsa

Traditional salsa with a kick! Use whatever type of chili peppers your family prefers — and add hot pepper sauce if your tastes are even more daring.

TIPS

If you don't mind heat, you can leave the seeds and veins in the chilis.

When you make your own salsa, you control the heat. Remember, you can always add heat, but cooling down a batch of prepared salsa is next to impossible. Taste it before packing in jars. If you are sure that your family prefers a hotter salsa, add extra spices before processing. For best results, adjust the heat with added hot pepper sauce or chopped hot peppers just before serving.

Salsa makes a flavorful barbecue sauce. Purée homemade salsa in a food processor or blender and stir in a touch of extra-virgin olive oil.

Makes about twelve 8-ounce (250 mL) jars or six pint (500 mL) jars

10 cups	chopped cored peeled tomatoes	2.5 L
5 cups	chopped seeded green bell peppers	1.25 L
5 cups	chopped onions	1.25 L
2½ cups	chopped seeded chili peppers, such as hot banana (yellow wax), Hungarian wax, serrano or jalapeño (see tip, at left)	625 mL
1¼ cups	cider vinegar	300 mL
3	cloves garlic, finely chopped	3
2 tbsp	finely chopped cilantro	30 mL
1 tbsp	salt	15 mL
1 tsp	hot pepper sauce (optional)	5 mL

1. Prepare canner, jars and lids. *(For more information, see page 415.)*

2. In a large stainless steel saucepan, combine tomatoes, green peppers, onions, chili peppers, vinegar, garlic, cilantro, salt and hot pepper sauce, if using. Bring to a boil over medium-high heat, stirring constantly. Reduce heat and boil gently, stirring frequently, until slightly thickened, about 10 minutes.

3. Ladle hot salsa into hot jars, leaving ½ inch (1 cm) headspace. Remove air bubbles and adjust headspace, if necessary, by adding hot salsa. Wipe rim. Center lid on jar. Screw band down until resistance is met, then increase to fingertip-tight.

4. Place jars in canner, ensuring they are completely covered with water. Bring to a boil and process both 8-ounce (250 mL) and pint (500 mL) jars for 15 minutes. Remove canner lid. Wait 5 minutes, then remove jars, cool and store. *(For more information, see pages 417–418.)*

Fiesta Salsa

The cool cucumber helps balance the heat from the peppers in this unusual salsa. With its festival of ingredients and flavors, the best way to enjoy Fiesta Salsa is to keep it simple by accompanying it with tortilla chips.

TIPS

If using field cucumbers, you may want to remove the seeds by cutting the cucumber in half lengthwise and scraping out the seeds with the tip of a spoon.

Anaheim peppers are mild green or red chilies, depending upon the variety. If you can't find them, you can substitute fresh poblano or New Mexico chilies or hot yellow banana peppers.

To roast Anaheim peppers, preheat oven to 400°F (200°C). Place peppers on a baking sheet and roast, turning two or three times, until the skin on all sides is blackened, about 20 minutes. Transfer peppers to a heatproof bowl. Cover with a plate and let stand until cool. Remove and, using a sharp knife, lift skins off. Discard skins and chop peppers.

Makes about eight 8-ounce (250 mL) jars or four pint (500 mL) jars

7 cups	chopped cored peeled tomatoes	1.75 L
2 cups	chopped peeled cucumbers (see tip, at left)	500 mL
2 cups	chopped sweet banana peppers	500 mL
1 cup	chopped green onions	250 mL
½ cup	chopped peeled roasted Anaheim pepper (see tips, at left)	125 mL
½ cup	chopped seeded jalapeño peppers	125 mL
½ cup	cider vinegar	125 mL
¼ cup	loosely packed finely chopped cilantro	50 mL
1 tbsp	finely chopped fresh marjoram or oregano	15 mL
1 tsp	salt	5 mL
2 tbsp	lime juice	30 mL

1. Prepare canner, jars and lids. *(For more information, see page 415.)*

2. In a large stainless steel saucepan, combine tomatoes, cucumbers, banana peppers, green onions, roasted Anaheim pepper, jalapeño peppers, vinegar, cilantro, marjoram, salt and lime juice. Bring to a boil over medium-high heat, stirring constantly. Reduce heat and boil gently, stirring frequently, until slightly thickened, about 10 minutes.

3. Ladle hot salsa into hot jars, leaving ½ inch (1 cm) headspace. Remove air bubbles and adjust headspace, if necessary, by adding hot salsa. Wipe rim. Center lid on jar. Screw band down until resistance is met, then increase to fingertip-tight.

4. Place jars in canner, ensuring they are completely covered with water. Bring to a boil and process both 8-ounce (250 mL) and pint (500 mL) jars for 15 minutes. Remove canner lid. Wait 5 minutes, then remove jars, cool and store. *(For more information, see pages 417–418.)*

Jalapeño Salsa

Here's a spicy salsa to satisfy those with bold tastes. Allow it to mature for 3 to 4 weeks to mellow and round out the outstanding flavor.

TIPS

If you don't mind heat, you can leave the seeds and veins in the jalapeños.

Any type of salsa or chutney is excellent served as a dip with grilled whole wheat flatbread.

Makes about six 8-ounce (250 mL) jars or three pint (500 mL) jars

3 cups	chopped cored peeled tomatoes	750 mL
3 cups	chopped seeded jalapeño peppers (see tip, at left)	750 mL
I cup	chopped onions	250 mL
I cup	cider vinegar	250 mL
6	cloves garlic, finely chopped	6
2 tbsp	finely chopped cilantro	30 mL
2 tsp	dried oregano	10 mL
I ½ tsp	salt	7 mL
½ tsp	ground cumin	2 mL

1. Prepare canner, jars and lids. *(For more information, see page 415.)*

2. In a large stainless steel saucepan, combine tomatoes, jalapeño peppers, onions, vinegar, garlic, cilantro, oregano, salt and cumin. Bring to a boil over medium-high heat, stirring constantly. Reduce heat and boil gently, stirring frequently, until slightly thickened, about 10 minutes.

3. Ladle hot salsa into hot jars, leaving ½ inch (1 cm) headspace. Remove air bubbles and adjust headspace, if necessary, by adding hot salsa. Wipe rim. Center lid on jar. Screw band down until resistance is met, then increase to fingertip-tight.

4. Place jars in canner, ensuring they are completely covered with water. Bring to a boil and process both 8-ounce (250 mL) and pint (500 mL) jars for 15 minutes. Remove canner lid. Wait 5 minutes, then remove jars, cool and store. *(For more information, see pages 417–418.)*

Salsa Verde

This spicy green tomato salsa certainly isn't a traditional salsa verde, which is usually made with tomatillos, but we think it's every bit as delicious. Enjoy it with grilled meats and fish or straight from the jar as a dip for tortilla chips. Or use it to create Mini Spuds (see box, below).

TIPS

Use a variety of hot peppers to regulate the heat in this salsa. Habanero and Scotch bonnet peppers are among the hottest chilies. Jalapeños are much milder. If you don't mind heat, you can leave the seeds and veins in the peppers.

Homemade salsas tend to be runnier than commercial salsas. If you wish to have a chunkier salsa, drain off the excess juice before serving. This juice is a wonderful addition to stews, soups or salad dressings.

Makes about six 8-ounce (250 mL) jars or three pint (500 mL) jars

7 cups	chopped cored peeled green tomatoes	1.75 L
5 to 10	jalapeño, habanero or Scotch bonnet peppers, seeded and finely chopped (see tip, at left)	5 to 10
2 cups	finely chopped red onions	500 mL
2	cloves garlic, finely chopped	2
½ cup	lime juice	125 mL
½ cup	loosely packed finely chopped cilantro	125 mL
2 tsp	ground cumin	10 mL
1 tsp	dried oregano	5 mL
1 tsp	salt	5 mL
1 tsp	freshly ground black pepper	5 mL

1. Prepare canner, jars and lids. *(For more information, see page 415.)*

2. In a large stainless steel saucepan, combine tomatoes, peppers, onions, garlic and lime juice. Bring to a boil over medium-high heat, stirring constantly. Stir in cilantro, cumin, oregano, salt and black pepper. Reduce heat and boil gently, stirring frequently, for 5 minutes. Remove from heat.

3. Ladle hot salsa into hot jars, leaving ½ inch (1 cm) headspace. Remove air bubbles and adjust headspace, if necessary, by adding hot salsa. Wipe rim. Center lid on jar. Screw band down until resistance is met, then increase to fingertip-tight.

4. Place jars in canner, ensuring they are completely covered with water. Bring to a boil and process both 8-ounce (250 mL) and pint (500 mL) jars for 20 minutes. Remove canner lid. Wait 5 minutes, then remove jars, cool and store. *(For more information, see pages 417–418.)*

> **Mini Spuds**
> For a delicious appetizer, halve cooked mini potatoes and remove some of the potato to create a shell. Set shells aside and mash the potato with shredded cheese and salsa to taste. Return mixture to shells. Top with extra cheese, if desired, and heat in the oven or microwave until cheese melts. (This also works with baked potatoes as a main course dish.)

Carrot Pepper Salsa

This delightfully different salsa is a mouthwatering addition to hot dogs and sausages. It also makes a delicious dip for fresh vegetables or tortilla chips. Stir it into potato or pasta salad to add color and flavor.

TIPS

If you don't mind heat, you can leave the seeds and veins in the jalapeños.

We recommend using freshly ground pepper because it is much more flavorful than pre-ground varieties.

Refer to the Produce Purchase Guide on pages 426–429 to determine how much produce you'll need to buy to prepare this recipe.

Makes about five 8-ounce (250 mL) jars

6 cups	coarsely chopped cored peeled tomatoes	1.5 L
3 cups	coarsely grated peeled carrots	750 mL
1 ½ cups	cider vinegar	375 mL
1 ¼ cups	lightly packed brown sugar	300 mL
½ cup	finely chopped onion	125 mL
½ cup	finely chopped seeded jalapeño peppers (see tip, at left)	125 mL
1 ½ tsp	salt	7 mL
½ tsp	freshly ground black pepper	2 mL
¼ cup	chopped cilantro	50 mL

1. In a large stainless steel saucepan, combine tomatoes, carrots, vinegar, brown sugar, onion, jalapeño peppers, salt and black pepper. Bring to a boil over medium-high heat, stirring constantly. Reduce heat and boil gently, stirring occasionally, until thickened, about 1 hour. Stir in cilantro and cook for 5 minutes.

2. Meanwhile, prepare canner, jars and lids. *(For more information, see page 415.)*

3. Ladle hot salsa into hot jars, leaving ½ inch (1 cm) headspace. Remove air bubbles and adjust headspace, if necessary, by adding hot salsa. Wipe rim. Center lid on jar. Screw band down until resistance is met, then increase to fingertip-tight.

4. Place jars in canner, ensuring they are completely covered with water. Bring to a boil and process for 15 minutes. Remove canner lid. Wait 5 minutes, then remove jars, cool and store. *(For more information, see pages 417–418.)*

Tomatillo Salsa

The combination of tomatillos, chilies and cilantro creates a salsa with an authentic Mexican taste. In addition to making a great dip for corn chips, this salsa works well as a condiment for fajitas, burritos and quesadillas.

TIPS

Both jalapeño and long green chili peppers work well in this recipe. If you are not a heat seeker, try milder poblano or Anaheim peppers.

Salsa flavors mellow and blend during shelf storage. Optimum flavor is achieved after 3 to 4 weeks.

Makes about four 8-ounce (250 mL) jars or two pint (500 mL) jars

5½ cups	chopped cored husked tomatillos	1.375 L
I cup	chopped onion	250 mL
I cup	chopped seeded green chili peppers (see tip, at left)	250 mL
½ cup	white vinegar	125 mL
4 tbsp	lime juice	60 mL
4	cloves garlic, finely chopped	4
2 tbsp	finely chopped cilantro	30 mL
2 tsp	ground cumin	10 mL
½ tsp	salt	2 mL
½ tsp	hot pepper flakes	2 mL

1. Prepare canner, jars and lids. *(For more information, see page 415.)*
2. In a large stainless steel saucepan, combine tomatillos, onion, chili peppers, vinegar, lime juice, garlic, cilantro, cumin, salt and hot pepper flakes. Bring to a boil over medium-high heat, stirring constantly. Reduce heat and boil gently, stirring frequently, for 10 minutes.
3. Ladle hot salsa into hot jars, leaving ½ inch (1 cm) headspace. Remove air bubbles and adjust headspace, if necessary, by adding hot salsa. Wipe rim. Center lid on jar. Screw band down until resistance is met, then increase to fingertip-tight.
4. Place jars in canner, ensuring they are completely covered with water. Bring to a boil and process both 8-ounce (250 mL) and pint (500 mL) jars for 15 minutes. Remove canner lid. Wait 5 minutes, then remove jars, cool and store. *(For more information, see pages 417–418.)*

Roasted Tomatillo–Chipotle Salsa

For a sensational entrée, marinate a pork shoulder blade roast in this salsa overnight in the refrigerator. Then slow-roast it for about 10 hours in a slow cooker, until it practically shreds itself. If you prefer, spoon it into warm kaiser or onion buns and enjoy a great meal of good-ole-boy pulled pork.

TIP

Always follow a tested home canning recipe for salsa. Do not add extra ingredients to the salsa prior to processing, as this can affect the acidity of the salsa, which is a critical factor in the safety of a home-canned product. You can always add ingredients before serving the salsa if you wish.

Makes about six pint (500 mL) jars

• *Preheat broiler*

12	dried chipotle chili peppers, stemmed	12
12	dried cascabel chili peppers, stemmed	12
2 lbs	husked tomatillos	900 g
2 lbs	Italian plum tomatoes	900 g
2	small onions	2
1	head garlic, broken into cloves	1
1 cup	white vinegar	250 mL
2 tsp	granulated sugar	10 mL
1 tsp	salt	5 mL

1. In a large dry skillet, over medium heat, working in batches, toast chipotle and cascabel chilies on both sides, about 30 seconds per side, until they release their aroma and are pliable. Transfer to a large glass or stainless steel bowl. When all chilies have been toasted, add 2 cups (500 mL) hot water. Weigh chilies down with a bowl or a weight to ensure they remain submerged, and soak until softened, about 15 minutes. Working in batches, transfer chilies and soaking liquid to a blender or a food processor fitted with a metal blade and purée until smooth. Set aside.

2. Meanwhile, under a broiler, roast tomatillos, tomatoes, onions and garlic, turning to roast all sides, until tomatillos and tomatoes are blistered, blackened and softened, and onions and garlic are blackened in spots, about 15 minutes. Set onions and garlic aside until cool. Place tomatillos and tomatoes in paper bags. Secure openings and set aside until cool enough to handle, about 15 minutes. Peel tomatoes, onions and garlic. Finely chop onion and garlic. Set aside.

3. In a blender or food processor, purée roasted tomatillos and tomatoes and reserved puréed chilies until smooth. Set aside.

4. Prepare canner, jars and lids. *(For more information, see page 415.)*

5. In a large stainless steel saucepan, combine tomatillo purée, roasted onion and garlic, vinegar, sugar and salt. Bring to a boil over medium-high heat, stirring constantly. Reduce heat and boil gently, stirring frequently, until slightly thickened, about 15 minutes.

6. Ladle hot salsa into hot jars, leaving $\frac{1}{2}$ inch (1 cm) headspace. Remove air bubbles and adjust headspace, if necessary, by adding hot salsa. Wipe rim. Center lid on jar. Screw band down until resistance is met, then increase to fingertip-tight.

7. Place jars in canner, ensuring they are completely covered with water. Bring to a boil and process for 15 minutes. Remove canner lid. Wait 5 minutes, then remove jars, cool and store. *(For more information, see pages 417–418.)*

Peppery Pear Salsa

Sweet juicy pears combine with red and green peppers to create a carnival of color in this tantalizingly spicy salsa. Use it as a dipping sauce for grilled flatbread or as a breakfast condiment with eggs. It also works well with grilled meat and poultry.

TIP

To prevent the pears from browning, we recommend measuring the vinegar into the saucepan before preparing the pears. As the pears are chopped, drop them into the vinegar, stirring to ensure all surfaces are covered. When all have been chopped, continue with Step 2.

Makes about six 8-ounce (250 mL) jars or three pint (500 mL) jars

I cup	white vinegar	250 mL
8 cups	coarsely chopped cored peeled pears (see tip, at left)	2 L
3	red bell peppers, seeded and coarsely chopped	3
3	green bell peppers, seeded and coarsely chopped	3
I cup	granulated sugar	250 mL
2 tbsp	salt	30 mL
2 tsp	dry mustard	10 mL
I tsp	ground turmeric	5 mL
½ tsp	ground allspice	2 mL
½ tsp	freshly ground black pepper	2 mL

1. Prepare canner, jars and lids. *(For more information, see page 415.)*

2. In a large stainless steel saucepan, combine vinegar and pears. Add red and green peppers, sugar, salt, mustard, turmeric, allspice and black pepper. Bring to a boil over medium-high heat, stirring constantly. Reduce heat and boil gently, stirring frequently, until slightly thickened, about 5 minutes.

3. Ladle hot salsa into hot jars, leaving ½ inch (1 cm) headspace. Remove air bubbles and adjust headspace, if necessary, by adding hot salsa. Wipe rim. Center lid on jar. Screw band down until resistance is met, then increase to fingertip-tight.

4. Place jars in canner, ensuring they are completely covered with water. Bring to a boil and process both 8-ounce (250 mL) and pint (500 mL) jars for 20 minutes. Remove canner lid. Wait 5 minutes, then remove jars, cool and store. *(For more information, see pages 417–418.)*

Peach Salsa

If you're tired of tomato salsa, try this fruity salsa for a refreshing change. Fruit salsas (which don't contain tomatoes) can be nutritious toppings for ice cream. For something quite different, try this on graham crackers, pancakes or waffles, or rolled up in a crêpe with a dollop of whipped cream.

TIPS

To prevent the peaches from browning, we recommend measuring the vinegar into the saucepan before preparing the peaches. As the peaches are chopped, drop them into the vinegar, stirring to ensure all surfaces are covered. When all have been chopped, continue with Step 2.

If you prefer milder salsas, remove the seeds and devein the jalapeños before chopping.

Makes about eight 8-ounce (250 mL) jars

1/2 cup	white vinegar	125 mL
6 cups	chopped pitted peeled peaches (see tip, at left)	1.5 L
1 1/4 cups	chopped red onion	300 mL
4	jalapeño peppers, finely chopped	4
1	red bell pepper, seeded and chopped	1
1/2 cup	loosely packed finely chopped cilantro	125 mL
2 tbsp	liquid honey	30 mL
1	clove garlic, finely chopped	1
1 1/2 tsp	ground cumin	7 mL
1/2 tsp	cayenne pepper	2 mL

1. Prepare canner, jars and lids. *(For more information, see page 415.)*
2. In a large stainless steel saucepan, combine vinegar and peaches. Add onion, jalapeño peppers, red pepper, cilantro, honey, garlic, cumin and cayenne. Bring to a boil over medium-high heat, stirring constantly. Reduce heat and boil gently, stirring frequently, until slightly thickened, about 5 minutes. Remove from heat.
3. Ladle hot salsa into hot jars, leaving 1/2 inch (1 cm) headspace. Remove air bubbles and adjust headspace, if necessary, by adding hot salsa. Wipe rim. Center lid on jar. Screw band down until resistance is met, then increase to fingertip-tight.
4. Place jars in canner, ensuring they are completely covered with water. Bring to a boil and process for 15 minutes. Remove canner lid. Wait 5 minutes, then remove jars, cool and store. *(For more information, see pages 417–418.)*

Variation

For added flavor, replace 1 cup (250 mL) of the peaches with chopped pitted peeled apricots.

Pineapple Chili Salsa

This tropical salsa is perfect for outdoor summer meals. Serve it with grilled pita bread brushed with olive oil for a simple but delicious appetizer.

TIPS

If fresh pineapple is not available, substitute canned pineapple. For easiest preparation, buy canned pineapple tidbits, or you can buy canned pineapple slices, drain (reserving juice) and chop. Measure 2 cups (500 mL).

Anaheim peppers are mild green or red chilies, depending upon the variety. If you can't find them, you can substitute fresh poblano or New Mexico chilies or hot banana (yellow wax) peppers.

Makes about six 8-ounce (250 mL) jars

4 cups	cubed seeded peeled papaya	I L
2 cups	cubed cored peeled fresh pineapple (see tip, at left)	500 mL
I cup	golden raisins	250 mL
I cup	lemon juice	250 mL
½ cup	lime juice	125 mL
½ cup	pineapple juice	125 mL
½ cup	chopped seeded Anaheim peppers (see tip, at left)	125 mL
2 tbsp	finely chopped green onion	30 mL
2 tbsp	finely chopped cilantro	30 mL
2 tbsp	packed brown sugar	30 mL

1. Prepare canner, jars and lids. *(For more information, see page 415.)*
2. In a large stainless steel saucepan, combine papaya, pineapple, raisins, lemon juice, lime juice, pineapple juice, Anaheim peppers, green onion, cilantro and brown sugar. Bring to a boil over medium-high heat, stirring constantly. Reduce heat and boil gently, stirring frequently, until slightly thickened, about 10 minutes.
3. Ladle hot salsa into hot jars, leaving ½ inch (1 cm) headspace. Remove air bubbles and adjust headspace, if necessary, by adding hot salsa. Wipe rim. Center lid on jar. Screw band down until resistance is met, then increase to fingertip-tight.
4. Place jars in canner, ensuring they are completely covered with water. Bring to a boil and process for 15 minutes. Remove canner lid. Wait 5 minutes, then remove jars, cool and store. *(For more information, see pages 417–418.)*

Relish

Relish, a delicious combination of chopped vegetables and/or fruits cooked in seasoned vinegar, is more of a traditional North American condiment than salsa and chutney. While relish may have originated as a way to use up an abundance of homegrown vegetables and fruit, these mixed pickles also served as an easy way for our pioneer ancestors to add variety to their plain and basic diets. These versatile condiments have almost limitless uses, from providing the perfect finish to hamburgers and hot dogs to adding zest to salads. For the best flavor, allow jars of relish to stand for 2 weeks before serving. This allows the flavors of all the ingredients to mellow.

Homemade Pickling Spice

Some of the relish and chutney recipes in this chapter, and several of the pickle recipes later in the book, call for pickling spice as an ingredient. You can buy prepared pickling spice at well-stocked supermarkets or make your own.

Makes about ¹/₂ cup (125 mL)

I	cinnamon stick (about 4 inches/10 cm), broken into pieces	I
5	bay leaves, crushed	5
2 tbsp	mustard seeds	30 mL
I tbsp	whole allspice	15 mL
I tbsp	coriander seeds	15 mL
I tbsp	whole black peppercorns	15 mL
I tbsp	ground ginger	15 mL
I tbsp	dill seeds	15 mL
2 tsp	cardamom seeds	10 mL
I to 2 tsp	hot pepper flakes	5 to 10 mL
I tsp	whole cloves	5 mL

1. In a small glass or stainless steel bowl, combine cinnamon stick pieces, bay leaves, mustard seeds, allspice, coriander seeds, peppercorns, ginger, dill seeds, cardamom seeds, hot pepper flakes and cloves. Stir well. Store in 4-ounce (125 mL) jars or an 8-ounce (250 mL) jar, or another airtight container, for up to 1 year.

Cucumber Relish

This cool and classic relish, which is beautiful in appearance, makes a great finish for any summer barbecue.

TIPS

Whether you seed cucumbers is based on personal preference and the type of cucumber you use. Field cucumbers have larger and more plentiful seeds, while English cucumbers are nearly seedless. If using field cucumbers, you may want to remove the seeds by cutting the cucumber in half lengthwise and scraping out the seeds with the tip of a spoon.

Refer to the Produce Purchase Guide on pages 426–429 to determine how much produce you'll need to buy to prepare this recipe.

Makes about twelve 8-ounce (250 mL) jars or six pint (500 mL) jars

8 cups	finely chopped peeled cucumbers (see tip, at left)	2 L
4 cups	finely chopped seeded green bell peppers	1 L
4 cups	finely chopped seeded red bell peppers	1 L
2 cups	finely chopped celery	500 mL
1 cup	finely chopped onion	250 mL
½ cup	pickling or canning salt	125 mL
3 cups	white vinegar	750 mL
2¼ cups	granulated sugar	550 mL
3 tbsp	celery seeds	45 mL
3 tbsp	mustard seeds	45 mL

1. In a large glass or stainless steel bowl, combine cucumbers, green and red peppers, celery, onion and pickling salt. Cover and let stand in a cool place (70 to 75°F/21 to 23°C) for 4 hours. Transfer to a colander placed over a sink and drain. Rinse with cool water and drain thoroughly. Using your hands, squeeze out excess liquid. Set aside.

2. Meanwhile, prepare canner, jars and lids. *(For more information, see page 415.)*

3. In a large stainless steel saucepan, combine vinegar, sugar, celery seeds and mustard seeds. Stir well and bring to a boil over medium-high heat. Add drained cucumber mixture and return to a boil, stirring frequently. Reduce heat and boil gently, stirring frequently, until vegetables are heated through, about 10 minutes.

4. Ladle hot relish into hot jars, leaving ½ inch (1 cm) headspace. Remove air bubbles and adjust headspace, if necessary, by adding hot relish. Wipe rim. Center lid on jar. Screw band down until resistance is met, then increase to fingertip-tight.

5. Place jars in canner, ensuring they are completely covered with water. Bring to a boil and process both 8-ounce (250 mL) and pint (500 mL) jars for 10 minutes. Remove canner lid. Wait 5 minutes, then remove jars, cool and store. *(For more information, see pages 417–418.)*

Dill Relish

Dill relish is a traditional relish that has been passed on from generation to generation.

TIPS

When measuring wet ingredients, use a liquid measuring cup (with a handle and spout and graduated markings for measures). Smaller measuring cups (1 or 2 cups/250 or 500 mL) are more accurate than many of the larger cups (4 or 8 cups/1 or 2 L), so it is better to use a smaller one several times than to use one larger cup.

A clear plastic ruler (kept solely for kitchen use) will help you determine the correct headspace. Each filled jar should be measured accurately, as the headspace can affect sealing and the preservation of the contents.

Makes about seven pint (500 mL) jars

8 lbs	pickling cucumbers	3.6 kg
½ cup	pickling or canning salt	125 mL
2 tsp	ground turmeric	10 mL
4 cups	water	1 L
2½ cups	finely chopped onions	625 mL
⅓ cup	granulated sugar	75 mL
2 tbsp	dill seeds	30 mL
4 cups	white wine vinegar	1 L

1. In a food processor fitted with a metal blade or a food grinder, working in batches, finely chop cucumbers, transferring batches to a glass or stainless steel bowl as they are completed. Sprinkle with pickling salt and turmeric. Add water, cover and let stand in a cool place (70 to 75°F/21 to 23°C) for 2 hours. Transfer to a colander placed over a sink and drain thoroughly. Rinse with cool water and drain thoroughly again. Using your hands, squeeze out excess liquid.

2. Meanwhile, prepare canner, jars and lids. *(For more information, see page 415.)*

3. In a large stainless steel saucepan, combine drained cucumbers, onions, sugar, dill seeds and vinegar. Bring to a boil over medium-high heat. Reduce heat and boil gently, stirring occasionally, until slightly thickened and vegetables are heated through, about 10 minutes.

4. Ladle hot relish into hot jars, leaving ½ inch (1 cm) headspace. Remove air bubbles and adjust headspace, if necessary, by adding hot relish. Wipe rim. Center lid on jar. Screw band down until resistance is met, then increase to fingertip-tight.

5. Place jars in canner, ensuring they are completely covered with water. Bring to a boil and process for 15 minutes. Remove canner lid. Wait 5 minutes, then remove jars, cool and store. *(For more information, see pages 417–418.)*

Grandmother's Golden Relish

Preserving a cherished family recipe can be a rewarding cross-generational activity. Unfortunately, many hand-me-down recipes are best left as keepsakes because they don't meet current food safety standards. Several years ago, when one Ontario grandmother retired from home canning, her granddaughter asked us to update her relish recipe. She and her family wanted to prepare this golden condiment knowing that the results would conform to current safety standards, in addition to being delicious.

TIPS

This recipe can be doubled to make about eight pint (500 mL) jars. Use ½ cup (125 mL) pickling or canning salt and process for 15 minutes.

English cucumbers can be used for this recipe, but field cucumbers produce the best results.

Makes about eight 8-ounce (250 mL) jars

6 cups	chopped seeded peeled field cucumbers (see tip, at left)	1.5 L
2 cups	chopped onions	500 mL
1 cup	chopped seeded red bell pepper	250 mL
1 cup	chopped seeded green bell pepper	250 mL
4 tbsp	pickling or canning salt	60 mL
3 cups	granulated sugar	750 mL
7 tsp	ClearJel® (see tip, page 225)	35 mL
2 tbsp	dry mustard	30 mL
1½ tsp	ground turmeric	7 mL
1½ tsp	celery seeds	7 mL
1½ tsp	mustard seeds	7 mL
2 cups	white vinegar	500 mL

1. In a large glass or stainless steel bowl, combine cucumbers, onions, red and green peppers and pickling salt. Cover and let stand in a cool place (70 to 75°F/21 to 23°C) for 12 hours or overnight. Transfer to a colander placed over a sink and drain. Rinse with cool water and drain thoroughly. Using your hands, squeeze out excess liquid. Set aside.

2. Meanwhile, prepare canner, jars and lids. *(For more information, see page 415.)*

3. In a large stainless steel saucepan, combine sugar, ClearJel®, dry mustard, turmeric, celery seeds and mustard seeds. Whisk in vinegar and bring to a boil over medium-high heat, stirring constantly, until thickened, about 1 minute. Add cucumber mixture and, stirring constantly, return to a boil that cannot be stirred down. Remove from heat.

4. Ladle hot relish into hot jars, leaving ½ inch (1 cm) headspace. Remove air bubbles and adjust headspace, if necessary, by adding hot relish. Wipe rim. Center lid on jar. Screw band down until resistance is met, then increase to fingertip-tight.

5. Place jars in canner, ensuring they are completely covered with water. Bring to a boil and process for 10 minutes. Remove canner lid. Wait 5 minutes, then remove jars, cool and store. *(For more information, see pages 417–418.)*

Chow-Chow Relish

Enjoy summer's harvest in a tangy relish that's perfect with barbecue fare. This recipe uses the old-fashioned method of soaking the vegetables in a salt-water brine instead of sprinkling them with salt. This may produce a slightly saltier relish than you're accustomed to.

TIPS

We don't peel the cucumber for use in this recipe because the skin brightens up the color of the relish, making it more visually appealing. Since the peel is left on, we specify the use of English cucumbers. Field cucumbers are often sold waxed to extend shelf life, and the pickling liquid cannot penetrate the wax.

On processing day, blanch the green beans and carrots for use in this recipe by dropping them in boiling water for 30 seconds. Immediately drain and set aside. Blanching inactivates enzymes that can cause undesirable changes in the color and texture of green beans and carrots.

Makes about seven 8-ounce (250 mL) jars

2 cups	coarsely chopped English cucumber (see tip, at left)	500 mL
1½ cups	chopped seeded red bell peppers	375 mL
1½ cups	chopped cabbage	375 mL
1½ cups	sliced onions	375 mL
1½ cups	chopped cored green tomatoes (unpeeled)	375 mL
9 cups	water, divided	2.25 L
1 cup	pickling or canning salt	250 mL
3 cups	white vinegar	750 mL
2½ cups	granulated sugar	625 mL
3 tbsp	mustard seeds	45 mL
2 tbsp	celery seeds	30 mL
1 tbsp	ground turmeric	15 mL
1½ cups	diced green beans, blanched (see tip, at left)	375 mL
1½ cups	diced peeled carrots, blanched (see tip, at left)	375 mL

1. In a large glass or stainless steel bowl, combine cucumber, red peppers, cabbage, onions and green tomatoes. Add 8 cups (2 L) of the water and pickling salt. Cover and let stand in a cool place (70 to 75°F/21 to 23°C) for 12 hours or overnight. Transfer to a colander placed over a sink and drain thoroughly. Rinse with cool water and drain thoroughly again. Using your hands, squeeze out excess liquid. Set aside.

2. In a large stainless steel saucepan, combine remaining 1 cup (250 mL) water, vinegar, sugar, mustard seeds, celery seeds and turmeric. Bring to a boil over medium-high heat. Add drained cucumber mixture, green beans and carrots and return to a boil. Reduce heat and boil gently, stirring frequently, until thickened to the consistency of a thin commercial relish, about 40 minutes.

3. Meanwhile, prepare canner, jars and lids. *(For more information, see page 415.)*

4. Ladle hot relish into hot jars, leaving ½ inch (1 cm) headspace. Remove air bubbles and adjust headspace, if necessary, by adding hot relish. Wipe rim. Center lid on jar. Screw band down until resistance is met, then increase to fingertip-tight.

5. Place jars in canner, ensuring they are completely covered with water. Bring to a boil and process for 10 minutes. Remove canner lid. Wait 5 minutes, then remove jars, cool and store. *(For more information, see pages 417–418.)*

Green Tomato Hot Dog Relish

Use this relish for traditional jobs such as garnishing hot dogs, or add it to sandwich spreads such as mayonnaise. It also makes a great dipping sauce for fish.

TIPS

Read a recipe all the way through, even before you go shopping for the ingredients. It's very important to have all of the ingredients and equipment ready before you start making preserves.

A jar lifter is very helpful for handling hot, wet jars. Because they are bulky and fit loosely, oven mitts — even water-resistent types — are not a wise choice. When filling jars, an all-purpose rubber glove, worn on your helper hand, will allow you to steady the jar.

Place a clean towel on your work surface to absorb water from the hot jars as you take them out of the boiling-water canner to be filled, and again once the jars are processed. The towel prevents hot jars from coming into contact with cooler countertops. Significant temperature differences can cause jar breakage.

Makes about six 8-ounce (250 mL) jars

6 cups	finely chopped cored green tomatoes (unpeeled)	1.5 L
2	onions, finely chopped	2
2	green bell peppers, seeded and chopped	2
1	red bell pepper, seeded and chopped	1
¼ cup	pickling or canning salt	50 mL
1 tsp	whole cloves	5 mL
1 tsp	celery seeds	5 mL
1	cinnamon stick (about 4 inches/10 cm), broken in half	1
2 cups	white vinegar	500 mL
1½ cups	lightly packed brown sugar	375 mL
1	clove garlic, finely chopped	1
1 tbsp	dry mustard	15 mL
½ tsp	salt	2 mL
½ tsp	ground ginger	2 mL

1. In a large glass or stainless steel bowl, combine green tomatoes, onions, green and red bell peppers and pickling salt. Cover and let stand in a cool place (70 to 75°F/21 to 23°C) for 12 hours or overnight. Transfer to a colander placed over a sink and drain. Rinse with cool water and drain thoroughly. Using your hands, squeeze out excess liquid. Set aside.

2. Tie cloves, celery seeds and cinnamon stick in a square of cheesecloth, creating a spice bag.

3. In a large stainless steel saucepan, combine vinegar, brown sugar, garlic, mustard, salt, ginger and spice bag. Bring to a boil over medium-high heat, stirring to dissolve sugar. Add drained tomato mixture, stir well and return to a boil. Reduce heat and boil gently, stirring frequently, until tomatoes are transparent, about 1 hour. Discard spice bag.

4. Meanwhile, prepare canner, jars and lids. *(For more information, see page 415.)*

5. Ladle hot relish into hot jars, leaving ½ inch (1 cm) headspace. Remove air bubbles and adjust headspace, if necessary, by adding hot relish. Wipe rim. Center lid on jar. Screw band down until resistance is met, then increase to fingertip-tight.

6. Place jars in canner, ensuring they are completely covered with water. Bring to a boil and process for 10 minutes. Remove canner lid. Wait 5 minutes, then remove jars, cool and store. *(For more information, see pages 417–418.)*

Bruschetta in a Jar

What could be more welcoming than warm, freshly toasted homemade bruschetta? Preserving tomatoes when they are in season lets you enjoy the convenience of ready-to-serve garden-fresh tomatoes all year long. Just spoon these zesty tomatoes onto a toasted baguette and garnish with grated cheese and a splash of olive oil, if desired.

TIP

Plum tomatoes work better than globe tomatoes in this recipe, as their flesh is firmer and holds its shape during processing, which is preferable for bruschetta. You can seed them if you prefer, but this is not essential. Plum tomatoes do not need to be drained because they yield little liquid. However, if you are unable to find plum tomatoes, you can use globe tomatoes. Chop tomatoes and drain in a colander placed over a sink for 30 minutes to remove excess liquid. Use liquid as a salad dressing.

Makes about seven 8-ounce (250 mL) jars

5	cloves garlic, finely chopped	5
1 cup	dry white wine	250 mL
1 cup	white wine vinegar	250 mL
1/2 cup	water	125 mL
2 tbsp	granulated sugar	30 mL
2 tbsp	dried basil	30 mL
2 tbsp	dried oregano	30 mL
2 tbsp	balsamic vinegar	30 mL
9 cups	chopped cored plum tomatoes (1 inch/2.5 cm pieces) (see tip, at left)	2.25 L

1. Prepare canner, jars and lids. *(For more information, see page 415.)*

2. In a large, deep stainless steel saucepan, combine garlic, wine, wine vinegar, water, sugar, basil, oregano and balsamic vinegar. Bring to a full rolling boil over high heat, stirring occasionally. Reduce heat, cover and boil gently, for 5 minutes, until garlic is heated through. Remove from heat .

3. Pack tomatoes into hot jars to within a generous 1/2 inch (1 cm) of top of jar. Ladle hot vinegar mixture into jar to cover tomatoes, leaving 1/2 inch (1 cm) headspace. Remove air bubbles and adjust headspace, if necessary, by adding hot liquid. Wipe rim. Center lid on jar. Screw band down until resistance is met, then increase to fingertip-tight.

4. Place jars in canner, ensuring they are completely covered with water. Bring to a boil and process for 20 minutes. Remove canner lid. Wait 5 minutes, then remove jars, cool and store. *(For more information, see pages 417–418.)*

Antipasto Relish

This Italian-style vegetable relish has all the delicious flavor of commercial antipasto. This combination of high-acid vegetables can be processed safely in a boiling-water canner.

TIP

To ripen tomatoes for canning, empty them from the basket or box onto a single layer of newspaper or a large mesh rack. Store in a cool (but not cold), dry place, out of direct sun. Turn tomatoes daily to prevent spoilage and soft spots. As the tomatoes ripen, sort into different stages of ripeness and use the ripest ones first.

Makes about six 8-ounce (250 mL) jars

7	whole black peppercorns	7
4	bay leaves	4
1¾ cups	white vinegar	425 mL
1 cup	lightly packed brown sugar	250 mL
2 tbsp	salt	30 mL
4	cloves garlic, finely chopped	4
1 tbsp	dried oregano	15 mL
6 cups	coarsely chopped cored peeled tomatoes	1.5 L
3	bell peppers (1 each green, red and yellow), seeded and chopped	3
2	carrots, peeled and diced	2
1	stalk celery, diced	1
1	large onion, coarsely chopped	1

1. Tie peppercorns and bay leaves in a square of cheesecloth, creating a spice bag.

2. In a large stainless steel saucepan, combine vinegar, brown sugar, salt, garlic, oregano and spice bag. Bring to a boil over high heat, stirring to dissolve sugar. Stir in tomatoes, peppers, carrots, celery and onion. Reduce heat and boil gently, stirring frequently, for 1 hour, until thickened to the consistency of a thin commercial relish. Discard spice bag.

3. Meanwhile, prepare canner, jars and lids. *(For more information, see page 415.)*

4. Ladle hot relish into hot jars, leaving ½ inch (1 cm) headspace. Remove air bubbles and adjust headspace, if necessary, by adding hot relish. Wipe rim. Center lid on jar. Screw band down until resistance is met, then increase to fingertip-tight.

5. Place jars in canner, ensuring they are completely covered with water. Bring to a boil and process for 10 minutes. Remove canner lid. Wait 5 minutes, then remove jars, cool and store. *(For more information, see pages 417–418.)*

Oranges in Cointreau (page 157)

Blackberries in Framboise (page 162)

Honey-Spiced Peaches (page 164)

Curried Fruit Compote (page 168)

Brandied Fruit Mincemeat (page 176)

Tart Cherry Pie Filling (page 174)

Chocolate Raspberry Sundae Topper (page 188)

Mango Chutney (page 246)

**Cranberry Ketchup (page 257),
Ginger-Garlic Mustard (page 272),
Sauerkraut (page 344)**

Strawberry Lemonade Concentrate (page 192)

Two-in-One Barbecue Sauce (page 262)

Homestyle Corn Relish

This old-fashioned relish is a perennial favorite. Adjust the ratio of red and green bell peppers to suit your preference, without exceeding the specified quantity.

TIPS

If using fresh corn, blanch husked ears in boiling water for 5 minutes before removing kernels. If using frozen corn, thaw kernels first.

ClearJel® is a cooking starch that is acceptable for use in home canning. Not all cooking starches are suitable for home canning, as reheating causes some to lose viscosity. Making mixtures too thick can interfere with required heat penetration during heat processing. In this recipe, ClearJel® is used to create a thicker, smoother texture. For more information, see the Glossary, page 431.

Makes about six pint (500 mL) jars

4 cups	white vinegar	1 L
1¼ cups	granulated sugar	300 mL
2 tbsp	salt	30 mL
8 cups	corn kernels (see tip, at left)	2 L
4 cups	diced seeded mixed red and green bell peppers	1 L
1¾ cups	diced celery	425 mL
1 cup	finely chopped onion	250 mL
2 tbsp	dry mustard	30 mL
2 tsp	celery seeds	10 mL
2 tsp	ground turmeric	10 mL
¼ cup	water	50 mL
2 tbsp	ClearJel® (see tip, at left)	30 mL

1. Prepare canner, jars and lids. *(For more information, see page 415.)*
2. In a large stainless steel saucepan, combine vinegar, sugar and salt. Bring to a boil over medium-high heat, stirring to dissolve sugar. Gradually add corn, red and green peppers, celery and onion, stirring constantly and maintaining the boil. Stir in mustard, celery seeds and turmeric. In a small bowl, combine water and ClearJel®, making a paste. Stir into vegetable mixture. Reduce heat and boil gently, stirring frequently, until thick enough to mound on a spoon, about 5 minutes.
3. Ladle hot relish into hot jars, leaving ½ inch (1 cm) headspace. Remove air bubbles and adjust headspace, if necessary, by adding hot relish. Wipe rim. Center lid on jar. Screw band down until resistance is met, then increase to fingertip-tight.
4. Place jars in canner, ensuring they are completely covered with water. Bring to a boil and process for 15 minutes. Remove canner lid. Wait 5 minutes, then remove jars, cool and store. *(For more information, see pages 417–418.)*

Sweet-and-Sour Pepper Relish

Use this zesty relish to add color and flavor to hot dogs and hamburgers. For those who like it spicy, add the red chili pepper and use hot banana (yellow wax) peppers in place of the sweet banana peppers.

TIPS

If using a red chili pepper, we recommend cayenne or Holland (Dutch) varieties. When cutting hot peppers, wear rubber gloves to keep your hands from being burned.

Refer to the Produce Purchase Guide on pages 426–429 to determine how much produce you'll need to buy to prepare this recipe.

Makes about seven 8-ounce (250 mL) jars

4 cups	finely chopped seeded green bell peppers	I L
3 cups	chopped cored peeled tart apples, such as Granny Smith	750 mL
2 cups	chopped cabbage	500 mL
I cup	finely chopped seeded sweet banana peppers	250 mL
2 tbsp	salt	30 mL
3 cups	cider vinegar	750 mL
3 cups	granulated sugar	750 mL
I tsp	mustard seeds	5 mL
I	red chili pepper, finely chopped (optional) (see tip, at left)	I

1. In a large glass or stainless steel bowl, combine green peppers, apples, cabbage, banana peppers and salt. Cover and let stand in a cool place (70 to 75°F/21 to 23°C) for 2 hours. Transfer to a colander placed over a sink and drain. Rinse with cool water and drain thoroughly. Using your hands, squeeze out excess liquid. Set aside.

2. Meanwhile, prepare canner, jars and lids. *(For more information, see page 415.)*

3. In a large stainless steel saucepan, combine vinegar, sugar, mustard seeds and red chili pepper, if using. Bring to a boil over medium-high heat, stirring to dissolve sugar. Reduce heat to medium-low, add drained pepper mixture and boil gently, stirring frequently, until vegetables are heated through, about 10 minutes.

4. Ladle hot relish into hot jars, leaving ½ inch (1 cm) headspace. Remove air bubbles and adjust headspace, if necessary, by adding hot relish. Wipe rim. Center lid on jar. Screw band down until resistance is met, then increase to fingertip-tight.

5. Place jars in canner, ensuring they are completely covered with water. Bring to a boil and process for 10 minutes. Remove canner lid. Wait 5 minutes, then remove jars, cool and store. *(For more information, see pages 417–418.)*

Piccalilli Relish

Recipes for this relish vary widely according to regional tastes and the availability of locally produced vegetables.

TIP

You can buy prepared pickling spice at well-stocked supermarkets or make your own (see page 217).

Makes six to seven 8-ounce (250 mL) jars

5 cups	finely chopped cabbage	1.25 L
4 cups	chopped cored green tomatoes (unpeeled)	1 L
1½ cups	chopped onions	375 mL
1 cup	chopped seeded red bell pepper	250 mL
1 cup	chopped seeded green bell pepper	250 mL
3 tbsp	salt	45 mL
¼ cup	pickling spice (see tip, at left)	50 mL
4 tbsp	coarsely chopped gingerroot	60 mL
2 tbsp	mustard seeds	30 mL
3 cups	white vinegar	750 mL
1¾ cups	water	425 mL
1 cup	granulated sugar	250 mL
2 tsp	ground turmeric	10 mL

1. In a large glass or stainless steel bowl, combine cabbage, green tomatoes, onions, red and green peppers and salt. Cover and let stand in a cool place (70 to 75°F/21 to 23°C) for 12 hours or overnight. Transfer to a colander placed over a sink and drain. Rinse with cool water and drain thoroughly. Using your hands, squeeze out excess liquid. Set aside.

2. Meanwhile, prepare canner, jars and lids. *(For more information, see page 415.)*

3. Tie pickling spice, gingerroot and mustard seeds in a square of cheesecloth, creating a spice bag.

4. In a large stainless steel saucepan, combine drained cabbage mixture, vinegar, water, sugar, turmeric and spice bag. Cover and bring to a boil over medium-high heat. Uncover and boil for 5 minutes, stirring frequently. Reduce heat and boil gently, stirring frequently, until thickened to the consistency of a thin commercial relish, about 20 minutes. Discard spice bag.

5. Ladle hot relish into hot jars, leaving ½ inch (1 cm) headspace. Remove air bubbles and adjust headspace, if necessary, by adding hot relish. Wipe rim. Center lid on jar. Screw band down until resistance is met, then increase to fingertip-tight.

6. Place jars in canner, ensuring they are completely covered with water. Bring to a boil and process for 10 minutes. Remove canner lid. Wait 5 minutes, then remove jars, cool and store. *(For more information, see pages 417–418.)*

Dixie Relish

This relish makes an ideal gift for those who love sweet-and-sour food. We decided to stick with tradition and use the old-fashioned method for soaking the vegetables in a salt-water brine, which was in the original recipe, instead of just sprinkling salt over the vegetables, as more contemporary recipes do. Just be aware that this relish may be slightly saltier than those you are accustomed to, as tastes have changed over the years, but it's delicious nonetheless.

TIP

Refer to the Produce Purchase Guide on pages 426–429 to determine how much produce you'll need to buy to prepare this recipe.

Makes about six 8-ounce (250 mL) jars

4 cups	finely chopped cabbage	1 L
1½ cups	chopped onions	375 mL
1½ cups	chopped seeded red bell peppers	375 mL
1½ cups	chopped seeded green bell peppers	375 mL
¼ cup	pickling or canning salt	50 mL
7 cups	lukewarm water	1.75 L
3 tbsp	mustard seeds	45 mL
2 tbsp	celery seeds	30 mL
1 tbsp	whole allspice	15 mL
1 tbsp	whole cloves	15 mL
1	cinnamon stick (about 4 inches/10 cm), broken into pieces	1
3 cups	white vinegar	750 mL
2 cups	granulated sugar	500 mL

1. In a large glass or stainless steel bowl, combine cabbage, onions and red and green peppers. Dissolve pickling salt in lukewarm water and pour over vegetables. Cover and let stand in a cool place (70 to 75°F/21 to 23°C) for 1 hour. Transfer to a colander placed over a sink and drain thoroughly. Rinse with cool water and drain thoroughly again. Using your hands, squeeze out excess liquid. Set aside.

2. Meanwhile, prepare canner, jars and lids. *(For more information, see page 415.)*

3. Tie mustard seeds, celery seeds, allspice, cloves and cinnamon stick in a square of cheesecloth, creating a spice bag.

4. In a large stainless steel saucepan, combine drained cabbage mixture, vinegar, sugar and spice bag. Cover and bring to a boil over medium-high heat. Uncover, reduce heat and boil gently, stirring frequently, until thickened to the consistency of a thin commercial relish, about 15 minutes. Discard spice bag.

5. Ladle hot relish into hot jars, leaving ½ inch (1 cm) headspace. Remove air bubbles and adjust headspace, if necessary, by adding hot relish. Wipe rim. Center lid on jar. Screw band down until resistance is met, then increase to fingertip-tight.

6. Place jars in canner, ensuring they are completely covered with water. Bring to a boil and process for 15 minutes. Remove canner lid. Wait 5 minutes, then remove jars, cool and store. *(For more information, see pages 417–418.)*

Red Root Relish

This zesty relish makes a delicious and colorful substitute for horseradish.

TIPS

To cook beets, scrub them thoroughly, leaving the root and 2 inches (5 cm) of the stem intact to prevent bleeding. Place in a saucepan and cover with cold water. Bring to a boil, reduce heat to medium-low and boil gently until tender, about 35 minutes, depending on the size of the beet. Drain, discard liquid and rinse well under cold running water. The skins should slip off easily. Remove roots and stems.

If you prefer a relish with a finer texture, shred the cooked beets rather than dicing them. Use 3½ cups (875 mL) lightly packed shredded beets.

Makes about four pint (500 mL) jars

4 cups	diced peeled cooked beets (see tips, at left)	1 L
4 cups	finely chopped red cabbage	1 L
3 cups	white vinegar	750 mL
1½ cups	granulated sugar	375 mL
1 cup	finely chopped onions	250 mL
1 cup	finely chopped seeded red bell pepper	250 mL
1 tbsp	prepared horseradish	15 mL
1 tbsp	salt	15 mL

1. Prepare canner, jars and lids. *(For more information, see page 415.)*

2. In a large stainless steel saucepan, combine beets, cabbage, vinegar, sugar, onions, red pepper, horseradish and salt. Bring to a boil over medium-high heat, stirring occasionally. Reduce heat and boil gently, stirring occasionally, until vegetables are tender and heated through, about 20 minutes.

3. Ladle hot relish into hot jars, leaving ½ inch (1 cm) headspace. Remove air bubbles and adjust headspace, if necessary, by adding hot relish. Wipe rim. Center lid on jar. Screw band down until resistance is met, then increase to fingertip-tight.

4. Place jars in canner, ensuring they are completely covered with water. Bring to a boil and process for 15 minutes. Remove canner lid. Wait 5 minutes, then remove jars, cool and store. *(For more information, see pages 417–418.)*

Fennel Relish

The light licorice notes of fennel subtly flavor this unusual relish. It is particularly delicious with grilled or baked salmon.

TIP

ClearJel® is a cooking starch that is acceptable for use in home canning. Not all cooking starches are suitable for home canning, as reheating causes some to lose viscosity. Making mixtures too thick can interfere with required heat penetration during heat processing. In this recipe, ClearJel® is used to create a thicker, smoother texture. For more information, see the Glossary, page 431.

Makes about five 8-ounce (250 mL) jars

I	large bulb fennel, including feathery leaves	I
⅓ cup	lightly packed brown sugar	75 mL
2 tbsp	ClearJel® (see tip, at left)	30 mL
I tbsp	dry mustard	15 mL
I tsp	salt	5 mL
I cup	cider vinegar	250 mL
½ cup	water	125 mL
2½ cups	finely chopped onions	625 mL
¼ cup	drained pickled capers	50 mL
I tsp	grated lemon zest	5 mL
I tsp	fennel seeds	5 mL
¼ tsp	freshly cracked black pepper	I mL

1. Prepare canner, jars and lids. *(For more information, see page 415.)*

2. Remove feathery leaves from fennel and finely chop leaves to measure 2 tbsp (30 mL) lightly packed. Set aside. Remove stalks and core from fennel bulb and discard. Pulse remainder of bulb in a blender or a food processor fitted with a metal blade until finely chopped, but not puréed. Measure 3 cups (750 mL) firmly packed. Set aside.

3. In a large stainless steel saucepan, combine brown sugar, ClearJel®, mustard and salt. Add vinegar and water and whisk until dry ingredients dissolve. (Whisking prevents ClearJel® from clumping.) Stir in onions, capers, lemon zest, fennel seeds and pepper. Bring to a boil over medium-high heat, stirring frequently. Reduce heat, cover and boil gently for 4 minutes. Add reserved fennel leaves and chopped bulb. Return to a boil over medium-high heat. Remove from heat.

4. Ladle hot relish into hot jars, leaving ½ inch (1 cm) headspace. Remove air bubbles and adjust headspace, if necessary, by adding hot relish. Wipe rim. Center lid on jar. Screw band down until resistance is met, then increase to fingertip-tight.

5. Place jars in canner, ensuring they are completely covered with water. Bring to a boil and process for 10 minutes. Remove canner lid. Wait 5 minutes, then remove jars, cool and store. *(For more information, see pages 417–418.)*

Jerusalem Artichoke Relish

Although Jerusalem artichokes carry the name "artichoke," they don't resemble an artichoke. Also known as a sunchoke, this vegetable looks very similar to ginger and has knobby roots. The thin beige skin can have a red or purple tint, and it is edible. The yellow-white flesh is crisp and juicy with a sweet flavor. Jerusalem artichokes make a delicious and unusual relish.

TIPS

Use lukewarm or room temperature water to help dissolve the salt.

To peel Jerusalem artichokes, use a sharp paring knife and remove thin brown outer layer. Jerusalem artichokes tend to oxidize rapidly when cut, so they need to be treated to prevent browning. Use a commercial produce protector and follow the manufacturer's instructions, or drop freshly chopped artichokes into a solution of lemon juice and water (see page 202).

Makes about ten 8-ounce (250 mL) jars

1 cup	pickling or canning salt	250 mL
16 cups	water (see tip, at left)	4 L
2 lbs	Jerusalem artichokes, peeled (see tip, at left)	900 g
3⅓ cups	granulated sugar	825 mL
4 cups	white vinegar	1 L
2 cups	finely chopped seeded red or green bell peppers	500 mL
2 cups	finely chopped onions	500 mL
2 tbsp	mustard seeds	30 mL
1 tbsp	ground turmeric	15 mL
¼ tsp	salt	1 mL

1. In a large glass or stainless steel bowl, dissolve pickling salt in water. Add artichokes. Cover and let stand in a cool place (70 to 75°F/21 to 23°C) for 12 hours or overnight. Transfer to a colander placed over a sink and drain thoroughly. Rinse with cool water, drain thoroughly again and dry. Transfer to a food processor fitted with a metal blade or a food grinder and finely chop. Treat to prevent browning (see tip, at left). Set aside. Drain before adding to the saucepan.

2. Meanwhile, prepare canner, jars and lids. *(For more information, see page 415.)*

3. In a large stainless steel saucepan, combine sugar and vinegar. Bring to a boil over high heat, stirring to dissolve sugar. Add drained artichokes, red and green peppers, onions, mustard seeds, turmeric and salt. Reduce heat to medium-high and return to a boil, stirring occasionally. Remove from heat.

4. Ladle hot relish into hot jars, leaving ½ inch (1 cm) headspace. Remove air bubbles and adjust headspace, if necessary, by adding hot relish. Wipe rim. Center lid on jar. Screw band down until resistance is met, then increase to fingertip-tight.

5. Place jars in canner, ensuring they are completely covered with water. Bring to a boil and process for 10 minutes. Remove canner lid. Wait 5 minutes, then remove jars, cool and store. *(For more information, see pages 417–418.)*

Zesty Zucchini Relish

Horseradish and hot peppers give this relish its zest. It's a great way to use up extra zucchini from the garden, and it makes a great accompaniment to bratwursts hot off the grill.

TIPS

We recommend using cayenne or Holland (Dutch) chili peppers if you prefer a hotter relish. If you like a milder relish, use varieties such as yellow wax or New Mexico.

When cutting hot peppers, wear rubber gloves to keep your hands from being burned.

Makes about five pint (500 mL) jars

12 cups	finely chopped zucchini	3 L
4 cups	chopped onions	1 L
2	red bell peppers, seeded and chopped	2
1	green bell pepper, seeded and chopped	1
1/3 cup	pickling or canning salt	75 mL
2 1/2 cups	granulated sugar	625 mL
2 1/2 cups	white vinegar	625 mL
1 tbsp	ground nutmeg	15 mL
1 tbsp	ground turmeric	15 mL
4 tbsp	prepared horseradish	60 mL
1	chili pepper, including seeds, chopped (see tips, at left)	1

1. In a large glass or stainless steel bowl, combine zucchini, onions, red and green peppers and pickling salt. Cover and let stand in a cool place (70 to 75°F/21 to 23°C) for 12 hours or overnight. Transfer to a colander placed over a sink and drain. Rinse with cool water and drain thoroughly. Using your hands, squeeze out excess liquid.

2. In a large stainless steel saucepan, combine drained zucchini mixture, sugar, vinegar, nutmeg, turmeric, horseradish and chili pepper. Bring to a boil over medium-high heat, stirring occasionally. Reduce heat and boil gently, stirring frequently, until liquid is reduced and mixture is the consistency of a thin commercial relish, about 45 minutes.

3. Meanwhile, prepare canner, jars and lids. *(For more information, see page 415.)*

4. Ladle hot relish into hot jars, leaving 1/2 inch (1 cm) headspace. Remove air bubbles and adjust headspace, if necessary, by adding hot relish. Wipe rim. Center lid on jar. Screw band down until resistance is met, then increase to fingertip-tight.

5. Place jars in canner, ensuring they are completely covered with water. Bring to a boil and process for 15 minutes. Remove canner lid. Wait 5 minutes, then remove jars, cool and store. *(For more information, see pages 417–418.)*

Achar (South Asian Pickle)

In some ethnic traditions, "pickles" are an essential side dish that completes both the look and the taste of the main entrée. This chunky pickle is meant to be served just so. It's great with tandoori chicken and similar fare.

TIP

This achar recipe was adapted from a traditional Indian recipe that required considerable quantities of peanut oil, nuts and other ingredients that would make it unacceptable for boiling-water processing. If desired, a small quantity of peanut or vegetable oil may be stirred into the product before serving to enhance the authenticity of the taste. We prefer the "lighter" version produced by this recipe.

Makes about seven pint (500 mL) jars

½ cup	unsalted roasted peanuts, ground	125 mL
4 tbsp	sesame seeds	60 mL
2	onions, quartered	2
15	small dried red chilies (about 1 inch/2.5 cm each)	15
1	1½-inch (4 cm) piece gingerroot, peeled	1
4	cloves garlic	4
2½ cups	white vinegar	625 mL
1 cup	granulated sugar	250 mL
2 tbsp	salt	30 mL
1 tbsp	ground turmeric	15 mL
5	English cucumbers, ends removed, cut into sticks (1½ inches/4 cm long and ½ inch/1 cm wide)	5
2	medium carrots, peeled and cut into sticks (1½ inches/4 cm long and ½ inch/1 cm wide)	2
5 cups	small cauliflower florets	1.25 L

1. In a skillet, over medium heat, combine ground peanuts and sesame seeds. Cook, stirring constantly, until fragrant and lightly browned, about 5 minutes. Immediately transfer to a bowl and set aside.

2. Prepare canner, jars and lids. *(For more information, see page 415.)*

3. In a blender or a food processor fitted with a metal blade, purée onions, chilies, gingerroot and garlic into a paste.

4. In a large stainless steel saucepan, combine puréed vegetables, vinegar, sugar, salt and turmeric. Bring to a full rolling boil over high heat, stirring frequently to prevent scorching. Reduce heat and boil gently until mixture thickens slightly, 5 to 10 minutes. Add cucumbers, carrots, cauliflower and reserved peanut mixture. Bring to a boil over medium-high heat, stirring constantly. Reduce heat and boil gently, stirring occasionally, for 5 minutes, until vegetables are heated through.

5. Pack hot achar into hot jars, leaving ½ inch (1 cm) headspace. Remove air bubbles and adjust headspace, if necessary, by adding hot achar. Wipe rim. Center lid on jar. Screw band down until resistance is met, then increase to fingertip-tight.

6. Place jars in canner, ensuring they are completely covered with water. Bring to a boil and process for 15 minutes. Remove canner lid. Wait 5 minutes, then remove jars, cool and store. *(For more information, see pages 417–418.)*

Chutney

Chutney — which comes from the East Indian word *chatni*, meaning "to be liked" or "to be tasted" — is a delicious combination of fruit, vinegar and sugar, cooked and seasoned with spices, onions, garlic or peppers. Chutneys can range from chunky to smooth and from mild to hot in seasoning. A traditional accompaniment to curried dishes, chutney also makes a great addition to cheese trays and complements a wide range of dishes, from omelets and soufflés to grilled fish. For maximum visual appeal, create chutneys that offer contrasting colors as well as flavors.

Green Tomato Chutney

Although you need to start this chutney the night before you are ready to cook it, it's worth the extra effort. Not only does it allow you to use up any unripe tomatoes from the garden, it is deliciously sweet. Among its uses, it does a terrific job of evening out the bite of spicy dishes that pack too strong a punch.

TIP

You can buy prepared pickling spice in well-stocked supermarkets or make your own (see page 217).

Makes about seven pint (500 mL) jars

16 cups	sliced cored peeled green tomatoes	4 L
½ cup	pickling or canning salt	125 mL
	Cold water	
3 tbsp	pickling spice (see tip, at left)	45 mL
4 cups	white vinegar	1 L
16 cups	chopped cored peeled apples (see tip, opposite)	4 L
3	onions, chopped	3
3	green bell peppers, seeded and chopped	3
6 cups	lightly packed brown sugar	1.5 L
1 tsp	chili powder	5 mL

1. In a large glass or stainless steel bowl, layer tomatoes and pickling salt. Add cold water to cover. Cover and refrigerate for 12 hours or overnight. Transfer to a colander placed over a sink. Rinse well with cold water and drain thoroughly.

2. Tie pickling spice in a square of cheesecloth, creating a spice bag. Set aside.

TIP

To prevent the apples from browning, we recommend measuring the vinegar into the saucepan before preparing the apples. As the apples are chopped, drop them into the vinegar, stirring to ensure all surfaces are covered. When all have been chopped, continue with Step 3.

3. In a large stainless steel saucepan, combine vinegar and apples. Add drained tomatoes, onions and green peppers. Bring to a boil over medium-high heat and boil for 30 minutes, stirring frequently. Stir in brown sugar and return to a boil, stirring to dissolve sugar. Reduce heat and boil gently, stirring frequently, for 30 minutes. Add reserved spice bag and chili powder and stir well. Boil gently, stirring frequently, until thick enough to mound on a spoon, about 30 minutes. Discard spice bag.

4. Meanwhile, prepare canner, jars and lids. *(For more information, see page 415.)*

5. Ladle hot chutney into hot jars, leaving $\frac{1}{2}$ inch (1 cm) headspace. Remove air bubbles and adjust headspace, if necessary, by adding hot chutney. Wipe rim. Center lid on jar. Screw band down until resistance is met, then increase to fingertip-tight.

6. Place jars in canner, ensuring they are completely covered with water. Bring to a boil and process for 15 minutes. Remove canner lid. Wait 5 minutes, then remove jars, cool and store. *(For more information, see pages 417–418.)*

Sweet Yellow Tomato Chutney

Compared to traditional red tomatoes, yellow tomatoes have a milder, sweeter and slightly fruity flavor. This colorful chutney uses the special characteristics of yellow tomatoes to create a sweet-and-sour flavor that goes particularly well with grilled fish.

TIPS

To prevent the apples from browning, we recommend measuring the vinegar into the saucepan before preparing the apples. As the apples are chopped, drop them into the vinegar, stirring to ensure all surfaces are covered. When all have been chopped, continue with Step 1.

Refer to the Produce Purchase Guide on pages 426–429 to determine how much produce you'll need to buy to prepare this recipe.

Makes about nine pint (500 mL) jars

4 cups	cider vinegar	1 L
9 cups	chopped cored peeled tart green apples (see tip, at left)	2.25 L
12 cups	chopped cored peeled yellow tomatoes	3 L
3 cups	golden raisins	750 mL
2½ cups	chopped onions	625 mL
1½ cups	granulated sugar	375 mL
1 cup	lightly packed brown sugar	250 mL
3	chili peppers, such as jalapeño or hot banana (yellow wax), finely chopped	3
2	cloves garlic, finely chopped	2
¼ cup	mustard seeds	50 mL
1 tbsp	finely chopped gingerroot	15 mL
1½ tsp	ground cinnamon	7 mL
1 tsp	salt	5 mL

1. In a large stainless steel saucepan, combine vinegar and apples. Add tomatoes, raisins, onions, granulated sugar, brown sugar, chili peppers, garlic, mustard seeds, gingerroot, cinnamon and salt. Bring to a boil over medium-high heat, stirring frequently. Reduce heat and boil gently, stirring frequently, until thick enough to mound on a spoon, about 60 minutes.

2. Meanwhile, prepare canner, jars and lids. *(For more information, see page 415.)*

3. Ladle hot chutney into hot jars, leaving ½ inch (1 cm) headspace. Remove air bubbles and adjust headspace, if necessary, by adding hot chutney. Wipe rim. Center lid on jar. Screw band down until resistance is met, then increase to fingertip-tight.

4. Place jars in canner, ensuring they are completely covered with water. Bring to a boil and process for 15 minutes. Remove canner lid. Wait 5 minutes, then remove jars, cool and store. *(For more information, see pages 417–418.)*

Tomato and Apple Chutney

Serve this tasty chutney warmed over baked Brie for an appealing appetizer. Allow a plentiful supply of crackers and apple slices for spreading the Brie.

TIPS

To prevent the apples from browning, we recommend measuring the vinegar into the saucepan before preparing the apples. As the apples are chopped, drop them into the vinegar, stirring to ensure all surfaces are covered. When all have been chopped, continue with Step 1.

You'll need to use an English cucumber in this recipe because it is not peeled. Field cucumbers are often waxed, which makes them unsuitable for preserving unless the skin is removed.

For a milder chutney, devein and seed the red chili pepper.

Makes about six pint (500 mL) jars

3 cups	white vinegar	750 mL
4 cups	chopped cored peeled apples (see tip, at left)	1 L
10 cups	chopped cored peeled tomatoes	2.5 L
3 cups	lightly packed brown sugar	750 mL
2 cups	chopped English cucumber (see tip, at left)	500 mL
1½ cups	chopped onions	375 mL
1½ cups	chopped seeded red bell peppers	375 mL
1 cup	raisins	250 mL
1	red chili pepper, such as serrano or Holland (Dutch), finely chopped (see tip, at left)	1
1	clove garlic, finely chopped	1
1 tbsp	ground ginger	15 mL
1 tsp	salt	5 mL
1 tsp	ground cinnamon	5 mL

1. In a large stainless steel saucepan, combine vinegar and apples. Add tomatoes, brown sugar, cucumber, onions, red peppers, raisins, chili pepper, garlic, ginger, salt and cinnamon. Bring to a boil over medium-high heat, stirring frequently. Reduce heat and boil gently, stirring frequently, until thick enough to mound on a spoon, about 30 minutes.

2. Meanwhile, prepare canner, jars and lids. *(For more information, see page 415.)*

3. Ladle hot chutney into hot jars, leaving ½ inch (1 cm) headspace. Remove air bubbles and adjust headspace, if necessary, by adding hot chutney. Wipe rim. Center lid on jar. Screw band down until resistance is met, then increase to fingertip-tight.

4. Place jars in canner, ensuring they are completely covered with water. Bring to a boil and process for 10 minutes. Remove canner lid. Wait 5 minutes, then remove jars, cool and store. *(For more information, see pages 417–418.)*

Curried Apple Chutney

The curry adds an Indian flavor experience to this apple chutney. Try serving it with chicken satay skewers.

TIPS

To prevent the apples from browning, we recommend measuring the vinegar into the saucepan before preparing the apples. As the apples are chopped, drop them into the vinegar, stirring to ensure all surfaces are covered. When all have been chopped, continue with Step 1.

The flavor of chutneys and salsas blends and mellows upon standing, so plan on storing your preserves for at least 2 to 3 weeks for the best flavor.

Makes about ten pint (500 mL) jars

4 cups	white vinegar	1 L
8 cups	chopped cored peeled apples (see tip, at left)	2 L
5½ cups	raisins	1.375 L
4 cups	lightly packed brown sugar	1 L
1 cup	chopped onions	250 mL
1 cup	chopped seeded red bell pepper	250 mL
3 tbsp	mustard seeds	45 mL
2 tbsp	ground ginger	30 mL
2 tsp	ground allspice	10 mL
2 tsp	curry powder	10 mL
2 tsp	salt	10 mL
2	chili peppers, such as hot banana (yellow wax) or jalapeño, chopped	2
1	clove garlic, finely chopped	1

1. In a large stainless steel saucepan, combine vinegar and apples. Add raisins, brown sugar, onions and red pepper. Bring to a boil over medium-high heat, stirring constantly. Reduce heat and boil gently, stirring frequently, for 30 minutes. Add mustard seeds, ginger, allspice, curry powder, salt, chili peppers and garlic. Boil gently, stirring frequently, until thick enough to mound on a spoon, about 15 minutes.

2. Meanwhile, prepare canner, jars and lids. *(For more information, see page 415.)*

3. Ladle hot chutney into hot jars, leaving ½ inch (1 cm) headspace. Remove air bubbles and adjust headspace, if necessary, by adding hot chutney. Wipe rim. Center lid on jar. Screw band down until resistance is met, then increase to fingertip-tight.

4. Place jars in canner, ensuring they are completely covered with water. Bring to a boil and process for 15 minutes. Remove canner lid. Wait 5 minutes, then remove jars, cool and store. *(For more information, see pages 417–418.)*

Apple Rhubarb Chutney

Richly colored, with just a hint of spice, this chunky chutney is as delicious on toast as it is alongside savory snacks such as cheese and grilled pork.

TIPS

For good-textured chutney, choose firm cooking apples that keep their shape during cooking, such as Golden Delicious or Spartan.

When boiling sauces, chutneys and salsas that thicken as the moisture is evaporated, you may need to gradually reduce the heat to maintain a low boil and prevent scorching.

Makes about four 8-ounce (250 mL) jars

4 cups	diced peeled cored apples, treated to prevent browning (see page 202) and drained	1 L
4 cups	granulated sugar	1 L
2 cups	diced rhubarb, fresh or frozen	500 mL
½ cup	water	125 mL
	Grated zest and juice of 1 lemon	
½ cup	dried cranberries	125 mL
1 tsp	ground cinnamon	5 mL
½ tsp	ground nutmeg	2 mL

1. In a large stainless steel saucepan, combine apples, sugar, rhubarb, water and lemon zest and juice. Bring to a boil over medium-high heat, stirring constantly. Reduce heat and boil gently, stirring frequently, for 15 minutes. Add cranberries, cinnamon and nutmeg. Boil gently, stirring frequently, until thick enough to mound on a spoon, about 15 minutes.

2. Meanwhile, prepare canner, jars and lids. *(For more information, see page 415.)*

3. Ladle hot chutney into hot jars, leaving ½ inch (1 cm) headspace. Remove air bubbles and adjust headspace, if necessary, by adding hot chutney. Wipe rim. Center lid on jar. Screw band down until resistance is met, then increase to fingertip-tight.

4. Place jars in canner, ensuring they are completely covered with water. Bring to a boil and process for 10 minutes. Remove canner lid. Wait 5 minutes, then remove jars, cool and store. *(For more information, see pages 417–418.)*

Apricot Chutney

Mellow, with a hint of spice, this flavorful chutney makes a great accompaniment to grilled meats and a tasty addition to a cheese tray.

TIPS

To prevent the apples from browning, we recommend measuring the vinegar into the saucepan before preparing the apples. As the apples are chopped, drop them into the vinegar, stirring to ensure all surfaces are covered. When all have been chopped, continue with Step 1.

Place a clean towel on your work surface to absorb water from the hot jars as you take them out of the boiling-water canner to be filled, and again once the jars are processed. The towel prevents hot jars from coming into contact with cooler countertops. Significant temperature differences can cause jar breakage.

Makes about seven 8-ounce (250 mL) jars

1 1/2 cups	cider vinegar	375 mL
2	tart green apples, peeled, cored and finely chopped (see tip, at left)	2
3 cups	chopped dried apricots	750 mL
3 cups	boiling water	750 mL
2	onions, finely chopped	2
1 cup	granulated sugar	250 mL
1 cup	lightly packed brown sugar	250 mL
4	cloves garlic, finely chopped	4
1/2 cup	raisins	125 mL
2 tbsp	finely chopped gingerroot	30 mL
2 tsp	mustard seeds	10 mL
1 1/2 tsp	ground cinnamon	7 mL
1 tsp	ground allspice	5 mL
1 tsp	freshly ground black pepper	5 mL
1/2 tsp	ground cloves	2 mL
1/4 tsp	salt	1 mL
1/4 tsp	cayenne pepper	1 mL

1. In a large stainless steel saucepan, combine vinegar and apples. Add apricots, boiling water, onions, granulated sugar, brown sugar, garlic, raisins and gingerroot. Bring to a boil over medium-high heat, stirring constantly. Reduce heat and boil gently, stirring occasionally, for 30 minutes. Add mustard seeds, cinnamon, allspice, black pepper, cloves, salt and cayenne. Boil gently, stirring frequently, until thick enough to mound on a spoon, about 15 minutes.

2. Meanwhile, prepare canner, jars and lids. *(For more information, see page 415.)*

3. Ladle hot chutney into hot jars, leaving 1/2 inch (1 cm) headspace. Remove air bubbles and adjust headspace, if necessary, by adding hot chutney. Wipe rim. Center lid on jar. Screw band down until resistance is met, then increase to fingertip-tight.

4. Place jars in canner, ensuring they are completely covered with water. Bring to a boil and process for 10 minutes. Remove canner lid. Wait 5 minutes, then remove jars, cool and store. *(For more information, see pages 417–418.)*

Mediterranean Apricot and Date Chutney

This dark golden chutney is delicious served with tagines (Moroccan stews). It has only a few ingredients, all of which are available year-round, making it a great recipe to prepare on a rainy day, filling your kitchen with enticing aromas as it simmers.

TIP

The flavors of chutneys and salsas blend and mellow upon standing, so plan on storing your preserves for at least 2 to 3 weeks for the best flavor.

Makes about twelve 8-ounce (250 mL) jars

2 lbs	dried apricots	900 g
	Water	
3 cups	lightly packed brown sugar	750 mL
2½ cups	chopped pitted dates	625 mL
2½ cups	raisins	625 mL
2 cups	white wine vinegar	500 mL
1 tbsp	mustard seeds	15 mL
1 tbsp	salt	15 mL
2 tsp	ground ginger	10 mL
1 tsp	ground coriander	5 mL

1. In a large bowl, combine apricots with water to cover. Let stand for 30 minutes. Drain, chop and place in large stainless steel saucepan. Add 2 cups (500 mL) water, brown sugar, dates, raisins, vinegar, mustard seeds, salt, ginger and coriander. Bring to a boil over medium-high heat, stirring frequently. Reduce heat and boil gently, stirring frequently, until thick enough to mound on a spoon, about 20 minutes.

2. Meanwhile, prepare canner, jars and lids. *(For more information, see page 415.)*

3. Ladle chutney into hot jars, leaving ½ inch (1 cm) headspace. Remove air bubbles and adjust headspace, if necessary, by adding hot chutney. Wipe rim. Center lid on jar. Screw band down until resistance is met, then increase to fingertip-tight.

4. Place jars in canner, ensuring they are completely covered with water. Bring to a boil and process for 10 minutes. Remove canner lid. Wait 5 minutes, then remove jars, cool and store. *(For more information, see pages 417–418.)*

Fruity Banana Chutney

Here's a chutney you can make at any time of year because it uses a combination of dried fruits and those that are available year-round. Try it with grilled chicken for a delicious treat.

TIPS

To prevent the apple from browning, we recommend measuring the vinegar into the saucepan before preparing the apple. As the apple is chopped, drop it into the vinegar, stirring to ensure all surfaces are covered. When all have been chopped, continue with Step 1.

A clear plastic ruler (kept solely for kitchen use) will help you determine the correct headspace. Each filled jar should be measured accurately, as the headspace can affect sealing and the preservation of the contents.

Makes about six 8-ounce (250 mL) jars

1 ½ cups	cider vinegar	375 mL
1 cup	chopped cored peeled apple (see tip, at left)	250 mL
1 ½ cups	mashed bananas	375 mL
1 cup	chopped pitted dates	250 mL
1 cup	chopped pitted prunes	250 mL
1 cup	chopped onions	250 mL
½ cup	chopped dried apricots	125 mL
½ cup	mixed candied peel	125 mL
3	cloves garlic, chopped	3
1 ½ cups	lightly packed dark brown sugar	375 mL
½ cup	water	125 mL
1 ½ tsp	ground coriander	7 mL
1 tsp	cayenne pepper	5 mL
1 tsp	ground allspice	5 mL
1 tsp	ground turmeric	5 mL
1 tsp	grated gingerroot	5 mL

1. In a large stainless steel saucepan, combine vinegar and apple. Add bananas, dates, prunes, onions, apricots, candied peel and garlic. Bring to a boil over medium-high heat. Reduce heat and boil gently, stirring occasionally, for 15 minutes. Add brown sugar, water, coriander, cayenne, allspice, turmeric and gingerroot, stirring to dissolve sugar. Boil gently, stirring frequently, until thick enough to mound on a spoon, about 15 minutes.

2. Meanwhile, prepare canner, jars and lids. *(For more information, see page 415.)*

3. Ladle hot chutney into hot jars, leaving ½ inch (1 cm) headspace. Remove air bubbles and adjust headspace, if necessary, by adding hot chutney. Wipe rim. Center lid on jar. Screw band down until resistance is met, then increase to fingertip-tight.

4. Place jars in canner, ensuring they are completely covered with water. Bring to a boil and process for 10 minutes. Remove canner lid. Wait 5 minutes, then remove jars, cool and store. *(For more information, see pages 417–418.)*

Simply Delicious Cherry Chutney

Capture the incomparable flavor of freshly picked cherries in this old-fashioned chutney. It's an ideal partner for pork and makes a fabulous finish for a cheese tray.

TIPS

Cheesecloth can be found at many retailers, such as grocery stores and other stores that carry kitchen supplies. Look in the area where kitchen utensils are located.

When boiling sauces, chutneys and salsas that thicken as the moisture is evaporated, you may need to gradually reduce the heat to maintain a low boil and prevent scorching.

The flavors of chutneys and salsas blend and mellow upon standing, so plan on storing your preserves for at least 2 to 3 weeks for the best flavor.

Makes about six 8-ounce (250 mL) jars

4½ tsp	whole allspice	22 mL
1	cinnamon stick (about 6 inches/15 cm), broken	1
10 cups	frozen red tart or sweet black cherries, partially thawed, coarsely chopped	2.5 L
2	large apples, peeled, cored and chopped	2
1½ cups	finely chopped red or other sweet onions, such as Vidalia	375 mL
1 cup	white vinegar	250 mL
2	cloves garlic, finely chopped	2
½ tsp	salt	2 mL
1 cup	lightly packed brown sugar	250 mL
1½ cups	raisins	375 mL

1. Tie allspice and cinnamon stick in a square of cheesecloth, creating a spice bag.

2. In a large stainless steel saucepan, combine cherries, apples, onions, vinegar, garlic, salt and spice bag. Bring to a boil over medium-high heat and boil hard, stirring frequently, for 20 minutes. Add brown sugar and stir to dissolve. Reduce heat and boil gently, stirring frequently, until thick enough to mound on a spoon, about 20 minutes. Add raisins and return to a boil, stirring constantly. Remove from heat. Discard spice bag.

3. Meanwhile, prepare canner, jars and lids. (*For more information, see page 415.*)

4. Ladle hot chutney into hot jars, leaving ½ inch (1 cm) headspace. Remove air bubbles and adjust headspace, if necessary, by adding hot chutney. Wipe rim. Center lid on jar. Screw band down until resistance is met, then increase to fingertip-tight.

5. Place jars in canner, ensuring they are completely covered with water. Bring to a boil and process for 10 minutes. Remove canner lid. Wait 5 minutes, then remove jars, cool and store. (*For more information, see pages 417–418.*)

Cranberry Chutney

Keep a few bags of cranberries in your freezer so you can make this luscious chutney at any time of year. It's a delicious substitute for commercially prepared cranberry condiments.

TIPS

Fresh or frozen cranberries can be used. Frozen are usually sold in perforated bags.

Candied pineapple is also known as crystallized or glacé pineapple.

Read a recipe all the way through, even before you go shopping for the ingredients. It's very important to have all of the ingredients and equipment ready before you start making preserves.

A jar lifter is very helpful for handling hot, wet jars. Because they are bulky and fit loosely, oven mitts — even water-resistent types — are not a wise choice. When filling jars, an all-purpose rubber glove, worn on your helper hand, will allow you to steady the jar.

Makes about six 8-ounce (250 mL) jars

3 cups	fresh or frozen cranberries (see tip, at left)	750 mL
1 ¼ cups	finely chopped onions	300 mL
1 ¼ cups	chopped candied pineapple (see tip, at left)	300 mL
3	cloves garlic, finely chopped	3
2 tbsp	finely chopped gingerroot	30 mL
1 tsp	grated orange zest	5 mL
¼ cup	freshly squeezed orange juice	50 mL
1 cup	red wine vinegar	250 mL
1 ½ cups	granulated sugar	375 mL
1 cup	golden raisins	250 mL
1 cup	water	250 mL
1 tsp	dry mustard	5 mL
1 tsp	ground cinnamon	5 mL
1 tsp	ground cloves	5 mL
½ tsp	cayenne pepper	2 mL

1. In a large stainless steel saucepan, combine cranberries, onions, pineapple, garlic, gingerroot, orange zest and juice and vinegar. Bring to a boil over medium-high heat, stirring occasionally. Reduce heat, cover and boil gently until cranberries soften and burst, about 15 minutes. Add sugar, raisins, water, mustard, cinnamon, cloves and cayenne. Boil gently, stirring frequently, for about 15 minutes. (Mixture should be slightly runny and will thicken upon cooling.)

2. Meanwhile, prepare canner, jars and lids. *(For more information, see page 415.)*

3. Ladle hot chutney into hot jars, leaving ½ inch (1 cm) headspace. Remove air bubbles and adjust headspace, if necessary, by adding hot chutney. Wipe rim. Center lid on jar. Screw band down until resistance is met, then increase to fingertip-tight.

4. Place jars in canner, ensuring they are completely covered with water. Bring to a boil and process for 10 minutes. Remove canner lid. Wait 5 minutes, then remove jars, cool and store. *(For more information, see pages 417–418.)*

Kiwi Chutney

This flavorful chutney is traditionally used as a condiment with poultry or meat, but it also makes a delicious accompaniment to cheese and crackers. If you prefer chutney with a fruitier flavor, reduce the spices by half.

TIPS

When preparing jars and lids, prepare a couple extra in case your yield is larger than you expect. If you don't have enough jars, place any leftover preserves in an airtight container, store in the refrigerator and use within a few weeks.

Before using jars, inspect them carefully for any chips, cracks or fractures. Discard any imperfect jars.

Makes about seven 8-ounce (250 mL) jars

6 cups	chopped peeled kiwifruit	1.5 L
3	tart green apples, peeled, cored and chopped	3
1½ cups	chopped onions	375 mL
1½ cups	cider vinegar	375 mL
1½ cups	granulated sugar	375 mL
¾ cup	lightly packed dark brown sugar	175 mL
½ cup	raisins	125 mL
4	cloves garlic, finely chopped	4
1 tsp	finely chopped gingerroot	5 mL
1½ tsp	ground cinnamon	7 mL
1 tsp	mustard seeds	5 mL
½ tsp	cayenne pepper	2 mL
½ tsp	ground cloves	2 mL
½ tsp	ground allspice	2 mL
¼ tsp	salt	1 mL
¼ tsp	freshly ground black pepper	1 mL

1. In a large stainless steel saucepan, combine kiwifruit, apples, onions, vinegar, granulated sugar, brown sugar, raisins, garlic and gingerroot. Bring to a boil over medium-high heat, stirring constantly. Reduce heat and boil gently, stirring frequently, for 30 minutes. Add cinnamon, mustard seeds, cayenne, cloves, allspice, salt and black pepper. Boil gently, stirring frequently, until thick enough to mound on a spoon, about 10 minutes.

2. Meanwhile, prepare canner, jars and lids. *(For more information, see page 415.)*

3. Ladle hot chutney into hot jars, leaving ½ inch (1 cm) headspace. Remove air bubbles and adjust headspace, if necessary, by adding hot chutney. Wipe rim. Center lid on jar. Screw band down until resistance is met, then increase to fingertip-tight.

4. Place jars in canner, ensuring they are completely covered with water. Bring to a boil and process for 10 minutes. Remove canner lid. Wait 5 minutes, then remove jars, cool and store. *(For more information, see pages 417–418.)*

Mango Chutney

TIPS

The best way to prepare the mango for this recipe is to make 4 lengthwise cuts to the pit. Cut away quarters, leaving about ¼ inch (0.5 cm) of fibrous flesh around the pit. Cut remaining fruit from the peel and chop. Repeat with remaining mangoes.

There are three different types of molasses, produced at different stages of the refining process. Each type may be labeled in different ways, depending on where you live. The first refinement produces a mild-flavored product that is labeled "mild-flavored," "light" or "fancy." The second refinement produces a somewhat stronger molasses and is called "full-flavored," "dark" or "cooking," and the third refinement produces the very strong blackstrap molasses. For this recipe, we recommend using molasses from the first refinement for the best flavor. If you prefer a stronger flavor, "dark," "full-flavored" or "cooking" molasses may be used. Avoid using blackstrap or any sugar-reduced product.

Makes about six 8-ounce (250 mL) jars

4 cups	chopped pitted peeled mangoes (see tip, at left)	I L
I cup	coarsely chopped onions	250 mL
I cup	lightly packed dark brown sugar	250 mL
I cup	cider vinegar	250 mL
¾ cup	golden raisins	175 mL
½ cup	chopped seeded peeled limes	125 mL
½ cup	chopped seeded peeled orange	125 mL
¼ cup	chopped seeded peeled lemon	50 mL
3	cloves garlic, finely chopped	3
½ cup	finely chopped gingerroot	125 mL
½ cup	mild-flavored or fancy molasses (see tip, at left)	125 mL
2 tbsp	finely chopped cilantro	30 mL
I tbsp	mustard seeds	15 mL
I tsp	hot pepper flakes	5 mL
I tsp	ground cinnamon	5 mL
¼ tsp	ground cloves	I mL
¼ tsp	ground allspice	I mL

1. In a large stainless steel saucepan, combine mangoes, onions, brown sugar, vinegar, raisins, limes, orange, lemon, garlic, gingerroot and molasses. Bring to a boil over medium-high heat, stirring constantly. Reduce heat and boil gently, stirring frequently, for 20 minutes. Add cilantro, mustard seeds, hot pepper flakes, cinnamon, cloves and allspice. Boil gently, stirring frequently, until thick enough to mound on a spoon, about 10 minutes.

2. Meanwhile, prepare canner, jars and lids. *(For more information, see page 415.)*

3. Ladle hot chutney into hot jars, leaving ½ inch (1 cm) headspace. Remove air bubbles and adjust headspace, if necessary, by adding hot chutney. Wipe rim. Center lid on jar. Screw band down until resistance is met, then increase to fingertip-tight.

4. Place jars in canner, ensuring they are completely covered with water. Bring to a boil and process for 10 minutes. Remove canner lid. Wait 5 minutes, then remove jars, cool and store. *(For more information, see pages 417–418.)*

Nectarine Chutney

Lime and chili pepper add South American flair to this golden chutney. Use it to garnish refried beans, adding color and flavor.

TIPS

To peel nectarines, place them in a pot of boiling water for 30 to 60 seconds or until the skins start to crack. Immediately dip in cold water. The skins will slip off easily.

When cutting hot peppers, wear rubber gloves to keep your hands from being burned.

If you have particularly hard water and use it in the boiling-water canner, it can leave a residue on jars. Use filtered or reverse-osmosis water to fill your canner instead.

Makes about three pint (500 mL) jars

8 cups	sliced pitted peeled nectarines (see tip, at left)	2 L
2 tsp	salt	10 mL
2½ cups	lightly packed brown sugar	625 mL
1½ cups	red wine vinegar	375 mL
¼ cup	Worcestershire sauce	50 mL
1 cup	finely chopped onions	250 mL
¾ cup	lime juice	175 mL
2	cloves garlic, finely chopped	2
1	chili pepper, such as jalapeño or hot banana (yellow wax), finely chopped	1
2 tbsp	chopped crystallized ginger	30 mL
¼ tsp	ground cloves	1 mL
¼ tsp	ground cinnamon	1 mL

1. In a large glass or stainless steel bowl, combine nectarines and salt. Let stand for 20 minutes.

2. In a large stainless steel saucepan, combine brown sugar, vinegar and Worcestershire sauce. Bring to a boil over medium-high heat, stirring to dissolve sugar. Stir in nectarines and return to a boil. Reduce heat and boil gently, stirring frequently, until nectarines are transparent, about 15 minutes. Using a slotted spoon, transfer nectarines to a bowl. Set aside.

3. To the saucepan, add onions, lime juice, garlic, chili pepper, ginger, cloves and cinnamon. Bring to a boil over medium-high heat. Reduce heat and boil gently, stirring occasionally, until onions are tender, about 10 minutes. Return nectarines to saucepan. Boil gently over medium heat, stirring frequently, until mixture is thick enough to hold its shape on a spoon, about 20 minutes.

4. Meanwhile, prepare canner, jars and lids. *(For more information, see page 415.)*

5. Ladle hot chutney into hot jars, leaving ½ inch (1 cm) headspace. Remove air bubbles and adjust headspace, if necessary, by adding hot chutney. Wipe rim. Center lid on jar. Screw band down until resistance is met, then increase to fingertip-tight.

6. Place jars in canner, ensuring they are completely covered with water. Bring to a boil and process for 15 minutes. Remove canner lid. Wait 5 minutes, then remove jars, cool and store. *(For more information, see pages 417–418.)*

Orange Rhubarb Chutney

The combination of rhubarb and this unique spice blend produces a great-tasting condiment that complements meat or poultry and makes an excellent addition to cheese trays.

TIPS

You can buy prepared pickling spice at well-stocked supermarkets or make your own (see page 217).

Read a recipe all the way through, even before you go shopping for the ingredients. It's very important to have all of the ingredients and equipment ready before you start making preserves.

Place a clean towel on your work surface to absorb water from the hot jars as you take them out of the boiling-water canner to be filled, and again once the jars are processed. The towel prevents hot jars from coming into contact with cooler countertops. Significant temperature differences can cause jar breakage.

Makes about six 8-ounce (250 mL) jars

10	whole black peppercorns	10
1 tbsp	mustard seeds	15 mL
1 tbsp	pickling spice (see tip, at left)	15 mL
4 tbsp	grated orange zest	60 mL
2/3 cup	freshly squeezed orange juice	150 mL
6 cups	chopped rhubarb	1.5 L
5 cups	lightly packed brown sugar	1.25 L
3½ cups	cider vinegar	875 mL
3 cups	coarsely chopped onions	750 mL
1½ cups	raisins	375 mL
2 tbsp	finely chopped garlic	30 mL
2 tbsp	finely chopped gingerroot	30 mL
1 tbsp	curry powder	15 mL
1 tsp	ground allspice	5 mL

1. Tie peppercorns, mustard seeds and pickling spice in a square of cheesecloth, creating a spice bag. Set aside.

2. In a large stainless steel saucepan, combine orange zest and juice, rhubarb, brown sugar, vinegar, onions, raisins, garlic and gingerroot. Bring to a boil over medium-high heat, stirring constantly. Reduce heat and boil gently, stirring occasionally, for 45 minutes. Add curry powder, allspice and reserved spice bag; stir well. Boil gently, stirring frequently, until thick enough to mound on a spoon, about 30 minutes. Discard spice bag.

3. Meanwhile, prepare canner, jars and lids. *(For more information, see page 415.)*

4. Ladle hot chutney into hot jars, leaving ½ inch (1 cm) headspace. Remove air bubbles and adjust headspace, if necessary, by adding hot chutney. Wipe rim. Center lid on jar. Screw band down until resistance is met, then increase to fingertip-tight.

5. Place jars in canner, ensuring they are completely covered with water. Bring to a boil and process for 10 minutes. Remove canner lid. Wait 5 minutes, then remove jars, cool and store. *(For more information, see pages 417–418.)*

Caribbean Peach Chutney

This chutney has a mellow flavor that is reminiscent of the Caribbean islands. If you prefer a chutney with a more traditional flavor, use the Calcutta spicing (see the variation).

TIPS

To prevent the peaches from browning, we recommend measuring the vinegar into the saucepan before preparing the peaches. As the peaches are chopped, drop them into the vinegar, stirring to ensure all surfaces are covered. When all have been chopped, continue with Step 2.

Any type of brown sugar works well in this recipe, but if you prefer a rich-colored chutney, use the dark brown variety.

Candied peel is also known as glacé or crystallized peel.

Makes about six pint (500 mL) jars

I cup	chopped gingerroot	250 mL
2 cups	malt vinegar	500 mL
10 cups	chopped pitted peeled peaches	2.5 L
2 cups	lightly packed brown sugar	500 mL
2	onions, finely chopped	2
2	green bell peppers, seeded and finely chopped	2
I	hot banana (yellow wax) pepper, seeded and finely chopped	I
I cup	dark raisins	250 mL
I cup	golden raisins	250 mL
I cup	mixed candied peel (see tip, at left)	250 mL
I tbsp	salt	15 mL
I tsp	ground cinnamon	5 mL
½ tsp	ground nutmeg	2 mL
¼ tsp	ground cloves	I mL

1. Tie gingerroot in a large square of cheesecloth, creating a spice bag. Set aside.

2. In a large stainless steel saucepan, combine vinegar and peaches. Bring to a boil over medium-high heat. Boil, stirring constantly, until peaches are tender, about 10 minutes. Add brown sugar, onions, green peppers, banana pepper, dark and golden raisins, candied peel and salt; return to a boil. Reduce heat and boil gently, stirring frequently, for 30 minutes. Add cinnamon, nutmeg, cloves and reserved spice bag. Boil gently, stirring frequently, until thick enough to mound on a spoon, about 15 minutes. Discard spice bag.

3. Meanwhile, prepare canner, jars and lids. *(For more information, see page 415.)*

4. Ladle hot chutney into hot jars, leaving ½ inch (1 cm) headspace. Remove air bubbles and adjust headspace, if necessary, by adding hot chutney. Wipe rim. Center lid on jar. Screw band down until resistance is met, then increase to fingertip-tight.

5. Place jars in canner, ensuring they are completely covered with water. Bring to a boil and process for 15 minutes. Remove canner lid. Wait 5 minutes, then remove jars, cool and store. *(For more information, see pages 417–418.)*

Plum Chutney

For the best results, use blue plums, such as Damson or Stanley, to make this flavorful chutney.

TIPS

When boiling sauces, chutneys and salsas that thicken as the moisture is evaporated, you may need to gradually reduce the heat to maintain a low boil and prevent scorching.

The flavors of chutneys and salsas blend and mellow upon standing, so plan on storing your preserves for at least 2 to 3 weeks for the best flavor.

Makes about six pint (500 mL) jars

16 cups	chopped pitted plums (unpeeled)	4 L
3 cups	lightly packed brown sugar	750 mL
3 cups	white vinegar	750 mL
2 cups	raisins	500 mL
1 cup	chopped onion	250 mL
2 tbsp	mustard seeds	30 mL
2 tsp	ground ginger	10 mL
1 tsp	salt	5 mL

1. In a large stainless steel saucepan, combine plums, brown sugar, vinegar, raisins, onions, mustard seeds, ginger and salt. Bring to a boil over high heat, stirring frequently. Reduce heat and boil gently, stirring frequently, until thick enough to mound on a spoon, about 30 minutes.

2. Meanwhile, prepare canner, jars and lids. *(For more information, see page 415.)*

3. Ladle hot chutney into hot jars, leaving ½ inch (1 cm) headspace. Remove air bubbles and adjust headspace, if necessary, by adding hot chutney. Wipe rim. Center lid on jar. Screw band down until resistance is met, then increase to fingertip-tight.

4. Place jars in canner, ensuring they are completely covered with water. Bring to a boil and process for 15 minutes. Remove canner lid. Wait 5 minutes, then remove jars, cool and store. *(For more information, see pages 417–418.)*

Tamarind Chutney

This sweet-and-sour, richly seasoned "runny" chutney pairs beautifully with any rice or curry meal. It also enlivens roast pork tenderloin or roast chicken. To add a layer of richness and cut the sweetness, swirl in a dollop of yogurt before serving.

TIPS

Tamarind is from a brown curved bean pod found on tamarind trees. The pods contain seeds and edible pulp with a sweet-and-sour flavor. Tamarind is available as a pressed fibrous slab, bottled concentrate or dried pods. We have used the pressed slab tamarind in this recipe.

Dried tamarind is available in Asian or Indian markets and specialty food stores.

Makes about five 8-ounce (250 mL) jars

1 ¼ lbs	dried tamarind, broken into chunks (see tip, at left)	570 g
4 cups	warm water	1 L
2 tbsp	cumin seeds	30 mL
3 cups	granulated sugar	750 mL
1 cup	sultana raisins, rinsed	250 mL
4 tsp	finely chopped gingerroot	20 mL
2 ½ tsp	salt	12 mL
¼ tsp	freshly ground black pepper	1 mL
1 tsp	cayenne pepper	5 mL

1. Prepare canner, jar and lids. *(For more information, see page 415.)*
2. In a medium bowl, combine tamarind and warm water. Let stand for at least 20 minutes, until tamarind is softened and easy to break. Using your fingers, squeeze tamarind under the water to break it up. Drain tamarind and discard soaking liquid. Transfer tamarind to a sieve placed over a non-metallic bowl. Press with the back of a spoon to extract all the liquid and pulp. Scrape the bottom of the sieve and remove any pulp clinging to it. Measure 3 cups (750 mL) of tamarind pulp and liquid and set aside.
3. In a large dry skillet, over medium heat, toast cumin seeds, stirring, until fragrant and just beginning to brown, about 3 minutes. Let cool slightly, then transfer to a mortar or a spice grinder and grind.
4. In a large stainless steel saucepan, combine reserved tamarind pulp and liquid, ground cumin seeds, sugar, raisins, gingerroot, salt, black pepper and cayenne. Bring to a boil over high heat, stirring frequently. Remove from heat.
5. Ladle hot chutney into hot jars, leaving ½ inch (1 cm) headspace. Remove air bubbles and adjust headspace, if necessary, by adding hot chutney. Wipe rim. Center lid on jar. Screw band down until resistance is met, then increase to fingertip-tight.
6. Place jars in canner, ensuring they are completely covered with water. Bring to a boil and process for 15 minutes. Remove canner lid. Wait 5 minutes, then remove jars, cool and store. *(For more information, see pages 417–418.)*

Golden Gossip Chutney

Spend an afternoon with a friend, making a batch of this delicious chutney with always-available carrots. Catch up on all the latest news while you prepare the ingredients, then share the results of your work.

TIPS

To prevent the grated apples from browning, we recommend measuring the vinegar into a large bowl before preparing the apples. Grate the apples into the bowl, stirring to ensure all surfaces are covered. When all the apples have been grated, continue with Step 2, adding the mixture to the recipe along with the onions and other ingredients.

To dice means to cut into ¼-inch (0.5 cm) cubes.

Be sure to use bottled, not freshly squeezed, lemon juice in this recipe because its acidity level is known and will ensure that the acid is sufficient to lower the pH of the recipe to the appropriate level for boiling-water processing.

Makes about nine 8-ounce (250 mL) jars

1	cinnamon stick (about 5 inches/12 cm), broken into pieces	1
2 tbsp	mustard seeds	30 mL
2 tsp	whole cloves	10 mL
4 cups	shredded peeled carrots	1 L
2½ cups	granulated sugar	625 mL
2¼ cups	water	550 mL
½ tsp	cayenne pepper	2 mL
1½ cups	malt vinegar	375 mL
3 cups	grated cored peeled apples (see tip, at left)	750 mL
2 cups	finely chopped onions	500 mL
1½ cups	coarsely chopped pitted dates	375 mL
3 tbsp	finely chopped gingerroot	45 mL
3	cloves garlic, finely chopped	3
1 tbsp	tomato paste	15 mL
2	small red bell peppers, seeded and diced (see tip, at left)	2
¼ cup	bottled lemon juice (see tip, at left)	50 mL

1. Tie cinnamon stick pieces, mustard seeds and cloves in a square of cheesecloth, creating a spice bag.

2. In a large stainless steel saucepan, combine carrots, sugar, water, cayenne and spice bag. Bring to a boil over medium-high heat, stirring constantly. Reduce heat and boil gently, stirring occasionally, until carrots are softened, about 5 minutes. Add vinegar, apples, onions, dates, gingerroot, garlic and tomato paste; stir well. Cover and boil gently until thick enough to mound on a spoon, about 20 minutes. Add red peppers and lemon juice. Boil gently, stirring frequently, until pepper is heated through, about 10 minutes. Discard spice bag.

3. Meanwhile, prepare canner, jars and lids. *(For more information, see page 415.)*

4. Ladle hot chutney into hot jars, leaving ½ inch (1 cm) headspace. Remove air bubbles and adjust headspace, if necessary, by adding hot chutney. Wipe rim. Center lid on jar. Screw band down until resistance is met, then increase to fingertip-tight.

5. Place jars in canner, ensuring they are completely covered with water. Bring to a boil and process for 10 minutes. Remove canner lid. Wait 5 minutes, then remove jars, cool and store. *(For more information, see pages 417–418.)*

Condiments

Condiments are the "something extra" that transform the ordinary into the extraordinary, with very little effort. This chapter contains recipes for everyday condiments such as ketchup and barbecue sauce, as well as more innovative recipes such as flavored mustards and vinegars. Whether your taste leans toward traditional or cutting edge, your mouth will be watering for more of these delicious treats.

Homemade condiments also make great gifts. The mustards and flavored vinegars are obvious choices, but also try giving more exotic items such as Singapore Chili Sauce or Thai Hot and Sweet Dipping Sauce. They are a great way to experience the flavors of different countries without leaving home.

Ketchups

Ketchup has been a staple condiment for hundreds of years. Although the main base for ketchup is tomatoes, the addition of other ingredients makes the flavors come to life. In addition to traditional ketchup, the recipes we've provided use ingredients from peppers to fruits to build on the natural flavor of tomatoes.

When making ketchup at home, be aware that it will have a thinner consistency than store-bought varieties. However, homemade ketchup is made from natural ingredients, without additives — which you and your family can appreciate while enjoying its superior taste.

....

Tomato Ketchup

Much tastier than store-bought, this ketchup is also lower in sugar and salt than commercial brands.

TIP

To ripen tomatoes for canning, empty them from the basket or box onto a single layer of newspaper or a large mesh rack. Store in a cool (but not cold), dry place, out of direct sun. Turn tomatoes daily to prevent spoilage and soft spots. As the tomatoes ripen, sort into different stages of ripeness and use the ripest ones first.

Makes about seven pint (500 mL) jars

3 tbsp	celery seeds	45 mL
4 tsp	whole cloves	20 mL
2	cinnamon sticks (each 4 inches/10 cm), broken into pieces	2
1½ tsp	whole allspice	7 mL
3 cups	cider vinegar	750 mL
24 lbs	tomatoes, cored and quartered	10.9 kg
3 cups	chopped onions	750 mL
1 tsp	cayenne pepper	5 mL
1½ cups	granulated sugar	375 mL
¼ cup	pickling or canning salt	50 mL

1. Tie celery seeds, cloves, cinnamon sticks and allspice in a square of cheesecloth, creating a spice bag.

2. In a stainless steel saucepan, combine vinegar and spice bag. Bring to a boil over high heat. Remove from heat and let stand for 25 minutes. Discard spice bag.

3. Meanwhile, in a large stainless steel saucepan, combine tomatoes, onions and cayenne. Bring to a boil over high heat, stirring frequently. Reduce heat and boil gently for 20 minutes. Add infused vinegar and boil gently until vegetables are soft and mixture begins to thicken, about 30 minutes.

. . . .

TIP

Tomatoes are very high in lycopene, an antioxidant that has been linked with reducing the risk of certain types of cancer. Interestingly, the lycopene in cooked or heat-processed tomatoes is more readily absorbed by the body than that contained in fresh tomatoes.

4. Working in batches, transfer mixture to a sieve placed over a glass or stainless steel bowl and press with the back of a spoon to extract all the liquid. (You can also do this in a food mill). Discard solids.

5. Return liquid to saucepan. Add sugar and salt. Bring to a boil over medium heat, stirring occasionally. Reduce heat and boil gently, stirring frequently, until volume is reduced by half and mixture is almost the consistency of commercial ketchup, about 45 minutes.

6. Meanwhile, prepare canner, jars and lids. *(For more information, see page 415.)*

7. Ladle hot ketchup into hot jars, leaving ½ inch (1 cm) headspace. Remove air bubbles and adjust headspace, if necessary, by adding hot ketchup. Wipe rim. Center lid on jar. Screw band down until resistance is met, then increase to fingertip-tight.

8. Place jars in canner, ensuring they are completely covered with water. Bring to a boil and process for 15 minutes. Remove canner lid. Wait 5 minutes, then remove jars, cool and store. *(For more information, see pages 417–418.)*

Fruit Ketchup

A delicious blend of tomatoes and fruit gives this ketchup a unique taste. Use it as you would any regular ketchup, but expect to taste fruity undertones. Kids will love this ketchup for dipping their chicken tenders.

TIPS

To peel tomatoes and peaches, place them in boiling water for 30 to 60 seconds or until the skins start to crack. Immediately dip in cold water. The skins will slip off easily.

If you have leftover liquid and pulp after it has been put through the sieve, cover and refrigerate for another purpose. It makes a nice addition to tomato-based soups or prepared spaghetti sauce. If you didn't get quite enough yield, add enough tomato juice to make the 5 cups (1.25 L).

Makes about four 8-ounce (250 mL) jars

4 cups	chopped cored peeled tomatoes (see tip, at left)	1 L
4 cups	chopped pitted peeled peaches (see tip, at left)	1 L
2 cups	chopped cored peeled apples	500 mL
1 cup	finely chopped onion	250 mL
3	cloves garlic, finely chopped	3
1 cup	liquid honey	250 mL
1/2 cup	white vinegar	125 mL
2 tsp	dry mustard	10 mL
1 tsp	salt	5 mL
1 tsp	freshly ground black pepper	5 mL
1 tsp	ground cloves	5 mL
1/2 tsp	ground allspice	2 mL
1/4 tsp	cayenne pepper	1 mL

1. In a large stainless steel saucepan, combine tomatoes, peaches and apples. Over low heat, using a large spoon or potato masher, mash the fruit until juices flow. Add onion and garlic. Increase heat to medium-high and bring to a boil, stirring frequently. Reduce heat, cover and boil gently until fruit is heated through and onions are transparent, about 10 minutes.

2. Working in batches, transfer mixture to a sieve placed over a glass or stainless steel bowl and press with the back of a spoon to extract all the liquid and pulp. (You can also do this in a food mill.) Measure out 5 cups (1.25 mL) (see tip, at left). Discard solids.

3. Return liquid and pulp to saucepan. Add honey, vinegar, mustard, salt, black pepper, cloves, allspice and cayenne. Bring to a boil over high heat, stirring occasionally. Reduce heat and boil gently, stirring occasionally, until mixture is almost the consistency of commercial ketchup, about 45 minutes.

4. Meanwhile, prepare canner, jars and lids. *(For more information, see page 415.)*

5. Ladle hot ketchup into hot jars, leaving 1/2 inch (1 cm) headspace. Remove air bubbles and adjust headspace, if necessary, by adding hot ketchup. Wipe rim. Center lid on jar. Screw band down until resistance is met, then increase to fingertip-tight.

6. Place jars in canner, ensuring they are completely covered with water. Bring to a boil and process for 15 minutes. Remove canner lid. Wait 5 minutes, then remove jars, cool and store. *(For more information, see pages 417–418.)*

Cranberry Ketchup

Cranberries yield a uniquely delicious sweet and tangy condiment that tastes remarkably similar to a popular British steak sauce. It goes particularly well with meat pies and egg dishes.

TIPS

Refer to the Produce Purchase Guide on pages 426–429 to determine how much produce you'll need to buy to prepare this recipe.

A clear plastic ruler (kept solely for kitchen use) will help you determine the correct headspace. Each filled jar should be measured accurately, as the headspace can affect sealing and the preservation of the contents.

Makes about eight 8-ounce (250 mL) jars

11 cups	cranberries (fresh or frozen)	2.75 L
2 cups	chopped onions	500 mL
5	cloves garlic, finely chopped	5
1½ cups	water	375 mL
3 cups	lightly packed brown sugar	750 mL
1 cup	vinegar	250 mL
2 tsp	dry mustard	10 mL
1 tsp	ground cloves	5 mL
1 tsp	salt	5 mL
1 tsp	freshly ground black pepper	5 mL
½ tsp	ground allspice	2 mL
½ tsp	cayenne pepper	2 mL

1. In a large stainless steel saucepan, combine cranberries, onions, garlic and water. Bring to a boil over high heat, stirring constantly. Reduce heat and boil gently for 6 to 10 minutes, until cranberries pop and become soft.

2. Working in batches, transfer mixture to a blender or food processor fitted with a metal blade and purée until smooth.

3. Return mixture to saucepan. Add brown sugar, vinegar, mustard, cloves, salt, black pepper, allspice and cayenne. Bring to boil over medium-high heat, stirring frequently. Reduce heat and boil gently, stirring frequently, until mixture is almost the consistency of commercial ketchup, about 30 minutes.

4. Meanwhile, prepare canner, jars and lids. *(For more information, see page 415.)*

5. Ladle hot ketchup into hot jars, leaving ½ inch (1 cm) headspace. Remove air bubbles and adjust headspace, if necessary, by adding hot ketchup. Wipe rim. Center lid on jar. Screw band down until resistance is met, then increase to fingertip-tight.

6. Place jars in canner, ensuring they are completely covered with water. Bring to a boil and process for 15 minutes. Remove canner lid. Wait 5 minutes, then remove jars, cool and store. *(For more information, see pages 417–418.)*

Red Hot Sauce

Serve this zesty sauce as a condiment, use it to baste barbecued meats during the final 15 minutes of cooking or add it to any recipe that requires a sweet, tangy accent.

TIPS

You can buy prepared pickling spice at well-stocked supermarkets or make your own (see page 217).

The best way to seed peppers is to trim off the stem end and then cut the pepper in half lengthwise. Scrape out the seeds and veins, using a spoon. Remember, when cutting or seeding hot peppers, wear rubber gloves to keep your hands from being burned.

Before using jars, inspect them carefully for any chips, cracks or fractures. Discard any imperfect jars.

Makes about four 8-ounce (250 mL) jars

2 tbsp	pickling spice (see tip, at left)	30 mL
8 cups	chopped cored peeled tomatoes	2 L
4 cups	white vinegar, divided	1 L
1½ cups	chopped seeded chili peppers, such as jalapeño, serrano, cayenne or Fresno (see tip, at left)	375 mL
1 cup	granulated sugar	250 mL
1 tbsp	pickling or canning salt	15 mL

1. Tie pickling spice in a square of cheesecloth, creating a spice bag. Set aside.

2. In a large stainless steel saucepan, combine tomatoes, 2 cups (500 mL) of the vinegar and chili peppers. Bring to a boil over medium-high heat, stirring constantly. Reduce heat and boil gently until vegetables are soft, about 15 minutes.

3. Working in batches, transfer mixture to a blender or a food processor fitted with a metal blade and purée until smooth.

4. Return mixture to saucepan. Add sugar, pickling salt and reserved spice bag. Return to a boil over medium-high heat, stirring frequently, until mixture begins to thicken. Add remaining 2 cups (500 mL) vinegar and boil gently, stirring frequently, until mixture is almost the consistency of commercial ketchup, about 45 minutes. Discard spice bag.

5. Meanwhile, prepare canner, jars and lids. *(For more information, see page 415.)*

6. Ladle hot sauce into hot jars, leaving ½ inch (1 cm) headspace. Remove air bubbles and adjust headspace, if necessary, by adding hot sauce. Wipe rim. Center lid on jar. Screw band down until resistance is met, then increase to fingertip-tight.

7. Place jars in canner, ensuring they are completely covered with water. Bring to a boil and process for 15 minutes. Remove canner lid. Wait 5 minutes, then remove jars, cool and store. *(For more information, see pages 417–418.)*

Brush-On Sauces

These sauces, which tend to be thicker in than most other sauces, are usually brushed onto food when barbecuing. They liven up the flavor of all kinds of food, from ribs, wings and kabobs to vegetables and seafood. The sauces in this section have a wide variety of flavor undertones, but all are finger-lickin' good.

· ·

Victorian Barbecue Sauce

Victorian cooks roasted their meat in huge kitchen fireplaces and enhanced it with homemade sauces concocted from garden staples such as rhubarb. Today's barbecue chefs can add the same fruity complements to grilled foods as they cook.

TIP

A jar lifter is very helpful for handling hot, wet jars. Because they are bulky and fit loosely, oven mitts — even water-resistent types — are not a wise choice. When filling jars, an all-purpose rubber glove, worn on your helper hand, will allow you to steady the jar.

Makes about four pint (500 mL) jars

8 cups	chopped rhubarb	2 L
3½ cups	lightly packed brown sugar	875 mL
1½ cups	chopped raisins	375 mL
½ cup	chopped onion	125 mL
½ cup	white vinegar	125 mL
1 tsp	ground allspice	5 mL
1 tsp	ground cinnamon	5 mL
1 tsp	ground ginger	5 mL
1 tsp	salt	5 mL

1. Prepare canner, jars and lids. *(For more information, see page 415.)*
2. In a large stainless steel saucepan, combine rhubarb, brown sugar, raisins, onion, vinegar, allspice, cinnamon, ginger and salt. Bring to a boil over high heat, stirring frequently. Reduce heat and boil gently, stirring frequently, until mixture is thickened to the consistency of a thin commercial barbecue sauce, about 30 minutes.
3. Ladle hot sauce into hot jars, leaving ½ inch (1 cm) headspace. Remove air bubbles and adjust headspace, if necessary, by adding hot sauce. Wipe rim. Center lid on jar. Screw band down until resistance is met, then increase to fingertip-tight.
4. Place jars in canner, ensuring they are completely covered with water. Bring to a boil and process for 15 minutes. Remove canner lid. Wait 5 minutes, then remove jars, cool and store. *(For more information, see pages 417–418.)*

Barbecue Sauce

Homemade barbecue sauce wins full marks for its rich tomato flavor. Use it to enhance the flavor of summer's grilled meats and add rays of sunshine to winter recipes.

TIPS

To peel tomatoes, place them in a pot of boiling water for 30 to 60 seconds or until the skins start to crack. Immediately dip in hot water. The skins will slip off easily.

If you don't have ground mace, you can substitute an equal quantity of ground nutmeg.

Refer to the Produce Purchase Guide on pages 426–429 to determine how much produce you'll need to buy to prepare this recipe.

Makes about three pint (500 mL) jars

20 cups	chopped cored peeled tomatoes (see tip, at left)	5 L
2 cups	finely chopped onions	500 mL
3	cloves garlic, finely chopped	3
I tbsp	hot pepper flakes	15 mL
I tbsp	celery seeds	15 mL
I ½ cups	lightly packed brown sugar	375 mL
I cup	white vinegar	250 mL
⅓ cup	lemon juice	75 mL
2 tbsp	salt	30 mL
I ½ tbsp	ground mace (see tip, at left)	22 mL
I tbsp	dry mustard	15 mL
I tsp	ground ginger	5 mL
I tsp	ground cinnamon	5 mL

1. In a large stainless steel saucepan, combine tomatoes, onions, garlic, hot pepper flakes and celery seeds. Bring to a boil over high heat, stirring constantly. Reduce heat, cover and boil gently until vegetables soften, about 30 minutes.

2. Working in batches, press mixture through a large-hole sieve or food mill or coarsely purée in a food processor. Discard any seeds that remain.

3. Return mixture to saucepan and boil, stirring occasionally, until cooked down by one-quarter. Add brown sugar, vinegar, lemon juice, salt, mace, mustard, ginger and cinnamon. Return to a boil over medium-high heat, stirring occasionally. Reduce heat and boil gently, stirring frequently, until mixture is thickened to the consistency of a thin commercial barbecue sauce, about 30 minutes.

4. Meanwhile, prepare canner, jars and lids. *(For more information, see page 415.)*

5. Ladle hot sauce into hot jars, leaving ½ inch (1 cm) headspace. Remove air bubbles and adjust headspace, if necessary, by adding hot sauce. Wipe rim. Center lid on jar. Screw band down until resistance is met, then increase to fingertip-tight.

6. Place jars in canner, ensuring they are completely covered with water. Bring to a boil and process for 20 minutes. Remove canner lid. Wait 5 minutes, then remove jars, cool and store. *(For more information, see pages 417–418.)*

Sombrero Barbecue Sauce

This jalapeño-spiked sauce is so good you'll want to buy a bushel of tomatoes when they are at their peak just to make it.

TIPS

Instead of peeling and chopping tomatoes by hand, you can put them through a food mill. Using this method, you will need about 16 cups (4 L) of tomato purée.

The best way to seed peppers is to trim off the stem end and then cut the pepper in half lengthwise. Scrape out the seeds and veins, using a spoon. Remember, when cutting or seeding hot peppers, wear rubber gloves to keep your hands from being burned.

Cheesecloth can be found at many retailers, such as grocery stores and other stores that carry kitchen supplies. Look in the area where kitchen utensils are located.

Makes about five pint (500 mL) jars

20 cups	chopped cored peeled tomatoes (see tip, at left)	5 L
2 cups	chopped celery	500 mL
2 cups	chopped onions	500 mL
1½ cups	chopped seeded green bell peppers	375 mL
2	jalapeño peppers, seeded and chopped	2
1 tsp	whole black peppercorns	5 mL
2½ cups	white vinegar	625 mL
1½ cups	lightly packed brown sugar	375 mL
2	cloves garlic, finely chopped	2
1 tbsp	dry mustard	15 mL
1 tbsp	paprika	15 mL
2 tsp	hot pepper sauce	10 mL
1½ tsp	salt	7 mL

1. In a large stainless steel saucepan, combine tomatoes, celery, onions, green peppers and jalapeño peppers. Bring to a boil over high heat, stirring frequently. Reduce heat, cover and boil gently until vegetables soften, about 30 minutes.

2. Working in batches, transfer mixture to a blender or food processor fitted with a metal blade and purée until smooth.

3. Return mixture to saucepan. Bring to a boil over medium-high heat, stirring occasionally. Reduce heat and boil gently, stirring frequently, until mixture is reduced by half, about 45 minutes.

4. Meanwhile, tie peppercorns in a square of cheesecloth, creating a spice bag.

5. Add vinegar, brown sugar, garlic, mustard, paprika, hot pepper sauce, salt and spice bag to tomato mixture. Increase heat to medium and boil gently, stirring frequently, until mixture is thickened to the consistency of a thin commercial barbecue sauce, about 1 hour. Discard spice bag.

6. Meanwhile, prepare canner, jars and lids. *(For more information, see page 415.)*

7. Ladle hot sauce into hot jars, leaving ½ inch (1 cm) headspace. Remove air bubbles and adjust headspace, if necessary, by adding hot sauce. Wipe rim. Center lid on jar. Screw band down until resistance is met, then increase to fingertip-tight.

8. Place jars in canner, ensuring they are completely covered with water. Bring to a boil and process for 35 minutes. Remove canner lid. Wait 5 minutes, then remove jars, cool and store. *(For more information, see pages 417–418.)*

Two-in-One Barbecue Sauce

The beauty of this recipe is that it allows you to create two different sauces from the same basic ingredients. The Stampede-Style Sauce is robust, perfect for red meats, while the Sweet 'n' Sour Sauce is a seductively flavored coating that works well with chicken and fish. Use either on grilled vegetables. If you prefer, you can double the ingredients of one variety and make six jars of that.

TIPS

To seed tomatoes, cut them in half and squeeze out seeds or scoop them out with a spoon or your fingers.

To purée tomatoes, either press them through a food mill or purée them in a blender or food processor after they have been peeled and seeded. Use a food processor to purée the green pepper and onion.

Makes about six pint (500 mL) jars

16 cups	puréed seeded peeled plum tomatoes (see tips, at left)	4 L
2¼ cups	puréed seeded green bell peppers (see tip, at left)	550 mL
2 cups	puréed onions (see tip, at left)	500 mL
3	cloves garlic, finely chopped	3
2 tbsp	mustard seeds, crushed	30 mL
1 tbsp	celery seeds	15 mL
2	dried chili peppers, seeded and crushed	2

Stampede-Style Sauce

¾ cup	mild-flavored or fancy molasses (see tip, page 246)	175 mL
¾ cup	malt vinegar	175 mL
⅓ cup	Worcestershire sauce	75 mL
2 tbsp	chili powder	30 mL
2 tsp	freshly ground black pepper	10 mL

Sweet 'n' Sour Sauce

1 tbsp	finely chopped gingerroot	15 mL
¾ cup	liquid honey	175 mL
¾ cup	cider vinegar	175 mL
½ cup	soy sauce	125 mL
2 cups	canned crushed pineapple, with juice	500 mL

1. To a large stainless steel saucepan, add half of the tomato purée. Over high heat, stirring frequently, bring to a full rolling boil. While maintaining the boil, gradually add remaining purée. Cook over high heat, stirring frequently, until reduced by half, about 1 hour. Add puréed green peppers and onions, garlic, mustard seeds, celery seeds and chili peppers. Return to a boil over high heat. Reduce heat to medium and boil gently, stirring frequently, until peppers and onions are tender, about 10 minutes.

2. Divide mixture equally between two stainless steel saucepans. Add ingredients for Stampede-Style Sauce to one pan; ingredients for Sweet 'n' Sour Sauce to the other. Bring both mixtures to a boil over high heat, stirring frequently. Reduce heat and boil gently, stirring frequently, until mixtures are thickened to the consistency of a thin commercial barbecue sauce, about 45 minutes.

3. Meanwhile, prepare canner, jars and lids. *(For more information, see page 415.)*

4. Ladle hot sauces into hot jars, leaving $\frac{1}{2}$ inch (1 cm) headspace. Remove air bubbles and adjust headspace, if necessary, by adding hot sauce. Wipe rim. Center lid on jar. Screw band down until resistance is met, then increase to fingertip-tight.

5. Place jars in canner, ensuring they are completely covered with water. Bring to a boil and process for 20 minutes. Remove canner lid. Wait 5 minutes, then remove jars, cool and store. *(For more information, see pages 417–418.)*

Zesty Peach Barbecue Sauce

Golden orange with red flecks, this barbecue sauce not only looks amazing, but tastes out of this world. Spoon some over your chicken or fish this summer!

TIP

To peel peaches, drop them in a pot of boiling water for 30 seconds. Immediately rinse under cold running water. The skins should lift off easily. You can chop the peaches by hand or, if you prefer, in a food processor.

Makes about eight 8-ounce (250 mL) jars

6 cups	finely chopped pitted peeled peaches (see tip, at left)	1.5 L
1 cup	finely chopped seeded red bell pepper	250 mL
1 cup	finely chopped onion	250 mL
3 tbsp	finely chopped garlic	45 mL
1¼ cups	liquid honey	300 mL
¾ cup	cider vinegar	175 mL
1 tbsp	Worcestershire sauce	15 mL
2 tsp	hot pepper flakes	10 mL
2 tsp	dry mustard	10 mL
2 tsp	salt	10 mL

1. Prepare canner, jars and lids. *(For more information, see page 415.)*

2. In a large stainless steel saucepan, combine peaches, red pepper, onion, garlic, honey, vinegar, Worcestershire sauce, hot pepper flakes, mustard and salt. Bring to a boil over medium-high heat. Reduce heat and boil gently, stirring frequently, until mixture is thickened to the consistency of a thin commercial barbecue sauce, about 25 minutes.

3. Ladle hot sauce into hot jars, leaving $\frac{1}{2}$ inch (1 cm) headspace. Remove air bubbles and adjust headspace, if necessary, by adding hot sauce. Wipe rim. Center lid on jar. Screw band down until resistance is met, then increase to fingertip-tight.

4. Place jars in canner, ensuring they are completely covered with water. Bring to a boil and process for 15 minutes. Remove canner lid. Wait 5 minutes, then remove jars, cool and store. *(For more information, see pages 417–418.)*

Chili Sauces

Chili sauce has long been a home-preserved favorite, often prepared annually from recipes handed down from generation to generation. This tasty condiment can range from mild to spicy in flavor and smooth to chunky in texture. The growing popularity of palate-searing foods has prompted a renewed interest in this time-honored treat.

Traditionally, chili sauce is served with hot dogs, meatloaf or grilled meats and seafood, and is made with juicy red tomatoes, onions, peppers, vinegar and a variety of spices and herbs, but contemporary cooks have been experimenting with the ingredients and uses for this versatile condiment. This section contains recipes for making chili sauce from unconventional ingredients such as green tomatoes, apples, peaches and even raisins. Given all these options, chili sauce is well on its way to becoming a multi-use condiment.

Chili Sauce

This sweet and spicy blend of tomato, peppers and spices can be used as an accompaniment to grilled meats. It's also delicious with tourtière, a meat pie traditionally served during the Christmas season in Quebec that has been gaining popularity elsewhere.

Makes about seven 8-ounce (250 mL) jars

I	cinnamon stick (about 4 inches/10 cm), broken in half	I
I	bay leaf	I
2 tsp	mustard seeds	10 mL
I tsp	celery seeds	5 mL
½ tsp	whole cloves	2 mL
½ tsp	whole black peppercorns	2 mL
12 cups	chopped cored peeled tomatoes	3 L
2 cups	chopped onions	500 mL
2 cups	chopped seeded green bell peppers	500 mL
I ½ cups	white vinegar	375 mL
I ½ cups	granulated sugar	375 mL
I cup	chopped seeded red bell pepper	250 mL
2 tbsp	chopped seeded jalapeño pepper	30 mL
I tsp	salt	5 mL
2	cloves garlic, finely chopped	2
½ tsp	ground ginger	2 mL
½ tsp	ground nutmeg	2 mL

· ·

TIPS

The best way to seed peppers is to trim off the stem end and then cut the pepper in half lengthwise. Scrape out the seeds and veins, using a spoon. Remember, when cutting or seeding hot peppers, wear rubber gloves to keep your hands from being burned.

To speed up the cooking time, after measuring the chopped tomatoes place them in a colander for 15 minutes and drain off excess liquid. The mixture will thicken in about 90 minutes.

1. Tie cinnamon stick, bay leaf, mustard seeds, celery seeds, cloves and peppercorns in a square of cheesecloth, creating a spice bag.

2. In a large stainless steel saucepan, combine tomatoes, onions, green peppers, vinegar, sugar, red pepper, jalapeño pepper, salt and spice bag. Bring to a boil over high heat, stirring frequently. Reduce heat and boil gently, stirring occasionally, until mixture is reduced by almost half, about 2 hours. Stir in garlic, ginger and nutmeg; boil gently, stirring frequently, until mixture mounds on a spoon, about 15 minutes. Discard spice bag.

3. Meanwhile, prepare canner, jars and lids. *(For more information, see page 415.)*

4. Ladle hot sauce into hot jars, leaving ½ inch (1 cm) headspace. Remove air bubbles and adjust headspace, if necessary, by adding hot sauce. Wipe rim. Center lid on jar. Screw band down until resistance is met, then increase to fingertip-tight.

5. Place jars in canner, ensuring they are completely covered with water. Bring to a boil and process for 15 minutes. Remove canner lid. Wait 5 minutes, then remove jars, cool and store. *(For more information, see pages 417–418.)*

Green Chili Sauce

This tasty chili sauce made with green tomatoes is a great sidekick for hot dogs.

TIPS

You can buy prepared pickling spice at well-stocked supermarkets or make your own (see page 217).

The best way to seed peppers is to trim off the stem end and then cut the pepper in half lengthwise. Scrape out the seeds and veins, using a spoon. Remember, when cutting or seeding hot peppers, wear rubber gloves to keep your hands from being burned.

A clear plastic ruler (kept solely for kitchen use) will help you determine the correct headspace. Each filled jar should be measured accurately, as the headspace can affect sealing and the preservation of the contents.

Makes about nine pint (500 mL) jars

2 tbsp	pickling spice (see tip, at left)	30 mL
18 cups	chopped cored peeled green tomatoes	4.5 L
3	onions, chopped	3
3	large stalks celery, chopped	3
1	green bell pepper, seeded and chopped	1
1	red bell pepper, seeded and chopped	1
1	red chili pepper, such as cayenne, seeded and finely chopped	1
3 cups	white vinegar	750 mL
2½ cups	lightly packed brown sugar	625 mL
2 tbsp	salt	30 mL

1. Tie pickling spice in a square of cheesecloth, creating a spice bag.
2. In a large stainless steel saucepan, combine green tomatoes, onions, celery, green and red bell peppers, chili pepper, vinegar, brown sugar, salt and spice bag. Bring to a boil over high heat, stirring frequently. Reduce heat and boil gently, stirring occasionally, until thickened and sauce begins to mound on a spoon, about 3 hours. Discard spice bag.
3. Meanwhile, prepare canner, jars and lids. *(For more information, see page 415.)*
4. Ladle hot sauce into hot jars, leaving ½ inch (1 cm) headspace. Remove air bubbles and adjust headspace, if necessary, by adding hot sauce. Wipe rim. Center lid on jar. Screw band down until resistance is met, then increase to fingertip-tight.
5. Place jars in canner, ensuring they are completely covered with water. Bring to a boil and process for 20 minutes. Remove canner lid. Wait 5 minutes, then remove jars, cool and store. *(For more information, see pages 417–418.)*

Grandma's Chili Sauce

Just like Grandma used to make! Try this classic chili sauce as a garnish to any dish.

TIPS

You can use either round globe or Italian plum tomatoes. Plum tomatoes are meatier and will cook down faster.

If you don't have ground mace, you can substitute an equal quantity of ground nutmeg.

The best way to seed peppers is to trim off the stem end and then cut the pepper in half lengthwise. Scrape out the seeds and veins, using a spoon.

Makes about seven pint (500 mL) jars

16 cups	chopped cored peeled tomatoes (see tip, at left)	4 L
6	onions, chopped	6
6	green bell peppers, seeded and chopped	6
2	red bell peppers, seeded and chopped	2
2 cups	white vinegar	500 mL
1 cup	lightly packed brown sugar	250 mL
1	clove garlic, finely chopped	1
1 tbsp	freshly grated or drained bottled horseradish (optional)	15 mL
1 tbsp	celery salt	15 mL
1 tbsp	mustard seeds	15 mL
1 tbsp	salt	15 mL
1 tsp	ground allspice	5 mL
1 tsp	ground mace (see tip, at left)	5 mL
1 tsp	ground cinnamon	5 mL
1/4 tsp	ground cloves	1 mL

1. In a large stainless steel saucepan, combine tomatoes, onions, green and red peppers, vinegar, brown sugar, garlic, horseradish, if using, celery salt, mustard seeds and salt. Bring to a boil over high heat, stirring frequently. Reduce heat and boil gently, stirring occasionally, for $1\frac{1}{2}$ hours, until sauce begins to thicken. Add allspice, mace, cinnamon and cloves. Continue to boil gently, stirring occasionally, until thickened and sauce begins to mound on a spoon, about 30 minutes.

2. Meanwhile, prepare canner, jars and lids. *(For more information, see page 415.)*

3. Ladle hot sauce into hot jars, leaving $\frac{1}{2}$ inch (1 cm) headspace. Remove air bubbles and adjust headspace, if necessary, by adding hot sauce. Wipe rim. Center lid on jar. Screw band down until resistance is met, then increase to fingertip-tight.

4. Place jars in canner, ensuring they are completely covered with water. Bring to a boil and process for 20 minutes. Remove canner lid. Wait 5 minutes, then remove jars, cool and store. *(For more information, see pages 417–418.)*

Hot 'n' Sweet Chili Sauce

This sweet and spicy chili sauce adds a delightful zing to barbecued chicken or pork.

TIPS

You can buy prepared pickling spice at well-stocked supermarkets or make your own (see page 217).

We've suggested a range in the quantity of chili peppers in this recipe so you can vary the sauce to suit your taste. If you like a zesty sauce with lots of heat, use 8 chilies. If you prefer a balance between sweetness and heat, use 6 chilies.

The best way to seed peppers is to trim off the stem end and then cut the pepper in half lengthwise. Scrape out the seeds and veins, using a spoon. Remember, when cutting or seeding hot peppers, wear rubber gloves to keep your hands from being burned.

Makes about four pint (500 mL) jars

¼ cup	pickling spice (see tip, at left)	50 mL
6 cups	chopped cored peeled plum tomatoes	1.5 L
2	small peaches, peeled, pitted and chopped	2
1	apple, peeled, cored and chopped	1
1	pear, peeled, cored and chopped	1
1	onion, chopped	1
1	red bell pepper, seeded and chopped	1
6 to 8	chili peppers, such as jalapeño, serrano, cayenne or Fresno, seeded and finely chopped	6 to 8
1½ cups	white vinegar	375 mL
1½ cups	granulated sugar	375 mL
½ cup	sultana raisins	125 mL
4 tsp	salt	20 mL

1. Tie pickling spice in a large square of cheesecloth, creating a spice bag.

2. In a large stainless steel saucepan, combine tomatoes, peaches, apple, pear, onion, red pepper, hot peppers, vinegar, sugar, raisins, salt and spice bag. Bring to a boil over high heat, stirring frequently. Reduce heat and boil gently, stirring occasionally, until thick enough to mound on a spoon, about 1½ hours. Discard spice bag.

3. Meanwhile, prepare canner, jars and lids. *(For more information, see page 415.)*

4. Ladle hot sauce into hot jars, leaving ½ inch (1 cm) headspace. Remove air bubbles and adjust headspace, if necessary, by adding hot sauce. Wipe rim. Center lid on jar. Screw band down until resistance is met, then increase to fingertip-tight.

5. Place jars in canner, ensuring they are completely covered with water. Bring to a boil and process for 20 minutes. Remove canner lid. Wait 5 minutes, then remove jars, cool and store. *(For more information, see pages 417–418.)*

Singapore Chili Sauce

This chili sauce could be described as an Asian version of Tabasco sauce. Although it makes a nice accompaniment to cold roast chicken or beef and is great on hot dogs, this sauce is particularly delicious with Asian dishes such as noodles. But use it sparingly: it is very hot.

TIPS

For this recipe, you'll need about 1 lb (500 g) of chili peppers.

If you prefer a milder sauce, devein and seed the peppers.

If you like an incendiary sauce, substitute red Thai peppers for the varieties listed in the recipe. When using Thai peppers, do not devein or seed them, as this would be very labor-intensive. Just remove the stem end and chop as usual.

Remember, when cutting or seeding hot peppers, wear rubber gloves to keep your hands from being burned.

Makes about twelve 4-ounce (125 mL) jars or six 8-ounce (250 mL) jars

2½ cups	white vinegar	625 mL
2½ cups	granulated sugar	625 mL
4 cups	chopped hot red chili peppers, such as Holland (Dutch), Fresno or jalapeño (see tip, at left)	1 L
1½ cups	sultana raisins, rinsed	375 mL
¼ cup	chopped garlic	50 mL
1 tbsp	grated gingerroot	15 mL
2 tsp	salt	10 mL

1. Prepare canner, jars and lids. *(For more information, see page 415.)*

2. In a large stainless steel saucepan, combine vinegar and sugar. Bring to a boil over high heat, stirring to dissolve sugar. Reduce heat and boil gently for 3 minutes. Add chili peppers, raisins, garlic, gingerroot and salt. Increase heat to high and bring to a boil. Reduce heat and boil gently until vegetables are heated through, about 5 minutes.

3. Ladle hot sauce into hot jars, leaving ½ inch (1 cm) headspace. Remove air bubbles and adjust headspace, if necessary, by adding hot sauce. Wipe rim. Center lid on jar. Screw band down until resistance is met, then increase to fingertip-tight.

4. Place jars in canner, ensuring they are completely covered with water. Bring to a boil and process for 10 minutes. Remove canner lid. Wait 5 minutes, then remove jars, cool and store. *(For more information, see pages 417–418.)*

Mustards

Mustard goes hand in hand with ketchup as a condiment for backyard favorites such as hamburgers and hot dogs. Although yellow "ballpark" mustard is still a household staple, over the years mustards infused with different flavors, such as herbs and spices — and even beer — have become popular. Making these more flavorful mustards at home is easy to do and economical, because such specialty items usually come with hefty price tags.

    When making mustards, be sure to blend the mustard seeds and other ingredients until a slightly grainy texture remains. Homemade mustard will have the consistency of a thin store-bought mustard. Do not cook until overly thickened, as this will prevent adequate heat penetration during processing.

....

Lemon-Sage Wine Mustard

Subtle lemon and sage accents enhance the flavor of this mild mustard. Stir it into vegetable salads or serve it with grilled vegetables and meats.

TIP

When picking herbs from the garden to use in preserves, pick them early in the morning, before they are warmed by the sun, for the most vibrant, fresh flavor.

Makes about five 4-ounce (125 mL) jars

I	bunch fresh sage	I
¾ cup	dry white wine	175 mL
¾ cup	yellow mustard seeds	175 mL
I cup	white wine vinegar	250 mL
	Grated zest and juice of 2 large lemons	
½ cup	liquid honey	125 mL
¼ tsp	salt	I mL

1. Finely chop enough sage leaves to measure ⅓ cup (75 mL) and set aside.

2. Coarsely chop remaining sage leaves and stems to measure ½ cup (125 mL) and place in a small stainless steel saucepan with white wine. Bring to a boil over medium heat, stirring and pressing sage to release flavor. Remove from heat. Cover tightly and let steep for 5 minutes.

3. Transfer sage infusion to a sieve placed over a glass or stainless steel bowl and press leaves with the back of a spoon to extract all the liquid. Discard solids and return liquid to saucepan. Add mustard seeds. Cover and let stand at room temperature until seeds have absorbed most of the moisture, about 2 hours.

4. Prepare canner, jars and lids. *(For more information, see page 415.)*

TIP

Read a recipe all the way through, even before you go shopping for the ingredients. It's very important to have all of the ingredients and equipment ready before you start making preserves.

5. In a blender or food processor fitted with a metal blade, combine marinated mustard seeds (with liquid) and vinegar. Process until blended and most seeds are well chopped. (You want to retain a slightly grainy texture.)

6. Transfer mixture to a stainless steel saucepan and add lemon zest, lemon juice, honey, salt and reserved finely chopped sage. Bring to a boil over high heat, stirring constantly. Reduce heat to low and boil gently, stirring frequently, until volume is reduced by a third, about 20 minutes.

7. Ladle hot mustard into hot jars, leaving ¼ inch (0.5 cm) headspace. Remove air bubbles and adjust headspace, if necessary, by adding hot mustard. Wipe rim. Center lid on jar. Screw band down until resistance is met, then increase to fingertip-tight.

8. Place jars in canner, ensuring they are completely covered with water. Bring to a boil and process for 10 minutes. Remove canner lid. Wait 5 minutes, then remove jars, cool and store. (*For more information, see pages 417–418.*)

Ginger-Garlic Mustard

Brown mustard seeds add extra pungency to this yellow mustard with Asian overtones.

TIPS

A jar lifter is very helpful for handling hot, wet jars. Because they are bulky and fit loosely, oven mitts — even water-resistent types — are not a wise choice. When filling jars, an all-purpose rubber glove, worn on your helper hand, will allow you to steady the jar.

Place a clean towel on your work surface to absorb water from the hot jars as you take them out of the boiling-water canner to be filled, and again once the jars are processed. The towel prevents hot jars from coming into contact with cooler countertops. Significant temperature differences can cause jar breakage.

Makes about five 4-ounce (125 mL) jars

1½ cups	water	375 mL
½ cup	coarsely grated peeled gingerroot	125 mL
2 tbsp	chopped garlic	30 mL
1 tsp	cracked black peppercorns	5 mL
½ cup	yellow mustard seeds	125 mL
¼ cup	brown mustard seeds	50 mL
1 cup	cider vinegar	250 mL
1 tbsp	soy sauce	15 mL
⅓ cup	dry mustard	75 mL
¼ cup	granulated sugar	50 mL

1. In a medium stainless steel saucepan, combine water, gingerroot, garlic and peppercorns. Bring to a boil over medium-high heat. Reduce heat to low and boil gently for 5 minutes.

2. Transfer mixture to a sieve placed over a glass or stainless steel bowl and press with the back of a spoon to extract all the liquid. Discard residue and return liquid to saucepan. Add yellow and brown mustard seeds. Cover and let stand at room temperature until seeds have absorbed most of the moisture, about 2 hours.

3. Prepare canner, jars and lids. *(For more information, see page 415.)*

4. In a blender or a food processor fitted with a metal blade, combine marinated mustard seeds with liquid, vinegar and soy sauce. Process on medium speed until blended and most seeds are well chopped. (You want to retain a slightly grainy texture.)

5. Transfer mixture to a stainless steel saucepan and whisk in dry mustard and sugar. Bring to a boil over medium heat, stirring constantly. Reduce heat to low and boil gently, stirring frequently, until volume is reduced by a third, about 15 minutes.

6. Ladle hot mustard into hot jars, leaving ¼ inch (0.5 cm) headspace. Remove air bubbles and adjust headspace, if necessary, by adding more hot mustard. Wipe rim. Center lid on jar. Screw band down until resistance is met, then increase to fingertip-tight.

7. Place jars in canner, ensuring they are completely covered with water. Bring to a boil and process for 10 minutes. Remove canner lid. Wait 5 minutes, then remove jars, cool and store. *(For more information, see pages 417–418.)*

Cranberry Mustard

This fruity mustard is particularly delicious with ham and adds color and interest to meat and fish entrées.

TIPS

A clear plastic ruler (kept solely for kitchen use) will help you determine the correct headspace. Each filled jar should be measured accurately, as the headspace can affect sealing and the preservation of the contents.

If you have particularly hard water and use it in the boiling-water canner, it can leave a residue on jars. Use filtered or reverse-osmosis water to fill your canner instead.

Makes about seven 4-ounce (125 mL) jars

1 cup	red wine vinegar	250 mL
⅔ cup	yellow mustard seeds	150 mL
1 cup	water	250 mL
1 tbsp	Worcestershire sauce	15 mL
2¾ cups	cranberries (fresh or frozen)	675 mL
¾ cup	granulated sugar	175 mL
¼ cup	dry mustard	50 mL
2½ tsp	ground allspice	12 mL

1. In a medium stainless steel saucepan, bring vinegar to a boil over high heat. Remove from heat and add mustard seeds. Cover and let stand at room temperature until seeds have absorbed most of the moisture, about 1½ hours.

2. Prepare canner, jars and lids. *(For more information, see page 415.)*

3. In a blender or food processor fitted with a metal blade, combine marinated mustard seeds (with liquid), water and Worcestershire sauce. Process until blended and most seeds are well chopped. (You want to retain a slightly grainy texture.) Add cranberries and blend until chopped.

4. Transfer mixture to a stainless steel saucepan and bring to a boil over medium heat, stirring constantly. Reduce heat to medium-low and boil gently, stirring frequently, for 5 minutes. Whisk in sugar, dry mustard and allspice. Continue to boil gently over low heat, stirring frequently, until volume is reduced by a third, about 15 minutes.

5. Ladle hot mustard into hot jars, leaving ¼ inch (0.5 cm) headspace. Remove air bubbles and adjust headspace, if necessary, by adding more hot mustard. Wipe rim. Center lid on jar. Screw band down until resistance is met, then increase to fingertip-tight.

6. Place jars in canner, ensuring they are completely covered with water. Bring to a boil and process for 10 minutes. Remove canner lid. Wait 5 minutes, then remove jars, cool and store. *(For more information, see pages 417–418.)*

Oktoberfest Beer Mustard

Pair this tangy-sweet mustard with smoked meats, salami or well-marinated grilled meats. And, of course, bratwurst.

TIP

Any type of beer can be used to make this mustard. Use what you have on hand, or use your favorite specialty beer. Dark beers will produce a more robust flavor and color. The overall flavor of the beer will shine through, so be sure to choose a beer with a flavor you can appreciate.

Makes about five 4-ounce (125 mL) jars

1½ cups	beer (see tip, at left)	375 mL
1 cup	brown mustard seeds	250 mL
1 cup	water	250 mL
½ cup	malt vinegar	125 mL
½ cup	lightly packed brown sugar	125 mL
¼ cup	dry mustard	50 mL
1 tbsp	onion powder	15 mL

1. In a medium stainless steel saucepan, combine beer and brown mustard seeds. Bring to a boil over medium-high heat. Remove from heat, cover and let stand at room temperature until seeds have absorbed most of the moisture, about 2 hours.

2. Prepare canner, jars and lids. *(For more information, see page 415.)*

3. In a blender or a food processor fitted with a metal blade, purée marinated seeds and any remaining liquid until blended and most seeds are well chopped. (You want to retain a slightly grainy texture.)

4. Transfer mixture to a stainless steel saucepan and whisk in water, vinegar, brown sugar, dry mustard and onion powder. Bring to a boil over high heat, stirring constantly. Reduce heat to medium and boil gently, stirring frequently, until volume is reduced by a third, about 15 minutes.

5. Ladle hot mustard into hot jars, leaving ¼ inch (0.5 cm) headspace. Remove air bubbles and adjust headspace, if necessary, by adding hot mustard. Wipe rim. Center lid on jar. Screw band down until resistance is met, then increase to fingertip-tight.

6. Place jars in canner, ensuring they are completely covered with water. Bring to a boil and process for 10 minutes. Remove canner lid. Wait 5 minutes, then remove jars, cool and store. *(For more information, see pages 417–418.)*

Vinegars

Creating your own signature vinegars will provide you with a supply of unique flavor boosters at your fingertips, allowing you to save time and produce delicious meals every day of the week. These easy-to-make condiments also make versatile one-of-a-kind gifts. Preserve flavored vinegars in smaller 4- or 8-ounce (125 or 250 mL) jars and combine two or three to make a delightful gift pack.

Although flavored vinegar may be made with any vinegar, milder products such as wine, cider and rice vinegar allow the featured flavor to shine through. For homemade flavored vinegars, regular white vinegar produces a sharper-tasting product and requires the addition of very robust flavors.

Adding natural fruit and herb flavors to vinegar is a great way to mellow the tartness without adding a lot of calories. That means you don't need to use as much high-calorie oil when a making typical salad dressing.

Loganberry Vinegar

Loganberries, a cross between blackberries and raspberries, make a sweet complement to the tart red wine vinegar in this recipe. Loganberry Vinegar can be drizzled over fresh fruit salads for an added dimension of flavor. The acidity will also help prevent fruits from browning.

Makes about ten 4-ounce (125 mL) jars or five 8-ounce (250 mL) jars

4 cups	loganberries	1 L
4 cups	red wine vinegar, divided	1 L

1. In a large glass bowl, combine loganberries and 1 cup (250 mL) vinegar. Using a potato masher, lightly crush loganberries. Add remaining vinegar, stirring to combine. Cover tightly with plastic wrap and let stand in a dark, cool place (70 to 75°F/21 to 23°C) for 1 to 4 weeks, stirring every 2 to 3 days. Taste weekly until desired strength is achieved.

2. Prepare canner, jars and lids. *(For more information, see page 415.)*

3. Line a strainer with several layers of cheesecloth and place over a large stainless steel saucepan. Strain vinegar without squeezing cheesecloth. Discard cheesecloth and residue. Place saucepan over medium heat and heat vinegar to 180°F (82°C).

4. Ladle hot vinegar into hot jars, leaving ¼ inch (0.5 cm) headspace. Wipe rim. Center lid on jar. Screw band down until resistance is met, then increase to fingertip-tight.

5. Place jars in canner, ensuring they are completely covered with water. Bring to a boil and process for 10 minutes. Remove canner lid. Wait 5 minutes, then remove jars, cool and store. *(For more information, see pages 417–418.)*

Blueberry-Basil Vinegar

Use this robust vinegar to make a delicious salad dressing that is lower in calories and fat than store-bought versions (see box, below right).

TIPS

To crush basil leaves, place them in a mortar and, one layer at a time, crush with a pestle.

When picking herbs from the garden to use in preserves, pick them early in the morning, before they are warmed by the sun, for the most vibrant, fresh flavor.

Cheesecloth can be found at many retailers, such as grocery stores and other stores that carry kitchen supplies. Look in the area where kitchen utensils are located.

Makes about ten 4-ounce (125 mL) jars or five 8-ounce (250 mL) jars

4 cups	blueberries	I L
4 cups	white wine vinegar, divided	I L
I cup	loosely packed basil leaves, crushed (see tip, at left)	250 mL
	Grated zest of I lemon	

1. In a large glass bowl, combine blueberries and 1 cup (250 mL) of the vinegar. Using a potato masher, lightly crush blueberries. Add remaining 3 cups (750 mL) vinegar, crushed basil and lemon zest, stirring to combine. Cover tightly with plastic wrap and let stand in a dark, cool place (70 to 75°F/21 to 23°C) for up to 4 weeks, stirring every 2 to 3 days. Taste weekly until desired strength is achieved.

2. Prepare canner, jars and lids. *(For more information, see page 415.)*

3. Line a strainer with several layers of cheesecloth and place over a large stainless steel saucepan. Strain vinegar without squeezing cheesecloth. Discard cheesecloth and residue. Place saucepan over medium heat and heat vinegar to 180°F (82°C).

4. Ladle hot vinegar into hot jars, leaving ¼ inch (0.5 cm) headspace. Wipe rim. Center lid on jar. Screw band down until resistance is met, then increase to fingertip-tight.

5. Place jars in canner, ensuring they are completely covered with water. Bring to a boil and process for 10 minutes. Remove canner lid. Wait 5 minutes, then remove jars, cool and store. *(For more information, see pages 417–418.)*

Variation

If you wish to keep fresh whole blueberries in the vinegar, add ¼ cup (50 mL) fresh blueberries to the mixture before ladling into jars.

Blueberry-Basil Dressing
In a blender or a food processor fitted with a metal blade, combine 1 clove garlic, 1 tbsp (15 mL) chopped fresh basil, 2 tbsp (30 mL) each Blueberry-Basil Vinegar and olive oil and 1 tsp (5 mL) each Dijon mustard and granulated sugar, plus the zest of ½ a lemon. Process until smooth. Drizzle over a bed of spinach for a light and healthy salad.

Cranberry-Orange Vinegar

The warm and colorful flavors of cranberry and orange shine through in this tasty vinegar. Use it to make a delicious marinade for chicken or turkey (see box, below right).

TIPS

If using smaller jars, cut the orange slices into halves or quarters as required.

Before using jars, inspect them carefully for any chips, cracks or fractures. Discard any imperfect jars.

Makes about ten 4-ounce (125 mL) jars or five 8-ounce (250 mL) jars

4 cups	fresh cranberries, divided	1 L
½ cup	water	125 mL
4	whole cloves	4
2	cinnamon sticks (each 4 inches/10 cm), broken into pieces	2
1 cup	granulated sugar	250 mL
3 cups	white wine vinegar	750 mL
2	orange slices (see tip, at left)	2

1. Prepare canner, jars and lids. *(For more information, see page 415.)*

2. Measure ½ cup (125 mL) cranberries and set aside. In a large stainless steel saucepan, combine remaining cranberries and water. Bring to a boil over medium-high heat. Reduce heat and boil gently, stirring frequently, until cranberries burst. Remove from heat and, using a potato masher, lightly crush cranberries.

3. Meanwhile, tie cloves and cinnamon sticks in a square of cheesecloth, creating a spice bag. Set aside.

4. Line a strainer with several layers of cheesecloth and place over a glass measure. Strain juice without squeezing cheesecloth and measure 1 cup (250 mL). Discard cheesecloth and residue. Transfer cranberry juice to a large stainless steel saucepan and add sugar and reserved spice bag. Cook over medium-high heat, stirring until sugar dissolves. Add reserved cranberries and vinegar. Bring to a boil over medium-high heat. Reduce heat, cover and heat gently until cranberries are heated through but haven't burst, about 10 minutes. Discard spice bag.

5. Place 1 orange slice into each hot jar. Ladle hot vinegar into hot jars, leaving ¼ inch (0.5 cm) headspace. Wipe rim. Center lid on jar. Screw band down until resistance is met, then increase to fingertip-tight.

6. Place jars in canner, ensuring they are completely covered with water. Bring to a boil and process for 10 minutes. Remove canner lid. Wait 5 minutes, then remove jars, cool and store. *(For more information, see pages 417–418.)*

Cranberry Marinade
In a bowl, combine ¾ cup (175 mL) Cranberry-Orange Vinegar, ½ cup (125 mL) olive oil, 3 tbsp (45 mL) liquid honey and salt and cracked black pepper to taste. Use as a marinade for poultry. Marinate bone-in chicken or turkey in the refrigerator for 4 to 6 hours before grilling.

Mulled Blackberry Vinegar

The addition of spices intensifies the richness of blackberry flavor in this delicious vinegar, which makes an exquisite addition to a traditional ham glaze. Add 3 to 4 tablespoons (45 to 60 mL) of Mulled Blackberry Vinegar to your favorite glaze recipe.

TIPS

Wash berries gently in small batches in a colander under cool running water to make sure you remove all dirt and grit and to avoid bruising the soft fruit.

If desired, add ¼ cup (50 mL) washed and drained fresh berries to each jar before filling and processing.

Makes about ten 4-ounce (125 mL) jars or five 8-ounce (250 mL) jars

4 cups	blackberries	1 L
4 cups	cider vinegar, divided	1 L
2	cinnamon sticks (each 4 inches/10 cm) broken into pieces	2
1 tbsp	whole cloves	15 mL
1 tbsp	whole allspice	15 mL

1. In a large glass bowl, combine blackberries and 1 cup (250 mL) of the vinegar. Using a potato masher, lightly crush blackberries. Add remaining vinegar, cinnamon, cloves and allspice, stirring to combine. Cover tightly with plastic wrap and let stand in a dark, cool place (70 to 75°F/21 to 23°C) for up to 4 weeks, stirring every 2 to 3 days. Taste weekly until desired strength is achieved.
2. Prepare canner, jars and lids. *(For more information, see page 415.)*
3. Line a strainer with several layers of cheesecloth and place over a large stainless steel saucepan. Strain vinegar without squeezing cheesecloth. Discard cheesecloth and residue. Place saucepan over medium heat and heat vinegar to 180°F (82°C).
4. Ladle hot vinegar into hot jars, leaving ¼ inch (0.5 cm) headspace. Wipe rim. Center lid on jar. Screw band down until resistance is met, then increase to fingertip-tight.
5. Place jars in canner, ensuring they are completely covered with water. Bring to a boil and process for 10 minutes. Remove canner lid. Wait 5 minutes, then remove jars, cool and store. *(For more information, see pages 417–418.)*

Raspberry Vinegar

This old-fashioned favorite is a welcome addition to salad dressings. Combine with an equal quantity of balsamic vinegar and add a splash to fresh fruit.

Makes about twelve 4-ounce (125 mL) jars or six 8-ounce (250 mL) jars

4 cups	raspberries	1 L
5 cups	white wine vinegar, divided	1.25 L

1. In a large glass bowl, combine raspberries and 1 cup (250 mL) of the vinegar. Using a potato masher, lightly crush raspberries. Add remaining vinegar, stirring to combine. Cover tightly with plastic wrap and let stand in a dark, cool place (70 to 75°F/21 to 23°C) for 1 to 4 weeks, stirring every 2 to 3 days. Taste weekly until desired strength is achieved.
2. Prepare canner, jars and lids. *(For more information, see page 415.)*

Raspberry Dressing or Dip
Combine ½ cup (125 mL) light sour cream or vanilla-flavored yogurt and 2 tbsp (30 mL) each Raspberry Vinegar and liquid honey. Stir until combined. Sprinkle ground cinnamon over the top and serve!

3. Line a strainer with several layers of cheesecloth and place over a large stainless steel saucepan. Strain without squeezing cheesecloth. Discard cheesecloth and residue. Place saucepan over medium heat and heat vinegar until it reaches 180°F (82°C).

4. Ladle hot vinegar into hot jars, leaving ¼ inch (0.5 cm) headspace. Wipe rim. Center lid on jar. Screw band down until resistance is met, then increase to fingertip-tight.

5. Place jars in canner, ensuring they are completely covered with water. Bring to a boil and process for 10 minutes. Remove canner lid. Wait 5 minutes, then remove jars, cool and store. *(For more information, see pages 417–418.)*

Mixed Dried Herb Vinegar

When fresh herbs are not available, dried herbs and spices make wonderful flavored vinegars. Fresh, top-quality dried herbs and spices are essential to deliver a clear, sparkling flavor.

TIP

Cheesecloth can be found at many retailers, such as grocery stores and other stores that carry kitchen supplies. Look in the area where kitchen utensils are located.

Makes about eight 4-ounce (125 mL) jars or four 8-ounce (250 mL) jars or two pint (500 mL) jars

2 tsp	dried basil	10 mL
2 tsp	dried oregano	10 mL
1 tsp	hot pepper flakes	5 mL
4 cups	white wine vinegar	1 L

1. Place basil, oregano and hot pepper flakes in a clean quart (1 L) mason jar and set in a bowl of hot (not boiling) water to warm the glass.

2. In a medium stainless steel saucepan, bring vinegar to a boil over high heat. Slowly pour hot vinegar over dried herbs. Apply lid tightly and let stand in a dark, cool place (70 to 75°F/21 to 23°C) for 1 to 2 weeks, shaking jar every 3 days. Taste weekly until desired strength is achieved.

3. Prepare canner, jars and lids. *(For more information, see page 415.)*

4. Line a strainer with several layers of cheesecloth and place over a large stainless steel saucepan. Strain vinegar without squeezing cheesecloth. Discard cheesecloth and herbs. Place saucepan over medium heat and heat vinegar to 180°F (82°C).

5. Ladle hot vinegar into hot jars, leaving ¼ inch (0.5 cm) headspace. Wipe rim. Center lid on jar. Screw band down until resistance is met, then increase to fingertip-tight.

6. Place jars in canner, ensuring they are completely covered with water. Bring to a boil and process for 10 minutes. Remove canner lid. Wait 5 minutes, then remove jars, cool and store. *(For more information, see pages 417–418.)*

Fresh Tarragon Wine Vinegar

Herbed vinegars give you a jumpstart on flavorful vinaigrette dressings for vegetable, pasta or rice salads. Simply whisk a splash of olive oil and Dijon mustard into this herb-laced vinegar, then season to taste with salt and freshly ground pepper.

TIPS

When picking herbs from the garden to use in preserves, pick them early in the morning, before they are warmed by the sun, for the most vibrant, fresh flavor.

A cupboard or a paper bag works fine as a dark place. To develop the best flavor, don't forget to shake the jar periodically.

Makes about eight 4-ounce (125 mL) jars or four 8-ounce (250 mL) jars or two pint (500 mL) jars

8	sprigs tarragon	8
4 cups	red wine vinegar	I L
I tbsp	port wine or sweet vermouth (optional)	15 mL

1. Thoroughly wash tarragon in cool running water and shake off excess moisture. Using a mortar and pestle or the back of a spoon, bruise tarragon, one layer at a time, to release its flavor. Place sprigs in a clean quart (1 L) mason jar and set in a bowl of hot (not boiling) water to warm the glass.

2. In a medium stainless steel saucepan, bring vinegar to a boil over high heat. Slowly pour hot vinegar over tarragon. Add port wine, if using. Apply lid tightly and let stand in a dark, cool place (70 to 75°F/21 to 23°C) for 1 to 2 weeks, shaking jar every 3 days. Taste weekly until desired strength is achieved.

3. Prepare canner, jars and lids. *(For more information, see page 415.)*

4. Line a strainer with several layers of cheesecloth and place over a large stainless steel saucepan. Strain vinegar without squeezing cheesecloth. Discard cheesecloth and tarragon. Place saucepan over medium heat and heat vinegar to 180°F (82°C).

5. Ladle hot vinegar into hot jars, leaving ¼ inch (0.5 cm) headspace. Wipe rim. Center lid on jar. Screw band down until resistance is met, then increase to fingertip-tight.

6. Place jars in canner, ensuring they are completely covered with water. Bring to a boil and process for 10 minutes. Remove canner lid. Wait 5 minutes, then remove jars, cool and store. *(For more information, see pages 417–418.)*

Variations

In place of the tarragon, you can substitute other single herbs or combinations of herbs, such as rosemary, oregano and summer savory. For best results, use robustly flavored, freshly picked herbs of top quality.

Other Condiments

Condiments are popular around the world. The selection is diverse and most of the condiments in this chapter have exotic flavor profiles that represent various international sources. Some, such as Steak and Burger Sauce or Taco Sauce, you will recognize as household staples, which are usually store-bought. We encourage you to try your hand at making them yourself, as we think you'll be pleasantly surprised at the results. Others, such as Harissa Sauce, may not be as familiar, but we hope our suggestions for how to use them will encourage you to broaden your horizons and add them to your recipe repertoire. Because some of the ingredients may be difficult to find, we have given recommendations for where to locate them, as well as tips for substituting ingredients.

Thai Hot and Sweet Dipping Sauce

The perfect accompaniment for cold Thai rice paper rolls, this sauce is also delicious with any deep-fried Asian appetizer, such as spring rolls, chicken balls or wontons. It's also good with grilled chicken, and the addition of a tablespoon or two (15 or 30 mL) perks up classic oil-and-vinegar salad dressings.

TIP

The quantity of hot pepper flakes in this recipe yields a fairly spicy sauce. If you prefer less heat, adjust the amount of hot pepper flakes to suit your taste.

Makes about nine 8-ounce (250 mL) jars

½ cup	finely chopped garlic	125 mL
1 tbsp	salt	15 mL
6 cups	cider vinegar	1.5 L
6 cups	granulated sugar	1.5 L
½ cup	hot pepper flakes (see tip, at left)	125 mL

1. Prepare canner, jars and lids. *(For more information, see page 415.)*
2. In a small bowl, combine garlic and salt. Set aside.
3. In a large stainless steel saucepan, bring vinegar to a boil. Add sugar and stir until fully dissolved. Reduce heat and boil gently for 5 minutes. Remove from heat. Add garlic mixture and hot pepper flakes; stir well.
4. Ladle hot sauce into hot jars, leaving ½ inch (1 cm) headspace. Remove air bubbles and adjust headspace, if necessary, by adding hot sauce. Wipe rim. Center lid on jar. Screw band down until resistance is met, then increase to fingertip-tight.
5. Place jars in canner, ensuring they are completely covered with water. Bring to a boil and process for 15 minutes. Remove canner lid. Wait 5 minutes, then remove jars, cool and store. *(For more information, see pages 417–418.)*

Taco Sauce

Nothing store-bought
compares with the lip-
smacking tastes of
homemade, and taco
sauce is no exception.
Try this sauce over hard
or soft tacos or with
enchiladas, and you'll
never use prepared
sauce again. Taco
Sauce is also perfect
for finishing fajitas
and bean dip.

TIP

You will need
approximately 2 cans
(each 12 oz/375 mL)
tomato paste to make
this sauce. Buying larger
cans of tomato paste will
make measuring 3 cups
(750 mL) quicker and
easier. Or use your own
homemade tomato paste
(see recipe, page 361).

Makes about six 8-ounce (250 mL) jars

5 cups	water	1.25 L
3 cups	tomato paste (see tip, at left)	750 mL
1 cup	cider vinegar	250 mL
½ cup	corn syrup	125 mL
2 tbsp	chili powder	30 mL
1 tbsp	salt	15 mL
1 tsp	cayenne pepper	5 mL
½ tsp	hot pepper sauce	2 mL

1. Prepare canner, jars and lids. *(For more information, see page 415.)*

2. In a large stainless steel saucepan, combine water, tomato paste, vinegar, corn syrup, chili powder, salt, cayenne and hot pepper sauce. Bring to a boil over medium-high heat, stirring frequently. Reduce heat and boil gently, stirring frequently, until mixture is thickened to the consistency of a thin commercial barbecue sauce, about 30 minutes.

3. Ladle hot sauce into hot jars, leaving ½ inch (1 cm) headspace. Remove air bubbles and adjust headspace, if necessary, by adding hot sauce. Wipe rim. Center lid on jar. Screw band down until resistance is met, then increase to fingertip-tight.

4. Place jars in canner, ensuring they are completely covered with water. Bring to a boil and process for 30 minutes. Remove canner lid. Wait 5 minutes, then remove jars, cool and store. *(For more information, see pages 417–418.)*

Steak and Burger Sauce

Use this fruity sauce to baste grilled meats, or serve it with hearty cheese and onion sandwiches for a pub-style lunch.

TIPS

You can buy prepared pickling spice at well-stocked supermarkets or make your own (see page 217).

Refer to the Produce Purchase Guide on pages 426–429 to determine how much produce you'll need to buy to prepare this recipe.

Cheesecloth can be found at many retailers, such as grocery stores and other stores that carry kitchen supplies. Look in the area where kitchen utensils are located.

A clear plastic ruler (kept solely for kitchen use) will help you determine the correct headspace. Each filled jar should be measured accurately, as the headspace can affect sealing and the preservation of the contents.

Makes about five 8-ounce (250 mL) jars

2 tbsp	pickling spice (see tip, at left)	25 mL
4 cups	chopped pitted peeled plums	1 L
4 cups	chopped pitted peeled peaches	1 L
2 cups	chopped cored peeled apples	500 mL
1½ cups	cider vinegar	375 mL
3	hot banana peppers, seeded and chopped	3
2 tbsp	grated gingerroot	30 mL
2 tbsp	finely chopped garlic	30 mL
3 cups	granulated sugar	750 mL
1 tbsp	ground cinnamon	15 mL
1 tbsp	dry mustard	15 mL
1 tsp	ground cloves	5 mL
½ tsp	ground allspice	2 mL

1. Tie pickling spice in a square of cheesecloth, creating a spice bag. Set aside.

2. In a large stainless steel saucepan, combine plums, peaches, apples, vinegar, banana peppers, gingerroot and garlic. Bring to a boil over high heat, stirring frequently. Reduce heat and boil gently, stirring occasionally, until fruit is tender, about 10 minutes.

3. Working in batches, transfer mixture to a blender or food processor fitted with a metal blade and purée until smooth.

4. Return mixture to saucepan and stir in sugar, cinnamon, mustard, cloves, allspice and reserved spice bag. Bring to a boil over high heat, stirring frequently. Reduce heat and boil gently, stirring frequently, until mixture is the consistency of a thin commercial ketchup, about 40 minutes. Discard spice bag.

5. Meanwhile, prepare canner, jars and lids. *(For more information, see page 415.)*

6. Ladle sauce into hot jars, leaving ½ inch (1 cm) headspace. Remove air bubbles and adjust headspace, if necessary, by adding hot sauce. Wipe rim. Center lid on jar. Screw band down until resistance is met, then increase to fingertip-tight.

7. Place jars in canner, ensuring they are completely covered with water. Bring to a boil and process for 15 minutes. Remove canner lid. Wait 5 minutes, then remove jars, cool and store. *(For more information, see pages 417–418.)*

Harissa Sauce

TIPS

An equal quantity of ancho, mulato or guajillo chilies can be substituted for the New Mexico chilies.

For easier preparation, or if supplies of fresh tomatoes are limited, an equal quantity of drained canned tomatoes may be substituted for fresh. Drain thoroughly before using.

Makes about twelve 4-ounce (125 mL) jars or six 8-ounce (250 mL) jars

4 oz	dried New Mexico chili peppers (see tip, at left), seeded and stems removed	125 g
	Warm water	
4 cups	chopped seeded cored peeled plum tomatoes (see tip, at left)	1 L
2 cups	chopped onions	500 mL
¾ cup	lightly packed brown sugar	175 mL
1 cup	cider vinegar	250 mL
½ cup	chopped seeded red bell pepper	125 mL
2½ tsp	ground cumin	12 mL
1¼ tsp	ground coriander	6 mL
4 tbsp	finely chopped garlic	60 mL
1 tbsp	salt	15 mL

1. In a large glass or stainless steel bowl, cover chili peppers with warm water. Weigh chilies down with a bowl or weight to ensure they remain submerged, and soak until softened, at least 20 minutes. Drain, reserving water, and coarsely chop.

2. In a large stainless steel saucepan, combine tomatoes, onions, sugar, vinegar, red pepper, cumin and coriander. Bring to a boil over high heat, stirring frequently. Reduce heat and boil gently, stirring frequently, until mixture is the consistency of a thin commercial ketchup, about 25 minutes.

3. Meanwhile, prepare canner, jars and lids. *(For more information, see page 415.)*

4. In a blender or food processor fitted with a metal blade, combine chilies, garlic, salt and 3 tbsp (45 mL) of the reserved chili soaking water. Process until a smooth paste is formed. Add paste to tomato mixture and boil gently for 5 minutes, stirring frequently.

5. Ladle hot sauce into hot jars, leaving ½ inch (1 cm) headspace. Remove air bubbles and adjust headspace, if necessary, by adding hot sauce. Wipe rim. Center lid on jar. Screw band down until resistance is met, then increase to fingertip-tight.

6. Place jars in canner, ensuring they are completely covered with water. Bring to a boil and process for 10 minutes. Remove canner lid. Wait 5 minutes, then remove jars, cool and store. *(For more information, see pages 417–418.)*

Plum Sauce

This sweet and slightly spicy sauce is perfect with Asian-style foods, as well as chicken and pork, and is tastier than similar store-bought sauces.

TIPS

The kind of chili pepper you use will determine the degree of heat in your sauce. Of those suggested, jalapeño is the hottest, so if you prefer a spicier sauce, use it when making this recipe. Or you can use 1 tbsp (15 mL) chopped jalapeño and 1 tbsp (15 mL) chopped Anaheim, New Mexico or poblano for a bit more zest than you would achieve using any of the others.

The best way to seed peppers is to trim off the stem end and then cut the pepper in half lengthwise. Scrape out the seeds and veins, using a spoon. Remember, when cutting or seeding hot peppers, wear rubber gloves to keep your hands from being burned.

Makes about four pint (500 mL) jars

2 cups	lightly packed brown sugar	500 mL
1 cup	granulated sugar	250 mL
1 cup	cider vinegar	250 mL
¾ cup	finely chopped onion	175 mL
2 tbsp	finely chopped seeded green chili pepper, such as Anaheim, New Mexico green chili, poblano or jalapeño (see tips, at left)	30 mL
2 tbsp	mustard seeds	30 mL
1 tbsp	salt	15 mL
2	cloves garlic, finely chopped	2
1 tbsp	finely chopped gingerroot	15 mL
10 cups	finely chopped pitted plums	2.5 L

1. In a large stainless steel saucepan combine brown sugar, granulated sugar, vinegar, onion, chili pepper, mustard seeds, salt, garlic and gingerroot. Bring to a boil over high heat, stirring constantly. Add plums and return to a boil. Reduce heat and boil gently, stirring occasionally, until thick and syrupy, about 1¾ hours.

2. Meanwhile, prepare canner, jars and lids. *(For more information, see page 415.)*

3. Ladle hot sauce into hot jars, leaving ½ inch (1 cm) headspace. Remove air bubbles and adjust headspace, if necessary, by adding hot sauce. Wipe rim. Center lid on jar. Screw band down until resistance is met, then increase to fingertip-tight.

4. Place jars in canner, ensuring they are completely covered with water. Bring to a boil and process for 20 minutes. Remove canner lid. Wait 5 minutes, then remove jars, cool and store. *(For more information, see pages 417–418.)*

Roasted Red Pepper Spread

The roasted vegetables in this spread have a wonderful robust flavor that can be enjoyed on toasted crusty breads. We recommend using it instead of tomatoes to make your favorite bruschetta.

TIPS

When picking herbs from the garden to use in preserves, pick them early in the morning, before they are warmed by the sun, for the most vibrant, fresh flavor.

When preparing jars and lids, prepare a couple extra in case your yield is larger than you expect. If you don't have enough jars, place any leftover preserves in an airtight container, store in the refrigerator and use within a few weeks.

Makes about five 8-ounce (250 mL) jars

• *Preheat broiler or grill*

6 lbs	red bell peppers	2.7 kg
I lb	Italian plum tomatoes	500 g
2	large cloves garlic (unpeeled)	2
I	small white onion	I
½ cup	red wine vinegar	125 mL
2 tbsp	finely chopped fresh basil	30 mL
I tbsp	granulated sugar	15 mL
I tsp	salt	5 mL

1. Under a broiler or on a grill at 425°F (220°C), roast red peppers, tomatoes, garlic and onion, turning to roast all sides, until tomatoes and peppers are blistered, blackened and softened and garlic and onion are blackened in spots, about 15 minutes. Remove from heat. Let garlic and onion cool. Place peppers and tomatoes in paper bags. Secure openings and let cool enough to handle, about 15 minutes. Peel papery skins off garlic and onion. Finely chop garlic and set aside. Finely chop onion, measure ¼ cup (50 mL) and set aside. Peel and seed peppers and tomatoes. Working in batches, place peppers and tomatoes in a blender or food processor fitted with a metal blade and purée until smooth.

2. Prepare canner, jars and lids. *(For more information, see page 415.)*

3. In a large stainless steel saucepan, combine tomato and pepper purée, garlic, onion, vinegar, basil, sugar and salt. Bring to a boil over medium-high heat, stirring frequently to prevent sticking. Reduce heat and boil gently until mixture thickens and mounds on a spoon, about 20 minutes.

4. Ladle hot spread into hot jars, leaving ½ inch (1 cm) headspace. Remove air bubbles and adjust headspace, if necessary, by adding hot spread. Wipe rim. Center lid on jar. Screw band down until resistance is met, then increase to fingertip-tight.

5. Place jars in canner, ensuring they are completely covered with water. Bring to a boil and process for 10 minutes. Remove canner lid. Wait 5 minutes, then remove jars, cool and store. *(For more information, see pages 417–418.)*

Perfect Pickles

From dill pickles to sauerkraut, pickling brings a burst of flavor and summer sunshine to winter meals. While dills are perhaps the most common pickle in North America, the scope of homemade fruit and vegetable pickles is very broad. The variety and flavor of pickles is determined not only by the ingredients, but also by the pickling method you use. In this chapter, we have included three types of pickles: refrigerated pickles, fresh-pack or quick-process pickles and brined and fermented pickles. Relish, chutney and other condiments are included in other chapters.

• •

Pickling Essentials

Although most of the ingredients used in pickles qualify as low-acid foods (which means that they need to be processed in a pressure canner), pickling recipes add sufficient acid to elevate the acidity of the final product to that of a high-acid food (pH of 4.6 or lower). The pickling process does this in one of two ways: through fermentation, which naturally creates lactic acid, or through the addition of vinegar. Either way, the acid level of pickles helps to preserve the food. It does not, however, eliminate the need to process the filled jars of pickles in a boiling-water canner — that step is essential for destroying microorganisms that can cause spoilage. Processing also inactivates enzymes that affect the flavor, color and texture of your pickles. Contrary to popular opinion, heat-processed pickles can be crisp. Top-quality produce, preserved as quickly as possible after harvesting, produces the crunch and bite we all want.

Equipment and Utensils

Because pickling involves high-acid ingredients, such as vinegar, you need to use non-reactive utensils, bowls and cooking pots. Stainless steel and glass are the best choices, although food-grade plastic and chip-free enamelware may also be used. Utensils made of zinc, iron, brass, copper, galvanized metal or chipped enamelware may react with the acid and salt, producing an unsatisfactory result. Also, wooden spoons shouldn't be used to stir pickle mixtures as they will absorb the flavors.

Ingredients and Preparation

Pickling, like any home canning technique, should begin with the highest-quality ingredients. Equally important are accurate measurements and, where appropriate, daily maintenance and temperature control. Although you may be following a recommended procedure, if you don't use the correct proportions of sugar, salt, vinegar and spices, the quality and safety of your pickles will be affected.

Vinegar is a preservative. When pickling, always use high-quality commercial white distilled or cider vinegar with 5% acidity (also listed as 50-grain) unless other types of vinegar are specified. Never decrease or dilute the quantity of vinegar when pickling. Doing either may alter its preservative effect and undermine the safety of the final product.

Although white distilled vinegar has a pungent flavor, it does not compete with the distinctive flavors of herbs and spices in brine. Cider vinegar, which is also acceptable for use in pickling, has a more mellow taste. However, cider vinegar may discolor or darken the produce, especially white or light-colored fruits and vegetables. If you wish to maintain the natural color of the produce you are pickling, use white distilled vinegar. This is especially important when pickling onions, cauliflower and pears.

Salt also plays an integral part in preserving produce. During the brining process, salt is mixed with water to create a solution that draws juices and sugar from foods to form lactic acid, which acts as a preservative. Salt also adds flavor and crispness to pickles.

Pickling recipes require a pure granulated salt known as pickling or canning salt. Table and iodized salt contain an anti-caking agent that will create cloudy, unappealing brine. Iodized salt also contains iodine, which may darken pickles. Do not alter the quantity of salt when making fermented pickles or sauerkraut. Correct proportions of salt and water are essential for proper fermentation.

Spices and herbs add flavor to pickles. For the best results, use only new spices and herbs. Spices and herbs that have been on hand for longer than a year will not deliver the same flavor. They may also produce pickles with an off-flavor or musty taste. Whole dried spices are preferable. Powdered spices or herb salts may create cloudy brine or darken the produce. Whole seasonings can be added directly to pickling mixtures, or they can be tied in a spice bag or a square of cheesecloth, which is placed in the pickling liquid.

Soft water is essential for making the best pickles, especially when preparing brined or fermented pickles. Hard water contains minerals that can negatively affect the quality of pickles. The minerals in hard water may cause darkening or discoloration and can cloud the liquid.

Softening Water

If soft water is not readily available, you can soften your water using this technique: Bring hard water to a boil in a large stainless steel saucepan and boil for 15 minutes. Remove from heat, cover and let stand for 24 hours. Skim off any scum that has formed on the surface and carefully decant or ladle into another container, without disturbing the sediment that collects at the bottom.

Crisping and firming agents. Some older recipes call for adding pickling lime, alum or grape leaves to pickles to make them crisper. Because these agents may have negative side effects, we have not used them in any of our recipes. In most cases, if you use fresh, high-quality produce, the correct ingredient quantities and a current, tested home canning recipe, you will achieve excellent results without the addition of crisping agents. However, the texture of some quick-process or fresh-pack pickles can be enhanced with the use of a product called Pickle Crisp™. This crisping agent uses calcium chloride, a naturally occurring salt found in some natural mineral deposits. Pickle Crisp™ may be added to jars of fresh-pack pickles before processing. Look for it where canning supplies are sold.

Tips for Picking and Preparing Perfect Cucumbers

- Select only fresh, firm, high-quality cucumbers with no signs of deterioration.
- Use cucumbers within 24 hours of harvesting. Store them in the refrigerator before using, as pickling cucumbers deteriorate rapidly at room temperature.
- Use only pickling cucumbers, such as Kirbys. Other varieties, such as field or English cucumbers, are better used in relishes or chutneys.
- Field cucumbers are usually peeled and seeded before use in pickling recipes. Do not use English cucumbers unless the recipe specifies this type of cucumber.
- Do not use waxed cucumbers. The pickling brine will not be able to penetrate the wax coating.

- When making dill pickles, select pickling cucumbers that are no longer than 6 inches (15 cm). Larger cucumbers are best used in relishes or recipes that require sliced or chunked cucumbers.
- Before using, scrub pickling cucumbers thoroughly with a soft brush in lots of cold running water. The soil can harbor bacteria, which may cause soft pickles.
- Before using, remove $\frac{1}{16}$ inch (0.2 cm) from each end of pickling cucumbers. The blossom ends contain enzymes that can cause soft pickles. Although the stem end does not need to be removed, it is preferable to do so for aesthetic reasons.

Refrigerator Pickles

Because refrigerator pickles are not heat-processed, they must be stored in the refrigerator. Refrigeration, combined with vinegar, aids preservation, but the absence of heat processing means the pickles will not keep for a long period of time. For best results, allow cucumbers to marinate in the refrigerator for at least 2 weeks and use within 3 months.

Easy Zesty Bread and Butter Chunks

The "zest" in these pickles comes from the addition of horseradish. They are quick and easy to make and have a delicious taste unlike any ordinary bread and butter pickle. Enjoy them on barbecued pork sandwiches or straight out of the jar!

TIPS

You can buy prepared pickling spice at well-stocked supermarkets or make your own (see page 217).

When pickling cucumbers are not available, substitute seeded peeled field cucumbers. To prepare, peel cucumbers, cut in half lengthwise and scoop out seeds, then out into $1/2$-inch (1 cm) slices. English cucumbers are not recommended for pickling.

Look for Pickle Crisp™ where canning supplies are sold.

Makes about four pint (500 mL) jars or two quart (1 L) jars

$1/4$ cup	pickling spice (see tip, at left)	50 mL
6 cups	sliced trimmed pickling cucumbers ($1/2$-inch/1 cm slices)	1.5 L
1	onion, peeled and sliced ($1/4$-inch/0.5 cm slices)	1
3 cups	white vinegar	750 mL
$2/3$ cup	granulated sugar	150 mL
2 tbsp	pickling or canning salt	30 mL
1 tbsp	prepared horseradish	15 mL
1 tbsp	celery seeds	15 mL
1 tbsp	Pickle Crisp™ (see tip, at left)	15 mL
2 tsp	ground ginger	10 mL
1 tsp	ground turmeric	5 mL

1. Tie pickling spice in a square of cheesecloth, creating a spice bag. Set aside.
2. In a large glass or stainless steel bowl, combine cucumbers and onion.
3. In a medium stainless steel saucepan, combine vinegar, sugar, salt, horseradish, celery seeds, Pickle Crisp™, ginger, turmeric and reserved spice bag. Bring mixture to a boil over medium-high heat. Reduce heat, cover and boil gently for 5 minutes.
4. Pour pickling liquid over cucumber mixture. Cover with waxed paper and set aside until cooled to room temperature, about 30 minutes. Discard spice bag.
5. Pack cucumbers and onions into jars to within a generous $1/2$ inch (1 cm) of top. Ladle pickling liquid into jar to cover vegetables, leaving $1/2$ inch (1 cm) headspace. Apply lids. Refrigerate for at least 24 hours before serving. For best results, allow cucumbers to marinate in refrigerator for at least 2 weeks and use within 3 months.

Refrigerated Dill Slices

Add crisp dill flavor to sandwiches with these tasty slices.

TIPS

You can slice the cucumbers using a knife, but you'll get beautifully even slices in much less time using a mandoline.

You can buy prepared pickling spice at well-stocked supermarkets or make your own (see page 217).

To ensure top quality and taste, always use new spices. If your spices are not sufficiently aromatic and/or smell even slightly musty, discard them and purchase new ones.

Pickle fruits and vegetables within 24 hours of harvest. If your schedule does not accommodate this brief time window, refrigerate the produce and use it as soon as possible.

All vinegars used for pickling must have 5% acidity.

Makes about five pint (500 mL) jars

8¼ cups	sliced trimmed pickling cucumbers (¼-inch/0.5 cm slices)	2.05 L
2 cups	white vinegar	500 mL
2 cups	water	500 mL
6 tbsp	pickling or canning salt	90 mL
¼ cup	granulated sugar	50 mL
2 tbsp	pickling spice (see tip, at left)	30 mL
7½ tsp	dill seeds	37 mL
5 tsp	mustard seeds	25 mL
1¼ tsp	whole black peppercorns	6 mL
5	cloves garlic, halved (optional)	5

1. Place cucumber slices in a large glass or stainless steel bowl. Set aside.

2. In a medium stainless steel saucepan, combine vinegar, water, pickling salt, sugar and pickling spice. Bring to a boil over medium-high heat, stirring to dissolve salt and sugar. Reduce heat, cover and boil gently for 10 minutes.

3. Pour pickling liquid over cucumber slices. Cover with waxed paper and set aside until cooled to room temperature, about 30 minutes.

4. In each jar, place 1½ tsp (7 mL) dill seeds, 1 tsp (5 mL) mustard seeds, ¼ tsp (1 mL) peppercorns and two garlic clove halves, if using. Add cucumber slices to within a generous ½ inch (1 cm) headspace of top of jar. Ladle pickling liquid into jar to cover cucumbers, leaving ½ inch (1 cm) headspace. Apply lids. For best results, allow cucumbers to marinate in refrigerator for at least 2 weeks and use within 3 months.

Variation

Instead of slicing the cucumbers, you can cut them lengthwise into quarters to create spears. Use about 2½ lbs (1.1 kg) or about 15 medium pickling cucumbers to make this quantity of pickles. Select cucumbers that are uniform in length, preferably the same length as the depth of your jars.

Crunchy Mixed Refrigerator Pickles

Everyone loves these pickled mixed vegetables, and they have never been easier to make. This refrigerated pickle requires no processing and yields one quart (1 L) jar. If you wish to make more of these delicious pickled vegetables, double or triple the recipe.

TIPS

To wash cucumbers, hold them under cool running water and scrub with a vegetable brush to remove all grit from the crevices. Drain well.

When cutting or seeding hot peppers, wear rubber gloves to keep your hands from being burned.

Look for Pickle Crisp™ where canning supplies are sold.

If pickling liquid is fresh and has not been used to make pickles, pour it into a canning jar, cover with a plastic lid and refrigerate for use in your next batch of pickles. For best results, use within 2 weeks. Excess pickling liquid can also be added to coleslaw dressing, marinades or barbecue sauces.

Makes one quart (1 L) jar

1 cup	sliced trimmed pickling cucumbers (1-inch/2.5 cm slices)	250 mL
1 cup	cauliflower florets	250 mL
1/3 cup	sliced peeled carrots (1 1/2-inch/4 cm slices)	75 mL
1/3 cup	sliced trimmed green beans (1 1/2-inch/4 cm slices)	75 mL
1/3 cup	peeled pearl or pickling onions	75 mL
1/2	red bell pepper, seeded and cut into wide strips	1/2
1/2	green bell pepper, seeded and cut into wide strips	1/2
1	hot red pepper, such as cayenne or Fresno, halved lengthwise	1
2 cups	white vinegar	500 mL
2/3 cup	granulated sugar	150 mL
1 tbsp	mustard seeds	15 mL
1 1/2 tsp	celery seeds	7 mL
1 1/2 tsp	Pickle Crisp™ (see tip, at left)	7 mL

1. In a large glass or stainless steel bowl, combine cucumbers, cauliflower, carrots, green beans, onions, red and green bell pepper and hot pepper. Stir to mix evenly. Set aside.

2. In a stainless steel saucepan, combine vinegar, sugar, mustard seeds, celery seeds and Pickle Crisp™, stirring to dissolve Pickle Crisp™. Bring to a boil over medium-high heat. Reduce heat and boil gently for 3 minutes.

3. Pour pickling liquid over vegetable mixture. Cover with waxed paper and let stand until cooled to room temperature, about 30 minutes.

4. Pack vegetables into jar to within a generous 1/2 inch (1 cm) of top of jar. Ladle pickling liquid into jar to cover vegetables, leaving 1/2 inch (1 cm) headspace. Apply lids. For best results, allow cucumbers to marinate in refrigerator for at least 2 weeks and use within 3 months.

Traditional Preserved Limes

These limes can be used as a condiment or as part of a relish tray, salad or rice dish. Whether you leave the limes whole or cut them into wedges is simply a matter of taste.

TIPS

Be sure to pack the limes in threes as you go to make sure they all fit.

Store preserved limes in a container with an airtight lid. Cover and refrigerate for up to 6 months.

If desired, during refrigerator storage, a jar of limes may be topped with ¼ inch (0.5 cm) vegetable oil. Such products should be used within 1 month.

Makes one quart (1 L) jar

20	limes, divided	20
½ cup	pickling or canning salt, divided	125 mL
4	jalapeño peppers, stemmed and sliced lengthwise into eighths (optional)	4
6	cloves garlic (optional)	6

1. Prepare jar and lid. *(For more information, see page 415.)* For this recipe, the jar needs to be sterilized prior to packing. Boil jar in water for 10 minutes and keep hot until ready to use.

2. Wash 9 of the limes in warm water, scrubbing well to remove any dirt and wax, and dry well, using paper towels. Cut a thin (⅛-inch/0.25 cm) slice off the stem end. From stem end, cut each lime into quarters, without cutting through the bottom end and leaving it intact. Juice the remaining 11 limes to measure 1½ cups (375 mL) juice.

3. Sprinkle 1 tbsp (15 mL) pickling salt over the bottom of sterilized jar. Working over a bowl, pack 1 heaping tsp (5 mL) salt into each lime before placing in the jar, stem end up. When 3 limes have been salted and packed, sprinkle 1 heaping tbsp (15 mL) salt over the top. Slip about 8 jalapeño slices, if using, against sides of the jar and add 2 cloves garlic, if using. Repeat twice with remaining limes, salt, jalapeños and garlic. Cover with the remaining salt.

4. Fill jar with lime juice to within ½ inch (1 cm) of top of jar. Center lid on jar. Screw band down until resistance is met, then increase to fingertip-tight.

5. Place jar in a dark, cool cupboard for 2 weeks, shaking every day to distribute the salt. After 2 weeks, the limes are ready to use. Remove pulp and membrane, using only the peel. Rinse under water to remove excess salt and dry with a paper towel. Store preserved limes in the refrigerator.

Variation

If you prefer, you can cut the limes into quarters. Combine in a large bowl with the salt. Toss to mix. Half fill the jar, add the jalapeño slices and garlic, then continue until the jar is filled, pushing the limes well down to squeeze in as many as possible.

Traditional Preserved Lemons

Preserved in salt and lemon juice and flavored with bay leaf, cinnamon and black peppercorns, these tasty lemons, which are a staple of Middle Eastern cuisine, are a welcome addition to many dishes. Use in tagines, stews or diced as a condiment on top of curries.

TIPS

Store preserved lemons in a container with an airtight lid. Cover and refrigerate for up to 6 months.

When purchasing limes or lemons for these preserved recipes, select top-quality fruit that is heavy for its size and shows no blemishes. Organic produce may be a good choice, as it is less likely to be waxed or coated.

Place jar in a paper bag to ensure that it is kept in the dark during the marinating time.

Makes one quart (1 L) jar

10	lemons, divided	10
½ cup	pickling or canning salt, divided	125 mL
4	bay leaves	4
4	cinnamon sticks (each about 4 inches/10 cm)	4
1 tsp	whole black peppercorns (optional)	5 mL

1. Prepare jar and lid. *(For more information, see page 415.)* For this recipe, the jar needs to be sterilized prior to packing. Boil jar in water for 10 minutes and keep hot until ready to use.

2. Wash 5 of the lemons in warm water, scrubbing well to remove any dirt and wax, and dry well, using paper towels. Cut a thin (⅛-inch /0.25 cm) slice off the stem end. From stem end, cut each lemon into quarters, without cutting through the bottom end and leaving it intact. Juice the remaining 5 lemons to measure 1½ cups (375 mL) juice.

3. Sprinkle 1 tbsp (15 mL) pickling salt over the bottom of sterilized jar. Working over a bowl, pack 1 heaping tbsp (15 mL) salt into each lemon before placing in the jar, stem end up. When 3 lemons have been salted and packed, slip bay leaves and cinnamon sticks against sides of the jar and add peppercorns, if using. Repeat with remaining lemons and salt. Cover with the remaining salt.

4. Fill jar with lemon juice to within ½ inch (1 cm) of top of jar. Center lid on jar. Screw band down until resistance is met, then increase to fingertip-tight.

5. Place jar in a dark, cool cupboard for 2 weeks, shaking every day to distribute the salt. After 2 weeks, the lemons are ready to use. Remove pulp and membrane, using only the peel. Rinse under water to remove excess salt and dry with a paper towel. Store preserved lemons in the refrigerator.

Variation

If you prefer, you can cut the lemons into quarters. In a large bowl, combine lemon quarters with salt and toss to mix. Fill the jar halfway, add the bay leaves, cinnamon sticks and peppercorns, if using, then continue until the jar is filled, pushing the lemons well down to squeeze in as many as possible.

Fresh-Pack or Quick-Process Pickles

Compared to brined or fermented products, fresh-pack or quick-process pickles require less preparation time and waiting, which is why beginning home canners often start by making this type of pickle. In this type of pickle, vegetables or fruit are packed in jars with a spicy vinegar solution. Some recipes may require the ingredients to stand for several hours or overnight in a salt and/or ice water solution to enhance texture, but the lengthy brining process particular to fermented pickles is eliminated.

For best flavor, store all fresh-pack pickles for 4 to 6 weeks in a cool, dry, dark place after processing. This standing time allows the flavors to mellow and blend, creating a full-bodied pickle taste.

Fruit Pickles — Single-Day

Pickled Plums

Let this rich, dark, spicy pickle age for at least 2 weeks. Serve it as an accompaniment to grilled chops, ham or cold roast beef. Save the syrup to use as a basting sauce for spareribs.

TIP

Cheesecloth can be found at many retailers, such as grocery stores and other stores that carry kitchen supplies. Look in the area where kitchen utensils are located.

Makes about six pint (500 mL) jars

• *Preheat oven to 275°F (140°C)*
• *Large covered baking dish*

I	3-inch (7.5 cm) piece gingerroot, peeled and coarsely chopped	I
2	cinnamon sticks (each about 4 inches/10 cm), broken into pieces	2
I tsp	whole cloves	5 mL
2	dried red chili peppers (see tip, opposite)	2
I	small piece of nutmeg, cracked	I
5 cups	lightly packed brown sugar	1.25 L
2 cups	cider vinegar	500 mL
½ cup	water	125 mL
	Peel of I orange, removed in a continuous spiral	
5 lbs	blue plums (about 50)	2.3 kg

I. Tie gingerroot, cinnamon stick pieces, cloves, chili peppers and nutmeg in a square of cheesecloth, creating a spice bag.

TIPS

Simple red cayenne chili peppers work well in this recipe, but you can vary the flavor by substituting an equal number of ancho or New Mexico peppers.

Why confine pickling to cucumbers? Fruits and other vegetables make delicious pickles. The brilliant colors produce pickles that are beautiful to look at, and their crisp texture and robust flavors make enjoyable treats.

2. In a large stainless steel saucepan, combine brown sugar, vinegar, water, orange zest and spice bag. Bring to a boil over medium-high heat, stirring constantly. Reduce heat and boil gently for 10 minutes.

3. Prick plums all over with a toothpick. In baking dish, combine plums and syrup. Cover and cook in preheated oven until plums are tender but firm, about 30 minutes. Discard spice bag and orange zest.

4. Meanwhile, prepare canner, jars and lids. *(For more information, see page 415.)*

5. Pack hot plums into hot jars to within a generous ¹⁄₂ inch (1 cm) of top of jar. Ladle hot syrup into jar to cover plums, leaving ¹⁄₂ inch (1 cm) headspace. Remove air bubbles and adjust headspace, if necessary, by adding more hot syrup. Wipe rim. Center lid on jar. Screw band down until resistance is met, then increase to fingertip-tight.

6. Place jars in canner, ensuring they are completely covered with water. Bring to a boil and process for 20 minutes. Remove canner lid. Wait 5 minutes, then remove jars, cool and store. *(For more information, see pages 417–418.)*

Dilly Peach Pickles

Although we tend to think of peaches as a sweet preserve, they make excellent pickles. These tangy treats are wonderful on their own or served with roasted and barbecued meats. During the winter months, create an appetizing salad by combining these peach halves with green vegetables and a creamy dressing. Look for good-quality, ripe but firm freestone peaches for these pickles.

TIPS

To peel peaches and treat to prevent browning, see page 140.

For this recipe, use the dill flower head, which is the yellow flower portion.

Makes about five pint (500 mL) jars

1 cup	granulated sugar	250 mL
2 cups	white vinegar	500 mL
2 tbsp	pickling or canning salt	30 mL
16 cups	halved pitted peeled peaches, treated to prevent browning and drained	4 L
5	cloves garlic	5
5	heads fresh dill (see tip, at left)	5

1. Prepare canner, jars and lids. *(For more information, see page 415.)*

2. In a large stainless steel saucepan, combine sugar, vinegar and salt. Bring to a boil over medium-high heat, stirring constantly. Add peach halves and return to a boil. Reduce heat and boil gently for 3 to 5 minutes, until heated through. Remove from heat.

3. Place 1 clove garlic and 1 head of dill in each hot jar. Pack peach halves, cavity side down, into hot jars to within a generous $\frac{1}{2}$ inch (1 cm) of top of jar. Ladle hot syrup into jar to cover peaches, leaving $\frac{1}{2}$ inch (1 cm) headspace. Remove air bubbles and adjust headspace, if necessary, by adding hot syrup. Wipe rim. Center lid on jar. Screw band down until resistance is met, then increase to fingertip-tight.

4. Place jars in canner, ensuring they are completely covered with water. Bring to a boil and process for 20 minutes. Remove canner lid. Wait 5 minutes, then remove jars, cool and store. *(For more information, see pages 417–418.)*

Cantaloupe Pickles

Cinnamon, cloves and allspice add warmth to these colorful cubes. For best results, choose a melon that is just ripe.

TIPS

When preparing jars and lids, prepare a couple extra in case your yield is larger than you expect. If you don't have enough jars, place any leftover preserves in an airtight container, store in the refrigerator and use within a few weeks.

Cheesecloth can be found at many retailers, such as grocery stores and other stores that carry kitchen supplies. Look in the area where kitchen utensils are located.

Makes about six pint (500 mL) jars

1	cinnamon stick (about 4 inches/10 cm), broken into pieces	1
2	whole cloves	2
1 tsp	whole allspice	5 mL
3 cups	white vinegar	750 mL
2 cups	water	500 mL
13 cups	cubed seeded peeled cantaloupe (1-inch/2.5 cm cubes)	3.25 L
4½ cups	granulated sugar	1.125 L

1. Tie cinnamon stick pieces, cloves and allspice in a square of cheesecloth, creating a spice bag.

2. In a large stainless steel saucepan, combine vinegar, water and spice bag. Bring to a boil over medium-high heat. Reduce heat and boil gently for 5 minutes. Remove from heat.

3. Add melon to saucepan. Cover and set aside for 30 minutes.

4. Stir sugar into cantaloupe mixture and return to medium-high heat. Bring to a boil, stirring occasionally. Reduce heat and boil gently, stirring occasionally, until melon becomes transparent, about 45 minutes. Discard spice bag.

5. Meanwhile, prepare canner, jars and lids. *(For more information, see page 415.)*

6. Pack cantaloupe into hot jars to within a generous ½ inch (1 cm) of top of jar. Ladle hot syrup into jar to cover cantaloupe, leaving ½ inch (1 cm) headspace. Remove air bubbles and adjust headspace, if necessary, by adding hot syrup. Wipe rim. Center lid on jar. Screw band down until resistance is met, then increase to fingertip-tight.

7. Place jars in canner, ensuring they are completely covered with water. Bring to a boil and process for 20 minutes. Remove canner lid. Wait 5 minutes, then remove jars, cool and store. *(For more information, see pages 417–418.)*

Pickled Pineapple

These sweet-and-sour spears of pickled pineapple have just a hint of spice. Eat them straight from the jar or serve them as a condiment.

TIPS

A jar lifter is very helpful for handling hot, wet jars. Because they are bulky and fit loosely, oven mitts — even water-resistent types — are not a wise choice. When filling jars, an all-purpose rubber glove, worn on your helper hand, will allow you to steady the jar.

Place a clean towel on your work surface to absorb water from the hot jars as you take them out of the boiling-water canner to be filled, and again once the jars are processed. The towel prevents hot jars from coming into contact with cooler countertops. Significant temperature differences can cause jar breakage.

Makes about four pint (500 mL) jars

3	cinnamon sticks (each about 4 inches/10 cm), broken into pieces	3
½ tsp	whole allspice	2 mL
¼ tsp	whole cloves	1 mL
2 cups	lightly packed brown sugar	500 mL
1 cup	red wine vinegar	250 mL
1 cup	unsweetened pineapple juice	250 mL
2	fresh pineapples, peeled, cored and cut into 1-inch (2.5 cm) spears	2

1. Prepare canner, jars and lids. *(For more information, see page 415.)*
2. Tie cinnamon stick pieces, allspice and cloves in a square of cheesecloth, creating a spice bag.
3. In a large stainless steel saucepan, combine sugar, vinegar, pineapple juice and spice bag. Bring to a boil over medium-high heat, stirring occasionally. Reduce heat, cover and boil gently for 20 minutes. Add pineapple and boil gently until pineapple is heated through. Using a slotted spoon, remove pineapple from syrup. Place in a large glass or stainless steel bowl and cover with foil to keep hot. Return syrup to a boil over medium-high heat. Discard spice bag.
4. Pack pineapple into hot jars to within a generous ½ inch (1 cm) of top of jar. Ladle hot syrup into jar to cover pineapple, leaving ½ inch (1 cm) headspace. Remove air bubbles and adjust headspace, if necessary, by adding hot syrup. Wipe rim. Center lid on jar. Screw band down until resistance is met, then increase to fingertip-tight.
5. Place jars in canner, ensuring they are completely covered with water. Bring to a boil and process for 10 minutes. Remove canner lid. Wait 5 minutes, then remove jars, cool and store. *(For more information, see pages 417–418.)*

Sweet Pumpkin Pickles

Pickled pumpkin has long been a tradition in many homes across North America. Warmly spiced and gorgeous golden orange in color, these pickles seem too good to eat.

TIPS

Before using jars, inspect them carefully for any chips, cracks or fractures. Discard any imperfect jars.

A clear plastic ruler (kept solely for kitchen use) will help you determine the correct headspace. Each filled jar should be measured accurately, as the headspace can affect sealing and the preservation of the contents.

Makes about six pint (500 mL) jars

2	cinnamon sticks (each about 4 inches/10 cm), halved	2
12	whole allspice	12
10	whole cloves	10
1	lemon	1
6 cups	granulated sugar	1.5 L
4 cups	white vinegar	1 L
24 cups	cubed seeded peeled pie pumpkin or butternut squash (¾-inch/2 cm cubes)	6 L

1. Prepare canner, jars and lids. *(For more information, see page 415.)*
2. Tie cinnamon stick halves, allspice and cloves in a square of cheesecloth, creating a spice bag. Set aside.
3. Zest lemon, using a fine-toothed grater, and set aside. Remove and discard white pith. Separate segments from membrane and coarsely chop. Squeeze any juice from membrane and add to segments. Set aside. Discard membrane.
4. In a large stainless steel saucepan, combine lemon zest, pulp and juice, sugar, vinegar and reserved spice bag. Bring to a boil over medium-high heat, stirring occasionally. Cover, reduce heat and boil gently for 10 minutes. Add pumpkin, return to a boil and cook for 3 minutes, until heated through. Discard spice bag.
5. Pack hot pumpkin into hot jars to within a generous ½ inch (1 cm) of top of jar. Ladle hot syrup into jar to cover pumpkin, leaving ½ inch (1 cm) headspace. Remove air bubbles and adjust headspace, if necessary, by adding more hot syrup. Wipe rim. Center lid on jar. Screw band down until resistance is met, then increase to fingertip-tight.
6. Place jars in canner, ensuring they are completely covered with water. Bring to a boil and process for 20 minutes. Remove canner lid. Wait 5 minutes, then remove jars, cool and store. *(For more information, see pages 417–418.)*

Dill Sandwich Slices

No hamburger is complete without the tangy zest of a dill pickle. Because these have already been cut into slices, they are easy to use.

TIPS

Always use fresh (not old and musty) pickling spice to ensure quality and taste. Whole spices should be used within 3 to 4 years of purchase.

You can buy prepared pickling spice at well-stocked supermarkets or make your own (see page 217).

For this recipe, use the dill flower head, which is the yellow flower portion.

If fresh dill is not available, use 1 to 2 tsp (5 to 10 mL) dill seeds or 2 tsp (10 mL) dried dillweed for each head of fresh dill.

Makes about five pint (500 mL) jars

3 tbsp	pickling spice (see tips, at left)	45 mL
4 cups	cider vinegar	1 L
4 cups	water	1 L
¾ cup	granulated sugar	175 mL
½ cup	pickling or canning salt	125 mL
5	bay leaves	5
5	cloves garlic	5
2½ tsp	mustard seeds	12 mL
5	heads fresh dill (see tips, at left)	5
13⅓ cups	sliced trimmed pickling cucumbers (¼-inch/0.5 cm lengthwise slices)	3.325 L

1. Prepare canner, jars and lids. *(For more information, see page 415.)*
2. Tie pickling spice in a square of cheesecloth, creating a spice bag.
3. In a large stainless steel saucepan, combine vinegar, water, sugar, pickling salt and spice bag. Bring to a boil over medium-high heat, stirring to dissolve sugar and salt. Reduce heat and boil gently for 15 minutes, until spices have infused the liquid.
4. Place 1 bay leaf, 1 garlic clove, ½ tsp (2 mL) mustard seeds and 1 head of dill into each jar. Pack cucumber slices into hot jars to within a generous ½ inch (1 cm) of top of jar. Ladle hot pickling liquid into jar to cover cucumbers, leaving ½ inch (1 cm) headspace. Remove air bubbles and adjust headspace, if necessary, by adding hot pickling liquid. Wipe rim. Center lid on jar. Screw band down until resistance is met, then increase to fingertip-tight.
5. Place jars in canner, ensuring they are completely covered with water. Bring to a boil and process for 15 minutes. Remove canner lid. Wait 5 minutes, then remove jars, cool and store. *(For more information, see pages 417–418.)*

Traditional Bread and Butter Pickles

Bread and butter pickles are the perfect accompaniment to a sandwich. You can use this recipe to create a traditional pickle, just like Grandma's, or use the variations to create something different — zesty pickles, pickles with a hint of garlic or a sweet golden brown British-style pickle. Try all three and see which suits your taste.

TIPS

Use Pickle Crisp™ to make fresh-pack pickles crisper. Add ¾ tsp (3 mL) to pint (500 mL) jars and 1 ½ tsp (7 mL) to quart (1 L) jars before processing.

When making pickles, select uniformly sized fruits and vegetables and/or cut them into pieces of similar size. During processing, each piece of produce should be heated to the same degree. If the pieces vary too much in size, smaller pieces will soften and larger pieces may not be heated sufficiently. In addition to reduced quality, inadequate heat penetration can become a safety issue.

Makes about five pint (500 mL) jars

10 cups	sliced trimmed pickling cucumbers (¼-inch/0.5 cm slices)	2.5 L
4	medium onions, thinly sliced	4
½ cup	pickling or canning salt	125 mL
3 cups	white vinegar	750 mL
2 cups	granulated sugar	500 mL
2 tbsp	mustard seeds	30 mL
1 tsp	celery seeds	5 mL
1 tsp	ground turmeric	5 mL

1. In a glass or stainless steel bowl, combine cucumbers, onions and salt. Mix well, cover with cold water and let stand at room temperature for 2 hours. Transfer to a colander placed over a sink, rinse with cool running water and drain thoroughly.

2. Meanwhile, prepare canner, jars and lids. *(For more information, see page 415.)*

3. In a large stainless steel saucepan, combine vinegar, sugar, mustard seeds, celery seeds and turmeric. Bring to a boil over medium-high heat, stirring to dissolve sugar. Stir in vegetables and return to a boil.

4. Pack vegetables into hot jars to within a generous ½ inch (1 cm) of top of jar. Ladle hot pickling liquid into jar to cover vegetables, leaving ½ inch (1 cm) headspace. Remove air bubbles and adjust headspace, if necessary, by adding hot pickling liquid. Wipe rim. Center lid on jar. Screw band down until resistance is met, then increase to fingertip-tight.

5. Place jars in canner, ensuring they are completely covered with water. Bring to a boil and process for 10 minutes. Remove canner lid. Wait 5 minutes, then remove jars, cool and store. *(For more information, see pages 417–418.)*

Variations

British Bread and Butter Pickles: Substitute 3 cups (750 mL) cider vinegar for the white vinegar and 2 cups (500 mL) packed brown sugar for the granulated sugar. Add 1 tsp (5 mL) ground ginger along with the turmeric.

Zesty Bread and Butter Pickles: Substitute 2 tbsp (30 mL) prepared horseradish for the celery seeds and 2 tbsp (30 mL) grated gingerroot for the turmeric.

Garlic Bread and Butter Pickles: Add 1 clove garlic to each hot jar.

Chunky Mustard Pickles

Here's a delicious answer to a bumper crop of garden cucumbers. These tasty pickles add color and flavor to any meal.

TIPS

Pickle fruits and vegetables within 24 hours of harvest. If your schedule does not accommodate this brief time window, refrigerate the produce and use it as soon as possible.

ClearJel® is a cooking starch that is acceptable for use in home canning. Not all cooking starches are suitable for home canning, as reheating causes some to lose viscosity. Making mixtures too thick can interfere with required heat penetration during heat processing. In this recipe, ClearJel® is used to create a thicker, smoother texture. For more information, see the Glossary, page 431.

Makes about seven pint (500 mL) jars

14 cups	cubed seeded peeled pickling or field cucumbers (½-inch/1 cm cubes)	3.5 L
6 cups	finely chopped onions	1.5 L
¼ cup	pickling or canning salt	50 mL
3 cups	granulated sugar	750 mL
4 tbsp	ClearJel® (see tip, at left)	60 mL
¼ cup	dry mustard	50 mL
1 tbsp	ground ginger	15 mL
1 tsp	ground turmeric	5 mL
½ cup	water	125 mL
2 cups	white vinegar	500 mL
1	red bell pepper, seeded and finely chopped	1

1. In a large glass or stainless steel bowl, combine cucumbers and onions. Sprinkle with pickling salt, cover and let stand at room temperature for 1 hour. Transfer to a colander placed over a sink and drain thoroughly.

2. Meanwhile, prepare canner, jars and lids. *(For more information, see page 415.)*

3. In a large stainless steel saucepan, combine sugar, ClearJel®, mustard, ginger and turmeric. Stir well. Gradually blend in water. Add vinegar and red pepper. Bring to a boil over medium-high heat, stirring frequently to dissolve sugar and prevent lumps from forming. Reduce heat and boil gently, stirring frequently, until mixture thickens, about 5 minutes. Add drained cucumber mixture and return to a boil.

4. Ladle cucumber mixture into hot jars, leaving ½ inch (1 cm) headspace. Remove air bubbles and adjust headspace, if necessary, by adding hot cucumber mixture. Wipe rim. Center lid on jar. Screw band down until resistance is met, then increase to fingertip-tight.

5. Place jars in canner, ensuring they are completely covered with water. Bring to a boil and process for 10 minutes. Remove canner lid. Wait 5 minutes, then remove jars, cool and store. *(For more information, see pages 417–418.)*

Variation

Chunky Zucchini Pickles: Substitute unpeeled, seeded zucchini for the cucumber.

Cucumber Sandwich Pickles

Among their other uses, these sandwich pickles are a great addition to homemade grilled panini sandwiches. Lay pickles between slices of smoked turkey, provolone cheese, beefsteak tomatoes and romaine lettuce. Serve with honey Dijon mustard on the side and enjoy.

TIPS

When packing fruits or vegetables into jars for pickles, pack tightly, but not too tightly. Leave room for the pickling liquid, since that is where the flavor comes from.

If pickling liquid is fresh and has not been used to make pickles, cover it and refrigerate for use in your next batch of pickles. For best results, use within 2 weeks. Excess pickling liquid can also be added to coleslaw dressing, marinades or barbecue sauces.

Makes about three pint (500 mL) jars

2 lbs	pickling cucumbers, trimmed and sliced lengthwise (1/4-inch/0.5 cm slices)	900 g
1/2 cup	pickling or canning salt	125 mL
12 cups	water, divided	3 L
5 cups	white vinegar, divided	1.25 L
1 cup	lightly packed brown sugar	250 mL
1 cup	granulated sugar	250 mL
1/2 tsp	celery seeds	2 mL
1/2 tsp	mustard seeds	2 mL
1/2 tsp	ground turmeric	2 mL

1. Place cucumbers in a clean crock or glass or stainless steel container.

2. In a large glass or stainless steel bowl, combine pickling salt and 8 cups (2 L) of the water, stirring until salt dissolves. Ladle over cucumbers and let stand in a cool place (70 to 75°F/21 to 23°C) for 3 hours. Drain cucumbers and discard liquid. Rinse cucumbers under cool running water and drain thoroughly.

3. In a large stainless steel saucepan, combine 3 cups (750 mL) of the vinegar and 3 cups (750 mL) of the water. Bring to a boil over medium-high heat. Add drained cucumber slices and return to a boil. Reduce heat and boil gently for 8 minutes, until cucumbers are heated through but not soft. Drain well, discarding liquid, and set aside.

4. Prepare canner, jars and lids. *(For more information, see page 415.)*

5. In a clean large stainless steel saucepan, combine remaining 2 cups (500 mL) vinegar, remaining 1 cup (250 mL) water, brown sugar, granulated sugar, celery seeds, mustard seeds and turmeric. Bring to a boil over medium-high heat, stirring to dissolve sugar. Reduce heat and boil gently for 10 minutes. Add drained cucumber slices, increase heat to medium-high and return to a boil. Remove from heat.

6. Pack hot cucumber slices into hot jars to within a generous 1/2 inch (1 cm) of top of jar. Add hot pickling liquid, leaving 1/2 inch (1 cm) headspace. Remove air bubbles and adjust headspace, if necessary, by adding hot pickling liquid. Wipe rim. Center lid on jar. Screw band down until resistance is met, then increase to fingertip-tight.

7. Place jars in canner, ensuring they are completely covered with water. Bring to a boil and process for 10 minutes. Remove canner lid. Wait 5 minutes, then remove jars, cool and store. *(For more information, see pages 417–418.)*

Lemon Cucumber Pickles

If you find traditional pickles too astringent, try this refreshing alternative. Lemon juice provides a unique flavor, and a touch of sugar takes the bite out of the vinegar. For best flavor, let these pickles "mature" for 4 to 6 weeks before using.

TIPS

Make pickles with a variety of fruits or vegetables, or a combination of both. Select tender vegetables and firm fruit.

Use Pickle Crisp™ to make fresh-pack pickles crisper. Add ¾ tsp (3 mL) to pint (500 mL) jars and 1½ tsp (7 mL) to quart (1 L) jars before processing.

Makes about six pint (500 mL) jars

14 cups	sliced peeled pickling cucumbers (¼-inch/0.5 cm slices)	3.5 L
4	red bell peppers, seeded and thinly sliced	4
2 tbsp	pickling or canning salt	30 mL
	Ice water	
7	bay leaves, divided	7
1 tbsp	whole black peppercorns	15 mL
1 tsp	whole allspice	5 mL
1⅓ cups	white vinegar	325 mL
1¼ cups	granulated sugar	300 mL
¾ cup	freshly squeezed lemon juice	175 mL
1	lemon, sliced	1
6	cloves garlic	6

1. In a large glass or stainless steel bowl, combine cucumbers, red peppers and salt. Mix well, cover with ice water and let stand at room temperature for 3 hours.
2. Meanwhile, prepare canner, jars and lids. *(For more information, see page 415.)*
3. Tie 1 bay leaf, peppercorns and allspice in a square of cheesecloth, creating a spice bag. Set aside.
4. In a large stainless steel saucepan, combine vinegar, sugar, lemon juice and reserved spice bag. Bring to a boil over medium-high heat, stirring to dissolve sugar. Reduce heat and boil gently for 7 minutes, until spices have infused the liquid.
5. In a colander placed over a sink, drain vegetables. Add to liquid in saucepan and return to a full boil, stirring occasionally. Discard spice bag.
6. Place 1 bay leaf, 1 lemon slice and 1 clove garlic in each hot jar. Pack vegetables into hot jars to within a generous ½ inch (1 cm) of top of jar. Ladle hot pickling liquid into jar to cover vegetables, leaving ½ inch (1 cm) headspace. Remove air bubbles and adjust headspace, if necessary, by adding hot pickling liquid. Wipe rim. Center lid on jar. Screw band down until resistance is met, then increase to fingertip-tight.
7. Place jars in canner, ensuring they are completely covered with water. Bring to a boil and process for 10 minutes. Remove canner lid. Wait 5 minutes, then remove jars, cool and store. *(For more information, see pages 417–418.)*

Pickled Asparagus

Having pickled asparagus on hand is an easy way to add flavor and color to your meals. It also makes a charming alternative to celery in a Bloody Mary or Caesar.

TIPS

When you cut asparagus into uniform, jar-sized spears, you'll end up with a lot of short pieces. These pieces can be pickled, but they are perhaps best cooked and used for soup or blanched and frozen for use in other vegetable recipes.

Asparagus is packed with the tips facing down in the jar so that the fragile tips are not damaged when the asparagus is removed from the jar.

Makes about six pint (500 mL) jars

7 lbs	asparagus	3.2 kg
	Ice water	
4 tbsp	finely chopped seeded red bell pepper	60 mL
2 tbsp	finely chopped seeded green bell pepper	30 mL
2 tbsp	finely chopped seeded hot chili pepper, such as jalapeño or cayenne	30 mL
3 tbsp	finely chopped garlic	45 mL
5 cups	white vinegar	1.25 L
1²⁄₃ cups	water	400 mL
1²⁄₃ cups	granulated sugar	400 mL
4 tsp	pickling or canning salt	20 mL
2 tbsp	dill seeds	30 mL
2 tbsp	mustard seeds	30 mL

1. Trim tough ends from asparagus and cut spears into uniform lengths about ¾ inch (2 cm) shorter than the inside height of the jars you are using. In a large shallow dish, cover asparagus with ice water and refrigerate for 1 hour. Drain well.

2. Meanwhile, prepare canner, jars and lids. *(For more information, see page 415.)*

3. In a small bowl, combine red and green bell pepper, hot pepper and garlic. Mix well and set aside.

4. In a large stainless steel saucepan, combine vinegar, water, sugar and salt. Stir well and bring to a boil over medium-high heat. Reduce heat and boil gently for 5 minutes. Add asparagus and return to a boil. Boil for 2 minutes or until asparagus is heated through.

5. Place 2 tbsp (30 mL) chopped pepper mixture, 1 tsp (5 mL) dill seeds and 1 tsp (5 mL) mustard seeds into each hot jar. Pack asparagus, tips down, into hot jars to within a generous ½ inch (1 cm) of top of jar. Ladle hot pickling liquid into jar to cover asparagus, leaving ½ inch (1 cm) headspace. Remove air bubbles and adjust headspace, if necessary, by adding hot pickling liquid. Wipe rim. Center lid on jar. Screw band down until resistance is met, then increase to fingertip-tight.

6. Place jars in canner, ensuring they are completely covered with water. Bring to a boil and process for 10 minutes. Remove canner lid. Wait 5 minutes, then remove jars, cool and store. *(For more information, see pages 417–418.)*

Dilled Beans

Green and yellow wax beans steeped in zesty dill brine make delicious and colorful pickles. Use them in salads, on relish trays or as garnishes. Mixed with a bit of salad oil, the brine makes a flavorful vinaigrette dressing.

TIPS

When preparing beans for preserving, cut them into jar-size or shorter lengths for ease of packing.

The dill head is made up of many sprigs. If a recipe calls for dill sprigs, cut the sprigs from the head using kitchen scissors.

If fresh dill is not available, use ½ tsp (2 mL) dill seeds per jar.

Makes about six pint (500 mL) jars

3 tbsp	pickling or canning salt	45 mL
3 cups	white vinegar	750 mL
3 cups	water	750 mL
2¼ lbs	green beans, trimmed and cut into jar-length pieces	1 kg
2¼ lbs	yellow wax beans, trimmed and cut into jar-length pieces	1 kg
3	small red bell peppers, seeded and sliced into thin strips	3
18	whole black peppercorns	18
6	sprigs fresh dill (see tips, at left)	6
6	cloves garlic	6

1. Prepare canner, jars and lids. *(For more information, see page 415.)*

2. In a large stainless steel saucepan, combine salt, vinegar and water. Bring to a boil over medium-high heat, stirring to dissolve salt. Add green and yellow beans and red peppers. Return to a boil. Remove from heat.

3. Place 3 peppercorns, 1 sprig of dill and 1 clove garlic in each hot jar. Pack beans and pepper strips into hot jars to within a generous ½ inch (1 cm) of top of jar. Ladle hot pickling liquid into jar to cover beans and peppers, leaving ½ inch (1 cm) headspace. Remove air bubbles and adjust headspace, if necessary, by adding more hot pickling liquid. Wipe rim. Center lid on jar. Screw band down until resistance is met, then increase to fingertip-tight.

4. Place jars in canner, ensuring they are completely covered with water. Bring to a boil and process for 10 minutes. Remove canner lid. Wait 5 minutes, then remove jars, cool and store. *(For more information, see pages 417–418.)*

Mustard Beans

Green and yellow wax beans make delicious, colorful pickles. Mustard combined with this blend of spices creates a zesty pickle that is equally at home as a side dish or added to potato or pasta salad.

TIP

ClearJel® is a cooking starch that is acceptable for use in home canning. Not all cooking starches are suitable for home canning, as reheating causes some to lose viscosity. Making mixtures too thick can interfere with required heat penetration during heat processing. In this recipe, ClearJel® is used to create a thicker, smoother texture. For more information, see the Glossary, page 431.

Makes about seven pint (500 mL) jars

3 cups	granulated sugar	750 mL
4 tbsp	ClearJel® (see tip, at left)	60 mL
¼ cup	dry mustard	50 mL
¼ cup	pickling or canning salt	50 mL
1 tbsp	ground ginger	15 mL
1 tsp	ground turmeric	5 mL
2½ cups	white vinegar	625 mL
½ cup	water	125 mL
4 cups	chopped onions	1 L
1¼ cups	finely chopped seeded red bell pepper	300 mL
11 cups	chopped trimmed green or yellow beans or a mixture of the two (1½-inch/4 cm pieces)	2.75 L

1. Prepare canner, jars and lids. *(For more information, see page 415.)*

2. In a large stainless steel saucepan, combine sugar, ClearJel®, mustard, pickling salt, ginger and turmeric. Gradually blend in vinegar and water. Add onions and red pepper. Bring to a boil over medium-high heat, stirring frequently to dissolve sugar and salt and prevent lumps from forming. Reduce heat and boil gently, stirring frequently, until mixture thickens, about 5 minutes. Stir in beans and return to a boil.

3. Ladle bean mixture into hot jars, leaving ½ inch (1 cm) headspace. Remove air bubbles and adjust headspace, if necessary, by adding hot bean mixture. Wipe rim. Center lid on jar. Screw band down until resistance is met, then increase to fingertip-tight.

4. Place jars in canner, ensuring they are completely covered with water. Bring to a boil and process for 15 minutes. Remove canner lid. Wait 5 minutes, then remove jars, cool and store. *(For more information, see pages 417–418.)*

Pickled Three-Bean Salad

In some circles, it is practically a tradition to have three-bean salad as part of a picnic spread. This staple has a robust flavor that is unique. Having some on hand allows for easy preparation for any party!

TIP

Refer to the Produce Purchase Guide on pages 426–429 to determine how much produce you'll need to buy to prepare this recipe.

Makes five to six pint (500 mL) jars

4½ cups	sliced trimmed green beans (1½-inch/4 cm slices)	1.125 L
4½ cups	sliced trimmed yellow wax beans (1½-inch/4 cm slices)	1.125 mL
1 lb	lima beans, shelled	500 g
2 cups	sliced celery (¾-inch/2 cm slices)	500 mL
1⅔ cups	sliced onions (¼-inch/0.5 cm slices)	400 mL
1 cup	diced seeded red bell pepper	250 mL
	Boiling water	
2½ cups	granulated sugar	625 mL
1 tbsp	mustard seeds	15 mL
1 tsp	celery seeds	5 mL
4 tsp	pickling or canning salt	20 mL
3 cups	white vinegar	750 mL
1¼ cups	water	300 mL

1. Prepare canner, jars and lids. *(For more information, see page 415.)*

2. In a large stainless steel saucepan, combine green and yellow beans, lima beans, celery, onions and red pepper. Add boiling water to cover and bring to a boil over medium-high heat. Reduce heat and boil gently for 5 minutes, until vegetables are heated through.

3. Meanwhile, in a seperate stainless steel saucepan, combine sugar, mustard seeds, celery seeds, salt, vinegar and water. Bring to a boil over medium-high heat, stirring to dissolve sugar. Reduce heat and boil gently for 5 minutes, until spices have infused the liquid.

4. Drain hot vegetables and pack into hot jars to within a generous ½ inch (1 cm) of top of jar. Ladle hot pickling liquid into jar to cover vegetables, leaving ½ inch (1 cm) headspace. Remove air bubbles and adjust headspace, if necessary, by adding hot pickling liquid. Wipe rim. Center lid on jar. Screw band down until resistance is met, then increase to fingertip-tight.

5. Place jars in canner, ensuring they are completely covered with water. Bring to a boil and process jars for 15 minutes. Remove canner lid. Wait 5 minutes, then remove jars, cool and store. *(For more information, see pages 417–418.)*

Pickled Beets

Pickled beets are a staple on most pantry shelves, and many people have clear preferences in terms of spicing. We've written this recipe using a traditional spice blend and provided two variations so you can adjust the flavors to suit your family's taste.

TIPS

You can buy prepared pickling spice at well-stocked supermarkets or make your own (see page 217).

To prepare beets for use in this recipe, leave the root and 2 inches (5 cm) of stem intact to prevent bleeding. Scrub thoroughly and sort by size, placing larger beets on the bottom of a saucepan and smallest on top. Add water to cover, bring to a boil and cook until tender, 20 to 40 minutes, depending upon the size of the beets. Remove beets from saucepan as they are cooked and run under cool running water. Drain. Slip off the skins and remove tap root and stems. Leave baby beets whole and slice or quarter larger beets.

Makes about six pint (500 mL) jars

3 tbsp	pickling spice (see tip, at left)	45 mL
2½ cups	white vinegar	625 mL
I cup	water	250 mL
I cup	granulated sugar	250 mL
I0 cups	prepared beets (see tip, at left)	2.5 L

1. Prepare canner, jars and lids. *(For more information, see page 415.)*
2. Tie pickling spice in a square of cheesecloth, creating a spice bag.
3. In a large stainless steel saucepan, combine vinegar, water, sugar and spice bag. Bring to boil over medium-high heat, stirring to dissolve sugar. Reduce heat and boil gently for 15 minutes, until spices have infused the liquid. Discard spice bag. Add beets and return mixture to a boil.
4. Using a slotted spoon, ladle beets into hot jars to within a generous ½ inch (1 cm) of top of jar. Ladle hot pickling liquid into jar to cover beets, leaving ½ inch (1 cm) headspace. Remove air bubbles and adjust headspace, if necessary, by adding more hot pickling liquid. Wipe rim. Center lid on jar. Screw band down until resistance is met, then increase to fingertip-tight.
5. Place jars in canner, ensuring they are completely covered with water. Bring to a boil and process for 30 minutes. Remove canner lid. Wait 5 minutes, then remove jars, cool and store. *(For more information, see pages 417–418.)*

Variations

Sweet Pickled Beets: Substitute 10 whole cloves and 2 cinnamon sticks (each about 4 inches/10 cm), broken, for the pickling spice.

Caraway Beets: Substitute 2 tbsp (30 mL) caraway seeds and 2 tsp (10 mL) whole black peppercorns for the pickling spice.

Pickled Beets and Onions: Add 3 cups (750 mL) sliced onions to the vinegar, water, sugar and spice solution. Cook as directed above, discard spice bag and add 8 cups (2 L) prepared beets, then proceed as directed above.

Dilled Carrots

These brightly colored pickled carrots make a great garnish for sandwiches and liven up relish trays.

TIPS

For this recipe, use the dill flower head, which is the yellow flower portion.

If fresh dill is not available, use ½ tsp (2 mL) of dill seeds per jar.

For quick and easy dilled carrots, use baby carrots, available in bags in the produce department of grocery stores.

Makes about seven pint (500 mL) jars

6 cups	white vinegar	1.5 L
2 cups	water	500 mL
½ cup	pickling or canning salt	125 mL
4	cloves garlic, halved	4
14	heads of dill (see tip, at left)	14
3½ tsp	hot pepper flakes (optional)	17 mL
5 lbs	carrots (25 to 30 medium), ends removed, peeled and cut into sticks (1 inch/2.5 cm long and ¾ inch/2 cm wide)	2.3 kg

1. Prepare canner, jars and lids. *(For more information, see page 415.)*
2. In a large stainless steel saucepan, combine vinegar, water and salt. Stir well and bring to a boil over medium-high heat, stirring to dissolve salt.
3. Place ½ clove of garlic, 1 head of dill and ½ tsp (2 mL) of hot pepper flakes, if using, in each hot jar. Pack carrot sticks into hot jars to within a generous ½ inch (1 cm) of top of jar. Top with second head of dill. Ladle hot pickling liquid into jar to cover carrots, leaving ½ inch (1 cm) headspace. Remove air bubbles and adjust headspace, if necessary, by adding hot pickling liquid. Wipe rim. Center lid on jar. Screw band down until resistance is met, then increase to fingertip-tight.
4. Place jars in canner, ensuring they are completely covered with water. Bring to a boil and process for 10 minutes. Remove canner lid. Wait 5 minutes, then remove jars, cool and store. *(For more information, see pages 417–418.)*

Vietnamese Carrot and Daikon Pickle

These pretty strands of orange and white pickle are the perfect accompaniment to any Southeast Asian meal, whether it is simply fried rice or curry served over a bed of rice.

TIP

The job will go faster if you have a mandoline to julienne the vegetables.

Makes about six pint (500 mL) jars

3 cups	white vinegar	750 mL
3 cups	water	750 mL
1½ cups	granulated sugar	375 mL
2 tsp	grated gingerroot	10 mL
2 lbs	carrots, julienned (2 inches/5 cm long and ⅛ to ¼ inch/0.25 to 0.5 cm wide)	900 g
2 lbs	daikon, julienned (2 inches/5 cm long and ⅛ to ¼ inch/0.25 to 0.5 cm wide)	900 g
6	whole star anise (optional)	6

1. Prepare canner, jars and lids. *(For more information, see page 415.)*

2. In a large stainless steel saucepan, combine vinegar, water, sugar and gingerroot. Bring to a boil over medium-high heat, stirring to dissolve sugar. Add carrot and daikon and stir for 1 minute. Remove from heat.

3. Place 1 star anise, if using, into each hot jar. Pack vegetables into hot jars to within a generous ½ inch (1 cm) of top of jar. Ladle hot pickling liquid into jar to cover vegetables, leaving ½ inch (1 cm) headspace. Remove air bubbles and adjust headspace, if necessary, by adding hot pickling liquid. Wipe rim. Center lid on jar. Screw band down until resistance is met, then increase to fingertip-tight.

4. Place jars in canner, ensuring they are completely covered with water. Bring to a boil and process for 10 minutes. Remove canner lid. Wait 5 minutes, then remove jars, cool and store. *(For more information, see pages 417–418.)*

Pickled Garlic

Makes about five 8-ounce (250 mL) jars

2½ cups	white vinegar	625 mL
I cup	dry white wine	250 mL
I tbsp	pickling or canning salt	15 mL
I tbsp	granulated sugar	15 mL
I tbsp	dried oregano	15 mL
12	large heads garlic, separated and peeled	12
5	dried chili peppers, such as cayenne, chile de arbol or Japanese dried chili (optional)	5

1. Prepare canner, jars and lids. *(For more information, see page 415.)*

2. In a large stainless steel saucepan, combine vinegar, wine, salt, sugar and oregano. Bring to a boil over medium-high heat, stirring to dissolve sugar. Reduce heat and boil gently for 1 minute. Add garlic and cook for 1 minute.

3. Pack garlic and 1 chili pepper, if using, into hot jars to within a generous ½ inch (1 cm) of top of jar. Ladle hot pickling liquid into jar to cover garlic, leaving ½ inch (1 cm) headspace. Remove air bubbles and adjust headspace, if necessary, by adding hot pickling liquid. Wipe rim. Center lid on jar. Screw band down until resistance is met, then increase to fingertip-tight.

4. Place jars in canner, ensuring they are completely covered with water. Bring to a boil and process for 10 minutes. Remove canner lid. Wait 5 minutes, then remove jars, cool and store. *(For more information, see pages 417–418.)*

Aubergine Pickles

Aubergine is the French/British word for eggplant. Although Chinese eggplant works best in this recipe, the larger variety may also be used.

TIPS

Boiling the eggplant before pickling removes the air and bitter flavor from its pulp. Take extra care in handling it, as eggplant bruises and falls apart easily after it has been boiled.

When packing fruits or vegetables into jars for pickles, pack tightly, but not too tightly. Leave room for the pickling liquid, since that is where the flavor comes from.

Makes about six pint (500 mL) jars

4½ cups	water	1.125 L
5 lbs	eggplant (about 4 large)	2.3 kg
1½ cups	white vinegar	375 mL
½ cup	balsamic vinegar	125 mL
3 tbsp	granulated sugar	45 mL
1 tbsp	dried oregano	15 mL
2 tsp	pickling or canning salt	10 mL
6	cloves garlic	6

1. In a stockpot, bring water to a rapid boil. Working quickly to prevent browning, peel and remove ends from eggplants. Cut into sticks approximately 3 inches (7.5 cm) long and ¾ inch (2 cm) wide. Immediately add to stockpot and return to a boil. Reduce heat and boil gently for 10 minutes, pressing the eggplant under the water every 2 minutes to remove air, until eggplant is tender. Transfer to a colander placed over a sink and rinse with cold running water to stop the cooking process. Let drain for 1 minute without pressing out excess liquid. Set aside.

2. Prepare canner, jars and lids. *(For more information, see page 415.)*

3. In a large stainless steel saucepan, combine white vinegar, balsamic vinegar, sugar, oregano and salt. Bring to a boil over medium-high heat, stirring to dissolve sugar. Add eggplant and return to a boil. Remove from heat.

4. Place 1 clove garlic in each hot jar. Pack hot eggplant into hot jars to within a generous ½ inch (1 cm) of top of jar. Ladle hot pickling liquid into jar to cover eggplant, leaving ½ inch (1 cm) headspace. Remove air bubbles and adjust headspace, if necessary, by adding hot pickling liquid. Wipe rim. Center lid on jar. Screw band down until resistance is met, then increase to fingertip-tight.

5. Place jars in canner, ensuring they are completely covered with water. Bring to a boil and process for 15 minutes. Remove canner lid. Wait 5 minutes, then remove jars, cool and store. *(For more information, see pages 417–418.)*

Marrow 'n' Onion Mustard Pickles

A green-and-yellow-hued member of the summer squash family, vegetable marrow is a time-honored side dish in some families. Here it is transformed into a chunky pickle that makes a zesty complement to grilled entrées, sandwiches and salad plates. Any firm summer squash, such as zucchini, may be substituted for the marrow.

TIPS

To remove onion skins with ease, blanch onions in boiling water until the center is heated through, 3 to 7 minutes, then immerse in cold water. Drain and peel off skins.

Be sure to squeeze excess moisture from salted, rinsed vegetables before adding them to remaining recipe ingredients.

Makes about six pint (500 mL) jars

12 cups	cubed seeded peeled vegetable marrow (3/4-inch/2 cm cubes)	3 L
1/4 cup	pickling or canning salt	50 mL
1 3/4 cups	granulated sugar	425 mL
8 tsp	ClearJel® (see tip, page 309)	40 mL
1/3 cup	mustard seeds	75 mL
1 1/2 tsp	celery seeds	7 mL
1 1/2 tsp	ground turmeric	7 mL
1/2 cup	water	125 mL
2 cups	white vinegar	500 mL
2 cups	large sweet red peppers, such as Shepherd or red bell, seeded and chopped	500 mL
8 cups	pickling or pearl onions, peeled (see tip, at left)	2 L

1. In a large glass or stainless steel bowl, layer marrow with pickling salt. Cover and let stand at room temperature for 3 hours. Transfer to a colander placed over a sink, rinse under cool water and drain thoroughly.

2. Meanwhile, prepare canner, jars and lids. *(For more information, see page 415.)*

3. In a large stainless steel saucepan, combine sugar, ClearJel®, mustard seeds, celery seeds and turmeric. Gradually blend in water, mixing well. Add vinegar and red peppers. Bring to a boil over medium-high heat, stirring frequently to dissolve sugar and prevent lumps from forming. Reduce heat and boil gently, stirring frequently, until mixture thickens, about 5 minutes. Stir in drained marrow and onions and return to a boil.

4. Ladle hot marrow mixture into hot jars, leaving 1/2 inch (1 cm) headspace. Remove air bubbles and adjust headspace, if necessary, by adding hot marrow mixture. Wipe rim. Center lid on jar. Screw band down until resistance is met, then increase to fingertip-tight.

5. Place jars in canner, ensuring they are completely covered with water. Bring to a boil and process for 15 minutes. Remove canner lid. Wait 5 minutes, then remove jars, cool and store. *(For more information, see pages 417–418.)*

Variation

If you like spicier pickles, substitute 2 tbsp (30 mL) chopped and seeded hot red chili peppers for some of the sweet red peppers.

Okra Pickles

Tired of the same old relish trays? Try substituting these okra pickles for small dill pickles. They make a delicious change.

TIPS

When trimming okra, remove the stems, taking care not to cut the pods.

When cutting or seeding hot peppers, wear rubber gloves to prevent hands from being burned.

Makes about four pint (500 mL) jars

3 cups	water	750 mL
3 cups	white vinegar	750 mL
1/3 cup	pickling or canning salt	75 mL
2 tsp	dill seeds	10 mL
3 1/2 lbs	small whole okra pods, trimmed (see tip, at left)	1.6 kg
4	cloves garlic	4
2	small hot red peppers, stems removed, halved lengthwise and seeded	2

1. Prepare canner, jars and lids. (For more information, see page 415.)
2. In a large stainless steel saucepan, combine water, vinegar, pickling salt and dill seeds. Bring to a boil over medium-high heat, stirring to dissolve salt. Reduce heat to low and keep hot until ready to use.
3. Pack okra into hot jars to within a generous 1/2 inch (1 cm) of top of jar. Put 1 clove garlic and 1/2 pepper in each jar. Ladle hot pickling liquid into jar to cover okra, leaving 1/2 inch (1 cm) headspace. Remove air bubbles and adjust headspace, if necessary, by adding hot pickling liquid. Wipe rim. Center lid on jar. Screw band down until resistance is met, then increase to fingertip-tight.
4. Place jars in canner, ensuring they are completely covered with water. Bring to a boil and process for 15 minutes. Remove canner lid. Wait 5 minutes, then remove jars, cool and store. (For more information, see pages 417–418.)

Red Onions in Vinegar

These onion rings are a perfect addition to fresh salads. Try adding them to a bed of romaine lettuce or spinach. Add strawberries and candied walnuts and dress with a mild vinaigrette.

Makes about seven 8-ounce (250 mL) jars

4 cups	red wine vinegar	1 L
1	clove garlic	1
10 cups	sliced peeled red onions (1/4-inch/0.5 cm thick rings)	2.5 L

1. Prepare canner, jars and lids. (For more information, see page 415.)
2. In a large stainless steel saucepan, combine vinegar and garlic. Bring to a boil over medium-high heat. Reduce heat and boil gently for 5 minutes, until garlic flavor has infused the liquid. Add onion rings, increase heat to medium-high and bring to a boil. Reduce heat and boil gently, covered, for 5 minutes, until onions are heated through. Discard garlic.

3. Pack hot onion rings into hot jars to within a generous $\frac{1}{2}$ inch (1 cm) of top of jar. Ladle hot pickling liquid into jar to cover onions, leaving $\frac{1}{2}$ inch (1 cm) headspace. Remove air bubbles and adjust headspace, if necessary, by adding hot pickling liquid. Wipe rim. Center lid on jar. Screw band down until resistance is met, then increase to fingertip-tight.

4. Place jars in canner, ensuring they are completely covered with water. Bring to a boil and process for 10 minutes. Remove canner lid. Wait 5 minutes, then remove jars, cool and store. *(For more information, see pages 417–418.)*

Pickled Roasted Red Peppers

These versatile peppers can be used in spaghetti sauce, as a sandwich filling, to garnish a salad, to add a twist to an antipasto platter or as a gourmet pizza topping.

TIPS

Roast peppers and garlic cloves over hot coals, on a grill at 425°F (220°C) or under the broiler until charred, turning to roast all sides. Once the skin of the peppers wrinkles and chars and garlic has charred spots, remove from heat. Place peppers in a paper bag until cool enough to handle, about 15 minutes, then lift off skins. Cool garlic. Squeeze roasted garlic cloves to remove from peel.

Other colors of bell peppers may be prepared and pickled as directed in this recipe.

Makes about four pint (500 mL) jars

4	large cloves garlic, roasted, removed from skin and mashed (see tip, at left)	4
1 $\frac{1}{2}$ cups	white vinegar	375 mL
1 $\frac{1}{2}$ cups	cider vinegar	375 mL
1 $\frac{1}{2}$ cups	dry white wine	375 mL
$\frac{1}{2}$ cup	water	125 mL
1 cup	coarsely chopped onion	250 mL
$\frac{1}{2}$ cup	granulated sugar	125 mL
2 tbsp	dried oregano	30 mL
4 tsp	pickling or canning salt	20 mL
20	medium sweet red peppers, such as red bell or Shepherd, roasted, peeled, seeded, deveined and cut lengthwise into serving-size pieces (see tip, at left)	20

1. Prepare canner, jars and lids. *(For more information, see page 415.)*

2. In a large stainless steel saucepan, combine roasted garlic, white vinegar, cider vinegar, white wine, water, onion, sugar, oregano and salt. Bring to a boil over medium-high heat, stirring to dissolve sugar. Reduce heat and boil gently for 5 minutes, until garlic and oregano flavors have infused the liquid.

3. Pack room temperature peppers into hot jars to within a generous $\frac{1}{2}$ inch (1 cm) of top of jar. Ladle hot pickling liquid into jar to cover peppers, leaving $\frac{1}{2}$ inch (1 cm) headspace. Remove air bubbles and adjust headspace, if necessary, by adding hot pickling liquid. Wipe rim. Center lid on jar. Screw band down until resistance is met, then increase to fingertip-tight.

4. Place jars in canner, ensuring they are completely covered with water. Bring to a boil and process for 15 minutes. Remove canner lid. Wait 5 minutes, then remove jars, cool and store. *(For more information, see pages 417–418.)*

Pickled Hot Peppers

These hot peppers really pack a punch. Stack them on sub sandwiches or chop and sprinkle over pizza to add pizzazz.

TIPS

For this recipe, you'll need about 1 1/2 lbs (680 g) of hot banana peppers, about 1 lb (500 g) of jalapeño peppers and about 4 oz (125 g) of serrano peppers.

Cut peppers into 1/2-inch (1 cm) thick rings. Discard stems. Remove seeds, if desired.

When cutting or seeding hot peppers, wear rubber gloves to keep your hands from being burned.

Makes about five pint (500 mL) jars

6 cups	sliced hot banana peppers (see tips, at left)	1.5 L
4 cups	sliced jalapeño peppers (see tips, at left)	1 L
1 cup	sliced serrano peppers (see tips, at left)	250 mL
6 cups	white vinegar	1.5 L
2 cups	water	500 mL
3	cloves garlic, crushed	3

1. Prepare canner, jars and lids. *(For more information, see page 415.)*
2. In a large glass or stainless steel bowl, combine peppers. Mix well and set aside.
3. In a large stainless steel saucepan, combine vinegar, water and garlic. Bring to a boil over medium-high heat. Reduce heat and boil gently for 5 minutes, until garlic flavor has infused the liquid. Discard garlic.
4. Pack peppers into hot jars to within a generous 1/2 inch (1 cm) of top of jar. Ladle hot pickling liquid into jar to cover peppers, leaving 1/2 inch (1 cm) headspace. Remove air bubbles and adjust headspace, if necessary, by adding hot pickling liquid. Wipe rim. Center lid on jar. Screw band down until resistance is met, then increase to fingertip-tight.
5. Place jars in canner, ensuring they are completely covered with water. Bring to a boil and process for 10 minutes. Remove canner lid. Wait 5 minutes, then remove jars, cool and store. *(For more information, see pages 417–418.)*

Summer Squash Pickles

These pickled cubes of squash have great eye appeal, as well as taste, when added to a summer pasta salad.

Makes about four to five 8-ounce (250 mL) jars

4 cups	cubed seeded peeled summer squash, such as yellow squash or zucchini (1/2-inch/1 cm cubes)	1 L
1 1/3 cups	sliced onion	325 mL
2 cups	water	500 mL
1 1/4 cups	granulated sugar	300 mL
1 cup	white vinegar	250 mL
1 tsp	pickling or canning salt	5 mL
1 tsp	dry mustard	5 mL
1/2 tsp	ground turmeric	2 mL
1/2 tsp	ground ginger	2 mL

Before using jars, inspect them carefully for any chips, cracks or fractures. Discard any imperfect jars.

1. Prepare canner, jars and lids. (*For more information, see page 415.*)
2. In a large glass or stainless steel bowl, combine squash and onion. Mix well and set aside.
3. In a large stainless steel saucepan, combine water, sugar, vinegar, salt, mustard, turmeric and ginger. Bring to a boil over medium-high heat, stirring to dissolve sugar. Add squash and onions. Return to a boil and boil for 10 minutes, until vegetables are heated through and slightly tender.
4. Pack hot vegetables and liquid into hot jars, leaving ½ inch (1 cm) headspace. Remove air bubbles and adjust headspace, if necessary, by adding hot liquid. Wipe rim. Center lid on jar. Screw band down until resistance is met, then increase to fingertip-tight.
5. Place jars in canner, ensuring they are completely covered with water. Bring to a boil and process for 10 minutes. Remove canner lid. Wait 5 minutes, then remove jars, cool and store. (*For more information, see pages 417–418.*)

Dilled Green Tomatoes

These flavorful green tomato wedges are a wonderful addition to ordinary salads. Use them in place of red tomatoes anytime you get a chance.

TIPS

One head of fresh dill is equivalent to 1 to 2 tsp (5 to 10 mL) dill seeds or 2 tsp (10 mL) dried dillweed.

The yield for pickled small whole vegetables, such as cherry tomatoes and baby beets, will vary depending on the size of the vegetables being used.

Makes six to seven pint (500 mL) jars

3½ cups	vinegar	875 mL
3½ cups	water	875 mL
¼ cup	pickling or canning salt	50 mL
5 lbs	small, firm green tomatoes, halved or quartered, or green cherry tomatoes	2.3 kg
6 to 7	cloves garlic	6 to 7
6 to 7	heads fresh dill (or ¼ cup/50 mL dill seeds or dried dillweed)	6 to 7
6 to 7	bay leaves	6 to 7

1. Prepare canner, jars and lids. (*For more information, see page 415.*)
2. In a large stainless steel saucepan, combine vinegar, water and pickling salt. Bring to a boil over medium-high heat, stirring to dissolve salt. Remove from heat.
3. Pack tomatoes into hot jars to within a generous ½ inch (1 cm) of top of jar. Add 1 clove garlic, 1 head dill (or 2 tsp/10 mL dill seeds or dillweed) and 1 bay leaf to each jar. Ladle hot pickling liquid into jar to cover tomatoes, leaving ½ inch (1 cm) headspace. Remove air bubbles and adjust headspace, if necessary, by adding hot pickling liquid. Wipe rim. Center lid on jar. Screw band down until resistance is met, then increase to fingertip-tight.
4. Place jars in canner, ensuring they are completely covered with water. Bring to a boil and process for 15 minutes. Remove canner lid. Wait 5 minutes, then remove jars, cool and store. (*For more information, see pages 417–418.*)

Pickled Green Tomato–Hot Pepper Mix

This combination of green tomatoes and hot peppers makes an excellent salsa-style sauce that is particularly delicious with grilled chicken. Drain the liquid from the jar and chop the vegetables coarsely in a food processor fitted with a metal blade. Use to generously garnish the top of the chicken and serve lime wedges alongside.

TIPS

You can buy prepared pickling spice at well-stocked supermarkets or make your own (see page 217).

Cut peppers into ½-inch (1 cm) thick rings, discarding stems and seeds.

When cutting or seeding hot peppers, wear rubber gloves to keep your hands from being burned.

If Anaheim, poblano or fresh New Mexico peppers are not available, substitute 3½ cups (875 mL) sliced, seeded Cubanelle or green bell peppers and ½ cup (125 mL) sliced, seeded jalapeño peppers.

Makes about five quart (1 L) jars

¼ cup	pickling spice (see tip, at left)	50 mL
2 tbsp	mustard seeds	30 mL
7 lbs	green tomatoes, cored and cut into eighths	3.2 L
4 cups	sliced seeded Hungarian or red bell peppers (see tip, at left)	1 L
4 cups	sliced seeded hot yellow banana peppers (see tips, at left)	1 L
4 cups	sliced seeded Anaheim, poblano or fresh New Mexico peppers (see tips, at left)	1 L
2 cups	pickling or pearl onions, peeled	500 mL
5	cloves garlic	5
1 tbsp	pickling or canning salt	15 mL
8 cups	white vinegar	2 L
4 cups	water	1 L
1 cup	granulated sugar	250 mL

1. Prepare canner, jars and lids. (*For more information, see page 415.*)
2. Tie pickling spice and mustard seeds in a square of cheesecloth, creating a spice bag. Set aside.
3. In a large glass or stainless steel bowl, combine tomatoes, peppers, onions, garlic and salt. Mix well and set aside.
4. In a large stainless steel saucepan, combine vinegar, water and sugar. Bring to a boil over medium-high heat, stirring to dissolve sugar. Add reserved spice bag, reduce heat and boil gently for 10 minutes, until spices have infused the liquid. Add vegetables and boil gently for 10 minutes, until vegetables are heated though and slightly tender. Remove from heat. Discard spice bag.
5. Pack hot vegetables into hot jars to within a generous ½ inch (1 cm) of top of jar, making sure 1 clove garlic is added to each jar. Ladle hot pickling liquid into jar to cover vegetables, leaving ½ inch (1 cm) headspace. Remove air bubbles and adjust headspace, if necessary, by adding hot pickling liquid. Wipe rim. Center lid on jar. Screw band down until resistance is met, then increase to fingertip-tight.
6. Place jars in canner, ensuring they are completely covered with water. Bring to a boil and process for 15 minutes. Remove canner lid. Wait 5 minutes, then remove jars, cool and store. (*For more information, see pages 417–418.*)

Peach Salsa (page 215),
Roasted Tomato–Chipotle Salsa (page 206),
Salsa Verde (page 210)

Homestyle Corn Relish (page 225),
Red Root Relish (page 229),
Zesty Zucchini Relish (page 232)

Jardinière (page 322),
Dilled Carrots (page 312),
Grandma's Dill Pickles
(page 328)

Seafood Cocktail Sauce (page 369),
Thai Hot and Sweet Dipping Sauce (page 281)

Blueberry-Basil Vinegar (page 276),
Raspberry Vinegar (page 278),
Fresh Tarragon Wine Vinegar (page 280)

Pickled Asparagus (page 307),
Red Onions in Vinegar (page 316)

Pickled Roasted Red Peppers (page 317)

Pickled Three-Bean Salad (page 310)

Chili (page 405)

Tomatoes Packed in Water (page 354)

Cinnamon Watermelon Rind Pickles (page 327)

Hot Pickle Mix

This zesty pickle is not for the timid! Adjust the quantity of jalapeño peppers to provide the level of heat you prefer.

TIPS

Make pickles with a variety of fruits or vegetables, or a combination of both. Select tender vegetables and firm fruit.

Refer to the Produce Purchase Guide on pages 426–429 to determine how much produce you'll need to buy to prepare this recipe.

Pickle fruits and vegetables within 24 hours of harvest. If your schedule does not accommodate this brief time window, refrigerate the produce and use it as soon as possible.

Makes about six pint (500 mL) jars

4 cups	sliced trimmed pickling cucumbers (¼-inch/0.5 cm slices)	1 L
2 cups	cauliflower florets	500 mL
1	green bell pepper, seeded and cut into strips	1
1	red bell pepper, seeded and cut into strips	1
1 cup	sliced peeled carrots (¼-inch/0.5 cm slices)	250 mL
1 cup	peeled pearl or pickling onions	250 mL
⅔ cup	pickling or canning salt	150 mL
8½ cups	water, divided	2.125 L
3 cups	sliced seeded hot yellow banana peppers (1½-inch/4 cm slices)	750 mL
1	clove garlic	1
8½ cups	white vinegar	2.125 L
¾ cup	granulated sugar	175 mL
2 tbsp	prepared horseradish	30 mL
3 to 9	jalapeño peppers, halved and seeded	3 to 9

1. In a large glass or stainless steel bowl, combine cucumbers, cauliflower, green and red peppers, carrots and onions.

2. In another large glass or stainless steel bowl, dissolve pickling salt in 7 cups (1.75 L) of the water. Pour over vegetables. Cover and let stand at room temperature for 1 hour.

3. Meanwhile, prepare canner, jars and lids. *(For more information, see page 415.)*

4. In a colander placed over a sink, drain vegetables. Rinse with cool running water and drain thoroughly. Add hot yellow peppers and mix well.

5. In a large stainless steel saucepan, combine garlic, remaining 1½ cups (375 mL) water, vinegar, sugar and horseradish. Bring to a boil over medium-high heat, stirring to dissolve sugar. Reduce heat and boil gently for 15 minutes, until liquid is infused with garlic flavor. Discard garlic clove.

6. Pack vegetables and 1 to 3 jalapeño pepper halves into hot jars to within a generous ½ inch (1 cm) of top of jar. Ladle hot pickling liquid into jar to cover vegetables, leaving ½ inch (1 cm) headspace. Remove air bubbles and adjust headspace, if necessary, by adding hot pickling liquid. Wipe rim. Center lid on jar. Screw band down until resistance is met, then increase to fingertip-tight.

7. Place jars in canner, ensuring they are completely covered with water. Bring to a boil and process for 10 minutes. Remove canner lid. Wait 5 minutes, then remove jars, cool and store. *(For more information, see pages 417–418.)*

Jardinière

This tasty pickle combines a colorful array of vegetables and makes a satisfying snack or addition to any meal. The word "jardinière" comes from the French jardin, meaning "garden," so this recipe could be described as "pickles from the garden."

TIPS

Why confine pickling to cucumbers? Fruits and other vegetables make delicious pickles. The brilliant colors produce pickles that are beautiful to look at, and their crisp texture and robust flavors make enjoyable treats.

Use Pickle Crisp™ to make fresh-pack pickles crisper. Add ¾ tsp (3 mL) to pint (500 mL) jars and 1½ tsp (7 mL) to quart (1 L) jars before processing.

Makes about five pint (500 mL) jars

3	bay leaves	3
6	whole black peppercorns	6
3	cloves garlic, thinly sliced	3
4 cups	white vinegar	1 L
2 cups	water	500 mL
2 cups	granulated sugar	500 mL
1 tbsp	pickling or canning salt	15 mL
2 cups	small cauliflower florets	500 mL
1½ cups	peeled pickling or pearl onions	375 mL
3	stalks celery, cut into ¼-inch (0.5 cm) slices	3
2	carrots, peeled and cut into sticks (1½ inches/4 cm long and ½ inch/1 cm wide)	2
1	small zucchini, cut into ¼-inch (0.5 cm) slices	1
2	large red bell peppers, seeded and cut into ¼-inch (0.5 cm) strips	2
1	large yellow bell pepper, seeded and cut into ¼-inch (0.5 cm) strips	1
1	large green bell pepper, seeded and cut into ¼-inch (0.5 cm) strips	1

1. Prepare canner, jars and lids. *(For more information, see page 415.)*
2. Tie bay leaves, peppercorns and garlic in a square of cheesecloth, creating a spice bag.
3. In a large stainless steel saucepan, combine vinegar, water, sugar, salt and spice bag. Bring to a boil over medium-high heat, stirring to dissolve sugar. Reduce heat, cover and boil gently for 5 minutes, until spices have infused the liquid. Add cauliflower, onions, celery, carrots and zucchini and return to a boil. Remove from heat and stir in red, yellow and green peppers. Discard spice bag.
4. Pack vegetables into hot jars to within a generous ½ inch (1 cm) of top of jar. Ladle hot pickling liquid into jar to cover vegetables, leaving ½ inch (1 cm) headspace. Remove air bubbles and adjust headspace, if necessary, by adding hot pickling liquid. Wipe rim. Center lid on jar. Screw band down until resistance is met, then increase to fingertip-tight.
5. Place jars in canner, ensuring they are completely covered with water. Bring to a boil and process for 10 minutes. Remove canner lid. Wait 5 minutes, then remove jars, cool and store. *(For more information, see pages 417–418.)*

End of Garden Pickles

These pickles take full advantage of the garden's bounty of summer vegetables. Its fresh taste is particularly delicious alongside grilled fish or chicken.

TIPS

Refer to the Produce Purchase Guide on pages 426–429 to determine how much produce you'll need to buy to prepare this recipe.

When making pickles, select uniformly sized fruits and vegetables and/or cut them into pieces of similar size. During processing, each piece of produce should be heated to the same degree. If the pieces vary too much in size, smaller pieces will soften and larger pieces may not be heated sufficiently. In addition to reduced quality, inadequate heat penetration can become a safety issue.

Makes about five pint (500 mL) jars

3 cups	sliced zucchini (¼-inch/0.5 cm slices)	750 mL
3 cups	sliced trimmed green beans (1-inch/2.5 cm slices)	750 mL
1½ cups	sliced peeled carrots (¼-inch/0.5 cm slices)	375 mL
2 cups	peeled pickling or pearl onions	500 mL
2	large green bell peppers, seeded and cut into ½-inch (1 cm) strips	2
1	large red bell pepper, seeded and cut into ½-inch (1 cm) strips	1
3 cups	cider vinegar	750 mL
1 cup	lightly packed brown sugar	250 mL
1 cup	granulated sugar	250 mL
2 tbsp	dry mustard	30 mL
2 tbsp	mustard seeds	30 mL
4½ tsp	pickling or canning salt	22 mL
1 tsp	ground cinnamon	5 mL
1 tsp	ground ginger	5 mL

1. Prepare canner, jars and lids. *(For more information, see page 415.)*

2. In a large glass or stainless steel bowl, combine zucchini, beans, carrots, onions and green and red peppers. Stir well and set aside.

3. In a large stainless steel saucepan, combine vinegar, brown sugar, granulated sugar, dry mustard, mustard seeds, salt, cinnamon and ginger. Bring to a boil over medium-high heat, stirring to dissolve sugar. Add vegetables and return to a boil. Reduce heat and boil gently for 15 minutes, until vegetables are heated through and slightly tender.

4. Pack hot vegetables and liquid into hot jars, leaving ½ inch (1 cm) headspace. Remove air bubbles and adjust headspace, if necessary, by adding hot pickling liquid. Wipe rim. Center lid on jar. Screw band down until resistance is met, then increase to fingertip-tight.

5. Place jars in canner, ensuring they are completely covered with water. Bring to a boil and process for 15 minutes. Remove canner lid. Wait 5 minutes, then remove jars, cool and store. *(For more information, see pages 417–418.)*

Zany Zucchini Pickles

*These zesty pickles
are so easy to make,
you'll welcome an
overabundance of
zucchini in the garden.*

TIPS

When packing fruits or
vegetables into jars for
pickles, pack tightly, but
not too tightly. Leave
room for the pickling
liquid, since that is where
the flavor comes from.

If pickling liquid is fresh
and has not been used to
make pickles, cover it and
refrigerate for use in your
next batch of pickles. For
best results, use within
2 weeks. Excess pickling
liquid can also be
added to coleslaw
dressing, marinades or
barbecue sauces.

Makes about six pint (500 mL) jars

14 cups	diagonally sliced zucchini (¼-inch/0.5 cm slices)	3.5 L
½ cup	pickling or canning salt	125 mL
	Cool water	
6 cups	white vinegar	1.5 L
4 cups	granulated sugar	1 L
4 tsp	mustard seeds	20 mL
2 tsp	celery seeds	10 mL
2 tsp	ground turmeric	10 mL

1. In a glass or stainless steel bowl, layer zucchini slices with pickling salt. Add cool water to cover, cover and let stand at room temperature for 2 hours. Transfer to a colander placed over a sink and drain zucchini. Rinse with cool running water and drain thoroughly.

2. In a large stainless steel saucepan, combine vinegar, sugar, mustard seeds, celery seeds and turmeric. Bring to a boil over medium-high heat, stirring to dissolve sugar. Reduce heat and boil gently for 5 minutes, until spices have infused the liquid. Stir in zucchini. Remove from heat, cover and let stand for 1 hour.

3. Meanwhile, prepare canner, jars and lids. *(For more information, see page 415.)*

4. Return saucepan to medium-high heat and bring zucchini mixture to a boil, stirring occasionally. Reduce heat and boil gently for 5 minutes, until zucchini is heated through.

5. Pack zucchini into hot jars to within a generous ½ inch (1 cm) of top of jar. Ladle hot pickling liquid into jar to cover vegetables, leaving ½ inch (1 cm) headspace. Remove air bubbles and adjust headspace, if necessary, by adding hot pickling liquid. Wipe rim. Center lid on jar. Screw band down until resistance is met, then increase to fingertip-tight.

6. Place jars in canner, ensuring they are completely covered with water. Bring to a boil and process for 10 minutes. Remove canner lid. Wait 5 minutes, then remove jars, cool and store. *(For more information, see pages 417–418.)*

Fruit Pickles — 2-Day

Peach Pickles

These mellow pickles are an excellent complement to roasted and barbecued meats.

TIPS

To peel peaches and treat to prevent browning, see page 140.

When pickling, use a current, thoroughly tested home canning recipe and follow it carefully. Pay particular attention to the quality of ingredients, their size and their degree of ripeness. For example, slightly under-ripe pears, peaches and green tomatoes produce the best pickles.

Pickle fruits and vegetables within 24 hours of harvest. If your schedule does not accommodate this brief time window, refrigerate the produce and use it as soon as possible.

Makes about five pint (500 mL) jars

2	cinnamon sticks (each about 4 inches/10 cm), broken into pieces	2
2 tbsp	whole cloves	30 mL
1 tbsp	grated gingerroot	15 mL
6 cups	granulated sugar	1.5 L
4 cups	white vinegar	1 L
16 cups	halved pitted peeled peaches, treated to prevent browning and drained	4 L

Day 1

1. Tie cinnamon stick pieces, cloves and gingerroot in a square of cheesecloth, creating a spice bag.
2. In a large stainless steel saucepan, combine sugar, vinegar and spice bag. Bring to a boil over medium-high heat, stirring to dissolve sugar. Reduce heat and boil gently for 5 minutes, until spices have infused the liquid. Add peaches and boil gently until just tender, about 7 minutes. Remove from heat, cover and refrigerate overnight.

Day 2

1. Prepare canner, jars and lids. *(For more information, see page 415.)*
2. Over medium-high heat, bring peaches and pickling liquid to a boil. Discard spice bag.
3. Pack peaches, cavity side down, into hot jars to within a generous ½ inch (1 cm) of top of jar. Ladle hot pickling liquid into jar to cover peaches, leaving ½ inch (1 cm) headspace. Remove air bubbles and adjust headspace, if necessary, by adding hot pickling liquid. Wipe rim. Center lid on jar. Screw band down until resistance is met, then increase to fingertip-tight.
4. Place jars in canner, ensuring they are completely covered with water. Bring to a boil and process for 20 minutes. Remove canner lid. Wait 5 minutes, then remove jars, cool and store. *(For more information, see pages 417–418.)*

Pear Pickles

A delicate blend of spices enhances the pear flavor of these tasty pickles. Serve them chilled as a palate cleanser between courses of a large meal, or as a light dessert with cheese and biscuits.

TIPS

You can buy prepared pickling spice at well-stocked supermarkets or make your own (see page 217).

The yield will vary somewhat depending on the size of the pears. Smaller pears work best for this recipe. Select pears that are quite firm and just ripe.

When pickling, use a current, thoroughly tested home canning recipe and follow it carefully. Pay particular attention to the quality of ingredients, their size and their degree of ripeness. For example, slightly under-ripe pears, peaches and green tomatoes produce the best pickles.

Makes about three pint (500 mL) jars

1 tbsp	pickling spice (see tip, at left)	15 mL
1 tsp	whole cloves	5 mL
1 tbsp	coarsely chopped gingerroot	15 mL
3 cups	granulated sugar	750 mL
2½ cups	water	625 mL
1½ cups	white vinegar	375 mL
½	lemon, cut into ¼-inch (0.5 cm) slices	½
6 lbs	firm just-ripe pears, such as Asian, peeled, cored, halved and treated to prevent browning (see page 140)	2.7 kg

Day 1

1. Tie pickling spice, cloves and gingerroot in a square of cheesecloth, creating a spice bag.
2. In a large stainless steel saucepan, combine sugar, water, vinegar, lemon slices and spice bag. Bring to a boil over medium-high heat, stirring to dissolve sugar. Reduce heat, cover and boil gently for 5 minutes, until spices have infused the liquid.
3. Working in batches, one layer at a time, add pears to pickling liquid and poach over medium-low heat until tender, about 7 minutes. Do not overcook. Using a slotted spoon, transfer to large bowl and cover with hot pickling liquid. When all pears are poached, ladle remaining pickling liquid over them. Cover and let stand in a cool place for at least 12 hours, but no longer than 18 hours.

Day 2

1. Prepare canner, jars and lids. *(For more information, see page 415.)*
2. Remove pears from pickling liquid and set aside. Discard spice bag. Transfer pickling liquid to a stainless steel saucepan and bring to a boil over medium-high heat.
3. Pack pears into hot jars to within a generous ½ inch (1 cm) of top of jar. Ladle hot pickling liquid into jar to cover pears, leaving ½ inch (1 cm) headspace. Remove air bubbles and adjust headspace, if necessary, by adding hot pickling liquid. Wipe rim. Center lid on jar. Screw band down until resistance is met, then increase to fingertip-tight.
4. Place jars in canner, ensuring they are completely covered with water. Bring to a boil and process for 20 minutes. Remove canner lid. Wait 5 minutes, then remove jars, cool and store. *(For more information, see pages 417–418.)*

Cinnamon Watermelon Rind Pickles

Make the most of your watermelon! After eating the juicy red watermelon pulp, use the peeled rind to make this sweet, cinnamon-flavored pickle. These are perfect for summertime picnics and barbecues or to perk up cold-weather meals.

TIPS

To prepare watermelon rind, remove dark green peel from watermelon rind and discard. Cut rind into 2- by 1-inch (5 by 2.5 cm) slices.

When preparing jars and lids, prepare a couple extra in case your yield is larger than you expect. If you don't have enough jars, place any leftover preserves in an airtight container, store in the refrigerator and use within a few weeks.

Place a clean towel on your work surface to absorb water from the hot jars as you take them out of the boiling-water canner to be filled, and again once the jars are processed. The towel prevents hot jars from coming into contact with cooler countertops. Significant temperature differences can cause jar breakage.

Makes four to five pint (500 mL) jars

16 cups	sliced peeled watermelon rind (2- by 1-inch/5 by 2.5 cm slices) (see tip, at left)	4 L
1 cup	pickling or canning salt	250 mL
8 cups	cool water, divided	2 L
6 cups	granulated sugar	1.5 L
4 cups	white vinegar	1 L
3	cinnamon sticks (each about 4 inches/10 cm), broken in half	3

Day 1

1. In a large crock, glass or stainless steel bowl, layer watermelon rind and salt. Add 4 cups (1 L) of the cold water. Place a large clean inverted plate on top of the rind and weigh down with two or three quart (1 L) jars filled with water and capped. Cover with plastic wrap or a clean towel and refrigerate for 8 hours or overnight.

Day 2

1. Transfer rind to a colander placed over a sink. Drain and rinse in cool running water. Drain and rinse again. Drain thoroughly.

2. In a large stainless steel saucepan, combine rind with remaining 4 cups (1 L) cool water. Bring to a boil over medium-high heat. Reduce heat and boil gently until rind is fork-tender, about 10 minutes. Drain and set aside.

3. In clean large stainless steel saucepan, combine sugar, vinegar and cinnamon stick halves. Bring to a boil over medium-high heat, stirring to dissolve sugar. Reduce heat and boil gently for 5 minutes, until cinnamon has infused the liquid. Add drained rind and return to a boil. Reduce heat and boil gently, stirring occasionally, for 1 hour, until watermelon is translucent. Discard cinnamon sticks.

4. Meanwhile, prepare canner, jars and lids. (*For more information, see page 415.*)

5. Pack hot rind into hot jars to within a generous 1/2 inch (1 cm) of top of jar. Ladle hot pickling liquid into jar to cover rind, leaving 1/2 inch (1 cm) headspace. Remove air bubbles and adjust headspace, if necessary, by adding more hot syrup. Wipe rim. Center lid on jar. Screw band down until resistance is met, then increase to fingertip-tight.

6. Place jars in canner, ensuring they are completely covered with water. Bring to a boil and process for 10 minutes. Remove canner lid. Wait 5 minutes, then remove jars, cool and store. (*For more information, see pages 417–418.*)

Vegetable Pickles — 2-Day

Grandma's Dill Pickles

Just like Grandma used to make! Bring back the memories of summertime pickling with Grandma with this traditional dill pickle recipe.

TIPS

Smaller pickling cucumbers yield crisper pickles. If you use pickles larger than 4 inches (10 cm), you will get a softer-textured product.

You can buy prepared pickling spice at well-stocked supermarkets or make your own (see page 217).

Use Pickle Crisp™ to make fresh-pack pickles crisper. Add ¾ tsp (3 mL) to pint (500 mL) jars and 1½ tsp (7 mL) to quart (1 L) jars before processing.

Makes seven pint (500 mL) jars

8 lbs	pickling cucumbers (3 to 4 inches/ 7.5 to 10 cm), trimmed	3.6 kg
16 cups	ice cubes or chipped ice	4 L
1¼ cups	pickling or canning salt, divided	300 mL
12 cups	water, divided	3 L
2 tbsp	pickling spice (see tip, at left)	30 mL
6 cups	white vinegar	1.5 L
¼ cup	granulated sugar	50 mL
7 tsp	mustard seeds	35 mL
10½	fresh dill heads (or 7 tbsp/105 mL dill seeds or finely chopped dillweed), divided	10½
7	cloves garlic, divided (optional)	7

Day 1

1. In a large clean crock, glass or stainless steel container, layer cucumbers and ice.

2. In a large glass or stainless steel bowl, dissolve ½ cup (125 mL) of the pickling salt in 4 cups (1 L) of the water. Pour over cucumbers and add cold water to cover cucumbers, if necessary. Place a large clean inverted plate on top of the cucumbers and weigh down with two or three quart (1 L) jars filled with water and capped. Refrigerate (or let stand in a cool place) for at least 12 hours, but no longer than 18 hours.

Day 2

1. Prepare canner, jars and lids. *(For more information, see page 415.)*

2. Tie pickling spice in a square of cheesecloth, creating a spice bag.

3. In a large stainless steel saucepan, combine remaining 8 cups (2 L) water, vinegar, remaining ¾ cup (175 mL) pickling salt, sugar and spice bag. Bring to a boil over medium-high heat, stirring to dissolve salt and sugar. Reduce heat, cover and boil gently for 15 minutes, until spices have infused the liquid.

4. Transfer cucumbers to a colander placed over a sink and drain. Rinse with cool running water and drain thoroughly. Pack cucumbers into jars to within a generous ½ inch (1 cm) of top of jar. Add 1 tsp (5 mL) mustard seeds, 1½ fresh dill heads (or 1 tbsp/15 mL dill seeds or finely chopped dillweed) and 1 clove garlic, if using, to each hot jar. Ladle hot pickling liquid into hot jar to cover cucumbers, leaving ½ inch (1 cm) headspace. Remove air bubbles and adjust headspace, if necessary, by adding more hot pickling liquid. Wipe rim. Center lid on jar. Screw band down until resistance is met, then increase to fingertip-tight.

5. Place jars in canner, ensuring they are completely covered with water. Bring to a boil and process for 10 minutes. Remove canner lid. Wait 5 minutes, then remove jars, cool and store. *(For more information, see pages 417–418.)*

Variation

You can also use this recipe to make seven quart (1 L) jars. Simply double the quantities for all ingredients except the cucumber purchase weight, which becomes 14 lbs (6.4 kg), and ice cubes, which remains constant. Process quart (1 L) jars for 15 minutes.

Spiced Red Cabbage

Eastern Europeans have thousands of delicious ways to serve cabbage. This colorful pickled cabbage is but one of many.

TIPS

To prepare cabbage heads, remove outer leaves. Core and then shred using a knife or mandoline.

When packing fruits or vegetables into jars for pickles, pack tightly, but not too tightly. Leave room for the pickling liquid, since that is where the flavor comes from.

A jar lifter is very helpful for handling hot, wet jars. Because they are bulky and fit loosely, oven mitts — even water-resistent types — are not a wise choice. When filling jars, an all-purpose rubber glove, worn on your helper hand, will allow you to steady the jar.

Makes about five quart (1 L) jars

12 lbs	red cabbage (about 3 large heads), cored and shredded (see tip, at left)	5.5 kg
½ cup	pickling or canning salt	125 mL
¼ cup	whole cloves	50 mL
¼ cup	whole allspice	50 mL
¼ cup	whole black peppercorns	50 mL
¼ cup	celery seeds	50 mL
2	cinnamon sticks (each about 4 inches/10 cm), broken into pieces	2
8 cups	red wine vinegar	2 L
1 cup	lightly packed brown sugar	250 mL
½ cup	mustard seeds	125 mL
¼ cup	ground mace or nutmeg	50 mL

Day 1

1. In a large clean crock, glass or stainless steel bowl, layer cabbage and salt. Cover and let stand in a cool place for 24 hours.

Day 2

1. Transfer cabbage to a colander placed over a sink and drain. Rinse with cool running water. Drain thoroughly on trays lined with paper towels, about 6 hours.
2. Prepare canner, jars and lids. *(For more information, see page 415.)*
3. Tie cloves, allspice, peppercorns, celery seeds and cinnamon stick pieces in a square of cheesecloth, creating a spice bag.
4. In a large stainless steel saucepan, combine vinegar, brown sugar, mustard seeds, mace and spice bag. Bring to a boil over medium-high heat, stirring to dissolve sugar. Reduce heat and boil gently for 5 minutes, until spices have infused the liquid. Discard spice bag.
5. Pack cabbage into hot jars to within a generous ½ inch (1 cm) of top of jar. Ladle hot pickling liquid into jar to cover cabbage, leaving ½ inch (1 cm) headspace. Remove air bubbles and adjust headspace, if necessary, by adding hot liquid. Wipe rim. Center lid on jar. Screw band down until resistance is met, then increase to fingertip-tight.
6. Place jars in canner, ensuring they are completely covered with water. Bring to a boil and process for 20 minutes. Remove canner lid. Wait 5 minutes, then remove jars, cool and store. *(For more information, see pages 417–418.)*

Pickled Onions

These tasty onions are the perfect addition to a martini, among other uses.

TIPS

To remove onion skins with ease, blanch onions in a large quantity of rapidly boiling water until the skins loosen, 3 to 7 minutes, then immerse in cool water. Drain and peel off skins.

When cutting or seeding hot peppers, wear rubber gloves to keep your hands from being burned.

If pickling liquid is fresh and has not been used to make pickles, cover it and refrigerate for use in your next batch of pickles. For best results, use within 2 weeks. Excess pickling liquid can also be added to coleslaw dressing, marinades or barbecue sauces.

Makes about fourteen 8-ounce (250 mL) jars or seven pint (500 mL) jars

16 cups	peeled pickling or pearl onions (see tip, at left)	4 L
1 cup	pickling or canning salt	250 mL
	Water	
8 cups	white vinegar	2 L
2 cups	granulated sugar	500 mL
1/4 cup	mustard seeds	50 mL
7 tsp	prepared horseradish	35 mL
7	small red chili peppers, such as cayenne, slit twice, lengthwise, and halved	7
7	bay leaves, broken in half	7

Day 1

1. In a large clean crock, glass or stainless steel bowl, combine onions and pickling salt. Add water to cover. Cover and let stand in a cool place for at least 12 hours, but no longer than 18 hours.

Day 2

1. Transfer onions to a colander placed over a sink and drain. Rinse with cool running water and drain thoroughly.
2. Prepare canner, jars and lids. *(For more information, see page 415.)*
3. In a large stainless steel saucepan, combine vinegar, sugar, mustard seeds and horseradish. Bring to a boil over medium-high heat, stirring to dissolve sugar. Reduce heat and boil gently for 15 minutes, until spices have infused the liquid.
4. Pack onions into hot jars to within a generous 1/2 inch (1 cm) of top of jar. Add 1/2 pepper and 1/2 bay leaf to each 8-ounce (250 mL) jar, or two 1/2 peppers and 1/2 bay leaves to each pint (500 mL) jar. Ladle hot pickling liquid into jar to cover onions, leaving 1/2 inch (1 cm) headspace. Remove air bubbles and adjust headspace, if necessary, by adding hot pickling liquid. Wipe rim. Center lid on jar. Screw band down until resistance is met, then increase to fingertip-tight.
5. Place jars in canner, ensuring they are completely covered with water. Bring to a boil and process for 10 minutes. Remove canner lid. Wait 5 minutes, then remove jars, cool and store. *(For more information, see pages 417–418.)*

Variation

Sour Pickled Onions: Omit sugar (or some of it, to taste) and bay leaves.

Mixed Vegetable Pickles

Use these tasty pickles to make a delicious vegetable pasta salad. Simply add them to chilled cooked pasta such as orecchiette or farfalle, stir in Italian dressing or your favorite vinaigrette and top with Parmesan cheese.

TIPS

Refer to the Produce Purchase Guide on pages 426–429 to determine how much produce you'll need to buy to prepare this recipe.

When cutting or seeding hot peppers, wear rubber gloves to prevent hands from being burned.

When making pickles, select uniformly sized fruits and vegetables and/or cut them into pieces of similar size. During processing, each piece of produce should be heated to the same degree. If the pieces vary too much in size, smaller pieces will soften and larger pieces may not be heated sufficiently. In addition to reduced quality, inadequate heat penetration can become a safety issue.

Makes about six pint (500 mL) jars

1 ¼ lbs	pickling cucumbers, trimmed and cut into 1-inch (2.5 cm) slices	570 g
2 cups	sliced peeled carrots (1 ½-inch/4 cm slices)	500 mL
2 cups	sliced celery (1 ½-inch/4 cm slices)	500 mL
2 cups	peeled pickling or pearl onions	500 mL
2	large red bell peppers, seeded and cut into ½-inch (1 cm) strips	2
3 cups	cauliflower florets	750 mL
2	hot red peppers, seeded and cut into ½-inch (1 cm) thick rings	2
1 cup	pickling or canning salt	250 mL
	Water	
6 ½ cups	white vinegar	1.625 L
2 cups	granulated sugar	500 mL
¼ cup	mustard seeds	50 mL
2 tbsp	celery seeds	30 mL

Day 1

1. In a large clean crock, glass or stainless steel bowl, combine cucumbers, carrots, celery, onions, red peppers, cauliflower and hot peppers. Set aside.

2. In a large glass or stainless steel bowl, combine pickling salt and 4 quarts (1 L) water, stirring to dissolve. Pour over vegetables. Cover and let stand in a cool place for 12 to 18 hours.

Day 2

1. Transfer vegetables to a colander placed over a sink. Drain, rinse with cool running water and drain thoroughly. Set aside.

2. Prepare canner, jars and lids. *(For more information, see page 415.)*

3. In a large stainless steel saucepan, combine vinegar, sugar, mustard seeds and celery seeds. Bring to a boil over medium-high heat, stirring to dissolve sugar. Boil for 3 minutes. Add reserved vegetables and return to a boil. Reduce heat and boil gently for 5 minutes, until vegetables are heated through.

4. Pack hot vegetables and liquid into hot jars, leaving ½ inch (1 cm) headspace. Remove air bubbles and adjust headspace, if necessary, by adding more hot pickling liquid. Wipe rim. Center lid on jar. Screw band down until resistance is met, then increase to fingertip-tight.

5. Place jars in canner, ensuring they are completely covered with water. Bring to a boil and process for 15 minutes. Remove canner lid. Wait 5 minutes, then remove jars, cool and store. *(For more information, see pages 417–418.)*

Mixed Mustard Pickles

This is a quick and easy way to preserve your garden vegetables. The results are unexpectedly delicious and allow you to enjoy fresh-tasting vegetables year-round.

TIPS

Refer to the Produce Purchase Guide on pages 426–429 to determine how much produce you'll need to buy to prepare this recipe.

ClearJel® is a cooking starch that is acceptable for use in home canning. Not all cooking starches are suitable for home canning, as reheating causes some to lose viscosity. Making mixtures too thick can interfere with required heat penetration during heat processing. In this recipe, ClearJel® is used to create a thicker, smoother texture. For more information, see the Glossary, page 431.

Makes eight pint (500 mL) jars or four quart (1 L) jars

5 cups	sliced trimmed pickling cucumbers (½-inch/1 cm slices)	1.25 L
4 cups	green tomato wedges	1 L
3 cups	cauliflower florets	750 mL
3 cups	chopped seeded green bell peppers	750 mL
3 cups	chopped seeded red bell peppers	750 mL
2 cups	peeled pickling or pearl onions	500 mL
1 cup	pickling or canning salt	250 mL
	Water	
1½ cups	granulated sugar	375 mL
4 tbsp	ClearJel® (see tip, at left)	60 mL
1 tbsp	ground turmeric	15 mL
½ cup	prepared mustard	125 mL
5 cups	white vinegar	1.25 L

Day 1

1. In a large clean crock, glass or stainless steel bowl, combine cucumbers, green tomato wedges, cauliflower, green and red bell peppers and onions. Set aside.

2. In a large glass or stainless steel bowl, combine pickling salt and 4 quarts (4 L) water, stirring to dissolve salt. Pour over vegetables. Cover and let stand in a cool place for 12 to 18 hours.

Day 2

1. Transfer vegetables to a colander placed over a sink and drain. Rinse with cool running water and drain thoroughly. Set aside.

2. Prepare canner, jars and lids. *(For more information, see page 415.)*

3. In a large stainless steel saucepan, combine sugar, ClearJel® and turmeric. Gradually add ½ cup (125 mL) water, stirring until smooth. Stir in mustard and vinegar. Bring to a boil over medium-high heat, stirring constantly. Reduce heat and boil gently, stirring frequently, until mixture thickens. Add vegetables and return to a boil. Reduce heat and boil gently, stirring occasionally, for 15 minutes, until vegetables are heated through and slightly tender.

4. Pack hot pickles and liquid into hot jars, leaving ½ inch (1 cm) headspace. Remove air bubbles and adjust headspace, if necessary, by adding hot liquid. Wipe rim. Center lid on jar. Screw band down until resistance is met, then increase to fingertip-tight.

5. Place jars in canner, ensuring they are completely covered with water. Bring to a boil and process for 10 minutes. Remove canner lid. Wait 5 minutes, then remove jars, cool and store. *(For more information, see pages 417–418.)*

Brined and Fermented Pickles

Fermented pickles are made using vegetables, usually cucumbers, that are submerged in a salt-water brine to ferment or cure for up to 6 weeks. Dill, garlic and other herbs or spices are often added to the pickling brine for flavoring. Fermented pickles undergo a fermentation process that produces lactic acid to help preserve the product. During fermentation, the salt in the brine solution draws juices and sugar from foods and forms lactic acid. Sauerkraut and deli-style dills are two well-known fermented pickle products (see recipes, pages 344 and 346).

If a food is brined or cured but not fermented, acid in the form of vinegar is added later in the pickling process to aid with preservation.

The curing process for brined or fermented pickles causes favorable color, flavor and texture changes. So, although these pickles may require more time and steps to complete, the unique results offer special rewards.

··

Sweet Crisp Pickles

Pickle Crisp™, a natural calcium chloride (salt), firms the cellular structure of cucumbers to yield this sweet pickle. It eliminates the need to soak cucumbers in a lime solution — a method that can be hazardous if very strict instructions are not followed precisely.

TIP

You can buy prepared pickling spice at well-stocked supermarkets or make your own (see page 217).

Makes about eight pint (500 mL) jars

7 lbs	pickling cucumbers (3 to 4 inches/ 7.5 to 10 cm long), trimmed and sliced in half lengthwise	3.2 kg
2	pouches (each 26 g) Pickle Crisp™ (see tip, opposite)	2
	Water	
	Ice cubes	
1 tbsp	celery seeds	15 mL
1 tbsp	whole cloves	15 mL
1 tbsp	pickling spice (see tip, at left)	15 mL
9 cups	granulated sugar	2.25 L
1 tbsp	pickling or canning salt	15 mL
8 cups	white vinegar	2 L

Stage 1

1. Place cucumbers in a large clean crock or glass or stainless steel container.
2. In a large glass or stainless steel bowl, combine Pickle Crisp™ and 8 quarts (8 L) water, stirring to dissolve Pickle Crisp™. Ladle over cucumbers. Cover and refrigerate for 12 hours.

Stage 2

1. Drain cucumbers and discard liquid. Rinse crock. Return cucumbers to clean crock. Add ice cubes to cover and let stand in a cool place (70 to 75°F/21 to 23°C) for 3 hours, adding additional ice cubes as needed. Drain and discard liquid. Rinse crock. Return pickles to crock.
2. Meanwhile, tie celery seeds, cloves and pickling spice in a square of cheesecloth, creating a spice bag.
3. In a large stainless steel saucepan, combine sugar, salt, vinegar and spice bag. Bring to a boil over medium-high heat, stirring to dissolve sugar and salt. Ladle over pickles. Cover tightly with plastic wrap and let stand in a cool place (70 to 75°F/21 to 23° C) for 8 to 12 hours.

Stage 3

1. Prepare canner, jars and lids. *(For more information, see page 415.)*
2. Remove spice bag and discard. Transfer pickles with liquid to a large stainless steel saucepan. Bring to a boil over medium-high heat. Reduce heat and boil gently for 30 minutes, until cucumbers are heated through.
3. Pack hot cucumbers into hot jars to within a generous ½ inch (1 cm) of top of jar. Ladle hot pickling liquid into jar to cover cucumbers, leaving ½ inch (1 cm) headspace. Remove air bubbles and adjust headspace, if necessary, by adding more hot syrup. Wipe rim. Center lid on jar. Screw band down until resistance is met, then increase to fingertip-tight.
4. Place jars in canner, ensuring they are completely covered with water. Bring to a boil and process for 10 minutes. Remove canner lid. Wait 5 minutes, then remove jars, cool and store. *(For more information, see pages 417–418.)*

Sweet Gherkin Pickles

Small and sweet, just the way kids love them! These sweet gherkins are the perfect addition to a relish tray. Their small size is visually appealing.

TIPS

To wash cucumbers, hold them under cool running water and scrub with a vegetable brush to remove all grit from the crevices. Drain well.

You can buy prepared pickling spice at well-stocked supermarkets or make your own (see page 217).

Ingredient quantities are approximate. Variations in the sizes of pickling cucumbers and jars dictate the number of pickles that can be placed in each jar. This, in turn, affects the quantity of liquid required.

When preparing jars and lids, prepare a couple extra in case your yield is larger than you expect. If you don't have enough jars, place any leftover preserves in an airtight container, store in the refrigerator and use within a few weeks.

Makes about seven pint (500 mL) jars

8 lbs	small pickling cucumbers (1½ to 2½-inches/4 to 6 cm long), trimmed	3.6 kg
½ cup	pickling or canning salt, divided	125 mL
	Water	
2 tsp	celery seeds	10 mL
2 tsp	pickling spice (see tip, at left)	10 mL
2	cinnamon sticks (each about 4 inches/10 cm)	2
½ tsp	whole allspice	2 mL
8 cups	granulated sugar, divided	2 L
6 cups	white vinegar, divided	1.5 L
½ tsp	ground turmeric	2 mL

Stage 1

1. Place cucumbers in a large clean crock or glass or stainless steel container.
2. In a large stainless steel saucepan, combine half of the pickling salt and 6 quarts (6 L) water. Bring to a boil over medium-high heat, stirring to dissolve salt. Ladle over cucumbers. Cover and let stand in a cool place (70 to 75°F/21 to 23°C) for 8 to 12 hours.

Stage 2

1. Drain cucumbers and discard brine. Rinse crock. Return cucumbers to crock. In a large stainless steel saucepan, combine remaining pickling salt and 6 quarts (6 L) water. Bring to a boil over medium-high heat, stirring to dissolve salt. Ladle over cucumbers. Cover and let stand in a cool place for 8 to 12 hours.

Stage 3

1. Drain cucumbers and discard brine. Rinse crock. Using a toothpick, prick cucumbers in several places and return to crock.
2. Tie celery seeds, pickling spice, cinnamon sticks and allspice in a square of cheesecloth, creating a spice bag.

Before using jars, inspect them carefully for any chips, cracks or fractures. Discard any imperfect jars.

Read a recipe all the way through, even before you go shopping for the ingredients. It's very important to have all of the ingredients and equipment ready before you start making preserves.

A jar lifter is very helpful for handling hot, wet jars. Because they are bulky and fit loosely, oven mitts — even water-resistent types — are not a wise choice. When filling jars, an all-purpose rubber glove, worn on your helper hand, will allow you to steady the jar.

Place a clean towel on your work surface to absorb water from the hot jars as you take them out of the boiling-water canner to be filled, and again once the jars are processed. The towel prevents hot jars from coming into contact with cooler countertops. Significant temperature differences can cause jar breakage.

3. In a large stainless steel saucepan, combine 3 cups (750 mL) of the sugar, 3 cups (750 mL) of the vinegar, turmeric and spice bag. Bring to a boil over medium-high heat, stirring to dissolve sugar. Ladle over cucumbers. Place a large clean inverted plate on top of cucumbers and weigh down with two or three quart (1 L) jars filled with water and capped. Cover with a clean heavy towel. Let stand in a cool place for 8 to 12 hours.

Stage 4

1. Drain cucumbers, reserving liquid and spice bag. Rinse crock. Return cucumbers to crock. In a large stainless steel saucepan, combine 2 cups (500 mL) of the sugar, 2 cups (500 mL) of the vinegar, reserved liquid and spice bag. Bring to a boil over medium-high heat, stirring to dissolve sugar. Ladle over cucumbers. Weigh down as in Stage 3, Step 3, and let stand in a cool place for 8 to 12 hours.

Stage 5

1. Drain cucumbers, reserving liquid and spice bag. Rinse crock. Return cucumbers to crock. In a large stainless steel saucepan, combine 2 cups (500 mL) of the sugar, remaining 1 cup (250 mL) vinegar, reserved liquid and spice bag. Bring to a boil over medium-high heat, stirring to dissolve sugar. Ladle over cucumbers. Weigh down as in Stage 3, Step 3, and let stand in a cool place for 8 to 12 hours.

Stage 6

1. Prepare canner, jars and lids. *(For more information, see page 415.)*
2. Remove spice bag and discard. Drain cucumbers, reserving liquid. In a large stainless steel saucepan, combine remaining 1 cup (250 mL) sugar and reserved liquid. Bring to a boil over medium-high heat, stirring to dissolve sugar.
3. Pack pickles into hot jars to within a generous ½ inch (1 cm) of top of jar. Ladle hot pickling liquid into jar to cover pickles, leaving ½ inch (1 cm) headspace. Remove air bubbles and adjust headspace, if necessary, by adding more hot liquid. Wipe rim. Center lid on jar. Screw band down until resistance is met, then increase to fingertip-tight.
4. Place jars in canner, ensuring they are completely covered with water. Bring to a boil and process for 10 minutes. Remove canner lid. Wait 5 minutes, then remove jars, cool and store. *(For more information, see pages 417–418.)*

Sweet Icicle Pickles

Although this recipe requires small tasks over several days, pickle lovers believe the distinctly tangy flavors that result are well worth the extra effort. These pickles got the name "icicle" because of the way they are cut, into small spears.

TIPS

You can buy prepared pickling spice at well-stocked supermarkets or make your own (see page 217).

Additional brine may be needed to ensure that the cucumbers are completely submerged. To make brine, combine 4½ tsp (22 mL) salt with 4 cups (1 L) water, stirring to dissolve salt. Bring to a boil over medium-high heat. Remove from heat and let cool to room temperature.

To wash cucumbers, hold them under cool running water and scrub with a vegetable brush to remove all grit from the crevices. Drain well.

Makes about six pint (500 mL) jars or three quart (1 L) jars

4 lbs	pickling cucumbers (4 to 6 inches/10 to 15 cm long), trimmed and cut lengthwise into quarters or small icicles	1.8 kg
1 cup	pickling or canning salt	250 mL
8 cups	water	2 L
4½ tsp	pickling spice (see tip, at left)	22 mL
5 cups	granulated sugar	1.25 L
5 cups	white vinegar	1.25 L

Stage 1

1. Place cucumbers in a large clean crock or glass or stainless steel container.

2. In a large stainless steel saucepan, combine pickling salt and water. Bring to a boil over medium-high heat, stirring to dissolve salt. Ladle over cucumbers, ensuring they are submerged in the brine (see tip, at left).

3. Place a clean inverted plate on top of the cucumbers and weigh down with two or three quart (1 L) jars filled with water and capped. Cover with a clean heavy towel. Let stand in a cool place (70 to 75°F/21 to 23°C) for 1 week. Every day, remove any scum that has formed.

Stage 2

1. Drain cucumbers and discard brine. Rinse crock. Rinse cucumbers in cold running water and drain thoroughly. Return to crock. Cover with boiling water, cover and let stand in a cool place for 24 hours.

Stage 3

1. Drain cucumbers and discard liquid. Rinse crock. Return cucumbers to crock.

2. Tie pickling spice in a square of cheesecloth, creating a spice bag.

3. In a large stainless steel saucepan, combine sugar, vinegar and spice bag. Bring to a boil over medium-high heat, stirring to dissolve sugar. Ladle over cucumbers. Cover and let stand in a cool place for 24 hours.

When making pickles, select uniformly sized fruits and vegetables and/or cut them into pieces of similar size. During processing, each piece of produce should be heated to the same degree. If the pieces vary too much in size, smaller pieces will soften and larger pieces may not be heated sufficiently. In addition to reduced quality, inadequate heat penetration can become a safety issue.

Ingredient quantities are approximate. Variations in the sizes of pickling cucumbers and jars dictate the number of pickles that can be placed in each jar. This, in turn, affects the quantity of liquid required.

Stage 4

1. Drain cucumbers, reserving liquid and spice bag. Rinse crock. Return cucumbers to crock. In a large stainless steel saucepan, bring reserved liquid and spice bag to a boil over medium-high heat. Ladle over cucumbers. Cover and let stand in a cool place for 24 hours.

Stage 5

1. Repeat Stage 4 daily for 3 days.

Stage 6

1. Prepare canner, jars and lids. *(For more information, see page 415.)*

2. Remove spice bag and discard. Drain cucumbers, reserving liquid. In a large stainless steel saucepan, bring reserved pickling liquid to a boil over medium-high heat.

3. Pack cucumbers into hot jars to within a generous $\frac{1}{2}$ inch (1 cm) of top of jar. Ladle hot pickling liquid into jar to cover cucumbers, leaving $\frac{1}{2}$ inch (1 cm) headspace. Remove air bubbles and adjust headspace, if necessary, by adding hot pickling liquid. Wipe rim. Center lid on jar. Screw band until resistance is met, then increase to fingertip-tight.

4. Place jars in canner, ensuring they are completely covered with water. Bring to a boil and process for 10 minutes. Remove canner lid. Wait 5 minutes, then remove jars, cool and store. *(For more information, see pages 417–418.)*

Sweet Red Cucumber Rings

Not only do these cucumber rings have a wonderful sweet yet hot cinnamon flavor, their color is visually appealing. They are beautiful as an edible garnish for a ham roast or even tossed in a salad with a sweet fruit vinaigrette.

TIPS

For the best results, use pickling cucumbers in this recipe. To make cucumber rings, peel cucumbers and trim the ends. Cut in half crosswise. Using an apple corer, remove the middle portion of each cucumber half, including seeds. Cut each half into ¼-inch (0.5 cm) to ½-inch (1 cm) rings.

If desired, this recipe can be prepared using small field cucumbers to create half-moons. Peel cucumbers, cut in half lengthwise and scoop out seeds with a spoon. Cut cucumber halves into ½-inch (1 cm) slices; measure and proceed as directed for pickling cucumber rings.

Look for Pickle Crisp™ where canning supplies are sold.

Makes about seven quart (1 L) jars

32 cups	pickling cucumber rings (see tip, at left)	8 L
2	pouches (each 26 g) Pickle Crisp™	2
	Water	
	Ice cubes	
4½ cups	cider vinegar, divided	1.125 L
1	small bottle (1 oz/28 mL) red food coloring	1
10 cups	granulated sugar (approx.)	2.5 L
8	cinnamon sticks (each about 4 inches/10 cm)	8
1 cup	red hot cinnamon candies	250 mL

Stage 1

1. Place cucumber rings in a large clean crock or glass or stainless steel container.
2. In a large glass or stainless steel bowl, combine Pickle Crisp™ and 8 quarts (8 L) water, stirring to dissolve Pickle Crisp™. Ladle over cucumber rings. Cover and refrigerate for 24 hours.

Stage 2

1. Drain cucumbers and discard liquid. Rinse crock. Return cucumbers to crock. Add ice to cover and let stand in a cool place for 3 hours, adding ice as necessary. Drain and discard liquid. Rinse crock.
2. In a large stainless steel saucepan, combine cucumber rings, 1 cup (250 mL) of the vinegar and food coloring. Add just enough cold water to cover. Bring to a boil over medium-high heat. Reduce heat and boil gently for 2 hours, until cucumbers are red throughout. Drain and discard liquid. Return cucumbers to crock.
3. In a clean large stainless steel saucepan, combine 3½ cups (875 mL) water, remaining 3½ cups (875 mL) vinegar, 10 cups (2.5 L) sugar, cinnamon sticks and red hot cinnamon candies. Bring to a boil over medium-high heat, stirring to dissolve sugar and candies. Ladle over cucumber rings. Cover tightly with plastic wrap and let stand in a cool place (70 to 75°F/21 to 23°C) for 8 to 12 hours.

TIPS

When packing fruits or vegetables into jars for pickles, pack tightly, but not too tightly. Leave room for the pickling liquid, since that is where the flavor comes from.

When measuring wet ingredients, use a liquid measuring cup (with a handle and spout and graduated markings for measures). Smaller measuring cups (1 or 2 cups/250 or 500 mL) are more accurate than many of the larger cups (4 or 8 cups/1 or 2 L), so it is better to use a smaller one several times than to use one larger cup.

If you have particularly hard water and use it in the boiling-water canner, it can leave a residue on jars. Use filtered or reverse-osmosis water to fill your canner instead, or add a small amount of vinegar to the water in the canner to cut the film that develops.

Stage 3

1. Drain cucumbers, reserving liquid. Rinse crock. Return cucumbers to crock.

2. In a large stainless steel saucepan, combine reserved liquid and up to 1 cup (250 mL) granulated sugar if you prefer sweeter pickles. Bring to a boil over medium-high heat, stirring to dissolve sugar. Ladle over cucumber rings. Cover tightly with plastic wrap and let stand in a cool place for 24 hours.

Stage 4

1. Repeat Stage 3 daily for 2 days, adding a bit of sugar every day if you prefer a sweeter product.

Stage 5

1. Prepare canner, jars and lids. *(For more information, see page 415.)*

2. Remove cinnamon sticks and discard. Transfer cucumber rings and syrup to a large stainless steel saucepan. Bring to a boil over medium-high heat.

3. Pack hot cucumber rings into hot jars to within a generous ½ inch (1 cm) of top of jar. Ladle hot syrup into jar to cover rings, leaving ½ inch (1 cm) headspace. Remove air bubbles and adjust headspace, if necessary, by adding hot syrup. Wipe rim. Center lid on jar. Screw band down until resistance is met, then increase to fingertip-tight.

4. Place jars in canner, ensuring they are completely covered with water. Bring to a boil and process for 10 minutes. Remove canner lid. Wait 5 minutes, then remove jars, cool and store. *(For more information, see pages 417–418.)*

Cucumber Chips

The robust flavor of these cucumber chips is the perfect finish for your juicy quarter-pound cheeseburger, hot off the grill!

TIPS

Refer to the Produce Purchase Guide on pages 426–429 to determine how much produce you'll need to buy to prepare this recipe.

To wash cucumbers, hold them under cool running water and scrub with a vegetable brush to remove all grit from the crevices. Drain well.

Cheesecloth can be found at many retailers, such as grocery stores and other stores that carry kitchen supplies. Look in the area where kitchen utensils are located.

When packing fruits or vegetables into jars for pickles, pack tightly, but not too tightly. Leave room for the pickling liquid, since that is where the flavor comes from.

Makes about three pint (500 mL) jars

20 cups	sliced trimmed pickling cucumbers (¼-inch/0.5 cm slices)	5 L
½ cup	pickling or canning salt	125 mL
7 cups	white vinegar, divided	1.75 mL
5 cups	water, divided	1.25 L
1 tbsp	ground turmeric	15 mL
2	cinnamon sticks (each about 4 inches/10 cm)	2
1	piece gingerroot (¼ by 1 inch/0.5 by 2.5 cm)	1
1 tbsp	mustard seeds	15 mL
1 tsp	whole cloves	5 mL
2 cups	granulated sugar	500 mL
2 cups	lightly packed brown sugar	500 mL

Stage 1

1. In a large clean crock or glass or stainless steel bowl, combine cucumbers and pickling salt. Mix thoroughly and let stand in a cool place (70 to 75°F/21 to 23°C) for 3 hours.

2. Drain cucumbers and discard liquid. Rinse crock. Rinse cucumbers in cold running water and drain thoroughly. Return to crock.

3. In a large stainless steel saucepan, combine 3 cups (750 mL) of the vinegar, 4 cups (1 L) of the water and turmeric. Bring to a boil over medium-high heat. Ladle over cucumbers and let cool to room temperature. Drain, discarding liquid. Rinse crock. Taste cucumbers and, if they are too salty, rinse in cold running water and drain thoroughly. Return to crock.

4. Meanwhile, tie cinnamon sticks, gingerroot, mustard seeds and cloves in a square of cheesecloth, creating a spice bag.

5. In a large stainless steel saucepan, combine granulated sugar, remaining 4 cups (1 L) vinegar, remaining 1 cup (250 mL) water and spice bag. Bring to a boil over medium-high heat, stirring to dissolve sugar. Reduce heat and boil gently for 15 minutes, until spices have infused the liquid. Ladle over cucumbers. Cover and let stand in a cool place (70 to 75°F/21 to 23°C) for at least 12 hours, but no longer than 24 hours.

TIPS

When making pickles, select uniformly sized fruits and vegetables and/or cut them into pieces of similar size. During processing, each piece of produce should be heated to the same degree. If the pieces vary too much in size, smaller pieces will soften and larger pieces may not be heated sufficiently. In addition to reduced quality, inadequate heat penetration can become a safety issue.

Pickle fruits and vegetables within 24 hours of harvest. If your schedule does not accommodate this brief time window, refrigerate the produce and use it as soon as possible.

Stage 2

1. Prepare canner, jars and lids. *(For more information, see page 415.)*

2. Remove spice bag and discard. Drain pickles, reserving liquid. In a large stainless steel saucepan, combine brown sugar and reserved liquid. Bring to a boil over medium-high heat, stirring to dissolve sugar.

3. Pack cucumbers into hot jars to within a generous ½ inch (1 cm) of top of jar. Ladle hot pickling liquid into jar to cover cucumbers, leaving ½ inch (1 cm) headspace. Remove air bubbles and adjust headspace, if necessary, by adding hot pickling liquid. Wipe rim. Center lid on jar. Screw band down until resistance is met, then increase to fingertip-tight.

4. Place jars in canner, ensuring they are completely covered with water. Bring to a boil and process for 10 minutes. Remove canner lid. Wait 5 minutes, then remove jars, cool and store. *(For more information, see pages 417–418.)*

Sauerkraut

Sauerkraut is linked with the traditional German celebration of Oktoberfest. Along with mustard, it's the perfect finish to a juicy grilled bratwurst.

TIPS

A 4-quart (4 L) container is needed for every 5 pounds (2.3 kg) of fresh vegetables. Thus, when making sauerkraut with 25 lbs (11.4 kg) of cabbage, you will need a 20-quart (20 L) container such as a stone crock or glass or food-grade plastic container. We do not recommend using multiple smaller containers, because there will be greater spoilage loss.

If brine does not cover cabbage, bring 4½ tsp (22 mL) pickling or canning salt and 4 cups (1 L) water to a boil over medium-high heat, stirring to dissolve salt. Let cool to room temperature, then ladle over sauerkraut to cover.

When making sauerkraut, be sure to follow the processing times your recipe specifies. Different-sized jars and raw-pack or hot-pack methods affect processing time.

Makes about twelve pint (500 mL) or six quart (1 L) jars

25 lbs	white cabbage (about 5 large heads), outer leaves discarded, cored and quartered	11.4 kg
1 cup	pickling or canning salt, divided	250 mL

Stage 1

1. In a food processor fitted with a slicing attachment, in batches as necessary, cut cabbage into thin shreds, about $\frac{1}{16}$ inch (0.2 cm) thick. (You can also do this with a sharp knife or mandoline.) Remove any large pieces and discard.

2. In a large stone crock or glass or food-grade plastic container (see tip, at left), working in 5-lb (2.3 kg) batches, combine shredded cabbage and 3 tbsp (45 mL) of the pickling salt. Mix thoroughly. Let stand for 15 minutes or until juices start to flow and cabbage wilts slightly. Using a wooden spoon or your hands, press down firmly on the cabbage until the juice comes to the surface. Repeat four times, until all the cabbage is used up, leaving at least 4 inches (10 cm) of space between cabbage and rim of container. Sprinkle remaining pickling salt on top. If not enough juice has been produced to cover cabbage, add brine (see tip, at left).

3. Place a large clean inverted plate over the cabbage mixture and weigh down with two or three quart (1 L) jars filled with water and capped. (Keep cabbage under brine by 1 to 2 inches (2.5 to 5 cm) throughout fermentation.) Cover with a clean heavy towel. Let stand in a cool place (70 to 75°F/21 to 23°C). Every day, remove and discard any scum that has formed. During fermentation, gas bubbles will form. When bubbling ceases, fermentation is complete (see tip, page 346).

Fermentation may take up to 6 weeks, depending on atmospheric conditions and variations in the cabbage itself.

A jar lifter is very helpful for handling hot, wet jars. Because they are bulky and fit loosely, oven mitts — even water-resistent types — are not a wise choice. When filling jars, an all-purpose rubber glove, worn on your helper hand, will allow you to steady the jar.

A clear plastic ruler (kept solely for kitchen use) will help you determine the correct headspace. Each filled jar should be measured accurately, as the headspace can affect sealing and the preservation of the contents.

Stage 2

RAW-PACK METHOD

1. Prepare canner, jars and lids. *(For more information, see page 415.)*
2. Pack sauerkraut, with brine, into hot jars, leaving ½ inch (1 cm) headspace. Remove air bubbles and adjust headspace, if necessary, by adding more brine. Wipe rim. Center lid on jar. Screw band down until resistance is met, then increase to fingertip-tight.
3. Place jars in canner, ensuring they are completely covered with water. Bring to a boil and process pint (500 mL) jars for 20 minutes and quart (1 L) jars for 25 minutes. Remove canner lid. Wait 5 minutes, then remove jars, cool and store. *(For more information, see pages 417–418.)*

HOT-PACK METHOD

1. Prepare canner, jars and lids. *(For more information, see page 415.)*
2. In a large stainless steel saucepan, bring sauerkraut, with brine, to a simmer over medium-high heat. Do not boil. Pack hot sauerkraut and brine into hot jars, leaving ½ inch (1 cm) headspace. Remove air bubbles and adjust headspace, if necessary, by adding more brine. Wipe rim. Center lid on jar. Screw band down until resistance is met, then increase to fingertip-tight.
3. Place jars in canner, ensuring they are completely covered with water. Bring to a boil and process pint (500 mL) jars for 10 minutes and quart (1 L) jars for 15 minutes. Remove canner lid. Wait 5 minutes, then remove jars, cool and store. *(For more information, see pages 417–418.)*

Deli Dills

Recreate the flavor of your favorite deli with these tangy fermented dills. Although they take time, your patience will be rewarded with their unique flavor, which is unlike any fresh-pack pickles.

TIPS

You can buy prepared pickling spice at well-stocked supermarkets or make your own (see page 217).

Fermentation takes place best at a cool temperature, between 70 and 75°F (21 and 23°C). At this temperature, fermentation should take about 3 weeks. At a slightly lower temperature, between 60 and 65°F (16 and 18°C), fermentation may take 5 to 6 weeks to complete. If the storage temperature is below 60°F (16°C), fermentation may not take place. At temperatures higher than 75°F (23°C), pickles may become soft.

Cut off the blossom end of all pickling cucumbers, as it contains an enzyme that can soften pickles. If you are unsure of which end is the blossom end, simply remove a ⅛-inch (0.3 cm) slice from each end of the cucumber.

Makes about six quart (1 L) jars

¾ cup	pickling spice (see tip, at left), divided	175 mL
2 to 3	bunches fresh dill, divided	2 to 3
10 lbs	pickling cucumbers (4 inches/ 10 cm long), trimmed	4.5 kg
1½ cups	pickling or canning salt	375 mL
2 cups	white vinegar	500 mL
32 cups	water	8 L
6	garlic cloves (optional)	6

Stage 1

1. In a large clean crock or glass or stainless steel container, place half the pickling spice and one bunch of dill. Add cucumbers, leaving at least 4 inches (10 cm) of space between cucumbers and rim of container. Set aside.

2. In a large stainless steel pot, combine pickling salt, vinegar and water. Bring to a boil over medium-high heat, stirring to dissolve salt. Remove from heat and let cool to room temperature.

3. Ladle pickling liquid over cucumbers to cover. Place remaining dill and remaining pickling spice over the top. Add garlic, if using. Place a large clean inverted plate on top of the cucumbers and weigh down with two or three quart (1 L) jars filled with water and capped. Cover with a clean heavy towel. Let stand in a cool place (70 to 75°F/21 to 23°C) for about 3 weeks, until cucumbers are well flavored with dill and clear throughout. Every day, remove any scum that has formed. During fermentation, gas bubbles will form. When bubbling ceases, fermentation is complete (see tip, at left).

Stage 2

1. Prepare canner, jars and lids. *(For more information, see page 415.)*

2. Drain pickles, reserving brine. Set pickles aside. Strain brine into a large stainless steel pot. Bring to a boil over medium-high heat. Reduce heat and boil gently for 5 minutes.

3. Pack pickles into hot jars to within a generous ½ inch (1 cm) of top of jar. Ladle hot pickling liquid into jar to cover pickles, leaving ½ inch (1 cm) headspace. Remove air bubbles and adjust headspace, if necessary, by adding hot pickling liquid. Wipe rim. Center lid on jar. Screw band down until resistance is met, then increase to fingertip-tight.

4. Place jars in canner, ensuring they are completely covered with water. Bring to a boil and process for 15 minutes. Remove canner lid. Wait 5 minutes, then remove jars, cool and store. *(For more information, see pages 417–418.)*

Pickles Problem Solver

PROBLEM	CAUSE	PREVENTION/SOLUTION
Pickling liquid is cloudy.	Food spoilage caused by underprocessing.	Use only tested recipes and process for the recommended length of time.
	Minerals present in the water used.	Use soft water. Hard water contains minerals. For instructions on softening hard water, see page 289.
	Anti-caking agent, an additive found in table salt.	When canning, use canning and pickling salt, which does not contain additives.
Pickling liquid is pink.	Overmature dill used.	Always use the freshest ingredients when home canning. The product is still safe, however.
	Yeast growth caused by underprocessing. Yeast growth may also make pickles cloudy or slimy. *Discard the pickles.*	Follow a tested recipe and process jars for the recommended length of time.
Pickles are darkened or discolored.	Minerals present in the water used.	Use soft water. For instructions on softening hard water, see page 289.
	Brass, iron, copper, aluminum or zinc utensils used.	Use unchipped enamelware, glass, stainless steel or stoneware utensils when making pickles. The minerals in materials react with the acid in the pickling liquid.
	Ground spices used.	Use whole spices.
	Whole spices left in jar of pickles.	Whole spices used to flavor pickling liquid, including those contained in a spice bag, should be removed before canning.
Pickles are hollow.	Faulty growth of cucumbers.	None. To identify if cucumbers are hollow before using them, place in a bowl of water. Hollow cucumbers will float. These cucumbers are best suited to making relish.

PROBLEM	CAUSE	PREVENTION/SOLUTION
Pickles are spotted, dull or faded.	Cucumbers were not well brined.	Use the recommended ratio of water to salt. Complete the fermentation process.
	Excessive exposure to light during storage.	Store home-canned food in a dark, dry, cool place (70 to 75°F/21 to 23°C).
	Poor-quality cucumbers used.	Always use high-quality produce, good enough to eat.
Pickles are shriveled.	Too much salt, sugar or vinegar was added to the cucumbers at once.	Gradually add salt, sugar or vinegar until the full amount has been incorporated.
	Cucumbers were brined in a solution that was too strong, using syrup that was too heavy or using vinegar with more than 5% acidity.	Follow a current, tested recipe, using the recommended amounts of salt, sugar and vinegar at 5% acidity.
	Cucumbers were not fresh when brined.	Brine cucumbers within 24 hours of harvest, or refrigerate until ready to use. Pickling cucumbers deteriorate very rapidly, especially at room temperature.
	Whole cucumbers were not pricked before canning.	Prick whole cucumbers before canning to allow the brine to saturate and plump the flesh of the cucumbers.
	Cucumbers had a wax coating that prevented the brine from penetrating the peel.	Check to make sure your cucumbers are unwaxed. Pickling cucumbers and English cucumbers are not waxed, but some field cucumbers are.
	Overcooking or overprocessing.	Follow recommended cooking and processing times in a current, tested recipe.
There is white sediment on the bottom of the jar.	Harmless yeasts have grown on the surface and then settled to the bottom.	None. The presence of a small amount of white sediment is normal.
	Additives in table salt.	When canning, use a canning and pickling salt, which does not contain additives.

PROBLEM	CAUSE	PREVENTION/SOLUTION
Pickles lack crispness.	Poor-quality cucumbers used.	Choose high-quality cucumbers and use them within 24 hours of harvest.
	A cucumber variety used that is not recommended for pickling and canning.	Use only pickling cucumbers. Other varieties may be good choices for relishes or chutneys.
	A crisping agent not used.	Use a crisping agent such as Pickle Crisp™ (see page 289).
Pickles are soft or slippery.	Blossom ends of cucumbers were not removed.	Cut 1/16 inch (0.2 cm) off blossom ends of pickling cucumbers. The blossom end contains enzymes that may cause softening.
	Brine or vinegar was too weak.	Use pickling or canning salt and vinegar with 5% acidity. Follow a current, tested recipe for proper ratios of salt to vinegar.
	Scum was not removed daily from the top of the brine during fermentation.	Completely remove scum daily during fermentation.
	Pickles were not completely covered with brine during fermentation.	Pickles must be completely covered with brine during fermentation and in the jar.
	Pickles were underprocessed and spoilage is occurring. *Discard the pickles.*	Follow the recommended processing time in a current, tested recipe using a boiling-water canner.
Pickles have a strong, bitter taste.	Spices were old, they were cooked too long in the vinegar or the quantity was excessive.	Use fresh spices — whole spices should be used within 3 to 4 years of purchase. Follow current, tested recipes to ensure quantities and times are correct.
	Vinegar used was too strong.	Use vinegar with the proper strength for home canning: 5% acidity.
	Salt substitutes used in place of pickling or canning salt.	Salt substitutes contain potassium chloride, which is naturally bitter.

PROBLEM	CAUSE	PREVENTION/SOLUTION
There is scum on the brine.	Surface scum that forms during fermentation is a result of yeast, mold and bacteria feeding on the acid. If they are allowed to accumulate, they will reduce its concentration.	Completely remove scum daily from the surface of the brine during fermentation.
Garlic cloves are green, blue or bluish-green.	Immature garlic used.	Cure immature bulbs for 2 to 4 weeks at 70°F (21°C). Garlic and pickles are safe to eat.
	A chemical reaction caused by the interaction of the pigments in the garlic with the iron, tin or aluminum in a reactive cooking pot, hard water or water pipes.	None. Garlic and pickles are safe to eat. Using soft water may help.
	Garlic may naturally have more blue pigment, and this may become more evident after pickling.	None.
Cauliflower is pink.	A chemical reaction caused by the interaction of pickling liquid acid with the pigment of the cauliflower.	None. Pink cauliflower is safe to eat.

Tomatoes

From whole tomatoes to juice and sauces, tomatoes are among the most popular and versatile of home-canned foods. Preserving tomatoes at home opens a treasure chest of possibilities for delicious and nutritious meals prepared with the very best ingredients Mother Nature has to offer.

● ●

Tomato Essentials

Choosing Tomatoes for Home Canning

Select tomatoes that are disease-free, uniformly colored, firm but not hard, and heavy for their size. Vine-ripened tomatoes will produce the most flavorful results. Tomatoes should also have a good fragrance and be free of bruises, cracks and discoloration. Do not use tomatoes from vines that have been subjected to frost. Because their natural acidity is lower, frost-touched tomatoes will not produce the required degree of acid. They can be used for cooking or freezing, but not for home canning.

Both globe (round) and oblong (plum or paste) tomatoes are suitable for home canning. Although round tomatoes are noted for their juicy eating quality, they require extra cooking to reach the thicker consistencies home canners expect. Because plum tomatoes are meatier and less juicy, they create thicker sauces in less cooking time. Plum tomatoes contain elevated levels of sugar, acid and pectin, which also makes them preferable for home canning.

While green (unripe) tomatoes can be safely used as an ingredient in many home canning recipes, we don't recommend preserving them as a stand-alone item. Green tomatoes contain a compound called solanine, which can be toxic if consumed in large amounts. Moreover, solanine — like other alkaloids, such as caffeine — contributes an astringent taste to foods that must be balanced by sweeter fruits, vegetables or sugar. The darker the green, the higher the tomato's solanine content. The safest strategy is to use only pale green tomatoes or those tinged with red. If you have a supply of green tomatoes, you can ripen them considerably by placing them in a brown paper bag or between layers of newspaper until the intense green pales. (Some varieties of tomatoes, such as certain heirloom varieties, are green when ripe.)

When purchasing tomatoes for home canning, store them in a cool place, away from direct sunlight, until you're ready to prepare them. Do not refrigerate. Cold storage destroys the flavor of tomatoes, stops their natural ripening cycle and leads to a mealy texture.

Preparing Tomatoes

When preparing tomatoes, it is particularly important to use only stainless steel saucepans and utensils. The acid in tomatoes can react with aluminum, copper, brass, galvanized or iron equipment, creating bitter flavors and undesirable colors. Avoid wooden utensils, as they can absorb flavor and colors and carry them to other foods.

When preparing large quantities of tomato sauce, a food mill (see Glossary, page 432) or Victorio strainer (see Glossary, page 437) is a wise investment. This mechanical device, available in both hand-turned and electric models, separates tomato pulp and juice from the seeds and peel and finely grinds the tomatoes. Quartering tomatoes (in small quantities to prevent the loss of liquid) before pressing speeds the procedure. Fully ripe tomatoes are the best choice when using a food mill or Victorio strainer. If your tomatoes are slightly under-ripe, you may need to quarter and heat them (in small batches to slow liquid loss) before passing them through the mill.

When your recipe calls for whole or chopped tomatoes, the quickest and easiest way to remove the skins is by blanching. Fill a large deep stainless steel saucepan to the halfway level with water and bring to a boil over high heat. Cut an X in the bottom (opposite stem end) of each tomato. Working in small batches, immerse tomatoes in boiling water for 30 to 60 seconds, just until the skins loosen or curl. Immediately plunge tomatoes into ice cold water. The skins should slip off easily.

Separation of Juice from Solids

When tomatoes are cut or crushed before being heated, exposure to the air activates a natural enzyme. This enzyme breaks down pectin, which causes the liquids and solids to separate. This phenomenon is the cause of watery sauces. It is also the villain that causes solids to separate from liquids in jars of processed tomato products.

Heating tomatoes immediately after they are cut or crushed inactivates this enzyme. That's why many of our recipes direct you to cut small quantities of tomatoes and heat them in batches.

Using the hot-pack method when packing tomatoes or canning them whole also helps to inactivate this enzyme.

Acidification

Although tomatoes are classified as high-acid foods, they have a pH of 4.6, which falls very close to the dividing line between high- and low-acid foods. Differences among varieties of tomatoes, growing conditions, their maturity and how they are handled can cause their natural acidity level to vary. As a result, homemade tomato products must be "acidified" by adding bottled lemon juice or citric acid before they are heat-processed. We specify the use of bottled lemon juice rather than freshly squeezed because the commercial product has a known and consistent pH. Fresh lemons produce juice of variable acidity.

Adding Salt

Whether to add salt to tomatoes is a matter of taste. Salt is added only as a seasoning, since the quantity used does not have a preservative effect. Because canned tomatoes are usually used as an ingredient in recipes, it probably makes sense to omit the salt and other flavorings, such as herbs, and add these seasonings at the time of preparation.

Heat Processing

When home-canning tomatoes, you can use either a boiling-water canner or a pressure canner. However, as a general rule, tomato products that include added vegetables are too low in acidity to be processed in boiling water and must be processed in a pressure canner. Furthermore, any tomato recipe that includes meat or fish *must* be processed in a pressure canner.

Acidification is required for all jars of home-canned tomatoes, regardless of whether they are processed in a boiling-water canner or a pressure canner.

Tomatoes Processed in a Boiling-Water Canner

Tomatoes that do not have added vegetables can be safely home-canned in a boiling-water canner. We have included a few special tomato-based recipes that contain a small quantity of added vegetables but that still can be safely processed in a boiling-water canner. The acidity of these mixtures and the processing times have been scientifically determined to ensure a safe result. Remember, these recipes are exceptions, and ingredient quantities must not be altered.

....

Tomatoes Packed in Water

Whole, halved or quartered tomatoes can be hot- or raw-packed in water, in tomato juice (see variation) or with no added liquid (see recipe, page 356). You'll need about 3 lbs (1.37 kg) of tomatoes for each quart (1 L) jar.

TIP

For the best-quality product and vacuum seal, pack tomatoes one jar at a time. For each jar, add the lemon juice or citric acid, then the salt, if using. Then pack the tomatoes as indicated in Step 6 and place the jar in the canner. Repeat until all jars are filled.

Tomatoes
Bottled lemon juice or citric acid
Salt (optional)

1. Prepare canner, jars and lids *(for more information, see page 415)*.
2. Working in small batches, immerse tomatoes in boiling water for 30 to 60 seconds or until the skins start to loosen or crack. Immediately plunge into a bowl of cold water and slip the skins off. Remove cores and any bruised or discolored portions that become apparent after blanching. Leave whole, halve or quarter.
3. Prepare tomatoes for packing:

   RAW-PACK METHOD
   Bring about 4 cups (1 L) water to a boil and keep hot (you will use it to fill the jars). Do not heat tomatoes.

   HOT-PACK METHOD
   Place tomatoes in a large stainless steel saucepan. (For best results when canning whole tomatoes, do not layer them in the pan. Quartered and halved tomatoes can be layered.) Add water to cover. Bring to a boil over medium-high heat, stirring gently. Reduce heat and boil gently for 5 minutes.

1.5 L jars are available only in Canada. These jars may be used to process tomatoes in a boiling-water canner, but only in those recipes for which a specific time is stated for this size of jar. 1.5 L jars are not recommended for processing tomatoes or any food in a pressure canner, as suitable heat processing studies to determine safe processing times have not been established.

To ripen tomatoes for canning, empty them from the basket or box onto a single layer of newspaper or a large mesh rack. Store in a cool (but not cold), dry place, out of direct sun. Turn tomatoes daily to prevent spoilage and soft spots. As the tomatoes ripen, sort into different stages of ripeness and use the ripest ones first.

4. Before packing each jar of tomatoes (see tip, at left), add lemon juice or citric acid to the hot jar in the quantity specified below:

Acidification Ingredient Options	Jar Size		
	Pint (500 mL)	Quart (1 L)	1.5 L (see tip)
Bottled lemon juice	1 tbsp (15 mL)	2 tbsp (30 mL)	3 tbsp (45 mL)
Citric acid	¼ tsp (1 mL)	½ tsp (2 mL)	¾ tsp (4 mL)

5. Add salt, if using, in the quantity specified below:

	Pint (500 mL)	Quart (1 L)	1.5 L (see tip)
	½ tsp (2 mL)	1 tsp (5 mL)	1½ tsp (7 mL)

6. Pack tomatoes into prepared jars to within a generous ½ inch (1 cm) of top of jar. Ladle hot cooking liquid (or boiling water if using the raw-pack method) into jar to cover tomatoes, leaving ½ inch (1 cm) headspace. Remove air bubbles and adjust headspace, if necessary, by adding hot liquid. Wipe rim. Center lid on jar. Screw band down until resistance is met, then increase to fingertip-tight.

7. Place jars in canner, ensuring they are completely covered with water. Bring to a boil and process pint (500 mL) jars for 40 minutes and quart (1 L) and 1.5 L jars for 45 minutes. Remove canner lid. Wait 5 minutes, then remove jars, cool and store. *(For more information, see pages 417–418.)*

Variation

Tomatoes Packed in Tomato Juice: Packing tomatoes in tomato juice concentrates and enhances the flavor of the end product. However, the processing times must be increased. Use either the hot- or raw-pack method and follow the steps above, substituting commercially prepared or homemade (see recipe, page 360) heated tomato juice for the water. Increase processing time to 85 minutes for both pint (500 mL) and quart (1 L) jars. We do not recommend using 1.5 L jars for tomatoes packed in tomato juice.

Raw-Packed Tomatoes with No Added Liquid

Packing tomatoes raw with no added liquid produces the most concentrated flavor. However, this method requires extended processing times to ensure that the heat fully penetrates to the center of the jars. You'll need about 3 lbs (1.37 kg) of tomatoes for each quart (1 L) jar.

TIPS

You'll need about 21 lbs (9.5 kg) of tomatoes to produce seven quart (1 L) jars. A bushel of tomatoes weighs 53 lbs (24 kg) and yields fifteen to twenty-one quart (1 L) jars.

For the best-quality product and vacuum seal, pack tomatoes one jar at a time. For each jar, add the lemon juice or citric acid, then the salt, if using. Then pack the tomatoes as indicated in Step 5 and place the jar in the canner. Repeat until all jars are filled.

Tomatoes
Bottled lemon juice or citric acid
Salt (optional)

1. Prepare canner, jars and lids *(for more information, see page 415).*

2. Working in small batches, immerse tomatoes in boiling water for 30 to 60 seconds or until the skins start to loosen or crack. Immediately plunge into a bowl of cold water and slip the skins off. Remove cores and any bruised or discolored portions that become apparent after blanching. Leave whole, halve or quarter.

3. Before packing each jar of raw tomatoes (see tip, at left), add lemon juice or citric acid to the hot jar in the quantity specified below:

Acidification Ingredient Options	Jar Size	
	Pint (500 mL)	Quart (1 L)
Bottled lemon juice	1 tbsp (15 mL)	2 tbsp (30 mL)
Citric acid	¼ tsp (1 mL)	½ tsp (2 mL)

4. Add salt, if using, in the quantity specified below:

	Pint (500 mL)	Quart (1 L)
	½ tsp (2 mL)	1 tsp (5 mL)

5. Pack raw tomatoes into prepared jars to within a generous ½ inch (1 cm) of top of jar. Press tomatoes into the jar until the spaces between them fill with juice, leaving ½ inch (1 cm) headspace. Remove air bubbles and adjust headspace, if necessary, by adding tomatoes. Wipe rim. Center lid on jar. Screw band down until resistance is met, then increase to fingertip-tight.

6. Place jars in canner, ensuring they are completely covered with water. Bring to a boil and process pint (500 mL) or quart (1 L) jars for 85 minutes. (This recipe is not recommended for 1.5 L jars.) Remove canner lid. Wait 5 minutes, then remove jars, cool and store. *(For more information, see pages 417–418.)*

Crushed Tomatoes

Crushed tomatoes
resemble whole or
halved tomatoes in
flavor, but since they
are crushed they're
ideal for sauce, soup
and stew recipes.
You will need about
2¾ lbs (1.25 kg) of
tomatoes for each quart
(1 L) jar.

TIPS

For the best-quality
product and vacuum seal,
pack tomatoes one jar at
a time. For each jar, add
the lemon juice or citric
acid, then the salt, if using.
Then pack the tomatoes
as indicated in Step 6
and place the jar in the
canner. Repeat until all
jars are filled.

Tomatoes are very high
in lycopene, an antioxidant
that has been linked with
reducing the risk of
certain types of cancer.
Interestingly, the
lycopene in cooked
or heat-processed
tomatoes is more readily
absorbed by the body
than that contained in
fresh tomatoes.

Tomatoes	
Bottled lemon juice or citric acid	
Salt (optional)	

1. Prepare canner, jars and lids *(for more information, see page 415)*.

2. Working in small batches, immerse tomatoes in boiling water for 30 to 60 seconds or until the skins start to loosen or crack. Immediately plunge into a bowl of cold water and slip the skins off. Remove cores and any bruised or discolored portions that become apparent after blanching.

3. Working in batches, quarter enough tomatoes to measure about 2 cups (500 mL). Transfer to a large stainless steel saucepan and bring to a boil over medium-high heat. Using a potato masher, crush tomatoes to release juices. While maintaining a gentle boil and stirring to prevent scorching, quarter additional tomatoes and add to the saucepan as you work. (The remaining tomatoes do not need to be crushed, as they will soften with heating and stirring.) Continue until all tomatoes are added, then boil gently for 5 minutes.

4. Before packing each jar of tomatoes (see tip, at left), add lemon juice or citric acid to the hot jar in the quantity specified below:

Acidification Ingredient Options	Jar Size	
	Pint (500 mL)	Quart (1 L)
Bottled lemon juice	1 tbsp (15 mL)	2 tbsp (30 mL)
Citric acid	¼ tsp (1 mL)	½ tsp (2 mL)

5. Add salt, if using, in the quantity specified below:

	Pint (500 mL)	Quart (1 L)
	½ tsp (2 mL)	1 tsp (5 mL)

6. Pack hot tomatoes into prepared jars to within a generous ½ inch (1 cm) of top of jar. Press tomatoes in the jar until spaces between them fill with juice, leaving ½ inch (1 cm) headspace. Remove air bubbles and adjust headspace, if necessary, by adding hot tomatoes. Wipe rim. Center lid on jar. Screw band down until resistance is met, then increase to fingertip-tight.

7. Place jars in canner, ensuring they are completely covered with water. Bring to a boil and process pint (500 mL) jars for 35 minutes and quart (1 L) jars for 45 minutes. Remove canner lid. Wait 5 minutes, then remove jars, cool and store. *(For more information, see pages 417–418.)*

Herbed Seasoned Tomatoes

Adding dried herbs and spices to home-canned tomatoes gives you a head start on recipes that require seasoned tomatoes. Choose the spice blend (see recipes, opposite) that suits the kind of recipes you are likely to make, or make two jars of each to meet a variety of needs.

TIPS

To peel tomatoes, place them in a pot of boiling water for 30 to 60 seconds or until the skins start to crack. Immediately dip in cold water. The skins will slip off easily.

For the best-quality product and vacuum seal, pack tomatoes one jar at a time. For each jar, add the lemon juice or citric acid, then the salt, if using, then the spice blend. Then pack the tomatoes and place the jar in the canner. Repeat until all jars are filled.

Makes about six pint (500 mL) jars

12 cups	halved cored peeled tomatoes (see tips, at left)	3 L
	Spice blend(s) (see recipes, opposite)	
	Bottled lemon juice or citric acid	
	Salt (optional)	

1. Prepare canner, jars and lids. *(For more information, see page 415.)*
2. Choose desired spice blend(s). Prepare the quantity that suits your needs and set aside.
3. Place tomatoes in a large stainless steel saucepan. (For best results, do not layer tomatoes in pan). Add water to cover. Bring to a boil over medium-high heat, stirring gently. Reduce heat and boil gently for 5 minutes.
4. Before packing each jar of tomatoes (see tip, at left), add 1 tbsp (15 mL) lemon juice or ¼ tsp (1 mL) citric acid and ¼ tsp (1 mL) salt to the hot jar. Add the specified quantity of your chosen spice blend. Pack hot tomatoes into prepared jars to within a generous ½ inch (1 cm) of top of jar. Ladle hot liquid into jar to cover tomatoes, leaving ½ inch (1 cm) headspace. Remove air bubbles and adjust headspace, if necessary, by adding hot liquid. Wipe rim. Center lid on jar. Screw band down until resistance is met, then increase to fingertip-tight.
5. Place jars in canner, ensuring they are completely covered with water. Bring to a boil and process for 40 minutes. Remove canner lid. Wait 5 minutes, then remove jars, cool and store. *(For more information, see pages 417–418.)*

Spice Blends

Before you start preparing the tomatoes, choose your spice blend(s) in the quantity that suits your needs, prepare and set aside. Treat these recipes as guidelines and adjust the proportion of ingredients within the blend to suit your preferences.

Italian Spice Blend

Dried herbs and spices	2 Jars	6 Jars
Basil	I tsp (5 mL)	4 tsp (20 mL)
Thyme	I tsp (5 mL)	2 tsp (10 mL)
Oregano	I tsp (5 mL)	2½ tsp (12 mL)
Rosemary	½ tsp (2 mL)	1½ tsp (7 mL)
Sage	½ tsp (2 mL)	1½ tsp (7 mL)
Garlic powder	¼ tsp (1 mL)	I tsp (5 mL)
Hot pepper flakes (optional)	¼ tsp (1 mL)	I tsp (5 mL)

For each pint (500 mL) jar, use 2¼ tsp (11 mL) of spice blend. If omitting hot pepper flakes, use only 2 tsp (10 mL) per jar.

Mexican Spice Blend

Dried herbs and spices	2 jars	6 jars
Chili powder	2 tsp (10 mL)	6 tsp (30 mL)
Ground cumin	I tsp (5mL)	2 tsp (10 mL)
Oregano	I tsp (5 mL)	2 tsp (10 mL)
Garlic powder	I tsp (5 mL)	2 tsp (10 mL)
Ground coriander	I tsp (5 mL)	2 tsp (10 mL)
Seasoned salt (optional)	½ tsp (2 mL)	1½ tsp (7 mL)

For each pint (500 mL) jar, use 2½ tsp (12 mL) of spice blend. If omitting seasoned salt, use only 2 tsp (10 mL) per jar.

Cajun Spice Blend

Dried herbs and spices	2 jars	6 jars
Chili powder	I tsp (5 mL)	3 tsp (15 mL)
Paprika	I tsp (5 mL)	2 tsp (10 mL)
Onion flakes	½ tsp (2 mL)	1½ tsp (7 mL)
Garlic powder	½ tsp (2 mL)	1½ tsp (7 mL)
Ground allspice	½ tsp (2 mL)	1½ tsp (7 mL)
Thyme	½ tsp (2 mL)	1½ tsp (7 mL)
Cayenne pepper	¼ tsp (1 mL)	I tsp (5 mL)

For each pint (500 mL) jar, use 2 tsp (10 mL) of spice blend.

Tomato Juice

On average, it takes
3 to 3¼ lbs (1.37 to
1.5 kg) of tomatoes
to make 1 quart (1 L)
of juice.

TIPS

If juice separation is not a concern, in Step 2 simply quarter tomatoes into a large stainless steel saucepan. Crush and boil gently for 5 minutes before pressing through a sieve, food mill or Victorio strainer.

It is very important that you reheat the tomato juice before filling the jars. Processing times are based on hot juice in a hot jar. If the juice is tepid, the processing time won't be sufficient to vent the excess headspace gases and/or destroy spoilage microorganisms.

1.5 L jars are available only in Canada. These jars may be used to process tomatoes in a boiling-water canner, but only in those recipes for which a specific time is stated for this size of jar. 1.5 L jars are not recommended for processing tomatoes or any food in a pressure canner, as suitable heat processing studies to determine safe processing times have not been established.

| Tomatoes, cored |
| Bottled lemon juice or citric acid |
| Salt (optional) |

1. Prepare canner, jars and lids *(for more information, see page 415)*.
2. Wash and sort tomatoes, removing any bruised or discolored product. Quarter 6 tomatoes and place in a large stainless steel saucepan. Bring to a boil over high heat. Using a potato masher, crush tomatoes to release juices, stirring constantly. While maintaining a boil and stirring to prevent burning, quarter additional tomatoes, adding them to the saucepan as you work. Make sure the mixture continues to boil vigorously while you add, stir and crush the remaining tomatoes. When all tomatoes have been added, reduce heat to medium and boil gently until tomatoes are soft and juicy, about 10 minutes. Remove from heat.
3. Working in batches, press tomatoes through a fine sieve, food mill or Victorio strainer to remove skins and seeds. Discard skins and seeds. Return juice to saucepan and bring to a boil over medium-high heat. Remove from heat.
4. Before filling each jar with tomato juice, add lemon juice or citric acid to the hot jar in the quantity specified below:

Acidification Ingredient Options	Jar Size		
	Pint (500 mL)	Quart (1 L)	1.5 L (see tip)
Bottled lemon juice	1 tbsp (15 mL)	2 tbsp (30 mL)	3 tbsp (45 mL)
Citric acid	¼ tsp (1 mL)	½ tsp (2 mL)	¾ tsp (4 mL)

5. Add salt, if using, in the quantity specified below:

	Pint (500 mL)	Quart (1 L)	1.5 L (see tip)
	½ tsp (2 mL)	1 tsp (5 mL)	1½ tsp (7 mL)

6. Ladle hot juice into prepared jars, leaving ½ inch (1 cm) headspace. Wipe rim. Center lid on jar. Screw band down until resistance is met, then increase to fingertip-tight.
7. Place jars in canner, ensuring they are completely covered with water. Bring to a boil and process pint (500 mL) jars for 35 minutes, quart (1 L) jars for 40 minutes and 1.5 L jars for 50 minutes. Remove canner lid. Wait 5 minutes, then remove jars, cool and store. *(For more information, see pages 417–418.)*

Tomato Paste

A perfect pantry item, tomato paste can be used year-round to jazz up soups, stews and tomato-based sauces.

TIPS

For the best-quality product and vacuum seal, pack tomato paste one jar at a time. For each jar, add the lemon juice or citric acid, then pack the tomato paste and place the jar in the canner. Repeat until all jars are filled.

To ripen tomatoes for canning, empty them from the basket or box onto a single layer of newspaper or a large mesh rack. Store in a cool (but not cold), dry place, out of direct sun. Turn tomatoes daily to prevent spoilage and soft spots. As the tomatoes ripen, sort into different stages of ripeness and use the ripest ones first.

Makes about nine 8-ounce (250 mL) jars

50	large plum tomatoes, cored	50
1½ cups	chopped seeded red bell peppers	375 mL
2	bay leaves	2
1 tsp	salt	5 mL
1	clove garlic (optional)	1
	Bottled lemon juice or citric acid	

1. Wash and sort tomatoes, removing any bruised or discolored product. Quarter 6 tomatoes to measure about 2 cups (500 mL). Transfer to a large stainless steel saucepan and bring to a boil over medium-high heat. Using a potato masher, crush tomatoes to release juices. While maintaining a boil and stirring to prevent burning, quarter additional tomatoes, adding them to the saucepan as you work. Make sure the mixture continues to boil vigorously while you add, stir and crush the remaining tomatoes. When all tomatoes have been added, stir in red peppers and bring to a boil. Reduce heat and boil gently, stirring occasionally, until tomatoes are very soft, about 1 hour.

2. Working in batches, press mixture through a fine sieve, food mill or Victorio strainer to remove skins and seeds. Discard skins and seeds.

3. Return mixture to saucepan. Add bay leaves, salt and garlic, if using. Return to boil over medium heat. Reduce heat and boil gently, stirring frequently, until mixture is thick enough to mound on a spoon, about 2½ hours. Discard bay leaves and garlic clove.

4. Meanwhile, prepare canner, jars and lids. *(For more information, see page 415.)*

5. Before filling each jar with tomato paste (see tip, at left), add 1½ tsp (7 mL) lemon juice or ¼ tsp (1 mL) citric acid to the hot jar. Ladle hot paste into prepared jars, leaving ½ inch (1 cm) headspace. Remove air bubbles and adjust headspace, if necessary, by adding hot paste. Wipe rim. Center lid on jar. Screw band down until resistance is met, then increase to fingertip-tight.

6. Place jars in canner, ensuring they are completely covered with water. Bring to a boil and process for 45 minutes. Remove canner lid. Wait 5 minutes, then remove jars, cool and store. *(For more information, see pages 417–418.)*

Basic Tomato Sauce

Jars of this tomato sauce are like a painter's canvas — ready to be transformed, in this case into a wide variety of delicious sauces and entrées. For each quart (1 L) jar of thin sauce, you'll need about 5 lbs (2.3 kg) of tomatoes.

TIPS

For a thin sauce, you'll need an average of 35 lbs (15.9 kg) of tomatoes to produce 7 quart (1 L) jars of sauce. For a thick sauce, you'll need an average of 46 lbs (20.9 kg) to yield 7 quart (1 L) jars.

For the best-quality product and vacuum seal, pack tomato sauce one jar at a time. For each jar, add the lemon juice or citric acid, then the salt and dried herbs, if using. Then ladle in hot sauce as indicated in Step 8 and place the jar in the canner. Repeat until all jars are filled.

| Tomatoes, cored (see tip, at left) |
| Bottled lemon juice or citric acid |
| Salt (optional) |
| Dried herbs (optional) |

1. Prepare canner, jars and lids *(for more information, see page 415)*.
2. Wash and sort tomatoes, removing any bruised or discolored product. Quarter 6 tomatoes and place in a large stainless steel saucepan. Bring to a boil over medium-high heat. Using a potato masher, crush tomatoes to release juices, stirring constantly. While maintaining a boil and stirring to prevent burning, quarter additional tomatoes, adding them to the saucepan as you work. Make sure the mixture continues to boil vigorously while you add, stir and crush the remaining tomatoes. When all tomatoes have been added, boil, stirring occasionally, until tomatoes are soft and juicy, about 10 minutes. Remove from heat.
3. Working in batches, press tomatoes through a fine sieve, food mill or Victorio strainer to remove skins and seeds. Discard skins and seeds.
4. Return mixture to saucepan and bring to a boil over high heat, stirring frequently. Reduce heat to medium-high and boil until volume is reduced by at least one-third for a thin sauce. For a thicker sauce, cook until reduced by half.
5. Before filling each jar with tomato sauce (see tip, at left), add lemon juice or citric acid to the hot jar in the quantity specified below.

Acidification Ingredient Options	Jar Size		
	Pint (500 mL)	Quart (1 L)	1.5 L (see tip)
Bottled lemon juice	1 tbsp (15 mL)	2 tbsp (30 mL)	3 tbsp (45 mL)
Citric acid	¼ tsp (1 mL)	½ tsp (2 mL)	¾ tsp (4 mL)

6. Add salt, if using, in the quantity specified below.

	Pint (500 mL)	Quart (1 L)	1.5 L (see tip)
	½ tsp (2 mL)	1 tsp (5 mL)	1½ tsp (7 mL)

1.5 L jars are available only in Canada. These jars may be used to process tomatoes in a boiling-water canner, but only in those recipes for which a specific time is stated for this size of jar. 1.5 L jars are not recommended for processing tomatoes or any food in a pressure canner, as suitable heat processing studies to determine safe processing times have not been established.

Dried basil, oregano, rosemary, thyme and Italian seasoning mixes are excellent seasonings for this sauce. Use those preferred by your family. Add the dried herbs to each jar, rather than trying to season the entire batch of tomatoes. Start with ½ tsp (2 mL) per pint (500 mL) jar — you can always add more when using the sauce. Many families like to add a fresh basil leaf to each jar. This is acceptable, but remember to use only unblemished leaves that have been thoroughly rinsed.

7. Add dried herbs, if using, to each jar (see tip, at left).

8. Ladle hot sauce into prepared jars, leaving ½ inch (1 cm) headspace. Remove air bubbles and adjust headspace, if necessary, by adding hot sauce. Wipe rim. Center lid on jar. Screw band down until resistance is met, then increase to fingertip-tight.

9. Place jars in canner, ensuring they are completely covered with water. Bring to a boil and process pint (500 mL) jars for 35 minutes, quart (1 L) jars for 40 minutes and 1.5 L jars for 50 minutes. Remove canner lid. Wait 5 minutes, then remove jars, cool and store. *(For more information, see pages 417–418.)*

Preventing Siphoning

Considerable pressure builds up inside jars of tomatoes and other home-canned foods while they are being heat-processed. Improper packing and processing procedures can lead to liquid loss, or siphoning, which, in turn, can lead to seal failure. Seal failure is caused when food particles pass between the sealing compound and the rim of the jar, preventing formation of a secure seal. Siphoning is a greater danger when you are processing jars with larger volumes.

To prevent siphoning, first make sure to follow headspace guidelines precisely. When packing whole foods such as tomatoes, peaches and pickles into jars, pack them firmly, but not too tightly. Food expands when heated and can "boil over" if too tightly packed, causing siphoning.

Finally, be careful to follow the correct heating and cooling procedures associated with processing. To prevent siphoning in a boiling-water canner, when the processing time has been completed, turn the heat off, remove the canner lid and wait 5 minutes, then remove jars. To prevent siphoning in a pressure canner, monitor the pressure closely during processing, making only gradual adjustments to the heat level. Allow the pressure canner to cool completely and naturally before releasing the lid (see page 383). Once the lid is removed, let the jars cool inside the pressure canner for a further 10 minutes. In either case, when removing jars, be sure to lift them straight up, without tilting, and cool them upright, undisturbed, for 24 hours.

Seasoned Tomato Sauce

Even though onions, a low-acid food, are included in this sauce, this recipe can be processed safely in a boiling-water canner because the acidity of the mixture and a safe processing time have been scientifically determined. However, it is crucial that you do not alter the ingredients or quantities or you may produce a product that isn't safe to eat.

TIPS

It is very important that you reheat the tomato sauce before filling the jars. Processing times are based on hot sauce in a hot jar. If the sauce is tepid, the processing time won't be sufficient to vent the excess headspace gases and/or destroy spoilage microorganisms.

For the best-quality product and vacuum seal, pack tomatoes one jar at a time. For each jar, add the lemon juice, then ladle in hot sauce and place the jar in the canner. Repeat until all jars are filled.

Makes about six pint (500 mL) jars

10 lbs	tomatoes, cored	4.5 kg
2½ cups	finely chopped onions	625 mL
3	cloves garlic, finely chopped	3
1½ tsp	dried oregano	7 mL
2	bay leaves	2
1 tsp	salt	5 mL
1 tsp	freshly ground black pepper	5 mL
1 tsp	granulated sugar	5 mL
½ tsp	hot pepper flakes	2 mL
	Bottled lemon juice or citric acid	

1. Wash and sort tomatoes, removing any bruised or discolored product. Quarter 6 tomatoes and place in a large stainless steel saucepan. Bring to a boil over high heat. Using a potato masher, crush tomatoes to release juices, stirring constantly. While maintaining a boil and stirring to prevent burning, quarter additional tomatoes, adding them to the saucepan as you work. Make sure the mixture continues to boil vigorously while you add, stir and crush the remaining tomatoes. When all tomatoes have been added, stir in onions, garlic, oregano, bay leaves, salt, black pepper, sugar and hot pepper flakes. Return to a boil, stirring occasionally. Reduce heat to medium and boil, stirring frequently, until sauce is reduced by half and thickens slightly, about 2 hours.

2. Meanwhile, prepare canner, jars and lids. *(For more information, see page 415.)*

3. Working in batches, press tomato mixture through a fine sieve or food mill to remove skins and seeds. Discard peel and seeds.

4. Return mixture to saucepan and bring to a full rolling boil over medium-high heat, stirring occasionally. Remove from heat.

5. Before filling each jar with tomato sauce (see tip, at left), add 1 tbsp (15 mL) lemon juice or ¼ tsp (1 mL) citric acid to the hot jar. Ladle hot sauce into prepared jars, leaving ½ inch (1 cm) headspace. Remove air bubbles and adjust headspace, if necessary, by adding hot sauce. Wipe rim. Center lid on jar. Screw band down until resistance is met, then increase to fingertip-tight.

6. Place jars in canner, ensuring they are completely covered with water. Bring to a boil and process for 35 minutes. Remove canner lid. Wait 5 minutes, then remove jars, cool and store. *(For more information, see pages 417–418.)*

Italian-Style Tomato Sauce

This recipe delivers traditional Italian flavor with no oil and balances the quantity of low-acid vegetables with added acid, in this case lemon juice. It has been scientifically tested to yield a home-canned product that can be safely processed in a boiling-water canner. Do not alter the ingredients or quantities, as this may result in an unsafe product.

TIPS

You'll need about 4½ lbs (2 kg) of plum tomatoes to make the tomato purée for this recipe.

To make fresh tomato purée, pass quartered tomatoes through a food mill or Victorio strainer. If you do not have a food mill or Victorio strainer, blanch, peel, core, seed and chop tomatoes. Place in a colander and let stand for 15 minutes. Discard liquid and purée tomatoes in a food processor fitted with a metal blade.

When you're reheating this sauce to use in recipes, add a little olive oil for flavor.

Makes about three pint (500 mL) jars

8 cups	fresh plum tomato purée (see tips, at left)	2 L
⅔ cup	finely chopped onion	150 mL
⅔ cup	finely chopped celery	150 mL
½ cup	finely chopped carrot	125 mL
2	cloves garlic, finely chopped	2
4 tbsp	bottled lemon juice	60 mL
2 tsp	salt	10 mL
½ tsp	freshly ground black pepper	2 mL
½ tsp	hot pepper flakes	2 mL

1. Prepare canner, jars and lids. *(For more information, see page 415.)*

2. In a large stainless steel saucepan, combine 1 cup (250 mL) of the tomato purée, onion, celery, carrot and garlic. Bring to a boil over medium-high heat, stirring frequently. Reduce heat, cover and boil gently until vegetables are tender, about 5 minutes. While maintaining a steady boil, add remaining tomato purée, 1 cup (500 mL) at a time, stirring frequently. Stir in lemon juice, salt, black pepper and hot pepper flakes. Increase heat to high and bring to a full rolling boil; boil hard, stirring frequently, until mixture is reduced by one-third, about 15 minutes.

3. Ladle hot sauce into hot jars, leaving ½ inch (1 cm) headspace. Remove air bubbles and adjust headspace, if necessary, by adding hot sauce. Wipe rim. Center lid on jar. Screw band down until resistance is met, then increase to fingertip-tight.

4. Place jars in canner, ensuring they are completely covered with water. Bring to a boil and process for 35 minutes. Remove canner lid. Wait 5 minutes, then remove jars, cool and store. *(For more information, see pages 417–418.)*

Pizza Sauce

Why order out for pizza when you've got this terrific sauce on hand? Spread it over a pre-made crust and add your favorite toppings for a quick, easy supper. Feel free to add more oregano, pepper and garlic powder, but do not change the proportion of tomato purée to lemon juice.

TIPS

You'll need about 9 lbs (4.1 kg) of plum tomatoes to make the tomato purée for this recipe.

To make fresh tomato purée, pass quartered tomatoes through a food mill or Victorio strainer. If you do not have a food mill or Victorio strainer, blanch, peel, core, seed and chop tomatoes. Place in a colander and let stand for 15 minutes. Discard liquid and purée tomatoes in a food processor fitted with a metal blade.

Makes about four pint (500 mL) jars

13 cups	fresh plum tomato purée (see tips, at left)	3.25 L
½ cup	bottled lemon juice	125 mL
2 tsp	dried oregano	10 mL
1 tsp	freshly ground black pepper	5 mL
1 tsp	salt	5 mL
1 tsp	garlic powder	5 mL

1. Prepare canner, jars and lids. (For more information, see page 415.)

2. Place half of the tomato purée in a large stainless steel saucepan. Bring to a boil over high heat, stirring occasionally. Maintaining a constant boil, add remaining tomato purée, 1 cup (250 mL) at a time. Stir in lemon juice, oregano, pepper, salt and garlic powder. Boil hard, stirring frequently, until mixture is the consistency of a thin commercial sauce, about 15 minutes. Remove from heat.

3. Ladle hot sauce into hot jars, leaving ½ inch (1 cm) headspace. Remove air bubbles and adjust headspace, if necessary, by adding hot sauce. Wipe rim. Center lid on jar. Screw band down until resistance is met, then increase to fingertip-tight.

4. Place jars in canner, ensuring they are completely covered with water. Bring to a boil and process for 35 minutes. Remove canner lid. Wait 5 minutes, then remove jars, cool and store. (For more information, see pages 417–418.)

Creole Sauce

This spicy Southern sauce is ideal for baking and barbecuing chicken or fish. If it's too hot for your taste, tame it with a bit of sour cream or yogurt, which will give a slightly charred result to your meat or fish, similar to blackened chicken.

TIP

To peel tomatoes, place them in a pot of boiling water for 30 to 60 seconds or until the skins start to crack. Immediately dip in cold water. The skins will slip off easily.

Makes about nine 8-ounce (250 mL) jars

11 cups	coarsely chopped cored peeled tomatoes (see tip, at left)	2.75 L
1	green bell pepper, seeded and chopped	1
1 cup	chopped green onions	250 mL
4 tbsp	red wine vinegar	60 mL
3	cloves garlic, finely chopped	3
2 tbsp	Worcestershire sauce	30 mL
1 tbsp	dried oregano	15 mL
2 tsp	hot pepper sauce	10 mL
1 tsp	freshly ground black pepper	5 mL
1/2 tsp	salt	2 mL
1/2 tsp	cayenne pepper	2 mL

1. In a large stainless steel saucepan, combine tomatoes, green pepper, green onions, vinegar, garlic, Worcestershire sauce, oregano, hot pepper sauce, black pepper, salt and cayenne. Bring to a boil over high heat, stirring frequently. Reduce heat and boil gently, stirring occasionally, until mixture is the consistency of a thin commercial ketchup, about 40 minutes.

2. Meanwhile, prepare canner, jars and lids. *(For more information, see page 415.)*

3. Ladle hot sauce into hot jars, leaving 1/2 inch (1 cm) headspace. Remove air bubbles and adjust headspace, if necessary, by adding hot sauce. Wipe rim. Center lid on jar. Screw band down until resistance is met, then increase to fingertip-tight.

4. Place jars in canner, ensuring they are completely covered with water. Bring to a boil and process for 20 minutes. Remove canner lid. Wait 5 minutes, then remove jars, cool and store. *(For more information, see pages 417–418.)*

Chicken Wing Sauce

Use this delicious, shelf-stable tomato sauce as a dipping sauce with grilled chicken wings or as a time-saving ingredient. Spoon the ready-to-use sauce over browned chicken pieces and simmer or bake until done. If you prefer a sauce with more "heat," feel free to add 2 to 3 tbsp (30 to 45 mL) of your favorite hot sauce along with the vinegar and spices.

TIPS

To peel tomatoes, place them in a pot of boiling water for 30 to 60 seconds or until the skins start to crack. Immediately dip in cold water. The skins will slip off easily.

Refer to the Produce Purchase Guide on pages 426–429 to determine how much produce you'll need to buy to prepare this recipe.

Makes about eight 8-ounce (250 mL) jars

10 cups	chopped cored peeled tomatoes (see tip, at left)	2.5 L
2 cups	chopped onions	500 mL
1/3 cup	lightly packed brown sugar	75 mL
1/2 tsp	cayenne pepper	2 mL
1 1/2 cups	white vinegar	375 mL
4 tsp	salt	20 mL
2	cloves garlic, minced	2
1 tsp	ground allspice	5 mL
1 tsp	ground cinnamon	5 mL
1 tsp	ground cloves	5 mL
1 tsp	ground ginger	5 mL

1. Prepare canner, jars and lids. *(For more information, see page 415.)*

2. In a large stainless steel saucepan, combine tomatoes, onions, brown sugar and cayenne. Bring to a boil over high heat, stirring constantly. Reduce heat and boil gently, stirring occasionally, for 30 minutes. Remove from heat and let cool slightly.

3. Working in batches, transfer mixture to a blender or a food processor fitted with a metal blade and purée until smooth.

4. Return purée to saucepan. Stir in vinegar, salt, garlic, allspice, cinnamon, cloves and ginger. Bring to a boil over high heat, stirring constantly. Reduce heat and boil gently, stirring occasionally, until mixture is the consistency of a thin commercial sauce, about 1 hour.

5. Ladle hot sauce into hot jars, leaving 1/2 inch (1 cm) headspace. Remove air bubbles and adjust headspace, if necessary, by adding hot sauce. Wipe rim. Center lid on jar. Screw band down until resistance is met, then increase to fingertip-tight.

6. Place jars in canner, ensuring they are completely covered with water. Bring to a boil and process for 15 minutes. Remove canner lid. Wait 5 minutes, then remove jars, cool and store. *(For more information, see pages 417–418.)*

Seafood Cocktail Sauce

Don't limit this zesty sauce to shrimp alone — use it to accompany any seafood.

TIPS

You'll need about 9 lbs (4.1 kg) of plum tomatoes to make the tomato purée for this recipe.

To make fresh tomato purée, pass quartered tomatoes through a food mill or Victorio strainer. If you do not have a food mill or Victorio strainer, blanch, peel, core, seed and chop tomatoes. Place in a colander and let stand for 15 minutes. Discard liquid and purée tomatoes in a food processor fitted with a metal blade.

Peel fresh horseradish root with a vegetable peeler to remove outer skin. (You can also do this by scraping the skin with a spoon.) Discard any bruised or brown portions, as well as the hard, woody core. Finely grate with a hand grater or a food processor fitted with a fine metal grating blade. Be aware that horseradish, like onions, has a strong aroma; using a food processor will reduce the production of tears.

Makes about nine 8-ounce (250 mL) jars

13 cups	fresh plum tomato purée (see tips, at left)	3.25 L
	Zest and juice of 2 lemons	
3	cloves garlic, minced	3
1¼ cups	granulated sugar	300 mL
1 cup	white vinegar	250 mL
2 tbsp	salt	30 mL
2 tbsp	Worcestershire sauce	30 mL
2 tsp	dry mustard	10 mL
1 tsp	cayenne pepper	5 mL
1 tsp	onion powder	5 mL
½ tsp	freshly ground black pepper	2 mL
3 cups	finely grated peeled horseradish	750 mL

1. Prepare canner, jars and lids. *(For more information, see page 415.)*

2. Place half of the tomato purée in a large stainless steel saucepan. Bring to a boil over high heat, stirring occasionally. Maintaining a constant boil, add remaining tomato purée, 1 cup (250 mL) at a time. Reduce heat and boil gently, stirring occasionally, until mixture is reduced by half, about 30 minutes. Add lemon zest and juice, garlic, sugar, vinegar, salt, Worcestershire sauce, mustard, cayenne, onion powder and black pepper. Increase heat to high and bring to a full rolling boil, stirring frequently. Remove from heat and immediately stir in horseradish.

3. Ladle hot sauce into hot jars, leaving ½ inch (1 cm) headspace. Remove air bubbles and adjust headspace, if necessary, by adding hot sauce. Wipe rim. Center lid on jar. Screw band down until resistance is met, then increase to fingertip-tight.

4. Place jars in canner, ensuring they are completely covered with water. Bring to a boil and process for 15 minutes. Remove canner lid. Wait 5 minutes, then remove jars, cool and store. *(For more information, see pages 417–418.)*

Tomatoes Processed in a Pressure Canner

Processing tomatoes in a pressure canner may produce a more nutritious and higher-quality product because the tomatoes are heated to a higher temperature but are processed for a shorter period of time. The longer a food product is exposed to heat, the greater the loss of nutrients and overall product quality. If you have a pressure canner, it may be the best choice when processing tomatoes. Before preparing any of the pressure canner recipes that follow, review the general information on pressure canning on pages 380–384.

Tomatoes Packed in Water

Select fresh tomatoes at the peak of quality and flavor. Use firm tomatoes free of cracks, spots and growths. Prepare only enough for one canner load. You'll need about 3 lbs (1.37 kg) of tomatoes for each quart (1 L) jar.

TIP

For the best-quality product and vacuum seal, pack tomatoes one jar at a time. For each jar, add the lemon juice or citric acid, then the salt, if using. Then pack the tomatoes as indicated in Step 6 and place the jar in the canner. Repeat until all jars are filled.

Tomatoes
Bottled lemon juice or citric acid
Salt (optional)

1. Prepare weighted-gauge pressure canner, jars and lids. *(For more information, see page 382.)*
2. Working in small batches, immerse tomatoes in boiling water for 30 to 60 seconds or until the skins start to loosen or crack. Immediately plunge into a bowl of cold water and slip the skins off. Remove cores and any bruised or discolored portions that become apparent after blanching. Leave whole, halve or quarter.
3. Prepare tomatoes for packing:

   RAW-PACK METHOD
   Bring about 4 cups (1 L) water to a boil and keep hot (you will use it to fill the jars). Do not heat tomatoes.

   HOT-PACK METHOD
   Place tomatoes in a large stainless steel saucepan. (For best results when canning whole tomatoes, do not layer them in the pan. Quartered and halved tomatoes can be layered.) Add water to cover. Bring to a boil over medium-high heat, stirring gently. Reduce heat and boil gently for 5 minutes.

4. Before packing each jar of tomatoes (see tip, at left), add lemon juice or citric acid to the hot jar in the quantity specified opposite:

To ripen tomatoes for
canning, empty them from
the basket or box onto a
single layer of newspaper
or a large mesh rack.
Store in a cool (but not
cold), dry place, out of
direct sun. Turn tomatoes
daily to prevent spoilage
and soft spots. As the
tomatoes ripen, sort
into different stages of
ripeness and use the
ripest ones first.

Botanically, tomatoes are
a fruit (a berry, the edible,
seed-containing part of
a plant). Legally, however,
tomatoes are vegetables,
thanks to a U.S. Supreme
Court ruling that favored
their "common use" over
their botanical origin.

Tomatoes are very
high in lycopene, an
antioxidant that has been
linked with reducing the
risk of certain types of
cancer. Interestingly, the
lycopene in cooked or
heat-processed tomatoes
is more readily absorbed
by the body than
that contained in
fresh tomatoes.

Acidification Ingredient Options	Jar Size	
	Pint (500 mL)	Quart (1 L)
Bottled lemon juice	1 tbsp (15 mL)	2 tbsp (30 mL)
Citric acid	¼ tsp (1 mL)	½ tsp (2 mL)

5. Add salt, if using, in the quantity specified below:

	Pint (500 mL)	Quart (1 L)
	½ tsp (2 mL)	1 tsp (5 mL)

6. Pack tomatoes into prepared jars to within a generous 1 inch (2.5 cm) of top of jar. Ladle hot cooking liquid (or boiling water if using the raw-pack method) into jar to cover tomatoes, leaving 1 inch (2.5 cm) headspace. Remove air bubbles and adjust headspace, if necessary, by adding hot liquid. Wipe rim. Center lid on jar. Screw band down until resistance is met, then increase to fingertip-tight.

7. Place jars in pressure canner. Adjust water level, lock lid and bring to a boil over medium-high heat. Vent steam for 10 minutes, then close vent. Continue heating to achieve 10 lbs (68 kPa) pressure. Process both pint (500 mL) and quart (1 L) jars for 10 minutes.

8. Turn off heat. Let pressure return to zero naturally. Wait 2 minutes longer, then open vent. Remove canner lid. Wait 10 minutes, then remove jars, cool and store. *(For more information, see pages 383–384.)*

Variations

Tomatoes Packed in Tomato Juice: Packing tomatoes in tomato juice concentrates and enhances the flavor of the end product. However, the processing times need to be increased. Use either the raw- or hot-pack method and follow the steps above, substituting commercially prepared or homemade (see recipe, page 360) tomato juice for the water. Increase processing time to 25 minutes for both pint and quart jars.

Raw-Packed Tomatoes with No Added Liquid: You'll get the most concentrated tomato flavor by packing tomatoes raw with no added liquid. However, this method requires a longer processing time to ensure that the heat fully penetrates to the centers of the jars. Use the raw-pack method, but do not boil any water. Follow the steps above, filling jars with raw tomatoes. After removing air bubbles, adjust headspace, if necessary, by adding tomatoes. Increase processing time to 25 minutes for both pint and quart jars.

Tomato Juice

On average, it takes 3 to 3¼ lbs (1.37 to 1.5 kg) of tomatoes to make 1 quart (1 L) of juice.

TIPS

If juice separation is not a concern, in Step 2, simply quarter tomatoes into a large stainless steel saucepan. Crush and boil gently for 5 minutes before pressing through a sieve, food mill or Victorio strainer.

It is very important that you reheat the tomato juice before filling the jars. Processing times are based on hot juice in a hot jar. If the juice is tepid, the processing time won't be sufficient to vent the excess headspace gases and/or destroy spoilage microorganisms.

Fill jars and place them in the canner one at a time. For each jar, add the lemon juice or citric acid, then the salt, if using. Then ladle in hot juice as indicated in Step 7 and place the jar in the canner. Repeat until all jars are filled.

| Tomatoes, cored |
| Bottled lemon juice or citric acid |
| Salt (optional) |

1. Prepare weighted-gauge pressure canner, jars and lids. *(For more information, see page 382.)*
2. Wash and sort tomatoes, removing any bruised or discolored product. Quarter 6 tomatoes and place in a large stainless steel saucepan. Bring to a boil over high heat. Using a potato masher, crush tomatoes to release juices, stirring constantly. While maintaining a boil and stirring to prevent burning, quarter additional tomatoes, adding them to the saucepan as you work. Make sure the mixture continues to boil vigorously while you add, stir and crush the remaining tomatoes. When all tomatoes have been added, reduce heat to medium and boil gently until tomatoes are soft and juicy, about 10 minutes. Remove from heat.
3. Working in batches, press tomatoes through a fine sieve, food mill or Victorio strainer to remove skins and seeds. Discard skins and seeds.
4. Return juice to saucepan and bring to a boil over medium-high heat. Remove from heat.
5. Before filling each jar with tomato juice (see tip, at left), add lemon juice or citric acid to the hot jar in the quantity specified below:

Acidification Ingredient Options	Jar Size	
	Pint (500 mL)	Quart (1 L)
Bottled lemon juice	1 tbsp (15 mL)	2 tbsp (30 mL)
Citric acid	¼ tsp (1 mL)	½ tsp (2 mL)

6. Add salt, if using, in the quantity specified below:

	Pint (500 mL)	Quart (1 L)
	½ tsp (2 mL)	1 tsp (5 mL)

7. Ladle hot juice into prepared jars, leaving 1 inch (2.5 cm) headspace. Wipe rim. Center lid on jar. Screw band down until resistance is met, then increase to fingertip-tight.

8. Place jars in pressure canner. Adjust water level, lock lid and bring to a boil over medium-high heat. Vent steam for 10 minutes, then close vent. Continue heating to achieve 10 lbs (68 kPa) pressure. Process both pint (500 mL) and quart (1 L) jars for 15 minutes.

9. Turn off heat. Let pressure return to zero naturally. Wait 2 minutes longer, then open vent. Remove canner lid. Wait 10 minutes, then remove jars, cool and store. *(For more information, see pages 383–384.)*

Variation

Herbed Tomato Juice: Prepare as directed above, adding one well-rinsed sprig of your favorite fresh herb to each jar before ladling in the hot juice.

Basic Tomato Sauce

Jars of this tomato sauce are like a painter's canvas — ready to be transformed, in this case into a wide variety of delicious sauces and entrées. For each quart (1 L) jar of thin sauce, you'll need about 5 lbs (2.3 kg) of tomatoes.

TIPS

For a thin sauce, you'll need an average of 35 lbs (15.9 kg) of tomatoes to produce seven quart (1 L) jars of sauce. For a thick sauce, you'll need an average of 46 lbs (20.9 kg) to yield seven quart (1 L) jars.

For the best-quality product and vacuum seal, pack tomato sauce one jar at a time. For each jar, add the lemon juice or citric acid, then the salt and dried herbs, if using. Then ladle in hot sauce as indicated in Step 8 and place the jar in the canner. Repeat until all jars are filled.

Tomatoes, cored (see tip, at left)
Bottled lemon juice or citric acid
Salt (optional)
Dried herbs (optional)

1. Prepare weighted-gauge pressure canner, jars and lids. *(For more information, see page 382.)*

2. Wash and sort tomatoes, removing any bruised or discolored product. Quarter 6 tomatoes and place in a large stainless steel saucepan. Bring to a boil over medium-high heat. Using a potato masher, crush tomatoes to release juices, stirring constantly. While maintaining a boil and stirring to prevent burning, quarter additional tomatoes, adding them to the saucepan as you work. Make sure the mixture continues to boil vigorously while you add, stir and crush the remaining tomatoes. When all tomatoes have been added, boil, stirring occasionally, until tomatoes are soft and juicy, about 10 minutes. Remove from heat.

3. Working in batches, press tomatoes through a fine sieve, food mill or Victorio strainer to remove skins and seeds. Discard skins and seeds.

4. Return mixture to saucepan and bring to a boil over high heat, stirring frequently. Reduce heat to medium-high and boil until volume is reduced by at least one-third for a thin sauce. For a thicker sauce, cook until reduced by half.

5. Before filling each jar with tomato sauce (see tip, at left), add lemon juice or citric acid to the hot jar in the quantity specified below:

Acidification Ingredient Options	Jar Size	
	Pint (500 mL)	Quart (1 L)
Bottled lemon juice	1 tbsp (15 mL)	2 tbsp (30 mL)
Citric acid	¼ tsp (1 mL)	½ tsp (2 mL)

6. Add salt, if using, in the quantity specified below:

	Pint (500 mL)	Quart (1 L)
	½ tsp (2 mL)	1 tsp (5 mL)

7. Add dried herbs, if using, to each jar (see tip, opposite).

8. Ladle hot sauce into prepared jars, leaving 1 inch (2.5 cm) headspace. Remove air bubbles and adjust headspace, if necessary, by adding hot sauce. Wipe rim. Center lid on jar. Screw band down until resistance is met, then increase to fingertip-tight.

9. Place jars in pressure canner. Adjust water level, lock lid and bring to a boil over medium-high heat. Vent steam for 10 minutes, then close vent. Continue heating to achieve 10 lbs (68 kPa) pressure. Process both pint (500 mL) and quart (1 L) jars for 15 minutes.

10. Turn off heat. Let pressure return to zero naturally. Wait 2 minutes longer, then open vent. Remove canner lid. Wait 10 minutes, then remove jars, cool and store. *(For more information, see pages 383–384.)*

Crushed Tomatoes

Crushed tomatoes resemble whole or halved tomatoes in flavor, but since they are crushed they are ideal for sauces, soups and stews. You'll need about 2¾ lbs (1.25 kg) of tomatoes for every quart (1 L) jar.

TIPS

For the best-quality product and vacuum seal, pack tomatoes one jar at a time. For each jar, add the lemon juice or citric acid, then the salt, if using. Then pack the tomatoes as indicated in Step 6 and place the jar in the canner. Repeat until all jars are filled.

To ripen tomatoes for canning, empty them from the basket or box onto a single layer of newspaper or a large mesh rack. Store in a cool (but not cold), dry place, out of direct sun. Turn tomatoes daily to prevent spoilage and soft spots. As the tomatoes ripen, sort into different stages of ripeness and use the ripest ones first.

Tomatoes
Bottled lemon juice or citric acid
Salt (optional)

1. Prepare weighted-gauge pressure canner, jars and lids. *(For more information, see page 382.)*
2. Working in small batches, immerse tomatoes in boiling water for 30 to 60 seconds or until the skins start to loosen or crack. Immediately plunge into a bowl of cold water and slip the skins off. Remove cores and any bruised or discolored portions that become apparent after blanching.
3. Working in batches, quarter enough tomatoes to measure about 2 cups (500 mL). Transfer to a large stainless steel saucepan and bring to a boil over medium-high heat. Using a potato masher, crush tomatoes to release juices. While maintaining a gentle boil and stirring to prevent scorching, quarter additional tomatoes and add to saucepan as you work. (The remaining tomatoes do not need to be crushed, as they will soften with heating and stirring.) Continue until all tomatoes are added, then boil gently for 5 minutes.
4. Before packing each jar of tomatoes (see tip, at left), add lemon juice or citric acid to the hot jar in the quantity specified below:

Acidification Ingredient Options	Jar Size	
	Pint (500 mL)	Quart (1 L)
Bottled lemon juice	1 tbsp (15 mL)	2 tbsp (30 mL)
Citric acid	¼ tsp (1 mL)	½ tsp (2 mL)

5. Add salt, if using, in the quantity specified below:

	Pint (500 mL)	Quart (1 L)
	½ tsp (2 mL)	1 tsp (5 mL)

6. Pack hot tomatoes into prepared jars to within a generous 1 inch (2.5 cm) of top of jar. Press tomatoes in the jar until spaces between them fill with juice, leaving 1 inch (2.5 cm) headspace. Remove air bubbles and adjust headspace, if necessary, by adding hot tomatoes. Wipe rim. Center lid on jar. Screw band down until resistance is met, then increase to fingertip-tight.

TIP

Before using jars, inspect them carefully for any chips, cracks or fractures. Discard any imperfect jars.

7. Place jars in pressure canner. Adjust water level, lock lid and bring to a boil over medium-high heat. Vent steam for 10 minutes, then close vent. Continue heating to achieve 10 lbs (68 kPa) pressure. Process both pint (500 mL) and quart (1 L) jars for 15 minutes.

8. Turn off heat. Let pressure return to zero naturally. Wait 2 minutes longer, then open vent. Remove canner lid. Wait 10 minutes, then remove jars, cool and store. *(For more information, see pages 383–384.)*

Tomatoes and Celery

Celery adds a robust flavor to tomatoes and reduces the number of ingredients and time required when preparing tomato-based savory dishes. However, preserving tomatoes and celery in equal quantities reduces the acidity of this recipe, so it must be processed in a pressure canner. You will need about 1½ lbs (680 g) of tomatoes and 4 stalks of celery for each quart (1 L) jar.

Tomatoes, cored, peeled and chopped
Celery, sliced
Salt (optional)
Boiling water

1. Prepare weighted-gauge pressure canner, jars and lids. *(For more information, see page 382.)*

2. In a large stainless steel saucepan, combine equal measures of tomatoes and celery. Bring to a boil over medium-high heat. Reduce heat and boil gently for 15 minutes.

3. Pack hot vegetables into hot jars to within a generous 1 inch (2.5 cm) of top of jar. If using salt, add ½ tsp (2 mL) to each pint jar or 1 tsp (5 mL) to each quart jar. Ladle boiling water into jar to cover vegetables, leaving 1 inch (2.5 cm) headspace. Remove air bubbles and adjust headspace, if necessary, by adding boiling water. Wipe rim. Center lid on jar. Screw band down until resistance is met, then increase to fingertip-tight.

4. Place jars in pressure canner. Adjust water level, lock lid and bring to a boil over medium-high heat. Vent steam for 10 minutes, then close vent. Continue heating to achieve 10 lbs (68 kPa) pressure. Process pint (500 mL) jars for 30 minutes and quart (1 L) jars for 35 minutes.

5. Turn off heat. Let pressure return to zero naturally. Wait 2 minutes longer, then open vent. Remove canner lid. Wait 10 minutes, then remove jars, cool and store. *(For more information, see pages 383–384.)*

TIP

A jar lifter is very helpful for handling hot, wet jars. Because they are bulky and fit loosely, oven mitts — even water-resistent types — are not a wise choice. When filling jars, an all-purpose rubber glove, worn on your helper hand, will allow you to steady the jar.

Variation

Tomatoes and Okra: Substitute sliced okra for the celery. In Step 2, bring tomatoes to a boil over medium-high heat. Reduce heat and boil gently for 15 minutes. Add okra and boil gently for 5 minutes.

Stewed Tomatoes and Vegetables

These naturally preseasoned tomatoes reduce the number of added seasonings required for casseroles and other recipes. Remember, the proportion of vegetables to tomatoes reduces the overall acidity of this recipe, so it must be processed in a pressure canner.

TIPS

For the best-quality product and vacuum seal, pack tomatoes one jar at a time. For each jar, add the lemon juice or citric acid, then pack the tomato mixture and place the jar in the canner. Repeat until all jars are filled.

Refer to the Produce Purchase Guide on pages 426–429 to determine how much produce you'll need to buy to prepare this recipe.

Makes about seven pint (500 mL) jars or three quart (1 L) jars

16 cups	chopped cored peeled tomatoes	4 L
1 cup	chopped celery	250 mL
½ cup	chopped onion	125 mL
¼ cup	chopped seeded green bell pepper	50 mL
1 tbsp	granulated sugar	15 mL
2 tsp	salt	10 mL
	Bottled lemon juice or citric acid	

1. Prepare weighted-gauge pressure canner, jars and lids. *(For more information, see page 382.)*

2. In a large stainless steel saucepan, combine tomatoes, celery, onion, green pepper, sugar and salt. Bring to a boil over medium heat, stirring to break up tomatoes. Cover and boil gently, stirring occasionally to prevent sticking, until vegetables begin to soften, about 10 minutes.

3. Before packing each jar of tomatoes (see tip, at left), add lemon juice or citric acid to the hot jar in the quantity specified below:

Acidification Ingredient Options	Jar Size	
	Pint (500 mL)	Quart (1 L)
Bottled lemon juice	1 tbsp (15 mL)	2 tbsp (30 mL)
Citric acid	¼ tsp (1 mL)	½ tsp (2 mL)

4. Using a slotted spoon, pack hot tomato mixture into prepared jars to within a generous 1 inch (2.5 cm) of top of jar. Ladle in hot cooking liquid to cover tomato mixture, leaving 1 inch (2.5 cm) headspace. Remove air bubbles and adjust headspace, if necessary, by adding hot cooking liquid. Wipe rim. Center lid on jar. Screw band down until resistance is met, then increase to fingertip-tight.

5. Place jars in pressure canner. Adjust water level, lock lid and bring to a boil over medium-high heat. Vent steam for 10 minutes, then close vent. Continue heating to achieve 10 lbs (68 kPa) pressure. Process pint (500 mL) jars for 15 minutes and quart (1 L) jars for 20 minutes.

6. Turn off heat. Let pressure return to zero naturally. Wait 2 minutes longer, then open vent. Remove canner lid. Wait 10 minutes, then remove jars, cool and store. *(For more information, see pages 383–384.)*

Pressure Canning:
Low-Acid Foods

Unlike fruits and pickled foods, low-acid foods — vegetables, meat, poultry, seafood and recipes using these ingredients — require greater heat exposure to destroy harmful toxin-producing bacterial spores. Research in the mid- and late 1900s revealed that processing jars of low-acid foods in boiling water (212°F/100°C) is neither practical nor adequate to destroy toxin-producing bacterial spores. The only practical and recommended method today is to process low-acid foods using a pressure canner, which (at or below 1,000 feet/305 m above sea level) elevates temperatures to 240°F (116°C). When canning low-acid foods, it is particularly important to follow tested, up-to-date home canning recipes that provide the correct processing method, time and temperature, to ensure that spoilage microorganisms are destroyed.

Stocking your pantry with jars of green beans, roasted peppers, fresh tomatoes, rosy beets or other vegetables is a great way to get dinner on the table quickly and be assured that you and your family and friends are enjoying the highest-quality produce without additives. You can also preserve tomato sauce, soups, entrées, meat and seafood. Although we didn't have room in this book to include recipes for a broad range of specialty items, our websites (in Canada: **www.homecanning.ca***; in the United States:* **www.homecanning.com***) provide recipes for preserving these foods.*

• •

Preserving Low-Acid Foods

The acidity of foods is measured on the pH scale, which runs between 1 (strongest acidity) and 14 (weakest acidity). Vegetables, meat, poultry and seafood are low-acid foods. That means they have an acidity greater than a pH of 4.6. Unlike high-acid foods, which have a pH of 4.6 or less, low-acid foods contain little natural acid. This is an important factor in preserving, because acid guards against bacterial growth that is a risk for public health. If foods do not have enough natural acid, they must be heated to very high temperatures to be preserved safely. These high temperatures are essential when preserving low-acid foods so that all of the bacteria that can pose a danger to your health will be destroyed.

Pressure Canning

Low-acid foods must be processed at 240°F (116°C) to kill harmful bacteria and their toxin-producing spores. To safely preserve low-acid foods, a device called a pressure canner must be used. This equipment has a lid that is locked in place. As a result, when water in the canner is heated to the boiling point, it produces steam faster than the steam can escape from the vent and thus pressurizes the canner. The pressurized steam creates hotter temperatures, which surround the jars and cause the temperature of the food within to rise to 240°F (116°C).

Pressure Canners

A pressure cooker (or pressure saucepan) and a pressure canner are not synonymous. Pressure cookers and saucepans are smaller and differ in design and function from canners. Pressure cookers and saucepans are not safe for home canning low-acid foods.

A pressure canner is a tall pot with a lid that locks in place and a pressure-regulating device. To be considered a pressure canner, the pot must hold a minimum of 4 quart (1 L) jars. Most pressure canners are designed to hold 7 quart (1 L) jars or 8 to 9 pint (500 mL) jars. Some large pressure canners hold 18 pint (500 mL) jars in two layers, but hold only 7 quart (1 L) jars.

There are two types of pressure canners. Recipes in this book use a weighted-gauge pressure canner specifically designed for home canning. It is fitted with different weights for each required pressure level. The second type of canner used for low-acid foods is a dial-gauge pressure canner, which has a visual gauge to indicate the pressure level.

Before using any pressure canner, carefully read the manufacturer's instruction manual. Each type and brand of canner is different.

Weighted-Gauge Pressure Canners

A weighted-gauge canner is fitted with either a three- or a one-piece weight unit with 5-, 10- and 15-lb (34, 69 and 103 kPa) pressure adjustments. (Only 10- and 15-lb/69 and 103 kPa pressure weights are used in home canning. The 5-lb/34 kPa weight is used for cooking, but not preserving.) Steam, exhausted throughout the processing period, causes the weights to rock, indicating that the pressure level has been achieved or is being maintained.

A weighted-gauge pressure canner requires 10 lbs (69 kPa) of pressure when used at or below 1,000 feet (305 m) above sea level. At higher elevations, the canner requires 15 lbs (103 kPa) of pressure.

A one-piece weighted-gauge canner that does not adjust for different pressure levels is designed to process only at 15 lbs (103 kPa) pressure. Follow the manufacturer's guidelines for important operating instructions for this type of canner.

The weighted-gauge canner does not require testing for accuracy, but if the weights are damaged in any way, they must be replaced.

Dial-Gauge Pressure Canners

A dial-gauge canner is fitted with a one-piece pressure regulator and a gauge to indicate the correct pressure level. Small amounts of steam are exhausted from the regulator throughout the processing period. Based on the reading on the dial gauge, you adjust the heat to maintain the required pressure level. The dial gauge must be visually monitored throughout the processing period to ensure that accurate pressure is being maintained and sufficient processing takes place.

Dial-gauge pressure canners require 11 lbs (76 kPa) of pressure when used at or below 1,000 feet (305 m) above sea level. For higher elevations, please consult the Low-Acid Altitude Adjustment Chart on page 382.

Dial-gauge canners must be tested for accuracy prior to each canning season. Your canner manufacturer will be able to tell you where the dial gauge can be tested.

Parts of a Pressure Canner
Lid

The lid locks or clamps securely onto the base of the canner. The lid may be fitted

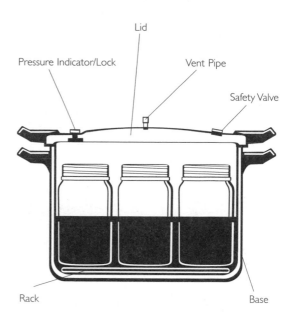

with a gasket, a rubber ring that sits along the inside circumference of the lid and comes in contact with the base when locked into place. The gasket assists in providing a seal between the lid and the base to minimize steam leakage. This gasket must be checked before each use to make sure it is still fully functional.

The lid houses a vent pipe and safety valve. The vent pipe is a short hollow pipe that sticks up above the canner lid. When the vent pipe is open, air and steam can escape from the closed canner. When the vent is closed and the weight is in place, the amount of steam that can escape is restricted, and pressure builds up inside the canner. Pressure canners are made with a safety valve designed to prohibit over-pressurization. If a canner becomes over-pressurized, the safety valve is forced open, allowing steam to escape from the hole and the pressure to decrease inside the canner.

Gauge

The gauge measures pressure inside the canner, as described above, under

Weighted-Gauge Pressure Canners and Dial-Gauge Pressure Canners.

Base

A pressure canner base is a heavy, specialized pot with a minimum capacity of four quart (1 L) jars. The base must be deep enough that the jars to be processed do not obstruct the locking of the lid.

Rack

This flat disk with perforated holes sits on the canner bottom. It elevates jars from the bottom of the canner.

Altitude Adjustments

When low-acid foods are canned at elevations higher than 1,000 feet (305 m), the recommended processing time remains constant, but the required pressure is increased. The pressure levels for the low-acid recipes in this book are based on the use of a weighted-gauge canner at or below 1,000 feet (305 m) above sea level. To process low-acid food at altitudes higher than 1,000 feet (305 m) above sea level, use the chart below to adjust processing pressure. *When using any canner, never reduce the processing times.*

Low-Acid Altitude Adjustment Chart

ALTITUDE		WEIGHTED-GAUGE		DIAL-GAUGE	
(Feet)	(Meters)	(lb)	(kPa)	(lb)	(kPa)
0 to 1,000	0 to 305	10	69	11	76
1,001 to 2,000	306 to 609	15	103	11	76
2,001 to 4,000	610 to 1,219	15	103	12	83
4,001 to 6,000	1,220 to 1,828	15	103	13	90
6,001 to 8,000	1,829 to 2,438	15	103	14	97
8,001 to 10,000	2,439 to 3,048	15	103	15	103

How to Use a Pressure Canner, Step by Step

1. Wash jars, lids and screw bands in hot, soapy water. Rinse well.
2. Place rack in the pressure canner and place jars on the rack. Fill jars halfway with water and add 2 to 3 inches (5 to 7.5 cm) of water to the canner. Bring water to a simmer (180°F/82°C) over medium heat and maintain the simmer until you're ready to use the jars. Do not boil. *Note:* When preserving chilled foods, such as fish, do *not* heat jars or water in canner prior to filling the jars. (Raw-packed vegetables are placed in hot jars as they must be covered with hot liquid.)
3. Set screw bands aside. Place lids in a saucepan, cover with water and bring to a simmer (180°F/82°C) over medium heat. Keep lids hot until you're ready to use them. Do not boil.

4. Prepare recipe. Working with one jar at a time, remove jar from canner, pouring hot water back into canner. Place the jar on a protected work surface (see page 414). If using, place funnel in jar. Ladle prepared food into jar, leaving 1 inch (2.5 cm) headspace. Slide a nonmetallic utensil, such as a rubber spatula, down between food and the inside of the jar several times to release air bubbles.

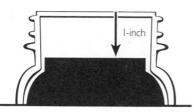

Low-acid foods require 1-inch (2.5 cm) headspace

Adjust headspace, if necessary, by adding hot food and/or liquid. With a clean damp cloth or paper towel, wipe jar rim and threads. (For meat, fish, soups, etc., dampen the cloth with diluted vinegar to help remove any fat that may be on the rim.) Center hot lid on jar and screw band down until resistance is met, then increase to fingertip-tight. Return jar to canner rack and repeat until all jars are filled.

5. When all jars are filled, adjust water level in canner as directed by the manufacturer. Place lid on canner and lock it into place. Leave weight off vent pipe. Over medium-high heat, bring water to a boil. (You'll know the water is boiling when steam starts

coming out of the vent in a steady stream.) Vent steam from the canner for 10 minutes. Place weight on vent.

6. If using a weighted-gauge pressure canner at altitudes at or below 1,000 feet (305 m) above sea level, bring pressure to 10 lbs (69 kPa). (If using a dial-gauge canner and/or canning in higher-altitude areas, refer to the Low-Acid Altitude Adjustment Chart, opposite.) After the gauge indicates that the recommended pressure level has been reached, begin counting the processing time. Regulate heat slowly but continuously to maintain pressure without necessitating drastic changes to the heat level.

7. When processing time is complete, turn off heat and let canner cool naturally. During this time, the canner will become depressurized and pressure will return to zero. (Follow the canner manufacturer's guidelines to determine when the pressure has returned to zero.) Do not remove the weight from the vent until the canner is completely cooled and pressure has returned to zero.

8. When the pressure has returned to zero, wait 2 additional minutes, then remove the weight from the vent. Unlock and remove lid, making sure that the steam escapes away from you. Let jars sit in the canner for 10 minutes to adjust to the lower temperature in the room.

9. Remove jars from canner, without tilting. Place jars upright, 1 to 2 inches (2.5 to 5 cm) apart, on a dry towel or wooden cutting board in a draft-free place and let cool, undisturbed, for 24 hours. Do not tighten screw bands if they have loosened during processing.

10. After 24 hours, check lids for seal. Remove screw bands and press down on the center of each lid with your finger. Sealed lids will be concave (they'll curve downward) and will show no movement when pressed (for more information, see page 418). Jars that haven't sealed properly must be refrigerated or reprocessed immediately (see page 418). Rinse and dry screw bands. Wipe jars and, if desired, loosely reapply screw bands. Label jars and store in a cool, dry, dark place (see page 418).

Vegetables

Home-canned vegetables add color, variety and nutritional value to any meal. Vegetables for canning can come from your own garden, farmers' markets or grocery stores. When choosing vegetables to can, look for crisp, brightly colored produce that is heavy for its size. Avoid vegetables that are bruised, wilted, moldy or blemished. These are all signs of deterioration. For the best results, be sure to preserve your vegetables immediately after harvest or purchase. If produce cannot be preserved immediately, refrigerate until ready for use.

Packing Vegetables

For certain vegetables, you can use either the raw-pack or the hot-pack method to pack the jars. In the recipes in this section, if you have the option, both methods will be listed. If only one method is satisfactory for a particular vegetable, only the relevant method will be listed.

Raw-Pack Method

The food is left uncooked. If you use this method, be sure to firmly pack the vegetables into the jar. Raw vegetables are not as pliable. During processing, the vegetables will shrink or soften, which may result in a jar that is not as full as you expected. Food is also more likely to float when the raw-pack method has been used. This method is recommended only for foods that become more delicate after they are cooked.

Hot-Pack Method

The food is precooked in water, making it more pliable. This method permits a tighter pack and requires fewer jars. The hot-pack method is usually preferred for vegetables that are relatively firm and easy to handle.

Method for Pressure Canning Vegetables

These instructions are based on using a weighted-gauge pressure canner at altitudes at or below 1,000 feet (305 m) above sea level.

If you are using a dial-gauge pressure canner or canning at higher altitudes, please consult the instruction manual for your pressure canner and/or review the instructions at the beginning of this chapter (pages 380–384).

TIP

Pack raw vegetables as tightly as possible in jars, unless otherwise noted in the recipe. Raw vegetables shrink slightly and soften during processing.

1. Prepare weighted-gauge pressure canner, jars and lids. *(For more information, see page 382.)*

2. Prepare selected raw-pack or hot-pack vegetables as directed in the recipe.

3. Pack vegetables into jars to within a generous 1 inch (2.5 cm) of top of jar. Add salt, if using, as specified in chart below. Ladle boiling water or cooking liquid into jar to cover vegetables, leaving 1 inch (2.5 cm) headspace. Remove air bubbles and adjust headspace, if necessary, by adding more hot liquid. Wipe rim. Center lid on jar. Screw band down until resistance is met, then increase to fingertip-tight.

4. Place jars in pressure canner. Adjust water level, lock lid and bring to a boil over medium-high heat. Vent steam for 10 minutes, then close vent. Continue heating to achieve 10 lbs (69 kPa) pressure and maintain pressure to process for time indicated in the recipe for specific vegetable and jar size.

5. Turn off heat. Let pressure return to zero naturally. Wait 2 minutes longer, then open vent. Remove canner lid. Wait 10 minutes, then remove jars, cool and store. *(For more information, see pages 383–384.)*

QUANTITIES OF ADDED SALT PER JAR	
Mason Jar Size	Salt
Pint (500 mL)	½ tsp (2 mL)
Quart (1 L)	1 tsp (5 mL)

Asparagus

Choose tender spears, 4 to 6 inches (10 to 15 cm) long. You'll need about 3½ lbs (1.6 kg) of asparagus, or about 70 medium spears, for each quart (1 L) jar.

Preparation: Wash asparagus and drain. Remove tough ends and peel off scales, if desired. Wash again.

Raw-pack: Leave spears whole or cut into 1-inch (2.5 cm) pieces. Tightly pack asparagus (tips down, if packing whole) into hot jars, without crushing, as directed in Step 3 (see page 385).

Hot-pack: Cut asparagus into 1-inch (2.5 cm) pieces. In a stainless steel saucepan, combine asparagus with boiling water to cover. Bring to a boil over medium-high heat and boil for 3 minutes, until tender-crisp. Drain, reserving cooking liquid for packing, if desired. Pack hot asparagus into hot jars as directed in Step 3 (see page 385).

For both methods: Continue with Steps 4 and 5 (see page 385), processing pint (500 mL) jars for 30 minutes and quart (1 L) jars for 40 minutes.

Green Beans

Select young, crisp beans. Discard diseased or rusted beans. You'll need 1½ to 2½ lbs (680 g to 1.14 kg) of beans for each quart (1 L) jar.

TIP

A clear plastic ruler (kept solely for kitchen use) will help you determine the correct headspace. Each filled jar should be measured accurately, as the headspace can affect sealing and the preservation of the contents.

Preparation: Wash beans and drain. Trim ends and cut or break into 2-inch (5 cm) pieces.

Raw-pack: Tightly pack beans into hot jars as directed in Step 3 (see page 385).

Hot-pack: In a stainless steel saucepan, combine beans with boiling water to cover. Bring to a boil over medium-high heat and boil for 5 minutes, until tender-crisp. Drain, reserving cooking liquid for packing, if desired. Pack hot beans into hot jars as directed in Step 3 (see page 385).

For both methods: Continue with Steps 4 and 5 (see page 385), processing pint (500 mL) jars for 20 minutes and quart (1 L) jars for 25 minutes.

Variations

Substitute French beans, Romano or Italian beans, yellow wax beans or purple snap beans for the green beans. For a particularly attractive presentation, combine green and yellow beans.

Fresh Lima (Butter), Pinto or Soy Beans

Select bright-colored, firm and uniformly shaped beans. Do not use beans that have been stored dry for prolonged periods. Avoid bruised or scarred beans with brown spots. You'll need 3 to 5 lbs (1.37 kg to 2.3 kg) of beans for each quart (1 L) jar.

Preparation: Wash and shell beans. Wash again and drain.

Raw-pack: Loosely pack beans into hot jars as directed in Step 3 (see page 385). Do not press or shake down.

Hot-pack: In a stainless steel saucepan, combine beans with boiling water to cover. Bring to a boil over medium-high heat and boil for 3 minutes, until heated through. Drain, reserving cooking liquid for packing, if desired. Pack hot beans into hot jars as directed in Step 3 (see page 385).

For both methods: Continue with Steps 4 and 5 (see page 385), processing pint (500 mL) jars for 40 minutes and quart (1 L) jars for 50 minutes.

Beets

Choose firm, ripe, freshly harvested beets with roots intact to prevent bleeding. Beets should be 1 to 2 inches (2.5 to 5 cm) in diameter. Larger beets may be fibrous. You'll need 2 to $3^1/_2$ lbs (900 g to 1.6 kg) of beets for each quart (1 L) jar.

Preparation: Trim beet tops, leaving 2 inches (5 cm) of stem and root. Scrub well. In a stainless steel saucepan, combine beets with boiling water to cover. Bring to a boil over medium-high heat and boil until skins slip off easily, 15 to 25 minutes. Drain, discarding cooking liquid. Rinse in cold water. Remove skins and trim stems and roots. Leave baby beets whole. Slice or dice larger beets.

Hot-pack: Pack into hot jars as directed in Step 3 (see page 385), ladling in fresh boiling water to cover beets. Continue with Steps 4 and 5 (see page 385), processing pint (500 mL) jars for 30 minutes and quart (1 L) jars for 35 minutes.

Okra

Choose small, crisp, bright-colored pods. Discard diseased, shriveled or discolored pods. You'll need $1^1/_2$ to 2 lbs (680 g to 900 g) of okra for each quart (1 L) jar.

Preparation: Wash and drain okra. Remove stem and blossom ends without cutting into pod. Leave whole or cut into 1-inch (2.5 cm) slices. In a stainless steel saucepan, combine okra with hot water to cover. Bring to a boil over medium-high heat and boil for 2 minutes, until heated through. Drain, discarding cooking liquid.

Hot-pack: Pack hot okra into hot jars as directed in Step 3 (see page 385), ladling in fresh boiling water to cover okra. Continue with Steps 4 and 5 (see page 385), processing pint (500 mL) jars for 25 minutes and quart (1 L) jars for 40 minutes.

Cream-Style Corn

Use eating-quality corn with slightly immature kernels. You'll need about 4 medium ears of corn for each pint (500 mL) jar. Do not process in jars larger than a pint (500 mL).

Preparation: Husk corn and remove silk. Wash ears. Blanch in a large pot of boiling water for 4 minutes, until tender-crisp. Drain, discarding cooking liquid, and let cool slightly. Using a serrated knife, cut kernels from the center of cobs. Do not cut kernels from the tip ends. Scrape cobs to extract pulp and milk. Measure kernels, pulp and milk together. For every 2 cups (500 mL) corn mixture, add 1 cup (250 mL) boiling water.

Hot-pack: Transfer corn mixture to a stainless steel saucepan and bring to a boil over medium-high heat. Reduce heat and boil gently for 3 minutes, until heated through. Ladle corn and liquid into hot pint (500 mL) jars as directed in Step 3 (see page 385). Continue with Steps 4 and 5 (see page 385), processing for 85 minutes.

Whole Kernel Corn

Use eating-quality corn with slightly immature kernels. You'll need about 8 medium ears of corn for each quart (1 L) jar.

TIPS

The sugar content in young ears and sweet varieties of corn may cause browning. This does not affect the safety of the product.

Before using jars, inspect them carefully for any chips, cracks or fractures. Discard any imperfect jars.

Preparation: Husk corn and remove silk. Wash ears. Using a serrated knife, cut kernels from the center of cobs. Do not cut kernels from the tip ends.

Raw-pack: Loosely pack kernels into hot jars as directed in Step 3 (see page 385). Do not press or shakje down.

Hot-pack: Measure corn. For every 4 cups (1 L) kernels, add 1 cup (250 mL) boiling water. In a stainless steel saucepan, combine corn and water. Bring to a boil over medium-high heat. Reduce heat and boil gently for 5 minutes, until heated through. Ladle hot corn and liquid into hot jars as directed in Step 3 (see page 385).

For both methods: Continue with Steps 4 and 5 (see page 385), processing pint (500 mL) jars for 55 minutes and quart (1 L) jars for 85 minutes.

Carrots

Use small carrots, 1 to 1¼ inches (2.5 to 3 cm) in diameter. Larger carrots may be fibrous. You'll need 2 to 3 lbs (900 g to 1.37 kg) of carrots for each quart (1 L) jar.

Preparation: Wash carrots and drain. Peel and wash again. Leave baby carrots whole. Slice or dice larger carrots.

Raw-pack: Tightly pack carrots into hot jars as directed in Step 3 (see page 385).

Hot-pack: In a stainless steel saucepan, combine carrots with boiling water to cover. Bring to a boil over medium-high heat. Reduce heat and boil gently for 5 minutes, until tender-crisp. Drain, reserving cooking liquid for packing, if desired. Pack hot carrots into hot jars as directed in Step 3 (see page 385).

For both methods: Continue with Steps 4 and 5 (see page 385), processing pint (500 mL) jars for 25 minutes and quart (1 L) jars for 30 minutes.

Leafy Greens

These instructions work for beet greens, mustard greens, turnip greens, spinach, Swiss chard, collard greens and kale. Choose only freshly harvested greens with tender and appealing leaves. Discard any wilted, discolored, diseased or insect-damaged leaves. You'll need about 4 lbs (1.8 kg) of greens for each quart (1 L) jar.

Preparation: Wash greens thoroughly in several changes of water. Trim and discard large tough stems. In a stainless steel saucepan of boiling water, working in batches (1 lb/500 g at a time), blanch greens until they are well wilted, 3 to 5 minutes. Drain, discarding cooking liquid. Using tongs, transfer greens to a cutting board. Using a sharp knife, coarsely chop.

Hot-pack: Pack hot greens into hot jars as directed in Step 3 (see page 385), ladling in fresh boiling water to cover greens. Continue with Steps 4 and 5 (see page385), processing pint (500 mL) jars for 70 minutes and quart (1 L) jars for 90 minutes.

Cultivated Mushrooms

Choose brightly colored domestic mushrooms that are small to medium in size with small, closed caps. You'll need about 2 lbs (900 g) of mushrooms for each pint (500 mL) jar. Do not process in jars larger than a pint (500 mL).
Caution: Do not can wild mushrooms.

Preparation: Trim stem ends and any discolored parts. Fill sink or large glass or stainless steel bowl with cold water. Soak mushrooms in cold water for 10 minutes. Drain and rinse well in clean, cold water. Leave small mushrooms whole and cut larger ones in half. Put cut pieces in a color protection solution (see page 202) to prevent browning.

Hot-pack: In a stainless steel saucepan, combine mushrooms with water to cover. Bring to a boil over medium-high heat and boil for 5 minutes, until heated through. Drain, discarding cooking liquid. Pack hot mushrooms into hot jars as directed in Step 3 (see page 385), ladling in fresh boiling water to cover mushrooms. Continue with Steps 4 and 5 (see page 385), processing both 8-ounce (250 mL) and pint (500 mL) jars for 45 minutes.

Black-Eyed Peas

These instructions also work for crowder or field peas. You'll need 2 to 2¼ lbs (900 g to 1 kg) of pea pods for each quart (1 L) jar.

Preparation: Wash pea pods and drain. Shell peas. Wash again.

Raw-pack: Loosely pack peas into hot jars as directed in Step 3 (see page 385). Do not press or shake down.

Hot-pack: In a stainless steel saucepan, combine peas with boiling water to cover. Bring to a boil over medium-high heat and boil for 3 minutes, until heated through. Ladle hot peas and cooking liquid into hot jars as directed in Step 3 (see page 385).

For both methods: Continue with Steps 4 and 5 (see page 385), processing pint (500 mL) jars for 40 minutes and quart (1 L) jars for 50 minutes.

Sweet Green Peas

These are also known as English peas. Select well-filled, plump pods containing young, tender, sweet peas. You'll need about 4½ lbs (2 kg) of pea pods for each quart (1 L) jar.

Preparation: Wash pea pods, drain. Shell peas. Wash again.

Raw-pack: Loosely pack peas into hot jars as directed in Step 3 (see page 385). Do not shake or press down.

Hot-pack: In a stainless steel saucepan, combine peas with boiling water to cover. Bring to a boil over medium-high heat. Boil small peas (less than ¼ inch/0.5 cm) for 3 minutes and larger peas for 5 minutes, until heated through. Drain, reserving cooking liquid for packing, if desired. Rinse peas in hot water and drain again. Pack hot peas into hot jars as directed in Step 3 (see page 385).

For both methods: Continue with Steps 4 and 5 (see page 385), processing both pint (500 mL) and quart (1 L) jars for 40 minutes.

Bell Peppers

Select mature, firm peppers that are bright in color. For an attractive presentation, combine two or more colors. Avoid shriveled, diseased or broken peppers. You'll need about 1 lb (500 g) of peppers for each pint (500 mL) jar. Do not process in jars larger than a pint (500 mL).

Preparation: Wash peppers and drain. Remove stem and seeds and cut into quarters.

Hot-pack: In a large pot of boiling water, blanch peppers for 3 minutes, just until tender-crisp. Drain, discarding cooking liquid. Pack hot peppers into hot jars as directed in Step 3 (see page 385), ladling in fresh boiling water to cover peppers. Continue with Steps 4 and 5 (see page 385), processing both 8-ounce (250 mL) and pint (500 mL) jars for 35 minutes.

Pimientos and Hot Peppers

Use these instructions to can any variety of hot pepper, from milder banana peppers to hot chili peppers such as jalapeños. Choose mature, firm peppers that are bright in color. Avoid shriveled, bruised, or broken peppers. You'll need about 1 lb (500 g) of hot peppers for each pint (500 mL) jar. Do not process in jars larger than a pint (500 mL).

TIP

When seeding and cutting hot peppers, wear rubber gloves to keep your hands from being burned.

Preparation: *Pimientos:* In a large pot of boiling water, cook peppers for 10 to 20 minutes, until skins are loosened and can be peeled off. Drain and let cool. Or roast as for chili peppers, above, let cool and remove skins, stems, blossom ends and seeds. Flatten.

Chilies and other tough-skinned peppers: Wash and dry peppers. Cut two small slits in each pepper. Preheat oven to 400°F (200°C) or set to broil. Place chilies on a baking sheet in a single layer. Roast in preheated oven or under broiler until skins blister, turning to roast all sides, about 6 to 8 minutes. Place peppers in a paper bag; secure opening and let cool for 15 minutes. Remove skins, stems and seeds.

Other hot peppers: Wash and dry peppers. Remove stems and seeds (for small peppers, remove stem and scoop out seeds from the top). In a large pot of boiling water, blanch peppers for 3 minutes, until skins loosen. Remove skins. Small peppers can be left whole, large peppers quartered.

Hot-pack: Pack peppers loosely into hot jars as directed in Step 3 (see page 385), ladling in fresh boiling water to cover peppers. Continue with Steps 4 and 5 (see page 385), processing both 8-ounce (250 mL) and pint (500 mL) jars for 35 minutes.

Sweet Potatoes

Select small to medium sweet potatoes that are firm and mature but not too fibrous. Look for smooth, unblemished skins. You'll need 2 to 3 lbs (900 g to 1.37 kg) of sweet potatoes for each quart (1 L) jar.

Preparation: Wash sweet potatoes and drain. In a large stainless steel saucepan of boiling water or in a steamer, boil or steam potatoes for 15 to 20 minutes or just until the potatoes are cooked enough to easily remove the skin (the interior of the potato will still be fairly firm). Drain, if necessary, and let cool slightly. Peel and cut into quarters or small uniform cubes. Do not mash or purée.

Hot-pack: Pack hot sweet potatoes into hot jars as directed in Step 3 (see page 385), ladling in fresh boiling water to cover sweet potatoes. Continue with Steps 4 and 5 (see page 385), processing pint (500 mL) jars for 65 minutes and quart (1 L) jars for 90 minutes.

White Potatoes

Select small to medium potatoes of ideal eating quality with smooth, unblemished skins. Avoid those that have green spots or are shriveled. You'll need 2 to 3 lbs (900 g to 1.37 kg) of potatoes, or 15 medium, for each quart (1 L) jar.

Preparation: Wash potatoes and drain. Peel and wash again. Leave small potatoes whole and cut large potatoes into quarters or small uniform cubes, placing in a stainless steel saucepan of cold water as you chop to prevent browning.

Hot-pack: Bring to a boil over medium-high heat. Boil small cubes for 2 minutes and small whole potatoes or quartered potatoes for 10 minutes, until heated through but not soft. Drain, discarding cooking liquid. Pack hot potatoes into hot jars as directed in Step 3 (see page 385), ladling in fresh boiling water to cover potatoes. Continue with Steps 4 and 5 (see page 385), processing pint (500 mL) jars for 35 minutes and quart (1 L) jars for 40 minutes.

Pumpkin or Winter Squash

These instructions work for all varieties of winter squash, including acorn, banana, buttercup, butternut, Golden Delicious and Hubbard, as well as pumpkin. Choose pumpkin or squash with hard rinds and mature pulp. Small sugar or pie pumpkins yield the best results. You'll need about 2¼ lbs (1 kg) of pumpkin or winter squash for each quart (1 L) jar.

Preparation: Wash pumpkin or squash, cut in half and remove seeds. Remove peel or rind and cut flesh into 1-inch (2.5 cm) cubes. Do not mash or purée.

Hot-pack: In a stainless steel saucepan, combine pumpkin or squash with boiling water to cover. Bring to a boil over medium-high heat and boil for 2 minutes, until heated through but not soft. Drain, discarding cooking liquid. Pack hot pumpkin or squash into hot jars as directed in Step 3 (see page 385), ladling in fresh boiling water to cover pumpkin or squash. Continue with Steps 4 and 5 (see page 385), processing pint (500 mL) jars for 55 minutes and quart (1 L) jars for 90 minutes.

Root Vegetables

These instructions work for parsnips or turnips. Choose root vegetables that are firm and seem heavy for their size and look for smooth skins, free of blemishes. You'll need 1½ to 2 lbs (680 g to 900 g) of vegetables for each quart (1 L) jar.

TIP

We don't recommend canning rutabagas, as they usually discolor and develop a strong flavor in the process. If you do choose to can them, you can use the process outlined here.

Preparation: Scrub vegetables and drain. Peel and slice or dice, as desired.

Hot-pack: In a stainless steel saucepan, combine vegetables with boiling water to cover. Bring to a boil over medium-high heat and boil for 5 minutes, until heated through. Drain, reserving cooking liquid for packing, if desired. Pack hot vegetables into hot jars as directed in Step 3 (see page 385). Continue with Steps 4 and 5 (see page 385), processing pint (500 mL) jars for 30 minutes and quart (1 L) jars for 35 minutes.

Seafood

Prepare fish for home canning as you would for cooking. Leave the backbone in small fish and debone larger fish. Soak fish in a salt-water brine before canning. Because seafood and fish are very low in acidity, you must can them in 8-ounce (250 mL) or pint (500 mL) jars. Heat penetration of larger jars may be inadequate to destroy bacterial spores.

....

Fish

Preserving a fisherman's catch extends the pleasure of a successful fishing trip with ready-to-use fish from your pantry. This recipe works for all varieties of fish, including salmon and shad, with the exception of tuna (see www.homecanning.com or www.homecanning.ca for a home-canned tuna recipe). **Process fish only in 8-ounce (250 mL) or pint (500 mL) jars.**

TIP

Clean fish within 2 hours after it is caught. Keep cleaned fish chilled until ready to can.

1 cup	pickling or canning salt	250 mL
16 cups	water	4 L
	Fresh fish, bones removed if fish is large	

1. In a large stainless steel bowl, dissolve pickling salt in water to make salt-water brine. Cut fish into pieces just long enough to fit into jars. Place fish in brine and let soak in the refrigerator for 1 hour. Drain well for about 10 minutes.

2. Prepare weighted-gauge pressure canner and lids 30 minutes before ready to pack fish. *(For more information, see page 382.)* Wash jars but do not heat. (Because fish is packed chilled, it must be packed into room temperature jars to prevent jar breakage.)

3. Pack fish, skin side next to glass, into jars to within a generous 1 inch (2.5 cm) of top of jar. Do not add liquid. Remove any visible air bubbles. Wipe rim with a paper towel moistened with vinegar. Center lid on jar. Screw band down until resistance is met, then increase to fingertip-tight.

4. Place jars in pressure canner. Adjust water level, lock lid and bring to a boil over medium-high heat. Vent steam for 10 minutes, then close vent. Continue heating to achieve 10 lbs (69 kPa) pressure. Process both 8-ounce (250 mL) and pint (500 mL) jars for 100 minutes.

5. Turn off heat. Let pressure return to zero naturally. Wait 2 minutes longer, then open vent. Remove canner lid. Wait 10 minutes, then remove jars, cool and store. *(For more information, see pages 383–384.)*

Clams

Keep clams alive, moist and chilled until ready to can. Preserving clams gives you a head start on making delicious homemade clam chowder year-round. Remember that pressure canning is the only safe method for preserving clams. Do not attempt to preserve them in a boiling-water canner. Process clams only in 8-ounce (250 mL) or pint (500 mL) jars.

TIP

To create a vacuum seal, a clean sealing surface is essential. Since many low-acid foods contain fat, use a paper towel dampened with vinegar to clean jar rims after filling jars. The vinegar helps to remove any fat that may have touched the rim while food was being added to the jar.

	Fresh clams	
	Water, divided	
½ cup	pickling or canning salt	125 mL
2 tbsp	bottled lemon juice	30 mL

1. Prepare weighted-gauge pressure canner, jars and lids. *(For more information, see page 382.)*

2. Scrub clams thoroughly under cold running water. In a large stainless steel saucepan, combine clams with water to cover. Cook over medium heat, shaking the saucepan occasionally, until all the clams open. Discard any that do not open. Transfer to a colander placed over a large bowl and drain, reserving juice. Open shells, remove meat and set aside. Strain juice through a fine sieve or cheesecloth-lined strainer. Place juice in a stainless steel saucepan and keep warm over low heat until ready to use.

3. In a large stainless steel bowl, dissolve pickling salt in 4 quarts (4 L) water. Add clam meat. Stir well, then transfer to a colander placed over a sink and drain. Rinse thoroughly.

4. In a clean large stainless steel saucepan, bring 4 quarts (4 L) water to a boil over high heat. Add lemon juice and clam meat and boil for 2 minutes. Drain, discarding liquid.

5. Pack hot clam meat into hot jars to within a generous 1 inch (2.5 cm) of top of jar. Ladle hot reserved clam juice into jar to cover clam meat, leaving 1 inch (2.5 cm) headspace. If there is not enough juice to cover clam meat, use boiling water. Remove air bubbles and adjust headspace, if necessary, by adding hot clam juice or water. Wipe rim with a paper towel moistened with vinegar. Center lid on jar. Screw band down until resistance is met, then increase to fingertip-tight.

6. Place jars in pressure canner. Adjust water level, lock lid and bring to a boil over medium-high heat. Vent steam for 10 minutes, then close vent. Continue heating to achieve 10 lbs (69 kPa) pressure. Process 8-ounce (250 mL) jars for 60 minutes and pint (500 mL) jars for 70 minutes.

7. Turn off heat. Let pressure return to zero naturally. Wait 2 minutes longer, then open vent. Remove canner lid. Wait 10 minutes, then remove jars, cool and store. *(For more information, see pages 383–384.)*

Meat and Poultry

The flavor and texture of home-canned meat and poultry is dependent upon the quality of the starting product. Home canning does not improve the quality of the meat, it only preserves the existing quality. Select lean cuts of fresh, good-quality meat. Excess fat from fattier cuts may cause the meat to develop a strong flavor and can cause seal failure.

When preparing meat, cut across the grain, making uniform slices about 1 inch (2.5 cm) thick. Then cut with the grain into jar-size pieces or cubes suitable for cooking and canning. Be sure to trim away gristle, bruised spots and fat.

Soak strong-flavored game meats in a salt-water brine for 1 hour before canning. Do not allow meat to stand longer in brines or water. To make a salt-water brine for soaking fresh game meats, add 1 tbsp (15 mL) salt for every 4 cups (1 L) of water and stir until dissolved. If brining meat, do not add salt to each jar.

Roast Beef, Lamb, Mutton, Pork, Veal or Venison

Select lean cuts of good-quality meat appropriate for roasting. The quantity of meat required for each jar will vary depending on the type of meat used and the size of the strips.

TIP

Instead of roasting meat in Step 2, you could brown it in a skillet, over medium heat, using no more than 1 tbsp (15 mL) added fat or vegetable oil.

• Preheat oven to 400°F (200°C)

| Boneless beef, lamb, mutton, pork, veal or venison |
| Salt (optional) |
| Hot broth (see tip, opposite) |

1. Prepare weighted-gauge pressure canner, jars and lids. *(For more information, see page 382.)*
2. Cut meat into ½- to 1-inch (1 to 2.5 cm) thick strips just long enough to fit in jars. In a large roasting pan, spread meat strips out in a single layer. Sear in preheated oven just until browned but still rare inside (the cooking time will vary depending on the type of meat used and the size of the strips).
3. Pack hot meat into hot jars to within a generous 1 inch (2.5 cm) of top of jar. If using salt, add ½ tsp (2 mL) to each pint jar or 1 tsp (5 mL) to each quart jar. Ladle hot broth into jar to cover meat, leaving 1 inch (2.5 cm) headspace. Remove air bubbles and adjust headspace, if necessary, by adding hot broth. Wipe rim with a paper towel moistened with vinegar. Center lid on jar. Screw band down until resistance is met, then increase to fingertip-tight.

TIP

To make broth for canning meat, remove meat from cooking pan. Add 1 cup (250 mL) boiling water or stock for each 1 to 2 tbsp (15 to 30 mL) fat in the pan. Bring to a boil over medium-high heat; boil for 2 to 3 minutes, scraping up any bits stuck to pan. Do not thicken broth with flour or standard cornstarch before canning. However, if desired, ClearJel® (see the Glossary, page 431) can be used to lightly thicken the broth in this recipe.

4. Place jars in pressure canner. Adjust water level, lock lid and bring to a boil over medium-high heat. Vent steam for 10 minutes, then close vent. Continue heating to achieve 10 lbs (69 kPa) pressure. Process pint (250 mL) jars for 75 minutes and quart (500 mL) jars for 90 minutes.

5. Turn off heat. Let pressure return to zero naturally. Wait 2 minutes longer, then open vent. Remove canner lid. Wait 10 minutes, then remove jars, cool and store. *(For more information, see pages 383–384.)*

Variation

Ground Beef, Lamb, Mutton, Pork, Veal or Venison: Substitute chopped beef, lamb, mutton, pork, veal or venison for the boneless meat. Grind meat in a meat grinder or a food processor fitted with a metal blade. Instead of roasting meat in Step 2, brown meat in batches in a skillet over medium-high heat. For every 4 cups (1 L) browned meat, add 1 to 1½ cups (250 to 375 mL) boiling water, broth or tomato juice. Continue with Step 3, using a slotted spoon to pack hot meat into hot jars, then ladling boiling water, broth or tomato juice over meat.

Chicken, Duck, Goose, Turkey or Game Birds

One- to two-year-old fowl is the best for canning. After washing fowl, cut skin between legs and body. Bend legs until hip joints snap. Slip knife under ends of shoulder blades and cut up to wings. Pull breast and back apart and remove entrails. Rinse and dry; do not salt. Before canning, allow fowl to chill for 6 to 12 hours.

TIPS

Before using jars, inspect them carefully for any chips, cracks or fractures. Discard any imperfect jars.

A clear plastic ruler (kept solely for kitchen use) will help you determine the correct headspace. Each filled jar should be measured accurately, as the headspace can affect sealing and the preservation of the contents.

To help remove any fat that may be on the jar rim, dampen the cloth or paper towel used to clean the rim with diluted vinegar.

Poultry or game bird
Hot water or broth (see tip, page 397)

1. Prepare weighted-gauge pressure canner, jars and lids. *(For more information, see page 382.)* If using the raw-pack method, do not heat jars.

2. Prepare meat for packing:

   RAW-PACK METHOD
   Separate poultry or game bird at joints. Bones may be left in or removed.

   HOT-PACK METHOD
   Boil, steam or bake poultry or game bird until about two-thirds done. Separate at joints. Bones may be left in or removed.

3. Pack poultry into room temperature jars (for raw-pack) or hot jars (for hot-pack) to within a generous 1 inch (2.5 cm) of top of jar. Ladle hot water or broth into jar to cover poultry, leaving 1 inch (2.5 cm) headspace. Remove air bubbles and adjust headspace, if necessary, by adding hot liquid. Wipe rim with a paper towel moistened with vinegar. Center lid on jar. Screw band down until resistance is met, then increase to fingertip-tight.

4. Place jars in pressure canner. Adjust water level, lock lid and bring to a boil over medium-high heat. Vent steam for 10 minutes, then close vent. Continue heating to achieve 10 lbs (69 kPa) pressure. Process pint (500 mL) jars of bone-in poultry for 65 minutes; boneless poultry for 75 minutes. Process quart (1 L) jars of bone-in poultry for 75 minutes; boneless poultry for 90 minutes.

5. Turn off heat. Let pressure return to zero naturally. Wait 2 minutes longer, then open vent. Remove canner lid. Wait 10 minutes, then remove jars, cool and store. *(For more information, see pages 383–384.)*

Soups, Stews and Sauces

Recipes that contain both low-acid and high-acid ingredients but have an overall pH higher than 4.6 must be processed as a low-acid food product using a pressure canner. Ingredients used in combination recipes should be cut into uniform pieces to allow for even heat penetration during processing. Evenly heating the food prevents small pieces from becoming soft-textured and mushy and ensures that larger pieces are heated through.

Chicken Stock

Use this chicken stock instead of water when preparing stuffing and rice. It's a quick and easy way to add flavor and interest to these comfort foods!

TIP

A clear plastic ruler (kept solely for kitchen use) will help you determine the correct headspace. Each filled jar should be measured accurately, as the headspace can affect sealing and the preservation of the contents.

Makes about eight pint (500 mL) jars or four quart (1 L) jars

1	chicken (4 lbs/1.8 kg), cut into pieces	1
16 cups	water	4 L
2	stalks celery	2
2	medium onions, quartered	2
10	whole black peppercorns	10
2	bay leaves	2
1 tbsp	salt	15 mL

1. In a large stainless steel saucepan, combine chicken and water. Bring to a boil over medium-high heat. Add celery, onions, peppercorns, bay leaves and salt. Reduce heat and boil gently for 2 hours, or until chicken is tender. Using a slotted spoon, remove chicken and reserve for another use. Strain stock through a cheesecloth-lined sieve. Let cool until fat solidifies, then skim fat from stock. Return stock to a boil before ladling into jars

2. Prepare weighted-gauge pressure canner, jars and lids 30 minutes before stock is ready. *(For more information, see page 382.)*

3. Ladle hot stock into hot jars, leaving 1 inch (2.5 cm) headspace. Wipe rim with a paper towel moistened with vinegar. Center lid on jar. Screw band down until resistance is met, then increase to fingertip-tight.

4. Place jars in pressure canner. Adjust water level, lock lid and bring to a boil over medium-high heat. Vent steam for 10 minutes, then close vent. Continue heating to achieve 10 lbs (69 kPa) pressure. Process pint (500 mL) jars for 20 minutes and quart (1 L) jars for 25 minutes.

5. Turn off heat. Let pressure return to zero naturally. Wait 2 minutes longer, then open vent. Remove canner lid. Wait 10 minutes, then remove jars, cool and store. *(For more information, see pages 383–384.)*

Beef Stock

This rich and flavorful stock is a perfect base for soups and stews. Try using it to make French dip sandwiches. Place your leftover or deli-style roast beef in the stock, add your favorite herbs and spices, and heat. Serve on kaiser rolls, and use the extra juice for dipping.

TIP

Place a clean towel on your work surface to absorb water from the hot jars as you take them out of the pressure canner to be filled, and again once the jars are processed. The towel prevents hot jars from coming into contact with cooler countertops. Significant temperature differences can cause jar breakage.

Makes about four pint (500 mL) jars or two quart (1 L) jars

4 lbs	meaty beef bones	1.8 kg
8 cups	water	2 L
1	medium onion, finely chopped	1
1	carrot, sliced	1
1	stalk celery, sliced	1
1	bay leaf	1
	Salt	
	Beef bouillon cubes or granules (optional)	

1. In a large stainless steel saucepan, combine beef bones and water. Bring to a boil over high heat. Reduce heat to medium-low and skim foam. Add onion, carrot, celery, bay leaf and salt to taste. Cover and boil gently for 2 to 3 hours or until desired flavor is reached. (If a stronger flavor is desired, boil longer or add beef bouillon cubes.) Remove beef bones and discard. Strain stock through a fine sieve or cheesecloth-lined strainer. Discard vegetables and bay leaf. Let cool until fat solidifies, then skim fat from stock. Return stock to a boil before ladling into jars.

2. Prepare weighted-gauge pressure canner, jars and lids 30 minutes before stock is ready. *(For more information, see page 382.)*

3. Ladle hot stock into hot jars, leaving 1 inch (2.5 cm) headspace. Wipe rim with a paper towel moistened with vinegar. Center lid on jar. Screw band down until resistance is met, then increase to fingertip-tight.

4. Place jars in pressure canner. Adjust water level, lock lid and bring to a boil over medium-high heat. Vent steam for 10 minutes, then close vent. Continue heating to achieve 10 lbs (69 kPa) pressure. Process pint (500 mL) jars for 20 minutes and quart (1 L) jars for 25 minutes.

5. Turn off heat. Let pressure return to zero naturally. Wait 2 minutes longer, then open vent. Remove canner lid. Wait 10 minutes, then remove jars, cool and store. *(For more information, see pages 383–384.)*

Vegetable Stock

Homemade stock adds
naturally delicious
flavor to foods and
allows you to avoid
unwanted additives in
commercial products.
Small jars of stock
are especially handy
for use in sauces
for sautéed or
pan-broiled foods.

TIP

A jar lifter is very helpful
for handling hot, wet jars.
Because they are bulky
and fit loosely, oven mitts
— even water-resistent
types — are not a wise
choice. When filling jars,
an all-purpose rubber
glove, worn on your
helper hand, will allow
you to steady the jar.

**Makes about eight pint (500 mL) jars or
four quart (1 L) jars**

1 lb	carrots, cut into 1-inch (2.5 cm) pieces	500 g
6	stalks celery, cut into 1-inch (2.5 cm) pieces	6
3	medium onions, quartered	3
2	red bell peppers, cut into 1-inch (2.5 cm) pieces	2
2	large tomatoes, cored, seeded and chopped	2
2	medium turnips, chopped	2
3	cloves garlic, crushed	3
3	bay leaves	3
1 tsp	crushed dried thyme	5 mL
8	whole black peppercorns	8
28 cups	water	7 L

1. In a large stainless steel saucepan, combine carrots, celery, onions, red peppers, tomatoes, turnips, garlic, bay leaves, thyme, peppercorns and water. Bring to a boil over medium-high heat. Reduce heat, cover and boil gently for 2 hours. Uncover and boil gently for 2 hours. Strain stock through a fine sieve or cheesecloth-lined strainer. Discard vegetables and seasonings. Return stock to a boil before ladling into jars.

2. Prepare weighted-gauge pressure canner, jars and lids 30 minutes before stock is ready. *(For more information, see page 382.)*

3. Ladle hot stock into hot jars, leaving 1 inch (2.5 cm) headspace. Wipe rim with a paper towel moistened with vinegar. Center lid on jar. Screw band down until resistance is met, then increase to fingertip-tight.

4. Place jars in pressure canner. Adjust water level, lock lid and bring to a boil over medium-high heat. Vent steam for 10 minutes, then close vent. Continue heating to achieve 10 lbs (69 kPa) pressure. Process pint (500 mL) jars for 30 minutes and quart (1 L) jars for 35 minutes.

5. Turn off heat. Let pressure return to zero naturally. Wait 2 minutes longer, then open vent. Remove canner lid. Wait 10 minutes, then remove jars, cool and store. *(For more information, see pages 383–384.)*

Vegetable Soup

In this soup, vegetables cook together to create a delicious broth. Making soup from scratch can be a time-consuming process, but with a large batch of Vegetable Soup on hand, you can heat up homemade, delicious soup at a moment's notice.

TIP

A jar lifter is very helpful for handling hot, wet jars. Because they are bulky and fit loosely, oven mitts — even water-resistent types — are not a wise choice. When filling jars, an all-purpose rubber glove, worn on your helper hand, will allow you to steady the jar.

Makes about fourteen pint (500 mL) jars or seven quart (1 L) jars

8 cups	chopped cored peeled tomatoes	2 L
6 cups	cubed peeled potatoes	1.5 L
6 cups	thickly sliced carrots	1.5 L
4 cups	cooked lima beans	1 L
4 cups	fresh or frozen corn kernels	1 L
2 cups	sliced celery (1-inch/2.5 cm slices)	500 mL
2 cups	chopped onions	500 mL
6 cups	water	1.5 L
	Salt and freshly ground black pepper	

1. Prepare weighted-gauge pressure canner, jars and lids. *(For more information, see page 382.)*

2. In a large stainless steel saucepan, combine tomatoes, potatoes, carrots, beans, corn, celery, onions and water. Bring to a boil over medium-high heat. Reduce heat and boil gently for 15 minutes. Season with salt and pepper to taste.

3. Ladle hot soup into hot jars, leaving 1 inch (2.5 cm) headspace. Remove air bubbles and adjust headspace, if necessary, by adding hot soup. Wipe rim. Center lid on jar. Screw band down until resistance is met, then increase to fingertip-tight.

4. Place jars in pressure canner. Adjust water level, lock lid and bring to a boil over medium-high heat. Vent steam for 10 minutes, then close vent. Continue heating to achieve 10 lbs (69 kPa) pressure. Process pint (500 mL) jars for 55 minutes and quart (1 L) jars for 85 minutes.

5. Turn off heat. Let pressure return to zero naturally. Wait 2 minutes longer, then open vent. Remove canner lid. Wait 10 minutes, then remove jars, cool and store. *(For more information, see pages 383–384.)*

Split Pea Soup (Habitant Soup)

Our forebears knew and appreciated the nutritional qualities and delicious flavors that can be created with economical split peas. This recipe is ideal for warming body and soul on cold, dreary winter days.

TIP

Stick blenders make quick work of the purée step in most preserving recipes. Cook the mixture as directed until the food is softened. Turn heat off, then purée the mixture in the saucepan and proceed as directed.

Makes about five pint (500 mL) jars or two quart (1 L) jars

2 cups	dried split peas	500 mL
8 cups	water	2 L
1 ½ cups	sliced carrots	375 mL
1 cup	chopped onion	250 mL
1 cup	diced cooked ham	250 mL
1	bay leaf	1
¼ tsp	ground allspice	1 mL
	Salt and freshly ground black pepper	

1. In a large stainless steel saucepan, combine peas and water. Bring to a boil over medium-high heat. Reduce heat, cover and boil gently for about 1 hour or until peas are tender.

2. Prepare weighted-gauge pressure canner, jars and lids. *(For more information, see page 382.)*

3. If a smooth soup is desired, working in batches, purée peas and liquid in a food mill or a food processor fitted with a metal blade. Return purée to saucepan.

4. Add carrots, onion, ham, bay leaf and allspice to saucepan. Bring to a boil over medium-high heat. Reduce heat and boil gently for 30 minutes. If soup is too thick, thin with boiling water. Season with salt and pepper to taste. Remove bay leaf.

5. Ladle hot soup into hot jars, leaving 1 inch (2.5 cm) headspace. Remove air bubbles and adjust headspace, if necessary, by adding hot soup. Wipe rim with a paper towel moistened with vinegar. Center lid on jar. Screw band down until resistance is met, then increase to fingertip-tight.

6. Place jars in pressure canner. Adjust water level, lock lid and bring to a boil over medium-high heat. Vent steam for 10 minutes, then close vent. Continue heating to achieve 10 lbs (69 kPa) pressure. Process pint (500 mL) jars for 75 minutes and quart (1 L) jars for 90 minutes.

7. Turn off heat. Let pressure return to zero naturally. Wait 2 minutes longer, then open vent. Remove canner lid. Wait 10 minutes, then remove jars, cool and store. *(For more information, see pages 383–384.)*

Chicken Soup

A hot, steaming bowl of chicken soup is sure to cure the winter blahs. To make this soup more substantial before serving, add soup pasta, broken bits of vermicelli or rice while heating.

TIPS

A jar lifter is very helpful for handling hot, wet jars. Because they are bulky and fit loosely, oven mitts — even water-resistent types — are not a wise choice. When filling jars, an all-purpose rubber glove, worn on your helper hand, will allow you to steady the jar.

Place a clean towel on your work surface to absorb water from the hot jars as you take them out of the pressure canner to be filled, and again once the jars are processed. The towel prevents hot jars from coming into contact with cooler countertops. Significant temperature differences can cause jar breakage.

Makes about eight pint (500 mL) jars or four quart (1 L) jars

16 cups	chicken stock (store-bought or see recipe, page 399)	4 L
3 cups	diced cooked chicken (about 1 ½ lbs/680 g raw boneless)	750 mL
1 ½ cups	diced celery	375 mL
1 ½ cups	diced carrots	375 mL
1 cup	diced onions	250 mL
	Salt and freshly ground black pepper	
3	chicken bouillon cubes (optional)	3

1. Prepare weighted-gauge pressure canner, jars and lids. *(For more information, see page 382.)*
2. In a large stainless steel saucepan, combine chicken stock, chicken, celery, carrots and onions. Bring to a boil over medium-high heat. Reduce heat and boil gently for 30 minutes. Season with salt and pepper to taste. Add bouillon cubes, if using, and cook until bouillon cubes are dissolved.
3. Ladle hot soup into hot jars, leaving 1 inch (2.5 cm) headspace. Remove air bubbles and adjust headspace, if necessary, by adding hot soup. Wipe rim with a paper towel moistened with vinegar. Center lid on jar. Screw band down until resistance is met, then increase to fingertip-tight.
4. Place jars in pressure canner. Adjust water level, lock lid and bring to a boil over medium-high heat. Vent steam for 10 minutes, then close vent. Continue heating to achieve 10 lbs (69 kPa) pressure. Process pint (500 mL) jars for 75 minutes and quart (1 L) jars for 90 minutes.
5. Turn off heat. Let pressure return to zero naturally. Wait 2 minutes longer, then open vent. Remove canner lid. Wait 10 minutes, then remove jars, cool and store. *(For more information, see pages 383–384.)*

Chili

Jars of homemade chili make wonderful last-minute meals when your day evaporates, leaving no time for cooking. Serve it in bowls or spoon it over cornbread, bean-filled tortillas or even toast.

TIPS

If you like your chili good and hot, don't seed and devein the red hot chili pepper. If you prefer a milder chili, remove the seeds and veins.

When seeding and cutting hot peppers, wear rubber gloves to prevent hands from being burned.

To serve, pour chili into a saucepan, add cooked or canned pinto or kidney beans, heat and enjoy.

Adjust chili flavor to your taste using a combination of dried herbs and spices. Do not, however, use commercial chili seasoning mixes, as they may contain thickeners that are not recommended for home canning.

Makes about six pint (500 mL) jars or three quart (1 L) jars

5 lbs	ground beef	2.3 kg
2 cups	chopped onions	500 mL
2	cloves garlic, minced	2
6 cups	canned tomatoes, with juice	1.5 L
½ cup	chili powder	125 mL
4½ tsp	salt	22 mL
1	red chili pepper, finely chopped (see tip, at left)	1
1 tsp	cumin seeds	5 mL

1. Prepare weighted-gauge pressure canner, jars and lids. *(For more information, see page 382.)*

2. In a large stainless steel saucepan, over medium-high heat, brown ground beef. Drain off fat. Add onions and garlic; cook until onion is tender. Add tomatoes, chili powder, salt, chili pepper and cumin seeds. Increase heat to medium-high and bring to a boil. Reduce heat and boil gently for 20 minutes. Skim off excess fat.

3. Ladle hot chili into hot jars, leaving 1 inch (2.5 cm) headspace. Remove air bubbles and adjust headspace, if necessary, by adding hot chili. Wipe rim with a paper towel moistened with vinegar. Center lid on jar. Screw band down until resistance is met, then increase to fingertip-tight.

4. Place jars in pressure canner. Adjust water level, lock lid and bring to a boil over medium-high heat. Vent steam for 10 minutes, then close vent. Continue heating to achieve 10 lbs (69 kPa) pressure. Process pint (500 mL) jars for 75 minutes and quart (1 L) jars for 90 minutes.

5. Turn off heat. Let pressure return to zero naturally. Wait 2 minutes longer, then open vent. Remove canner lid. Wait 10 minutes, then remove jars, cool and store. *(For more information, see pages 383–384.)*

Variation

Alternative Chili Seasoning: In place of the dry seasonings and chili pepper, substitute this seasoning blend: ⅓ cup (75 mL) chili powder, 2 tsp (10 mL) ground cumin, 2 tsp (10 mL) salt, 1 tsp (5 mL) dried oregano, 1 tsp (5 mL) ground coriander, 1 tsp (5 mL) crushed hot pepper flakes and ½ tsp (2 mL) freshly ground black pepper.

Spaghetti Sauce with Meat

Jars of this homemade, ready-to-eat, hearty sauce make excellent meals when unexpected guests arrive or you've run out of ideas or time to prepare family meals. Remember, this is a low-acid food that must be processed in a pressure canner.

TIPS

Lean ground beef or sausage will yield the best flavor, but extra-lean or medium can also be used.

Feel free to adjust the types and amounts of herbs and seasonings to suit your preference. Taste sauce before ladling it into jars and add seasoning, if desired.

Makes about nine pint (500 mL) jars or five quart (1 L) jars

30 lbs	tomatoes	13.6 kg
2½ lbs	ground beef or sausage (see tip, at left)	1.14 kg
5	cloves garlic, minced	5
1 cup	chopped onions	250 mL
1 cup	chopped seeded green bell pepper or celery	250 mL
1 lb	mushrooms, sliced (optional)	500 g
4 tbsp	chopped fresh parsley	60 mL
¼ cup	lightly packed brown sugar	50 mL
2 tbsp	dried oregano	30 mL
4 tsp	salt	20 mL
2 tsp	freshly ground black pepper	10 mL

1. Wash tomatoes, removing stems and any bruised or discolored portions. Core and quarter 6 tomatoes and place in a large stainless steel saucepan. Bring to a boil over high heat. Using a potato masher, crush tomatoes to release juices, stirring constantly. While maintaining a boil and stirring to prevent scorching, core and quarter additional tomatoes, adding them to the saucepan as you work. Make sure the mixture continues to boil vigorously while you add, stir and crush the remaining tomatoes. When all tomatoes have been added, reduce heat and boil gently until tomatoes are soft, about 10 minutes.

2. Working in batches, press tomato mixture through a fine sieve or food mill. Discard peels and seeds. Set purée aside.

3. Prepare weighted-gauge pressure canner, jars and lids. *(For more information, see page 382.)*

4. In a large stainless steel skillet, over medium heat, brown ground beef, breaking it up with a fork, until no longer pink. Drain off excess fat. Add garlic, onions, green pepper and mushrooms, if using. Sauté until vegetables are tender, about 3 minutes.

5. In a large stainless steel saucepan, combine reserved tomato purée, meat mixture, parsley, brown sugar, oregano, salt and pepper. Add water to make a thinner sauce, if desired. Bring to a boil over medium-high heat and boil, stirring occasionally, for 5 minutes, until heated through.

6. Ladle hot sauce into hot jars, leaving 1 inch (2.5 cm) headspace. Remove air bubbles and adjust headspace, if necessary, by adding hot sauce. Wipe rim. Center lid on jar. Screw band down until resistance is met, then increase to fingertip-tight.

7. Place jars in pressure canner. Adjust water level, lock lid and bring to a boil over medium-high heat. Vent steam for 10 minutes, then close vent. Continue heating to achieve 10 lbs (69 kPa) pressure. Process pint (500 mL) jars for 60 minutes and quart (1 L) jars for 70 minutes.

8. Turn off heat. Let pressure return to zero naturally. Wait 2 minutes longer, then open vent. Remove canner lid. Wait 10 minutes, then remove jars, cool and store. *(For more information, see page 383–384.)*

Beef Stew with Vegetables

When you're in the mood for true comfort food, serve this hearty stew with crusty bread or sweet corn muffins.

TIPS

Refer to the Produce Purchase Guide on pages 426–429 to determine how much produce you'll need to buy to prepare this recipe.

A clear plastic ruler (kept solely for kitchen use) will help you determine the correct headspace. Each filled jar should be measured accurately, as the headspace can affect sealing and the preservation of the contents.

Makes about fourteen pint (500 mL) jars or seven quart (1 L) jars

1 tbsp	vegetable oil	15 mL
4 to 5 lbs	stewing beef, cut into 1½-inch (4 cm) cubes	1.8 to 2.3 kg
12 cups	cubed peeled potatoes	3 L
8 cups	sliced peeled carrots	2 L
3 cups	chopped celery	750 mL
3 cups	chopped onions	750 mL
4½ tsp	salt	22 mL
1 tsp	dried thyme	5 mL
½ tsp	freshly ground black pepper	2 mL
	Boiling water	

1. Prepare weighted-gauge pressure canner, jars and lids. *(For more information, see page 382.)*

2. In a large nonstick skillet, heat oil over medium-high heat. Working in batches, brown beef, adding oil if absolutely needed. Transfer beef to a large stainless steel saucepan and add potatoes, carrots, celery, onions, salt, thyme, pepper and boiling water to cover. Bring to a boil, stirring frequently.

3. Ladle hot stew into hot jars, leaving 1 inch (2.5 cm) headspace. Remove air bubbles and adjust headspace, if necessary, by adding hot stew. Wipe rim with a paper towel moistened with vinegar. Center lid on jar. Screw band down until resistance is met, then increase to fingertip-tight.

4. Place jars in pressure canner. Adjust water level, lock lid and bring to a boil over medium-high heat. Vent steam for 10 minutes, then close vent. Continue heating to achieve 10 lbs (69 kPa) pressure. Process pint (500 mL) jars for 75 minutes and quart (1 L) jars for 90 minutes.

5. Turn off heat. Let pressure return to zero naturally. Wait 2 minutes longer, then open vent. Remove canner lid. Wait 10 minutes, then remove jars, cool and store. *(For more information, see pages 383–384.)*

Beef in Wine Sauce

Last-minute cooks will appreciate this delicious meal starter to serve over rice or pasta. Dress it up with a garnish of fresh herbs and add a vegetable. You'll have a delicious homemade meal on the table in less than 30 minutes.

TIPS

Browning and seasoning sauce is made up of a blend of spices, vegetable stock and caramel coloring. It is used to enhance the flavor of food and to add a rich, appealing color. Look for it near the gravies and marinades at your local grocery store.

To serve, pour into a saucepan and stir in 2 tsp (10 mL) cornstarch for each pint (500 mL). Cook over medium-high heat, stirring frequently, for about 5 minutes, until mixture thickens. Do not add cornstarch before canning.

Makes about three pint (500 mL) jars or one quart (1 L) jar

1 tbsp	vegetable oil	15 mL
2 lbs	boneless round steak, cut into 1-inch (2.5 cm) cubes	900 g
1 cup	grated cored apple (unpeeled)	250 mL
1 cup	grated peeled carrot	250 mL
¾ cup	sliced onion	175 mL
½ cup	water	125 mL
½ cup	dry red wine	125 mL
1 tsp	salt	5 mL
2	cloves garlic, minced	2
2	beef bouillon cubes	2
2	bay leaves	2
½ tsp	browning and seasoning sauce (see tip, at left)	2 mL

1. In a large nonstick skillet, heat oil over medium-high heat. Working in batches, brown steak, adding oil if absolutely needed. Transfer steak to a large stainless steel saucepan and add apple, carrot, onion, water, wine, salt, garlic, bouillon cubes and bay leaves. Bring to a boil over medium-high heat, stirring occasionally. Reduce heat and boil gently, stirring frequently, for about 1 hour, until meat is tender and sauce is thickened. Remove bay leaves. Add browning and seasoning sauce.

2. Prepare weighted-gauge pressure canner, jars and lids 30 minutes before sauce is ready. *(For more information, see page 382.)*

3. Ladle hot beef and sauce into hot jars, leaving 1 inch (2.5 cm) headspace. Remove air bubbles and adjust headspace, if necessary, by adding hot sauce. Wipe rim with a paper towel moistened with vinegar. Center lid on jar. Screw band down until resistance is met, then increase to fingertip-tight.

4. Place jars in pressure canner. Adjust water level, lock lid and bring to a boil over medium-high heat. Vent steam for 10 minutes, then close vent. Continue heating to achieve 10 lbs (68 kPa) pressure. Process pint (500 mL) jars for 75 minutes and quart (1 L) jars for 90 minutes.

5. Turn off heat. Let pressure return to zero naturally. Wait 2 minutes longer, then open vent. Remove canner lid. Wait 10 minutes, then remove jars, cool and store. *(For more information, see pages 383–384.)*

The Art and Science of Home Food Preservation

The air we breathe, the water we drink and the soil in which food grows — all contain microorganisms, such as yeasts, molds and bacteria. They are a naturally occurring part of all foods. Although invisible to the human eye, uncontrolled microorganism growth causes food to deteriorate and spoil unless the food is preserved in some way. Off-flavors, offensive odors and color changes are signs of spoilage.

One way to control food spoilage is to expose the microorganisms in food to heat and hermetically seal the heated food. Heat kills microorganisms and inactivates enzymes in food to prevent further deterioration. Hermetically sealing the food in a jar prevents recontamination. This is the process commonly called home canning.

> "Hermetic" means "completely airtight"; therefore, when a jar has a hermetic seal, no air can get in to recontaminate the food.

Proper, safe home canning procedures interrupt the normal cycle of food spoilage and decay. Knowing how and why preserving food in mason jars works will help you achieve successful results in each home canning session.

When food is properly harvested, prepared correctly, then placed in jars that are "heat-processed" (heated to the correct temperature and held for a time determined in scientifically established heat penetration studies), potentially harmful food microorganisms can be destroyed. In addition, heat processing inactivates naturally occurring enzymes that lead to deterioration in food.

Together with the use of home canning jars and two-piece metal closures, heat processing also creates an airtight seal that prevents recontamination of food during storage. Here's how that happens: heating causes gases and food to expand, leading to a buildup of pressure inside the jar. The pressure is relieved or reduced as air (gases) from the headspace and food escapes from under the lid. The pressure buildup and release of gases occurs repeatedly throughout the processing time. The release of gases, called venting, creates a vacuum inside a sealed and cooled jar.

Once a product has been heat-processed and cooled to room temperature, the pressure outside the jar is greater than that inside the jar. The greater outside pressure pushes the lid down, and the softened sealing compound inside the lid conforms to the rim of the jar, creating a hermetic seal. This seal prevents other microorganisms from entering or contaminating the food during storage.

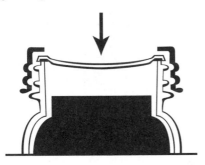

Heat-processing home-canned food is not optional! It is essential for destroying food spoilage microorganisms and creating an adequate hermetic seal. This is important not just for delicious taste and quality, but also for food safety. Failure to adequately heat-process jars for the amount of time and at the temperature specified in the recipe can result in seal failure, food spoilage and substantial health risks.

Acidity Determines the Heat Processing Method

Some spoilage microorganisms, as outlined below, are affected by foods' inherent acidity level. Therefore, acidity,

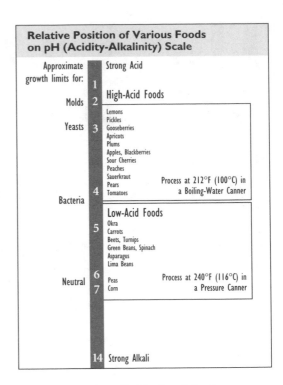

or pH, is used to divide food for home canning into two groups: high- and low-acid foods. Each group requires a specific heat processing method.

Acidity is determined by the level of acid naturally present in a food or added to a recipe mixture (for example, the addition of vinegar or lemon juice to borderline or low-acid foods such as pickling vegetables).

High-Acid Foods

Foods or recipes with a pH of 4.6 or lower are considered high-acid foods. These can be safely heat-processed in boiling water. A boiling-water canner heats food to 212°F (100°C), a temperature sufficient to kill molds, yeasts and some bacteria found in high-acid foods. Fruits, jams, jellies and fruit spreads are high-acid foods. Some, such as figs and tomatoes, sit on the borderline between high- and low-acid status and therefore require acidification (the addition of an acidic ingredient, such as vinegar or lemon juice) to be safely processed in a boiling-water canner. Fermented foods such as sauerkraut and fermented pickles are also high-acid foods. Other recipes combine high- and low-acid ingredients, but are sufficiently high in added acidic ingredients to achieve a pH of 4.6 or lower. Examples include pickles, relishes, chutney and condiments.

Low-Acid Foods

Low-acid foods have very little natural acid. This group includes vegetables, meats, poultry and seafood, as well as soups, stews, tomato-vegetable mixtures, tomato-meat mixtures and meat sauces. Any food or recipe that has a pH greater than 4.6 is a low-acid food. All low-acid foods must be heat-processed in a pressure canner, which heats food to 240°F (116°C), the temperature required to destroy toxin-producing bacterial spores. Botulism, a potentially deadly form of food poisoning, is caused by consumption of the toxins produced by the spores of the bacterium *Clostridium botulinum*. This bacterium thrives on low-acids foods in the absence of air in moist environments — the exact conditions inside a home canning jar.

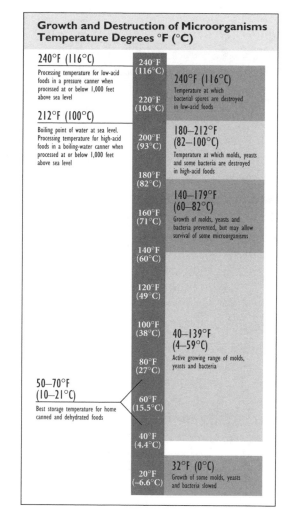

Growth and Destruction of Microorganisms
Temperature Degrees °F (°C)

240°F (116°C)
Processing temperature for low-acid foods in a pressure canner when processed at or below 1,000 feet above sea level

212°F (100°C)
Boiling point of water at sea level. Processing temperature for high-acid foods in a boiling-water canner when processed at or below 1,000 feet above sea level

50–70°F (10–21°C)
Best storage temperature for home canned and dehydrated foods

240°F (116°C)
220°F (104°C)
200°F (93°C)
180°F (82°C)
160°F (71°C)
140°F (60°C)
120°F (49°C)
100°F (38°C)
80°F (27°C)
60°F (15.5°C)
40°F (4.4°C)
20°F (-6.6°C)

240°F (116°C)
Temperature at which bacterial spores are destroyed in low-acid foods

180–212°F (82–100°C)
Temperature at which molds, yeasts and some bacteria are destroyed in high-acid foods

140–179°F (60–82°C)
Growth of molds, yeasts and bacteria prevented, but may allow survival of some microorganisms

40–139°F (4–59°C)
Active growing range of molds, yeasts and bacteria

32°F (0°C)
Growth of some molds, yeasts and bacteria slowed

Spoilage Microorganisms

To understand why different food processing methods are recommended for high- and low-acid foods, it helps to know how acid and temperature affect molds, yeasts, bacteria and enzymes.

Molds and Yeasts

Molds are fungi that grow as silken threads and appear as fuzz on food. Some molds produce mycotoxins, which are harmful to eat. Molds thrive on the acids that are a protection against bacteria. Yeasts, which are also fungi, cause food to ferment, rendering it unfit for consumption (with the exception of purposefully fermented foods such as pickles). Molds and yeasts are easily destroyed when food is heated to temperatures between 140 and 190°F (60 and 88°C). Temperatures in a boiling-water canner reach 212°F (100°C), more than sufficient to kill molds and yeasts.

Bacteria

Bacteria are much harder to destroy. Certain bacteria, especially those found in low-acid foods, actually thrive at temperatures that destroy molds and yeasts.

- Salmonella is destroyed when held at 140°F (60°C).

- *Staphylococcus aureus*, or "staph," is destroyed when food is kept above 140°F (60°C). However, staph bacteria produce a toxin that must be destroyed by heating the product to 240°F (116°C) for the time specified in tested home canning recipes.
- Boiling water (water at a temperature of 212°F/100°C) can kill *Clostridium botulinum* but does not affect its toxin-producing spores. The only practical way to destroy these spores is to heat low-acid food to a temperature of 240°F (116°C), which can only be done in a pressure canner, using the specific times and pressure established in scientific heat penetration studies.

Enzymes

Enzymes are present in all living things. They promote the normal organic changes necessary to the life cycle, but their action changes food flavor, texture and color, making it unappetizing. Like molds and yeasts, enzymes are easily inactivated by temperatures higher than 140°F (60°C). They are therefore effectively treated in a boiling-water canner.

Ensuring Quality Foods

Remember, preserving food does not improve its quality. Always select the best-quality produce and freshest ingredients. Preserve fruits and vegetables as soon as possible after they are harvested or purchased. Refrigerate any food that cannot be canned within a few hours; refrigeration slows down the natural deterioration process.

When preserving, carefully remove any diseased areas or bruised spots. Do not use heavily diseased, moldy, insect-damaged or overripe produce, as it has a higher microorganism count. Heat processing times are developed for properly harvested and prepared foods. A given processing time may not be sufficient to destroy microorganisms if proper harvesting and preparation procedures were not followed.

Equipment

The majority of the most popular home-canned foods — jams and jellies, pickles, fruits and tomatoes — can be prepared and preserved using utensils you are likely to already have in your kitchen. To get started, of course, you will need canning jars and two-piece metal closures, as well as a canner for heat-processing the filled jars.

Boiling-Water Canner

Most of the recipes in this book are heat-processed in a boiling-water canner. This is not something you necessarily need to run out and buy: most kitchens have pots that can double as boiling-water canners, especially if you're using smaller jars. A boiling-water canner is simply a large, deep saucepan equipped with a lid

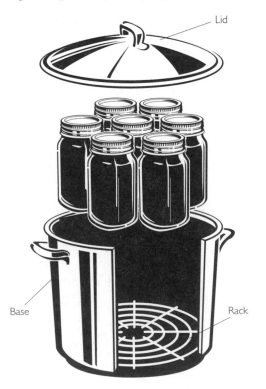

Lid

Base

Rack

and a rack. Cooking equipment stores do stock commercial boiling-water canners, but before you purchase this specialized equipment, check to see if one of your existing pots might be a suitable substitute. (Note: Ceramic stovetops require heavy, flat-bottomed pots for effective heat transfer. Unfortunately, most commercial boiling-water canners are made of light-weight metal that tends to warp with use.)

Any pot used as a boiling-water canner must be large enough to fully surround and completely immerse the jars in water. Ideally, the pot will be at least 3 inches (7.5 cm) deeper than the height of the jars. This depth allows space for the jars to be covered by at least 1 inch (2.5 cm) of water, while leaving sufficient extra pot height (1 to 2 inches/2.5 to 5 cm) for the water to boil rapidly.

The rack simply lifts the jars off the bottom of the pot, keeping the glass away from direct heat and allowing water to heat the entire jar. Racks designed specifically for boiling-water canners have handles that

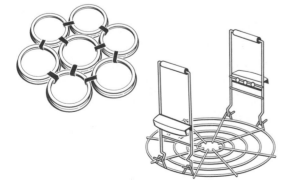

allow the rack to be lifted and secured to the rim of the pot. When the rack is filled with jars, do not remove it from the pot. You can also use a cake cooling rack, or you can tie extra screw bands together to cover the bottom of the pot.

Pressure Canner

To heat-process vegetables, meat, poultry or fish — or recipes that include any of these foods — you'll need a special piece of equipment called a pressure canner. Pressure canners are available in cooking supply stores. They are tall, usually heavy pots with two special features: a lid that can be locked in place and a pressure-regulating device. To learn more about pressure canners and how to use them, see pages 380–384.

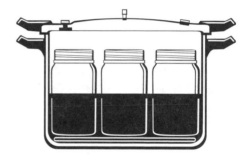

Canning Jars

Glass canning jars, often called mason jars, are the only containers recommended for safe home canning. Authentic canning jars have a unique threaded neck designed to engage with home canning screw bands. The top of the jar must be smooth, without chips, and flat to accommodate the sealing compound in the flange of the lid. The shape and volume capacity of canning jars must also comply with well-established heat processing methods and times. Canning jars and lids may be purchased in grocery, hardware and general merchandise stores that stock home preserving and cooking supplies.

While some commercial jars may look like canning jars and may even be embossed with the word "mason," not all such jars are designed and manufactured to withstand the repeated heating, cooling and handling demanded by the home canning process. These jars are designed for single use and recycling. Such jars may not withstand home canning temperatures, may not provide proper engagement with two-piece closures and may not have the shape or volume capacity that allows for the required heat penetration during processing. Look for the qualities specified above when purchasing canning jars.

Do not use older canning jars that cannot be fitted with current two-piece metal closures for home canning. Use such jars creatively for crafts, as decorative objects, or to store nonperishable foods or collectibles. Some older jars may have monetary value among antiques collectors.

While canning jars are designed to withstand high temperatures in moist environments, such as those in a canner, they are not suitable for use in the dry heat of an oven. In an oven, glass jars heat unevenly, creating hot and cold spots. When they are transferred to a work surface or filled with food, the clash of temperatures can lead to breakage. Unlike Pyrex utensils, canning jars are not manufactured to withstand extreme or sudden temperature changes. Pouring very hot liquid into a cool or room temperature jar can cause thermal shock, which weakens jars and can cause the bottom to break out. *To prevent breakage,*

always pour hot food into hot jars. Heat clean jars on a rack in water, not in an oven. Jars may be washed and heated in a dishwasher, provided they can be kept hot until you are ready to fill them with hot food. If you are processing in a boiling-water canner but heating your jars in the dishwasher, be sure to heat the water in the canner to a simmer before adding the hot filled jars.

Always place hot jars on a protected surface to avoid exposing the hot glass to temperature differentials, which can lead to jar breakage. A wooden cutting board or a heatproof tray is an excellent choice. Placing a hot jar on a cold stainless steel counter can create a temperature differential that can lead to thermal shock and jar breakage.

To avoid scratching glass canning jars, which can also lead to breakage, use only plastic or coated metal utensils when cleaning, filling, emptying or lifting mason jars.

Home-Canning Closures

These two-piece metal closures include a screw band and a flat metal lid.

Lids are constructed of tin-plated steel that has been protected with food-safe coatings. On the underside of the lid is a channel coated with a unique food-safe sealing compound specifically formulated for preserving food at home. Flat canning lids are not reusable. Vacuum seals create permanent impressions in the lid's sealing compound, so it cannot re-form to seal onto a second jar.

The threaded metal screw band fits over the threaded neck of the jar. Holding the lid securely in place during heat processing is the sole purpose of a screw band. Once the jar is cooled and the seal has been confirmed, the screw band can — and, in fact, should — be removed. When jars of food are heat-processed, moist gases are vented from the jar, leaving a residue under the screw band. If the screw band is not removed so that it and the jar rim can be cleaned and dried, the food residue can make later removal difficult and can cause the screw band to rust prematurely. Once the screw band and jar rim have been cleaned, you may, if you wish, reapply the screw band. Some people prefer to reapply the screw band, especially if they intend to transport the jars. Screw bands can be reused many times. Discard any screw bands that have become deformed or show signs of rusting.

Canning Utensils

While they are not essential, there are a number of specialty kitchen tools that make canning easier and safer. Look for these handy tools where cooking utensils are sold in grocery, hardware and general merchandise stores.

- **Jar lifters.** Used to lift jars into and out of canners, these look like large tongs, but their metal jaws are coated with soft plastic. Regular metal kitchen tongs are not recommended for use in home canning, as they can easily scratch the glass jars or the protective surfaces on lids. Moreover, regular tongs are not large or strong enough to lift filled jars.
- **Canning funnels.** Available in plastic and stainless steel, canning funnels have wide openings and sit inside the mouth of the jar to make filling jars easier and tidier.
- **Magnetic wands.** These simple utensils, basically just a magnet affixed to the end of a plastic stick, are super handy for lifting prepared lids from hot water without scratching the coating or burning your fingers.
- **Nonmetallic spatulas.** A narrow, long-handled rubber or silicone spatula facilities the gentle release of air bubbles trapped in filled jars. A plastic chopstick also works well, as does a special "bubble

remover" tool, available where home canning supplies are sold.

When selecting tools to use for filling or cleaning jars, remember to choose nonmetallic utensils; metal utensils can easily damage canning jars, resulting in seal failure or breakage.

Boiling-Water Heat Processing, Step by Step

Jars of high-acid foods are processed in a boiling-water canner, which heats the jar and its contents at 212°F (100°C). High-acid foods include soft spreads (jam, jelly, fruit butter, conserve, preserves, marmalade), fruits and fruit juices, salsa, relish, chutney, condiments (ketchup, barbecue sauce, chili sauce, mustard, vinegar), pickles and basic tomatoes. The higher temperatures of a pressure canner are required to deal with microorganisms that thrive in foods with lower acidity. If you're preserving vegetables, meat, poultry, fish or combinations of these foods, refer to pages 382–384.

When preserving high-acid foods, follow these simple steps:

> *Note:* Assembling all utensils and inspecting and washing jars and lids before beginning the recipe preparation will prevent unwanted delays as you move through the recipe.

1. **Clean the jars and closures:** Wash jars, lids and screw bands in hot, soapy water. Rinse well and drain. You don't need to dry them. *If using jars from previous canning projects, carefully examine jars. Discard any jars that have nicks, cracks, uneven rim surfaces or other damage or defects.*
2. **Heat the jars:** Place a rack in the bottom of a boiling-water canner, then place the

required number of mason jars on the rack. When using 8-ounce (250 mL) or smaller jars, add water to the jars and the canner until it reaches the top of the jars. For pint (500 mL) and larger jars, add water to the jars and the canner until the jars are about two-thirds full. Cover the canner and bring the water to a simmer (180°F/82°C) over medium heat. Do not boil the jars; boiling jars, or presterilization, is unnecessary. *Heat processing destroys any microorganisms, not only in the food but also in the containers and closures.* Keep jars hot until you're ready to use them.

3. **Prepare the closures:** Set screw bands aside — they do not require heating or sterilizing. *You want the screw bands to be at room temperature for easy handling when you apply them to the jars.* Place lids — the flat, round portion of the two-piece closures — in a small saucepan, cover with water and bring to a simmer (180°F/82°C) over medium heat. Do not boil. Keep lids hot until you're ready to use them.

4. **Prepare the recipe.** *(If the recipe preparation and cooking time is more than 30 minutes, you can wait until the recipe is prepared and in the cooking stage before beginning to heat the jars and lids as outlined in Steps 2 and 3.)*

5. **Fill the jars:**
   a) Working with one jar at a time, remove a jar from the canner, pouring hot water back into canner. Place the jar on a heat-protected work surface, such as a wooden cutting board, a towel or a heatproof tray (see page 414 for information on jar breakage due to thermal shock).

   b) If using, place funnel in jar.

   c) Ladle prepared food into hot jar, leaving the amount of headspace specified in the recipe. *Headspace is the space between the top of the jar and the top of the food.*

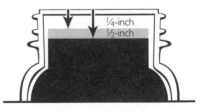

   ¼-inch
   ½-inch

Pickles, tomatoes, fruit, relishes, chutneys and condiments require ½ inch (1 cm) headspace

Soft spreads and fruit juices require ¼ inch (0.5 cm) headspace.

d) Slide a nonmetallic utensil, such as a rubber spatula, down between the food and the inside of the jar two or three times to release the air bubbles. *Failure to remove air bubbles can cause seal failure and will influence the color and storage quality of the preserved product.* Adjust headspace, if necessary, by adding hot food and/or liquid.

e) With a clean damp cloth or paper towel, wipe jar rim and threads. *Particles of food that remain on the rim of the jar can prevent formation of a vacuum seal.*

f) Using a magnetic or nonmetallic utensil, lift a hot lid from the water and place it on the jar, centering the sealing compound on the rim of the jar.

g) Place a screw band on the jar. With your fingers, screw band down until resistance is met, then increase to fingertip-tight. Do not use a tool or excessive force to tighten the screw bands. *Over-tightening screw bands can prevent jars from venting and can lead to seal failure.*

h) Return jar to the rack in the hot water-filled canner. Repeat filling steps until all jars are filled.

6. **Heat-process the filled jars:** When all of the jars are in the canner, adjust the water level in the canner so that it covers the jars by at least 1 inch (2.5 cm). Cover the canner with a lid and bring water to a full rolling boil over high heat. Once the water is boiling hard and continuously, begin counting the processing time specified in the recipe. *The rapid boil must continue for the duration of the processing time.*

7. **Cool the jars:** At the end of the processing time, turn the heat off and remove the canner lid. Let the canner cool for 5 minutes. *This short standing time allows the pressure inside the jars to stabilize and reduces the likelihood of liquid loss that could otherwise occur when the jars are moved.* After 5 minutes, remove the jars, lifting them out of the hot water without tilting

them. *Don't worry about water on the tops of the jar lids; it will evaporate during the cooling period.* Don't dry lids or jars at this point. You don't want to disturb the lids while the seal is being formed. Place jars upright on a towel in a draft-free place and let cool, undisturbed, for 24 hours. *If desired, drape a tea towel over the jars: it will prevent drafts from reaching the jars.*

After Processing

Checking the Vacuum Seal

When processed jars have cooled for 24 hours, check lids for seal. Remove the screw bands. With your fingers, press down on the center of each lid. Sealed lids will be concave (they'll curve downward) and will show no movement when pressed. If you are still uncertain of the seal, grasp the edges of the lid and lift the jar while supporting the jar with your other hand. A cooled, sealed lid will stay firmly attached to the jar, regardless of its weight. Jars that have not sealed properly must be refrigerated or reprocessed immediately (see page 419). Use unsealed refrigerated product within a few days.

Storing Home-Canned Foods

Jars that have good seals need to be cleaned and labeled before storage. With a damp cloth, thoroughly wipe lids, jar threads and jar surfaces to remove any water residue or food particles. If you have hard water, you may notice a mineral residue on the jars and lids. A cloth dampened in vinegar will help remove the residue, but you will want to wipe the jars a second time with clean water. Wash screw bands, removing any food residue on the threads inside the band. Dry the bands and store them separately for your next preserving project. *If desired, screw bands may be loosely reapplied to jars.*

Store sealed and labeled home-canned foods in a cool, dark place such as a pantry or cupboard. Basement storage is ideal, as basements usually offer cooler and more consistent temperatures. Avoid high-humidity areas, and do not store jars in areas with elevated temperatures. Arrange your jars in a manner that will allow you to use those that have been stored for the longest period first.

For best quality, use home-canned foods within 1 year. (This storage recommendation relates only to sealed jars that have been processed following tested recipes and correct processing methods and times.) After 1 year, natural chemical changes can occur that can diminish the eating quality, flavor, color, texture or nutritional value of the product. Foods stored for longer than 1 year are not necessarily bad, but the quality will be reduced.

When Jars Don't Seal Properly

If lids have not sealed within 24 hours, the product must be either refrigerated immediately or reprocessed using the method specified in the original recipe. (Note that reprocessing can lead to reduced product quality due to the secondary heat exposure, so refrigerating the unsealed product may be a better choice. Larger quantities of unsealed product can be transferred to freezer containers and frozen.)

To reprocess unsealed product, remove food and/or liquid from jars and reheat it as recommended in the original recipe. Wash, rinse and heat jars as directed on pages 415–416. *Use new lids* and heat them as directed on page 416. Pack hot food and/or liquid into hot jars, leaving the amount of headspace recommended in the original recipe. Remove air bubbles, clean jar rims and place new hot lids on the jars. Apply screw bands until resistance is met. Place jars in the canner and reprocess using the canning method and full length of processing time recommended by the recipe.

Using Home-Canned Food

Jars of foods that have been prepared and processed using the up-to-date methods recommended in this book can be used as you would commercial foods. However, it is always a good idea to visually examine each jar before it is opened to ensure that unexpected changes in the condition of the seal or the food have not occurred during storage. Do not use any product that has come unsealed or that shows signs of spoilage. If you follow the instructions in this book, this circumstance will be extremely rare, but if for any reason you doubt the product quality or vacuum seal, the age-old axiom "when in doubt, throw it out" is the wisest course of action (see the following to learn how to safely dispose of spoiled foods).

To open jars with vacuum-sealed lids, release the vacuum by gently lifting the edge of the lid with a can opener. Some can openers have a sharp pointed edge that may be used to puncture the center of the lid, releasing the vacuum seal. The objective is to break the seal without damaging the jar's sealing surface.

Once home-canned foods have been opened, any leftovers must be refrigerated until the contents are used.

Identifying and Disposing of Spoiled Foods

Food spoilage produces gases that cause the lids to swell and/or break the seal. Do not use a product unless it requires considerable force to break the seal. Other spoilage indicators include mold, gassiness, cloudiness, spurting liquid, seepage, yeast growth, fermentation, slime and disagreeable odors.

Jars displaying any of these indicators must be discarded in a manner that does not endanger the health of humans or animals. Spoiled high-acid foods may be disposed of as you would any refrigerated or fresh food. Spoiled low-acid foods and their containers must be handled carefully and detoxified before disposal to prevent possible contamination from any botulin that may be present. To detoxify the product, jar, lid and screw band, place all items in a deep saucepan. (It is not necessary to remove the contents from the jar.) Carefully cover with 1 to 2 inches (2.5 to 5 cm) of water. Cover the saucepan. Bring the water to a boil and boil hard for 30 minutes, being careful not to splash water or food product outside the saucepan. Let cool. Discard all contents of the saucepan.

Use a solution of one part chlorine bleach to five parts water to clean the saucepan and any other surface that has come in contact with the suspect product. Allow the cleaning solution to stand for 5 minutes before rinsing. Dispose of dishcloths and sponges used in the detoxification process.

Altitude

Just as it does in baking, higher altitude affects home canning recipes. As elevation — or altitude above sea level — increases, water boils at lower temperatures that are less effective for killing harmful spoilage microorganisms.

Heat processing directions in this book are stated for elevations of 0 to 1,000 feet (0 to 305 m), at which water boils at 212°F (100°C). When preserving at elevations higher than 1,000 feet (305 m), processing needs to be adjusted to extend the food's exposure to adequate heat to destroy microorganisms. The method of adjustment differs between high- and low-acid foods:

For high-acid foods processed in a boiling-water canner, processing time is increased as indicated below.

For low-acid foods processed in a pressure canner, processing time remains constant, but the level of pressure is increased. This increase must be based on the specific elevation and type of pressure canner (see Low-Acid Altitude Adjustment Chart, page 382).

Do you know the altitude of your home? Many people are unaware that they live at a high altitude. The list that follows highlights cities across North America with elevations greater than 1,000 feet (305 m) — areas considered high-altitude for home canning purposes. It is not, however, a complete list of locations considered high-altitude. Aviation charts list elevation, so checking with your local airport is an excellent way to determine the general altitude of your area. As well, local elevation information is often available through U.S. county extension offices and through government health or municipal agencies in Canada.

Altitude Adjustment Chart for High-Acid Foods Processed in a Boiling-Water Canner

Feet	Meters	Increase in Processing Time
1,001–3,000	306–915	5 minutes
3,001–6,000	916–1,830	10 minutes
6,001–8,000	1,831–2,440	15 minutes
8,001–10,000	2,441–3,050	20 minutes

* For low-acid food processed in a pressure canner, see page 382.

UNITED STATES

Arizona	Massachusetts	North Dakota
Bisbee, 4,780 feet (1,457 m)	Pittsfield, 1,194 feet (364 m)	Bismarck, 1,661 feet (506 m)
Flagstaff, 6,999 feet (2,133 m)	**Michigan**	Devil's Lake, 1,455 feet (443 m)
Nogales, 3,955 feet (1,205 m)	Marquette, 1,221 feet (372 m)	Jamestown, 1,498 feet (457 m)
Phoenix, 1,135 feet (346 m)	**Minnesota**	Minot, 1,716 feet (523 m)
Prescott, 5,045 feet (1,538 m)	Duluth, 1,428 feet (435 m)	Williston, 1,982 feet (604 m)
Tucson, 2,643 feet (806 m)	Mankato, 1,020 feet (311 m)	**Ohio**
Arkansas	Rochester, 1,317 feet (401 m)	Akron, 1,228 feet (374 m)
Bentonville, 1,296 feet (395 m)	**Missouri**	Youngstown, 1,196 feet (365 m)
Fayetteville, 1,251 feet (381 m)	Kansas City, 1,026 feet (313 m)	**Oklahoma**
California	**Montana**	Boise City, 4,178 feet (1,273 m)
Mojave, 2,791 feet (851 m)	Billings, 3,652 feet (1,113 m)	Elk City, 2,002 feet (610 m)
Colorado	Butte, 5,550 feet (1,692 m)	Lawton, 1,110 feet (338 m)
Aspen, 7,820 feet (2,384 m)	Glendive, 2,456 feet (749 m)	Oklahoma City, 1,295 feet (395 m)
Boulder, 5,288 feet (1,612 m)	Great Falls, 3,677 feet (1,121 m)	
Burlington, 4,219 feet (1,286 m)	Helena, 3,877 feet (1,182 m)	**Oregon**
Colorado Springs, 6,874 feet (2,095 m)	Kalispell, 2,932 feet (894 m)	Klamath Falls, 4,095 feet (1,248 m)
	Nebraska	
Cortez, 5,918 feet (1,804 m)	Chadron, 3,297 feet (1,005 m)	La Grande, 2,717 feet (828 m)
Denver, 5,280 feet (1,609 m)	Grand Island, 1,847 feet (563 m)	Medford, 1,335 feet (407 m)
Greeley, 4,697 feet (1,432 m)	Hastings, 1,961 feet (598 m)	Redmond, 3,077 feet (938 m)
Grand Junction, 4,858 feet (1,481 m)	Lincoln, 1,219 feet (372 m)	**Pennsylvania**
	Omaha, 1,325 feet (404 m)	Altoona, 1,504 feet (458 m)
Sterling, 4,038 feet (1,230 m)	Scottsbluff, 3,967 feet (1,209 m)	Pittsburgh, 1,204 feet (367 m)
Georgia	Valentine, 2,591 feet (790 m)	**South Carolina**
Atlanta, 1,026 feet (313 m)	**Nevada**	Greenville, 1,048 feet (319 m)
Gainesville, 1,275 feet (389 m)	Carson City, 4,697 feet (1,432 m)	**South Dakota**
Idaho	Elko, 5,140 feet (1,567 m)	Aberdeen, 1,302 feet (397 m)
Boise, 2,871 feet (875 m)	Ely, 6,259 feet (1,908 m)	Pierre, 1,742 feet (531 m)
Idaho Falls, 4,740 feet (1,445 m)	Las Vegas, 2,181 feet (665 m)	Rapid City, 3,204 feet (977 m)
Lewiston, 1,438 feet (438 m)	Reno, 4,415 feet (1,346 m)	Sioux Falls, 1,429 feet (436 m)
Pocatello, 4,452 feet (1,357 m)	**New Hampshire**	Watertown, 1,748 feet (533 m)
Twin Falls, 4,151 feet (1,265 m)	Berlin, 1,161 feet (354 m)	**Tennessee**
Iowa	**New Mexico**	Bristol, 1,519 feet (463 m)
Dubuque, 1,076 feet (328 m)	Albuquerque, 5,355 feet (1,632 m)	**Texas**
Sioux City, 1,098 feet (335 m)		El Paso, 3,958 feet (1,206 m)
Kansas	Carlsbad, 3,295 feet (1,004 m)	Midland, 2,871 feet (875 m)
Abilene, 1,152 feet (351 m)	Roswell, 3,671 feet (1,119 m)	San Angelo, 1,919 feet (585 m)
Goodland, 3,656 feet (1,114 m)	Santa Fe, 6,348 feet (1,935 m)	**Utah**
Hutchinson, 1,543 feet (470 m)	Taos, 7,091 feet (2,161 m)	Cedar City, 5,622 feet (1,714 m)
Topeka, 1,078 feet (329 m)	**North Carolina**	Moab, 4,555 feet (1,388 m)
Wichita, 1,333 feet (406 m)	Asheville, 2,165 feet (660 m)	Ogden, 4,473 feet (1,363 m)

UNITED STATES

Utah (continued)	Washington	Wyoming
Provo, 4,497 feet (1,371 m)	Spokane, 2,372 feet (723 m)	Casper, 5,347 feet (1,630 m)
Salt Lake City, 4,227 feet (1,288 m)	**West Virginia**	Cheyenne, 6,156 feet (1,876 m)
	Beckley, 2,504 feet (763 m)	Cody, 5,102 feet (1,555 m)
Vermont	Bluefield, 2,857 feet (871 m)	Gillette, 4,365 feet (1,330 m)
Lyndonville, 1,188 (362 m)	Clarksburg, 1,217 feet (371 m)	Laramie, 7,284 feet (2,220 m)
Virginia	Wheeling, 1,195 feet (364 m)	Riverton, 5,525 feet (1,684 m)
Roanoke, 1,175 feet (358 m)	**Wisconsin**	Rock Springs, 6,760 feet (2,060 m)
	Rhinelander, 1,624 feet (495 m)	

CANADA

Alberta	British Columbia	North Bay, 1,215 feet (370 m)
Calgary, 3,557 feet (1,084 m)	Kamloops, 1,133 feet (345 m)	**Saskatchewan**
Edmonton 2,373 feet (723 m)	Kelowna, 1,409 feet (429 m)	Regina, 1.894 feet (577 m)
Red Deer, 2,968 feet (904 m)	Prince George, 2,268 feet (691 m)	Saskatoon, 1,653 feet (503 m)
Lethbridge 3,047 feet (928 m)	**Manitoba**	Swift Current, 2,683 feet (817 m)
Medicine Hat, 2,352 feet (716 m)	Brandon, 1,343 feet (409 m)	
	Ontario	**Yukon**
Vermillion, 2,025 feet (617 m)	Kenora, 1,344 feet (409 m)	Whitehorse, 2,317 feet (706 m)

Home Canning Problem Solver

PROBLEM	CAUSE	PREVENTION/SOLUTION
Seal fails. *Use food immediately, refrigerate immediately or correct cause and reprocess within 24 hours.*	Failure to heat-process filled jars using the correct method and an adequate length of time.	Heat-process *all* filled jars using the method and time recommended in a tested home canning recipe for the specific food and jar size.
	Improper preparation of lids and/or adjustment of screw bands.	a) Carefully follow manufacturer's preparation directions for lids and jars. (Heat lids in hot water; do not boil.) b) Using your fingers, screw bands down until resistance is met, then increase to fingertip-tight. Do not force. Do not use a lid wrench to apply bands.
	Improper headspace.	Use headspace recommended in recipe for food product being canned.
	Food particles on jar rim.	Carefully clean jar rims and threads with a clean, damp cloth before applying lids and screw bands.
	Failure to adjust processing time or pressure for high altitude.	Know the altitude of your home and adjust processing time or pressure as needed.
Jars seals, or appears to seal, and then unseals. *If spoilage is evident, do not use.*	Minimum or inadequate vacuum, caused by underprocessing or not heat-processing filled jars.	Heat-process *all* filled jars using the method and time recommended in a tested home canning recipe
	for the specific food and jar size. Particles of food left on sealing	surface.
	Carefully clean jar rims before applying closures.	Crack or chip in jar rim.
	Check jars before packing and discard any with uneven, chipped sealing surfaces. Excess air left in jar.	Use headspace recommended in recipe and slide a nonmetallic utensil between food and jar to release trapped air before applying lids and screw bands.

PROBLEM	CAUSE	PREVENTION/SOLUTION
Lid buckles, appearing to warp or bulge upward under the screw band. *If spoilage is evident, do not use food.*	When buckling is apparent immediately after heat processing, cause is overly tight application of screw bands.	Using your fingers, screw bands down until resistance is met, then increase to fingertip-tight. Do not force. Do not use a lid wrench to apply bands.
	When buckling becomes apparent during storage, cause is food spoilage; heat processing has been insufficient to destroyed all spoilage microorganisms.	a) Heat-process *all* filled jars using the method and time recommended in a tested home canning recipe for the specific food and jar size. b) Adjust processing time or pressure for higher altitudes. *Note:* Foods on which lids buckle during storage must be discarded in a way that prevents consumption by both humans and animals.
Liquid is lost during processing. *Do not open jar to replace liquid.*	Food not heated before being packed into jars.	Use the hot-pack method.
	Food packed too tightly.	Pack food loosely when using the hot-pack method.
	Air bubbles not removed before lids and screw bands were applied.	Slide a nonmetallic utensil between food and jar to release trapped air. Repeat 2 to 3 times.
	Light band torque: screw bands applied too loosely.	With your fingers, screw bands down until resistance is met, then increase to fingertip-tight. Do not force.
	Pressure canner not operated correctly.	Regulate heat continuously so that pressure does not fluctuate, avoiding sudden changes to the heat level.
	Starchy foods absorbed liquid.	Pack starchy foods, such as corn, loosely.
Liquid is lost immediately after processing (siphoning).	Jars removed from canner before internal pressure/temperature could stabilize/acclimate to outside temperature.	a) For boiling-water canner, when processing time is complete, remove lid and turn heat off. Before removing jars, wait 5 minutes. b) For pressure canner, follow manufacturer's directions for cooling prior to removing canner lid.

PROBLEM	CAUSE	PREVENTION/SOLUTION
Food darkens in top of jar.	Liquid does not cover food.	Completely cover food solids with liquid, making sure headspace is adequate, before applying closures.
	No heat processing to inactivate enzymes.	Heat-process *all* filled jars using the method and time recommended in a tested home canning recipe for the specific food and jar size.
	Packing and processing does not expel air.	Use the hot-pack method when indicated in recipe. Heat-process *all* filled jars using the method and time recommended in a tested home canning recipe for the specific food and jar size.
	Excess air sealed in jar due to improper headspace or bubble removal.	Use headspace recommended in recipe and slide a nonmetallic utensil between food and jar to release trapped air before applying lids and screw bands.
Food becomes black, brown or gray.	Natural chemical substances (tannins, sulfur compounds and acids) in food react with minerals in water or with metal containers or utensils used in preparing the food.	a) Use soft water. b) Use stainless steel cooking pans, stainless steel or glass bowls, and heat-resistant nonmetallic utensils. Avoid using brass, copper, iron, aluminum, zinc or chipped enamelware.
Black spots appear on underside of metal lid.	Natural compounds in some foods cause brown or black deposits on the underside of the lid. *This deposit is harmless and does not mean the food is unsafe to eat.*	None.
Rust appears on underside of metal lid.	Improper coating or scratches on underside of lid.	a) Use lids made by an established, reputable manufacturer. b) Use only nonmetallic utensils when handling lids. Use a magnetic wand, rather than tongs, to lift lids from hot water.

Produce Purchase Guide

Approximate, average weights and volume yields of common fruits and vegetables. Actual yields will vary based on size of selected items and preparation technique.

| VEGETABLES | PURCHASE UNIT | WEIGHT | | PREPARED YIELD VOLUME | | |
		Imperial	Metric	Preparation	Imperial	Metric
Asparagus, green	16 to 20 medium	1 lb	500 g	tough ends removed, sliced	3 cups	750 mL
Beans, green or yellow		1 lb	500 g	tips removed, sliced	3 cups	750 mL
Beans, dried (legumes)	kidney beans	1 lb	500 g	dried	2½ cups	625 mL
	pea/navy beans	1 lb	500 g	dried	2⅓ cups	575 mL
Beets	without tops	1 lb	500 g	peeled, diced	2 cups	500 mL
Broccoli	1 medium bunch	1 lb	500 g	florets	2 cups florets	500 mL
Cabbage		1 lb	500 g	shredded (quantity varies by size of shred)	4 to 6 cups	1 to 1.5 L
Carrots	5 to 6 medium without tops	1 lb	500 g	sliced	3 cups	750 mL
				shredded	2½ cups	625 mL
Cauliflower		1 lb	500 g	florets	1½ cups florets	375 mL
Celery	1 stalk			sliced	½ cup	125 mL
Corn on the cob	1 medium ear			kernels cut from ear	½ cup	125 mL
Cucumber, English or field	1 medium	8 oz	250 g	sliced or diced	2 cups	500 mL
Cucumber, pickling	6 to 7 medium	1 lb	500 g	sliced	3⅓ cups	825 mL
Jalapeño peppers	20 medium	1 lb	500 g	sliced	4 cups	1 L
Onions, cooking	3 to 4 medium	1 lb	500 g	chopped	2½ cups	625 mL
	1 medium			chopped	¾ cup	175 mL
Onions, pearl or pickling	about 50 (¾ to 1 inch/ 2 to 2.5 cm)	1 lb	500 g	whole, peeled	4 cups	1 L
Onions, red	2 medium	1 lb	500 g	sliced	3⅓ cups	825 mL
Mushrooms		1 lb	500 g	sliced	5 to 6 cups	1.25 to 1.5 L
Parsnips	4 medium	1 lb	500 g	peeled and chopped	2 cups	500 mL
Peas, green, fresh in pods		1 lb	500 g	shelled	1 cup	250 mL

| VEGETABLES | PURCHASE UNIT | WEIGHT | | PREPARED YIELD VOLUME | | |
		Imperial	Metric	Preparation	Imperial	Metric
Sweet bell peppers, red, green, orange or yellow	1 large	6 to 8 oz	175 to 250 g	chopped	1¼ cups	300 mL
Potatoes	3 medium	1 lb	500 g	diced	2¼ cups	550 mL
Pumpkin, pie		1 lb	500 g	peeled, cubed	4 cups	1 L
Squash, butternut		1 lb	500 g	peeled, cubed	3¼ cups	800 mL
Tomatoes, round garden or globe	3 medium	1 lb	500 g	chopped	2½ to 3 cups	625 to 750 mL
	3 medium	1 lb	500 g	peeled and crushed or put through food mill	1½ cups	375 mL
	1 bushel	53 lbs	24 kg			
Tomatoes, Italian plum (Roma)	5 medium	1 lb	500 g	chopped	2 cups	500 mL
	5 medium	1 lb	500 g	crushed or puréed	1½ cups	375 mL
	1 bushel	53 lbs	24 kg			
Turnips, Rutabaga		1 lb	500 g	cubed	2½ cups	625 mL
Zucchini	3 medium	1 lb	500 g	sliced	3 cups	750 mL
	1 medium			sliced	1 cup	250 mL

| FRUITS | PURCHASE UNIT | WEIGHT | | PREPARED YIELD VOLUME | | |
		Imperial	Metric	Preparation	Imperial	Metric
Apples	3 medium	1 lb	500 g	peeled and sliced	3 cups	750 mL
	1 medium			diced	1 cup	250 mL
Apricots	8 to 12 medium	1 lb	500 g	sliced	2 to 3 cups	500 to 750 mL
	1 medium			sliced and pitted	¼ cup	50 mL
Bananas	3 medium	1 lb	500 g	sliced	2 cups	500 mL
	3 medium	1 lb	500 g	mashed	1 cup	250 mL
Blackberries		1 lb	500 g	whole, fresh	2⅔ cups	650 mL
		1 lb	500 g	crushed	1⅔ cups	400 mL
Black currants, fresh		1 lb	500 g	whole, fresh	4 cups	1 L
Black currants, dried		1 lb	500 g	dried	3¼ cups	800 mL
Blueberries		1 lb	500 g	whole	2⅔ cups	650 mL
		1 lb	500 g	crushed	1¾ cups	425 mL

| FRUITS | PURCHASE UNIT | WEIGHT | | PREPARED YIELD | | |
| | | | | VOLUME | | |
		Imperial	Metric	Preparation	Imperial	Metric
Cherries, fresh		1 lb	500 g	stemmed but not pitted	3 cups	750 mL
		1 lb	500 g	pitted	2½ cups	625 mL
Red tart pitted cherries, frozen	10-lb (4.5 kg) bucket	10 lbs	4.5 kg		16 cups	4 L
Crabapples	45 to 50 small	1 lb	500 g	whole	3⅔ cups	900 mL
Cranberries		1 lb	500 g	whole, fresh	4 cups	1 L
Elderberries		1 lb	500 g	whole, fresh	3¼ cups	800 mL
Figs, fresh	9 medium	1 lb	500 g	whole, fresh	2½ cups	625 mL
Figs, dried	40 medium	1 lb	500 g	dried, chopped	3 cups	750 mL
Gooseberries		1 lb	500 g	whole, fresh	3¼ cups	800 mL
Grapefruit	1 to 2 medium	1 lb	500 g			
	1 medium			juice	⅔ cup	150 mL
	1 medium			sections, membrane removed	10 to 12 sections	10 to 12 sections
Grapes		1 lb	500 g	whole, stems removed	2½ to 3 cups	625 to 750 mL
		1 lb	500 g	seeds removed	2 to 2½ cups	500 to 625 mL
Lemons	2 to 3 medium	1 lb	500 g			
	1 medium			juice, approx.	2½ to 3 tbsp	37 to 45 mL
	1 medium			grated zest	1 tbsp	15 mL
Limes	6 to 8 medium	1 lb	500 g			
	1 medium			juice, approx.	1 to 3 tbsp	15 to 45 mL
	1 medium			grated zest	1 to 2 tsp	5 to 10 mL
Melon	One 6-inch (15 cm) melon	3 lbs	1.4 kg			
	cantaloupe	3 lbs	1.4 kg	peeled, seeded and cubed	6 to 7 cups	1.5 to 1.75 L
	honeydew	3 lbs	1.4 kg	peeled, seeded and cubed	4 to 5 cups	1 to 1.25 L
Mulberries		1 lb	500 g	whole, fresh	3¼ cups	800 mL
Nectarines	3 medium	1 lb	500 g	sliced	2½ cups	625 mL
Oranges	2 to 3 medium	1 lb	500 g			
	1 medium			juice	⅓ cup	75 mL
	1 medium			chopped sections, membrane removed	½ cup	125 mL
	1 medium			grated zest	4 tsp	20 mL

| FRUITS | PURCHASE UNIT | WEIGHT | | PREPARED YIELD | | |
| | | | | VOLUME | | |
		Imperial	Metric	Preparation	Imperial	Metric
Peaches	3 medium	1 lb	500 g	peeled, pitted and sliced	2¼ cups	550 mL
	3 medium	1 lb	500 g	crushed	1¾ cups	425 mL
Pears	3 medium	1 lb	500 g	peeled, cored and sliced	2¼ cups	550 mL
Pineapple	1 medium	about 4 lbs	about 1.8 kg	peeled, cored and cubed	5 cups	1.25 L
		1 lb	500 g	peeled, cored cubes	2½ cups	625 mL
Plums	10 large yellow or medium purple (prune) plums	1 lb	500 g			
	2 medium plums			pitted and sliced	⅓ cup	75 mL
Prunes, dried	pitted	1 lb	500 g	whole, pitted	2½ cups	625 mL
Raisins	seedless	1 lb	500 g	whole	3 cups	750 mL
Red currants		1 lb	500 g	whole, fresh	4 cups	1 L
Rhubarb	4 to 8 stalks	1 lb	500 g	sliced into 1-inch pieces	3 cups	750 mL
Raspberries	2 pint containers	1 lb	500 g	whole, fresh	4 cups	1 L
	2 pint containers	1 lb	500 g	crushed	1¾ to 2 cups	425 to 500 mL
Saskatoon berries	1 pint container	1 lb	500 g	whole	3¼ cups	800 mL
Strawberries, medium berries		1 lb	500 g	whole, fresh	2⅔ cups	650 mL
		1 lb	500 g	sliced	2 to 2⅓ cups	500 to 575 mL
		1 lb	500 g	crushed	1⅔ cups	400 mL

Glossary

acetic acid. A pungent, colorless liquid acid that is the primary acid in vinegar (vinegar is 5% acetic acid). Acetic acid is what makes vinegar sour.

acid. A substance in a class of sour compounds.

alum. An ingredient used in older pickling recipes to add crispness and firmness to pickles. Alum, if consumed in large doses, may cause nausea and/or gastrointestinal problems and is no longer recommended for use in pickling recipes. If used, it must be thoroughly rinsed away. The chemical name is potassium aluminum sulfate.

altitude. The vertical elevation (distance in feet or meters) of a location above sea level.

antioxidant. A substance, such as citric acid (lemon or lime juice), ascorbic acid (vitamin C) or a blend of citric and ascorbic acids, that inhibits oxidation and controls browning of light-colored fruits and vegetables. Antioxidants are believed to neutralize free radicals, harmful particles in your body that can cause long-term damage to cells and lead to disease.

artificial sweetener. Any one of many synthetically produced non-nutritive sweet substances. Artificial sweeteners vary in sweetness but are usually many times sweeter than granulated sugar.

ascorbic acid. The chemical name for vitamin C, a natural, water-soluble vitamin that is commercially available in a concentrated form as white, odorless crystals or powder. It is used as an antioxidant to inhibit oxidation and control browning of light-colored fruits and vegetables.

bacteria. Microorganisms, some of which are harmful, found in the soil, water and air around us. Some bacteria thrive in conditions common in low-acid canned food and produce toxins that must be destroyed by heating to 240°F (116°C) for a specified length of time. For this reason, low-acid foods must be processed in a pressure canner.

band. See *screw band.*

blanch. To submerge a food in boiling water or steam for a short period of time, done to loosen the skin or peel or to inactivate enzymes. Blanching is immediately followed by rapidly cooling the food in ice water.

boil. To heat a liquid until bubbles break the surface. At sea level, this happens at 212°F (100°C). At elevations above 1,000 feet (305 m), the boiling point is reached at a lower temperature (see Altitude, page 420). A boil is achieved only when the liquid is continuously rolling or actively bubbling. See also *boil gently or simmer; boil, full rolling.*

boil gently or simmer. To cook food gently just below the boiling point (180 to 200°F/82 to 93°C). Bubbles rise from the pot bottom, only slightly disturbing the surface of the food.

boil, full rolling. A rapid boil, usually foaming or spurting, that cannot be stirred down, achieved at a temperature of 220°F (104°C). This stage is essential for attaining a gel when making cooked jams or jellies.

boiling point. The temperature at which liquid reaches a boil (212°F/100°C at sea level).

boiling-water canner. A large, deep saucepan with a lid and a rack to lift jars off direct heat. The pot must be large enough to immerse jars in water. It must be deep enough to allow canning jars to be covered by at least 1 inch (2.5 cm) of water and leave sufficient extra pot height (1 to 2 inches /2.5 to 5 cm) to allow water to boil rapidly.

boiling water method. The home canning method used to process high-acid foods. Heat is transferred to the food product by the boiling water, which completely surrounds the jar and two-piece closure. A temperature of 212°F (100°C) is reached and must be maintained for the time specified by the recipe. This method is adequate to destroy molds, yeasts and some bacteria, as well as to inactivate enzymes. The boiling-water method must *not* be used to process low-acid foods.

botulism. Food poisoning caused by ingestion of the toxin produced by spores of the bacterium *Clostridium botulinum*. Botulism can be fatal. The spores are usually present in the dust, wind and soil clinging to raw food. They belong to a species of bacteria that cannot grow in the presence of air, and they do not normally thrive in high-acid foods. The spores can survive and grow in any tightly sealed jar of low-acid food that has not been processed correctly. Using the correct processing temperature and time to preserve low-acid foods will destroy toxin-producing spores.

bouquet garni. A spice bag, or a square of cheesecloth tied into a bag, that is filled with whole herbs and spices and is used to flavor broth, soup, pickling liquid and other foods. This method allows for easy removal of the herbs and spices after cooking.

brine. A salt-water solution used in pickling or when preserving foods. Although salt and water are the main ingredients, sugar and spices are sometimes added.

brined pickles. See *fermented pickles*.

browning. The unfavorable color change caused when the cut surface of some fruits and vegetables is exposed to the oxygen in the air. The reaction is called oxidation.

bubble remover. A nonmetallic utensil used in home canning to remove or free air bubbles trapped inside the jar. To ensure appropriate headspace, air bubbles should be removed before the two-piece lid is applied.

butter. See *fruit butter*.

calcium chloride. A naturally occurring salt found in some mineral deposits, and used as a crisping agent. The food-safe ingredient is added to the jar before processing or used in a solution with water as a presoak. Calcium chloride is used commercially to produce crisp, firm pickles. See also *Pickle Crisp™*.

candy or jelly thermometer. A kitchen thermometer that usually comes with adjustable hooks or clips to allow it to be attached to the pan. During the preparation of soft spreads without added pectin, it is used to determine when the gel stage is reached (this occurs at 220°F/104°C, or 8°F/4°C above

the boiling point of water). Always insert the thermometer vertically into the jelly and ensure that it does not contact the pot surface.

canner. Either one of two pieces of equipment used in home canning to process jars filled with a food product and covered with a two-piece closure. The two types of canners recommended for use in home canning are a boiling-water canner for high-acid foods and a pressure canner for low-acid foods.

canning liquid. Any one of many types of liquids, such as water, cooking liquid, pickling liquid, broth, juice or syrup, used to cover solid food products. Adding liquid prevents darkening of food exposed to the surface and allows for heat penetration.

canning salt. See *salt, pickling or canning*.

cap. See *two-piece closure*.

cheesecloth. A lightweight, woven cloth that has many uses in the kitchen. For home canning, it can be used in place of a jelly bag to strain juice from fruit pulp when making jelly or homemade juice, or it can be formed into a bag to hold whole herbs and spices during the cooking process, aiding in easy removal.

chutney. A combination of vegetables and/or fruits, spices and vinegar cooked for a long period of time to develop favorable flavor and texture. Chutneys are highly spiced and have a sweet-sour blending of flavors.

citric acid. A natural acid derived from citrus fruits, such as lemons and limes. It is available as white crystals or granules and is used as an ingredient in commercial produce protectors to prevent oxidation and in pectin products to aid in gel formation by increasing the acidity of the jam or jelly.

ClearJel®. A commercially available modified food starch that is approved for use in home canning. Unlike regular cornstarch, products thickened with ClearJel® do not break down when heated to high temperatures and/or cooled and reheated. ClearJel® can be ordered from online sources or by mail order. For ordering information in your area, type "ClearJel" as the keyword in an Internet search engine.

closure. See *two-piece closure.*

cold-packing. See *raw-pack method.*

condiment. A sweet or savory sauce used to enhance or garnish entrées.

conserve. A soft spread similar to jam, made with a combination of two or more fruits, along with nuts and/or raisins. If nuts are used, they are added during the last five minutes of cooking.

cool place. A term used to describe the best storage temperature for home-canned products. The ideal temperature is 50 to 70°F (10 to 21°C).

crisping agent. Any one of many substances that make pickles crisp and firm. Some older pickling recipes call for pickling lime, alum or grape leaves to crisp pickles, but these are no longer recommended. Using fresh, high-quality produce, the correct ingredient quantities and a current, tested home canning recipe will produce firm pickles without the addition of crisping agents. The texture of some quick-process or fresh-pack pickles, however, can be enhanced with the use of a product called Pickle Crisp™.

cucumber, pickling. A small variety of cucumber used to make pickles. Pickling cucumbers are usually no more than 6 inches (15 cm) in length. Cucumbers deteriorate rapidly at room temperature and should be stored in the refrigerator and used within 24 hours of harvest.

dextrose. A naturally occurring form of glucose. Dextrose is available as a white crystal or powder and is less sweet than granulated sugar. It is also called corn sugar or grape sugar. Dextrose is widely used as an ingredient in commercial food products. It is found in commercial pectin and produce protectors and functions as a bulking agent or filler.

dial-gauge pressure canner. A pressure canner fitted with a one-piece pressure regulator and a gauge to visually indicate the correct pressure level.

dill. A pungent, aromatic herb that can be used fresh or dried. Fresh dill has feathery green leaves. The most useful dried form is dill seeds. In home canning, dill is primarily used for pickling. One head of fresh dill is equivalent to 1 to 2 tsp (5 to 10 mL) dill seeds or 2 tsp (10 mL) dried dillweed.

E. coli. A species of bacteria that is normally present in the human intestines. A common strain, *Escherichia coli* 0157:H7, produces high levels of toxins and, when consumed, can cause symptoms such as diarrhea, chills, headaches and high fever. In some cases, it can be deadly.

enzyme. A protein that acts as a catalyst in organisms. In food, enzymes start the process of decomposition, changing the flavor, color and texture of fruits and vegetables. Enzyme action can be neutralized by following recommended food preservation methods.

exhausting. See *venting.*

ethylene gas. An odorless, colorless gas that occurs naturally in nature. It is produced by and released from fruits during the ripening process. In turn, the ethylene gas acts as a ripening agent and, when exposed, speeds up the ripening of under-ripe fruits.

fermentation. A reaction caused by yeasts that have not been destroyed during the processing of canned food. Bubble formation and scum are signs that fermentation is taking place. With the exception of some pickles that use intentional fermentation in preparation, do not consume fermented home-canned foods.

fermented pickles. Vegetables, usually cucumbers, that are submerged in a salt-water brine to ferment or cure for up to 6 weeks. Dill, garlic and other herbs and spices are often added to the brine for flavoring. Fermented pickles are also called "brined pickles."

firming agent. See *crisping agent.*

fingertip-tight. The degree to which screw bands are properly applied to home canning jars. Use your fingers to screw band down until resistance is met, then increase to fingertip-tight. Do not use a utensil or the full force of your hand to over-tighten bands.

food mill. A mechanical sieve used to purée soft or cooked foods. Seeds and skins are retained in the upper portion, and purée is collected in a bowl below.

food poisoning. Any illness caused by the consumption of harmful bacteria and their toxins. The symptoms are usually gastrointestinal.

fresh-pack pickles. Cucumbers that are canned in a spicy vinegar solution without fermenting, although they are frequently brined for several hours or overnight. All fresh-pack pickles should stand for 4 to 6 weeks after processing to cure and develop optimal flavor.

fruit butter. A soft spread made by slowly cooking fruit pulp and sugar to a consistency thick enough to mound on a spoon and spread easily. Spices may be added.

fruit pickle. Fruit, usually whole, that is simmered in a spicy, sweet-sour syrup until it becomes tender or transparent.

funnel. A plastic utensil that is placed in the mouth of a home canning jar to allow for easy pouring of a food product into the jar. Funnels help prevent spillage and waste.

gasket. A rubber ring that sits along the inside circumference of a pressure canner lid and comes in contact with the base when locked into place. The gasket provides a seal between the lid and the base so steam cannot escape.

gelling agent. Any substance that acts to form a gel-like structure by binding liquid.

gel stage. The point at which a soft spread becomes a full gel. The gelling point is 220°F (104°C), or 8°F (4°C) above the boiling point of water.

headspace. The unfilled space in a home canning jar between the top of the food or liquid and the underside of the lid. The correct amount of headspace is essential to allow for food expansion as the jars are heated and for the formation of a strong vacuum seal as jars cool.

heat penetration/heat processing. See *processing*.

hermetic seal. A seal that secures a food product against the entry of microorganisms and maintains commercial sterility.

high-acid food. A food or food mixture that contains sufficient acid — naturally or added as an ingredient — to provide a pH value of 4.6 or lower. Fruits, fruit juices, tomatoes, jams, jellies and most soft spreads are naturally high-acid foods. Food mixtures such as pickles, relishes, salsas and chutneys contain added vinegar or citric acid, which lowers their pH, making them high-acid foods. High-acid foods can be safely processed in a boiling-water canner.

home canning. The process of preserving fresh or prepared foods in glass jars with two-piece closures, using heat processing to destroy microorganisms that cause spoilage.

hot-pack method. Filling jars with preheated, hot food prior to heat processing. Preheating food expels air, permits a tighter pack in the jar and reduces floating. This method is preferred over the raw-pack method, especially for firm foods.

inversion. A home canning method in which hot foods are ladled into jars, two-piece closures are applied and the jars are turned upside down (inverted) for a period of time. Since no heat processing takes place, *this method is not recommended*.

jam. A soft spread made by combining crushed or chopped fruits with sugar and cooking to form a gel. Commercial pectin may or may not be added. Jams can be made with a single fruit or with a combination of fruits. They should be firm but spreadable. Jams do not hold the shape of the jar.

jar. A glass container used in home canning to preserve food and/or liquids. For safe home canning, jars must be designed to seal with two-piece metal closures and to withstand the temperatures and reuse associated with home canning. See also *mason jar*.

jelly. A soft spread made by combining fruit juice or acidified vegetable juice with sugar and cooking to form a gel. Commercial pectin may or may not be added.

jelly bag. A mesh or cloth bag used to strain juice from fruit pulp when making jellies. A strainer lined with several layers of cheesecloth may be substituted. Both the jelly bag and cheesecloth need to be dampened before use.

jelly strainer. A stainless steel tripod stand fitted with a large ring. A jelly bag is placed over the ring. The stand has feet that hold it above a bowl to allow juice to drain or drip from the bag into the bowl.

kosher salt. See *salt, kosher*.

kPa (kilopascal). A metric unit of atmospheric pressure (force).

L (liter). A metric unit of volume. One liter is similar in volume to 1 U.S. quart.

lactic acid. The acid produced during fermentation. The fermentation process converts the natural sugars in food to lactic acid, which, in turn, controls the growth of undesirable microorganisms by lowering the pH (increasing the acidity) of the food product and its environment. Lactic acid also adds a distinctive tart flavor and transforms low-acid foods into high-acid foods that can be safely processed in a boiling-water canner.

lemon juice. Juice extracted from lemons that is added to food products to increase the acidity. Lemon juice can also be purchased commercially. In home canning, lemon juice is added to certain foods to increase acidity and ensure proper processing. In some soft spread recipes, especially those prepared with added pectin, the acid in the lemon juice also aids with gelling. The acidity of freshly squeezed lemon juice is variable, depending on the lemon variety and harvest conditions, whereas bottled lemon juice is produced to consistent acidity standards. In recipes that specify bottled lemon juice, it is crucial for the success of the final product not to use freshly squeezed lemon juice. Where bottled is not specified, either freshly squeezed or bottled lemon juice may be used.

lid. A flat metal disc with a flanged edge lined with sealing compound used in combination with a metal screw band for vacuum-sealing home canning jars.

lime. See *pickling lime.*

long-boil soft spread. A sugar and fruit mixture boiled to concentrate fruit's natural pectin and evaporate moisture until a thick or gelled texture is achieved. Long boiling works best with fruits containing naturally high pectin levels. It yields smaller quantities per amount of fruit used and creates a caramelized fruit flavor. It may require a smaller measure of sugar as an ingredient, but the final cooked-down product isn't necessarily lower in sugar than other products.

low-acid food. A food that contains little natural acid and has a pH higher than 4.6.

Vegetables, meat, poultry and seafood are all low-acid foods. Bacteria thrive in low-acid foods. The only recommended and practical means of destroying bacteria naturally found in low-acid foods is to heat the food to 240°F (116°C) (at sea level) for a specified time in a pressure canner.

marmalade. A soft spread that contains pieces of citrus fruit and peel evenly suspended in transparent jelly. Marmalade is cooked in small batches and brought rapidly to, or almost to, the gelling point. Marmalades are similar in structure to jam.

mason jar. A glass jar that is suitable for heat processing food and/or liquids using a boiling-water canner or a pressure canner. Mason jars are designed to seal with two-piece metal lids and to withstand the temperatures and reuse associated with home canning. True mason jars also conform to specific shapes and capacities compatible with established safe heat processing methods and times. The jars are available in regular (70 mm) and wide-mouthed (86 mm) styles and in capacities ranging from 4 ounces (125 mL) to 1 quart (1 L). (In Canada, a 1.5 L jar is also available.) Most mason jars have rounded shoulders, but some have straight walls. Straight-walled mason jars can be used for freezing as well as home canning.

measures or measuring cups. Standard kitchen utensils used to accurately measure liquid or dry ingredients. Liquid measures are commonly glass or plastic and have a handle and a pour spout. Dry measures can be either stainless steel or plastic. Both types are available in imperial (cups) and metric (mL) sizes.

metal band. See *screw band.*

microorganism. A living plant or animal of microscopic size, such as molds, yeasts or bacteria, that can cause spoilage in canned or frozen foods.

mL (milliliter). A metric unit of volume, $1/1000$th of a liter. Measures for dry ingredients are available in 1, 2, 5 and 25 mL spoons and 50, 125 and 250 mL dry measures. Metric liquid measures, usually glass or plastic, show levels for quantities divisible by 10.

mold. Microscopic fungi that grow as silken threads and appear as fuzz on food. Molds thrive on acids and can produce mycotoxins. Mold is easily destroyed at processing temperatures between 140 and 190°F (60 and 88°C).

mycotoxins. Toxins (poisons) produced by some species of molds that grow on high-acid foods.

open-kettle canning. A home canning method in which hot foods are ladled into jars and two-piece closures are applied. Since no heat processing takes place, *this method is not recommended.*

oven canning. A home canning method in which jars are placed in the oven and heated. *This method is not recommended.*

overnight. A period of time from 8 to 12 hours.

oxidation. The reaction that takes place when cut fruits and vegetables are exposed to the oxygen in the air. Oxidation causes the cut surface of the produce to brown and can also lead to texture changes.

paraffin wax. A pure, refined wax used in an older home canning method. The wax was melted and poured over soft spreads in the jar. It is not a reliable method of preventing contamination by microorganisms, and in many instances mold growth will occur. Since no heat processing takes place, paraffin wax has not been recommended as a safe closure for soft spreads for many years.

pectin. A naturally occurring carbohydrate found in fruits and vegetables that is responsible for cell structure. The natural pectin content decreases as fruits and vegetables ripen. Thus, they become soft and lose their structure. Pectin is available commercially in powdered and liquid forms. Commercial pectin is used to make jams, jellies and other soft spreads.

pH (potential of hydrogen). A measuring system in chemistry for determining the acidity or alkalinity of a solution. In canning, foods are separated into high-acid and low-acid. A boiling-water canner is used for processing high-acid foods; a pressure canner must be used for processing low-acid foods.

Pickle Crisp™. A crisping agent that uses calcium chloride, a naturally occurring salt found in some mineral deposits, to enhance the texture of pickles. Pickle Crisp™ may be added to jars of quick-process or fresh-pack pickles before processing. Look for it where canning supplies are sold.

pickling. Preserving food, especially cucumbers and vegetables, in a high-acid (vinegar) solution, often with spices added for flavor. Pickled foods must be processed in a boiling-water canner.

pickling lime (calcium hydroxide). A white, almost insoluble powder, also known as slaked lime, used in some older pickling recipes to add crispness to pickles. Due to its caustic nature, pickling lime is no longer recommended for making homemade pickles. Failure to remove lime adequately may increase the risk of botulism. Lime can also cause gastrointestinal problems if too much is ingested.

pickling or canning salt. See *salt, pickling or canning.*

preserves. A soft spread in which the fruit is preserved with sugar so it retains its shape and is transparent, shiny, tender and plump. The syrup varies from the thickness of honey to that of soft jelly. A true preserve does not hold its shape when spooned from the jar.

preserve. To prepare foods to prevent spoilage or deterioration for long periods of time. Some methods of preservation are home canning, freezing, dehydration, pickling, salting, smoking and refrigeration. The method used determines the length of time the food will be preserved.

pressure canner. A tall, usually heavy pot with a lid that is locked in place and a pressure-regulating device. The lid is fitted with a safety valve, a vent and a pressure gauge. Pressure canners are used to process low-acid foods, because steam at 10 lbs (68 kPa) of pressure (at sea level) will reach 240°F (116°C), the temperature needed to destroy harmful bacteria that thrive in low-acid foods.

pressure canning method. The home canning method used to heat-process low-acid foods. Low-acid foods must be processed in a pressure canner to destroy potentially harmful bacteria, their spores and the toxins they produce. In practical terms, this can only be done at 240°F (116°C). Because the steam inside the canner is pressurized, its temperature can exceed the boiling point of water (212°F/100°C). In a weighted-gauge canner at sea level, the temperature will reach 240°F (116°C) at 10 lbs (68 kPa) of pressure.

pretreatment. Blanching or treating produce with an antioxidant to prevent browning, slow enzyme action or destroy bacteria.

processing or heat processing. Heating filled jars of food to a specified temperature for a specified time to inactivate enzymes and destroy harmful molds, yeasts and bacteria. Heat processing is essential for the food safety of all home-canned foods. Processing destroys microorganisms that are naturally present in food and/or enter the jar upon filling. It also allows gases or air to be vented from the jar to create an airtight vacuum seal as the product cools, thus preventing recontamination of the food.

processing time. The time in which filled jars are heated in a boiling-water canner or a pressure canner. The processing time must be sufficient to heat the coldest spot in the jar. The processing time is specified for every current, tested home canning recipe and depends on several factors, such as acidity, type of food product and size of jar.

produce protector. A commercially available antioxidant that prevents cut fresh produce from browning when exposed to the oxygen in the air, a reaction known as oxidation.

raw-pack method. Filling jars with raw, unheated food prior to heat processing.

refrigeration. The process of decreasing the temperature for cold storage of produce. Refrigeration slows the growth of microorganisms and prolongs deterioration for a short period of time.

relish. A pickled product prepared using chopped fruits and/or vegetables cooked in a seasoned vinegar solution. If a sweet relish is desired, sugar is added. Hot peppers or other spices may also be added for flavor.

reprocessing. Repeating the heat processing of filled, capped jars when a lid does not seal within 24 hours. The original lid must be removed and the food and/or liquid reheated as recommended by the recipe. The food and/or liquid must be packed into clean hot jars and covered with a new clean lid with the screw band adjusted. The filled jars must then be reprocessed using the canning method and full length of processing time recommended by the recipe.

rubber gasket. See *gasket.*

salt, kosher. A coarse-grained, textured salt that is free of additives. Kosher salt may be used when making pickles. Because of the variance in density and form, contact kosher salt packers for information regarding equivalencies.

salt, pickling or canning. A fine-grained salt used in pickling and home canning. It is free of anti-caking agents, which can cause the pickling liquid to turn cloudy, and iodine, which can darken the pickles.

salt, table. A free-flowing, fine-grained salt. Table salt is the most common salt and is used as a table seasoning. It contains additives that may yield unfavorable results when pickling. Iodized table salt (sodium iodide) is not recommended for pickling because it contains an anti-caking ingredient that can make brines cloudy, as well as iodine, which may darken the pickles. Non-iodized table salt can be used for pickling. The pickling liquid may be cloudy, but the pickles will not be dark.

salt, sea. A type of salt produced by the evaporation of seawater. It comes in fine- and coarse-grained textures and is usually more costly than other types of salt. Sea salt should not be used for pickling because it may contain minerals that could darken the pickles.

saucepan, large. An 8- to 10-quart (8 to 10 L) heavy pot essential for cooking soft spreads. The pot must have a broad, flat bottom for good heat distribution and deep sides to prevent food from boiling over.

screw band. A threaded metal band used in combination with a flat metal lid to create vacuum seals for home-preserved food. The band holds the lid in place during processing.

sealing compound. The red, shiny material found in the exterior channel on the underside of the flat metal lid. The sealing compound comes in contact with the lip of the jar and forms a seal when the jar cools after processing.

simmer. See *boil gently or simmer.*

skimmer. A metal kitchen utensil that has a long handle attached to a wide, flat surface with perforated holes. Skimmers are used to skim foam from soft spreads after cooking or to drain hot liquid from hot vegetables.

smoke curing. A preservation method achieved by smoking food, usually meat or fish, at a certain temperature to partially or fully cook it and to impart a smoky flavor. Even if meat or fish is smoke-cured prior to canning, it must go through heat processing in a pressure canner to become shelf-stable.

spice bag. A small muslin bag used to hold whole herbs and spices during cooking. The bag allows the flavor of the herbs and spices to seep into the food or liquid, and makes removing the spices easy when cooking is complete. Spice bags come in various sizes. If a spice bag is not available, tie herbs and spices in a square of cheesecloth.

spoilage. The evidence that a food product has not been completely rid of micro-organisms. If microorganisms are present, the nutrients in the food product will allow them to grow and multiply. Spoilage occurs when food products have not been processed correctly. Signs of spoilage include broken seals, mold, gassiness, cloudiness, spurting liquid, seepage, yeast growth, fermentation, slime and disagreeable odors. See page 419 for details on safely discarding spoiled foods, especially low-acid foods.

steam-pressure canner. See *pressure canner*.

steam-pressure canning method. See *pressure canning method*.

sterilization. The process of killing all living microorganisms. In home canning, this is achieved by heating food in capped jars to a high enough temperature for a length of time sufficient to destroy the most heat-resistant microorganism known to be associated with that food.

storage. A cool, dry, dark place where home-canned goods can be kept until ready to be consumed.

syneresis. The separation of liquid from a gel. In home canning, this can happen to soft spreads, usually during storage. It is not a safety concern.

syrup or canning syrup. A mixture of water (or juice) and sugar used to add liquid to canned food, usually fruit.

thermal shock breakage. Stress exerted on canning jars when glass is exposed to sudden temperature differentials. This stress weakens the glass and can lead to glass breakage, commonly by the bottom breaking out.

two-piece closure. A two-piece metal closure for vacuum-sealing home canning jars. The set consists of a metal screw band and a flat metal lid with a flanged edge lined with sealing compound.

vacuum seal. The state of negative pressure in properly heat-processed jars of home-canned foods. When a jar is closed at room temperature, the atmospheric pressure is the same inside and outside the jar. When the jar is heated, the air and food inside expand, forcing air out. As the jar cools and the contents shrink, a partial vacuum forms. The sealing compound found on the underside of home canning lids prevents air from re-entering.

venting. 1) Forcing air to escape from a closed jar by applying heat. As a food or liquid is heated, it expands upward and forces air from the jar through pressure buildup in the headspace. 2) Permitting air to escape from a pressure canner (also called exhausting).

Victorio strainer. A hand-turned or electrical device that separates seeds and skins while grinding pulp to create a purée. Used with fully ripe soft fruit or soft cooked foods.

vinegar, distilled white. The standard form of vinegar. It is a clear, colorless acidic liquid derived from grain alcohol that has a sharp, pungent flavor. Unlike apple cider vinegar or malt vinegar, distilled white vinegar does not compete with the distinctive flavors of herbs and spices in a brine. Because it is clear, it does not change the color of white or light-colored fruits and vegetables. In home canning, use 5% acidity (50 grain).

vinegar, cider. A type of vinegar derived from apples that is light golden in color and has a tart fruit flavor. Cider vinegar has a milder flavor than distilled white vinegar. Because it has color, it may darken white or light-colored fruits and vegetables. In home canning, use 5% acidity (50 grain).

vinegar, red or white wine. A type of vinegar derived from wine. The flavor reflects the source of the wine.

weighted-gauge pressure canner. A pressure canner that is fitted with either a three- or a one-piece weight unit with 5-, 10- and 15-lb (35, 69 and 103 kPa) pressure adjustments. (Only 10- and 15-lb/69 and 103 kPa pressure weights are used in home canning. The 5-lb/35 kPa weight is used for cooking, but not preserving.) Steam, exhausted throughout the processing period, causes the weight(s) to rock, indicating that the pressure level has been achieved or is being maintained.

yeast. Microscopic fungi grown from spores that cause fermentation in foods. Yeasts are inactive in foods that are frozen and are easily destroyed by heat-processing at a temperature of 212°F (100°C).

Acknowledgments

This book is a salute to the generations of North Americans who have home-canned the bounty of land and sea to sustain their families, and to those who have more recently discovered the rewards and satisfaction of preserving food at home.

Prompted by consumer queries and requests, the information and recipes between these covers represent the work of a host of Ball® and Bernardin® home economists and technologists too numerous to name individually. Special thanks, however, go to the following individuals (listed alphabetically), whose varied and valued contributions made this book possible: Lee Caward, Kevin Cockburn, Bob Dees, Charlene Erricson, Colin Erricson, Judith Finlayson, Tempo Hamm, Judy Harrold, Paulette Hillier, Cheryl Holliday, Marian Jarkovich, Matt Johannsson, Jennifer MacKenzie, Janet Magee, Teresa Makarewicz, Charlene Samples, Mark Shapiro, Izabella Snider, Andrew Smith, Sue Sumeraj, Dave Watson, Gillian Watts, Sheila Wawanash.

— Judi and Lauren

Index